The **Rough Guide** to

Cancún and
the Yucatán

written and researched by
Zora O'Neill and John Fisher

ROUGH GUIDES

www.roughguides.com

Contents

Colour section   1

Introduction 4
Where to go 5
When to go 9
Things not to miss 11

Basics   17

Getting there............................ 19
Getting around........................ 23
Accommodation....................... 27
Eating and drinking.................. 29
The media................................ 33
Festivals.................................... 33
Sport and outdoor activities..... 36
Culture and etiquette 38
Shopping 39
Travelling with children............. 40
Travel essentials 41

Guide   49

1 Cancún, Isla Mujeres
   and Isla Holbox 49
2 Playa del Carmen, Cozumel
   and the Caribbean coast..... 77
3 Tulum and around 105
4 The Costa Maya and the
   Río Bec 125
5 Valladolid and Chichén Itzá ...149

6 Mérida and around........... 171
7 Uxmal and the Ruta Puuc ...195
8 Campeche 213
9 Tabasco and Chiapas........ 235

Contexts   269

History 271
Environment and wildlife........ 283
The Maya belief system 287
Books 290

Language   297

Mexican Spanish 299
Rules of pronunciation........... 299
Useful words and phrases 299
Food and drink terms............ 302
Glossary................................. 307

Small print & Index   309

Yucatán food colour section following p.112

Maya culture colour section following p.208

3

Introduction to

Cancún and the Yucatán

The eastern tip of the curving horn of Mexico, facing the Caribbean Sea to the east and the Gulf of Mexico to the west and north, is known for major tourist attractions like the beaches of Cancún and the astonishing pyramid at Chichén Itzá. But the Yucatán Peninsula, as this area is known, is also still very much the frontier, a swathe of untamed greenery that forms a place apart from the rest of Mexico.

Until the 1960s, this was literally the case, as no road connected the Yucatán with central Mexico. As a result, residents were left to develop their own world-view, one that looked to Europe and Cuba for cultural cues while taking pride in the indigenous Maya culture. Today, it's not uncommon for people born in this region to identify themselves first and foremost as *orgullosamente yucateco* (proudly Yucatecan) and as mexicano a distant second.

More than anywhere else in Mexico, the Yucatán and the northeastern part of Chiapas reflect native American culture at every level of society: **Maya tradition** is palpable in remote, timeless villages of thatch-roof homes (palapas), but also in shopping malls, political campaigns and TV advertisements. Although the Maya as a people are by no means free of the poverty borne disproportionately by indigenous cultures throughout the country, many Maya have prospered, and their culture is widely influential. All *yucatecos* use Maya vocabulary, eat Maya cuisine and generally take pride in living in "the land of the pheasant and the deer", as the Maya have for centuries called their richly forested region.

Travel in the Yucatán and the Maya parts of Chiapas can be blazingly easy, along smooth toll highways in ultra-cushy buses. But the more remote you are, the more likely you are to be aboard something like a rattletrap minivan packed with machete-carrying farmers. But even if that minivan gets mired in a rainy season pothole, you may be the only passenger upset. The Yucatán is known for its *tranquilo* outlook – a **laidback sense** that minor annoyances really are

minor, and that there's always something else to do in the meantime. This attitude can be frustrating – but also wonderfully relaxing, if you give in to it.

The tranquillity extends to the **cities**, even the largest of which have the pace of overgrown villages – and certainly none of Mexico City's smog and slums. Modesty and near-formal politeness are the norm; violent crime is almost nonexistent. Women travellers in particular will appreciate the overall lack of machismo culture that's so common in central Mexico.

From the powdery white Caribbean **beaches** to the wild, dense rainforest that covers the inland peninsula and the muggy river valleys of Chiapas and Tabasco, you'll find a huge variety of attractions. Some, such as the ancient **Maya cities** or the mega-clubs of Cancún, are man-made, while others are natural – UNESCO has established five biosphere reserves in this area, the largest being the 1.7-million-acre Calakmul Biosphere Reserve. Travellers who prefer **urban** life will enjoy both the sprawling energy of Villahermosa and the gracious tranquillity of Mérida.

Where to go

C ancún, the largest tourist destination in the Yucatán, has a reputation as a spring-breaker's bacchanal, but it offers much more: as a built-from-scratch city carved out of the jungle in the 1970s, it's an interesting urban experiment that also happens to have beautiful beaches and world-class hotels and restaurants. Surrounding resorts such as **Playa del Carmen** are highly developed these days, but continuing down the

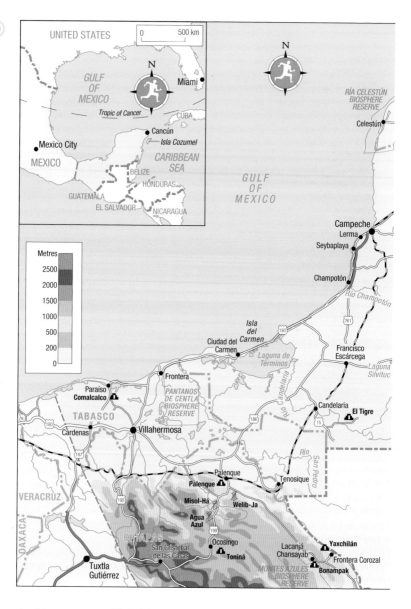

Caribbean coast you'll find less frenetic towns, such as **San Miguel**, on the reef-ringed island of **Cozumel**, **Tulum** and eventually the isolation of the **Costa Maya**, near Mexico's border with Belize.

Away from the Caribbean, you can choose to visit some of the scores of captivating ancient **Maya sites** (see the *Maya culture* colour section) or a number of thriving cities, the largest of which is **Mérida**, the capital of Yucatán State and a beautiful mix of Spanish colonial and French- and Italian-inspired architecture. On the Gulf coast of the peninsula, the city of **Campeche**, with its historic core of pastel-painted buildings, is a tiny gem. South and west of Campeche lies the state of Tabasco, where the Olmecs – considered the

Beach needs

The crystalline white sands and turquoise water of the Yucatán's **Caribbean coast** are so transfixing that many visitors never go further than their sun chairs. The coast between Cancún and Tulum, known as the **Riviera Maya** (see p.77), has seen intense development, and isolated beaches are a rarity. Farther south, the **Costa Maya** (see p.149) around Mahahual and Xcalak offers isolation, but the beaches are a shade less picturesque. Another less crowded alternative is the **Gulf coast** (see p.213 & p.235), along the north and west sides of the peninsula, where the water is not as clear but the sands are empty. In any case, all of the beaches in Mexico are technically public, so you may lay down your towel anywhere you like. If none of that satisfies, head for **Laguna Bacalar** (see p.133), an enormous, clear lake that eerily resembles the Caribbean.

originators of all Mesoamerican cultures – flourished more than a millennium before the first Maya cities were built. You can see the gigantic stone heads they carved, along with other relics, in the city of **Villahermosa**. Chiapas, directly south of Tabasco, was the centre of the Zapatista uprising in the 1990s. The strength of indigenous traditions here, together with the opening-up of a number of lesser-known Maya ruins near the majestic city of **Palenque**, continues to lure travellers.

If it's wildlife you're after, a number of nature reserves are sanctuaries for countless colourful birds and mammals. The **Sian Ka'an Biosphere Reserve**, on the Caribbean coast, comprises a particularly diverse range of eco-systems, while **Ría Celestún** and **Ría Lagartos** (on the west and north Gulf coasts, respectively) are bird-filled estuaries. The **Calakmul Biosphere Reserve**, in

◄ Kids at play in the Caribbean

the jungle at the heart of the peninsula, encompasses the vast Maya city of Calakmul as well as numerous lesser sites, where howler monkeys can often be heard, if not always seen, among the ruins. Divers shouldn't miss Cozumel, where the coast is lined with lush coral gardens. These are outlying parts of the **Mesoamerican Barrier Reef**, the longest barrier reef in the western hemisphere, running along the Caribbean coast from just south of Cancún all the way to Honduras.

The majority of visitors base themselves on the Caribbean beaches and venture no further than day-tripping distance. But it takes only a little more effort to leave the crowds behind and see an entirely different side of local life. A typical travel route through the Yucatán Peninsula begins in Cancún and goes counter-clockwise around the main highways, via Chichén Itzá, Mérida and the surrounding sights, then on to Campeche, with a dip into Tabasco State to see the Olmec ruins, and down to Palenque in Chiapas. A completist will finish the Maya circuit via the **Río Bec** ruins in the southern parts of Campeche and Quintana Roo. Any of these can also be included as a shorter side-trip of a day or so.

When to go

The majority of the Yucatán Peninsula is low-lying and tropical, with daytime temperatures in the 30s (around 80–90°F) year-round. Near the coast, the heat and humidity are tempered by the proximity of the water and its sea breezes. Inland, it's noticeably warmer and stickier, while the south – the Costa Maya and inland rainforests – is hotter and wetter than the northern areas around Cancún and Mérida.

Summer, from late May to October, can be uncomfortably hot and is in theory the **rainy season**, though just how wet it is varies from place to place. In the heart of the Yucatán you can expect muggy air and a heavy but short-lived

Traditional house, Isla Mujeres

downpour virtually every afternoon, which can come as a relief at the hottest time of year. Chiapas is the wettest state, with many minor roads washed out by autumn. On the Caribbean coast, the rains culminate in **hurricane season** from mid-September to mid-October – you'll get wet weather and choppy seas (as well as plenty of mosquitoes), if not an actual storm.

Winter is the traditional tourist season, with drier air, milder temperatures and clear skies, and in the beach resorts like Cancún and Playa del Carmen, hotels are packed from late December to April. In the early part of the season, through to February, there is still the chance of rainy or stormy days, though these are rarely very long-lasting. Only in the Chiapas highlands, on the very fringes of this area, does it get significantly chilly.

Average temperatures and rainfall

	Jan	Mar	May	Jul	Sep	Nov
Cancún						
Max/Min °F	81/67	84/71	88/77	90/78	89/76	84/72
Max/Min °C	27/19	29/22	31/25	32/26	32/24	29/22
Rainfall (inches/mm)	3.5/88.9	1.6/40.6	4.6/116.8	4.3/109.2	9/228.6	3.8/96.5
Mérida						
Max/Min °F	82/64	90/68	93/70	91/73	90/73	84/66
Max/Min °C	28/18	32/20	34/21	33/23	32/23	29/19
Rainfall (inches/mm)	1.2/30.5	0.6/15.2	2.9/73.7	5.0/127	7.7/195.6	1.4/35.6
Villahermosa						
Max/Min °F	76/66	83/69	89/73	86/74	85/73	79/68
Max/Min °C	24/18	28/20	31/22	30/23	29/22	26/20
Rainfall (inches/mm)	3.6/91.4	1.9/48.3	3.3/83.8	5.2/132.1	13.1/332.7	9.4/238.8

17

things not to miss

It's not possible to see everything the Yucatán has to offer in one trip – and we don't suggest you try. What follows, in no particular order, is a selective and subjective taste of the peninsula's highlights, from stunning ancient ruins and spectacular beaches to folk dancing and traditional crafts. They're arranged in five colour-coded categories, so you can browse through to find the very best things to see, do and experience. All highlights have a page reference to take you straight into the Guide, where you can find out more.

01 **Palenque ruins** Page **250** • The biggest Maya site in Chiapas is remarkable for both its well-preserved architecture and its setting atop jungle-covered hills, with waterfalls below.

03 **Mérida en domingo** Page 187 • Every Sunday, Mérida's central plaza is closed to cars for a fantastic street party for young and old alike.

02 **Haciendas** Page **198** • Many of the crumbling grand houses of the Yucatán's agricultural elite have been restored in recent years, as luxury hotels, restaurants or museums.

04 **Sian Ka'an Biosphere Reserve** Page **122** • The peninsula's most diverse nature sanctuary contains more than one million acres of empty beaches, vibrant reefs, tangled mangroves and lush forest. Birders flock here.

05 **Swim with whale sharks** Page 76 • From midsummer to early fall, hundreds of these enormous, gentle fish gather off the north Gulf coast.

06 **Playa del Carmen nightlife** Page **92** • Come sundown, this beach town's main pedestrian strip is one long street party. Bars and clubs pulse with music, and out on the sand the scene can be (quite literally) hot.

07 **Uxmal** Page **200** • Just south of Mérida, this ancient city complex features odd lore (one origin story involves a magical dwarf) and even odder buildings, such as the bulging Pirámide del Adivino, which rises from a unique oval base.

08 Central Campeche Page **223** • The centre of Campeche is a UNESCO World Heritage Site, a jewel box of colonial history from the 17th century, when it was fortified against pirates; each house is painted a different gem-like hue.

09 Smaller sites Page **231** • Lesser-known Maya ruins, such as Hochob (shown here), are often just as spectacular as the big names. Drive off the typical route to the Ruta Puuc, the Río Bec or the Chenes ruins, and you'll likely have the whole site to yourself.

10 Cochinita pibil Page **30** • Sample this rich dish that combines vivid orange annatto, exotic allspice, garlic and pork, all slow-roasted in a banana leaf – traditionally done in a pit in the ground.

11 Cenote X'keken Page **157** • Filled with cool, crystal-clear water, Cenote X'keken is just one of the many caverns and sinkholes that dot the Yucatán's limestone bedrock. A swim in one of them is an otherworldly experience.

12 Hammocks Page **185** • Take a quintessential piece of Yucatecan relaxation home with you. The best hammocks are found in Izamal and Mérida.

14 Traditional textiles Page **267** • San Cristóbal de las Casas is known for its exceptional embroidery and weaving, as craftspeople come from many surrounding villages to sell their work.

13 Chichén Itzá Page **161** • El Castillo, the pyramid that towers over this iconic ruined city, is a symbol of ancient Maya power in the Yucatán Peninsula.

15

15 Yaxchilán
Page **257** •
Half the fun of visiting these remote Maya ruins is the journey downriver, with Mexico on one bank and Guatemala on the other.

16 Calakmul
Page **146** • The Yucatán's largest ruined city is also the most remote, near the border with Guatemala and deep in a jungle where howler monkeys and jaguars roam.

17 Undersea exploring
Page **106** • Below the surface of the Caribbean, all along the Mesoamerican Barrier Reef, lies some of the most diverse and vivid marine life in the world. Scuba divers and snorkellers shouldn't miss the coral atolls around Cozumel.

Basics

Basics

Getting there 19

Getting around 23

Accommodation... 27

Eating and drinking 29

The media 33

Festivals 33

Sport and outdoor activities 36

Culture and etiquette 38

Shopping.. 39

Travelling with children.. 40

Travel essentials... 41

Getting there

The quickest and easiest way to get to the Yucatán is to fly, although you can also reach the peninsula by travelling overland from central Mexico, Guatemala or Belize as part of a longer trip. Cruise ships provide the only water transport.

The cost of travel to the Yucatán, particularly if you are flying into Cancún, fluctuates according to the season: tickets are at a premium from December to April, when the beach resorts are packed, but they can often be had for a song in autumn. Flights to Mérida and Villahermosa are more stable, but generally more expensive. There are no direct flights to Cancún from Europe – expect to transfer in the US (with all the immigration hassle) or Canada, or fly to Mexico City and backtrack.

You can occasionally cut costs by going through a **consolidator** or a **discount agent**, who have a line on charter flights to Cancún; however, departure dates are fixed and withdrawal penalties are high.

Flights from the US and Canada

The cheapest and most frequent flights to Cancún are from the southern "gateway" cities of Dallas, Houston and Miami, and from New York City (Jet Blue) and Philadelphia (US Airways). United/Continental also serves **Mérida, Ciudad del Carmen and Villahermosa** (the latter two flights are for oilmen and often expensive), and was starting service to Tuxtla Gutiérrez (the nearest airport to San Cristóbal de las Casas in Chiapas) in 2011. Air Canada flies direct to Cancún from all major cities, if not always daily. Cheaper charters are plentiful in winter. From both the US and Canada, deals often include a few nights' lodging at a beach resort. Coming from the west coast of the US or Canada, it is sometimes cheaper to book one flight to Mexico City, then continue to the Yucatán on a domestic airline (see p.23).

Flights from the UK and Ireland

Aside from charter flights in winter, there's only one direct flight between **Britain** and the Yucatán Peninsula: London Gatwick to Cancún (British Airways). European national airlines fly only to Mexico City, but check low-cost carriers Condor and Air Berlin for Cancún. Or fly to the cheapest destination in the US – usually New York – then take a budget airline such as Jet Blue to Cancún; allow a full day's transfer time for immigration. It's virtually never cheaper to fly to Mexico City and backtrack. Websites in the UK are not as geared to finding Mexican destinations as their US counterparts, so a specialist such as North South or Journey Latin America (see p.22) can sometimes work wonders. For charter flights try My Travel (☎0870/238 7777, ⓦwww.mytravel.com).

From Ireland, there are no direct flights to anywhere in Mexico. You can either fly via London (from most big cities) or via the US from Dublin or Shannon. Ticket prices often depend more on advance purchase, rather than the time of year.

Flights from Australia, New Zealand and South Africa

High season for Mexico flights **from Australia and New Zealand** is mid-June to mid-July, and December to January.

Airfare to Cancún

Typical return fares in winter high season are from around:
US US$325–500
Canada Can$650
UK £550–700
Ireland €550–700; £700 from Belfast
Australia Aus$2900
New Zealand NZ$2800
South Africa SA$13,500

Prices also depend on routing. You can often find a cheaper itinerary from Sydney to Mexico City, then book a separate internal ticket (unfortunately, this doesn't work from New Zealand).

From South Africa, you have to connect in Europe or the US – the latter is almost always less expensive. South African Airways flies to Atlanta, connecting with a Delta flight to Cancún, a route that is usually the cheapest, as well as the most direct.

Flights from Central America

To bypass the potential bureaucratic hassles that come with isolated posts on Mexico's southern borders, you can of course fly. Maya Island Air (🌐www.mayaregional.com) connects Belize and Guatemala with the Yucatán. Once-daily flights connect Cancún to Guatemala City (US$175/£110 one-way) and Belize (US$140/£90). Taca International (🌐www.grupotaca.com) flies to Mexico City.

Overland from central Mexico, Belize and Guatemala

If you plan to travel by bus to the peninsula from Mexico City or any point south and east, visit 🌐www.ticketbus.com.mx, where you can check schedules and buy tickets for most first-class and deluxe routes, as well as some second-class services. As many bus stations are located outside town, this website will spare you an extra trip to the terminal.

Mérida, capital of Yucatán state, is also its transport hub. The main bus route to the city from Mexico City is via Villahermosa, then through Campeche, a twenty-hour ride (definitely opt for ADO GL, the semi-luxe bus line). Villahermosa is just ten hours from the capital, with frequent services all day. From Oaxaca, you transfer in Villahermosa for points east.

Travellers have several choices when arriving by car from Guatemala. The easiest, most frequented checkpoint is at the

Six steps to a better kind of travel

At Rough Guides we are passionately committed to travel. We feel strongly that only through travelling do we truly come to understand the world we live in and the people we share it with – plus tourism has brought a great deal of **benefit** to developing economies around the world over the last few decades. But the extraordinary growth in tourism has also damaged some places irreparably, and of course **climate change** is exacerbated by most forms of transport, especially flying. This means that now more than ever it's important to **travel thoughtfully** and **responsibly**, with respect for the cultures you're visiting – not only to derive the most benefit from your trip but also to preserve the best bits of the planet for everyone to enjoy. At Rough Guides we feel there are six main areas in which you can make a difference:

- Consider what you're contributing to the **local economy**, and how much the services you use do the same, whether it's through employing local workers and guides or sourcing locally grown produce and local services.
- Consider the **environment** on holiday as well as at home. Water is scarce in many developing destinations, and the biodiversity of local flora and fauna can be adversely affected by tourism. Try to patronize businesses that take account of this.
- Travel with a purpose, not just to tick off experiences. Consider **spending longer** in a place, and getting to know it and its people.
- Give thought to how often you **fly**. Try to avoid short hops by air and more harmful night flights.
- Consider **alternatives to flying**, travelling instead by bus, train, boat and even by bike or on foot where possible.
- Make your trips "**climate neutral**" via a reputable carbon offset scheme. All Rough Guide flights are offset, and every year we donate money to a variety of charities devoted to combating the effects of climate change.

Airpasses to Mexico

If you also want to fly to other parts of the Americas in addition to Mexico, Hahn Air's **All America Air Pass** (⊛ www.allairpass.com) is worth considering. The pass links Mexico with all the major cities of North, Central and South America and the Caribbean, with the total price calculated on the legs you choose (usually between US$150 and US$300, depending on distance). You could also omit a leg and cover that by land. Flights into the Yucatán are not typically available, but the pass can still save you money over a standard ticket with a complex routing. The pass is available only from travel agents.

Talismán Bridge to Tapachula in southern Chiapas, Mexico (beyond the scope of this book). An international **bus** runs from Guatemala City through to Tapachula (4 daily; 5–6hr); you have to get off the bus at the border, then reboard on the Mexico side after having your passport inspected. If you arrive at the checkpoint on a second-class Guatemalan bus, you can take one of the many combis waiting on the Mexico side.

A more remote but direct crossing is at Bethél, Guatemala, on the Río Usumacinta, opposite Frontera Corozal in Mexico. Buses run from Flores to Bethél (5hr), where you take a thirty-minute boat ride across the river (about US$36 for up to four people). From Frontera Corozal, you can head directly to Palenque or stop at Bonampak and Yaxchilán. Less desirable (for the complex transport connections and odd location), yet possible, is the crossing at El Naranjo, which requires an hour-long boat ride to the village of El Ceibo in Mexico; combis run on to Tenosique in Tabasco. It's a good idea to get your passport stamped in Flores before proceeding to the border, or, coming the other way, in Tenosique.

Crossing from Belize, buses run frequently to Chetumal from Corozal, twenty minutes from the border (and not to be confused with Frontera Corozal, in Chiapas, Mexico). They deposit passengers at either the Chetumal bus station or the market just northeast of the centre. If you're out in the cays, you can take a water taxi (1hr 30min) from San Pedro on Ambergris Cay to Chetumal: San Pedro Water Taxi (⊛ www.sanpedrowatertaxi.com) and San Pedro Belize Express (⊛ www.sanpedrobelizeexpress.com) both have daily departures in the morning. Immigration is at the docks on both sides.

No matter where you're coming from, you will need a Mexico-issued tourist card (see p.43) in addition to your passport to enter Mexico. They can be scarce at out-of-the-way border crossings, so if you have the opportunity, visit a consulate in Guatemala City or Belize City to obtain one in advance. Allow plenty of time in your schedule; **posts typically close by 8pm**. Also note that Mexico observes daylight saving time, while Guatemala does not. Keep your passport handy once in Mexico, as buses near the border are often stopped in immigration sweeps.

By cruise ship

Several **cruise lines** ply the Caribbean from Florida, taking in Cozumel or the more remote port of Mahahual (often called Puerta Maya in cruise literature). A few cruises also dock at Progreso. Sometimes off-season or last-minute prices for three-day Cozumel cruises are so low (down to US$190 per person) that it can be worth using the ship as one-way transport. Agencies specializing in cruises include Cruise World (☎ 1-800/228-1153, ⊛ www.cruiseworldtours.com) and The Cruise Professionals (☎ 1-800/265-3838, ⊛ www.cruiseworldtours.com).

Airlines, agents and operators

Airlines

Air Berlin ⊛ www.airberlin.com. Dusseldorf and Munich to Cancún, winter only.
Air Canada ⊛ www.aircanada.com.
☎ 01-800/719-2827 in Mexico. Calgary, Edmonton, Halifax, Montreal, Ottawa, Toronto, Vancouver and Winnipeg to Cancún. Toronto to Cozumel.

American Airlines ⓦ www.aa.com. ☏ 01-800/904-6000 in Mexico. Chicago, Dallas, Miami and New York to Cancún. Chicago and Dallas to Cozumel.

British Airways ⓦ www.ba.com. ☏ 01-866/835-4133 in Mexico. Gatwick (London) to Cancún.

Condor ⓦ www.condor.com. Frankfurt to Cancún.

Continental Airlines ⓦ www.continental.com. ☏ 01-800/523-3273 in Mexico. Cleveland, Houston and Newark (New York) to Cancún; Houston to Cozumel, Mérida, Ciudad del Carmen and Villahermosa. Merging with United at end of 2011.

Delta Air Lines ⓦ www.delta.com. ☏ 01-800/123-4710 in Mexico. Numerous US cities to Cancún; Atlanta, Detroit, Memphis and Minneapolis to Cozumel.

JetBlue ⓦ www.jetblue.com. ☏ 01-800/861-3372 in Mexico. Boston, Ft. Lauderdale, New York, Orlando and Washington to Cancún.

Lufthansa ⓦ www.lufthansa.com. ☏ 55/4738-6561 in Mexico. Frankfurt to Mexico City.

Spirit ⓦ www.spiritair.com. Detroit or Ft. Lauderdale to Cancún.

United ⓦ www.united.com. ☏ 01-800/003-0777 in Mexico. Los Angeles, San Francisco, Denver, Chicago and Washington to Cancún; Chicago to Cozumel.

US Airways ⓦ www.usair.com. ☏ 01-800/843-3000 in Mexico. Boston, Charlotte, Philadelphia and Phoenix to Cancún; Charlotte to Cozumel.

Virgin America ⓦ www.virginamerica.com. Los Angeles and San Francisco to Cancún.

Agents and operators

For culinary tours, see p.32; for cycling tours, see p.26.

Aerosaab Mexico ☏ 984/873-0804, ⓦ www.aerosaab.com. Charter flights from Cancún, Cozumel and Playa del Carmen to Chichén Itzá and Holbox.

Amerika Venture US & Canada ☏ 1-866/679-7070, ⓦ www.amerikaventure.com. French-run ecotourism operator with a fifteen-day "Ruta Maya" tour including Guatemala and Belize that costs US$2995.

Bamba Experience UK ☏ 020/8144 2949, Mexico ☏ 01-800/GO-BAMBA; ⓦ www.bambaexperience.com. Hop-on, hop-off backpackers' bus service

between Mexico City and Cancún, and elsewhere in Latin America.

Catherwood Travels ⓦ www.catherwoodtravels.com. Sister company to a group of impeccably luxurious haciendas, this custom tour company can arrange many behind-the-scenes visits – for a price.

Cathy Matos Mexican Tours UK ☏ 020/8492 0000, ⓦ www.cathymatosmexico.co.uk. A specialist in Mexico for three decades, Cathy can arrange almost any sort of Yucatán trip, favouring the unusual and the upmarket.

EcoColors US ☏ 1-866/376-5056, Canada ☏ 1-866/984-6574, Mexico ☏ 01-800/326-5677, ⓦ www.ecotravelmexico.com. Cancún-based eco-adventure group with several circuit tours.

Global Exchange US ☏ 415/255-7296, ⓦ www.globalexchange.org. "Reality Tours" to increase travellers' awareness of issues in developing countries. Trips to Chiapas to learn about indigenous rights cost US$1000.

Journey Latin America UK ☏ 020/8747 8315, ⓦ www.journeylatinamerica.co.uk. Latin America experts with a wide range of mix-and-match tours and holidays, as well as language courses in Mérida.

MayaSites Travel Services US ☏ 877/620-8715, ⓦ www.mayasites.com. Excellent operation focused on the Maya world, run by an American and two Yucatecans, all with archeology backgrounds. Special offerings include Carnaval-season tours.

MexicaChica Getaways US ☏ 214/613-9663, Mexico ☏ 999/901-5430, ⓦ www.mexicachica.com. Women-only learning vacations: culinary tours, Spanish classes and arts workshops, based in Mérida.

North South Travel UK ☏ 01245/608 291, ⓦ www.northsouthtravel.co.uk. Travel agency offering discounted fares worldwide; profits support projects in the developing world and sustainable tourism.

Trailfinders UK ☏ 0845/058 5858, Republic of Ireland ☏ 01/677 7888, Australia ☏ 1300/780 212, ⓦ www.trailfinders.com. One of the best-informed and most efficient agents for independent travellers.

Getting around

Although distances in Mexico can be huge, if you're just travelling within the Yucatán Peninsula and Chiapas, the longest slog you might face is an overnight bus between Mérida and Palenque, between seven and ten hours. Ground transport is frequent and reasonably efficient everywhere, though you might want to take an internal flight if you'll be travelling on to (or from) central Mexico.

By air

Cancún, Cozumel, Mérida, Ciudad del Carmen and Villahermosa all receive domestic flights. There's no connection between cities within the peninsula, though; all flights originate in Mexico City or elsewhere in central Mexico. Tickets are not terribly cheap, but the time saved over bus travel can make them worthwhile.

Domestic airlines

Aeromar Mexico ☏ 01-800/237-6627; ⓦ www .aeromar.us. Poza Rica or Reynosa to Villahermosa.
Aeroméxico US ☏ 01-800/237-6639, Mexico ☏ 01-800/021-4010; ⓦ www.aeromexico.com. All major cities, usually via Mexico City.
InterJet Mexico ☏ 1-800/011-2345, ⓦ www .interjet.com.mx. Mexico City to Cancún, Chetumal, Mérida, Ciudad del Carmen and Villahermosa.
Magnicharters Mexico ☏ 01-800/201-1404, ⓦ www.magnicharters.com. Mexico City to Cancún and Mérida.
Vivaaerobus.com US ☏ 1-888/935-9848, Mexico ☏ 55/4777-5050; ⓦ www.vivaaerobus.com. Mexico City to Cancún and Villahermosa; Monterrey to Cancún, Mérida and Villahermosa; Guadalajara to Mérida.
Volaris US ☏ 1-866/988-3527, Mexico ☏ 01-800/7-VOLARIS; ⓦ www.volaris.com.mx. Guadalajara to Cancún; Toluca (Mexico City) to Cancún and Mérida; Puebla to Cancún.

By bus

Long-distance **buses** (*camiones*, as distinct from city *autobuses*) are by far the most common and efficient form of transport. A multitude of companies run them, connecting even the smallest of villages. Services between major cities use comfortable and dependable vehicles; remote villages may be connected by more rattletrap conveyances.

There are **two basic classes of bus**: first (*primera*) and second (*segunda*). First-class vehicles have reserved seats, videos and air conditioning, and an increasing number of second-class lines on the most popular inter-city routes have the same comforts. One difference is in the fare, which is at least ten percent higher on first-class services. More important, though, is the number of stops – second-class buses go *intermedio*, stopping at every possible junction, while first-class *directo* services blow through tiny towns. Most people choose first class for any appreciably long distance, but don't be put off second class if the timing or location of the station seems more convenient – and it may even prove less crowded. **Air conditioning** is not necessarily a boon; there's nothing more uncomfortable than a bus with sealed windows and a broken air-conditioner, or a bus chilled to 16°C/60°F.

Deluxe buses form a separate class, running only on important inter-city routes; ADO GL and UNO are the two services in the Yucatán. Fares are around thirty percent higher than for first-class buses, but they have few if any stops, snacks and drinks on hand and air conditioning that works (be sure to keep a sweater handy, as it can get very cold); they may also be emptier. The UNO buses have more fully reclining seats with leg rests, comparable to business-class seats on airlines, as well as movies audible only through headphones (supplied in a little amenities package), which is an improvement over standard service, where blaring family flicks are the norm. Both ADO GL and UNO have computerized reservations and accept credit cards.

Most towns of any size have a modern bus station, known as the **Camionera**, or just **El ADO** ("el ah-day-oh"), as that's usually the primary company operating there. Don't let the word "central" fool you, though, as they can be located a long way from the town centre. Where there is no unified terminus you may find separate first- and second-class terminals, or individual ones for each company. In almost every bus station, there is some form of **baggage storage** office (guardería), which charges about US$0.50/£0.30 per item per hour. Before leaving anything, make sure that the place will be open when you come to collect.

To get the best seats, buy **tickets** in advance from the bus station, the central TicketBus office (when the terminal is at the edge of town) or online (www.ticketbus.com .mx). You'll rarely have any problem getting a place on a bus from its point of origin or from really big towns. In smaller, mid-route places (where buses coming through are marked *de paso*), however, you may have to wait for the bus to arrive to learn if there are any seats.

Holiday seasons, school breaks and festivals can overload services to certain destinations; the only real answer is to buy tickets in advance. However, you could also try the second-class lines, where they'll pack you in standing, or take whatever's going to the next big town along the way and try for another one departing from there.

A common alternative to scheduled buses is the shared passenger vans or taxis called **colectivos**. These serve heavily trafficked routes on short hops, such as the highway between Playa del Carmen and Tulum; they depart when full, usually from a designated spot near the main bus station. They also connect very small towns where there is a less frequent or no bus service — in these cases, they usually operate on a more fixed schedule, with departures once or twice a day. In general, they're marginally cheaper than buses, and they have all the flexibility of a second-class bus: you can be let off anywhere, and flag them down on the highway. They can be less comfortable, though, as they usually run packed to capacity.

Within smaller towns, instead of taxis, **triciclos** – pedicab tricycles – can take you where you need to go. In more modern towns, *triciclos* are giving way to motorized minicabs, similar to tuktuks or auto rickshaws. As with any taxi, agree on a fare before you hop on; at tourist-heavy destinations (Celestún, for example), it's typical for fares to be charged per person.

By car

Although most people approach the idea of driving in Mexico with some apprehension, doing so in the Yucatán can be a pleasure. The stereotypical "fine"-levying policeman is rare here; likewise, Yucatecan drivers are more courteous than most visitors expect, and roads are in good condition. Care and concentration will almost guarantee a safe trip: as long as you learn the basic road rules, obey the speed limit and stay off the roads after dark, you should not encounter any real problems.

Rental agencies

Renting a car is virtually required for seeing some sites at your own pace. Local agencies are recommended in the "Listings" section of larger cities. Among international agencies, Auto Europe (Ⓦwww.autoeurope .com) and Hertz (Ⓦwww.hertz.com) typically have the best rates, and everything is cheaper if you rent from Playa del Carmen rather than Cancún. If you use an international operation, you may be able to skip added insurance and simply use the collision coverage provided by your credit card (an option for many Americans). In this case, the rental agency will put a hold of several thousand dollars on your card, and if you are involved in an accident, you will have to pay all costs up front and file a claim upon returning home. An added risk is if you are in an accident in which someone is injured; Mexico's Napoleonic code (guilty until proven innocent) means you could be held at a police station until the situation is sorted – and only Mexico-issued insurance provides any sort of help. In a serious incident, contact your consulate and your Mexican insurance company as soon as possible.

Daily **rates** with all insurance and unlimited mileage start at around US$50/£26. If you are travelling to Xcalak or Punta Allen during or right after the rainy season, a four-wheel-drive vehicle is a good idea; anywhere else, though, it's unnecessary – fortunately, because some readers have reported hiring a jeep to be difficult. Bring thorough documentation of your reservation and confirmed rate (including insurance – or not), and any portion you've already paid, as some agencies have been known to change rates in their favour. It can also help to have the national or international customer service number at hand.

Licences from the US, Canada, Britain, Ireland, Australia and New Zealand are valid in Mexico, though an International Driving Permit (basically a translation of your licence) can be useful if your domestic one has no photo on it (contact AAA in the US, ⓦ www .aaa.org, or the equivalent auto association in your home country).

Road rules and conditions

Mexican **roads and traffic** can seem alarming at first, but ease once you know the basic courtesies. Traffic circulates on the right, and the normal speed limit is 40kph (25mph) in built-up areas, 70kph (43mph) in open country and between 90kph (56mph) and 110kph (68mph) on highways. Most important of the **road rules** is that a left-turn signal often means it's clear to overtake – slow-moving trucks simply leave their signal on, or a driver may indicate it's clear to pass by turning on his blinker. If you actually want to make a left turn (assuming there is no separate left-turn bay), put on your left-turn signal but pull into the farthest *right* lane, or the hard shoulder if possible – then turn when all lanes are clear. A driver who wants to pass will flash his headlights; you're expected to pull to the right and slow a bit. Another convention is that the first driver to flash his lights at a junction, or where only one vehicle can pass, has the right of way. Mexican drivers also use their hazard lights liberally – to signal that they are going slow, or if they are passing loose gravel, say. Don't count on clear highway signage, especially on Hwy-307 along the coast south of Cancún, where signs pointing to specific resorts don't always align with new left-turn lanes.

The new highways are excellent, and the toll (*cuota*) **superhighways**, such as the one between Cancún and Mérida, are better still, though expensive. Away from the major population centres, roads are often narrow and occasionally potholed, and cyclists weave along the nonexistent hard shoulder. Rural roads (including the free highway to Chichén Itzá) are punctuated by large **speed bumps** (*topes*) in every town or village: the most important road sign to recognize is the *tope* warning, represented as three or four humps – though they are not always marked. If not crossed at a crawl, *topes* can do serious damage to your car's undercarriage. If you have to drive at night, proceed with care and look out for wildlife, pedestrians and cyclists.

In towns, streets are often one-way, but **signage** can be poor (look for small arrows affixed to lampposts or street signs, or arrows painted on buildings). **Theft** is a small threat, so lock everything that might look enticing out of sight. **Petrol stations** (all operated by the national company Pemex) are fairly widespread, but it's always a good idea to fill up before you leave a major town. Standard unleaded is called "Magna", and all stations are full service. While 99 percent of attendants are scrupulously honest, do stay alert while your tank is being filled and when you're paying. An occasional scam is for one attendant to distract the driver with idle chatter while a second diverts some of the fuel into another container. The once-popular scam of not resetting the pump to zero is far less common now that pumps have gone digital; but some attendants will still make a point of showing you the zero setting. Tip all attendants M$5 or M$10, especially if they wash your windscreen. If you're in a remote area and need petrol, look out for hand-painted signs advertising *se vende gasolina*.

A free highway mechanic service, **Ángeles Verdes** (Green Angels), patrols major routes looking for beleaguered motorists. They can be reached by phone on ☏01-800/903-9200 or ☏078 and usually speak some English. Service is free, though of course they welcome small tips.

Hitching

It's possible **to hitch** your way around the Yucatán, but it's not the ideal strategy. Most drivers expect you to contribute to their expenses, which can rather defeat the purpose. The standard risks apply: robbery is not unheard of, and women in particular (but also men) are advised **not to hitch alone**. Learn where the driver is going before getting in, rather than stating your own destination first. Sit by a door and keep your baggage to hand in case you need to leave in a hurry (feigned carsickness is one way to get a driver to stop). That said, you'll probably come across genuine friendliness and certainly meet people you wouldn't otherwise encounter. It does help if your Spanish will stretch to a conversation.

Hitching is common among Yucatecans in the interior of the peninsula, where bus services are less frequent, and if you're driving this way, you may want to pick up people just to pass the time. Riders will typically ask how much they should pay as they get out.

Local transport

Public transport within Mexican towns and cities, usually in the form of buses, is plentiful and inexpensive, though crowded and, except in Cancún, not particularly transparent – don't expect published route maps. The main destinations of the bus are painted on the windscreen, which helps. In bigger places, **combis** offer a faster alternative, usually for the same price. These minibuses or vans run along a fixed route to set destinations; they'll pick you up and drop you off wherever you like along the way, and you pay for the distance travelled.

Regular **taxis** can also be good value, but be aware of rip-offs – meters are used only in a few taxis in Mérida; otherwise drivers apply a zone system. In the latter case, fix a price before you get in. In the big cities, rate tables of fixed prices are posted at prominent spots, such as hotel lobbies, and at the central taxi depot. At airports, a booth sells vouchers for taxis into town at a fixed price; sometimes there's an option of paying less for a shared car. You should know the name of a hotel to head for, or the driver may seize the opportunity to take you to the one that pays the biggest commission. Never accept a ride in an unofficial or unmarked taxi.

Cycling

Getting around by **bicycle** is popular with locals – small roads between villages are often crowded with creaky bikes piled high with firewood. For this reason, many drivers are more bike-aware than in other countries, but smaller roads have very narrow shoulders, or none at all, often with a sharp drop-off into a ditch. The terrain is almost completely flat, and some municipalities have added paved paths alongside main roads. ADO buses will also load bicycles on buses for a small fee.

!El Tour (⊛www.bikemexico.com) specializes in budget bike trips, running four or five each year. Its seven-day Yucatán tour is a bargain US$795. For a little more comfort, Ecocolors (p.66) runs a similar trip for US$1350. Ecoturismo Yucatán (☎999/920-2772, ⊛www.ecoyuc.com) runs daylong

---

Addresses in Mexico

An address such as Hidalgo 39 8° 120, means Hidalgo no. 39, 8th floor, room 120 (a ground-floor address is denoted PB, for *planta baja*). Abbreviations sometimes used before the street name are C (Calle, Street), Av (Avenida), Blv (Bulevar); Calzada and Paseo are other common terms; note that these are omitted in listings sections of this guide unless the street name is a number (such as C 8).

Most colonial towns have streets laid out in a numbered grid, with odd-numbered streets running east–west, and even ones north–south. The main plaza at the centre of town is usually at a point where all the numbers converge: calles 59, 60, 61 and 62 in Mérida, for example. In some places a suffix – Ote (for Oriente, East), Pte (for Poniente, West), Nte (for Norte, North), or Sur (South) – may be added to the address to tell you which side of the two central dividing streets it lies.

bike trips out of Mérida, and MexiGO Tours (☎985/856-0777, www.mexigotours.com) has an excellent Maya-village day-trip on bikes. **Within cities**, you will see some local bicycle riders, but hardly anyone cycles for leisure or as a daily commute. If you do ride, stick to smaller streets. Mérida has an admirable programme called the Bici-Ruta, which closes many downtown streets to car traffic on Sundays (see p.179).

Accommodation

Hotels in Mexico can describe themselves as *posadas*, *hostales*, *casas de huéspedes* and plain *hoteles* – terms used more or less interchangeably, though the first three are usually reserved for budget operations. Options can range from rustic sand-floor cabañas to luxurious pleasure palaces.

Travellers looking for **smaller hotels** have plenty of choice; in Cancún's zona hotelera, though, "small" means fewer than three hundred rooms. Enormous **resorts** are a dime a dozen, and if you want a week of tanning, with only occasional sightseeing, you can usually find very good package deals that may include the airfare; in this case, it can be worth spending a few days in a discount resort in Cancún, say, then striking out on your own.

Finding a room is rarely difficult – in most well-established towns, the cheap hotels are concentrated around the main plaza, with others near the bus station (or where the bus station used to be, before it moved to the outskirts). The more modern and expensive places often lie on the edge of town, accessible only by car or taxi. And in colonial towns like Mérida, Valladolid and San Cristóbal de las Casas, you'll have a hard time choosing among stylishly redone colonial bed-and-breakfasts. The only times you really need to book ahead are in coastal resorts over the peak Christmas season, at

Accommodation price codes

All hotel rooms are subject to a twelve-percent **tax**. The quoted rates at some hotels – generally those under US$40/£22 per night – include this, while most others add it on. Prices listed in this guide are in Mexican pesos, don't include tax and are typically based on **the cheapest available room for two people/one bed in high season** (January–April in all of the beach areas, plus July and August in Playa del Carmen and points south). Additional price hikes apply everywhere for the week between Christmas and New Year, and in Semana Santa, the week before Easter. For larger, chain-owned resorts and hotels, online rates can be up to half the official rate. All the accommodation listed in this book has been categorized into one of nine **price codes**, as set out below. Options in the ❶ category are rare, found only in Chiapas; ❷–❹ covers basic beach cabañas or simple rooms in small towns, while ❺–❻ is midrange, usually ensuring air conditioning and comfortable beds; anything above creeps into luxury, except on prime beaches, where it just gets your foot in the door of an average room.

❶ M$249 and under	❹ M$500–699	❼ M$1100–1499
❷ M$250–349	❺ M$700–899	❽ M$1500–1999
❸ M$350–499	❻ M$900–1099	❾ M$2000 and over

Easter, on Mexican holidays, and almost anywhere during a local fiesta.

Price is not always a reliable guide – a filthy fleapit and a well-run converted mansion may charge exactly the same. To guarantee value, see your room first. A room with one double bed (*cama matrimonial*) is almost always cheaper than a room with two singles (*doble* or *con dos camas*), and most hotels have large family rooms with several beds, which are tremendous value. In the Yucatán, virtually all budget hotel rooms also have **hammock hooks**, so you can often sling up an extra person that way. A little gentle haggling rarely goes amiss (*¿Tiene un cuarto más barato?*).

Air conditioning (*aire acondicionado* or *clima*) inflates prices and is frequently optional. An older air-conditioning unit can be noisy and inefficient – switch it on when you're first checking the room. Also check its **insect-proofing**. Cockroaches and ants are common, and there's not much anyone can do about them, but decent netting or window-screens will keep out mosquitoes and worse and allow you to sleep. Bedbugs are so far uncommon here, but do look out for signs of squashed bugs on the walls or furniture.

If you're travelling on a budget, you may want to invest in a hammock for convenience and comfort. Mattresses at low-end hotels (and some midrange places) can be quite firm, as they're set on concrete slabs. But these same hotels often have hooks for hammocks installed in the walls. See p.39 for tips on buying a hammock.

All-inclusive resorts

All-inclusives are one of the most popular lodging choices in the Yucatán, and the package deals they offer, which include lodging, all meals and gratuities, can be enticing even to travellers who ordinarily wouldn't consider them. For parents with younger children, a package provides a fuss-free programme of activities to keep kids occupied. If you're considering this option, though, don't skimp – cheaper places may seem like a bargain, but the facilities can be run down and the meals bordering on inedible. It also bears mentioning that all-inclusive resorts are perhaps the most

useless form of tourism for the Mexican economy. In Cancún, less than ten percent of tourism dollars stay in the country. These resorts are also the least likely (at least so far) to be mindful of their environmental impact.

Haciendas

These **grand manors** are one of the great treats of the Yucatán. Many ranches or henequen plantations built in the nineteenth century went to ruin, but in recent years have been restored, complete with long verandas, tile floors, lofty ceilings and lush gardens. Most are within an hour's drive of Mérida, though there are a few in Campeche state as well. *Hacienda Temozón* (see p.199), for instance, between Mérida and Uxmal, has incorporated many of the typical henequen-processing outbuildings into its layout, and hosted Vicente Fox and Bill Clinton. Even if you're not up for a US$300 room, you can enjoy the colonial ambience of other sprawling places for less than US$100 per night – try *Hacienda Yaxcopoil* (see p.198), south of Mérida. In addition to the haciendas mentioned in this book, visit ⓦwww.yucatantoday.com (search for "Hacienda Hotels").

Eco-resorts

A growing trend on the Yucatán Peninsula is the **eco-resort**. But "eco-" is a freely used prefix, often just meaning the setting is relatively rural. And often hotels will tout their solar panels and wind turbines not because they've chosen this option but because they don't have access to the electric grid – as at most of the beach places in Tulum. A truly environmentally sound hotel will also have a wastewater treatment system, a composting procedure and a building plan that minimizes impact on plant and animal life – as well as an economic and social relationship with the surrounding native culture. *Genesis Retreat* near the ruins of Ek-Balam north of Valladolid (see p.159) is an excellent example, as is *Boca Paila Camps* in the Sian Ka'an Reserve (p.122). It's not necessarily less expensive to run a hotel using wind and solar power; "eco" isn't synonymous with "bargain". Visit the International Ecotourism Society at ⓦwww.ecotourism.org for the full list of guidelines, as well as recommended tour operators and lodges.

Campsites, hammocks and cabañas

Camping is technically possible on beaches that are not protected natural areas – but limited access along the Caribbean make this practically quite difficult. There are few organized campsites, though you can still find a few beach hideaways in Tulum, and *Los Pinos* (see p.86) in Punta Bete, and several ecotourism groups offer camping (often with tent included) – see Cenote Yokdzonot (p.167) and Manglares de Dzinitún (p.193), as well as *El Panchán* in Palenque (p.249). If you have a van or RV, *Acamaya Reef Park* (p.81) and *Paamul* (p.108) have good facilities.

Cabañas, are found at the more rustic, backpacker-oriented beach resorts (Mahahual and a dwindling number in Tulum) and sometimes inland. Usually just wood-pole walls with a **palapa** (palm-frond) roof, the shacks have a cot or hammock. They are frequently without electricity, though as a beach becomes more popular, they tend to transform into sturdier beach bungalows with modern conveniences and higher prices.

Youth hostels

There are six Hostelling International hostels (Ⓦ www.hostellingmexico.com) in the Yucatán and Chiapas, and a number of unaffiliated ones maintain excellent standards. You typically pay around US$10/£7 per person for single-sex or shared dorm facilities.

Eating and drinking

Whatever your preconceptions about Mexican food, they will almost certainly be proved wrong. The cuisine bears little resemblance to what's served in "Mexican" restaurants in other parts of the world. Some dishes are spicy (picante), but on the whole you add your own seasoning from bowls of chile sauce on the table. For a menu glossary, see p.302.

Where to eat

Basic meals are served at **restaurantes**, but you can get breakfast, snacks and often full meals at **cafés**, too, and plenty of **takeout** and **fast-food** places serve sandwiches, tortas (sandwiches on fluffy rolls) and tacos. **Jugerías** are devoted to juices and fruit salads, and every city **market** (*mercado*) has hot-food vendors, too.

Anywhere you dine, even in the fanciest places, you shouldn't feel obliged to order any more than you're hungry for; wasting food is frowned upon. If you do get too much, it's acceptable to have your leftovers wrapped up to go (*para llevar*).

What to eat

The Yucatecan diet is essentially one of corn and its products, supplemented by beans and chiles. There are at least a hundred different types of **chile**. Each has a distinct flavour, and by no means are all hot (which is why we don't use the British term "chilli"), although the most common, *chile habañero*, small and either green or orange (similar to Jamaica's Scotch bonnets), is deadly when eaten straight. Chile is also the basic ingredient in more complex sauces, notably *mole*, a blend of spices that could be called Mexico's version of curry, traditionally served with turkey or chicken. *Mole* isn't native to the Yucatán, though rich *mole poblano*, which involves bitter chocolate, is common. Another novel use of chiles is *chiles en nogada*, in which *poblano* peppers are stuffed with a fruit-laced meat ragout, then covered in creamy walnut sauce and garnished with pomegranate seeds. The colours reflect the Mexican flag, and it's served especially in August and September during the build-up to Independence Day.

Pinto or black **beans** (*frijoles*) usually accompany every dish and are frequently served *refritos*, which means not "refried", but "really fried". **Corn** (*maíz*), in some form or another, also features in virtually everything. Boiled or roasted on the cob, slathered with mayonnaise, crumbly *cotija* cheese, chile-salt and lime, it is known as *elote* (a cupful of kernels is sold as *esquites*). Chewy, puffed, hulled kernels (*pozole*) are put in meaty soups and stews. Most commonly, though, corn is treated with lye and ground into *masa*, then formed into tortillas: flat maize pancakes served in stacks to accompany your meal. Wheat flour ones (*tortillas de harina*) are a sign of a restaurant that's either authentically northern Mexican, or pretentious and expensive, or simply bad.

Masa forms the basis of a category of Mexican dishes called *antojitos*, eaten as snacks or for light dinners or breakfasts. Simplest of these are tacos – soft tortillas filled with anything from grilled beef to the red pork-and-pineapple combo called *al pastor*. **Enchiladas** are rolled, filled tortillas covered in chile sauce and baked; enchiladas *suizas* are the mildest, with chicken and cheese and topped with a green tomatillo sauce. Tortillas torn up and topped with meat or egg and mild salsa are called *chilaquiles*, common at breakfast. *Huaraches*, so named because they resemble sandals, are thick ovals of *masa* lightly fried on a griddle and topped with vegetables or meats and cheese.

Masa is also the basis of **tamales**, cornmeal pudding stuffed, flavoured and cooked in banana leaves. They can be either savoury, with shredded pork, or sweet when made with something like coconut and raisins. Steamed tamales (*colados*) are soft, whereas oven-baked ones (*horneados* or *rostados*) have a chewy, crunchy shell.

Northern Yucatán is cattle country, and the **meat** is delicious as long as you're not craving a melt-in-your-mouth slab of steak. Typical cuts like skirt steak (*arrachera*) are sliced thin, grilled to medium and garnished with grilled onions. (For thick steaks, head to an Argentine restaurant.) Pork is ubiquitous, usually shredded and used in small portions as flavouring; turkey is also very common. **Eggs** feature on every menu, in the classic Mexican combinations of *huevos rancheros* (fried eggs on a tortilla with red salsa) or *huevos a la mexicana* (scrambled with onion, tomato and chile), as well as the Yucatán-specific *huevos motuleños,* fried eggs on a tortilla with beans, mild tomato salsa, ham, cheese, peas and fried banana slices.

In coastal towns, you'll enjoy wonderfully fresh **fish**, shrimp and conch (*caracol*), simply grilled, fried with garlic (*en mojo de ajo*) or in **ceviche** – doused in lime and left to "cook" in the acidic juice with tomato, onion and plenty of coriander. A *cocktél* is seafood served in a cocktail glass with lime juice, ketchup and chopped onion and chile, usually with a side dish of Saltines. And shrimp tacos – lightly battered shrimp seasoned with mayo and chunky *pico de gallo* salsa – are an inexpensive treat. The season for rock lobster (*langosta*) on the Caribbean coast is only September to the end of February – outside that time, it's a frozen and imported product. Spring is the best time for fat, succulent pink shrimp.

Yucatecan specialities

Head inland for more typical **Yucatecan dishes** – see the "Yucatecan food" insert for descriptions of some of the most famous. Look especially for *pollo* or *cochinita pibil*, chicken or suckling pig wrapped in banana leaves and cooked in a *pib* (a pit in the ground), and anything *en relleno negro*, a black, burnt-chile sauce. Valladolid has its own specialities, including *longaniza*, a bright-red smoked sausage. In Campeche, *pan de cazón*, a casserole of tortillas and shredded shark meat, and shrimp fried in a coconut batter, are common.

The archetypal Yucatecan treat is the **salbute**, an *antojito* made of a crispy corn tortilla topped with shredded turkey, bright-pink pickled onions, avocado and radish slices and occasionally a salty tomato sauce. *Panuchos* are nearly identical but for an added dab of refried beans slipped inside the fried tortilla.

Vegetarian food

Vegetarians can eat well in the Yucatán, although it takes caution. Most restaurants serve vegetable soups and rice, and items like quesadillas, *chiles rellenos* and even tacos and enchiladas often come with non-meat fillings, such as cactus leaves (*nopal*), squash blossoms *(flor de calabaza)* and *huitlacoche*, a fungus that grows on corn – it even tastes a bit like bacon. *Queso fundido*, simply melted cheese, is served with tortillas and salsa, and a side of *rajas* (grilled strips of *poblano* peppers). Another boon is the leafy green *chaya* worked into many traditional dishes.

Vegetarianism, though growing, is not particularly common, and a simple cheese and chile dish may have some meat added to "improve" it. Additionally, the fat used for frying is often lard.

Meals

Mexicans eat a light breakfast early, a snack of tacos or eggs in mid-morning, lunch (the main meal of the day) around two o'clock or later and a light supper.

Breakfast (*desayuno*) in Mexico can consist simply of coffee and *pan dulce* – pastries often served in a basket (*canasta*); you pay for as many as you eat. More substantial breakfasts consist of eggs, and at fruit juice places you can have a simple *licuado*. You can eat a full meal in a restaurant at any time of day, but you'll eat better by adopting the local habit of taking your main meal at **lunchtime**, when a **comida corrida** or **comida corriente** (set meal, varied daily) is served, from around 1pm to 5pm. In more expensive places the same thing may be known as the *menú del día* or *menú turístico*. You get a soup, a main dish with a side of beans and a drink or dessert for US$5/£3 or less. The *comida* can include home-made soups, stews, local specialities, puddings and elusive vegetables. You'll find these set lunches at regular restaurants with broader menus, but also at *cocinas económicas*, open only for the midday meal. Usually managed by local women, they're often the best places to sample home-cooked food.

Drinking

Soft drinks (*refrescos*) – including Coke, Pepsi and Mexican brands such as apple-flavoured Sidral and the bubblegum-like Pino Negro, made in Mérida – are on sale everywhere. **Fruit juices** (*jugos*) are sold at shops and stalls known as *jugerías* or *licuaderías*. Orange (*naranja*) and carrot (*zanahoria*) are staples, and seasonal tropical fruits (such as spiky pink dragonfruit, *pitahaya*) are a treat. Combinations get complex and the names colourful: *el vampiro* involves beetroot juice, and *el viagra* combines everything in the shop. Juices mixed with water, for a lighter drink, are called *aguas frescas*, and this includes ubiquitous *limonada* (fresh limeade), *horchata* (rice milk with cinnamon), *jamaica* (hibiscus, or sorrel) and *tamarindo* (tamarind). *Licuados* are fruit blended with water (*con agua*) or milk (*con leche*). A banana-milk *licuado* with generous dashes of vanilla and cinnamon is a popular breakfast drink. Juice shops often double as ice-cream parlours (*neverías* or *paleterías*); La Flor de Michoacan is a chain with an impressive selection of refreshing cold drinks and ice pops.

Mexico grows coffee, but in most of the Yucatán it is served as weak *café americano* or *café de olla* (brewed in a clay pot, usually with cinnamon), and instant Nescafé is not uncommon, though it is growing rarer as espresso and Starbucks creep in. As for **tea** (*té*), typically it's some herb like *manzanillo* (camomile) or *yerbabuena* (mint), but basic *té negro* is available.

Alcohol

Though you can get all of the national brands, the standard **beers** in the Yucatán are the light pilsner Sol, amber León and Montejo, available in light (*clara*) and dark (*oscura*) brews. Look also for fuller-bodied (and more expensive) brews like Bohemia and Negra Modelo. A popular beer drink is the *michelada*, in which beer is poured into a salt-rimmed glass with ice, lime juice, hot sauce and Worcestershire sauce; a *chelada* is just the lime, ice and salt. When ordering, say what type of beer you'd like it with: a *michelada de Sol*, for example.

You'll normally be drinking in bars, but if you don't feel comfortable – this applies in particular to women (for more on which, see p.48) – you can also get takeaways from most shops, supermarkets and, cheapest of all, *agencias*, single-brand distributors. You pay a **deposit of about thirty to forty percent** of the purchase price: keep your receipt and return your bottles to the same store.

Mexican **wine** (*vino* – *tinto* is red, *blanco* is white) is improving. LA Cetto, in Baja California, is the largest producer, and its chardonnay is reasonably good; also look for smaller producers like Monte Xanic, Adobe Guadalupe and Liceaga (especially its merlot). In general, though, wine is expensive, poorly chosen and not very well cared-for.

Tequila, distilled from the cactus-like agave plant and produced in the state of Jalisco, is the most famous of Mexican spirits, served straight with lime and salt on the side. Lick the salt and bite into the lime, then take a swig of tequila (or the other way round). Silver (*plata*) is clear, young tequila, while *reposado* is somewhat aged, with a faint woody taste from their casks. Meant for sipping, *añejo* is aged longer; some approach Scotch in their smoky complexity. You can find inexpensive good bottles in the grocery store – Cazadores *reposado*, for instance, is smooth and a little sweet, with a slightly lower alcohol content than others.

Mescal (often spelled *mezcal*) is also made from agave; it's less refined and has a smoky flavour. The spurious belief that the worm in the mescal bottle is hallucinogenic is based on confusion between the drink and the peyote cactus, also called mescal; by the time you've got down as far as the worm, you wouldn't notice hallucinations

anyway. For other spirits, ask for *nacional* (locally produced) varieties for a bargain (and perhaps a bigger headache). **Rum** (*ron*), **gin** (*ginebra*) and **vodka** are made in Mexico, as are some very palatable **brandies** (*brandy* or *coñac* – try San Marcos or Presidente).

Whatever you order, if you do it in a more traditional bar or restaurant, you'll be served **botanas**, complimentary small dishes of snacks, which can be anything from a spicy ground-pumpkin-seed dip (*sikilp'aak*) to morsels of fried fish, or Lebanese ground-meat fritters (*kibi*) or hummus.

Traditional **cantinas** are for serious and excessive drinking; more often than not, there's a sign above the door prohibiting entry to "women, members of the armed forces and anyone in uniform". You can enjoy a lighter, mixed atmosphere at numerous modern bars.

Cooking classes and culinary tours

Los Dos cooking school (ⓦwww.los-dos .com) in Mérida offers daylong "Taste of Yucatan" classes for US$125, which includes a market tour. The chef, David Sterling, is an expert in regional Yucatecan food; he also leads street-food tours and multi-day trips to local artisanal producers. On the coast, **The Little Mexican Cooking School** (ⓦwww.thelittlemexican cookingschool.com) in Puerto Morelos does fun classes (US$110) with a personable chef who covers a range of Mexican cuisine, culminating in a big lunch; it also offers a weeklong package that includes accommodation.

The media

The majority of international coverage does not extend beyond Latin America. Papers can be lurid scandal sheets, brimming with violent crimes depicted in full colour, or have independent, solid reporting.

Probably the best **national paper** is *Reforma*, which has an excellent reputation for its independence and political objectivity. *La Jornada* is unabashedly left-wing. Subjects such as human rights, corruption and drug trafficking are increasingly tackled, but journalists face great danger if they speak out, not only from shady government groups but also from the drug traffickers. The worst incidents have been confined to northern Mexico. Yucatán and its press remains untouched by *narcotraficante* intrigue, and it supports several wide-ranging newspapers, from the conservative, long-established *El Diario* to the more liberal tabloids like *Por Esto*. In Cancún and along the coast, you can pick up the English-language *Cancun Today*, an insert in *USA Today*, but it's almost completely vacuous.

On Mexican **TV** you can watch any number of US shows dubbed into Spanish, but the most popular programmes are the *telenovelas*. These soap operas, produced in Mexico and elsewhere in Latin America, dominate the screens from 6pm to 10pm and pull in audiences of millions. Cable and satellite are now widespread, and even quite downmarket hotels offer numerous channels.

No **radio stations** in the Yucatán and Chiapas have regular English-language programmes. In Chiapas, though, you can tune in to the EZLN's broadcast, Radio Insurgente (Ⓦ www.radioinsurgente.org); the frequency depends on the area. The Universidad Autonoma de Yucatán broadcasts at 92.9 FM from Mérida, with a heavy rotation of classic *trova*.

Festivals

Stumbling onto some Yucatecan village fiesta may prove the highlight of your travels. Usually these are on the local saint's day, but many have pre-Christian origins. The most famous, spectacular or curious fiestas are listed on p.34.

The Maya of the Yucatán and Chiapas are not known for ceremonial **dancing** or the use of masks, so common in central Mexico. Instead, festive occasions are marked by dances that merge traditional Maya dress with Spanish or other folkloric forms and rhythms. A variation on the maypole dance, for instance, is common at rural fiestas. The most common is the *jarana*, featuring a complex and boisterous rhythm produced by a band of clarinets, a contra-bass and several brass instruments. Participants go all-out in their most festive *huipiles* and guayaberas and their best gold jewellery – and you might even see one of them bearing a roasted pig's head on a platter on his head.

Carnaval, the exuberant week before Lent, in February or early March, is celebrated with costumes, parades, eating and dancing, most spectacularly in Cozumel, Mérida, Campeche and Villahermosa, and works its way up to a climax on Shrove Tuesday. Cancún's festivities attract big-name bands, some of which don't even hit the stage until 5am. But smaller towns often have to wait well into Lent to celebrate because the travelling carnival rides have to make their way from bigger markets.

The country's biggest holiday is **Semana Santa** – Holy Week – beginning on Palm Sunday and continuing until Easter. Still a deeply religious festival in Mexico, it celebrates the resurrection of Christ, and has also become a veneration of the Virgin. In Mérida and the towns of Acanceh and Maní to the south, you can see rather vigorous and elaborate Passion plays (see opposite) that involve hundreds of people. Many businesses close for the whole week, and certainly from Thursday to Monday.

Independence Day (Sept 16) marks the historic day in 1810 when Manuel Hidalgo y Costilla issued *El Grito* (The Cry of Independence) from his parish church in Dolores Hidalgo. It's marked at midnight on September 15 with a Mass and an impassioned recitation of the *grito* (ending with "¡Viva México!") in the town plaza, followed by fireworks, music, dancing and parades.

Fall in the Yucatán is also the season for **gremios**. These are processions and dancing organized by each trade or social group (taxi drivers, plumbers, etc). Each group pays its respects at the local church, then parades through town with fireworks and a small band. If you follow the procession, you'll probably wind up at a big party that lasts until the wee hours. The biggest processions are in Mérida, but you'll see them in every small town from late September to October. In general, the fall is also when many villages have their town fiestas, marked with **bullfights** (*corridas*) in a bullring complete with stadium seats built entirely of sapling poles. Even if you're leery of the "fight" itself (only one bull is actually killed), these small-town events are boisterous fun, with every man who can muster a matador's costume (or a bizarre drag outfit) allowed to compete, and much drink consumed to bolster courage.

The Day of the Dead (**Día de los Muertos**, or **Hanal Pixan** in Maya) is when offerings are made to ancestors' souls, frequently with picnics and vigils at their graves. The festivities are not quite so gothic in the Yucatán, but homes and public squares are decorated with greenery-bedecked altars where candles, flowers and traditional foods honour departed relatives and local heroes. These usually go up on October 29 or 30, in preparation for a sunset dinner on October 31 in honour of children who have died; the next day, children's souls depart and adult spirits arrive, and their favourite foods are served until November 2. In Mérida, there's a lively street parade on October 31 that fuses central Mexican skeleton costumes with local traditions.

Christmas is a major holiday, and a time when people are on the move and transport is booked solid. Gringo influence is heavy nowadays, and after November 20 (the anniversary of the Mexican Revolution, commemorated with parades of children dressed as Pancho Villa) shop windows and storefronts are crammed with Santa Claus, fake Christmas trees and other Yankee trappings. But the Mexican festival remains distinct in many ways, with a much stronger religious element. It begins around December 16, when people set up Nativity scenes in their homes and perform Las Posadas, re-enactments of the Holy Family's search for lodgings, in town plazas. **New Year's Eve** is still largely an occasion to spend with family, with the actual hour celebrated by eating grapes, one for each strike of the clock.

A festival calendar

For events in smaller villages, ask at the Yucatán state tourism office in Mérida, which maintains a full list, or check the weekly events listings at ⓦwww.yucatanliving.com, which often mention nearby fiestas.

January

Fiesta de los Tres Reyes (Jan 1–6). In the cow town of Tizimín (Yucatán), a gathering involving lots of steak.

February

Día de la Candelaria (Feb 2). Candlemas: candlelight processions at Tecoh and Kantunil (Yucatán) and Ocosingo (Chiapas). The week prior is a fiesta in Valladolid (Yucatán).

March

Equinox (March 21). Huge gathering for the serpent shadow at Chichén Itzá.

April

Semana Santa (Holy Week, beginning Palm Sunday, variable March–April). Passion plays in Mérida, Acanceh and Maní.
Feria (second half of April). State fair in Villahermosa, with the crowning of La Flor Tabasco, the state beauty queen.
Fiestas de Santa Cruz (end of April). Two-week fair in El Cedral on Cozumel, ending on or near May 3.

May

Fiesta de la Cruz Parlante (May 12–18). Chancah Veracruz (Quintana Roo), near Felipe Carrillo Puerto, celebrates the Talking Cross of the Caste Wars.
Feria del Jipi (May 20). In Becal (Campeche), celebration of the Panama hat.
Torneo de Pesca (last weekend in May). Fishing tournament and party in Puerto Morelos.

June

Día de la Chispa (June 4). In Valladolid (Yucatán), re-enactment of the battle that sparked the 1910 Revolution.
Fiesta de San Pedro y San Pablo (June 26–30). On Cozumel and in Panaba (Yucatán), north of Tizimín.

July

Fiesta de Nuestra Señora del Carmen (July 15–30). Parties in Ciudad del Carmen and Motul (Yucatán).

Día de San Cristóbal (July 17). A week of festivities in San Cristóbal de las Casas.
Chac ceremony (dates variable). In Edzná (Yucatán), to encourage the spring rains.

August

Feria (Aug 10–16). Town celebration in Oxcutzcab (Yucatán).

September

Feria de San Roman (Sept 14–30). Campeche's city festival.
Equinox (Sept 21). Another serpent spectacle at Chichén Itzá (see March).
Día de San Miguel (Sept 29). A major festival in the main town on Cozumel.

October

El Cristo de Sitilpech (Oct 18–28). The miraculous Black Christ is paraded from Sitilpech (Yucatán) to neighbouring Izamal, where there's ten days of celebration.

November

Feria del Estado de Yucatán (first three weeks of Nov). Thrill rides, agricultural exhibits and fried foods at fairgrounds south of Mérida.
Feria de Motul (Nov 4–11). Festival in Motul (Yucatán) with bullfights.

December

Día de la Inmaculada Concepcíon (Dec 8). Widely celebrated, but especially in Izamal, where crowds gather to sing the entire night before.
Día de la Virgen de Guadalupe (Dec 12). Celebrated everywhere; roads are filled in the days prior with church groups running relays.
Christmas Fiesta (Dec 25–Jan 6). In Temax (Yucatán), featuring the procession of Las Pastorelas, in which images of the Holy Family are carried from house to house.

Sport and outdoor activities

The Yucatán is an active traveller's paradise, with scuba diving and snorkelling in reefs and caves as well as sailing and horseback riding. If you're just up for an afternoon's amble to appreciate the wildlife, you can do that, too.

Sport **fishing** is exceptionally good around Cancún and Cozumel and in Punta Allen, on the flat bays of the Sian Ka'an Biosphere Reserve; there's also good fishing on the Gulf coast. Isla Mujeres is a popular **yachting** port, as well as the finish line for the biennial Regatta del Sol (mid-May, even-number years) that begins in Pensacola, Florida. The peninsula is also becoming something of a centre for **kiteboarding**, with dedicated enthusiasts in Playa del Carmen and Tulum.

Although sand stirred up by hurricanes has had some impact on the Mesoamerican Barrier Reef that runs along the Caribbean coast, Cozumel remains a top **scuba-diving** destination, and Banco Chinchorro, off the coast from Mahahual, is a goal for wreck divers. The reef near Puerto Morelos is vibrant, but less visited. Cancún is not known for diving, though some spots are excellent for novices, with sandy floors, little current, easy access and plenty to see. Along the Gulf coast, the water is not nearly as clear. Certification courses are offered in every beach town, at scores of dive shops. Be clear and honest about your diving skills and experience; a respectable dive master should not push you to a more advanced dive. It helps if you can find a group of divers of roughly the same level and approach a shop together. Some old hands dive only with guides who have families, a good indicator that your leaders won't be taking unnecessary risks.

Cozumel has good wade-in **snorkelling**, and boat trips visit more remote coral gardens and walls; Puerto Morelos is also a good destination, though you must go with a guide. The trip from Isla Mujeres to Isla Contoy takes in several less-visited reefs, or you can take a much shorter trip just off the coast of Mujeres. And for the unforgettable experience of snorkelling with whale sharks, take a trip from Isla Holbox or Isla Mujeres between June and September.

The Yucatán also offers the unique experience of diving in freshwater sinkholes called **cenotes**, part of a vast network of underground rivers, caves and caverns that riddle the limestone bedrock of the peninsula. The spring water is pristine, and the elaborate rock formations otherworldly. Although many dive shops offer cenote diving packages, not all have the experience to back it up, and most cave-diving accidents have been the fault of guides who took the sport too lightly. Nonetheless, cavern diving (in which you explore a partially open space, with the entrance in clear view) requires only open-water certification; to go deeper into passageways and closed caves, you'll need excellent buoyancy control and further certification. **Anyone may snorkel** at a number of cenotes, where the proprietors often rent gear as well. An underwater torch can be a big help. Spelunkers can also explore quite a few **dry caves**.

Hiking and kayaking

The utterly flat Yucatán Peninsula doesn't yield interesting **hiking** or trekking, but you can take day-long or multi-day treks to remote areas in hillier Chiapas and around Calakmul. It helps to have a little Spanish, as the tours are geared to Mexicans, but the thrill of chancing upon unexcavated ruins in the midst of the jungle, or getting a behind-the-scenes look at closed sites, is unparalleled. Between November and February, Servidores Turísticos de Calakmul (☎983/871-6064, ⓦwww .ecoturismocalakmul.com) organizes **hiking trips** in the Calakmul Biosphere Reserve taking in the ruins of La Muñeca, which you can reach only on foot. Near Yaxchilán in

Reef behaviour

Coral reefs are among the richest and most complex ecosystems on earth, but they are also very fragile. The colonies grow at a rate of only around 5cm per year, so they must be treated with care and respect if they are not to be damaged beyond repair. Remember to follow these **simple rules** while you are snorkelling, diving or in a boat.

* **Never** touch or stand on corals, as the living polyps on their surface are easily damaged.
* **Avoid** disturbing the sand around corals. Apart from spoiling visibility, the cloud of sand will settle over the corals and smother them.
* **Don't** remove shells, sponges or other creatures from the reef, and avoid buying reef products from souvenir shops.
* **Don't** use suntan lotion in reef areas, as the oils are pollutants and will stifle coral growth; look for special biodegradable sunscreen for use while snorkelling.
* **Don't** anchor boats on the reef. Use the permanently secured buoys instead.
* **Don't** throw litter overboard.
* **Check** ahead of time where you are allowed to go fishing.
* **Review** your diving skills away from the reef first if you are an out-of-practice diver.

Chiapas, Siyaj Chan (☎502/5047-5908, in Guatemala; ⊛www.siyajchan.blogspot .com) leads six-hour hikes to Gruta Tzolkin, a cave deep in the forest.

In the flatlands, the scrub forest and jungle are filled with dazzling birds and other wildlife. The few trails where you can hike without a guide are mentioned in the relevant sections of the book, and will occupy only an hour or so. You're better off with a guide who can identify local flora and fauna. **Birdwatchers** will benefit from a tour with Mérida-based Ecoturismo Yucatán (☎999/920-2772, ⊛www.ecoyuc .com), which also organizes the annual Yucatán Bird Festival. Ecocolors (p.66), based in Cancún, also offers multi-day camping trips with naturalist guides and kayaking trips in the Sian Ka'an Biosphere Reserve. At less-visited Laguna Bacalar, Active Nature (⊛www.activenaturebacalar .com) runs four-day trips in kayaks down the Río Hondo to where manatees breed.

Spectator sports

Mexico's chief spectator sport is **soccer** (*fútbol*), and although there are no mega-stadiums in the Yucatán, going to a game can be a thrilling experience. Cancún got its first major team, the Atlante, in 2007 (moved from Mexico City); they play in a 20,000-seat stadium. The Mérida team goes by the wholesome nickname of Los Venados (the Deer). **Baseball** (*béisbol*) is also popular, with the minor-league Tigres playing in Cancún; the Piratas in Campeche; and the Leones de Yucatán in Mérida. Almost every town has one or two baseball fields where you can while away a summer night. The atmosphere at these is casual, and entrance fees are nominal or nonexistent.

Masked **wrestling** (*lucha libre*) is popular in the Yucatán, though not quite a major commercial enterprise here in the same way it is in central Mexico. Nonetheless, local matches can incite great passion – keep an eye out for flyers.

Culture and etiquette

Mexicans are generally very courteous, and in some ways rather formal. It is common, for example, to address people as *señor* or *señora*, and being too brusque can give a bad impression. Yucatecans use the formal *usted* address frequently, pepper their speech with such niceties as *para servirle* (at your service), and ask *¿Mande?* (rather than the more abrupt *¿Qué?*).

They typically dress as sharply as their income allows: no scruffy jeans, and men almost never wear shorts, while women prefer skirts or dresses. Formality, however, does not by any means equal coldness. Strangers may stand a bit closer than you're used to, and touch your arm while chatting.

Family, home and faith

Extended families often go everywhere together – on vacation, to restaurants – and celebrations involve every generation. Don't be surprised if a social invitation from a local turns into a trip back to the house to meet the entire family. Solo travellers in particular are seen as a little sad and lonely, so you might get some sympathy hospitality as a result. If you are invited to someone's house, bring a small gift such as sweets or flowers (though never marigolds – these are associated with the Day of the Dead). But more important, expect a lot of food that simply should not be refused. (Leaving a bit of food on your plate can help stop the flow – nature abhors a vacuum, as do Mexican hosts.) But when in doubt, the polite answer is "Yes, thank you".

Mexico is majority Roman Catholic, with a small evangelical minority. Religion is as much a matter of faith as a social norm that dictates everything from conservative behaviour between the sexes (you'll see young couples canoodling in parks at twilight, but that's usually as far as things go until marriage) to habits such as making the sign of the cross when passing a church. For your part, it is simply polite to avoid open criticism of religion unless you're sure of your company; also keep shoulders and knees covered when touring churches (though this isn't always followed by locals).

Catholicism in Mexico is not nearly as rigid as it appears, and major issues are under constant debate. Divorce laws vary by state, but it's fully legal and though certainly not a cause for celebration, it's more accepted than it used to be. In 2007, Mexico City legalized early-term abortion within its bounds; elsewhere in the country, the procedure is still available only to rape victims and women whose health is endangered by the pregnancy. Contraception is available in pharmacies, and condoms are openly encouraged for the sake of public health.

Time and appointments

Jaded expats often comment on the phenomenon of "Mexican time", and there is some truth to the fact that things move more slowly in the tropical heat. Punctuality is rarely a priority. Mexicans will say they are doing something *ahorita* – right now – but may not get to it for another hour. This can seem infuriating if you are processing paperwork or building a house, but fortunately travellers are unlikely to be doing these things. In fact, the relaxed attitude towards time can be a bit of a relief if you let yourself get into it. Don't get too slack, though: events usually start promptly, and business appointments run on schedule – though you may severely surprise someone if you show up at their home at the precise time invited. Just try not to make plans that rely on, say, dropping off the rental car as soon as the office opens.

Due to general courtesy rules, making social appointments can lead to misunderstandings. Mexicans find it impolite to say no, so that if you extend an invitation, you will almost certainly get a positive response – but that is no guarantee the person will turn up. If this seems *not* polite to you, remember that it can work in your favour as well. This is especially handy for women, who can smile sweetly and accept a date, then make a graceful exit.

Tipping

The *propina* (tip) is a standard part of Mexican culture. Ten percent is standard at restaurants – Mexicans usually leave any loose change – though fifteen percent is more common in American-oriented areas like Cancún. Always take a look at your bill first – service (*servicio*, usually ten percent, but sometimes fifteen) is sometimes included, especially at more formal places. In this case you're not expected to leave anything additional, though of course it's appreciated. In luxury **hotels**, tip as you would anywhere – M$10 or M$15 per bag to bellhops, M$10 or M$20 to parking attendants, plus M$20 or M$30 per day in the room. Staff at smaller, Mexican-run hotels don't generally expect tips, unless the clientele is largely foreign. Tips are also the norm at **petrol stations** – M$5 or M$10 to the attendant who pumps the fuel, as well as to the one who washes your windshield. **Restrooms** are usually staffed, and an M$5 tip is standard here – sometimes a sign is posted, sometimes not, and the attendant may or may not have a cup or towel laid out to collect change. One exception to tipping is **taxi drivers**, where only the flat fare is expected. If the driver helps with your bags, though, add another M$10 or M$20.

Smoking

A nationwide smoking ban in restaurants and public spaces went into effect in 2008, and seems to be largely adhered to – public smoking was rare in the Yucatán anyway.

Shopping

The craft tradition of Mexico, much of it from arts practised long before the Spanish arrived, is strong in the Yucatán. Regional and highly localized specialities survive, with villages boasting of their reputations for particular skills.

To buy **crafts**, there is no need these days to visit the place of origin; shops in all the big resorts gather the best and most popular items from around Mexico. On the other hand, it's more enjoyable to see where the articles come from, and the only way to get any real bargains. The good stuff is rarely cheap wherever you buy it, however.

In Mérida and Campeche, there are government-backed shops with very good quality wares and set prices; visit them at least to get an idea of what is available and at what price. Izamal and Valladolid both foster excellent crafts cultures; in Izamal, you can visit artists' workshops, and Valladolid is a centre for embroidery and tyre-tread-soled *huaraches* (sandals).

Good buys specific to the Yucatán include men's dapper, Cuban-style **guayabera shirts** and Panama hats (known here as *jipis*). Throughout the peninsula and Chiapas, Maya women wear flower-bedecked embroidered **huipiles**; the selection in Valladolid is especially vast. Silver **jewellery** (genuine sterling should be stamped ".925"), either made into fine filigree (Izamal has a good workshop) or set with colourful semiprecious stones, rich amber or milky Mexican opals, can be elegant and inexpensive.

The most popular souvenir of the Yucatán is a **hammock**, and Mérida is probably the best place to buy a respectable, inexpensive one (most are made in the nearby town of Tixkokob). Connoisseurs may appreciate double-weave ones made in Izamal and in prisons (sold on the highway outside Campeche and Valladolid). Don't buy from street vendors or market stalls until you've seen what a high-quality hammock really looks like (and what it costs). Junky, touristy ones have thicker strings woven loosely, so they're uncomfortable and don't hold their shape. Comfort is measured by the tightness of the weave and the breadth. Because you're supposed to lie in a hammock diagonally, to be relatively flat, the distance it stretches sideways is far more crucial than the length (although obviously the woven portion of the hammock, excluding the strings at each end, should be at least as long as you are tall). A good way to judge quality is by weight: a decent-size hammock (*doble* at least, preferably *matrimonial*) with cotton threads (*hilos de algodon*) will weigh more than a kilo and set you back about US$25/£13. Nylon (*nylon*) hammocks are sturdier and good for prolonged outdoor use, but they are not as cool to the skin as cotton. Street vendors often tout "traditional" sisal hammocks, but these are usually a sisal-cotton blend and don't merit the price markup. (Pure sisal hammocks are very rare, and rough on the skin besides.)

It is illegal to buy or sell antiquities, and even more criminal to try taking them out of the country. The town of Ticul specializes in reproductions (and in cheap and flashy shoes, should you be interested).

Markets

There's a **mercado** (market) in every Yucatecan town. *Mercados* are mainly dedicated to food and everyday necessities, but most have a section for crafts, or even a full separate crafts bazaar. You can also find a lot of fun smaller gift items and local foodstuffs, such as **coffee** (in Chiapas), inexpensive but fragrant **vanilla** and Yucatecan **honey.**

Crafts areas of markets are also about the only sphere in which **bargaining** is acceptable, and even then, it is a gentle process – nothing like a Middle Eastern bazaar, say. The standard tricks (never show the least sign of interest, let alone enthusiasm; walking away will always cut the price dramatically) hold true, and politeness helps a lot. Most important is to know what you want, its approximate value and how much you are prepared to pay. Never start negotiating for something you don't intend to buy. But overall don't let a quibble over a few dollars stop you from buying, and resist the urge to compare prices with fellow shoppers – ten pesos almost certainly means more to the seller than to you, and the best price is the one both you and the seller are happy with.

Travelling with children

Most Mexicans dote on children, and youngsters can often help break the ice with strangers. Some of the ritziest resort properties on the Caribbean have a no-kids policy, but you shouldn't have a problem staying at mid-range and budget places.

The biggest concern, especially with small children, is their **vulnerability**. Even more than their parents, children need protection from the sun, unsafe drinking water, heat and unfamiliar food. Diarrhoea can be dangerous for younger children; rehydration drinks such as Pedialyte are vital, and often available at convenience stores as well as pharmacies (Gatorade makes a decent

substitute). Also make sure, if possible, that your child is aware of the dangers of rabies and other animal-borne illnesses; keep kids away from all animals.

Public breast-feeding is almost never seen in cities, and only occasionally in villages, but it's possible in an emergency. Nappies, milk and standard medications are readily available in all but the tiniest towns, and while there may not be a lot of dedicated changing facilities, the inconvenience is largely made up for by the general tolerance and helpfulness toward parents and their little ones.

Some things you might want to make a special effort to show children include the monkeys at the reserve in Punta Laguna (see p.121) and any of the scores of cenotes. As for the haciendas, a livelier place like Hacienda Sotuta de Peón (see p.210) can engage younger kids who may not yet appreciate the ambience of a spooky abandoned place like Yaxcopoil (see p.198). The theme parks of Xcaret (see p.90) and Xel-Há (see p.110) are both a bit expensive, but safe environments in which younger kids can explore some of the natural elements of the Yucatán, such as cenotes and coral reefs. The cave tour at Río Secreto (see p.90) is open to children 6 and up, and older children will likely be fascinated with the caves at Loltún (see p.208) and Xpukil (see p.218). The latter, which lacks lights and defined paths, is probably best reserved for teenagers.

For customized and scheduled travel itineraries geared toward adventurous families, contact the US tour agency Rascals in Paradise (☎415/273-2224, ⓦwww .rascalsinparadise.com).

Travel essentials

Costs

Although in general costs are lower than you'll find at home, prices on the peninsula, compared with the rest of Central or South America, can come as something of a shock, especially on the Caribbean coast. Prices in the guide section are quoted in **Mexican pesos** (M$), but in the tourism-centric coastal areas, these prices change frequently, according to the exchange rate with the US dollar.

Wherever you go, you can probably get by on US$400/£250 a week, while on US$800/£500 you'd be living very comfortably. Prices can be affected by **season**, and hotels on the beaches raise their prices in the winter, from December through April. In every major tourist spot, prices go up in July and August, when Mexican (and European) tourists are out in force; the one exception is Cancún. The week between Christmas and New Year and the week before Easter (Semana Santa) command the highest rates. For more information on **accommodation** prices, see the box on p.27.

Food prices vary wildly, but you can get a substantial meal in a basic Mexican restaurant for around M$60/US$5/£3 – though such value is often available only at lunch. If you're keen to save money, make lunch your major meal, then have lighter snacks for dinner, as locals do. Restaurants charge fifteen percent IVA (*impuesto de valor añadido*, or value-added sales tax), but it is usually included in prices quoted on the menu.

Transport could be another major expense because distances are so large. On a per-kilometre basis, however, prices are still quite reasonable: the four-hour run between Cancún and Mérida starts at just M$239/US$19/£12 on a first-class bus.

Travelling with a group can save a lot. On the beaches, you can get apartments for up to six people for even greater savings. An **International Student or Youth Card** will not save you anything, however.

Crime and personal safety

Despite reports of sordid drug-cartel crimes coming out of Mexico, this part of the country is so far free from such violence, and the region cherishes its low rate of violent crime (Yucatán state has the lowest murder rate in the country, lower than most cities in the United States). You are unlikely to run into trouble in the Yucatán unless you go looking for it. It dismays locals to see travellers clutching their bags tightly and looking around suspiciously in such non-threatening areas as Cancún's zona hotelera or central Mérida.

The precautions to be taken against petty crime are common sense and would be second nature at home: don't wave money around; deposit valuables in the hotel safe. Drivers are likely to encounter problems only if they leave anything enticing visible in their car. The vehicle itself is less likely to be stolen than broken into for the valuables inside.

Checkpoints throughout the region can seem threatening due to all the visible guns, but officers are invariably polite, and with the exception of a very thorough check of any cars leaving Mahahual (where drug smugglers have been active), you will likely be waved through without any further questioning.

Police

Mexican police have a reputation for being quick to make up offences and ask for bribes. But this is not typically true of police in the Yucatán. Nonetheless, there are exceptions – and the easiest way to avoid trouble is simply to drive within the speed limit. If a policeman does accuse you of some violation, explain that you're a tourist, not used to the ways of the country – you may get off scot-free, but the subject of a fine may come up. You could simply pay up, but you would be perpetuating a system that the government is working hard to correct. If instead you insist that you are happy to proceed to the police station and pay your fine in person, the officer will likely drop the issue entirely. As everywhere in Mexico, it helps to be extremely polite (and perhaps play a little dumb).

If you are robbed, you will find the **tourist police** in the resort towns fairly sympathetic, if not particularly speedy in processing paperwork. Most insurance companies will insist on a **police report**. The department you need in order to *presentar una denuncia* (report the theft officially) is the **Procuradoría General de Justicia**.

The Mexican **legal system** is based on the Napoleonic code, which assumes your guilt until you can prove otherwise. Should you be jailed, your one phone call should be to your **consulate** – if nothing else, it will arrange an English-speaking lawyer. You can be held for up to 72 hours on suspicion before charges have to be brought.

Drugs

Drug offences are the most common cause of serious trouble between tourists and the authorities. Under heavy pressure from the US to stamp out the trade, local authorities are particularly happy to throw the book at foreign offenders.

Marijuana (known as *mota*) continues to be cultivated in Mexico. It's widely used, particularly along the Caribbean beaches, but it remains strictly illegal. For possession, you can expect a hefty fine, no sympathy and little help from your consulate. **Cocaine** and methamphetamine trafficking is a national problem, though fortunately meth use is so far rare in the Yucatán; cocaine is more common in the beach party towns, but the legal consequences are extreme. The cartels do not (yet) exert the social influence in the Yucatán that they do in the northern part of Mexico, but stories abound about suspicious packets washed up on the beaches south of Tulum, and equally suspicious sorts reclaiming them. A very thorough drug checkpoint is set up on the highway out of Mahahual.

Electricity

Voltage in Mexico is 110 volts AC, with two-flat-pin rectangular plugs, as in the US. Cuts in service and fluctuations in the current do occur, and in cheap hotels any sort of appliance that draws a lot of current may blow the fuses.

Emergency

General emergency number ℡080; Police ℡060; Green Angels (emergency highway breakdown) and Tourism ℡078 or ℡01-800/903-9200.

Entry requirements

Citizens of the US, Canada, the UK, Ireland, Australia, New Zealand and much of Western

Europe do not need a visa to visit Mexico as tourists for less than 180 days. Non-US citizens travelling via the US, however, may need a US visa. Visitors are subject to a M$260/US$22 entry fee, which will be included in your ticket if arriving by air. Effectively, your receipt for this fee is a **tourist card** or FMT (*folleto de migración turística*), which you'll receive on you're arriving flight or at a border crossing, and which you must keep on hand for the rest of your trip and turn over when you leave. At land borders, you'll need to pay the entry fee in cash at the border crossing. Note that it's not uncommon for border posts to run out of tourist cards.

A tourist card is valid for a single entry for **up to 180 days**, though officials will often write in thirty days or less. If you know you'll be visiting for a long stretch, be sure to specify you want the full time limit, as getting an extension can be time-consuming. For an extended visit, you may be asked to show bank statements or other proof of sufficient funds for your stay, about US$300 for every week you'll be in Mexico.

Should you lose your tourist card, head for the **Departamento de Migración**, or immigration department office; there are branches in the largest cities. For an extension, if you are near a border, it's simpler to cross for a day and get a new one upon re-entry than go into an office; if you do apply to the immigration department, it's wise to do so a couple of weeks in advance, though you may be told to come back nearer the actual expiry date.

Embassies in Mexico

All addresses are in Mexico City unless otherwise noted. Consulate locations in the Yucatán and Chiapas are under the "Listings" sections for the relevant cities in this book. For Mexican consulates and embassies in your home country or those bordering Mexico, see ⓦwww.sre.gob.mx under "Representaciones".
Australia Rubén Dario 55 ☎55/1101-2200, ⓦwww.mexico.embassy.gov.au.
Canada Schiller 529, Polanco ☎55/5724-7900, ⓦwww.canada.org.mx. Consulates in Cancún and Playa del Carmen.

Republic of Ireland Blvd Manuel Ávila Comacho 76, Lomas de Chapultepec ☎55/5520-5892, ⓦwww.embajadadeirlanda.com.mx.
New Zealand Jaime Balmas 8, Polanco ☎55/5283-9460, ⓦwww.nzembassy.com/mexico.
South Africa Andrés Bello 10, Edificio Forum, Polanco ☎55/1100-4970, ⓔsafrica@prodigy .net.mx. Consulate in Cancún.
UK Río Lerma 71, Cuauhtémoc ☎55/5207-2089, ⓦwww.embajadabritanica.com.mx. Consulate in Cancún.
US Paseo de la Reforma 305, Cuauhtémoc ☎55/5080-2000, ⓦwww.usembassy-mexico.gov. Consulates in Cancún, Playa del Carmen, Cozumel and Mérida.

Gay and lesbian travellers

Social acceptance of homosexuality is slowly spreading nationwide, and historically tolerant Maya culture makes the Yucatán a relatively welcoming place (a former governor of Quintana Roo state was openly bisexual). Gay marriage and gay adoption was legalized in Mexico City in 2010, and 2003 saw the passage of a federal law forbidding discrimination based on "appearance, mannerism and expression of one's sexual preference or gender". Beyond this, there's a surprisingly open subculture once you tap into it.

There are **gay bars and clubs** in Cancún, Playa del Carmen and Mérida (visit ⓦwww .sergay.com.mx for "Guia de Lugares", a basic directory, though it's not entirely up to date), and Cancún hosts annual gay festivals. Elsewhere, private parties are where it all happens, and you'll need a contact to find them.

Health

For minor medical problems, head for a **pharmacy** – look for a green cross and the "Farmacia" sign. Pharmacists are trained to diagnose and prescribe, and many speak English. They can also sell many more drugs over the counter than are available at home.

The quality of medical care in Mexico can be quite good and inexpensive; Mérida is a regional centre for medical treatment. Most towns have a state-run **health centre** (*centro de salud* or *centro médico*), where treatment is free. If you need advance planning, get a copy of *Yucatan: Healthy Travelers Handbook*, published by MedToGo (⑩www.medtogo.com); in Mexico, ask a large hotel or your consulate for a recommendation.

Travellers in Mexico face few grave health risks. "Montezuma's revenge" (**traveller's diarrhoea**, aka *turista*) is one of the commonest ailments. The bounty of fresh fruit is often enough to upset some people's systems, as is a steady diet of cheap margaritas. Watch this intake and wash your hands frequently (there is a sink for this in every restaurant), and you've cut the risk significantly. **Water**, too, is an issue, though you would have to be in an absolutely desperate rural situation to be served tap water (it makes the locals sick, too); by law, ice is always made with purified water. In Cancún and Cozumel, the tap water is purified, if not so tasty. If you do get a bout of *turista*, **rehydration drinks** such as Pedialyte are very useful. If you can't get these, dissolve half a teaspoon of salt and three of sugar in a litre of water. Yogurt and prickly-pear fruit (*tuna*) also help.

Protect against Mexico's sunny climate with strong **sunscreen** (look for biodegradable brands, as these are the only kind permitted in national marine parks, where oil-based sunscreens can smother the reefs) and wear a hat. Drink a litre or so of water or fruit juice a day, and don't exert yourself in the afternoon.

You're at virtually no risk for **malaria** unless you'll be spending an extended period in swampy areas along the border with Guatemala and Belize. In general, wear long sleeves and repellent (look for an effective natural formulation of essential oils in health stores in Mexico) around sunset. Special mosquito nets for hammocks are also available in Mexico. Mosquitoes carrying **dengue fever** have made occasional appearances in southern Chiapas. They fly during the day, so wear insect repellent all the time in this region. The only treatment is rest, with drugs to assuage the fever.

Other insects include **scorpions**, which can turn up in your shoes or bottoms of sleeping bags. Their sting is not dangerous, only painful; cold-pack the sting to reduce swelling, and seek medical treatment if pain does not lessen within six hours. Few **snakes** in the Yucatán are poisonous, and are unlikely to bite unless actively disturbed.

Insurance

As there are no reciprocal arrangements between Mexico and any other country, travel insurance with some medical coverage is essential. Most policies exclude so-called dangerous sports unless an extra premium is paid. In Mexico this can mean scuba diving, windsurfing, kiteboarding or trekking – check the fine print carefully. If you have anything stolen during your trip, you must make an official statement to the police and obtain a copy of the declaration (*copia de la declaración*) for your insurance company.

Internet

Internet cafés are common in all the larger cities and resort destinations, and service is usually excellent. Access typically costs no more than US$1/£0.65 an hour, though in tourist resorts, the price can be a little higher. Cancún's zona hotelera is the one web wasteland. Wireless (wi-fi) hot spots are increasingly prevalent (especially in Mérida,

Rough Guides travel insurance

Rough Guides has teamed up with WorldNomads.com to offer great travel insurance deals. Policies are available to residents of over 150 countries, with cover for a wide range of adventure sports, 24hr emergency assistance, high levels of medical and evacuation cover and a stream of travel safety information. As a roughguides.com user, you can take advantage of their policies online 24/7, from anywhere in the world – even if you're already travelling. And since plans often change when you're on the road, you can extend your policy and even claim online. Roughguides.com users who buy travel insurance with WorldNomads.com can also leave a positive footprint and donate to a community development project. For more information go to ⑩www.roughguides.com/shop.

where they're installed in most public parks), but don't count on them.

Laundry

Lavanderías are ubiquitous. They charge by the kilo, usually with a three-kilo minimum, and for a few dollars you'll get your clothes back clean, pressed and perfectly folded in less than 24 hours. Many hotels also offer laundry services that, although convenient, tend to charge by the item, adding up to a considerably greater cost.

Living in the Yucatán

Work permits are almost impossible to get hold of, but you can extend your time in Mexico with classes or volunteer work. Many **language schools** arrange homestays for around US$30 per night, including meals. We recommend the Institute of Modern Spanish in Mérida (Ⓦ www.modernspanish .com), where classes start at US$411 per week with a homestay. Also in Merida are the creative-arts-focused Habla (Ⓦ www.habla .org) and the Centro de Idiomas del Sureste (Ⓦ www.cisyucatan.com.mx), with rates from US$530 per week. El Bosque del Caribe (Ⓦ www.cancunlanguage.com) is based in downtown Cancún, and International House Riviera Maya (Ⓦ www.ihrivieramaya.com), Soléxico (Ⓦ www.solexico.com) and Playa-Lingua (Ⓦ www.playalingua.com) are in Playa del Carmen.

Volunteer programmes in the Yucatán include Global Vision International (Ⓦ www .gviusa.com), which organizes divers to gather data about reefs, and a jaguar preservation programme, and Willing Workers on Organic Farms (Ⓦ www.wwoof .org), which links volunteers with agricultural work; there are a couple of participating farms in the Yucatán.

Should you want to really settle in, Yucatan Expatriate Services (Ⓦ www.yucatanexpatri ateservices.com) can help with the details.

Mail

Mexican postal services (*correos*) are reasonably efficient. Anything sent abroad by air should have an **airmail** (*por avión*) stamp on it. Airmail postcards and letters under 20g cost M$10.50 to the US and Canada,

M$13 to Europe and South America and M$14.50 to the rest of the world. Letters should take around a week to North America and two to Europe or Australasia, but can take much longer. Dedicated airmail boxes in resorts and big cities tend to be more reliable than ordinary ones.

Sending **packages** out of the country requires examination by customs and much paperwork. Take your package (unsealed) to any post office and they'll set you on your way. Many stores will send your purchases home for you, which is a great deal easier.

Maps

Rough Guides, in conjunction with the World Mapping Project, have produced our own rip-proof, waterproof maps of Mexico and of the Yucatán, with roads, contours and physical features all clearly shown. You may also consider International Travel Maps' *Mexico South* (1:1,325,000), which includes Villahermosa and parts of Chiapas, and the *Yucatán Peninsula* (1:500,000), both available at Ⓦ www.itmb.com. For a full overview, the sturdy, laminated Yucatán map published by German mapmaker Borch is decent, as it covers much of Villahermosa and Chiapas.

For the Caribbean beach towns and around Chichén Itzá, also see the excellent maps produced by Can-Do Maps (Ⓦ www .cancunmap.com). They clearly label all hotels, restaurants and rental homes, as well as the usual sights.

In Mexico, Blue Maps are reasonably detailed and up-to-date; look for them in Oxxo stores and Walmart. Maps published by Patria and Guía Roji are also detailed, but not updated frequently, and newer or smaller roads in the Yucatán are often missing. Both are widely available, though – try large Pemex stations.

Money

The new Mexican peso, or **nuevo peso**, usually written $, was introduced in 1993 and is made up of 100 centavos (¢). Bills come in denominations of M$20, M$50, M$100, M$200 and M$500, with coins of 10¢, 20¢, 50¢, M$1, M$2, M$5, M$10 and M$20. The initials MN (*moneda nacional*, or national coin) are occasionally used. The exchange rate is typically around M$12 to US$1, or M$20 to £1. In Cancún and Cozumel (and to a lesser extent in Playa del Carmen), many businesses accept US dollars for items less than US$100 – but rates are not favourable.

US dollars, Canadian dollars, pounds sterling and euros can all be changed at *cambios* (exchanges) in large cities. An anti-money-laundering law introduced in 2010 theoretically restricts foreigners to exchanging no more than US$1500 per month, but at the time of press this wasn't being thoroughly enforced. Travellers' cheques are more trouble than they're worth, as they can be changed only at banks, and then only with lots of paperwork. Dump Guatemalan quetzales and Belize dollars before entering Mexico if possible.

Despite Mexico-side fees of about US$2 per transaction and at least a three percent charge from your own bank, **ATMs** (*cajeros automáticos*) still provide the best rates and convenience, as they can be found in all but the smallest towns. Avoid non-bank-affiliated machines, as their fees are exorbitant. You'll want to carry some backup cash just in case you encounter problems.

Credit cards are accepted at many better hotels and restaurants. Be sure that you are always charged in pesos, as any US dollar total will likely be at a poorer exchange rate.

Opening hours and public holidays

Only the smallest towns still take a siesta, and businesses are generally open from 9am to 5 or 6pm, and closed one day a week – usually Monday, but this can vary by town. **Post offices** set their own hours, but you can count on at least Monday to Thursday, 9am to 3pm. **Banks** are generally open Monday to Friday, 9.30am to 4pm, though HSBC branches are open until 7pm.

Phones

Many public phones require a phone card, matched to the brand of phone; coin phones (marked "monedas") are less ubiquitous, but more convenient. You can also visit a **caseta de teléfono** (phone office; look for "Larga

Distancia" signs), for only slightly more; most internet cafés are set up for Skype or another VOIP service.

Another alternative is a charge card or calling card that can be used in Mexico; you'll be connected to an English-speaking operator and billed at home at a rate that is predictable (for AT&T, dial ☏01-800/288-2872; for BT, ☏01-800/123-0244; for Canada Direct, ☏01-800/123-0200). To contact an operator for collect calls, dial ☏020 for numbers within Mexico and ☏090 for international calls.

The code for calls **to Mexico** is 52; mobile phones require a "1" before the area code. When calling land lines **in Mexico**, dial "01" followed by the two- or three-digit area code and the seven-digit phone number. Calls to mobile phones are preceded by "044" (for a number in the same area code) or "045" (for a number in a different area code), then the area code and number. When calling mobile numbers from another mobile, dial the area code and number directly.

Mexican GSM systems operate on 1900MHz, so European travellers will need

---

Public holidays

The main **public holidays**, when virtually everything will be closed, are listed below. Many places also close on January 6 (Twelfth Night/Reyes).

Jan 1 New Year's Day
Feb 5 Anniversary of the Constitution
March 21 Día de Benito Juárez
Variable Good Friday and Easter Saturday
May 1 Labour Day
May 5 Battle of Puebla
Sept 1 Presidential address to the nation
Sept 16 Independence Day
Oct 12 Día de la Raza (Columbus Day)
Nov 1–2 Día de los Muertos
Nov 20 Anniversary of the Revolution
Dec 12 Día de la Virgen de Guadalupe
Dec 24–26 Christmas

a multi-band model. The GSM network is relatively new in Mexico, and coverage can be spotty outside the big cities and beach areas. Renting a mobile costs US$4.50–6 per day for a pay-as-you-go phone (usually GSM only). You can buy a **SIM card** with a local number at Telcel and other mobile-phone stores, but you must register it with a national database in person at a Telcel service centre, with your passport. Cards cost about M$150 and usually include M$50 credit for calls or internet use, but rates are pricey, up to M$5/US$0.40/£0.25 per minute, with similarly priced data access.

Photography

Film is manufactured in Mexico and is not expensive. Camera hardware is prohibitively expensive, and digital accessories (memory cards, cords, etc) can be found only in bigger cities. Many internet cafés can download your photos to a CD. In general, more traditional people in the Yucatán and Chiapas do not like to be photographed, but in cities, people are more amenable. Public dances are usually fine to photograph, but be considerate if you encounter a more intimate ceremony.

Senior travellers

Mexico is not a country that offers any special difficulties to older travellers. The same considerations apply here as to anywhere else in the world. Senior citizens are often entitled to discounts, especially when visiting tourist sights, but also on occasion for accommodation and transport, something that's always worth asking about. The excellent senior-centric Road Scholar (Ⓦwww.roadscholar.org, formerly Elderhostel) runs a twelve-day ruins tour, and a Yucatán cycling tour.

Time

The area from the Yucatán to Chiapas is on GMT–6 in winter and GMT–5 in summer (the first Sun in April until the last Sun in Oct). This is the same as US Central Time – though note that the US now begins Daylight Saving Time one week earlier than Mexico and ends it one week later.

Toilets

Public toilets (*baños* or *sanitarios*) in Mexico are often staffed by an attendant (who is tipped M$5 or so or paid the signed fee) who keeps the place reasonably clean and hands out paper. (Also look for a large dispenser on the wall when you enter, as it's rarely in individual cubicles.) It's usually fine to use the toilets in a restaurant or bar without purchasing anything. The most common signs are Damas (Ladies) and Caballeros (Gentlemen), though you may find M (Mujeres) and H (Hombres), Señoras (Women) and Señores (Men) or, more confusing, the symbols of a moon (women) and sun (men).

Because almost every building in the Yucatán has its own septic tank (the limestone bedrock can't support sewage systems), people are scrupulous about not flushing toilet paper. A basket is invariably placed nearby for disposing of paper, and emptied frequently. You know you're in a very swanky hotel when the basket has gone missing.

Tourist information

The national Secretaría de Turismo's (Sectur) website (Ⓦwww.visitmexico.com) addresses most basic queries. In the Yucatán, **tourist offices** (*turismos*) are run by state and municipal authorities. Some are extremely helpful, with free information and leaflets by the cartload; others are barely capable of answering the simplest question. The more useful ones are listed in the relevant city and regional sections throughout the guide.

Other websites

You may find the following **websites** useful for travel planning in the Yucatán, Chiapas and Tabasco.

Backyard Nature Ⓦwww.backyardnature.net. Naturalist Jim Conrad spends half the year in the Yucatán and Chiapas. His weekly newsletters deliver sharp observations about local animals and plants.

Diario de Yucatán Ⓦwww.yucatan.com.mx. The oldest and largest newspaper on the peninsula, published daily in Mérida. In Spanish.

Exploring Colonial Mexico Ⓦwww.colonial-mexico.com. Run by Espadaña Press, this site concentrates on art and architecture from the colonial era, with an excellent archive of photos and information on Franciscan missions and haciendas in the Yucatán.

Mesoweb ⓦ www.mesoweb.com. A huge collection of articles on pre-Columbian Mexico and Central America, including archeological news, maps, timelines and articles about life in the Maya world.

Mexico Desconocido ⓦ www .mexicodesconocido.com. The online version of the popular magazine that explores Mexico's backcountry and heritage. A good portion is in English.

Mundo Maya ⓦ www.mayadiscovery.com. The online outlet of a now-defunct magazine devoted to Maya culture, with very readable short articles.

Ruins of Mexico ⓦ www.geocities.ws /atlantis01mx. An online guide to Mexico's archeological sites, with photos, plans and explanations.

Sac-Be ⓦ www.sac-be.com. Great resource for info on the Riviera Maya, with good events listings and an info-packed monthly newsletter.

Yucatan Living ⓦ www.yucatanliving.com. Site run by working expats in Mérida, full of news and informative articles on Yucatecan culture.

Yucatan Today ⓦ www.yucatantoday.com. Long-running tourist-info site, extending to all the major destinations in Yucatán state. Info is not always kept up to date, and "reviews" definitely favour advertisers, but for many details it's invaluable.

Travellers with disabilities

Mexico is not well equipped for people with disabilities, but things are improving all the time and, especially at the top end of the market, it shouldn't be too difficult to find accommodation and tour operators. Check beforehand that tour companies, hotels and airlines can accommodate you specifically.

If you stick to beach resorts and upmarket tourist hotels, you should certainly be able to find places that are wheelchair-friendly and accustomed to having guests who are disabled. American chains are very good for this.

Unless you have your own transport, the best way to travel inside the Yucatán may be by air, since buses rarely cater for disabilities, and certainly not for wheelchairs. Ramps are

rare, and streets and pavements are not in a very good state. Depending on your disability, you may want to find an able-bodied helper to accompany you.

Women travellers

Machismo may be one of the stereotypical factors in Mexican culture, but in the Yucatán, it's softened considerably by the gentler mores of Maya culture. *Yucatecos* are on the whole gentlemanly and gracious, and women needn't be too on guard. In the evenings, however, especially anywhere near bars, you're better off walking with a friend. Most hassles will be limited to **comments** in the street. These are generally meant as compliments, but you may soon tire of such astute observations as "Guera!" ("Blondie!"), in which case you'll have to simply tune them out. Chances are slim that any retorts on your part, in Spanish or otherwise, will reform a sidewalk lecher.

In the big resort areas, legendarily "easy" tourists attract droves of would-be gigolos, and the gap between wealthy visitors and the scraping-by population who actually built the place is quite distinct. There are occasional rapes reported in Cancún and Playa del Carmen, but it's hardly the epidemic that some guidebooks make it out to be. Simply be as sensible as you would ordinarily be: drink in moderation and have a plan with friends for extricating yourself from unwanted male attention.

Away from the cities, though, and especially in indigenous areas, there is rarely any problem. You may, as an outsider, be treated as an object of curiosity (or occasionally resentment), but not with any implied sexual threat. And wherever you come across it, such curiosity can also extend to great friendliness and hospitality.

Women are barred from the vast majority of **cantinas**, though some have adjoining "family" rooms. Dining alone in restaurants, on the other hand, is perfectly fine (and you can enjoy a drink with your meal), and the staff may take you under their wing.

Guide

Guide

1 Cancún, Isla Mujeres and Isla Holbox 49

2 Playa del Carmen, Cozumel and the Caribbean coast 77

3 Tulum and around 105

4 The Costa Maya and the Río Bec 125

5 Valladolid and Chichén Itzá 149

6 Mérida and around 171

7 Uxmal and the Ruta Puuc 195

8 Campeche 213

9 Tabasco and Chiapas 235

1

Cancún, Isla Mujeres and Isla Holbox

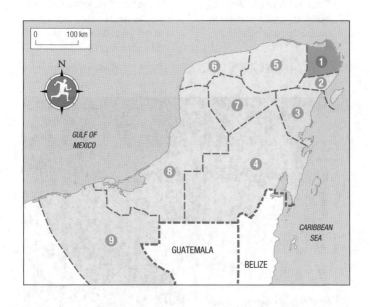

CHAPTER 1 # Highlights

* **Parque de las Palapas**
Downtown Cancún's social
centre comes to life after dark
with dancing, craft fairs and
vendors selling tasty snacks.
See p.58

* **Punta Cancún** Love it or
hate it, Cancún's (in)famous
nightlife is concentrated in
this wild corner of the zona
hotelera. See p.59

* **Playa Delfines** An amazingly
beautiful stretch of sand in
Cancún's zona hotelera.
See p.61

* **Playa Norte** What Caribbean
beach dreams are made of:
broad, fine sand, a mellow
atmosphere and even a
sunset view. See p.69

* **Isla Contoy** A large island
wildlife sanctuary that
makes the perfect place for
birdwatching, or just playing
at castaway. See p.71

* **Whale sharks** Swim with
these giant, peaceful fish
off the coast of Isla Holbox,
some up to 15m long.
See p.71 & p.75

▲ Playa Norte, Isla Mujeres

Cancún, Isla Mujeres and Isla Holbox

With its large airport and numerous hotels, **Cancún** is the place where most visitors' tours of the peninsula begin or end. Independent travellers usually skip this modern city, better known for package tours and megahotels, but it's a dynamic, prosperous place fringed with 20km of astoundingly beautiful **white beaches** and water so clear you can see your plane's shadow on the seafloor as you arrive. Also, contrary to expectation, Cancún can be culturally rewarding (and not painfully expensive) if you know where to look.

Isla Mujeres, a tiny island just across the bay from Cancún, affords a slightly more rustic experience, with small, candy-coloured wooden houses lining the narrow streets of the main town. Mujeres is definitely on the tourist route, but there's not a strip mall in sight, and the only entertainment is watching the water lap at the beach around the island's northern edge.

Inland, the rest of Quintana Roo's northern half is rural and barely touched by tourism. **Isla Holbox**, a dot of land off the northern Gulf coast, is a castaway island that has drawn more visitors in recent years because whale sharks gather off the coast in the summer. From Cancún, Isla Mujeres is just a half-hour ferry hop, but Isla Holbox is a three-hour bus trip from the airport, followed by a boat ride – precisely what keeps the place quiet.

Cancún

Built from scratch in 1970, **CANCÚN** entertains more than two million visitors a year with jet skis, top-volume mariachis and wet T-shirt contests at rowdy

A note about prices

Because Cancún, Cozumel and the other big towns along Quintana Roo's northern coast cater largely to tourists, local businesses often quote prices in US dollars, and peg them to the exchange rate, so a US$70 hotel room could be M$770 one week and M$840 the next. In this guide, we list prices in pesos, except when a business quotes a price solely in US dollars.

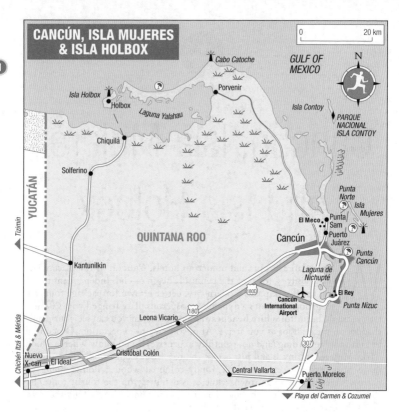

Playa del Carmen & Cozumel

mega-clubs. Restaurants are elaborate theatre, hotels are fantastical pleasure palaces in a constant state of reinvention and the crowds range from college kids to families to senior citizens.

Because of all this, Cancún has a poor reputation among independent travellers in search of "authentic" Mexico. For anyone who has been out in the rest of the Yucatán or is eager to get there, the abundance of concrete and apparent lack of local culture can be off-putting. But a night here doesn't have to be wasted time if you appreciate Cancún as an energetic, wildly successful urban experiment – a thriving city that just happens to have a staggeringly beautiful beach. A closer look reveals bohemian bars, bare-bones beach restaurants and inexpensive taco stands, all frequented by *cancunenses* who are proud of their city and its prosperity.

Orientation

The city has two separate parts: the *centro* (**downtown**) on the mainland and the **zona hotelera**, or hotel zone, the strip of hotels, malls, restaurants and other tourist facilities along a narrow barrier island shaped like a "7". The island is connected to the mainland at each end by causeways enclosing a huge lagoon.

Paseo Kukulcán runs the length of zona hotelera, from the airport up to **Punta Cancún** (where the road splits around the convention centre and a warren of bars) and back onto the mainland.

From Punta Cancún it's a half-hour bus ride to **Avenida Tulum**, the main north–south avenue downtown. It's lined with shops, banks, restaurants and travel agencies, as well as the city's most inexpensive hotels – up side streets, but in view.

On either side of Tulum, divided by intersecting avenues, are the giant city blocks known as *super-manzanas*. The oldest ones, part of the city plan laid out in the 1970s (and soon abandoned as growth outpaced the developers' time and budget), are distinguished by winding and looping streets leading to a central park or market. Each *super-manzana* (abbreviated SM) is known by a number; SM 22 contains Parque de las Palapas, the city's main park, along with many of the downtown area's restaurants and bars.

Some history

If nothing else, Cancún is proof of Mexico's remarkable ability to get things done fast, so long as the political will exists. In the late 1960s, the Mexican government decided to develop a new resort area to diversify the economy. Computers crunched weather data, and surveyors scouted the country's natural attractions to identify a 25-kilometre-long barrier island just off the northern Caribbean coast as the ideal combination of beautiful beaches, sparse population and accessible position. The largest settlement in the area was the village of Puerto Juárez, with about a hundred residents. The island that was to become Cancún's hotel zone had exactly one house, for the caretaker of the coconut plantation there.

Construction on the resort paradise began in 1970. Early workers struggled with dense forest, impossible deadlines and even an occasional jaguar attack. (Jules Siegel, an American who worked for the Mexican tourism ministry, recounts these early challenges in his excellent *Cancun Users Guide*; see Contexts, p.295.) When the first hotel opened in 1974, it relied on a generator for electricity and trucked in water.

In the twenty-first century, Cancún has managed to shed a bit of its reputation for tacky fun (spring break happens only a month a year, after all), and it has attracted more Mexican tourists. But since 2005, when Hurricane Wilma battered the city for three days, the city has struggled with beach erosion. Two massive rebuilding projects later, the sand seems to be holding steady – for now.

Arrival and information

Twenty kilometres south of the centre, the smoothly run **Cancún International Airport** (Ⓦwww.cancun-airport.com) has three terminals, only two of which tourists use. Most international flights arrive at terminal 3; domestic flights and some charter flights come into terminal 2. Both terminals have **currency exchange** desks, and in terminal 3, there are **ATMs** just past customs. In terminal 2, there's one in the departures hall; you'll also find luggage **lockers**.

An **airport bus** (M$42) runs roughly every thirty minutes to downtown (8.15am–12.40am; 30min); look for the ADO desk after customs, though a sign will likely direct you out the door to the bus bay itself (far to the right, near the end of the building, at terminal 2, and just past the palapa bar to the right at terminal 3). **Shared vans** take you to any part of the hotel zone for US$15/ M$150 per person. **Taxis**, for up to four passengers, are also flat-rate: US$60/ M$600 to the hotels or downtown, and US$65/M$650 to Gran Puerto, for the Isla Mujeres ferry. Tickets for vans and taxis are sold at the desks outside customs.

Arriving by bus (including the one from the airport), you'll pull in at Cancún's well-organized main **bus station**, at the centre of downtown. It has **luggage storage** (daily 6am–9.45pm). A city bus stops on Tulum, to your right as you walk out of the

Zona hotelera addresses

Street addresses in the beach zone are all kilometre markers on Paseo Kukulcán. The count starts on the north end, near the bridge over from downtown. It's not an exact science: two sets of markers exist, and are out of sync by about half a kilometre, so addresses are guidelines at best.

station. It runs either to the zona hotelera (southbound side of the avenue) or to the Isla Mujeres ferry docks (northbound side). The city does not have a walk-in tourist office, but no matter: **maps and brochures** are available at every hotel.

City transport

All the attractions in downtown Cancún are within walking distance, but you need transport to get to and around the zona hotelera. **Buses** marked "R-1 – Hoteles," run along Tulum every few minutes; the fare is M$8.50. (Several other bus routes go to the zona hotelera as well – all say "Hoteles" on the front window.) Others head north on Tulum to Gran Puerto and Puerto Juárez, for the ferry to Isla Mujeres; look for "Juárez" on the windscreen. Minivans (**combis**) also run this and other routes, but buses are plentiful enough and less cramped. In the zona hotelera, it's safest to stick with R-1 buses back. R-2 buses head due east into the commercial part of town; be ready to get off at the Chedraui store at the corner of Tulum and Cobá.

Taxis are plentiful and can be hailed almost anywhere. Fares are based on a zone system, and you should agree on the fare before getting in. Big hotels in the zona hotelera will have sample rates posted, which reflect a small surcharge; rates are cheaper if you flag a cab in the street. Anywhere in downtown is about M$40, and the trip between downtown and Punta Cancún costs around M$200; to Gran Puerto, the fare is M$50. A car isn't necessary, but it's not too much of a liability either, as **parking** is not too difficult.

Accommodation

If there's one thing Cancún has, it's hotel rooms. **Downtown** holds the only hope of a real budget room, and you're only a short bus ride from the public beaches. **Hostels** have proliferated, and there are several good ones (and many bad), as well as some solid midrange hotels, very convenient to the bus station.

The **zona hotelera**'s beachfront palaces can be prohibitively priced in high season (US$200 at the very least), but from May through November, rates can plummet by more than half. Online, you can often find excellent deals year-round, especially at the last minute. Try "opaque" booking sites like ⓦ www.hotwire.com, where you reserve without knowing the name of the hotel – you can't go wrong with any four- or five-star property, and even in high season, you might nab a beachfront room for less than US$150. If you're considering a big hotel investment here, also see "Cancún Beaches", p.61, for more tips on choosing the location.

Downtown Cancún

Alux Uxmal 21 ☎ 998/884-6613, ⓦ www .hotelalux.com.mx. Perfectly functional rooms are a bit dim but have a/c and TV. Its real appeal is the short walk to the bus station. ❷

Hostel Quetzal Orquideas 10 ☎ 998/883-9821. Super-friendly hostel with arty style – from the beautiful graffiti on the front wall to the gem-coloured sheets on the beds. Tucked in a rambling old house with a central courtyard, the private rooms are especially great (even for people who normally avoid hostels); each has private outdoor space and a/c. The big mixed-sex dorm (M$200) also has a/c, and nice big windows. Rates are a little higher than elsewhere because they include both breakfast and an exceptionally good dinner. ❷

Kin Mayab Tulum 75 at Uxmal ☎ 998/884-2999, Ⓦ www.hotelkinmayab.com. This centrally located hotel is clean and secure, with the most comfortable rooms and best pool in its price range (book ahead). Request the back section, by the pool and away from the street noise. ❺

Mundo Joven Uxmal 25 ☎ 998/898-2103, Ⓦ www .mundojovenhostels.com. Cancún's official HI hostel opened in 2010, and is nicely designed, and so far the all-white decor looks crisp, not dingy. There's free wi-fi and a/c everywhere, and both single-sex

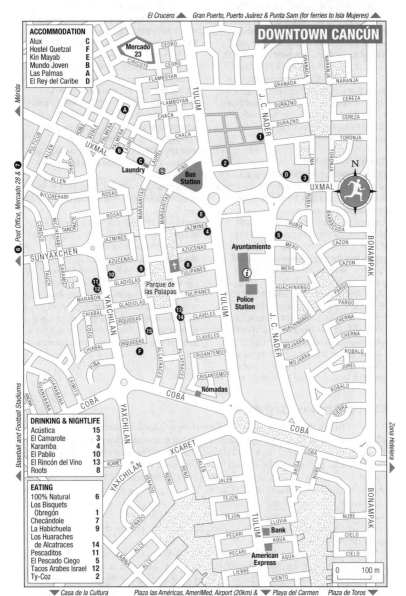

DOWNTOWN CANCÚN

El Crucero ▲   Gran Puerto, Puerto Juárez & Punta Sam (for ferries to Isla Mujeres) ▲

◄ Mérida

◄ Post Office, Mercado 28 & 7

◄ Baseball and Football Stadiums

Zona Hotelera ▶

ACCOMMODATION

Alux	C
Hostel Quetzal	F
Kin Mayab	E
Mundo Joven	B
Las Palmas	A
El Rey del Caribe	D

DRINKING & NIGHTLIFE

Acústica	15
El Camarote	3
Karamba	4
El Pabilo	10
El Rincón del Vino	13
Roots	8

EATING

100% Natural	6
Los Bisquets Obregón	1
Checándole	7
La Habichuela	9
Los Huaraches de Alcatraces	14
Pescaditos	11
El Pescado Ciego	5
Tacos Arabes Israel	12
Ty-Coz	2

Mercado 23

Laundry

Bus Station

Parque de las Palapas

Ayuntamiento

Police Station

Nómadas

Bank

American Express

N

0   100 m

▼ Casa de la Cultura   Plaza las Américas, AmeriMed, Airport (20km) & ▼   ▼ Playa del Carmen   Plaza de Toros ▼

and mixed dorms (from US$13), as well as private rooms. The hot tub on the roof says it all, though – this is a party place, for better or worse. ❸

🏃 **Las Palmas** Palmera 43 ☎ 998/884-2513, ⓔ hotelpalmascancun@hotmail.com. Catering as much to Mexican workers and travellers as to foreign backpackers, this place doesn't have the usual hostel party atmosphere. And at just M$120, the price for a bed in the big, single-sex dorms is the best in town for a/c. There are also a few huge private rooms, a basic communal kitchen and internet access. Continental breakfast included. ❷

🏃 **El Rey del Caribe** Uxmal 24 at Nader ☎ 998/884-2028, Ⓦ www.reycaribe.com. Sunny yellow rooms with kitchenettes, plus a pool, spa services and generous breakfast at this casual hotel that feels like it should be on a beach in Tulum. The only place in Cancún with a real ecofriendly sensibility. ❻

Zona hotelera

Club Med Cancun Punta Nizúc ☎ 998/881-8200, Ⓦ www.clubmed.com. One of the first all-inclusives in Cancún and still one of the best, on prime real estate at the zona hotelera's southern corner, with long beaches up both sides, snorkelling right off the coast and a west-facing pool for late-day sunning. Secluded suites in the Jade wing offer an escape from the gung-ho activities if you like. Thanks to the French influence, food is vastly superior to other all-ins. ❾

🏃 **Kin-Ha Beach** Paseo Kukulcán Km 7.5 ☎ 998/891-5400, Ⓦ www.kinhabeach.com. No-frills, but in the best possible way: big, clean rooms with two double beds, as well as family-friendly suites. Every room has a terrace or balcony, and the scenic beach is deep and palm-shaded – the best on the bay side. The handy location is walking distance from Punta Cancún. ❾

Mayapan Paseo Kukulcán Km 8.5, west end of Plaza Maya Fair ☎ 998/883-3227, Ⓦ www .hostalmayapan.com. The only hostel in the hotel zone, in a convenient location with inexpensive private rooms and nice smaller dorms (M$260). The large dorm (M$240) feels a bit gaol-like, though, and the whole place is oddly set in a wing of an abandoned mall. ❹

Le Meridien Retorno del Rey, near Paseo Kukulcán Km 14 ☎ 998/881-2200, Ⓦ www.starwood.com. Shares a great stretch of beach with the *Ritz*, but at half the price. It's also relatively small compared with other resorts here, and rooms match the standards of the Starwood chain. ❾

Ritz-Carlton Cancún Retorno del Rey 36, near Paseo Kukulcán Km 14 ☎ 998/881-0808, Ⓦ www .ritzcarlton.com. The last word in luxury in Cancún, with posh chandeliers and plush carpeting, for a faux-chateau look. The food and service are consistently the best in the city. You can get a taste of Mexico at cooking classes in the slick on-site culinary centre. ❾

Sina Suites Quetzal 33 ☎ 998/883-1017, Ⓦ www .sinasuitescancun.com. Personable staff preside over 33 large suites, each with either one or two bedrooms, a sofa bed in the living room and a full kitchen and dining room. The pool is huge, and a sundeck overlooks the lagoon. ❻

Westin Resort & Spa Cancún Paseo Kukulcán Km 20 ☎ 998/848-7400, Ⓦ www.westin.com. If you don't want to go the all-inclusive route, this is the next best location for sheer beauty after neighbouring *Club Med*, though it is isolated. The striking, minimalist hotel has decadent beds and powerful showers. Standard rooms actually feel a bit cosier than the austere, all-white ones in the club tower. An additional west-facing beach and pool on the lagoon get afternoon sun. ❾

Downtown Cancún

There's little in the way of sights in **downtown Cancún**, though it is a pleasant place to stroll in the evenings, particularly around the central **Parque de las Palapas**, which is ringed with food stalls and often serves as a venue for live music; smaller parks in the neighbourhood host craft or art shows. By day, for a sense of the city's hum away from the tourist trade, head for **Mercado 23**, north of the bus station off Avenida Tulum at Calle Cedro. The market is a small maze of stalls with the flavour of a village market, complete with butchers, herbalists and vegetable sellers. The bigger **Mercado 28**, west from the park on Avenida Sunyaxchén, was formerly the city's main general market, but now stocks primarily tourist tat; it's good for food stalls, though.

West from the park, **Avenida Yaxchilán** is the main nightlife strip. A few touts push menus, but the clientele at the bar-restaurants is mostly Mexican. Entertainment comes in the form of karaoke inside and serenades on the open terraces by roving *trovadores*, who have a musicians' clubhouse at Calle Nacchehabi.

The farthest north visitors will likely make it is the vaguely historical intersection of López Portillo and Tulum, known as **El Crucero** since it was the first crossroads in the city. A little bit west on Portillo, you reach a cluster of **market stalls** that cater solely to locals. Although not much of the merchandise may tempt you (meat smokers, underwear and fly-swatters are on offer), it's nice to stroll through a busy shopping area without getting the "Hey, amigo!" sales push.

The only Maya vestiges on the mainland, **El Meco** (8am–4pm; M\$37) is a small archeological site, recommended only for fanatics or anyone who won't get to any inland ruins. Head east on Portillo, then 3km north on the coast road. The ruins cover less ground than El Rey in the zona hotelera (see below), but the buildings, including a tall pyramid, are more substantial. The area was first inhabited in the Early Classic period, but the buildings are late Post-Classic, after 1100, similar in style to other coastal cities like San Gervasio on Cozumel and Tulum (see Contexts, p.274). Many pieces of jewellery and ceramics were found on the site, as well as a full human skeleton with its skull drilled with numerous holes. Eventually these will be on display in a new museum in the hotel zone, slated for completion in 2013.

Zona hotelera

Most visitors to Cancún head straight for the **zona hotelera** and its **beaches** (see box, p.61). The centre of the action is **Punta Cancún**, the cluster of malls, restaurants and bars around the convention centre at the bend in the "7" formed by the barrier island.

As in downtown, there are no major sights, but east of the main road at Punta Cancún, **Dreams Cancun** resort is a modernist landmark – and the closest thing Cancún has to a historic building. Built by noted Mexican architect Ricardo Legorreta, it was the first hotel to open in Cancún, in 1974 as *El Camino Real*. Architecture fans should try to talk their way in (say you're asking for info at reception) to admire the doors and windows framed with vibrant, typically Mexican colours. As a stylistic counterpoint, consider the **atrium lobby** of the **Gran Meliá Cancún** resort (Paseo Kukulcán Km 16.5), a neo-Maya pyramid built in the mid-eighties. From the giant Maya friezes outside to the interior overflowing with cascading plants and waterfalls, it's the pinnacle of Cancún's particular brand of excess, as a sort of proto-Dubai.

For waterfront leisure that's not a beach, head for the winding walkway along **Canal Sigfrido**, at Paseo Kukulcán Km 4. Especially nice at sunset, it gives an up-close view of the mangroves. Look for "Jardín del Arte" signs just east of the bridge by El Embarcadero.

Ruins

As if to round out the theme park that is Cancún's hotel zone, there are even a couple of requisite Maya **ruins**. The largest (which is not saying a lot) are **El Rey** (daily 8am–5pm; M\$37), at Km 18. With the glass-topped pyramid of the *Hilton* looming in the background, it's a quiet spot to contemplate the rise and fall of civilizations. Save for the enormous iguana population, you'll likely find yourself alone among the late Post-Classic buildings – contemporary with San Gervasio on Cozumel and Tulum. Along with El Meco, this was a stop on the highly developed sea-trade route around the peninsula, disrupted when the Spanish arrived in the early sixteenth century. The ruined structures are mostly small-scale residential buildings.

Sandwiched between a couple of hotels at Km 12.5 (walk down the beach or enter through the lobby of *Park Royal Pirámides*), the tiny site called **Yamil Lu'um** (free) consists of two very modest structures from the same period as El Rey; they likely served as lookout towers, and now provide a good view down the beach.

Watersports

Although Cancún isn't known for its stunning undersea life, the reef off **Punta Nizuc** is a decent **snorkelling** spot, with little live coral but lots of fish. This area is a national marine park; if you visit by boat, as most people do, a M$24 entrance fee is charged (though tour operators often don't include this in the quoted price). The typical outing is the so-called **"jungle tour"**, which entails riding two-passenger speedboats through the **lagoon mangroves**, then out to the reef (either at Punta Nizuc or to Angel Reef, a little further away but healthier).

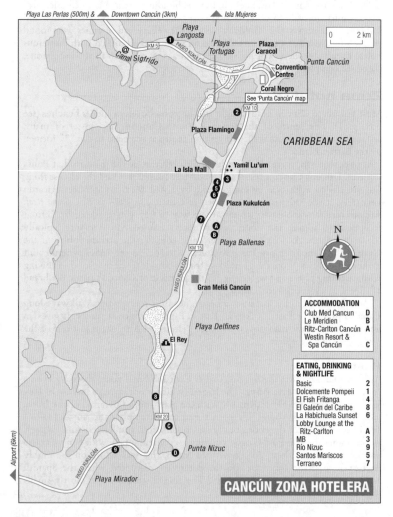

Playa Las Perlas (500m) & ▲ Downtown Cancún (3km)   ▲ Isla Mujeres

Playa Langosta

Playa Tortugas

Plaza Caracol

Punta Cancún

Convention Centre

Coral Negro

See 'Punta Cancún' map

Canal Sigfrido

PASEO KUKULCÁN

KM 5

KM 10

Plaza Flamingo

CARIBBEAN SEA

La Isla Mall

Yamil Lu'um

Plaza Kukulcán

Playa Ballenas

KM 15

Gran Meliá Cancún

Playa Delfines

El Rey

Playa Delfines

KM 20

Punta Nizuc

Airport (6km)

Playa Mirador

N

ACCOMMODATION

Club Med Cancun	D
Le Meridien	B
Ritz-Carlton Cancún	A
Westin Resort & Spa Cancún	C

EATING, DRINKING & NIGHTLIFE

Basic	2
Dolcemente Pompeii	1
El Fish Fritanga	4
El Galeón del Caribe	8
La Habichuela Sunset	6
Lobby Lounge at the Ritz-Carlton	A
MB	3
Río Nizuc	9
Santos Mariscos	5
Terraneo	7

CANCÚN ZONA HOTELERA

Cancún beaches

The legendary **beaches** of Cancún run along the barrier island's north and east shores. The north side of the island (the top portion of the "7") faces a bay, where the flat, pale-green water is often only knee-deep – great for children. Sea grass grows in some places, but it's no impediment to swimming and is often home to bright tropical fish. Rocks and cliffs break up the sand at Km 6 and Km 8.5 of Paseo Kukulcán, and continue around the point to Km 9.5 (hotels in these spots have very limited or man-made beaches).

The island's east side, where white sand stretches for more than ten kilometres, faces the Caribbean. The turquoise waters here are more inviting, but the waves are sometimes high and currents unpredictable; pay attention to the warning flags. Do your tanning in the morning, as the beach falls in shadow from the hotel towers by late afternoon.

All of Cancún's beaches are technically open to the public, but hotels guard their furniture against interlopers. At beachfront bars and clubs, you may use lounge chairs and umbrellas for the price of a drink. The ten designated **public beaches** are quieter, except on weekends, when locals descend. These are the ones worth seeking out, in order of their distance from downtown Cancún:

Playa Las Perlas Paseo Kukulcán Km 2.5. Small but family-friendly, with a playground. Also has changing stalls and palapas for shade.

Playa Langosta Paseo Kukulcán Km 5. Calm water for swimming and a few trees for shade. The adjacent shopping complex has bars and convenience stores.

Playa Tortugas Paseo Kukulcán Km 6. A lively scene, fairly built up, but with a particularly good rustic restaurant, Playa Tortugas Beach Club.

Playa Caracol Paseo Kukulcán Km 8.5. A deep, palm-shaded beach. Official access is farther east, by the Xcaret bus stop, but it's easier to walk through *Kinha Beach*, and its bar is a mellow place for a drink.

Playa Delfines Paseo Kukulcán Km 17.5. The longest and most gorgeous public beach – the reason Cancún was built. Vendors sell fruit and snacks, and there are a few chairs and umbrellas for rent.

Numerous tour operators run the trip (about US$60; 6hr); visit any of the numerous docks on the lagoon side. Less ethically, you can dodge the park fee and reach the reef by land: walk through the *Westin* (Km 20), then turn right and walk about ten minutes down the beach to Punta Nizuc (on *Club Med* property). From there you can cross the rocks and snorkel to your heart's content.

For a longer, more remote experience, you could also make the trip to the island bird sanctuary of **Isla Contoy** (see p.71), north of Isla Mujeres. Kolumbus Tours (T998/884-5333, Wwww.kolumbustours.com) is one good operator, with boats that are replicas of early exploratory sailing vessels. Tours cost US$80 and include lunch, drinks and snorkel gear; there's an additional US$10 park and dock fee.

Other reefs off Cancún's coast make good **diving** for beginners, with easy access and little current; contact Manta Divers (T998/849-4050, Wwww .mantadivers.com), at Paseo Kukulcán Km 13.5; open-water certification is around US$389. **Kiteboarding** is also popular. Ikarus (T984/803-3490, Wwww.ikaruskiteboarding.com), based in Playa del Carmen, gives classes (from US$140 per 2hr) on a remote beach north of Cancún.

Eating

Cancún is bursting with **restaurants**, and competition for customers is fierce. Downtown, the most popular eating places line Tulum and its side streets. You can eat from all over the globe – and from all over Mexico. For **budget food**, follow

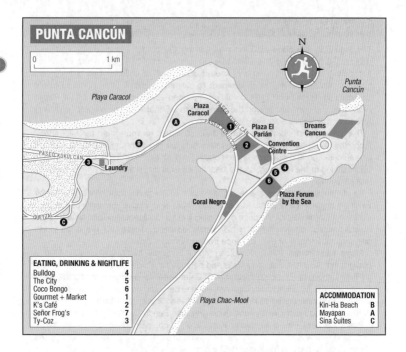

PUNTA CANCÚN

0   1 km

Playa Caracol

Plaza Caracol

Plaza El Parián

Dreams Cancun

Convention Centre

Laundry

Coral Negro

Plaza Forum by the Sea

Punta Cancún

N

Playa Chac-Mool

EATING, DRINKING & NIGHTLIFE	
Bulldog	4
The City	5
Coco Bongo	6
Gourmet + Market	1
K's Café	2
Señor Frog's	7
Ty-Coz	3

ACCOMMODATION	
Kin-Ha Beach	B
Mayapan	A
Sina Suites	C

the locals to the Parque de las Palapas (see p.58) and **Mercado 28** (see p.58), both of which serve various regional specialities. The stalls at the park are open until about 11pm; the market is better for lunch. **Zona hotelera** restaurants are largely a rip-off, but the exceptions noted here are solidly delicious.

Downtown Cancún

100% Natural Sunyaxchén 26 at Yaxchilán. Largely vegetarian and decidedly wholesome, with veggie burgers and granola, as well as fresh-tasting Mexican dishes. Breakfasts are especially nice, with lots of interesting juice combos.

Los Bisquets Obregón Nader 9. A national chain, this bustling diner serves excellent café con leche and Mexican pastries in the morning – just pick from the platter the waiter brings around. Open till midnight.

Checándole Xpuhil 6. A buzzing, popular restaurant that has been around since the earliest days, with a breezy terrace and a selection of satisfying and fresh-tasting Mexican classics. Entrees like enchiladas start at M$70; set lunch is M$60. Closed Sun.

La Habichuela Margaritas 25 ☎998/884-3158. Long-established French-Caribbean restaurant set in a walled garden in front of the park. It's a bit overpriced and old-fashioned, but the featured

cocobichuela (half a coconut filled with lobster and shrimp in a curry sauce, M$325) is pretty stunning. Neighbouring *Labná* applies the same elegant flair to Yucatecan specialities, with somewhat lower prices.

Los Huaraches de Alcatraces Alcatraces 31 (or enter on Claveles). This sparkling-clean cafeteria-style restaurant serves breakfasts and filling hot lunches for M$65 and up. But it's just as easy to fill up on the exceptionally chewy and fresh *huaraches* and quesadillas (from M$25). Fillings range from squash blossoms to cinnamon-laced chorizo sausage. Tues–Sun till 6pm.

Pescaditos Yaxchilán at Gladiolas. A bit of the beach downtown: light reggae vibe, with fantastic lightly battered fish and shrimp for a song (M$35 for a generous basket), as well as deadly shrimp-stuffed *chiles rellenos*. *Ceviches* are good too, if you don't want something fried.

El Pescado Ciego Nader 9. Creative seafood is the theme at this hip little restaurant, one of three in a row run by the same owners. Don't miss the house tacos (M$25), which are garnished with crushed Doritos – much more delicious than it sounds. Dinner only on Sun.

Tacos Arabes Israel Yaxchilán at Gladiolas. At this northern-style taco joint, pork is cooked on a shawarma skewer, with real charcoal. Cheap and tasty, though no real atmosphere to speak of.

🏃 **Ty-Coz** Tulum, behind Comercial Mexicana. This French sandwich shop is a treat. The huge and delicious M$15 *baguette económico*, stacked with ham, cheese, pickled jalapeños and a lip-smacking garlic sauce, is one of the most enticing options. Also good for breakfast, with buttery pastries and strong coffee. Till 10pm; closed Sun.

Zona hotelera

Dolcemente Pompeii Pez Volador 7, near Paseo Kukulcán Km 5.5 ☎ 998/849-4006. A rare casual restaurant catering to Mexican families and residents in the zona hotelera, serving mammoth portions of hearty Italian food, from handmade pastas (M$100 and up) to gelato. Hard to find because it's not affiliated with a mall or hotel: turn north in front of the giant Mexican flag. Closed Mon.

🏃 **El Fish Fritanga** Paseo Kukulcán Km 12.5. Hidden down some stairs behind a *Domino's*, this lagoon-side seafood joint is inexpensive, laidback and frequented by residents. There's a makeshift beach, so you can stick your feet in the sand while you eat, as well as a playground for kids. Great tacos (M$17) with fried fish or tangy octopus are served till 6pm, and for dinner, traditional Mexican dishes take over, in huge portions.

El Galeón del Caribe Paseo Kukulcán Km 19.2. A rustic restaurant (more like a campsite) off the lagoon side of the road, where fresh fish is grilled over a wood fire for M$120 or so. You're almost guaranteed to be the only non-Mexican there. The place can't be seen from the road – look for a small parking area and stairs leading down into the trees; if you get to the *Bel Air Collection*, you've gone too far south.

Gourmet + Market Paseo Kukulcán Km 8.5, east end of Plaza Caracol. At the east end of the mall (above Starbucks) this café is about the only non-hotel place to get breakfast in the hotel zone. The waffles are tremendous, and lunch sandwiches (M$120) are great too, with European meats and cheeses and fresh-baked bread.

K's Café Plaza El Parián, Paseo Kukulcán Km 8.7. Japanese-Mexican fusion is the byword at this tiny place hidden in the inner loop of this strip mall. Try cactus with soy and bonito, as well as rich miso ramen with fresh seafood.

MB Paseo Kukulcán Km 12.5, in *Live Aqua*. No sea view, but one of Cancún's best hotel restaurants. Miami chef Michelle Bernstein mixes Latin, Spanish and even Asian flavours in a stylish but not-too-formal atmosphere. Small but good wine list, too.

Río Nizuc Off Paseo Kukulcán, near Km 22. Few tourists find this seafood spot tucked amid the mangroves at the south end of the hotel zone. *Ceviche* (M$60) and *tikin-xic* fish (M$60) are popular with locals, who crowd in on weekends. Look for the turn just west of Puente Nizúc. Daily 11am–5pm.

Santos Mariscos Paseo Kukulcán Km 12.5. A cool seafood joint just south of *El Fish Fritanga* that serves West-coast-style seafood (wedges of crispy *jicama* topped with shrimp, for instance) at very reasonable prices. Open till midnight.

Ty-Coz Paseo Kukulcán Km 6.8. The zona hotelera branch of the French sandwich shop. Closes around 6pm.

Entertainment and nightlife

Cancún's goal is to encourage some two million visitors a year to have fun, with the **zona hotelera**'s huge dance clubs, vast theme bars and top-volume everything. **Downtown** offers a less frenetic scene, as locals dance on weekends to traditional Mexican tunes at Parque de las Palapas or at romantic cabarets. The Teatro de Cancún (☎ 998/849-5580, ⓦ www.teatrodecancun.com.mx), at Km 4 in the **zona hotelera**, hosts special events, including performances by the 84-member Orquesta Sinfónica de Quintana Roo. **Cinemas** show new American releases subtitled in Spanish; the largest one is Cinépolis (ⓦ www .cinepolis.com.mx) in Plaza Las Américas on Avenida Tulum, south of Avenida Cobá. In the zona hotelera, La Isla mall, at Paseo Kukulcán Km 12.5, also has a theatre (ⓦ www.cinemark.com.mx).

Bars

Downtown watering holes often have very good **live musicians** performing at some point in the evening. *Trova* is the traditional music of the Yucatán, dreamily romantic songs with a slower, Cuban-inspired rhythm.

Downtown Cancún

Acústica Alcatraces, south of Parque de las Palapas. Live *trova* or revolutionary folk music, usually played to a younger, emo-style crowd.

El Camarote, Uxmal 26, in the *Plaza Kokai* hotel ☎998/884-3218. Ignore the sports bar outside; in the small theatre inside, Yucatecan crooners perform romantic classics for an older crowd Thurs–Sat nights from 10:30pm (M$120 minimum).

El Pabilo Yaxchilán 31, in the *Xbalamqué* hotel. Not really a bar, but a literary coffee shop (dubbed a *"café-brería"*), very mellow and beatnik-cool, with folk singers or readings. A bulletin board has notices of art openings, concerts and the like.

El Rincón del Vino Alcatraces 29, south end of Parque de las Palapas ☎998/898-3187. A casual wine bar with a small terrace, this is a great place to sample the best from Mexican vineyards, along with savoury snacks. The scene gets buzzing around 9pm, when the live music starts – usually mellow *trova* or bossanova singers. Closed Sun.

Zona hotelera

La Habichuela Sunset Paseo Kukulcán Km 12.5 ☎998/885-0267. The hotel-zone outpost of this classic restaurant is a memorable spot for a sunset drink, with huge windows overlooking the lagoon.

Lobby Lounge at the Ritz-Carlton Retorno del Rey 36, near Paseo Kukulcán Km 14. Sink into big, comfortable chairs and sip delectable tequila cocktails (M$160) – try the one with carrot juice. On weekends, there's mellow live music.

Señor Frog's Paseo Kukulcán Km 10.5. Practically synonymous with the name Cancún, *Frog's* is the first stop off the plane for the spring-break hordes. Go for live reggae or karaoke, a wild ride down the water slide into the lagoon or just an anthropological experience. On weekends there's often a US$5 cover.

Terraneo Paseo Kukulcán Km 13.5. On the lagoon side of the road, this cool Spanish-inflected bar nonetheless feels as though it's on the beach, with a palapa roof, candlelight and some kind of hippie-ish jazz musicians most nights.

Clubs

In Punta Cancún, giant **nightclubs** with room for thousands face off across the street, and by about 11pm the road is clogged with scantily dressed thrill-seekers and hawkers flogging open-bar deals (expect to pay US$50 or so, or US$20 for cover only). Most clubs have some kind of floor show, segueing into fairly generic party anthems; the energy generally lasts, inside the clubs and out, till 4 or 5am. During spring break season or other festivals, you can catch some international pop and hip-hop stars performing for less than you'd pay at home.

Downtown Cancún

Karamba Tulum at Azucenas. The biggest gay disco in town, with room for four hundred to dance to pounding house and salsa beats, plus the requisite anthems. Most nights see drag acts, strippers and go-go boys galore. M$50 cover; closed Mon.

Roots Tulipanes 26 ☎998/884-2437. Intimate and funky, this partially open-air jazz and blues club has been Cancún's pre-eminent venue for live music for decades, and hosts a week-long jazz fest every year at the end of Sept. Also serves dinner. Cover is M$30–100.

Zona hotelera

Basic Paseo Kukulcán Km 10.5 ☎998/883-2180. The scene is young and the soundtrack heavy on techno and hip-hop at this club that's on a floating island just offshore. It's a little smaller (and sometimes cheaper) than the places in Punta Cancún. When the crowd gets overheated, water jets drench the dancers – keep that in mind when you're deciding what to wear.

Bulldog Paseo Kukulcán Km 9.5, south side of the *Krystal* hotel ☎998/848-9851. Outside the high season (when spring-breakers frolic in the hot tub), you'll probably find more local kids – and more good hip-hop and *rock en español*. It's the place to catch touring Mexican bands.

The City Paseo Kukulcán Km 9.5 ☎998/848-8380, ⓦwww.thecitycancun.com. Giant club that has hosted MTV's live spring-break party marathon in years past. For the floor show, *Coco Bongo* is better, but *The City* will occasionally host major international DJs, which means more variety in the music.

Coco Bongo Paseo Kukulcán Km 9.5, in Plaza Forum ☎ 998/883-5061, ⓦ www.cocobongo .com.mx. The epitome of the Cancún nightclub experience. The night warms up with a floor show involving trapeze acts, Beyoncé impersonators and roving candid cameras zooming in on the most shapely customers. Music, once it really gets started, is of the broadest, most crowd-pleasing variety – but you didn't come here to dance, did you?

Sport

Aside from golf (two courses in the hotel zone), all the action is downtown. Root for the local **baseball** team, the minor-league Tigres de Quintana Roo, at Estadio Beto Ávila, a bit southwest of the centre on Avenida Xcaret. During the season (March–Sept), there are usually eight or nine evening home games per month; check the schedule online at ⓦ www.tigresqr.com (click on "Calendario"). Cheap seats are M$20, and the best ones in the house are only M$80.

Cancún's **football** (soccer) team, the Atlante, arrived only in 2007, but it has a long history – including victory over the famous Guadalajara Chivas and a triumphant national win in their new stadium, just south and west of Beto Ávila, off Avenida Rojo Gómez.

The weekly **bullfight** at the Plaza de Toros (Dec–May Wed at 3.30pm; ☎ 998/884-8248; US$35), at the intersection of Bonampak and Sayil, is geared to tourists, but still goes in for the kill. To justify the steep entrance price, the

Moving on from Cancún

First- and second-class **buses** go from the terminal on Tulum at Uxmal. The shuttle to **Puerto Morelos** and **Playa del Carmen** (every 10min; 1hr) has its own lane and ticket desk, and there's a kiosk for tickets to the **airport** (every 30min 4:30am–10pm; 30min). Other destinations include **Mérida**, on the ultra-luxe ADO Platino service (7 daily, 5 of which arrive at the *Fiesta Americana*; 4hr), the not-quite-as-luxe ADO GL (13 daily; 4hr) and standard first and second class (hourly, round-the-clock; 4–6hr); **Campeche**, on ADO GL (5 daily 10am–11.30pm; 7hr) and first class (6 daily, 7.45am–10.30pm; 7hr); **Chetumal** on ADO GL (2 daily at 5.45pm & midnight; 5hr 30min), first class (hourly, 5am–12.30am; 6hr) and second class (roughly hourly, 4am–12.15pm; 7hr); **Chiquilá**, for Holbox (2 daily at 7.50am and 1.45pm, plus 12.40pm summer only; 4hr); **Izamal** on second class only (14 daily, 4am–2.30am; 4hr); **Mahahual** on first class (2 daily at 7.30am & 11.30pm, plus more in summer; 6hr); **Palenque** on ADO GL (1 daily at 5.45pm; 13hr), first class (1 daily at 7.30pm; 12hr) and second class (6 daily, 2–8.30pm; 13–15hr); **Tizimín**, all on second class (6 daily; 4hr); **Tulum** on first and second class (at least hourly, 4am–1am; 2hr 30min); **Valladolid** on first class (6 daily 5.15am–5.30pm; 2hr) and second class (hourly, 5am–3am; 3hr 30min); **Villahermosa** on ADO Platino (1 daily at 7.25pm; 12hr 30min), ADO GL (6 daily, 10am–8.15pm; 13hr 30min), first class (nearly hourly, 7.45am–9.15pm; 13hr 30min) and second class (12 daily, 3–8pm; 13hr 30min).

Heading west **by car** to Valladolid, Chichén Itzá and Mérida, you have a choice between the scenic but speed-bump-filled **free road** (*libre*) or the fast **toll highway** (*cuota*). From the bus station, drive north on Tulum about 1km, then turn left onto López Portillo; after a few kilometres you can get on the toll road. There's another entrance to the *cuota* (but not the free road) off Hwy-307, 1.5km south of the airport. You pay in advance, at the booths on the highway, for the sections you intend to travel along. The toll to Chichén Itzá is M$275; all the way to Mérida is M$355.

International **flights** and domestic connections to Mexico City leave regularly from Cancún; from downtown a taxi to the airport costs about M$250; from the zona hotelera, M$250 and up.

corrida is preceded by a rather cheesy folk dance show, as well as a bit of audience participation. You're better off trying to catch a (less bloody) fight at a village fiesta, but the ring here does have a certain dusty ambiance (and good traditional bars around the outside).

Listings

Airlines InterJet, Palenque, between Cobá and Xcaret, in Plaza Hollywood ☎ 998/892-0278. Aerosaab (☎ 998/865-4225, ⓦ www.aerosaab .com) runs charter flights and tours to Isla Holbox, Cozumel and Playa del Carmen.

American Express Tulum 208 at Agua (Mon–Fri 9am–5pm; ☎ 998/881-4025).

Banks Most banks (usually Mon–Fri 9.30am–3pm, Sat 9.30am–1pm) are along Tulum, between Uxmal and Cobá, and in the biggest hotel-zone shopping malls – La Isla, Kukulcán. The HSBC bank, downtown at Tulum 192, stays open until 7pm on weekdays.

Books and maps Sanborns (Paseo Kukulcán Km 11, in Plaza Flamingo, or downtown on Uxmal, opposite the bus station) and Fama (Tulum, between Tulipanes and Claveles) have basic maps and guides.

Car rental At the airport, most hotels and various locations downtown. Speed Car Rental, Uxmal 22 (☎ 998/892-0224, ⓦ www.carrentalspeed.com), is one option.

Consulates Canada: Centro Empresarial, Paseo Kukulcán Km 12 ☎ 998/883-3360; Cuba: Pecari 17 SM 20 ☎ 998/884-3423; South Africa: Granada 30, SM 2A ☎ 998/884-9513; UK: Paseo Kukulcán Km 13.5, at the *Royal Sands* ☎ 998/881-0100; US: Paseo Kukulcán Km 13, Torre La Europea ☎ 998/883-0272.

Internet Immediately across from the bus station and northwest on Uxmal are several internet cafés; some are casetas as well. In the zona hotelera, web access is significantly more expensive. There's one café at Paseo Kukulcán Km 4, opposite El Embarcadero.

Laundry Lavandería Las Palmas, on Uxmal just west of the bus station (daily 6am–9pm; M$13/kg). In the zona hotelera, at Paseo Kukulcán km 7.5, near *Ty-Coz* (see p.73).

Medical care The largest hospital close to the zona hotelera is AmeriMed, on Bonampak, behind Plaza las Américas (☎ 998/881-3400 or 881-3434 for emergencies, ⓦ www.amerimed.com.mx).

Post office Sunyaxchén at Xel-Há (Mon–Fri 8am–6pm, Sat 9am–1pm).

Shopping Of the hotel-zone malls, La Isla (Paseo Kukulcán Km 12.5) is the nicest, with international brands and plenty to occupy non-shoppers. For hammocks, El Aguacate in Plaza Bonita, next to Mercado 28 downtown (see p.58), is the only place that stocks quality ones that will hold up to serious travelling. Craft vendors (with a better selection than in the tacky "flea markets") often set up on Parque de las Palapas; they are usually happy to bargain. For more original artwork, go to an exhibition at the Casa de la Culture in downtown Cancún, west of the centre on Yaxchilán (☎ 998/884-8364), mounts new art exhibitions every couple of months.

Travel agencies and tours Most hotels in the zona hotelera have in-house agencies that can arrange day-trips to the chief Maya sites or other attractions along the coast. Otherwise, the student-friendly agency Nómadas has a branch at Cobá 5 (☎ 998/892-2320; ⓦ www.nomadastravel.com.mx) and leads affordable tours with guides to Chichén Itzá and other nearby attractions. EcoColors, Camarón 32, SM 27 (☎ 998/884-3667, ⓦ www .ecotravelmexico.com), runs single- and multi-day kayaking, birdwatching or cycling tours.

Isla Mujeres

Just a few kilometres off the coast of Mexico, in the startlingly clear Caribbean, **ISLA MUJERES** is substantially mellower than Cancún, drawing people for long stays despite the lack of tourist attractions and wild nightlife. A hippie hangout in the 1970s, the eight-kilometre-long patch of land is substantially built up – it's no desert island. But it retains a certain air of bohemian languor in its narrow streets lined with colourful wooden houses; it's a respite for anyone who has been slogging across Mexico, as well as a pleasant place to land, as the whole trip from the Cancún airport takes less than two hours.

Boats to Isla Mujeres

Two companies, Ultramar (⑳www.granpuerto.com.mx) and Magaña, run passenger **ferries** (M$70; 20min) to Isla Mujeres. Ultramar boats leave from Gran Puerto, at the end of Avenida López Portillo, and Magaña boats depart from Puerto Juárez, 250m north. Nothing distinguishes the services, which depart every thirty minutes (5am–12.30pm), so it's likely you'll just take the boat from Gran Puerto, which is the first you reach when coming from the centre. Catch a bus ("R-1 – Pto Juárez"; M$6) or a *combi* heading north on Avenida Tulum, or take a taxi from Avenida Tulum (around M$50). Boats also run from Playa Tortugas in the zona hotelera, for substantially more (US$15 one way).

Alternatively, you can hire a **private launch** next to Gran Puerto or at Puerto Juárez to stop to snorkel along the way. Rates are negotiable, but a typical trip costs about M$1500 for four passengers, with snorkelling gear.

The **car ferry** (M$220 per car, plus M$18 per additional passenger; 45min) leaves from Punta Sam, 6km north of Gran Puerto, with five departures daily (8am–8.15pm). But unless you're staying a long time, it's not worth taking a car to the island, which is quite small and has plenty of bicycles and mopeds for hire.

The attractions are simple: beach and sea – plus the fun of zipping around the island by bike, moped or golf cart, to more sea, more beaches and the tiny Maya temple that the conquistadors chanced upon, once full of female figures, which gave the place its name. But be back under the palms on **Playa Norte** by late afternoon: this big west-facing beach is one of the few places along Mexico's east coast where you can enjoy a glowing sunset over the water.

Arrival, information and transport

The passenger **ferries** (see box, above) arrive on Isla Mujeres at two adjacent piers; the car ferry comes in further south on Avenida Rueda Medina, at the end of Calle Bravo. From the pier, it's about a twenty-minute walk to the opposite side of the island and the most distant hotels. The **tourist office** (Mon–Fri 8am–8pm, Sat & Sun 9am–2pm) is on Rueda Medina just northwest of the passenger ferry piers. Here you can pick up leaflets and maps.

A **bus** runs every half-hour from Rueda Medina in the main town down to the southern end of the island (M$5). But a **moped** (M$100/ hr, M$350/24hr) or **bicycle** (M$100/day) is more flexible, and

ISLA MUJERES

Boats to Isla Contoy
Playa Norte
Punta Norte
Ferries to downtown Cancún
El Farolito
Bahía de Mujeres
Cuevas de los Tiburones Dormidos
Airstrip
Ferries to Cancún zona hotelera
Baseball Fields
Laguna Makax
Tortugranja
Salina Grande
CARIBBEAN SEA
Playa Lancheros
Artesanías de Mujeres
Hacienda Mundaca
0   1 km
El Garrafón de Castilla
Garrafón
ACCOMMODATION
Villa La Bella   B
Villa Rolandi   A
Punta Sur
EATING & DRINKING
Casa Rolandi   A
Lolo Lorena   2
Mango Café   3
El Varadero   1
Templo de Ixchel

the island is a very manageable size with few hills. With a group, hire a **golf cart** (M$150/hr, M$600/24hr). Virtually every other storefront rents out all three forms of transport, and prices vary little. You can also take a **taxi** – rates are posted at the stand between the ferry piers, starting at M$30 for hotels in the main town and running up to M$80 to the south end of the island; a tour costs M$180 per hour.

Accommodation

Isla Mujeres has a few solid **budget** places to stay, though they fill up in high season – advance reservations are recommended. The cheaper options are all on the northern edge of the island, and full apartments often give the best value (Ⓦ www.morningsinmexico.com has good listings). Note that on the east-facing coast, the sea is generally too rough to swim in. For **camping**, you can pitch your tent or sling up a hammock (US$6) on the grounds of the party-friendly *Poc-Na* **hostel**, Calle Matamoros at Calle Carlos Lazo (☎ 998/877-0090, Ⓦ www.pocna .com); dorm beds (US$9–14) and private rooms with air conditioning (❸) are a little less than spotless, and there's no kitchen.

Isla Mujeres town

Carmelina Guerrero 4 ☎ 998/877-0006, Ⓔ hotacarmelina@hotmail.com. The rooms at this budget operation are a steal, considering they have a/c and wi-fi. However, singles can be small. ❸

Casa El Pío Hidalgo 3, at Bravo Ⓦ www.casaelpio .com. The four rooms at this stylish hotel get booked up fast. All have one bed, plus a separate living room with a daybed. The owners' colour-saturated photos decorate the white walls, and the minimalist-cool wood furniture is made on the island. Three-night minimum. ❻

🏃 **Casa Sirena** Hidalgo, between Bravo and Allende Ⓦ www.sirena.com.mx. Very nicely redone home that has kept some old details, like tile floors, and added modern bathrooms, minimalist furniture and a breezy roof terrace with a panoramic view (ideal for the daily happy hour). Breakfasts are lavish, and there's even a small pool. Three-night minimum; advance reservations required. ❽

Francis Arlene Guerrero 7, at Abasolo ☎ 998/877-0310, Ⓦ www.francisarlene.com. Small family-owned hotel with well-tended courtyards, a roof terrace and clean, brightly painted rooms with plenty of comforts. A/c is an additional US$10. ❺

El Marcianito Abasolo 10 ☎ 998/877-0111. Ⓔ hotelmarcianito@hotmail.com. Though lacking *Vistalmar*'s view, this is otherwise a comparable budget option, with clean rooms with fans (upper floors are breezier) and well-maintained bathrooms. All have one double bed; an extra bed can be arranged for M$50. ❸

María Leticia Juárez 28, between Mateos and Matamoros ☎ 998/877-0832. Big, airy rooms with

or without kitchens and sitting rooms. It's great for long stays, but you absolutely must book ahead. ❹

Nautibeach Condos Playa Norte ☎ 998/877-0606 or 1-888/428-8599 in the US, Ⓦ www.nautibeach .com. Families look here first: enormous two-bedroom apartments, each with a balcony or veranda, in a modest, well-maintained complex facing the beach. If you don't need a kitchen, book one of the two studios (US$140). ❾

Las Palmas Guerrero 20 ☎ 998/236-5803, Ⓦ www.laspalmasonisla.com. Expat-run two-storey hotel built around a sociable courtyard with a communal kitchen. Rooms have very comfortable beds, fan and a/c; upstairs is a plunge pool and a great roof terrace. Five-night minimum Dec–April. ❻

🏃 **Villa La Bella** 2.5km south from the ferry, on the Caribbean side ☎ 998/888-0342, Ⓦ www.villalabella.com. This beautifully designed guesthouse is perched above dramatic crashing surf. Swim in the pretty pool instead, and sip a killer piña colada from the bar. The six rooms all have king-size beds and fantastic feather pillows. Delicious full breakfast is included. ❽

Villa Rolandi On the Sac Bajo Peninsula ☎ 998/999-2000, Ⓦ www.villarolandi.com. The fanciest hotel on the island by far, a European-feeling hideaway with huge, plush rooms with marble baths, a spa and a very good Italian-Swiss restaurant. The beach is relatively small, though, and it's far from the main town. ❾

🏃 **Vistalmar** Rueda Medina at Matamoros ☎ 998/877-0209, Ⓔ hotel_vistalmar1 @yahoo.com. Brightly painted hotel (the colours change every year or two) a couple of blocks northwest of the ferry pier. Good value, with choice of a/c or fan and big shared terraces with sea views. ❸

XS Hidalgo at northwest end, near Mateos ☎ 998/201-0203, ⓦ www.xshostel.com. This small, family-run place calls itself a hostel, but each of the six a/c rooms has only four beds. You can rent just one bed (US$19) and share, or rent the whole room. Good continental breakfast at the café, and on-site laundry.

The island

Isla Mujeres' main town occupies the northwestern third of the island. You can take a quick turn around the sixteen or so square blocks in just half an hour. The centre third of the island, referred to as *las colonias*, is a mainly locals' "suburb". Beyond, a single road runs along the west coast towards the southern tip, passing a ruined pirate abode, vacation homes and several small beaches with dead-calm waters. The road loops around and up the windswept, rocky east coast, where the surf crashes against the rocks. You can complete the circuit in a golf cart or by bicycle in just a few hours, or make a full day of it, taking time out for beach lounging and a leisurely lunch.

Isla Mujeres town and Punta Norte

Pedestrianized **Avenida Hidalgo**, lined with tequila bars, crochet-bikini vendors and family-friendly restaurants, cuts through the centre of **Isla Mujeres town**. The street's southeastern end opens onto the central **plaza**, where tamale and churro vendors set up shop in the evenings. On one side sits a church that's the site of week-long festivities every December; celebrating a legendary statue of the Virgin Mary on display inside (discovered in 1890 along with two others on the far north coast, the statue is said to walk on the beach occasionally).

Stretched around the northwestern edge of the town, **Playa Norte** is the archetypal Caribbean beach, with soft, deep sand, plenty of palm trees and bathtub-warm water stretching out at knee height for nearly a kilometre in some spots. The western side, just up from the ferry docks, is cluttered with fishing boats and ceviche stands; this is where *isleños* often swim and set up camp with the family on Sundays. At the northwestern tip, you can rent a chair and umbrella, with a drink from one of the mellow bars in perpetual happy hour. Across the northern side, close to the *Avalon Reef Club*, the all-inclusive resort on the promontory, you can **snorkel** a bit. The small bay in front of Casa Maya is particularly calm and a good spot for children to test the waters. (The shuttered house here belongs to one of the Mexican families who pioneered tourism on the island in the 1960s.)

Visit the town **cemetery**, on Calle Mateos at Calle Juárez, for the closing chapter of the saga of Fermín Antonio Mundaca (see below). The pirate's weather-worn grave, half-buried in sand, is empty: the lovelorn man died alone in Mérida. The grim traditional engraving, allegedly carved by the gloomy Mundaca himself, reads, "Lo que tu eres, yo fui. Lo que yo soy, tu serás" ("As you are, I was. As I am, you will be"). Just up Mateos, stop in at Artesanías Glenssy, a specialist in exceptionally beautiful **papier-mâché masks** and other objects.

South from town

Heading **south from town**, about halfway down the length of the island and a bit inland lurk the decaying remains of the **Hacienda Mundaca** (daily 9am–5pm; M$20), a ruined house and garden to which scores of romantic legends are attached. The most popular tale reports that in the mid-nineteenth century, the Spaniard Fermín Antonio Mundaca, a reputed swashbuckling pirate (though more likely a run-of-the-mill trader of sugar and slaves), fell in love with a young lovely nicknamed La Trigueña ("the brunette"). Attempting to woo her, he built an

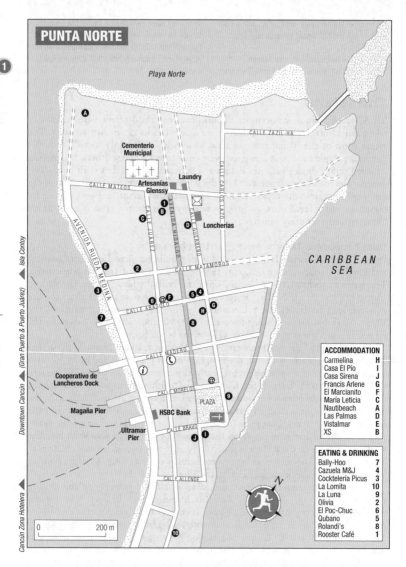

PUNTA NORTE

Playa Norte

CALLE ZAZIL-HA

Cementerio Municipal

Laundry

Artesanías Glenssy

Loncherías

CALLE MATEOS

CALLE JUÁREZ

AVENIDA HIDALGO

CALLE GUERRERO

CALLE CARLOS LAZO

AVENIDA RUEDA MEDINA

CALLE MATAMOROS

CARIBBEAN SEA

CALLE ABASOLO

CALLE MADERO

Cooperativo de Lancheros Dock

CALLE MORELOS

PLAZA

Magaña Pier

HSBC Bank

Ultramar Pier

CALLE BRAVO

CALLE ALLENDE

Downtown Cancún ◀ (Gran Puerto & Puerto Juárez) ◀ Isla Contoy

Cancún Zona Hotelera ◀

0   200 m

ACCOMMODATION
Carmelina	H
Casa El Pío	I
Casa Sirena	J
Francis Arlene	G
El Marcianito	F
María Leticia	C
Nautibeach	A
Las Palmas	D
Vistalmar	E
XS	B

EATING & DRINKING
Bally-Hoo	7
Cazuela M&J	4
Cocktelería Picus	3
La Lomita	10
La Luna	9
Olivia	2
El Poc-Chuc	6
Qubano	5
Rolandi's	8
Rooster Café	1

enormous hacienda in her honour; nonetheless, the lady spurned her suitor and ran off with someone her own age. Mundaca died alone and insane, and his glorious estate went to the dogs. Only one small house has been pieced together, with a few photos of old-time Isla Mujeres inside. There's also a somewhat random display of a traditional Maya hut. The best spot is the suitably gothic-feeling garden at the back of the property – where bug repellent is a must.

Across the roundabout, another road leads up the Sac Bajo Peninsula to the **tortugranja**, a government-run research centre (daily 9am–5pm; M$30) that protects eggs of endangered sea turtles and breeds them for release in the wild.

Farther on, Zama Beach Club is a nicely secluded patch of sand, with swimming pools and a bit of a stylish atmosphere.

Back at the roundabout, head about 100m south (just past the *Isla Mujeres Palace* resort) to **Playa Lancheros**, where the white sand is pleasantly shaded by palm trees. The rustic **restaurant** here produces some great seafood – its speciality is a fantastic *tikin-xic* fish, seasoned with achiote and grilled in banana leaves.

Shoppers may want to detour inland a few blocks from the roundabout, to visit the **Artesanías de Mujeres** (Mon–Sat 10am–5pm), a women's collective that makes beaded jewellery.

Punta Sur

Near the southern end of the island, the **Garrafón** reef is enclosed in a nature park (Sun–Fri 9am–6.30pm; ⓦwww.garrafon.com; US$59, including food and drink) to preserve what little is left of the coral. Even with gear, food and drink and activities like kayaking included, it's still a bit overpriced, though the fish are pretty. For the best snorkelling, you're better off on a tour from the piers in town or a trip to Isla Contoy (see below). Or, if you have small children, you can relax at the adjacent Garrafón de Castilla beach club (M$60), where colourful fish hang out in the small bay.

Just a bit farther south, turn right to reach an old **lighthouse**, which affords a decent view back up the coast. A rather rusted **sculpture park** occupies the land south of the lighthouse, apparently to add value to your ticket for the **Templo de Ixchel** (daily 9am–6.30pm; M$30 or free with Garrafón entry). When Francisco Hernández de Córdoba arrived in Mexico in the spring of 1517, here at the southernmost point of the island, the temple was filled with female fertility figures, dedications to the goddess Ixchel, which allegedly inspired the Spaniards to dub the place "the island of women". Today the temple is only a small blocky pile, but it is situated on low rocky cliffs where the waves crash dramatically. On New Year's Day, islanders come down here to watch the sun rise. The striking views continue as you head back north to the main town via the stark east-coast road, dotted with holiday villas (including a nifty one shaped like a conch shell) but still wild-feeling.

Offshore

Isla Mujeres is ringed with undersea attractions. **Las Cuevas de los Tiburones Dormidos** ("caves of the sleeping sharks"), a few kilometres from the northeast coast, is a popular dive spot where many species of sharks rest in an oxygen-rich freshwater current that lulls them into stasis. Trips here and to other nearby sites are easily booked through **dive shops** in town – recommended is Enrique's Unique Dives, Rueda Medina 1, by the PEMEX station (☎998/145-3594, ⓦwww.divingislamujeres.com).

For **snorkelling**, go with the *lancheros* cooperative, north of the passenger ferry landings (US$20; 2hr) at the end of Calle Madero. A popular destination is **El Farolito**, a shallow spot off the tip of the Sac Bajo Peninsula where you're mostly protected from the current. Aside from Isla Holbox (see p.73), Isla Mujeres is the only other official departure point for trips to snorkel with the **whale sharks** that gather off the Gulf coast between May and September. Boats usually leave at 8am, and the trip to the sharks takes a couple of hours; there's lunch and reef snorkelling on the way back. Every shop touts the trip, but only a small number of boats have a permit, so prices are all the same, about US$125.

If it's not whale-shark season, the next best day-trip is to **Isla Contoy**, 30km north. Designated a national park in 1961, the small island is home to some 150 bird species, including large colonies of pelicans, cormorants and frigates. Sea turtles nest on the calm western beaches, while the windy eastern coast is a mix of dunes and limestone cliffs. The boat trip out is leisurely, with stops to snorkel at reefs along the way; by lunchtime you're deposited on a small beach in a lagoon. Here you may find several other groups, which can dampen the isolated spirit a little, but the total number of daily visitors is limited to two hundred. You have the afternoon to relax in the sun or explore the wild setting. For an M$100 donation, you can take a birding tour with one of the resident biologists.

You can go with the *lancheros* cooperative, or with Captain Tony García, at Matamoros 7 (☎998/877-0229); both come highly recommended by island regulars. In either case, tours last the whole day and include a basic breakfast, grilled fish for lunch, soft drinks and snorkel gear for about US$55 per person. For more information on the reserve, contact Amigos de Isla Contoy (☎998/884-7483, ⓦ www.islacontoy.org), which has an office in the Plaza Bonita mall in downtown Cancún (see p.66).

Eating and drinking

The area along and around Avenida Hidalgo, between Morelos and Abasolo, is lined with **restaurants**. For inexpensive, basic Mexican food, head for the **loncherías** opposite *Las Palmas* hotel. At night, food **vendors** set up on the main plaza. For **nightlife**, the mellow palapa-roof **bars** on Playa Norte typically have cold beers and perhaps some Jimmy Buffett renditions by a local guitar player. Off the beach, *Bally-Hoo*, on the pier opposite Calle Abasolo, draws a yachtie crowd, and sprawling *La Luna*, on Calle Guerrero facing the plaza, hosts salsa bands and a Sunday reggae party.

Casa Rolandi At the *Villa Rolandi* hotel, at the end of the Sac Bajo Peninsula ☎998/877-0500, ⓦ www.rolandi.com. Elegant northern Italian restaurant, on a terrace overlooking the turquoise bay – one of the best spots on the island for a romantic dinner. The wood oven turns out specialities like suckling pig (M$320) and flaky fish (M$249).

Cazuela M&J Abasolo at Guerrero. Enjoy a fine ocean view at this casual café serving inexpensive (mostly Mexican) breakfasts. The signature egg dish is a sort of omelette baked in a *cazuela*, or earthenware casserole. Big glasses of green *chaya* juice are another healthy option. Tues–Sun 7am–2pm.

Cocktelería Picus Rueda Medina. Small beachfront hut just north of the ferry landings serving fresh and inexpensive *ceviches* and shrimp cocktails.

🏃 **La Lomita** Juárez 25-B. Locals line up for a helping of the chef-owner's daily special (M$60), anything from bean soup and *chiles rellenos* to pan-fried fish with salsa verde. Fantastic home cooking that's worth the hike up the small hill two blocks south of the plaza. Lunch only.

Lolo Lorena Rueda Medina, in the *colonias*. ⓦ www.lololorena.com. A Belgian woman cooks a creative set menu, usually Mediterranean-inspired, every night, served at one big convivial table in her home's courtyard (US$30 for five courses); reservations required. In high season, she also runs a small bakery in front, 8–10am and 1.30–5pm (closed Mon and Thurs).

Mango Café Payo Obispo (Perimetral Oriente), opposite Guadalupe Church ☎998/230-8489. A colourful restaurant in the *colonias*, best known for its breakfasts (fluffy French toast with seasonal fruit compotes; poblano chile stuffed with eggs and chaya, M$90), but it's also open for equally creative lunch and dinner. Hours scale back in low season – call to check.

Olivia Matamoros, between Juárez and Rueda Medina ☎998/877-1765. A wide-ranging Mediterranean menu, from Moroccan to Israeli flavours, is served in a pretty garden. Mains from M$80. Very popular, so reserve in high season. Tues–Sat 5–9.30pm.

El Poc-Chuc Abasolo at Juárez. This bargain *lonchería* with red vinyl tablecloths and a giant mural of Chichén Itzá is handily also open for dinner (although not all of the big meals are available at night). Fish soup (M$35) and crispy *panuchos* (M$25) are two reliable offerings.

Qubano Abasolo, between Hidalgo and Guerrero. The signature *tostón* sandwich here is a messy delight between two slabs of crispy-fried plantain slices, and the Hungarian potatoes are incongruous but tasty. Mon–Fri noon–5pm.

Rolandi's Hidalgo, between Madero and Abasolo. Part of a much-loved local chain, this casual place specializes in excellent pizza from a wood-fired oven.

🏃 Rooster Café Hidalgo, between Mateos and Matamoros. Chef Sergio cooked at big-name restaurants in the US – now he turns out beautifully presented, creative dinners: lobster with a grapefruit sauce, for instance, or roast duck with mango chutney (M$185). Breakfast and lunch are also strong (try the Isla omelet), and everything's reasonably priced.

El Varadero West coast, adjacent to Puerto Isla Mujeres. This super-casual Cuban restaurant is nestled among palm trees. Garlicky pork (M$95) and refreshing mojitos (M$50) are the specialities. Tell the cab driver "El Varadero del Burgos", as there's another place with a similar name nearby. Closed Mon.

Listings

Banks HSBC, on Rueda Medina opposite the ferry docks, has an ATM; another ATM is on the Ultramar pier.

Internet and telephone There are several cafés. The one next to *El Marcianito*, on Abasolo, between Rueda Medina and Juárez, can download photos from cameras; one on the northwest side of the plaza has cheap international calling too.

Laundry Lavandería Mis Dos Angelitos, Guerrero at Mateos (Mon–Sat 8am–11pm; M$10/kg, with 4-kilo minimum), and at *XS Hostel*.

Post office Guerrero at Mateos (Mon–Thurs 9am–4pm).

Isla Holbox

Near the northeastern corner of the peninsula, **ISLA HOLBOX** (pronounced "ol-BOSH") is sometimes touted as a new rustic beach hideaway to fill the place that Isla Mujeres once had in travellers' affections. The sole village has sand streets and a genuinely warm feel. The gulf waters here do not have the same glittering clarity as the Caribbean (nor the vibrant reefs), but they're warm and clean, and the beaches are all but empty. Development is of course on the rise, but much of the island remains wild and harbours all manner of **birds**, including flamingos. From mid-June to mid-September, visitors come to see the huge and rare **whale sharks** (see box, p.76) that congregate just off the cape. Sea turtles also nest here during the summer months.

One spot of trouble in paradise: potentially fearsome mosquitoes during the wet season (a popular Holbox souvenir T-shirt says "Blood Donor"). And after the bustle of whale-shark season, the island basically shuts down for the rest of September and October. Along with huge rain puddles in the streets, this can make the place feel a bit dreary until the weather turns dry and business picks up again near the end of November.

Getting there: Solferino and Chiquilá

The easiest way to reach Holbox is from Cancún, on the daily **bus** (4hr) for Chiquilá, the closest mainland town by ferry. The bus leaves Cancún at 7.50am (Mayab) and 1.45pm (Noreste), with an additional Mayab service at 12.40pm in June and July. Coming from the west is more difficult: buses leave Mérida (6hr) and Valladolid (3hr) in the middle of the night and arrive in time for the 6am ferry. Transferring in Tizimín (3hr) is a little easier, with a choice of three daytime buses. You can also take any second-class bus along Hwy-180 *libre* and get off at the tiny town of El Ideal; from there, you can take a taxi north to Chiquilá for about M$350, or, if you time it right, transfer to the bus coming from Cancún, which passes through around 10.30am and 4.15pm.

If you are **driving** from Cancún or Mérida, don't take the toll highway, as there's no convenient exit. You may want to stop in the village of **SOLFERINO**, 42km north of Hwy-180 and 15km south of Chiquilá, which is part of a regional ecotourism network that offers great opportunities to visit rural settlements and seldom-seen wild spots. Solferino's main contribution is a **buggy-and-kayak tour** to a nearby cork forest and lake. You can go for the afternoon (M$450; 4–5hr) or stay overnight at cabañas. The minimum group size is three people. Look for the operation on the west side of the road, on the south side of town, in a big palapa with a bridge leading to it. If no one's around, ask across the road or call the manager, José (mobile 984/879-1001). If you just want to stretch your legs, at least stop at the **orchid garden** (daily 8am–6pm; M$10) and giant ceiba tree (east from the highway – turn at the "Orquideario" sign). Next to the orchid garden is *Arboleta*, a small **café** and ad hoc gallery run by a friendly and talented Croatian woman. She also rents a beautiful **room**, with private bath (mobile 984/137-6409, ⓔarboleta@gmail.com; ❷); it's a bargain, especially by the week.

In **CHIQUILÁ**, the **ferry** for Holbox (M$60; 30min) leaves at least at 6am, 8am, 10am, 11am, noon, 2pm, 4pm, 5pm and 7pm, and more frequently in the summer. Holbox is also served by an unreliable **car ferry**, but there's no sense in taking a car to the tiny island. Secure parking is available near the pier (be certain you've set the price before you leave – about M$30 for any portion of a day). If you're with a group or arrive between ferries, you might want to hire a private boat (about M$350). But don't miss the last ferry: Chiquilá is not a place you want to get stranded. There's a restaurant, a basic hotel, a store and a petrol station, but little else. Buses **leave Chiquilá** for Cancún (2 daily at 7.30am & 1.45pm; 4hr) and Mérida, via Valladolid (1 daily at 5.30am; 6hr).

Arrival and information

The ferry moors at a dock on the south side of the island, where golf-cart and *triciclo* (pedicab) **taxis** wait to take you to the hotels in town or along the north coast. The maximum charge is M$60, to the furthest hotels. Otherwise, it's a ten-minute walk straight along Avenida Benito Juárez to the centre or, two blocks further, the beach. You'll usually receive a **map** on the ferry, though street names are seldom used.

On the modest main square, called the *parque*, you'll find a **post office, money-exchange** desk and, upstairs from the town hall, an **ATM**. It can run dry, though, so it's wise to bring extra cash. There's an **internet** café one block east, off the northeast corner of the plaza. Very few people have cars; walking distances (without luggage) are manageable, and locals also use the *triciclos* and electric **golf carts**. The latter are available to rent (about M$800/24hr) from several outlets near the *parque*, such as Rentadora Monkeys (☎984/875-2029). You can also get around by **bike** (M$25/hr), though they aren't always maintained very well.

Accommodation

Small-scale hotel development stretches east of town for a couple of kilometres. In early summer and before Christmas, rates for some of the upmarket rooms can fall by almost half; July and August, however, can be priced nearly as high as Christmas and Easter weeks. The **beachfront** hotels are all mid-range to luxury, but there are a few decent cheaper options away from the water. You can camp at *Ida y Vuelta* (US$7.50 per person).

Casa las Tortugas On the beach two blocks east of the plaza ☎984/875-2129, ⓦwww .holboxcasalastortugas.com. A great little collection of round, two-storey cabañas, beautifully decorated and tucked among dense greenery. Breakfast is included. A/c. ❼

Ida y Vuelta Escobedo east of the plaza, behind *Xaloc* ☎998/875-2358, ⓦwww.holboxhostel.com.

A friendly hostel with screened shelters for tents or hammocks (US$8) as well as a few beds (US$9), clean bathrooms and a shared kitchen. There's also a private house for rent. ⑤

La Palapa On the beach at Morelos (two blocks west of the plaza) ☏ 984/875-2121, ⓦ www.hotellapalapa.com. A consistently well-run beach hotel with very friendly staff. Rooms are whitewashed and simple, with tile floors and showers made of conch shells. A/c optional. ⑦

Posada Anhelyng Porfirio Díaz, three blocks west of the plaza ☏ 984/875-2006. Nine standard-issue but clean rooms around a small courtyard. A good alternative to Los Arcos if you want to be away from noise on the plaza; rooms here are also newer. ③

Posada Los Arcos West side of the plaza ☏ 984/875-2043. Clean, basic rooms, some with kitchenettes, around a small courtyard. Choice of fan or a/c (an additional M$100). ③

Posada Mawimbi On the beach next to *Casa las Tortugas* ☏ 984/875-2003, ⓦ www.mawimbi.net. Similar to *Casa las Tortugas* in layout, but with a few less expensive rooms. A/c in all rooms, but opt for an upstairs room if you like a breeze. ⑦

Tribu Coldwell, three blocks west of the plaza ☏ 984/875-2507, ⓦ www.tribuhostel.com. One of the best hostels in the Yucatán, and mostly hand-built by the owners. Facilities include a big kitchen, a cool bar and a movie room. Dorm beds are M$125–165, depending on room layout. Big fans and good cross-ventilation. Private rooms might convert non-hostel fans: tidy and simple, and a steal for being just a half-block off the beach. ③

Villas Los Mapaches Coldwell, four blocks west of the plaza ☏ 984/875-2090, ⓦ www.losmapaches.com. Comfortable bungalows tucked in among trees; almost all have kitchenettes, ideal for longer stays. Note there's no a/c, though. ⑥

The island

Uninhabited until the late nineteenth century (locals claim pirates as their forebears), Holbox today is home to only about two thousand people, most engaged in fishing, or selling fish to hungry visitors. All of the population is concentrated in a **small town** on the north coast. With sand streets, wooden houses and almost no cars, it's tranquil in the extreme. Most activities for visitors involve the wildlife on or around the island.

The biggest such natural attraction, literally and figuratively, is the group of **whale sharks** that cluster off the coast in late summer. You may see dolphins, rays and flying fish on the hour-long boat ride out to where the sharks gather, and tours often stop on the way back at Cabo Catoche, the northern cape, where there's a clutch of fishermen's shacks and a tall lighthouse. Operadora Turística Monkeys (☏ 984/875-2442, ⓦ www.holboxmonkeys.com) is one of the most established tour operators. The tour price (M$1000 per person, including lunch and snorkel gear; 5–6hr) is typically the same with every company, though it may change from season to season.

Other popular tours include **Isla Pájaros**, a very small island wildlife sanctuary inside Laguna Yalahau. A flamingo colony nests here between April and October, along with about 150 other species. Two observation towers give birdwatchers great views at sunset. Also in the lagoon, a freshwater **spring** wells up among the mangroves on the mainland side – a popular swimming hole that's a side destination for many trips. **Isla de Pasión** is a tiny dot of sand off the west end of the island; a big part of the trip is wading through the shallow water to reach it. Visits to these places, as well as to a cork-tree swamp near Solferino on the mainland, can be arranged through most hotels.

There's a **dive shop** at *Posada Mawimbi* (though the reefs aren't very remarkable), and **fly-fishing** is also big, as tarpon are here year-round (though the big ones come only April to August). Holbox Tarpon Club (☏ 984/875-2103, ⓦ www.holboxtarponclub.com) is a long-established guide service.

Eating and drinking

Your dining options on Holbox consist of seafood and Italian, and sometimes both. **Restaurants** are all very casual, and this can extend to opening hours as well – they

Visiting the whale sharks

The whale shark (*Rhincodon typus*, or *tiburón ballena* in Spanish) is a true shark, but it earns its name with its enormous size. The largest known fish, it can reach up to 14m in length, and typical adults are between 7m and 10m long. Another common name, domino shark, comes from its distinctive black skin covered in rows of white dots. The fish's lifespan is also remarkably long, as it can typically live well into its 70s.

Although whale sharks populate the tropical zone around the globe, the shallow waters off Isla Holbox are the only place in the world where such a large population gathers. The fish typically congregate in pods of ten or twenty, but researchers estimate the Holbox group at more than two hundred – perhaps because the swirling water here, where the Gulf of Mexico meets the Atlantic Ocean, teems with plankton, the whale sharks' primary food. Unlike sharks of the popular imagination, with their toothy maws, whale sharks are gentle filter-feeders. As they glide slowly in circles, they are sucking up whatever small sea life is in front of them. Swimming alongside the passive animals poses no risk, except perhaps of getting tossed about by the current from a turning or diving fish.

Whale shark tourism on Holbox has developed very recently, and regulations for visiting the creatures were applied for the first time in 2003. By law, Isla Holbox and Isla Mujeres are the only departure points for tours. Most of the area in which the fish swim is now a marine park, which requires visitors to be accompanied by trained guides, who should make sure swimmers get no closer than 2m to the sharks. Good captains should never attempt to "steer" the sharks with their boats. Take a hat and biodegradable sunscreen if you have it; as in other marine parks, regular sunblock is prohibited.

vary greatly depending on the season. Don't expect any **nightlife** – the closest thing to a full bar is *Carioca's*. Locals generally lounge around on the plaza, where there might be a traditional Mexican *lotería* runner, or some vendors or musicians.

Buena Vista Juárez at Coldwell. A very simple family-run fish restaurant, half a block back from the beach. Fried whole fish – straight from the water that day – is the thing to order.

Carioca's On the beach two blocks east of the plaza. If you want a drink, you'll probably wind up here – it's the only bar scene in town. And it's worth coming earlier for the "suxi" (pronounce it Maya-style) and other creative blends of Japanese and Mexican.

La Colibri Southwest corner of the plaza. This little wooden house, painted with flowers, is enticing – it's a nice place to start the morning with a big fruit juice. But for more substantial food, you're better off elsewhere.

La Conquista Juárez at Coldwell (one block north off the northwest corner of the plaza). This screened-in wood hut serves great empanadas and daily lunch specials.

La Parilla de Juan Igualdad at Bravo (one block east off the northeast corner of the plaza). Plant-filled, breezy upstairs Argentine-run restaurant, one of the more expensive in town (mains M$200 and up), but a nice creative break from the usual, with dishes like fresh snook in sun-dried tomato pesto or pastry stuffed with cheese and spinach. But skip the expensive margaritas (M$70!).

Los Pelones West side of the plaza. Authentic, handmade Italian food cooked by a friendly couple. There are familiar pasta dishes, such as ravioli with blue cheese and walnuts (all pasta is house-made, and perfectly toothsome), but also farther-reaching creations like couscous with seafood. Similar prices to *La Parilla de Juan*.

El Pollo Mago West side of the plaza. Good, inexpensive (M$60 for meat dishes; M$120 for seafood) home-cooked Mexican meals and snacks, similar to *La Conquista*, with a bit more variety.

Zarabanda Escobedo at Palomino (one block south off the southeast corner of the plaza). Long-established seafood place, not so bare-bones as *Buena Vista*. Soups here are particularly good, as are the ceviches. The non-fish Mexican options are solid too.

2

Playa del Carmen, Cozumel and the Caribbean coast

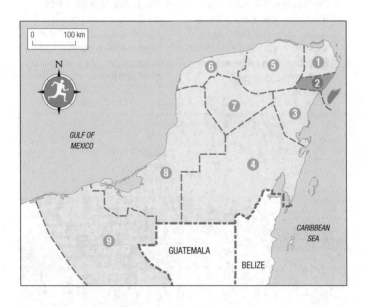

CHAPTER 2   # Highlights

* **Puerto Morelos Reef** The coral outcroppings off the coast of Puerto Morelos are a great place to snorkel or learn to dive. See p.83

* **La Quinta Avenida** With easily the best nightlife on the Caribbean coast, the central tourist artery through Playa del Carmen is an ever-evolving cosmopolitan party. See p.89

* **Río Secreto** Swim through this water-filled cave with nothing but your headlamp for light. A stunning natural attraction – and a great rainy-day activity. See p.90

* **Mamita's Beach Club** Playa del Carmen's best beach is also its most stylish social scene. See p.93

* **Faro Celarain Eco Park** The nature reserve at the southern tip of Cozumel is a must for birdwatchers (look for the Cozumel vireo), and its beaches are beautiful, too. See p.99

* **Colombia Shallows** This sandy-floor coral garden off Cozumel's southwest coast teems with colour and life – a mesmerizing place to snorkel. See p.101

▲ Crocodile lagoon in Faro Celarain Eco Park, Cozumel

Playa del Carmen, Cozumel and the Caribbean coast

evelopment along the spectacular white-sand beaches south of Cancún has reached fever pitch, as landowners have raced to cash in on the resort city's popularity. The tourist authorities granted the area south of Cancún the rather grandiose title **Riviera Maya**, and holidaymakers come in droves to the mammoth gated retreats that dot the coast. That said, finding a relatively deserted stretch of beach is by no means impossible. Immediately south of Cancún, in fact, lies one of the quieter spots: **Puerto Morelos**, a tiny town with clean beaches that has so far avoided unattractive development. (Its other big draw: offshore is the start of the vibrant **Mesoamerican Barrier Reef**, which stretches down to Honduras; the section here is a great, less-visited place to dive and snorkel.) A bit further south, **Punta Bete** is a little sandy point dotted with a couple of surprisingly affordable hotels. By contrast, the phenomenal growth of **Playa del Carmen**, formerly known only as the place where diving fanatics hopped on the ferry to **Isla de Cozumel**, has transformed a fishing camp into a major holiday destination in its own right, renowned for its nightlife and gorgeous beachfront.

A half-hour boat ride away, the island of Cozumel is ringed by some of the most beautiful **reefs** in Mexico. Since the early Sixties, the barely populated island has been a destination primarily for divers, but in the past two decades, the place has boomed like everywhere else, welcoming direct flights from the US as well as massive **cruise ships** at three piers. But you can still escape the crush of visitors and explore the island's rainbow-hued underwater gardens. And there's plenty to see on land as well, from the pretty town of **San Miguel** to the deserted eastern coast, known for its empty beaches and rustic bars, where you can while away the time with a margarita or enjoy some fresh grilled fish.

You can explore the mainland coast easily by car, or take cheap and efficient public transport along Hwy-307: both *colectivos* and second-class buses will stop anywhere you request, though at many points, the coast is between one and three kilometres from the highway. On Cozumel, though, there are no such options, so you'll have to rent a car to see the whole island, or join an organized tour.

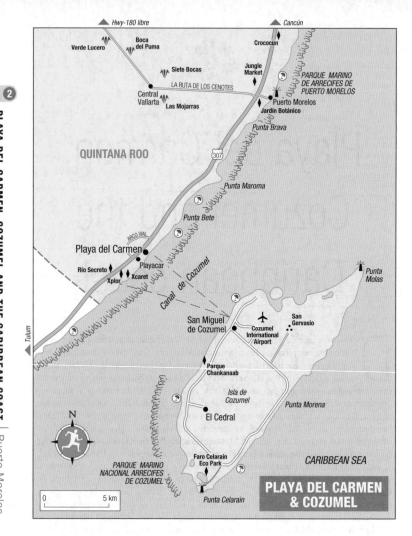

Verde Lucero
Boca del Puma
Siete Bocas
LA RUTA DE LOS CENOTES
Central Vallarta
Las Mojarras
Crococun
Jungle Market
PARQUE MARINO DE ARRECIFES DE PUERTO MORELOS
Puerto Morelos
Jardín Botánico
Punta Brava

Hwy-180 libre
Cancún

QUINTANA ROO

307

Punta Maroma

Punta Bete

ARCO VIAL

Playa del Carmen
Río Secreto
Playacar
Xplor   Xcaret

Canal de Cozumel

Punta Molas

San Miguel de Cozumel
Cozumel International Airport
San Gervasio

Parque Chankanaab

Isla de Cozumel

El Cedral

Punta Morena

N

PARQUE MARINO NACIONAL ARRECIFES DE COZUMEL

Faro Celarain Eco Park

Punta Celarain

CARIBBEAN SEA

PLAYA DEL CARMEN & COZUMEL

0   5 km

Tulum

Puerto Morelos

Leaving Cancún behind, **PUERTO MORELOS**, 20km south, is the first town on the coast. Even though it's practically in the shadow of Cancún's hotels, it feels wonderfully remote and barely developed. As the only working fishing village between Cancún and Tulum that hasn't been entirely consumed by tourism, it's so mellow that the afternoon siesta is still observed by most businesses. It can be extremely quiet in the summer, when many places shut entirely, but it isn't as dead as, say, Isla Holbox. The **beach** is pretty and broad, but the main draw here is the **reef**, which lies only half a kilometre offshore and is in healthy condition. For a population of roughly three thousand, the town offers a remarkable number of excellent **restaurants**, ranging from modern-fusion panache to hearty bargain lunches. Inland, on the road to Central Vallarta, some beautiful **cenotes** offer a place to swim and explore. With direct bus service from the airport, it's easy for visitors to bypass Cancún altogether, making Puerto Morelos their first stop along the Riviera Maya, or their last.

Arrival and information

Buses going down the coast leave the station in downtown Cancún every ten minutes, or leave directly from the airport (13 daily, 10am–8.45pm; 20min, M$55) and drop you at the highway junction. Taxis wait here to take you the 2km into town for M$20 (M$40 for some more distant hotels), or you might be lucky enough to meet up with the *colectivos* or buses that also make the trip, on no discernible schedule. There's no **info** office, but most hotels have copies of a booklet with a full map.

Accommodation

With a few exceptions, **hotels** in Puerto Morelos aren't fantastic, because most visitors rent apartments; the price threshold is also somewhat high, as there are no hostels or seriously low-end options. For **apartments**, check with the owners of Alma Libre bookstore (⑳www.almalibrebooks.com), who rent a few excellent places and recommend others as well. You can't **camp** on the beach in Puerto Morelos, as it's technically part of a marine park, but a good option is the pleasantly ramshackle *Acamaya Reef Park* (☏987/871-0131, ⑳www.acamayareef .com; US$15 per person), on the beach 5km north of town – look for a signposted turn near the entrance to the Crococun zoo. It also has six good-value cabañas, with shared or private bath (◐).

The Mesoamerican Barrier Reef

Mexico's Caribbean coast faces the **Mesoamerican Barrier Reef**, the second-longest reef in the world (Australia's Great Barrier Reef comes in first). Stretching from Puerto Morelos to the Bay Islands of Honduras, the reef hugs the shoreline for more than 700km. The complex eco-system also encompasses outlying atolls, such as those around Cozumel, the sea-grass beds close to shore and the mangrove swamps that help feed the coral and filter out pollutants from land. More than five hundred species, including the endangered West Indian manatee and extremely rare and slow-growing **black coral**, thrive here.

But like most coral systems around the world, the Mesoamerican Barrier Reef is under threat. Intense hurricanes have stirred up sand that smothers the coral. And the tourism boom onshore has had its own steady impact: some eighty percent of the oldest hard coral has died in just the past thirty years, and slick algae growth in many spots threatens essential reef organisms. Few building projects have directly attacked the reef, but careless development has destroyed swathes of mangrove swamps, which have been either torn out or used as dumping grounds.

Compared with other stretches of reef around the Caribbean, however, the Mesoamerican system is relatively healthy. As part of a larger trend along the coast, Puerto Morelos residents successfully campaigned to have their reef frontage designated a national park in 2000, in order to prevent overfishing and other harmful practices. Environmentally sensitive building codes are often ignored, though the government environmental agency has been to known to make crackdowns – unfortunately after damage is done. Still, the hope is that the tourism industry won't wind up killing off one of its most profitable attractions.

Amar Inn On the seafront, 500m north of the main plaza ☎998/871-0026, ✉amar_inn@hotmail.com. Bohemian, family-run hotel on the beach with six large rooms and three cabañas (fan only); some have high ceilings, loft beds and kitchenettes. Delicious Mexican breakfast included. ❺

Cabañas Puerto Morelos Rojo Gómez, north of the plaza ☎998/206-9064, ⓦwww .cancuncabanas.com. "Cabañas" sound rustic, but these are modern rooms with kitchenettes, all one block back from the beach (some have sea views) and centred on a pretty pool and garden. A/c optional (US$5 extra). ❻

Casa Cacahuate C 2 in the zona urbana. ☎998/208-9148, ⓦwww.mayaecho.com. With two spacious guestrooms, the "peanut house" is a great chance to be in the forest in relative comfort, as well as to interact with the non-touristy side of Puerto Morelos. It's also a handy place for solo travellers to get acclimatized, under the wing of hostess Sandra, a longtime Mexico resident (who also runs the Jungle Market, see p.84). ❹

Inglaterra Niños Héroes, half a block north of the plaza ☎998/206-9081, ⓦwww.hotelinglaterra .com. This budget place was in the middle of a complete overhaul in late 2010 – it will likely be a good-value spot. ❹

Marviya Rojo Gómez, 500m north of the plaza ☎998/871-0136, ⓦwww.marviya.com. Choose either a room in a big villa (weekly rates only) or one of the expansive studios with kitchens, rented by a friendly French couple. Two-night minimum in studios; one-week minimum in villa. ❹

Ojo de Agua On the seafront, 400m north of the plaza ☎987/840-3942, ⓦwww.ojo-de-agua.com. Bright, sunny rooms, all with a/c and colourful decor, most overlooking a giant pool; beyond lies a clean beach and a good bar-restaurant. One added perk: sea-view rooms don't cost more. ❻

Posada Amor Rojo Gómez, just south of the plaza ☎998/871-0033. One of the longest-running hotels in town, well-run and clean. Some of the quirky, individually decorated rooms are the least expensive around. A reasonable alternative if Posada El Moro is full, though try to get a room away from the bar. ❺

🏃 Posada El Moro Rojo Gómez 17, just north of the plaza ☎987/871-0159, ⓦwww .posadaelmoro.com. Sunny, spacious rooms with choice of fan or a/c (US$10 more). Suites have kitchens, and the weekly rates are a steal. Inside is a pretty little garden and even a small pool. Continental breakfast included. ❺

Rancho Sak-Ol 1km south of the plaza on the beach ☎987/871-0181, ⓦwww.ranchosakol.com. South of town, this is a pleasantly located, castaway-feeling mini-resort. A stay at these casual two-storey thatched cabañas with hanging beds includes a large breakfast buffet; guests can also use the communal kitchen. ❼

The beach town

A small, modern plaza sits in the centre of Puerto Morelos. The turn-off from Hwy-307 ends here, and **the town**'s only proper streets lead north and south from it, parallel to the beach. The plaza has a small church, a baseball court and a

---

Luxury Hotels in the Riviera Maya

Mexico's Caribbean coast is chockablock with resorts promising luxury, but not all of them live up to the name. For those in the mood for a really splendid resort experience, here's how the best of the best compare.

• **Banyan Tree Mayakoba** (ⓦwww.banyantree.com) Amazing service and huge suites from this Thailand-based operation, and warmer feeling than the neigh-bouring Mandarin Oriental.

• **Ceiba del Mar** (ⓦwww.ceibadelmar.com) Not quite as splendid as its competitors, but not so isolated either – you're just five minutes from Puerto Morelos. Also the only place that's less than US$500 in high season.

• **Esencia** (see p.109) Probably our favourite, as it genuinely feels like you're visiting at some wealthy friend's villa. Very small, and a great beach.

• **Maroma** (ⓦwww.maromahotel.com) Neck-and-neck with Esencia, Maroma is a bit bigger but still intimate, with a distinct, non-flashy style. So dedicated to mellow relaxation that rooms don't have TVs.

• **The Tides** (ⓦwww.tidesrivieramaya.com) The beach resort for shade-lovers: each totally private palapa-roof room has its own plunge pool. The beach is a bit rocky.

taxi rank. It's also home to the wonderful Alma Libre (Oct–May Mon–Sat 10am–3pm & 6–9pm, Sun 4–9pm; ☎998/252-2207, ⓦ www.almalibrebooks.com), probably Mexico's most extensive second-hand English-language **bookshop**, with some twenty thousand volumes to choose from, including a solid selection of books about the area's natural and archeological attractions. If you'll be visiting Puerto Morelos for a while, sign up for the owners' email newsletter on everything local, from restaurant openings to speed-bump news. They can also transfer the digital photos from your camera to a CD.

Off the east side of the plaza lies the **beach**, a long wooden **dock** and the old **lighthouse**, a squat little concrete structure knocked Tower of Pisa-style by a hurricane. A newer model has been built behind it, but the old one remains as a town icon. Even with a thriving stretch of **reef** only 600m offshore, Puerto Morelos sees nowhere near the traffic of Cozumel or Playa del Carmen. This also makes it a good spot to learn to **dive**. The reef can be visited only with a guide, who will take you to shallow coral gardens or, for more advanced divers, a couple of wreck sites. Long-established Almost Heaven Adventures (☎998/871-0230, ⓦ www.almostheavenadventures .com), just north of the plaza on Avenida Rojo Gómez, offers certification courses (US$350) and one- and two-tank dives (US$50–70), as well as **sport-fishing**

Ceiba del Mar & ▲ Acamaya Reef Park

ACCOMMODATION

Amar Inn	C
Cabañas Puerto Morelos	A
Casa Cacahuate	G
Inglaterra	E
Marviya	B
Ojo de Agua	D
Posada Amor	H
Posada El Moro	F
Rancho Sak-Ol	I

EATING & DRINKING

Al Chimichurri	9
Café d'Amancia	7
La Casa del Pescador	6
John Gray's Kitchen	2
Lonchería Mimi	3
Peskayitos	8
La Playita	1
T@cos.com	4
El Tío	5

PUERTO MORELOS

charters (from US$300). For **snorkelling**, you can go with Almost Heaven (which does night trips as well) or any of the boats at the two piers in town, for US$20 per person (2hr).

Very attractive and reasonably priced **craftwork**, such as hammocks and embroidered clothing, can be found at Hunab-Ku Artesanía, two blocks south of the plaza on Rojo Gómez. Here you can often see the artisans at work making their goods – and peek at the crocodiles that live in the mangroves behind. If all the restaurants in town make you curious, head to the Little Mexican Cooking School (☎998/251-8060, ⓦwww.thelittlemexicancookingschool.com; US$99), which runs half-day **cooking classes** in a sunny kitchen with an enthusiastic Mexican-Canadian chef. The school also has a small shop that sells cooking tools and locally produced foods.

Inland from the beach

The larger part of Puerto Morelos is actually on the inland side of Hwy-307. Few tourists make the trek here, but if you come, you'll find great places to eat, as well as the excellent **Jungle Market**, a craft sale and party run by a group of local women. Embroidery work is well priced, and there's also good food and music. It starts at 10.30am every Sunday December through Easter – you can ask most cab drivers for it by the English name, or say "Calle Dos, zona urbana" (M$50). The same group of women run a very affordable **spa** (massages US$40 for 1hr) Tuesday to Saturday; call (☎998/208-9148, ⓦwww.mayaecho.com) for reservations.

A bit farther afield, the so-called **Ruta de los Cenotes** is a road that runs inland past several swimming holes and caves (all are open daily 10am–5pm). Several spots have been built up as major group-tour attractions for day-trippers from Cancún, but there are a couple where independent travellers can relax. The best one is the first you reach, **Cenote Las Mojarras** (☎998/848-2831, ⓦwww .cenotelasmojarras.com; M$250), at Km 12.5. The cenote itself is a big open pool with a zipline. Entry fees can be lower if you're only staying a couple of hours, but with nature trails, lunch cooked over a wood fire and, best of all, an enthusiastic manager who knows everything about the local plants, you can easily spend all day here; you can even camp, with prior reservations. Several kilometres further is the turn for **Siete Bocas** (M$100), really a water-filled cave with seven points of entry; the facilities here are quite basic, and the cenote is more popular with divers than with snorkellers, as there's not much natural light to explore by. At Km 16, you reach **Boca del Puma** (☎998/886-9869, ⓦwww.bocadelpuma .com), the best of the big group-tour operations, with a three-hour bike tour to two cenotes (US$60), and a similar trip on horseback. At km 17.5, **Verde Lucero** (M$60) is a pretty, rustic-feeling pool with only basic facilities – some bathrooms and basic snacks. If you're driving in from the north, stay in the farthest-right, "local" lane when passing through Puerto Morelos, and turn at the large cement arch just south of town. Taxis from Puerto Morelos to any of the cenotes cost about M$180; a round-trip will depend on how much waiting time you want. Many dive shops in Puerto Morelos (see p.83) also run snorkelling and diving trips out here.

On the east side of the highway, opposite the turn for the cenote route, is the **Jardín Botánico Dr Alfredo Barrera Marín,** also signposted as Ya'ax Ché (May–Oct Mon–Sat 9am–5pm, Nov–April daily 8am–4pm; M$70). The 148-acre botanical gardens provide a good introduction to the peninsula's native flora. A three-kilometre path leads through medicinal plants, ferns, palms, some tumbledown Maya ruins and a mock-up *chiclero* camp, where you can see how the sap of the *zapote* (sapodilla) tree is tapped before being used in the production of gum. A longer trail leads through an untended chunk of forest (home to spider monkeys, though they usually keep out of sight) to a viewing platform above the canopy. Anyone particularly interested in botany should hire a guide at the site.

North of town

Just 2km north of town (head up any street from the centre), the *Ceiba del Mar* resort (see p.82) maintains a boardwalk that runs for about a kilometre through the **mangroves**. It's a great area for birding at dawn or dusk, with roseate spoonbills, herons and many migratory songbirds. This is a unique opportunity to walk among the trees and see this eco-system close up.

A bit further north, out on the east side of Hwy-307, **Crococun Zoo**; daily 9am–5pm; M$276 adults, M$168 kids) gives the chance to see crocodiles – from wee hatchlings up to grouchy old behemoths – at this reptile sanctuary. Kids can even handle and feed the little ones, along with snakes, birds, deer and some very sneaky monkeys, while the enthusiastic employees do a few slightly alarming stunts. The zoo is immediately next to the turn for *Excellence Riviera* resort. Buses running between Cancún and Playa del Carmen will stop here on request; a taxi from Puerto Morelos costs M$50.

Eating and drinking

Most of Puerto Morelos's **restaurants** are on the town plaza, a cheerful spot for dinner, followed by a cold beer or an evening stroll. There's also a lot of food sold out of people's houses and yards – keep an eye open for signs. Most restaurants close at least one night a week, but that seems to change on a whim (and some places are closed all summer). What little **nightlife** there is concentrates around the bar at *Posada Amor* and the neighbouring *Bara Bara*, both of which make good cocktails beyond the usual margaritas (though those are good too).

Al Chimichurri Rojo Gómez, south of the plaza. If you're on seafood overload, follow the smell of sizzling steak to this expert Argentine restaurant, where you can stock up on meat, hearty lasagne and *dulce de leche* crêpes. Closed Mon.

Café d'Amancia Southwest corner of the plaza. Come here for deadly strong coffee and a breakfast bagel or lunchtime sandwich, all in a great vantage point for watching the action on the square. Closed Tues.

La Casa del Pescador North side of the plaza. The restaurant run by the fishermen's cooperative (up the green spiral staircase) is simple and great value – a good place for lunch, or for dinner, when *La Petita* is shut. Fish filets from M$100.

John Gray's Kitchen Niños Héroes, north of the plaza ☏ 998/871-0665. Visitors from Cancún often make the short drive down for dinner at this small, casually elegant restaurant. The owner is an ex-*Ritz-Carlton* chef, and his gourmet background shows: the daily menu features simple, smart combos like pan-roasted duck breast with chipotle, tequila and honey (M$285), or macaroni and cheese with shrimp and truffle oil (M$265). Also open for breakfast, with tables in a shady garden. Closed Sun dinner.

Lonchería Mimi Niños Héroes, north of the plaza. Look for the pale-green facade on this tidy *cocina económica*, where a team of women cook up daily specials in a spotless open kitchen. Go early, as food tends to run out, and the four tables fill up fast.

Peskayitos Rojo Gómez, south of the plaza. Get your shrimp taco fix here: tempura-battered, fried and decked out with your choice of salsas. Sure, there's other stuff, but it's all about the tacos.

La Playita Melgar, half a block north of the plaza. This casual spot on the beach is where the town fishermen kick back and enjoy the fresh catch of the day, sold by the kilo and perfectly fried. A whole *pescado frito* for two and a few beers will set you back about M$250.

T@cos.com Rojo Gómez, north of the plaza. Improbable name, but very tasty and filling platters of tacos that are generous with the grilled meat, fried onions and creamy *habañero* salsa.

El Tío Melgar, just north of the plaza. Get shrimp tacos in the morning and *tortas* and *sopa de lima* at lunch at this hole in the wall that never seems to close. No energy has been wasted on decor; it all goes into the food.

Listings

ATM An HSBC machine is on the north side of the plaza; there is no actual bank. Avoid the other two non-bank-affiliated machines, as their fees are extortionate.

Buses Buses run every ten minutes from the stop on the highway to Cancún and Playa del Carmen, and fourteen times daily for the airport. Purchase tickets in advance, particularly for the airport, to make sure the bus stops and has a seat for you.

Cambios A couple of cambios can be found on the plaza, 7am–10pm.

Internet and telephone There are several pay phones (including one that takes coins) on the plaza by the taxi stand, as well as two internet cafés: one on the southwest corner of the plaza, next to the Oxxo, and another on the north side, next to the grocery store.

Laundry Lavaplus, on Niños Héroes, one block north of the plaza (M$12/kilo).

Punta Bete

Resorts almost solidly occupy the coast between Puerto Morelos and Playa del Carmen. But with some persistence (a car is required), you can still get access to the palm-shaded waterfront around **PUNTA BETE** (also called Xcalacoco). The drive from the highway can be challenging, as there's often construction, but it's fascinating to find a tiny castaway beach scene, with a few holdouts against development in the form of two particularly good-value **hotels**, as well as a nice place to spend the day in the sun. The turn is about 25km south of Puerto Morelos, marked with a sign for *The Tides Riviera Maya*, just south of the Cristal/Coca-Cola bottling plant.

About 2km along the road toward the coast, turn to the left and follow signs for ⚓ *Petit Lafitte* (☎984/877-4000, ⓦwww.petitlafitte.com; ➒), a small, somewhat rustic-feeling resort known for its excellent staff and scores of repeat guests; rates include breakfast and dinner. Or continue on to the Swiss-owned *Coco's Cabañas* (☎998/874-7056, ⓔmarsilhel@hotmail.com; ➏), just a bit back from the beach. It has five individual cabañas, a small pool and a really excellent **restaurant** (8am–9pm) with a varied menu – it makes a good lunch destination if you're at *Lafitte*, or just on the beach for the day. On the beach itself, just in front of *Coco's*, *Los Pinos* (☎984/873-1506; ➍) is a dull, basic hotel, but its **beach** is shaded with palms, and renting a chair (M$50) makes a good day out.

Playa del Carmen

Once a soporific fishing village where travellers camped out en route to Cozumel, **PLAYA DEL CARMEN** has mushroomed into a high-style party town for Europeans, South Americans and Mexico City jet-setters. Like Cancún 60km to the north, Playa – as it's commonly called – has no historic underpinnings. And like other beach towns, it can be a bit pricey as well as crowded. The town's main centre of activity, a pedestrian strip that runs nearly 2km along Avenida 5 (also called La Quinta Avenida, or Fifth Avenue), is often packed to capacity. But, thanks to low-rise development (no building is over four storeys tall) and a high number of Italian- and French-owned businesses, the place retains a certain mellow, chic atmosphere – and it seems positively cosmopolitan and calm when compared with hyperactive, Americanized Cancún. The **nightlife** in particular has a hip edge, the cuisine is sophisticated, and everywhere visitors will want to go is in a relatively by compact area.

Driving into or through Playa can be a bit of a chore, due to the traffic. An express overpass on Hwy-307 should be completed by the time you read this, but you still may find it faster and easier to take the *arco vial*, an express loop around the inland side of town (referred to as the *ejido*). The turn is well marked on the north edge of town, and it deposits you back on Hwy-307 at the south edge, south of Playacar, near a giant mall. If you're headed into Playa, it can still be faster to

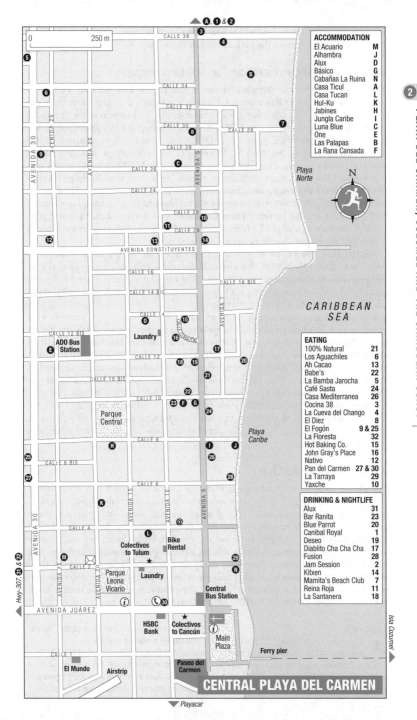

CALLE 38

CALLE 34

CALLE 32

CALLE 30

CALLE 28

CALLE 28

CALLE 26

CALLE 24

CALLE 22

CALLE 20

AVENIDA 25

AVENIDA 20

AVENIDA 30

AVENIDA 5

CALLE 28

Playa Norte

N

ACCOMMODATION
El Acuario	M
Alhambra	J
Alux	D
Básico	G
Cabañas La Ruina	N
Casa Ticul	A
Casa Tucan	L
Hul-Ku	K
Jabines	H
Jungla Caribe	I
Luna Blue	C
One	E
Las Palapas	B
La Rana Cansada	F

AVENIDA CONSTITUYENTES

CALLE 16

CALLE 14 BIS

CALLE 16 BIS

CALLE 4

AVENIDA 1

CARIBBEAN SEA

Laundry

CALLE 12 BIS

ADO Bus Station

CALLE 12

CALLE 10 BIS

CALLE 10

Parque Central

CALLE 8

CALLE 6 BIS

CALLE 6

AVENIDA 15

AVENIDA 10

AVENIDA 5

Playa Caribe

EATING
100% Natural	21
Los Aguachiles	6
Ah Cacao	13
Babe's	22
La Bamba Jarocha	5
Café Sasta	24
Casa Mediterranea	26
Cocina 38	3
La Cueva del Chango	4
El Diez	8
El Fogón	9 & 25
La Floresta	32
Hot Baking Co.	15
John Gray's Place	16
Nativo	12
Pan del Carmen	27 & 30
La Tarraya	29
Yaxche	10

DRINKING & NIGHTLIFE
Alux	31
Bar Ranita	23
Blue Parrot	20
Canibal Royal	1
Deseo	19
Diablito Cha Cha Cha	17
Fusion	28
Jam Session	2
Kitxen	14
Mamita's Beach Club	7
Reina Roja	11
La Santanera	18

CALLE 4

Colectivos to Tulum

Bike Rental

AVENIDA 20

CALLE 2

Parque Leona Vicario

Laundry

AVENIDA JUÁREZ

HSBC Bank

Colectivos to Cancún

Central Bus Station

Main Plaza

Ferry pier

CALLE 1

El Mundo

Airstrip

Paseo del Carmen

CENTRAL PLAYA DEL CARMEN

Hwy-307, 51 & 62

Playacar

Isla Cozumel

0   250 m

take the *arco vial* and turn toward the beach on the cross street you need, rather than inching through town on the surface road next to Hwy-307.

Arrival, information and transport

Most visitors arrive on short-haul buses at the central **bus station**, sometimes referred to as the *terminal turística*, on Avenida 5 at Juárez, the main street from the highway to the beach. (Another station, on Avenida 20, between calles 12 and 12 bis, handles longer-haul trips on ADO.) If you're heading to Playa directly from the international **airport** in Cancún, the ADO/Riviera bus (13 daily, 10am–8.45pm; 1hr) is the best deal, for M$120. Otherwise, any number of private minibus operators will take you directly to your hotel (about M$200/person), and a taxi costs about US$65. Upstairs at the bus station, there is short-term **luggage storage** (from M$10/hr) and longer-term lockers (M$60/24hr). There's also a small **airstrip** on the south edge of town, but it's used only for short hops to Cozumel or Chichén Itzá. If you're coming by **ferry from Cozumel**, you arrive at a pier at the end of Calle 1, the southern edge of Playa's main beachfront, and the town extends north and inland from here (for ferry details, see box, p.95).

Tourist info kiosks, on Juárez near Avenida 15 and on the main plaza (daily 9am–9pm; ☎ 984/873-2804, ✉ turismo@solidaridad.gob.mx), have bilingual staff who do their best to answer any enquiries. They stock the useful *Playa del Carmen*, with hotel and restaurant listings. Online, you can prep for your trip or get news on upcoming events at Ⓦ www.playa.info.

The central area of town is very walkable, but as Avenida 5 extends ever northward, it can be nice to ride a **bicycle** to the farthest points; a bike path runs along Avenida 10 (see p.94 for operators). You can hire **taxis** from stands on Avenida 5, or flag one down on the trafficked streets – it's about M$30 from the central bus station to hotels on the north side. To reach smaller towns or beaches just north and south of Playa, **colectivos** are the easiest option: the Cancún service (M$35) departs frequently from Juárez just west of the main bus station, and vans heading south to Tulum (M$35) leave from Calle 2, between avenidas 5 and 10. Taxis can also take you anywhere you need to go along the coast – they're more expensive than *colectivos*, but far cheaper than any tour company, even when you pay for waiting time.

Accommodation

Hotels are being built all the time in Playa del Carmen, so you'll have no difficulty finding a room. Prices, however, are somewhat inflated, especially along Avenida 5 and the beach. But these more central hotels are also noisy, due to general party ruckus (south of C 26 or so) or construction (on the ever-expanding north side). So heading inland a bit, to avenidas 15 and up, gets you both a better rate and a better night's sleep. High season in Playa includes the European vacation months of July and August, as well as mid-December to April; M$650 is the bare minimum for a room then. Of the **hostels**, we can't fully recommend any, but a promising new one, *Vive La Vida*, was set to open in early 2011. For **camping**, head to the tumbledown *Cabañas La Ruina* (☎ 984/873-0405; M$150), on Calle 2 at the beach.

Hotels

El Acuario Av 25, between C 2 and C 4 ☎ 984/873-2133, Ⓦ www.elacuariohotel .com.mx. Great example of the deals you can get by heading away from the beach: big rooms, all with a terrace or balcony, and some with kitchenettes, all clustered around a central pool and garden. There's also one full apartment available. ❹

Alhambra On the beach at C 8 ☎ 984/873-0735, Ⓦ www.alhambra-hotel.net. This gleaming-white, Moorish-style structure isn't what you'd expect in Playa, but it's one of the best-value hotels on the beach. Some of the equally white rooms are a bit small, but you'll be out on the beach, at the daily yoga classes or getting a massage at the spa. Rates include full breakfast. **8**

Alux Av 14, between Av 10 and Av 15 ☎984/803-2482, ⓦwww.hotelalux.com. *Alux* is a little frumpy, like its downtown Cancún counterpart, but it's also a good deal. A/c is optional, and some rooms have kitchenettes. **5**

Básico Av 5 at C 10 ☎984/879-4448, ⓦwww.hotelbasico.com. Cool industrial design meets an equally cool clientele. Rooms have fun details (Polaroid cameras, neon lighting) and floor-to-ceiling windows. Also check out the same owners' *Deseo* hotel, at C 12: it has an equally sharp style and is marginally quieter. On the very lowest end of **9**

Casa Ticul Av 5, between C 38 and C 40 ☎984/267-3501, ⓦwww.casaticul.com. Cool Playa style, but with a nice location – at the more residential end of La Quinta, a bit out of the noisy fray. Rooms are minimalist black and white, and there's a small pool and a breezy roof terrace. No kids. **8**

Casa Tucan C 4, between Av 10 and Av 15 ☎984/873-0283, ⓦwww.casatucan.de. A Playa institution, retaining a hippie atmosphere. Rooms can be a bit dark and musty – and you'll either love the elaborate murals or hate them. But with perks like laundry service, a big swimming pool and great coffee at the restaurant, it's hard to beat the price. Book ahead. **4**

Hul-Ku Av 20 no. 150, between C 4 and C 6 ☎984/873-0021, ⓦwww.hotelhulku.com. Remote location, but a big, deep pool and shady grounds. Rooms all have balconies, though furniture can be a little bit saggy. Nonetheless, excellent price, especially since some fan-only rooms are available. **4**

Jabines C 8, between Av 15 and Av 20 ☎984/873-0861. A reliable budget hotel filled with greenery, facing a modern plaza. Rooms are a little dark, but quieter than most. **2**

Jungla Caribe Av 5 at C 8 ☎984/873-0650, ⓦwww.jungla-caribe.com. On a prime corner on La Quinta, this quirky hotel has a jungly courtyard inside (so overgrown you can hardly see the pool). Stairs trimmed in black-and-white tiles ascend like an Escher etching to rooms with a similar black-and-white (and somehow Eighties-looking) style. A/c can be noisy (as can the street), but little balconies are fun for people-watching. **7**

Luna Blue C 26, between Av 5 and Av 10 ☎984/873-0990, ⓦwww.lunabluehotel.com. Built around a central garden with tall palms and other shady trees. Each room has a curvy, palapa-covered terrace, whitewashed walls, a/c and lots of windows – but no TV (though larger rooms have fridges). **6**

One Av 20, between C 12 and C 12 bis ☎984/877-3060, ⓦwww.onehotels.com. This somewhat generic business-class chain hotel near the long-distance bus depot opened in 2010. Ordinarily, it wouldn't be news, but in Playa, it's a rare spot of midrange value. Free wi-fi and full breakfast. **5**

Las Palapas C 34 at the beach ☎984/873-4260, ⓦwww.laspalapas.com. A small-scale beach resort, dense with greenery and in a sweet spot not far from the centre. The bungalows are rustic-chic but have a/c, TV and wi-fi. Rates include full breakfast. **9**

La Rana Cansada C 10 no. 132, between Av 5 and Av 10 ☎984/873-0389, ⓦwww.ranacansada.com. Like *Casa Tucan*, a throwback to "old Playa", though this place is more orderly, with spare, colourful rooms in various configurations (including a suite). Beds can be very firm, and ventilation isn't the greatest. Communal kitchen facilities. **5**

Central Playa del Carmen

Although Playa now stretches far inland from its namesake beach, visitors seldom stray far from **Avenida 5**, called La Quinta, the pedestrian zone that stretches more than 2km north from Avenida Juárez. It's lined with cocktail lounges, souvenir shops and stylish restaurants, and there's even a tiny Maya **ruin** hidden between the storefronts – look off the east side of La Quinta across from Calle Corazón. The scene generally gets mellower and less glitzy once you head north of Constituyentes, and especially above Calle 30.

For locals, the main public hangout spot in the centre is the terraced **main plaza** at the end of Juárez – one corner of which is dedicated to the **Capilla de Nuestra Señora del Carmen**, an attractive modern structure with rustic wood ceiling beams – and, to a lesser extent, the **Parque Central** in front of the town hall on Avenida 20, between calles 8 and 10. This concrete slab has a small amphitheatre that occasionally hosts performances. To one side of the park, six stelae are inscribed with the verses of the *Himno de Quintana Roo*, an ode to the fledgling state's pioneer spirit and its role as a refuge for the indigenous Maya – very inspiring, but really, all the attention is on the skateboarders who cruise the curving ramps here.

The beaches and beyond

One block east of La Quinta and running north from Calle 1 to Constituyentes, the main **town beach** has been rebuilt after severe erosion. As of late 2010, it was wonderfully deep, but only time will tell whether the sand stays put. Each hotel has its own bar and rents chairs and umbrellas, and you can take off on various water activities from here, or get a massage. But more serious beach-goers head to the area north of Constituyentes, called **Playa Norte**, where the deep, silky sand drops into waist-high green water with mid-size swells. Two beach clubs – *Mamita's* (see p.93) and *Kool by Tukan Beach* – form the major social scene in Playa. Glam sun-lovers park themselves all day on the chairs and lounge beds, sipping and snacking, while the DJs spin electronica. You can also wander further up the shore and stake out your own spot in the untended areas, or press even further north to the point, called Coco Beach, where you'll find kayaks for rent and an even hipper (but quieter) beach club, *Canibal Royal* (see p.92).

South of the centre (below C 1 and the Cozumel ferry pier) is **Playacar**, an 880-acre condo development. Where they're not fronting a big resort, the beaches here are often deserted. The lightly trafficked streets are a good place for a shady bike ride, or you can walk down from the centre of town in about half an hour.

For anyone interested in **diving**, Tank-Ha, on Avenida 5, between calles 8 and 10 (☎984/873-0302, ⓦwww.tankha.com), is a good place to start. The shop offers certification courses, one- and two-tank dives (US$40–70) and twice-daily **snorkelling** tours (9am & 1.30pm; 3hr; US$40). **Kiteboarding** specialists Ikarus give basic instruction on the beach in Playa, then take you up or down the coast for in-water lessons; visit the shop on Avenida 5 at Calle 20 (☎984/803-3490, ⓦwww.kiteboardmexico.com) for details.

South of Playa del Carmen

The huge, surprisingly pleasant theme park of **Xcaret** (daily 8.30am–9.30pm; US$69, kids US$34.50; ⓦwww.xcaret.com) is 6km south of Playa del Carmen. Budget travellers and anyone on a longer trip can skip it, but if your time is limited or you have children to entertain, the park is an opportunity to experience in one place all of the natural attractions of the Yucatán, such as snorkelling through underground caverns or in a fish-filled bay. There's also a vast butterfly habitat, a cave full of bats, a high-tech aquarium and an only slightly hokey "Maya village". Bus-and-entrance packages are available through every big hotel in Cancún and Playa del Carmen, though it's easy to get there on your own.

Adjacent to Xcaret is an elaborate zipline and outdoor-adventure park, **Xplor** (ⓦwww.xplor.travel; US$99), but it's expensive, and its natural features are not nearly as impressive as those of **Río Secreto** (ⓦwww.riosecretomexico.com; US$59, kids US$29.50), just to the south along Hwy-307. Here you don a wetsuit to explore water-filled caves – at times you clamber over rocks, and at other times you swim through sparkling-clear rivers. The only lights come from your guide's torch and your own headlamp, making the various rock formations loom out of the darkness dramatically. You may even see the occasional bat or spider crab. The slickness of the operation (and the price) might be a deterrent for some independent travellers, but it's a truly amazing experience, and unlike any other cave or cenote tour on the peninsula. And it's open to kids age six and up; you need not be a strong swimmer, either, as you're provided with a life jacket, and the rivers are not deep. Tours run daily at 9am, 11am, 1pm and 2pm – you can usually join one if you show up in the morning, but it's better to reserve ahead through the website.

All second-class (Mayab) buses stop on request near Xcaret or Río Secreto on Hwy-307, a ten-minute ride from Playa, or you can hop a dedicated ADO bus (4 daily at 9am, 9.40am, 10.40am & 11.30am) from Playa's central terminal. A taxi is about M$140.

Eating

Playa del Carmen practically bursts with **restaurants** of every kind, and even some of the traditional Mexican places here stay open late. The quality of food is often very good (particularly at the Italian and Argentine places), though rarely cheap, especially along **Avenida 5**. If you're on a **budget**, make a grazing breakfast from pastry at *Pan del Carmen* (Av 30 at C 6 or Juárez, between Av 10 and Av 15) and tacos from the vendors on the plaza by the bus station; for lunch or dinner, head for the strip of snack joints on Avenida 10, between calles 8 and 10; and just generally explore Avenida 15 and farther west. A warning: the turnover in restaurants in Playa is so high as to make a guidebook writer despair; many of these places may have closed by the time you go looking for them. The good news is that new places will have opened. For interesting developments, try the northern reaches of Avenida 5.

Cafés

Ah Cacao Av 5 at Constituyentes. If you prefer your caffeine in the form of chocolate, come to this hip little café for hot and cold cocoa-based drinks, plus truffles, ice cream and Mexican cacao nibs to go (a delicious souvenir). There's also espresso for traditionalists.

Café Sasta Av 5, between C 8 and C 10. Pastries and espresso are the main items at this Italian coffeehouse, and the sidewalk tables are an ideal spot for watching the fashion parade along La Quinta.

Hot Baking Co. C 12 bis, between Av 5 and Av 10. Bakery café with muffins, bagels slathered with cream cheese and giant cinnamon rolls. Those with heartier appetites can choose from omelettes and grilled sandwiches (M$60 and up).

🏃 **Nativo** Av 30, between Constituyentes and C 20. Delicious fresh-fruit smoothies and other healthy Mexican food, across the street from the similarly excellent *DAC* market.

Restaurants

100% Natural Av 5, between C 10 and C 12. Like the Cancún branch (see p.62), this link in the local mini-chain serves fresh, whole-grain-ified versions of Mexican food (lots of it vegetarian) and great fresh fruit juices. A good alternative to *La Cueva del Chango*, in a more central location.

🏃 **Los Aguachiles** C 34 at Av 25. Seven kinds of salsa arrive at your table along with the menu at this open-air seafood-snack place, and

the challenge is not ordering too many dishes to douse in them all. Even a simple *aguachido* (a tostada piled high with fish, cabbage and herbs) is a substantial snack, for only M$25. Daily 12.30–6.30pm.

Babe's C 10, between Av 5 and Av 10. This Swedish-owned Thai noodle house – which also serves a fine Cuban mojito – typifies Playa's international hotchpotch. Dishes like *pad thai* start at M$90 for a huge portion.

La Bamba Jarocha Av 30 at C 36. Savour super-fresh *ceviche*, seafood soup and shrimp *cocktel* in a non-gringo atmosphere. The place is very popular for long business lunches. Look for the beaded curtains on the doors.

🏃 **Casa Mediterranea** Av 5, between C 6 and C 8. Tucked inside the Jardín de Marieta, this modest little trattoria (there are only about six tables) does toothsome fresh pasta, such as fettuccine with shrimp and squash, for M$100 and up. Unpretentious and delicious.

Cocina 38 Av 5 at C 38 ☎984/873-0655. Minimalist and upscale, this chic little foodie haven does creative, confident seafood (sea bass with cardamom curry, say) as well as heartier items like pork belly. The short menu changes often, and even the smallest details, like the chocolates with the coffee and the Mexican house wine, are well chosen. Mains start at M$190. Closed Sun.

La Cueva del Chango C 38, between Av 5 and the beach. This garden restaurant serves till 11pm, but it's a local favourite especially for long, late breakfasts. The menu includes tasty empanadas and crêpes (about M$65) and house-roasted coffee. Closes at 2pm Sun.

El Diez Av 5 at C 30. Excellent Argentine restaurant with perfectly grilled steaks and good red wine – just what you want from South America, and well priced, with everything less than M$200. Look for the big numeral 10 on the sign.

La Floresta West side of Hwy-307, just north of Juárez. This big palapa next to the highway is a road-tripper's delight, serving overstuffed *tacos de camarón*, the perfect marriage of batter-fried shrimp, mayo and chunky tomato salsa. Should you need variety, seafood cocktails and *ceviches* are available, too.

El Fogón Av 30 at C 6 bis. Follow your nose to the meat-covered grill at this basic, brightly lit taco joint that's generally mobbed with locals. No booze is served, but you can wash down all the meat with a big selection of *aguas frescas*, all for less than M$100 per person. There's another branch on Av 30 near C 28.

John Gray's Place Corazón, west of Av 5, between C 12 and C 14 ☎984/803-3689. Like the original in Puerto Morelos (see p.85), this upscale restaurant has a simple but consistently satisfying menu, with items like spinach salad (M$95) and salmon with lentils (M$195). The cosy bar and lounge is great on its own – try the "smoky margarita" made with mescal.

La Tarraya On the seafront at C 2. A local institution that has been open for more than thirty years, well before Playa was even a gleam in a developer's eye. It still serves standard beach fare like *ceviches* and *pescado frito* (M$90 per kilo) with plenty of cold beer.

Yaxche Av 5 at C 22 ☎984/873-3011. Haute Maya is the theme at this gracious restaurant: (very) hot peppers stuffed with *cochinita pibil* (shredded roast pork), a Yucatecan shrimp gratin or lobster flambéed in *xtabentun*, a local liqueur. With entrees between M$170 and M$220, it's reasonably priced, considering the service and presentation.

Drinking and nightlife

At night, La Quinta becomes one long street party, and you can find any sort of music in the array of **bars**, though most people will wind up around the intersection with Calle 12, which has the highest concentration of cool **clubs** and **lounges**. If you're looking for a mellower atmosphere, head north of Calle 16, even as far up as Calle 40. Happy-hour specials can ease you into the night without depleting funds too rapidly.

Alux Juárez between Av 65 at Av 70, 400m west of Hwy-307 ☎984/803-2936. A trek out into the *ejido* – tell the cab driver "ah-LOOSH" – but worth a visit for its unique setting inside a large cave. Opens at 5.30pm for drinks, followed by dinner (overpriced, but fine); a DJ or a floor show of belly dancers and jazz musicians gets started around 10pm. Usually no cover, but drinks are M$70 and up.

Blue Parrot On the beach at C 12. This open-air bar has weathered decades of change in Playa but still sports rope swings instead of barstools. It has a popular happy hour (5–8pm), then attracts a crowd later in the night with assorted performers and musicians, and usually some dancing. No cover.

Canibal Royal C 48 at the beach ☎984/803-4506. On the far north side of Playa, this beach club rewards your long walk with a 1950s lounge vibe, creative food (super-fried calamari that somehow resembles crispy chunks of pork skin) and delectable eye candy, in the form of all the Mexico City hipsters who hang out here. 11am–7pm.

Deseo Av 5 at C 12. The outdoor bar at the stylish hotel draws its inspiration from Miami Beach, with beds to lounge on, easy-on-the-eyes bartenders and classic Mexican films projected on the blank wall over the pool.

Diablito Cha Cha Cha C 12 at Av 1. Mexico-goes-rockabilly is the loose theme at this retro-cool lounge furnished with Formica tables and vinyl chairs. Fuel up on Mexi-Asian snacks (tempura red snapper, spicy hand rolls), or just go straight for the tequila-mango cocktails (M$100).

Fusion C 6 at the beach. This mellow beach bar, with tables in the sand and the glow of kerosene lamps, is a great slice of old-fashioned, pre-club-scene Playa. There's live music most nights. Drinks from M$60.

Jam Session Av 5 at C 40 ☎984/803-4915. At this club hidden away at the north end of the strip, a house band plays blues, jazz and whatever else strikes their fancy, sometimes joined by visiting musicians. If you're feeling overwhelmed by the party scene down by C 12, this is a much mellower alternative. Wed–Sat 9am–2pm.

Kitxen Av 5, between Constituyentes and C 20. This cool bar-restaurant is owned by a member of legendary Mexican rock group Los Jaguares, so live bands often accompany good bar-snack food.

Mamita's Beach Club On the beach at C 28. The most popular hangout during the day, with plenty of room to spread out and a hip but not overbearing party atmosphere. Chairs and umbrellas are for rent, or you can spread a towel at the water's edge and still get waiter service for drinks; the food is very good (if a tad pricey), and better than *Kool*'s, next door.

Ranita C 10, between Av 5 and Av 10. A crew of regulars – mostly expats – hang out around the horseshoe-shaped bar. Unless there's a live band wedged into the small space, it's a mellow scene and a welcome break from other top-volume places.

Reina Roja C 20, between Av 5 and Av 10. You'll either love or hate the lounge in this hip hotel lobby – walking into the all-red-lit space is like entering a fever dream, and mannequins poised at the tables lend to the surreal feel.

La Santanera C 12, between Av 5 and Av 10. A super-stylish club with international DJ cred (Rob Garza of global mixmasters Thievery Corporation is a partner) that combines a comfortable, breezy lounge area with diverse music and good strong drinks. The scantily clad party crowd – equal parts visitors and residents – usually staggers out around 5am. No cover.

Shopping

Of all the beach towns, Playa offers the most interesting **shopping**, from folk art to designer flip-flops, though very little of it is cheap. Generally, shops get more specialized and interesting the further north you go on Avenida 5. Prices are fixed at speciality shops, but more general souvenir places (those selling the ubiquitous "jellyfish" lamps, for instance, or Mexican wrestler masks) can be open to a little bargaining.

Casita de la Música Av 5, between Juárez and C 2. Ignore the standard souvenirs – look instead at the third of the shop devoted to CDs of Mexican pop, and a decent selection of traditional Yucatecan *trova* ballads and other Mexican folk music.

El Jardín de Marieta Av 5, between C 6 and C 8. Look for the small stained-glass sign marking the entrance to this garden courtyard, where you'll find several excellent galleries and craft shops stocking contemporary paintings and ceramics from local artists, along with wood masks, beautiful weavings and a few gem antiques.

Paseo del Carmen Av 5 at C 1 Sur. Major attractions at this stylish open-air mall include hip Euro chains such as Pull & Bear and Bershka, as well as

Moving on from Playa del Carmen

Typically, short-haul **buses** leave from the central station at Juárez at Avenida 5, and long-haul services go from the station on Avenida 20, between calles 12 and 12 bis. You can buy tickets for all routes at either station; be sure to confirm the correct terminal. The most frequent service is **Cancún**, every ten minutes; **Cancún airport** buses run fourteen times a day 7.50am–7.15pm. Tourist-friendly ADO services also go from the central terminal to **Cobá** (2 daily at 8am & 9am, returning at 3.30pm; 2hr) and **Chichén Itzá** (1 daily at 8am, returning at 2.35pm & 4.30pm; 4hr); there are several other departures, especially for Cobá, from the long-haul terminal. Departures for **Tulum** (1hr) are several times an hour, nearly round-the-clock, and **Chetumal** (4hr), **Mérida** (5hr) and **Valladolid** (3hr) are at least hourly. You can also get to **San Cristóbal de las Casas** (3 daily; 17hr) via **Palenque** (12hr), and to **Villahermosa** (15 daily; 12–14hr). For **Cozumel**, see box, p.95.

The best way to reach smaller towns or beaches just north and south of Playa is by **colectivo**; the Cancún service departs frequently from Juárez in front of the main bus station, and vans heading south to Tulum leave from Calle 2, between avenidas 10 and 15. **Taxis** can also take you anywhere you need to go along the coast – they're more expensive than *colectivos*, but far cheaper than any tour company, even when you pay for waiting time.

a few cool bars and lounges like Havana import *La Bodeguita del Medio*, specializing in mojitos.
Shalom Av 5, between C 6 and C 8. This cool boutique will get you dressed for clubbing, Playa-style, with lots of drapey, avant-garde pieces as well as fun, shiny disco duds. Much of the clothing is handmade or one-of-a-kind.

La Sirena Av 5 at C 26. A folk-art shop with all the usual Frida Kahlo-theme items, but one highlight is the selection of small, candy-colour paintings of Chihuahua dogs and Mexican wrestlers – excellent unique gift items.

Listings

Airlines Aerosaab, Av 20 at C 1 ☎984/873-0804.
Banks HSBC, Juárez, between Av 10 and Av 15 (Mon–Fri 9am–7pm); Bancomer, Juárez, between Av 25 and Av 30 (Mon–Fri 9am–4pm). Both have ATMs.
Books El Mundo, C 1 Sur, between Av 20 and Av 25, has English and Spanish titles. Closed Sun.
Car and bike rental For cars, try Localiza, Juárez, between Av 5 and Av 10 (☎984/873-0580). For bicycles, look for shops on Av 10, such as Black Pearl, between C 2 and C 4; rates are M$100/24hr.
Consulates Canada: Av 10 at C 1, Plaza Paraíso ☎984/803-2411; US: C 1 Sur, between Av 15 and Av 20 ☎984/873-0303.

Internet access and telephones The streets off Av 5 hold numerous internet cafés; one on C 4, between Av 5 and Av 10, doubles as a caseta. There's also a Telmex caseta on Juárez between Av 10 and Av 15.
Laundry *Lavanderías* are scattered every other block on the side streets. Two are Giracaribe Laundry, on Av 10, between C 12 and C 14, and Gigalav, on C 2, between Av 10 and Av 15.
Post office Av 20 at C 2 (Mon–Fri 8am–2pm); geared to dealing with tourists.

Isla Cozumel

A forty-kilometre-long island directly off the coast from Playa del Carmen, **ISLA COZUMEL** is far larger than Isla Mujeres and has grown proportionately, particularly to cater to the mainstream tastes of the cruise-ship passengers that come ashore here. Nearly every day, up to ten liners, each with several thousand passengers, dock at one of the island's three piers, all just south of the main town of **San Miguel**. As a result, the town's population of seventy thousand comes close to doubling on the busiest cruise days in high season.

But don't be put off by the hordes: even in San Miguel, it's easy to escape into the blocks further from the sea or on the windswept eastern coast, with its deserted beaches and pounding waves. Or you can go underwater: the reefs that ring much of the coast have been dazzling visitors since Jacques Cousteau brought them to international attention in the early 1960s. The island, which the Maya dubbed *cuzamil* ("land of the swallows"), is also a destination for birdwatchers, as it's a stopover on migration routes and has several endemic species. Faro Celarain, a nature park on the southern tip of the island, is a haven for many of the rarest birds.

Some history

One of several communities along the Yucatán coast that survived the collapse of Classic Maya civilization after 1200, Cozumel isn't renowned for its architectural grandeur. But the scale of trade centred here was impressive, running via sea routes along the coast of Mexico and as far south as Honduras and perhaps even Panama, and the island may have been an early free-trade zone, where merchants from competing cities could trade peaceably. At the site of **San Gervasio**, the only excavated ruins on the island, there's also evidence of specialization in particular crafts and even a degree of mass production. Cozumel's later Maya rulers did not

The ferry to Cozumel

Two **passenger ferry** companies, Mexico Waterjets and Ultramar, depart from the pier at Calle 1 Sur in Playa del Carmen, for San Miguel in Cozumel, nearly every hour between 6am and 11pm. The price is the same (M$140), and the boats are roughly equivalent as well, so just pick whichever is departing soonest – and buy only a one-way ticket, so you have the same freedom on the return trip. The closest **parking** to the ferry terminal is the secure lot behind the Playa del Carmen bus station for about M$100 per day. Returning to Playa, the ferries depart Cozumel hourly, 5am–10pm.

Transbordadores del Caribe (☎987/872-7688, ⓦwww.transcaribe.com.mx) operates a **car ferry** to Cozumel from Puerta Calica (also called Punta Venado), 7km south of Playa del Carmen. Just past the entrance for Xcaret, follow signs for Calica – there is no indication of the ferry on the highway. The service for passenger cars runs twice a day (Mon 8am & 6pm, Tues–Sat 1.30pm & 6pm, Sun 6am & 6pm), with a crossing time of about 1hr 15min. At M$550 per car and M$60 per passenger, it's worthwhile only if you'll be staying on the island more than a few days, though there are occasional promotions – check the website.

wield power in the same grand style as their forebears, but the rest of an increasingly commercialized population was probably better off.

Whatever the truth, you get little opportunity to judge for yourself – an American air base, built here during World War II, erased all trace of Cozumel's largest ancient city, and the lesser ruins scattered across the roadless interior are mostly unrestored and inaccessible. (The airfield, converted to civilian use, remains the means by which most visitors arrive.)

After about 1600, Cozumel was virtually deserted, the territory of pirates with few settlers. In the mid-nineteenth century, though, as the bitter Caste Wars (see Contexts, p.278) between the rebel Maya and the Spanish colonists made life on the peninsula dangerous and unstable, the island became a refuge, and by the 1880s, the town of **San Miguel** was established as a home for the growing population. Over the years, island culture has developed distinct from that of the mainland, with *cozumeleños* relishing their lifestyle, which is somehow even more easygoing than on the rest of the coast. San Miguel hosts a particularly colourful celebration of **Carnaval**, the decadent week prior to Lent, with elaborate costumes, parades and exuberant bands and parties.

Arrival and information

Arriving by ferry, you're in the centre of San Miguel, with the plaza just across the street from the pier. The town is walkable, but blocks are larger than in Playa del Carmen, and if you're carrying luggage, you'll probably want a **taxi** to any hotel past Avenida 10 (M$40). From the **airport** (ⓦwww.asur.com.mx), which is at the northeast edge of town (around Av 65), a shared-van service (M$47) or taxis (M$209 per person) make the short drive into town, dropping you directly at your hotel. **Cruise ships** arrive at either the Punta Langosta pier on the southern edge of town or the International and Puerta Maya piers, both about 4km south; a taxi costs about M$70 to the centre. The **tourist office** (Mon–Sat 8.30am–5pm; ☎987/872-7585, ⓦwww.islacozumel.com.mx) is in the complex on the east side of the plaza, upstairs; there's also a kiosk by the ferry dock in Playa del Carmen.

Buses run around town (M$5), but the only one you might use is the one that runs about once an hour to the beaches and hotels just north and south of town. Look for the northbound bus on Avenida 10, and the southbound on Avenida 15, but note that the majority that go by are for other routes within San Miguel.

Island transport

No buses serve the east side of the island, so to get further afield you'll have to go on a tour, take a taxi (fares are posted by the rank at the ferry pier) or rent a vehicle. **Mopeds** are appealing, though roads can be dangerously slick in the rain and accidents are frequent. **Jeeps** are available from numerous outlets, but aren't really useful – rental contracts preclude your driving on dirt tracks. A convertible **VW Beetle** is the consummate Cozumel beach **car**, often still available from local companies. (But even international companies such as Hertz are flexible and rent by the half-day.) Mopeds cost M$400 or so; jeeps and cars, around M$650. Prices vary little, and vendors aren't always into haggling; for cars, you can almost always do better by booking ahead online.

Cycling is feasible in town; to the beaches to the north; to the south as far as Chankanaab, where there's a separate track for bikes and mopeds; and perhaps as far east as San Gervasio, if you don't have a strong headwind. But beyond that, the combination of heedless cars, wind and narrow hard shoulders make it fairly difficult. Sombrero Rentals (8.30am–1pm & 4–7pm; ☎987/857-0085, ⓦwww.sombrerorentals.com), on Avenida 10, between Juárez and Calle 2, has well-maintained mountain bikes and beach cruisers (about US$15/day), as well as mopeds.

Accommodation

Hotels in Cozumel are divided into two categories: expensive, usually all-inclusive resorts strung out along the coast on either side of San Miguel, and more affordable places in the town centre – though none of these, even the lone hostel, are very cheap. Along the beach, the hotels to the north require a taxi ride into town, while a few to the south are within walking distance from the action. At the town hotels, sea views are overrated, as they usually come with traffic noise from the **malecón** (San Miguel's seaside promenade) below.

San Miguel

Amaranto C 5, between Av 15 and Av 20 ☎987/872-3219, ⓦwww.tamarindoamaranto.com. Winding staircases and curving walls distinguish these three fanciful stucco palapas and two apartments stacked in a tile-trimmed tower. Rooms – all with fridge and microwave, some with a/c – are clustered around a cosy courtyard and small pool. ❹

Las Anclas Av 5 no. 325, between C 3 and C 5 ☎987/872-5476, ⓦwww.lasanclas.com. A cluster of two-storey suites with kitchenettes; each sleeps up to four, with a queen-size bed upstairs and two day-beds downstairs (though the latter are best for kids). The water pressure is probably the best in the whole Yucatán, and a lush central garden makes the place feel homey. ❼

La Casona Real Juárez at Av 25 ☎987/872-5471 ⓦwww.la-casona-real-hotel-cozumel.com. So long as you love bright colours (the fourteen rooms are all painted orange and yellow), you'll appreciate the excellent value at this modern hotel with a/c, a courtyard pool and free wi-fi. ❹

Flamingo C 6, between Melgar and Av 5 ☎987/872-1264, ⓦwww.hotelflamingo.com.

Popular with the scuba set, with a roof terrace and a bar (noise alert: occasional live salsa bands). "Courtyard" rooms aren't as breezy as the larger "superior" ones, but all have a nice modern style, and the full breakfast is very good. ❻

Hacienda San Miguel C 10, between Melgar and Av 5 ☎987/872-1986, ⓦwww.haciendasanmiguel.com. With a big central garden, towering palm trees and rustic wood furniture, this hotel feels almost rural, even though it's just on the quieter north side of town. ❼

Hostelito Av 10 no. 42, between Juárez and C 2 ☎987/869-8157, ⓔhostelitocozumelmx@gmail.com. Cozumel's only hostel. Dorms (M$150) are dim and fan-only, with slightly cramped bathrooms, but clean enough. Private rooms with a/c are also available. A great shared kitchen is an excellent amenity. ❸

Pepita Av 15 at C 1 ☎987/872-0098. One of the oldest hotels in town, and also one of the best kept, with clean, simple tile-floor rooms with a/c, fridge and TV. Amenities include a pretty courtyard and complimentary coffee in the morning. ❸

Saolima Salas 260, between Av 10 and Av 15 Ⓣated 987/872-0886. Basic and old-fashioned, but reasonably clean rooms, with optional a/c (M$50 extra). Although pretty unremarkable overall, it is the only decent option in this price range. ❷

Tamarindo B&B C 4 no. 421, between Av 20 and Av 25 Ⓣ 987/872-6190, Ⓦ www.tamarindocozumel .com. At this French-owned B & B, rooms have cosy nooks and whimsical touches. Two of the five rooms share a kitchen, while two bargain suites have kitchenettes. Full breakfast is included, and the owner's excellent cooking and island expertise put guests at ease. A/c is an option in some rooms. ❹

Elsewhere on the island

Blue Angel Resort Carretera Costera Sur Km 2.2 Ⓣ 987/872-7258, Ⓦ www.blueangelresort.com. Close to town, and with an excellent dive shop and shallow-dive training in the small pool and right off the hotel's small beach. All rooms have sea views and private balconies. ❻

El Presidente Inter-Continental Carretera Costera Sur Km 6.5 Ⓣ 987/872-9500, Ⓦ www.ihg .com. The sharp-edged modernist design of Cozumel's first luxury hotel, built in 1969, can feel a little severe, but the setting is flawless, with a pretty protected beach and accessible snorkelling from the long pier. All rooms have sea views. Just beware steep additional charges. ❾

Ventanas al Mar On the east coast, 5km south of *Mezcalito's* beach bar and the intersection with the Carretera Transversal Ⓦ www .ventanasalmar.com.mx. This hotel – the only one on the east coast – runs entirely on wind power. Bring groceries if you plan to stay a while (there's a two-night minimum). The giant rooms and the two-storey suites, which sleep four, have basic kitchenettes, as well as terraces overlooking crashing surf. Rates include full breakfast. ❼

San Miguel

The only major population centre on the island, **SAN MIGUEL** is clean and cheerful and a bit sprawling, with long blocks and low buildings, a few of which are little Caribbean-style clapboard houses that have somehow resisted decades of heavy weather. The primary drawback is that the wide seafront avenue, **Avenida Rafael Melgar**, is all too often a throng of day visitors traipsing from one duty-free diamond shop to the next. The weekends, though, are blissfully quiet – no cruise ships generally stop on Cozumel on Sunday, and only a couple arrive on Saturday and Monday.

The town's large main square, the **Plaza del Sol**, stands directly opposite the ferry dock, dominated by a tall clock tower. *Cozumeleños* come out on Sunday evenings, when there's live music. It's also popular to **stroll the malecón** (Melgar), which is graced with grand bronze statues commemorating Cozumel's Maya cultural heritage and long tradition of fishing.

On the malecón, between calles 4 and 6, the attractive **Museo de la Isla de Cozumel** (Mon–Sat 9am–5pm; M$36) has small exhibits on the flora and fauna of the island, its famous reefs and its history. You'll also see a good collection of Maya artefacts and old photos showing the colourful culture of Cozumel, all labelled in both English and Spanish. In the back on the ground floor, a traditional Maya hut is staffed by a friendly and informative local who can explain (primarily in Spanish) the uses of the various foodstuffs, herbs and accoutrements lying about. Overall, the place is a concise introduction to the primary points of Yucatán history. It occasionally hosts live music and theatre events, and there's a bustling café upstairs (see p.102).

San Miguel's name was chosen in the late 1800s, when construction workers unearthed a large, richly adorned statue of St Michael. Research suggests that the statue dates from the early sixteenth century, when Spanish explorer Juan de Grijalva likely brought it to the island as a gift for the native Maya. The discovery inspired townspeople to take San Miguel as their patron saint, and to build the **Iglesia de San Miguel** on the site where the statue was found, one block off the plaza at the corner of avenidas Juárez and 10. The statue of the winged archangel brandishing his sword is still on display on the church altar; Sunday Mass is at 7am, 9am, 6pm and 8pm.

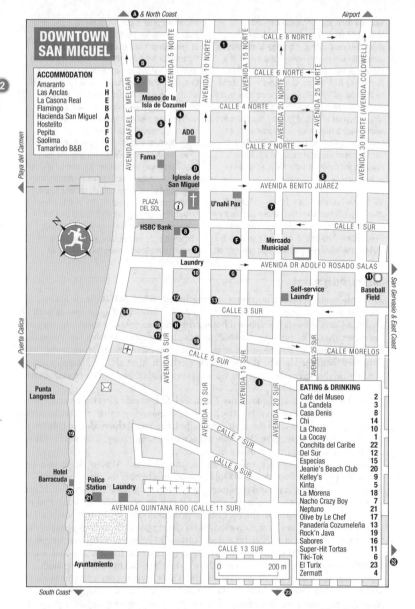

DOWNTOWN
SAN MIGUEL

ACCOMMODATION

Amaranto	I
Las Anclas	H
La Casona Real	E
Flamingo	B
Hacienda San Miguel	A
Hostelito	D
Pepita	F
Saolima	G
Tamarindo B&B	C

EATING & DRINKING

Café del Museo	2
La Candela	3
Casa Denis	8
Chi	14
La Choza	10
La Cocay	1
Conchita del Caribe	22
Del Sur	12
Especias	15
Jeanie's Beach Club	20
Kelley's	9
Kinta	5
La Morena	18
Nacho Crazy Boy	7
Neptuno	21
Olive by Le Chef	17
Panadería Cozumeleña	13
Rock'n Java	19
Sabores	16
Super-Hit Tortas	11
Tiki-Tok	6
El Turix	23
Zermatt	4

Inland past the church, the town gets more diverse. Avenida Coldwell (Av 30) is lined with a number of inexpensive restaurants and bars, as well as the main town **baseball field** (at Salas), which hosts games throughout the summer. The **central market** (*mercado municipal*) on Salas, between avenidas 20 and 25, is another outlying sight, and a refreshing counterpoint to all the seafront souvenir shops.

The north coast

This small hotel zone is the best place to go swimming close to town. Melgar runs **north out of San Miguel**, first passing a small **public beach** around Calle 16 (just north of the turn to the airport). It's popular with locals on the weekends, when food vendors set up along the malecón. The road then leads to a short strip of hotels and one small but well-kept **beach club**, Playa Azul (adjacent to the resort of the same name, 4km north of town; daily 10am–5pm), with a patch of clean sand, calm water and a few rocky spots for snorkelling. Here and at most other beach clubs, prices are fairly reasonable (beers no more than M$45, seafood mains about M$120), and the policy is just that you simply order something. There is usually no minimum or set cover. The beach here is all but empty on weekdays, but on Sunday afternoons it gets a little livelier with local families. The paved road continues 3km further, then bears slightly inland to end near the Cozumel Country Club (☎987/872-9570, ⓦwww.cozumelcountryclub.com.mx), a lush **golf course** set around a large lake.

The south coast

Heading south of San Miguel, Melgar turns into a small highway that passes several more hotels, all catering to divers, as the reef comes very close to shore here. This also makes for especially easy **walk-in snorkelling** at several points along the road (see box, p.102). A little more than 8km south of town, **Parque Chankanaab** (daily 8am–4pm; US$21, kids US$16 ⓦwww.cozumelparks.com) is the island's main tourist destination, a fun park built around a protected lagoon filled with fish. You'll probably want to skip it unless you have children, who will like the calm water. It's a bit overdeveloped, complete with mini-golf and dolphin pens, and can get very crowded on cruise-ship days.

After Chankanaab, the reef runs further from the coast, and swimming and sunning become the main entertainment at the beaches. To escape crowds, press on past the first clubs, which are usually sold as cruise ship day-trips, and can be quite hyperactive. A large arch on the inland side of the road at Km 17.5 marks the turn for the village of **El Cedral**, founded in 1847 and now primarily a vacation spot for San Miguel's better-off residents. With little more here than a small Maya site and a modern Spanish-style church filled with folk art, there's no reason to drive up, except in late April and early May, when the village hosts the ten-day-long **Fiesta de la Santa Cruz**, a huge fair commemorating the meeting of Maya and Spanish cultures, with bullfights, prize-winning livestock and dancing.

Immediately opposite the turn for El Cedral is **Alberto's** beach club (daily 10am–9pm), the most rustic option on the west coast. There's nothing but a small (very good) restaurant, which serves fresh fish caught with its own boats. (The lobster tail is great too, but it's not cheap.) The place isn't on many tourists' radar, so it stays pretty chilled out. You can take a snorkel trip from here (M$400; 3hr) to the best reefs (Palancar Shallows, Colombia Shallows; see p.101), though the boat trip is a bit shorter (and cheaper) just a couple of kilometres south at **Playa Palancar** (daily 9am–6pm), the last beach on the western side. The dive shop (closed Sun) runs reef tours (M$360; 2hr), and the beach area is attractively developed, with winding paths and palm trees. The restaurant serves good *tikin-xic* fish.

Faro Celarain Eco Park

At the southern end of the island, **Faro Celarain Eco Park** (daily 9am–4pm; US$10, kids US$5) encompasses 2750 acres of lagoons, lovely beaches and dense mangrove swamps. Visitors drive into the reserve on a very rutted road (treat your rental car kindly). The road passes a pier and viewing tower for admiring the lively crocodile population, as well as the tiny **Templo El Caracol**, which may have been built by the Maya as an ancient lighthouse. When the wind is right, you can hear it whistling through the conch shells embedded in the walls. The road ends at the modern Punta Celarain **lighthouse**, where you can climb to the top for amazing views. Installed in the former lighthouse-keeper's house at the base, the small **Museo de la Navegación** (daily 10am–4pm) has displays covering maritime history on the Yucatán coast and around the world.

From here, a creaking, wood-sided truck transports visitors to the gem of the park: a perfect little crescent of **beach** around a calm bay. Hang out in a hammock, tuck into fried fish at the restaurant (open only in high season) or take a kayak tour around the lagoon (US$40; 2hr). You can also rent **snorkel** gear (US$10) and paddle out to some small coral heads, dotted with sea fans and often home to hawksbill turtles.

Particularly in the winter, the park is a prime spot for **birdwatching**, as the mangroves host a number of migratory species, such as roseate spoonbills, giant frigates and various herons, as well as four endemic ones, including the vibrant Cozumel emerald, the widespread Cozumel vireo and the Cozumel thrasher, thought until recently to be extinct.

San Gervasio

Midway across the island, 6km north of the Carretera Transversal (the dead-straight road that runs east from San Miguel), is the largest excavated Maya site on the island. **San Gervasio** (daily 8am–5pm; US$7) was built to honour **Ixchel**, goddess of fertility and weaving, and was one of the many independent city-states that survived the fall of Chichén Itzá. It was also part of a larger trading community on the Yucatán coast, along with Tulum and El Rey in Cancún. Today the ruins are not very impressive to a casual visitor, but, as they are part of a larger nature reserve (which accounts for the high admission fee), they're worth a trip for their scenic setting in the jungle. Go early or late to see the most birds, butterflies and other wildlife.

Portions of San Gervasio appear to have been modelled on Chichén Itzá, with several small plazas connected by *sacbeob*, the limestone-paved white roads built by the Maya. One of the first buildings you reach, the **Manitas** structure, is a small residential room with red handprints all over it. The significance of this somewhat common motif, found at several other Maya sites, is still not understood. Off to the right stands the Chichan Nah, a dwarfish building probably used for ceremonial purposes, as it is similar in scale to the miniature temples at Tulum. By contrast, Structure 31, closer to the main plaza, is a relatively large residential building with a front portico, a style used primarily by the Chontal Maya of lowland Mexico and Guatemala. In the later centuries, it was likely the seat of the *halach uinic* (leader) of Cozumel. The main cluster of buildings, arranged around a compact plaza, formed the central administrative area. The principal shrine to Ixchel, the **Ka'na Nah**, lies 500m to the northwest along a *sacbé*. The site's tallest pyramid (though that's not saying a lot), it shows a few remnants of painted stucco. Along the northeast *sacbé*, which is marked by a delicate arch, you'll find the Post-Classic Nohoch Nah temple and the much older Casa de los Murciélagos ("house of bats"), a residential building started in 700 AD.

The east coast

Often impressively wild, Cozumel's **eastern shoreline** remains undeveloped because it faces the open sea, and in most places the water is too rough for swimming. The twenty-kilometre drive south along the Carretera Costera

Oriente, which runs along the seafront here, is a refreshing contrast to the busier west coast. Along the way, you'll pass tantalizing empty **beaches** (though you should swim only where you see others, and be wary of strong currents) and the occasional no-frills **beach bar**, open only till sundown because there's no electricity.

The first of these as you arrive via the cross-island road – and generally the busiest – is *Mezcalito's*, with *Señor Iguana's* just to the south handling the overflow. The food is decent and the party vibe strong, but the beaches here are a bit rocky. Heading south along the eastern coast highway, you pass a number of variations on the same beach-bar theme, and the further you go, the fewer people you see. **Punta Morena** is home to a bit of a surfer scene and a stylish bar-restaurant. The more casual (and usually busier) *Coconuts* bar follows, with a striking view from a tall bluff; the beach below is usually empty. **Chen Río**, a beach a little further on, has two protected coves where you can swim and snorkel (bring your own gear), and the bar serves great margaritas. The restaurant, *El Galeón*, consistently serves some of the best seafood on the strip as well. Just south, the relatively serene **Playa San Martín** is usually the best spot to swim: the currents are not too strong, the sand is kept relatively clean, flags mark the day's swimming conditions and there may even be a lifeguard on duty. Across the road from the beach, the bar *Andale* provides snacks and toilets.

Past about 2km of rocky bluffs, **Playa Punta Chiqueros** has a very good restaurant, *Playa Bonita*. The water out front is shallow, and you can rent umbrellas. Around a rocky curve is the scenic point called **El Mirador**, where the crashing waves have formed natural rock arches. Finally, the road turns inland at the entrance to Faro Celarian Eco Park and the bar *Rasta's*, known for its all-reggae soundtrack and savoury shrimp quesadillas.

Offshore excursions

The boundaries of Cozumel's vast **marine reserve**, the Parque Marino Nacional Arrecifes de Cozumel, encompass the beaches and most of the **reefs** edging the southern half of the island. The coral has grown into steep drop-offs, massive towers and deep canyons, as well as some beautiful shallow gardens. At the more remote reefs, you can see larger pelagic fish, even dolphins. On the west coast, the park boundary starts at Villa Blanca (just north of the International Pier and Puerta Maya) – south of here, you should be accompanied by a licensed dive guide (see p.102) and pay an additional M$24 park-maintenance fee (a wristband is your receipt).

As soon as you get off the ferry, you're offered **snorkelling** trips. Short tours (US$20–25; 1–2hr) go to nearby reefs such as Villa Blanca, which are fine but not spectacular. The best destination is **Palancar Shallows**, about 2km off the southwest coast, an area that ranges from five-metre-deep gardens to a mini-wall dropping 18m. The main strip reef is riddled with fissures and caves, providing nooks for all kinds of sea life as well as shelter from currents. Any boat tour here also usually stops at **Colombia Shallows**, a sprawling coral garden that dazzles with coral towers and vibrant sponges and anemones. You might spot rays, nurse sharks and eels. From the ferry, these tours take 4–5hr and cost US$45. But if you're planning to rent a car, go instead from *Playa Palancar* beach club (see p.99), where the boat ride is much shorter and the trip costs US$30.

Some of the top **dive spots** are **Colombia Deep**, which is as lush as the shallows but less crowded, and **Punta Sur**, directly south from the marshes on the southern tip. Strong currents (and an hour-long boat ride) deter all but the strongest divers, but those who make the trip are rewarded with a dramatic network of deep

Walk-in snorkelling

The coast just south of San Miguel has several convenient spots where you can snorkel without getting on a boat. Beach bars in this area rent gear for about M$120. But if you think you might visit a few spots, it's worth buying your own (about US$35 for a good-quality mask and snorkel) just for the convenience.

- Hotel Barracuda (Melgar 628, just north of C 11) Not the liveliest undersea life, but walking distance from the centre, and the *No Name Bar* here attracts interesting crew from the cruise ships.
- La Caletita (Carretera Sur Km 3) Look for a branch of *Alberto's* (see p.99). Enter the water here and drift north along the rock-and-coral wall, exiting at *Dive Paradise* hotel. Good for coral and sponges, but not many fish.
- Villa Blanca Shallows (Carretera Sur Km 3.5) Another spot for drift snorkelling – ask at the *Sunset Grill* which way the current is running.
- Airplane Wreck (In front of *El Cid La Ceiba* hotel, Carretera Sur Km 4.5) Walk through the hotel to the end of the pier: a plane was crashed here for a 1970s disaster movie.
- Paradise Shallows (Near Carretera Sur Km 5) South of town, bear right onto the moped road and turn at the road marked "Caleta"; then turn right at the marina and head to a parking area. There's no gear rental here; also wear water shoes, as there are lots of sea urchins in the rocks.
*Dzul-Ha (South of *El Presidente Inter-Continental*, on the moped road, at Km 6.5) Also called Las Palmas, this is probably the best walk-in spot, from the *Money Bar*. Swim north a bit and drift back south, as far as the *Fiesta Americana*, if you like. You're within marine park bounds here, and should buy a M$24 bracelet at the gear shop.

caverns and fissures, completely encrusted with vibrant corals and sea fans. **El Cedral** and **Las Palmas** (both just north of Palancar Shallows) are two other excellent spots for advanced divers. Of the dozens of **dive shops** in town, Deep Blue, on Salas at Avenida 10 (☏987/872-5653, ⊛www.deepbluecozumel.com), is one of the best, offering small-group tours to some of the most interesting and remote reefs off the island; a two-tank dive is US$73. For certification courses, Caribbean Divers (☏987/872-1145, ⊛www.caribbeandiverscozumel.com), on Avenida 5 at Calle 3, comes recommended.

Eating

Many of San Miguel's **restaurants** are tourist traps catering to a bland palate, but beyond the dull pasta-and-steakhouses, you can find some excellent bargain meals, as well as a couple of places worthy of throwing down the pesos. For a local-flavour lunch, you can do well just wandering several blocks back from the seafront – there are a surprising number of small family-run operations tucked in the back streets. The cheapest snacks of all can be had through the afternoon at the city **market**, on Salas, between avenidas 20 and 25.

Cafés

Café del Museo Melgar, between C 4 and C 6, at the Museo de la Isla de Cozumel. Enjoy a quiet breakfast or early lunch on the upstairs balcony of the city museum. The view of the sea is impressive, the coffee is spiked with cinnamon and the food – from *huevos rancheros* to club sandwiches – is fresh and filling. Closed Sun.

Jeanie's Beach Club Melgar at Quintana Roo (C 11). Big American breakfasts – especially waffles – are the attraction here. Plus, you can stick your feet in the sand at the little breakwater beach.
Nacho Crazy Boy Av 20, between C 1 and Juárez. The eponymous Nacho operates a battery of blenders and squeezers in front of his house, to create inexpensive and delicious juice drinks.

Panadería Cozumeleña C 3 at Av 10. Stop by this sweet-smelling bakery (entrance on C 3) to pick up *pan dulce* to go, or, for a more leisurely light breakfast, settle in at the adjacent coffee shop, a neighbourhood hangout (entrance on the corner).

Super-Hit Tortas Av 30 (Coldwell) at Salas. Meaty Mexican-style sandwiches with plenty of toppings for just M$20; in the summer, they make an ideal snack before going to a baseball game at the field behind. There's another branch on Av 30 at Xel-Ha (aka C 15).

Zermatt C 4 at Av 5. Bakery serving delectably light sugar doughnuts, among other sweet treats.

Restaurants

La Candela Av 5 at C 6. Home-cooked breakfast and lunch, with a half-Cuban twist (black beans and rice, mojitos). The "fish Candela" (in a tomatillo cream sauce; M$120) is just one of many tasty house dishes. Nice breezy terrace seating out back.

Casa Denis C 1, between Av 5 and Av 10. Open since 1945, *Casa Denis* occupies a little wood-frame house. The Yucatecan mains (*poc-chuc* for M$110) are occasionally a little bland, but are leagues better than any other restaurant around the plaza. The safest bet is a beer and some *panuchos* as you watch the action from your sidewalk table.

Chi Melgar at C 3. Cruise-ship crew love this second-floor restaurant for its Filipino specialities, but locals go for the Chinese; the chefs come from Hong Kong and Manila. Entrance is under the Pizza Hut awning. Mains from M$99.

La Choza Salas at Av 10. Busy and popular palapa-roof restaurant known for its Mexican home cooking, though it's inconsistent. The daily lunch special isn't on the menu; ask the waiter, and you could get a rib-sticking meal for about M$60.

La Cocay C 8, between Av 10 and Av 15 ☎ 987/872-5533. One of the few upscale places in town with real substance, "The Firefly" has excellent service and a seasonal menu with dishes such as fish in a fennel sauce or five-spice-roasted duck (mains $160–260). Closed Sun.

Conchita del Caribe Av 65, between C 13 and C 15. Well off the tourist track, this locally famous seafood spot – once housed in a renovated garage and now relocated to slightly classier digs – is inexpensive and delicious. *Ceviches* are particularly good (M$85 for a generous "small" portion). Closes at 6pm.

Del Sur Av 5 at C 3. At this Argentine restaurant styled to look like a Pampas farmhouse you might get stalled on the dozen varieties of empanadas (bacon and prune!), or fill up tender steaks (M$130) or grilled sausage, but hold out for delectably light and crumbly *alfajores* (sandwich cookies with caramel).

Especias C 3 at Av 5 ☎ 987/876-1558. Inexpensive Argentine, Mexican and even occasionally Thai dinners (M$15 for snacks like empanadas, about M$60 for salads and M$120 for more substantial main dishes). The dining room is upstairs on a roof terrace. Closed Sun.

Kinta Av 5, between C 2 and C 4 ☎ 987/869-0544. This "Mexican bistro" is gold-lit and cosy, even in the back garden, where tables are screened by greenery. The food is creative Mexican, but still familiar: pork with fruity pasilla chiles and mushrooms, for instance. With mains from M$120 to M$195, it's good value too.

Olive by Le Chef Av 5 at C 5. Charming, personal place where the chef-owner devises new specials every day, such as various pizzas and creative sandwiches (hard to argue with the lobster-bacon combo). Down the street, at C 7, the same owner runs *Le Bistro*, open for breakfast too.

Rock'n Java Melgar 602, between C 7 and Quintana Roo (C 11) ☎ 987/872-4405. At this American-owned seafront diner, healthy sandwiches, salads and veggie chili (between M$40–80) are balanced out by fantastically rich and delicious desserts, such as German chocolate cake. Delivery is available to hotels south of town.

Sabores Av 5, between C 3 and C 5. Real home cooking at this lunch-only cocina económica run out of the chef-owner's house. Just walk through the living room and kitchen and out to the huge shady garden, where you can choose from several entrees. The set price (usually about M$65) includes soup and an all-you-can-drink jug of agua de jamaica. Mon–Sat noon–4pm.

El Turix C 17, between Av 20 and Av 25, across from Corpus Christi church ☎ 987/872-5234. Chef Rafael Ponce promotes the ideals of Slow Food in the form of traditional Yucatecan dishes like *cochinita pibil*. He also does a great coconut pie. We'd make it an author pick, but the hours can be erratic – call ahead.

Drinking and nightlife

Evening entertainment in Cozumel is generally low-key, as the cruise ship crowd goes back aboard at night. The only real scene centres on the Plaza del Sol, where local families come out to chat and listen to strolling musicians or bands – it's especially lively on Sunday nights. As with everything else on the island, drinks can be a little pricey, at least in San Miguel, and happy hours are hard to come by. You could also check out what's happening at the Centro Cultural Ixchel, on Avenida 5, between Juárez and Calle 2, which hosts concerts and other events.

Kelley's Av 10, between Salas and C 1. A big open-air bar where you might see your divemaster or tour guide in their off-hours. Very friendly, with a pool table and live music on Fri. Serves big, tasty portions of American food during the day.

La Morena Av 10, between C 3 and C 5. A restaurant with a back garden serving earthy Yucatecan food, it's also a great place to hang out in the afternoon, when beers cost M$20 and you can fill up on the *botanas* served with each round.

Neptuno Melgar at Quintana Roo (C 11). Cozumel's only nightclub is heavy on the lasers, fog machines and ladies' drink specials. It's more popular with locals than tourists, and is relatively cheap. Thurs is reggaeton night; Fries are for salsa.

Tiki-Tok Melgar, between C 2 and C 4. This second-floor bar doles out the umbrella drinks, and the party gets started earlier than most, as this is one of the only bars in town with a sunset view over the water.

Listings

Banks HSBC is on Av 5 at C 1 (Mon–Fri 9am–7pm).

Books and maps Fama, Av 5, between Juárez and C 2.

Car rental Posted rates are the same everywhere, but you may be able to negotiate when business is slow. *Hotel Aguilar*, C 3 no. 98 at Av 5 (☎987/872-0307), also rents scooters and bicycles.

Cinema Cinépolis, Melgar 1001, between Xel-Há (C 15) and C 17.

Consulate US: Plaza Villamar, on the square ☎987/872-4574, ✉anne@cozumel.net.

Internet access Internet cafés are scarce in the centre of town; there is one place on Melgar near *Rock'n'Java*.

Laundry Self-service laundromat, Av 20, between Salas and C 3 (7am–9pm Mon–Sat, 8am–4pm Sun; M$229 per extra-large load). For drop-off

service, there are two *lavanderías* on Quintana Roo (C 11) just east of Melgar; the price is M$12/kilo.

Medical care Hyperbaric chamber and clinic on C 5, between Melgar and Av 5. 24-hour Centro de Salud, on Av 20 at C 11 (☎987/872-0140). Most doctors are accustomed to dealing with English-speaking patients and those with diving-related issues.

Post office Melgar at C 7 (Mon–Fri 9am–4pm, Sat 9am–1pm).

Shopping Avoid mark-ups in stores on Melgar by shopping on Sunday or Monday, when there are no or few ships in port and sales staff may be open to negotiation. U'nahi Pax (Juárez at Av 15) sells musical instruments, from pre-Columbian drums and rattles to elaborate harps and big-bellied guitars, plus folk music on CD.

3

Tulum and around

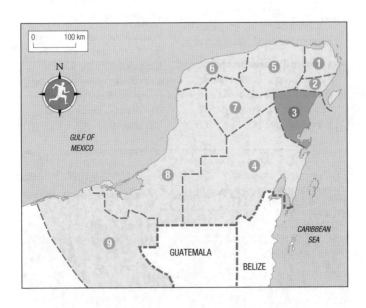

CHAPTER 3 # Highlights

✳ **Xel-Há** Despite the theme park appearance (and entry fee!), an area of exceptional natural beauty, teeming with fish and perfect for kids. See p. 110

✳ **Xcacel** The beautiful, empty beach here is a research station and protected area for nesting sea turtles. See p.111

✳ **Tulum** Visit the stirring seafront ruins then lounge at a cabaña along the gorgeous sand to the south. See p. 111

✳ **Cenotes** The area around Tulum has one of the highest concentrations of scenic cenotes and caverns on the peninsula. See p. 110 & p.119

✳ **Cobá** Rent a bicycle to explore these ruins, buried in dense jungle filled with wildlife, then climb the main pyramid for a stupendous view of green in every direction. See p. 119

✳ **Reserva de Monos Arañas de Punta Laguna** This reserve boasts a large population of spider monkeys as well as a tranquil lake great for canoeing. See p. 121

✳ **Punta Allen** Utter languor at literally the end of the road, surrounded by the wildlife and nature of the Sian Ka'an Biosphere Reserve, one of the largest protected areas in Mexico. See p.123

▲ Snorkelling among the fish at Xel-Há

3

Tulum and around

T
he heavily built-up **Riviera Maya** continues south of Playa del Carmen along Hwy-307, with all manner of grand resorts and condo villages lining the flawless sand – interspersed with the occasional, but increasingly rare, empty beach. As you head further south (and put more distance between yourself and Cancún's airport), the beach properties thin out a little. The accommodation here tends to cater to people willing to make the extra drive for a more isolated beach experience, culminating in the candle-lit, hippie-inflected cabañas of **Tulum**. On the inland side, the limestone shelf is riddled with some of the peninsula's most impressive **cenotes**, beautiful freshwater-filled caves that are refreshing and fascinating whether you want to swim, snorkel or scuba dive. Tulum, with its scenic Maya ruins and mellow beach-party scene, marks the southern border of Quintana Roo's tourist development. If you're not content just to lie on the beach, you can take a trip northwest to the grand ruins of **Cobá**, a vast Maya city buried in the forest.

After Tulum, the jungle thickens and Hwy-307 narrows and heads inland, skirting more than a million acres of wilderness that have been set aside in the **Sian Ka'an Biosphere Reserve**. This area forms a rich haven for marine and bird life, as well as larger forest mammals. The only village inside the reserve, tiny **Punta Allen**, is a destination for travellers looking for quiet isolation and great fishing. On the edge of the reserve, just off Hwy-307, the rambling ruins of **Chunyaxché** are often empty, while the ancient roads and canals the Maya built here are a great place to spot wildlife.

From Playa del Carmen to Tulum

Almost the entire sixty-kilometre stretch of coast between Playa del Carmen and Tulum has been transformed into resorts or condominium "villages" with gated entrances and little or no access for non-residents to the sea; the most egregious of these is the expensive, sterile **Puerto Aventuras**, 20km south of Playa, which feels like a theme park minus the rides. But amid the slick developments, a few less formal spots survive, along with some increasingly beleaguered hidden beaches. Everything here is relatively easy to reach; second-class buses and *colectivos* run almost constantly between Playa and Tulum and will stop anywhere along the highway. For more structured fun, you can stop off at **Xel-Há**, a semi-natural water park that's great for kids, or take a cenote and activity tour at **Hidden Worlds**, both just north of Tulum.

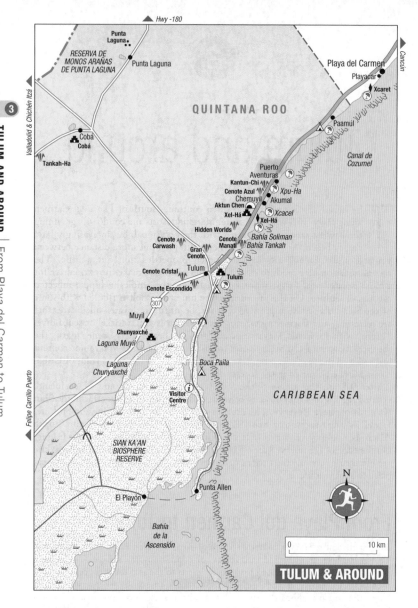

TULUM & AROUND

Paamul

The first community south of Playa, **PAAMUL** (☎984/875-1053, ⓦwww
.paamul.com) is a fancy RV park with an excellent **restaurant** that serves all the
standard *ceviches* and quesadillas, plus succulent main fish and meat dishes, prepared
with more care than at typical beach seafood joints. The reef runs very close to
shore here, making for some of the best wade-in **snorkelling** within the vicinity

of Playa, from a quiet, half-moon beach. The community also operates its own excellent dive centre (⑥ www.scubamex.com) and two overnight **lodging** options directly on the water – elegant, large rooms with three beds and stunning sea views (❼), or simpler wooden cabañas (❻), both with air conditioning, wi-fi and plenty of hot water.

Xpu-Ha

Twenty-five kilometres further south, a series of poorly signed tracks lead to **Xpu-ha**, whose perfectly white sand curves around in a large, gentle arc. Though the beach is gradually being taken over by development, it's still an especially lovely spot. *Esencia* (☎ 1-877/528-3490, or ☎ 1-713/528-7862 in the US, ⑥ www .hotelesencia.com; ❾), with 29 elegantly designed rooms, plunge pools and a spa, offers intimate luxury of the most elite kind (from US$600 a night). Just next door, the more affordable *Al Cielo* (☎ 984/840-9012, ⑥ www.alcielohotel .com; ❾) has four beautiful cabaña-style rooms and a duplex apartment with roof-top plunge pool. Even if the rooms are not in your price range, you can eat in the excellent Mediterranean restaurant (daily 12.30–9pm; reservation recommended), less pricey than it looks, which entitles you to use the beach facilities.

Towards the southern end of the beach, *La Playa XpuHa* restaurant and beach club (⑥ www.laplayaxpuha.com) is a friendly place with plenty of locals where for the price of a meal or a few drinks (minimum M$100) you can use the lounge chairs and other beach facilities; they also offer diving (⑥ www.bahiadivers.com) and have kayaks, jet-skis and snorkel gear to rent. The track immediately south of this leads to *Bonanza Xpu-ha* (no phone; ❺) a surviving budget place where you can stay in basic cabañas or **camp** (M$100); if you just want to visit the beach, there's a small charge for parking here.

Akumal

Akumal, about 10km south again, is primarily a condo community, but as one of the oldest and best established it has a number of excellent places to eat, interesting shops and several experienced dive and snorkelling establishments. Above all, its main beach offers superb snorkelling, with pretty much guaranteed sightings of turtles just a short way offshore. The Centro Ecológico de Akumal (☎ 984/875-9095, ⑥ www .ceakumal.org), just behind the beach, runs a programme monitoring and protecting the local turtle population, and organizes hatchling releases every evening in season. As you enter the community through the arch, the *Hotel Club Akumal* (☎ 984/875-9115, ⑥ www.akumalguide.com) is the best of several operations that rent bikes and offer local tours and services. Of the many places to eat in central Akumal, the chummy ⋇ *Turtle Bay* **restaurant** is highly recommended, especially for their home-baked goodies at breakfast. For more entertainment, head north up the coast road to *La Buena Vida* beach **bar and restaurant** on Half Moon Bay, a funky place with precarious tree-house seating, bedecked with fish skeletons. *Imelda's Ecocina*, in front of the Centro Ecológico, has an excellent value *comida* daily, plus an enjoyable Mayan buffet (M$240) with dancing on Wednesday and Friday evenings.

Accommodation in Akumal is mostly very pricey. *Vista del Mar* (☎ 984/875-9060, ⑥ www.akumalinfo.com; ❼), right next to the *Buena Vida*, has reasonable seafront rooms and more expensive condos; *Villas de Rosa* (☎ 984/875-9020, ⑥ www.cenotes.com) also has rooms (❻) and condos (❽) to the south on Aventuras beach (reached by a separate access road signed "Aventuras Akumal"). ⋇ *Que Onda* (☎ 984/875-9101, ⑥ www.queondaakumal.com; ❻), which is at the northernmost end of the coast road and not right on the beach, has slightly lower prices, and a more laidback, European vibe; there's a small pool and a good, Italian-influenced restaurant. *Que Onda* also offers private entry to the lagoon, **Yal-Ku** (daily 8am–5.30pm; M$110), which is almost a miniature Xel-Ha (see below) – fewer fish, but also far fewer people and much more natural surroundings. Of the **dive** places, both Akumal Dive Shop (T 984/875-9032, W www.akumaldiveshop.com, also snorkelling, fishing etc), right by the Centro Ecológico, and Aquatech Divers (T 984/875-9020, W www.cenotes.com), on Aventuras beach at the *Villas de Rosa*, are professional and experienced, offering cavern as well as offshore diving.

Xcacel

Directly south of the town of Chemuyil, poorly signed just beyond the Km. 247 marker, you'll find an exceptionally lovely, often empty beach at **Xcacel** (9am–5pm daily, M$10), a sea turtle research station and sanctuary where the animals come to lay their eggs. There are no services beyond a single shower – the attraction is the pristine bay with good waves for body-surfing, plus a small, open cenote behind the south end of the beach. If you're reliant on bus or *combi*, the beach is only 500m from the highway.

Xel-Há

Despite the sky-high entrance fee and the crowds and theme-park feel, **Xel-Há** (daily 8.30am–6pm; W www.xelha.com; US$79, kids between 1m and 1.40m US$40), 13km north of Tulum, remains one of the highlights of this coast, especially if you have children: you can easily spend an entire day here and, if you do, it can seem pretty good value. The price is genuinely all-inclusive – not just lockers, towels and snorkel gear, but all you can eat and drink (including a free bar) for the whole time you're here. The only extras are for photos and additional activities such as swimming with the dolphins (around US$100, but a very slick operation) or less enticing underwater tours. Centred around a natural formation of lagoons, inlets and underground caves, Xel-Há has wonderful snorkelling with large numbers of surprisingly big fish, and activities from kayaking to cliff jumping, rope swings to gently tubing down a river.

Across the highway, the small and only partly excavated **ruins of Xel Há** (daily 8am–5pm; M$37) are notable for the stucco paintings in the Grupo Pájaros and miniature, chest-high temples that resemble ones found at Tulum.

Cenotes along the highway

You'll see signs to cenotes (see box, opposite) all along the highway; some are highly developed sites, others mere roadside shacks. Perhaps the most spectacular of the organized cenote parks is **Hidden Worlds** (tours daily 9am–3pm; T 984/877-8535, W www.hiddenworlds.com), comprising a cluster of outstanding cenotes and caverns just south of Xel-Há. Guided group snorkelling (US$25–40) and diving (US$100 for two tanks) trips run every half hour or so: snorkellers pile into a jeep with a handful of other visitors and trundle through the forest to the enormous Tak Be Ha cavern and constricted Hilario's Well; open-water divers can experience some of the best cenote diving anywhere at the glimmering, sunlit Dos Ojos cenote and the Dreamgate, an awe-inspiring 61-metre-wide cavern. Other activities include zip-wires, a "sky cycle" through the trees and nature walks (packages $60–80).

Aktun Chen (daily 9am–5pm; W www.aktunchen.com; activities from US$21–38), between Akumal and Xel-Há, makes an interesting contrast as it's primarily a dry cave tour, though again there's a cenote and zip-lines plus a good chance of seeing wildlife, as they encourage animals with feeding. **Kantun-Chi** (daily 9am–5pm; tours M$200–500), further north between Puerto Aventuras and Xpu-Ha, also has wildlife and four spectacular cenotes. Immediately to the south

Exploring the cenotes

The area north and west of Tulum has one of the largest concentrations of **cenotes** on the peninsula, including Ox Bel Ha, which at almost 170km, is the longest water-filled cave system in the world. Many of them are easily accessible from Hwy-307 or off the road to Cobá (see p.119). Some have been developed as "eco-parks" or adventure centres, and for first-time visitors – especially those who might be leery of tight spaces and dark water – the guides and marked-out trails can be comforting. However, it's also worth visiting one of the less-developed alternatives, where for a small entry fee you are pretty much left to explore by yourself, and fewer visitors means a greater chance of encountering wildlife. If there's worthwhile snorkelling or diving, most will have equipment available to rent, and dive trips (and other visits) can be arranged in every resort. **Divers** must have open-water certification for **cavern diving** (in which you explore within the reach of daylight), while **cave diving** (in which you venture into closed passageways and halls) requires rigorous special training. Though local development threatens the cenotes and the fresh ground-water in the long term, inexperienced and clumsy visitors can do more damage in the short term: wear only **biodegradable sunscreen**; **do not touch** the surprisingly delicate stalactites; never break off anything as a souvenir; **mind your flippers**, as it's easy to kick up silt or knock into the rocks; and be very careful climbing in and out of the water – use the provided paths and ladders.

are three less organized and far less visited cenotes: Cristalino (daily 9am–7pm; M$40), Jardín del Edén (daily 7am–5pm; M$50) and Cenote Azul (daily 9am–5pm; M$50), great for swimming and snorkelling.

Soliman and Tankah bays

The final accessible beaches before Tulum are at adjacent **Bahía Soliman** and **Bahía Tankah**, two long crescents backed mainly by private houses and villas, many of which are available for rental. At Soliman bay it's increasingly hard for non-residents to get past the private security guards; for Tankah, follow the road signed to the *Blue Sky* restaurant. Behind Tankah beach, the **Cenote Manatí** (M$20) is a great place to snorkel – a network of seven pools that wind through the trees, with plenty of birdlife and supposedly even manatees, though you're unlikely to see the latter. The cenote is right by the *Casa Cenote* restaurant and hotel (Ⓦ www.casacenote .com; restaurant daily 8am–9pm, Texan-style barbecue on Sun), where you can eat well in a beautiful, chilled beachside setting; an underground outlet from the cenote emerges in the bay in front, discharging cool, fresh water.

Places to stay here include the *Tankah Inn* (Ⓣ 984/100-0703, Ⓦ www.tankah .com; ❼), a slightly dated but very friendly B&B guesthouse with wi-fi, a fridge in each room and many communal facilities, and *Tankah Villas* (Ⓣ 984/807-7390, Ⓦ www.sliceofparadise.com; ❼), with two beachfront cabañas and two small *casitas* with kitchen. The latter is near the northern end of the bay, where the reef meets the shore so that you can wade straight out to it.

Tulum

To visitors, **TULUM** can mean several things. First, it's arguably the most pictur-esque of all the ancient Maya sites, poised on fifteen-metre-high cliffs above an impossibly turquoise Caribbean. Tulum also refers to a stretch of broad, white **beach** that's the finest in the Riviera Maya, dotted with lodging options that range

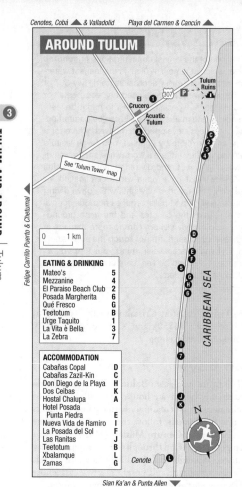

Cenotes, Cobá ▲ & Valladolid   Playa del Carmen & Cancún ▲

AROUND TULUM

Tulum Ruins

307

El Crucero ①

Acuatic Tulum

Ⓐ Ⓑ

See 'Tulum Town' map

0   1 km

Ⓒ ② ③ ④

Ⓓ

Ⓔ Ⓕ

Ⓖ ⑤ Ⓖ ⑥

CARIBBEAN SEA

Ⓘ ⑦

Ⓙ Ⓚ

N

Cenote Ⓛ

Sian Ka'an & Punta Allen ▼

EATING & DRINKING

Mateo's	5
Mezzanine	4
El Paraiso Beach Club	2
Posada Margherita	6
Qué Fresco	G
Teetotum	B
Urge Taquito	1
La Vita è Bella	3
La Zebra	7

ACCOMMODATION

Cabañas Copal	D
Cabañas Zazil-Kin	C
Don Diego de la Playa	H
Dos Ceibas	K
Hostal Chalupa	A
Hotel Posada Punta Piedra	E
Nueva Vida de Ramiro	I
La Posada del Sol	F
Las Ranitas	J
Teetotum	B
Xbalamque	L
Zamas	G

from bare-bones to ultra-swank; many of them, as well as several ultra-casual beach bars, still show their backpacker-friendly roots in style, if not in price. Finally, it's a booming town (often called **Tulum Pueblo** to distinguish it from the beach) that has evolved from roadside waystation to real population centre: as well as plenty of restaurants and budget accommodation, this is also the easiest place to line up a tour to the Sian Ka'an Biosphere Reserve (see p.122), or a diving or snorkelling excursion to one of the nearby cenotes (see p.119).

Arrival and information

Coming into the Tulum area on Hwy-307 from the north (it's 130km from Cancún), you arrive first at the well-marked pedestrian and bus entrances to the **ruins** – the site itself is on the water, 1km east. There's a dedicated long-haul bus stop here, so you don't have to double back from town.

Another kilometre or so south along the highway is a traffic light marking the main intersection, what locals call *El Crucero*. Turn left here to follow the road 3km to the **beach**, where most of the local accommodation is strung along a narrow road running alongside the water. To the north (left) are a few hotels (but see box, p.116), the better publicly accessible **beaches** and, after 2km, a back entrance to the ruins. To the south (right), hotels are scattered along the beach for seven kilometres; after that, you're at the border of the Sian Ka'an Biosphere Reserve and the road turns to dirt.

Back on Hwy-307 (here called Av Tulum), the centre of **town** is just a little further south. The **bus** station, open 24 hours, is near the southern end; **colectivos** stop almost next door. To get to the beach hotels, you'll need a **taxi** (starting at M$40); rates are posted in the median where taxis gather, just north of the station. Tulum's taxi drivers have a reputation for denying the existence of hotels that don't pay them commission; if you have planned on a particular hotel, insist on being taken there.

There's a **tourist info kiosk** with erratic hours on Avenida Tulum at Calle Osiris, just north of the HSBC bank, or you can pick up good free maps at the *Weary Traveler* hostel, just south of the bus station, as well as at many of the cafés, travel agencies and dive shops in town.

Yucatán food

"The Land of the Pheasant and the Deer" – as the Maya call the Yucatán Peninsula – is a bounteous place to eat. For millennia, the forest has augmented the basic diet of corn and beans with turkey, game meats, wild greens and luscious fruits. Locals have also embraced European products: pork, of course, but also Dutch cheese and novel spices. And the sea provides fresh ingredients, too, from succulent shrimp to enormous fish. It's all served up in a distinctive regional cuisine that's both earthy and delicate, as well as delicious, from breakfast till late-night.

The Yucatán table

Salbuches are the Yucatán's favourite snack ▲

Lightly battered shrimp make perfect tacos ▼

Before you even order, you'll see the **distinctive flavours** of the Yucatán set out in the middle of the table: commercial hot sauce is standard, plus bowls of gloriously pink pickled onions, grilled and pickled *habañero* peppers (the peninsula's most potent chile) and a raw chopped salsa of tomato, onion, cilantro (coriander leaves) and more *habañero*. That's what gives the salsa the name *xnipek*, Maya for "dog's nose", because it will make you damp with sweat.

By contrast, none of the food itself is innately spicy. It is, however, **colourful**: annatto lends a lurid orange stain to dishes like *tikin-xic* (pronounced "TIK-in sheek"; fish wrapped in banana leaves and grilled) and *poc-chuc*, for which pork is marinated in juice from the locally grown bitter orange. Food here can also be **staggeringly rich**. The Yucatecans embraced such European exotica as Dutch Edam cheese and concocted some of the world's first fusion food: *queso relleno*, a round of cheese hollowed out and filled with a delectable mix of beef, olives and raisins. On a less exotic note, Yucatecans are strangely enamoured with **mayonnaise**, which may or may not be a legacy of French fads in the nineteenth century.

Local ingredients are just as essential. **Pumpkin seeds** lend a nutty, creamy note to a salsa called *sikilpa'ak* and the sauce that douses *papadzules*, tortillas filled with hard-boiled egg. Shredded **turkey** (a bird the ancient Maya domesticated) adds body to the citrus-scented *sopa de lima*, and it tops *panuchos*, the small rounds of fried *masa* (the maize paste used for tortillas) that are as popular as tacos for an evening snack. **Seafood** has been an intrinsic part of the diet, too, and its preparation is usually simple: fried whole, or diced and mixed with lime juice to make a *ceviche*.

Bottled salsa adds a spicy kick ▼

Wash it all down with a shot of *xtabentun*, a honey-flavoured liqueur allegedly first distilled by the ancient Maya. Or opt for a fresh fruit juice – whatever time of year you visit, something delicious will be in season.

The Tabasco table

Tabasqueño cuisine is markedly different from Yucatecan food, dictated by the state's proximity to **rivers**. Locals revere, first and foremost, the alarming-looking *pejelagarto*, a long, skinny gar with nasty teeth; the big ones can be more than a metre long. It's a freshwater fish from the Grijalva river, often with a subtly muddy taste that you'll either love or hate. Served as a cold *ceviche*-style salad, the fish is nicely offset by bright lime juice and red onions. And it's packed in deep-fried empanadas to good effect. Inspiration also comes from the Gulf of Mexico – as in the hearty *chilpachole*, a spicy seafood stew, served with crab claws in season – and from the state's lush **tropical orchards**: dessert often features passionfruit (*maracuya*) and pineapple (*piña*).

▲ Bounty in a produce market near Progreso

▼ Fresh fried tortillas and *xnipek* salsa

Salsa style

A vital guide to the quality of a restaurant is its salsa – not just the standard condiments like pickled onions and *xnipek*, but also the **cooked salsas**, which can be either red (made with varieties of dried chiles) or green (with tomatillos). Grubby bowls refilled with canned supermarket products usually mean the place takes little pride in its food. But a good *comida casera* (home-cooking) operation will offer a freshly made salsa in a pretty dish. Look for little flecks of black in the mix – these indicate someone took the time to roast the ingredients, which adds a much deeper flavour.

▼ Dutch cheese shows the European influence

Colourful sweets at the Oxkutzcab market ▲

Freshly made tortillas for sale ▼

The miracle green

Yucatecan cuisine doesn't involve a lot of vegetables, except for one staple: **chaya**. Yucatecans use the leaves from the hardy, towering bushes at every meal, starting with an invigorating (and brilliantly coloured) **chaya-pineapple juice** for breakfast. It also winds up in tamales, scrambled eggs and soups and stews. And no wonder – aside from the small catch that it's toxic when eaten raw, it's incredibly healthful. Though its flavour is usually compared with spinach, it trumps that green as a source of iron, calcium, protein and vitamins A and B. Longtime chaya consumers swear by it as a cure for everything from diabetes to obesity to bad skin. Rarely has something so healthful also been so tasty.

In Tabasco, a good restaurant won't serve you the standard tortilla chips to start. Instead, you'll get a basket of thin fried patties made of plantain mash, starchy and a tiny bit sweet. It's all accented with a distinctive salsa made with **chiltepín chile peppers**. Tiny and green, they look deceptively like capers, but pack a serious punch.

The Chiapas table

Chiapanecos eat a huge range of things. Their diet varies depending on what valley or mountain town they live in, and what ethnic group they belong to. On menus, you can pick out regional goodies because they often start with t- or tl-. One great example is a cold drink called *tascalate*, a frothy blend of **chocolate** (a regional product), pine nuts, vanilla and sugar. Coffee from the Chiapas highlands is also worth trying. Cafés are getting better at preparing it to European tastes, though locals prefer it brewed weaker and spiced with cinnamon.

Accommodation

Although Tulum's beach is an obvious draw, you may want to stay in **town** if you arrive late in the day, have a limited amount of time (and money) or just prefer hot water round-the-clock. Hotels in the zona hotelera along the **beach road** do not connect to the electric grid, relying instead on varying combinations of solar panels, windmills and diesel generators; most have power for only about six hours in the evening. Depending on your point of view, the candle-lit ambience of the accommodation on the beach is either rustic charm or expensive primitivism.

Basic sand- or cement-floor **cabañas** made this area famous with hippie backpackers, but they're in short supply now (and are plagued with reports of theft), as ritzier places, with prices to match, take over; many describe themselves as eco-resorts, not always with much justification. There are several **camping** places on the beach road too, though none seem to survive long: *El Paraiso* (see p.115; M$150, or M$150 per person to hire a tent) is one of the more pleasant and secure locations.

TULUM TOWN

0   200 m

Laundry

Taxi office

Cenote Dive Center

Safari @

HSBC Bank

Bus Station

Riviera Movil

Laundry

Buster Car Rental

ACCOMMODATION

Casa del Sol	B
Don Diego de la Selva	E
L'Hotelito	A
Posada Luna del Sur	D
The Weary Traveler	C

& Felipe Carrillo Puerto

EATING & DRINKING

Azafran	1	Cetli	2	Pan del Carmen	6
El Camello		Divino Paraiso	7	Pepenero	9
Jr	11	Flor de		Pequeño	
La Casa del		Michoacan	8	Buenos Aires	5
Buen Pan	3	La Nave	4	El Tacoqueto	10

In town

Casa del Sol Polar Pte, about 300m south of the bus station, mobile ☎984/129-6424, ⓦwww.casa delsolhostels.com. Friendly, old-school backpacker hostel with ten-bed dorms (M$120), simple rooftop cabañas and rooms; breakfast, wi-fi and internet included; rental bikes and laundry available. ➋

Don Diego de la Selva Tulum, off the west side of Hwy-307, about 900m south of town, mobile ☎984/114-9744, ⓦwww.dtulum.com. Quiet, French-owned hideaway just out of town, with a pool, tranquil garden, French-influenced restaurant and big, white rooms with terraces; choice of fan or a/c. Use of beach facilities at *Don Diego de la Playa* (see p.114). ➏–➐

Hostal Chalupa On the road to the beach, 50m from Hwy-307 ☎984/128-8423, ⓦwww .chalupatulum.com. Excellent new hostel with rooftop bar and small pool; dorm beds (M$100) are in 3-or 4-bed dorms, all a/c and en-suite;

also available as private rooms. Vegetarian kitchen. ➍

L'Hotelito West side of Tulum, between Orion and Beta ☎984/136-1240, ⓦwww .hotelitotulum.com. Good value Italian-run hotel with palapa roofs and garden courtyard, quiet despite its location in the middle of town. Rooms have an old-fashioned, comfy feel: upstairs with high ceilings and fan or a/c; downstairs with a/c. ➌

Posada Luna del Sur Luna Sur 5 ☎984/871-2984, ⓦwww.posadalunadelsur .com. Exceptionally comfy, spotless, tranquil rooms set around a small garden. Welcoming and helpful owners and staff create an intimate B&B atmosphere. No children. ➏

Teetotum On the road to the beach, 100m from Hwy-307 ☎984/745-8827, ⓦwww .teetotumhotel.com. Four sharply designed rooms with iPod docks, quiet a/c and mod furniture.

Other perks include rooftop yoga classes, a small pool and a great café (breakfast included, see p.117). Its location on the road to the beach hits a sweet spot: quiet, but walking distance to town and an easy bike ride (on free bicycles) to the water. ⑧

The Weary Traveler Tulum, just south of the bus station ☎ 984/871-2390, ⓦ www .wearytravelerhostel.com. The best-known and most convenient hostel in town; basic, large dorms (M$120, a/c M$130) as well as private rooms with (④) or without bath (③). Very party-centric and not always the cleanest, but a great meeting place. DIY breakfast in the communal kitchen and shuttle to the beach included.

On the beach

Cabañas Copal 700m south of the junction with the highway access road ☎ 01-800/681-9537 in Mexico, ☎ 1-866/471-3472 in the US, ⓦ www .cabanascopal.com. The round, cement-floor, candle-lit cabañas are quite crowded in, but they're relatively well priced; if you're looking to go cheap, try to nab one of two shared-bath cabins (US$35). There's electricity only in public areas but plenty of hot water, and a clothing-optional beach. Services include restaurant and a good sauna. ⑦

Cabañas Zazil-Kin 2km north of the junction ☎ 984/124-0082, ⓦ www.zazilkintulum.com. Basic, concrete-floor cabañas, a couple with private bath – evening electricity and cold water only – plus a dozen a/c rooms in a new block. Perennially popular, with a lively bar scene – reserve or arrive early, as rooms go fast. ④, rooms ⑦

Don Diego de la Playa 2km south of the junction, mobile ☎ 984/114-9744, ⓦ www.dtulum.com. From the owners of *Don Diego de la Selva*, attractive permanent tents with a Bedouin feel and one two-storey cabaña right on the beach, all with shared bath. ⑥

Dos Ceibas 5.5km south of the junction ☎ 984/877-6024, ⓦ www.dosceibas.com. Colourful, spacious cabañas in front of a turtle-hatching beach. Solar power and recycling mean their "eco" label is more convincing than most; yoga and meditation classes offered. The

cheapest cabaña (US$65) has a bathroom outside. ⑥

Nueva Vida de Ramiro 4km south of the junction ☎ 984/157-5526, ⓦ www.tulumnv.com. Peaceful, quirky eco-hotel which relies entirely on wind turbines. Attractive wood cabins on stilts and newer cement cabins with big tiled bathrooms, are built over and around untamed greenery. The beach is great and the restaurant serves tasty seafood. With several suites and whole houses, it's a good choice for families. ⑧

La Posada del Sol 1.3km south of the junction ☎ 984/134-8874, ⓦ www.laposadadelsol.com. Beautifully designed high-ceiling rooms and cabañas; four on the jungle side of the road; six beachfront. There's also wi-fi and an excellent jewellery shop in the lobby. ⑦/⑨

Hotel Posada Punta Piedra 1.2km south of the junction ☎ 984/806-4502, ⓦ www .posadapuntapiedra.com. Half a dozen newly refurbished, luxurious cabañas plus a couple of family rooms, all with hot water and 24-hour electricity; bike rental and dive shop, too. ⑦

Las Ranitas 5km south of the junction ☎ 984/877-8554, ⓦ www.lasranitas.com. Long-established, understated but comfortable hotel with fourteen lovely (but expensive) breezy rooms and two family suites, plus tennis courts, a pool, wi-fi, an excellent library, 24-hour electricity and a great stretch of beach. ⑨

🏃 **Xbalamque** 7km south of the junction, on the inland side of the road just before the Sian Ka'an gate, mobile ☎ 984/131-5132, ⓦ www .xbalamquetulum.net. The idea here is to create a sort of hippie all-inclusive: very simple but clean back-to-nature cabañas come with shared bath and sporadic power; included are continental breakfast, use of communal outdoor kitchen, wi-fi, bikes and kayaks. Out back there's access to a cenote. ④

🏃 **Zamas** 1.8km south of the junction ☎ 1-415/387-9806 in the US, ⓦ www.zamas .com. Enormous, comfortable rooms, some right on the beach; one great family cabaña. Hot water and electricity are plentiful, but the style remains bohemian. Good restaurant on site (see p.118). ⑧

The town and the beach

Tulum **town** offers all the basic tourist services and an increasing number of good restaurants and bars, but it's not remotely attractive. By day there are generally few visitors because they've all decamped to the **beach**, one of the longest stretches of impeccable white sand along the Caribbean coast. The easiest access to the sea is at one of the **beach clubs**: there's no charge at these, though you'll pay for lounge chairs and drinks. Elsewhere the beach is open to all, but it can be hard to get to; there's free access if you head far enough south – especially inside the biosphere reserve – and many hotel bars and restaurants let you use their beach facilities for the price of a meal or drink. The most popular clubs are north on the beach road, in walking distance of the ruins: **El Paraiso**, much the biggest, draws crowds to its fully stocked bar, **kiteboarding** school (see p.118) and friendly vibe. If you're looking for more solitude, head further up to **Playa Maya**: you'll have to bring your own towels and refreshments, but local fishermen's co-ops offer snorkel tours taking in a view of the ruins (M$200/person) or fishing trips (M$2000 for the boat; book the day before).

For something more energetic than hammock-lounging, there are dive shops all along the beach and in town, plus more kiteboarding and plenty of places offering snorkelling and other tours. See "Listings", p.118, for details of these.

The ruins

On a sunny day, with the turquoise sea glittering behind the weather-beaten grey stones, the first view of the **Tulum ruins** (daily 8am–5pm, last entry 4.30; M$51) can be breathtaking, despite the small scale of its buildings, all clustered in a compact mass within fortified walls. When the Spaniards first set eyes on the place, in 1518, they considered it as large and beautiful as Seville. They were, perhaps, misled by their dreams of El Dorado and by the brightly painted facades of the buildings, for architecturally Tulum is no match for the great Maya cities. Mostly built after 1200, the structures seem haphazard because their walls flare outward and the doorways taper in – not the effect of time, but an intentional design, and one echoed in other Post-Classic sites along the coast like El Rey in Cancún and San Gervasio on Cozumel. Nevertheless, thanks to its location, Tulum sticks in the memory like no other site, and draws crowds second only to Chichén Itzá.

Tickets are sold at the site **entrance**, about 1km from the main highway and parking area, where there's also a warren of souvenir shops; a shuttle (M$20) runs between the parking area and the ruins. You can also approach from the south, parking at the dead-end of the beach road and walking in. The site itself takes only an hour or so to see, though you may want to allow time to **swim** at the tiny, perfect beach that punctuates the cliffs. Arrive in the early morning or late afternoon to avoid the worst crowds.

You walk in through a breach in the wall that surrounds the city on three sides; the fourth side faces the sea. This **wall**, some 5m high with a walkway along the top, may

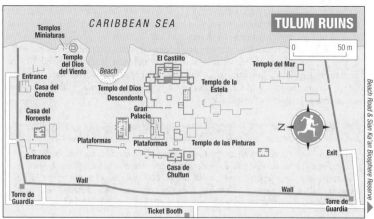

Visitor Centre, Hwy-307 (1km) & Tulum Town (2km)

Beach Road & Sian Ka'an Biosphere Reserve

have had a defensive purpose, but more likely it marked the boundary of the ceremonial and administrative precinct. Archeologists believe the towers that mark the corners of the wall were small temples rather than military structures. The walls did take on a defensive role around 1890, however, in the waning years of the Caste Wars, when Maya followers of the Talking Cross liberation movement (see box, p.129) reoccupied the site and held out against Mexican armies for more than 25 years.

Passing through the wall on the north side, you are in front of the **Casa del Noroeste**, one of the many small-scale buildings which typify the site, with their slanty walls and narrow windows. Closer to the sea sits the **Casa del Cenote**, a square structure straddling what was once a water-filled cave, the source of life for the settlement. On the bluff above and to the right are the **Templos Miniaturas**, several diminutive temples, complete with tiny lintels and mouldings, which were probably used as shrines. The nearby **Templo del Díos del Viento** (Temple of the Wind God) is a single-room structure set on a rounded platform; temples to wind gods were traditionally rounded in ancient Mexico so as to present no sharp obstacles to the wind – a design which, though common elsewhere, is seldom seen in this region. The temple finds its twin in a similar chamber, the **Templo del Mar**, which overlooks the water at the southern edge of the site.

Skirt the pocket-sized beach to reach the **Templo del Díos Descendente**. The diving (or descending) god, carved in stone above the narrow entrance of the temple, is one of Tulum's quirks: the small, upside-down winged figure appears all over the city, but in only a handful of places elsewhere in the Maya world. His significance is unclear – he may represent the setting sun, or rain or lightning, or he may be the bee god, since honey was one of the Maya's most important exports. Immediately adjacent to the temple, the imposing **Castillo**, on the highest part of the site, commands fine views in every direction, though visitors, prohibited from climbing it, can only look up at the building from the plaza at its base. The fortress-like pyramid probably served not just as a temple, but also as a beacon or lighthouse; even without a light it would have been an important landmark for mariners along an otherwise featureless coastline.

Just south of the Castillo, the squat, barely restored **Templo de la Estela** (Temple of the Stele) was named for a commemorative stone tablet found inside, which bears the date 564 AD. As that would have been well before the city's foundation, the tablet was presumably brought here from elsewhere.

Away from the sea, a cluster of buildings is arranged on a city-like grid, with the chief structures set on stone platforms along parallel streets. The most intriguing of these is the **Templo de las Pinturas** (Temple of the Paintings), whose intricate carvings slowly reveal themselves as you look closely. The corners form glowering masks trimmed with feather headdresses, and the "descending god" can be spotted in one niche. Unfortunately, you can no longer view the interior murals (actually on the *exterior* of an older, smaller temple, which has been preserved by the surrounding gallery), but one remarkable scene, created at a later date than the others, shows the rain god Chac seated on a four-legged animal – likely inspired by the conquistadors on horseback.

Hotel closures in Tulum

In Tulum – as indeed throughout the Riviera Maya – many hotels have allegedly been built illegally, either on land whose ownership is disputed or in breach of environmental and planning rules. Action is rarely taken, but in 2008 a number of hotels on the Tulum beach north of the junction (within the National Park area) were closed down; most promptly reopened, but as we went to press in 2011 several were closed again.

Eating and drinking

Because the accommodation in Tulum is spread over 10km and the town is so far from the beach, almost every hotel in the area has its own restaurant – ranging from cheap to very chic. Guests tend to stick to the restaurants in their own hotels, but a few **places to eat** along the coast road merit a special trip. In town there are plenty of inexpensive taco places, as well as a number of cafés and cheerful, mid-range places run by European expats. There's also an excellent **bakery**, *Pan del Carmen*, on Avenida Tulum at the corner of Osiris Norte, open daily from 6am to 11pm, which sells good bread and a huge variety of *pan dulce*.

As for **nightlife**, although many visitors tell tales of the ultimate beach party in Tulum, tracking down that elusive revel in the sand can be a little difficult. Look for flyers and posters in town, or ask around at cabaña camps and beach clubs like *Zazil-Kin* or *El Paraiso*; the latter usually has some kind of event around the full moon.

In town

Azafran Satélite Norte between Sagitario and Calle 2. Excellent breakfasts and home-made bagels and sandwiches served till about 3pm; off the beaten track but very popular with local expats.

El Camello Jr East side of Hwy-307 right at the southern edge of town. Unpretentious, plastic-table-and-chair place, but the crowds will tell you that the seafood is excellent and cheap – try the *ceviche*.

La Casa del Buen Pan Sagitario at Alfa. Savour the a/c along with organic coffee and a flaky croissant at this bakery that does both Mexican and European treats. Nice shaded garden area, too.

Cetli Polar at Orión ☎ 984/108-0681 ⓦ www.cetli.com.mx. Chef-owner Claudia trained in Mexico City's premier culinary academy; at her casual restaurant, try refined versions of Mexican classics (about M$180), such as a delicate green-almond *mole*. Evenings only, 5–10pm, closed Wed.

Divino Paraiso East side of Tulum, between Beta and Osiris. Terrace bar overlooking the main street, with a big sound system and occasional live music. Fun when it's busy, which is not every night.

Flor de Michoacan East side of Tulum, opposite the bus station. Handy branch of the nationwide chain serving fruit juices and *licuados*, as well as inexpensive Mexican *paletas* (home-made ice pops).

La Nave East side of Tulum between Orion and Beta. A busy hangout with fresh-fruit breakfasts, inexpensive pizza from a wood-fired oven (M$55 and up) and Italian staples like fresh gnocchi.

Pepenero East side of Tulum, across from *The Weary Traveler*. Chilled bar with lounge sounds and beanbag seating, a popular evening hang-out (Mon–Sat 6pm–2am). If mescal is your thing, check out *Juan y Jose Mescal Bar*, almost next door.

Pequeño Buenos Aires East side of Tulum at Beta. Giant Argentine steaks (M$150–250) and *parrilladas* (mixed grills), washed down with some excellent wines from an extensive list (by Tulum standards). The hamburger, using top-quality beef, is great value.

El Tacoqueto East side of Tulum at Acuario. A dependable *lonchería* with gut-busting daily specials (feel free to poke your head in the kitchen to see what looks good) for about M$50, or delicious hot-off-the-grill tacos for even less.

Teetotum On the road to the beach, 100m from Hwy-307. For breakfast, go big with French toast (with farmer's cheese and caramelized bananas), or smaller, with a basket of baked goods and home-made jam. The eclectic lunch menu includes both a BLT sandwich and a Vietnamese summer roll.

Urge Taquito West side of Hwy-307, one block north of *el crucero*. Roadside taco place specializing in shrimp tacos, which you can dress up with fixings from the salsa bar or the epic condiments rack. Mon–Sat noon–5pm.

On the beach

Mateo's 1.6km south of the junction. Very popular Tex-Mex style roadside diner with burgers, tacos, fajitas, coconut shrimp and the like. Service may be slow, as almost everything is cooked on a single oil-drum barbecue.

Mezzanine 1km north of the junction ⓦ www.mezzanine.com.mx. The restaurant is an elegant beachside setting for Thai curries and seafood, at prices not much higher than elsewhere. Meanwhile the super-cool bar-lounge, channelling Ibiza chic, does excellent cocktails and is the only place on the beach where you can regularly find a dance scene, every Fri in high season.

Posada Margherita 2km south of the junction at *Posada Margherita* hotel

⌂984/801-8493. Fantastic beachfront Italian restaurant with great seafood where everything, from bread to pasta, is home-made. The antipasto platter, served on a slice of a tree trunk, is a bounty of piquant cheeses, cured meats and olives. Prices are higher than the informal setting might suggest (around M$200 for mains), but the food is worth it. Reservations recommended.

Qué Fresco 1.8km south of the junction at Zamas. A good mid-range Italian/Mexican restaurant with great fish, fresh pastas and a wood-fired pizza oven. Its beachside setting makes it a perfect way to start the day, too. Daily 7.30am–10pm.

La Vita è Bella 1.6km north of the junction; just about walking distance from the ruins. Reasonably priced sandwiches and wood-oven pizzas are served throughout the day until 11pm, along with Italian-style steaks and seafood. A cocktail bar opens at 9.30pm, and a European party crowd often gets dancing later under the big palapa.

La Zebra 4km south of the junction. Live music Thurs through the weekend, but the Sun salsa party is the biggest draw, for both tourists and residents – hone your skills early with free classes at 6pm (coinciding with happy hour). There's a huge selection of tequilas, and the restaurant's Mexican food is good as well.

Listings

Bank HSBC, with an ATM, is in the middle of town, on the east side of Tulum between Osiris and Alfa; there are other ATMs at the bus station and nearby on the west side of Tulum.

Bike rental Many hostels have bikes, or try Iguana, Satélite at Andrómeda (⌂984/871-2357, ⓦwww.iguanabike.com), for good machines and organized tours to nearby cenotes and Playa Xcacel. At the beach, bikes are available at Posada Punta Piedra (see p.114).

Car rental National chains Hertz and Europcar are here, on Tulum, as is Buster (⌂01-800/728-8737, ⓦwww.busterrentacar.com), on Tulum at Jupiter, opposite the bus station and a little south.

Diving There are dozens of dive shops both in town and on the beach: reliable operators include Cenote Dive Center, at Andromeda and Centauro (⌂984/871-2232, ⓦwww.cenotedive.com) and Acuatic Tulum (⌂984/871-2508, ⓦwww.acuatic tulum.com.mx), with offices on the beach at Cabañas Zazil-Kin and just off Hwy-307 on the beach road.

Internet Plenty of places on Tulum offer internet access, and most hotels have wireless access.

Reliable downtown places include Riviera Movil, about two doors south of the ADO, and Safari (see "Tours and travel agents" below).

Kiteboarding Extreme Control (⌂984/745-4555, ⓦwww.extremecontrol.net), at El Paraiso Beach Club, and Morph Kiteboarding (mobile ⌂984/114-9524, ⓦwww.morphkiteboarding.com) with centres at the Playa Azul hotel (beach road about 4.3km south of the junction) and Xpu-Ha beach.

Laundry Several in town, including Lavandería Cheemil-Po, Tulum just south of the bus station, and Luzmar, Satélite at Polar.

Post office West side of Av Tulum, between Satélite and Centauro (Mon–Sat noon–3pm).

Taxis and transfers The main taxi office is on the west side of Tulum, between Centauro and Orion; most prices are shown on a board outside (M$40–100 to beach hotels and M$845 to Cancún, for example), but be sure to agree on the price before setting out, anyhow. Airport transfers can also be arranged with the Tucan Kin shuttle (⌂984/134-7535, ⓦwww.tucankin.com), with hotel pick-up from US$24.

Moving on from Tulum

Colectivo passenger vans run very frequently north from Tulum to Playa del Carmen, stopping anywhere en route on request. They gather near the bus station. There are also second-class buses to Cancún (2hr 30min) via Playa at least every hour, day and night, and first-class frequently through the day, from 7am to 9pm. The vast majority of these will call at the ruins stop. Heading south, colectivos run every hour or so to Felipe Carrillo Puerto; there are around fifteen second-class and eight first-class or pullman buses to Chetumal daily (3–4hr); four of the evening services continue direct to Palenque (10hr) and San Cristóbal de las Casas (15hr). Seven second-class buses a day and two first-class run to Cobá, the first around 7.15am, arriving in time for the site to open. All of these continue to Valladolid (2hr) and there are also direct services to Valladolid and Mérida (around 8 daily, 4hr) and three a day (all early) to Chichén Itzá (3hr).

Tours and travel agents Many tours can be arranged by your hotel, with pickup from the door. Safari, on the west side of Tulum between Osiris and Alfa, is a friendly place with internet and books as well as tours and airport transfers; Savana Travel Agency, on Tulum next to *La Nave*, is a full travel agency for flights and car rental as well as local tours. The best tours of Sian Ka'an, run by locals, are with the Centro Ecológico Sian Ka'an (☎984/871-2499, ⓦwww.siankaan.org), whose office is on Hwy-307 by the ruins entrance, in front of *El Crucero* hotel.

Cenotes near Tulum

As an alternative to the beach, there's a vast number of **cenotes** very close to Tulum. In addition to those to the north (see p.110), you can also check out **Grand Cenote** (daily 10am–6pm; M$100; gear rental available), just 4km from Tulum on the road to Cobá. A collapsed cavern that's good for swimming and snorkelling (as well as some spectacular dives), the pool can get very busy in the middle of the day, as it's a popular stop for tours. The dramatic stalagmites and stalactites are well worth braving crowds (and bats) for, though. **Zacil-Há** and **Cenote Carwash** are next to each other some 4km further (each M$50). The former is a local weekend hangout and a great beginner pool, as you can see the sandy bottom. Carwash, so-called because local taxi drivers used to wash their vehicles here, has spectacular underwater rock formations, touted as among the best on the peninsula, and is great for divers. All are easily accessible by second-class bus or a taxi, though you may have trouble carrying on to Cobá, as the buses are infrequent and often full.

For more solitude, head about 3km south of Tulum on Hwy-307, where **Cenote Escondido** lies about 1km east of the main road, and **Cenote Cristal** a similar distance west. These are secluded spots, open to the sky, good for snorkelling and rarely crowded; pay the joint entrance fee (M$50) at a small kiosk on the west side of Hwy-307.

Cobá

Some 50km northwest of Tulum lies the wonderfully isolated Maya site of **COBÁ** (daily 8am–6pm; M$51, parking M$40), set in dense, muggy inland forest amid several lakes. Although the ruins aren't as well restored as those at Tulum, their scale is much more impressive, and the dense greenery and wildlife make a good counterpoint to the coast. Again, it's far from undiscovered, and in the middle of the day the car park overflows with coaches. Few of these arrive before 10am, however, and most have left by 4pm; outside these hours you can still ramble through the forest in relative peace – and even at the busiest periods the huge scale of the site means it can absorb the visitors without feeling too crowded. There's even the possibility of seeing the local wildlife, including toucans, egrets, coatis and myriad tropical butterflies, such as the giant iridescent blue morpho. A visit here requires at least a couple of hours to see everything and a great deal of walking; renting a **bicycle** (M$30) just inside the site entrance is highly recommended. Otherwise *triciclo* cabs charge M$195 for the tour – many people end up hiring one to bring them back to the entrance when their energy runs out.

Occupied from about 100 AD until the arrival of the Spanish, Cobá was so long established and legendary that it was even mentioned in the *Chilam Balam* of Chumayel, the Maya book of prophecy and ritual lore written in the eighteenth century, well after the city had been abandoned. The city's zenith was in the Late Classic period, around 800 AD, when most of the larger pyramids were built and it grew wealthy thanks to close links with the great cities of Petén, in modern Guatemala. These cities influenced Cobá's architecture and its use of stelae, typically seen only in the southern Maya regions. Cobá also prospered later through its connections with coastal cities like Tulum, and several structures, built around 1200, reflect the style found at those sites.

The first cluster of buildings you reach, right by the entrance, is the compact **Grupo Cobá**, a residential and ceremonial complex where claustrophobia-inducing corbel-vault passages lead inside to tiny rooms. The large central pyramid, known as the **Iglesia** (church), was used for Maya ceremonies even after the city ceased to function. There's a small ball-court here, too, with worn carvings; on account of its size, local guides generally claim this was a training court. Up the main path, near the fork, the **Conjunto Pinturas**, named for the paintings inside the temple that sits atop the main building, is a complex assembled with recycled stones in the late Post-Classic era, after 1200.

A kilometre from the fork along the main route is the Nohoch Mul, Cobá's largest and most impressive structure. Along the way is a substantial **ball-court** where you can still see some of the original court markers – an almost 3-D human skull carved at the centre (a feature of many ball-courts, but rarely so well preserved) and a profile of a jaguar warrior with two eroded glyphs at the north end. There are also the rings through which the players would try to get the ball, and a fenced-off stele depicting the Maya calendar.

Just beyond the playing field is the **Xaibé** (Crossroads) pyramid, so named for its position at a major junction of *sacbeob*, the limestone-paved highways the Maya built to connect cities: there are more of them here than at any other site, including one which originally ran over 100km to Yaxuna. near Chichén Itzá. The pyramid's rounded, stepped design and exceptionally steep, impractical stairway is reminiscent of the Pirámide del Adivino at Uxmal (see p.202), in miniature.

At the end of the path, the looming **Nohoch Mul** reaches a height of 42m, taller than El Castillo at Chichén Itzá, and indeed one of the tallest Maya structures in the Yucatán. Perhaps because it is surrounded by lofty forest trees, it doesn't immediately look that impressive, but once you start to climb the narrow and precipitous stairway, the resemblance to the great pyramids at Tikal in Guatemala becomes more striking. The awesome view takes in nearby lakes as well as the jungle stretching uninterrupted to the horizon. The small temple at the top, similar to structures at Tulum, is a later addition, dating from around 1200 AD. There's a welcome cold-drinks stall at the bottom to reward your efforts.

Retrace your steps to the central fork, where another path leads 1km down a shady *sacbé* to **Grupo Macanxoc**, with a cluster of some twenty stelae, most carved during the seventh century AD. Stele 1 shows part of the Maya creation myth and the oldest date recorded in the Maya Long Count calendar system, which tracks the days since the moment of creation. Other stelae, all very worn, depict an unusually large number of women, suggesting that Cobá may have had female rulers. Clambering between the carvings, you're crossing not natural hills, but unreconstructed pyramids; in a way, these offer a more palpable sense of the civilization that thrived here than some of the more immaculately rebuilt structures.

Practicalities and Cobá village

For details of **buses** from Tulum, see p.118. The morning ADO bus leaves Cobá at 10.10am and continues to Chichén Itzá – by getting the first bus from Tulum you could theoretically cover both sites via public transport in a day, though you would be rushed. If you don't have a car and would like to visit everything around Cobá, including the cenotes (p.119 & opposite) and Reserva de Monos (opposite), check out small-group tours from Tulum.

The **village of Cobá**, where the bus stops, is little more than a cluster of houses and cabañas beside a small lake. There are a number of small **hotels**, however, and several restaurants. For a bit of tropical luxury, *Villa Arqueologica Coba* (☎01-800/557-7755, ⓦwww.villasarqueologicas.com.mx; ⓖ) overlooks the lake and comes complete with swimming pool, snooker table, wi-fi and air conditioning, though the rooms are on the small side. The *Hotelito Sac-bé* (☎984/206-7140, ⓦwww.hotelitosacbecoba.com; ❸), on the left side of the main street through the village, is a very friendly place with comfortable budget rooms, all ensuite and with TV, some with air conditioning. The restaurant here serves an excellent, generous breakfast. You will also find a couple of **restaurants** overlooking the lake – *La Pirámide*, which serves Yucatecan specialities like *cochinita pibil*, as well as other Mexican dishes, is good. There are additionally numerous no-frills **food stalls** adjacent to the site's entrance.

The lake at Cobá is home to a large population of **crocodiles** (so no swimming!) and turtles. Locals will charge you M$20 to watch them attract the crocodiles with pieces of chicken at the end of the jetty. But the crocs can often be seen simply basking on the shore right by the road, where they are routinely tormented by tour guides, a practice which you should not encourage. At the site car park there's a watchtower (M$30), from the top of which an impressive **zip-wire** (M$130) shoots across the lake.

Cenotes near Cobá

If you feel like a swim after a sweaty visit to the ruins, three nearby **cenotes** have been opened up by a village co-operative, about 6km southwest. With your own transport you can head straight out and buy tickets at the access road to the first cenotes (M$45 for one cenote, M$75 for two, M$100 for three); alternately you can arrange a taxi tour from the Cobá parking lot (from around M$250, inclusive). The first cenote, **Choo-Ha**, is the least good for swimming, though it does have some fine stalactites and stalagmites. The second, **Tankah-Ha**, is the most spectacular, but also the busiest as many small tours visit; here a wooden spiral stair with scarily high diving platforms leads down into a subterranean dome filled with deep, clear water. **Multún-Ha**, reached by a separate access road, is a similar, less visited dome – deeper still at around 20m below ground, where no natural light penetrates.

Reserva de Monos Arañas de Punta Laguna

From the roundabout outside Cobá, head northeast 18km (following signs for Nuevo X-Can) to reach the **Reserva de Monos Arañas de Punta Laguna**, at the small village of Punta Laguna. From the entrance kiosk, you're required to hike with a guide into the forest (M$40/person, plus M$200 for a guide for a group of up to ten people). As well as the **spider monkeys** here, which congregate in gregarious family groups, there are a few more solitary **howler monkeys** – there's no guarantee you'll see any monkeys at all, but the guides generally know where they are. They are at their liveliest in the early morning (preferably before 9am; the guides are locals who live here, so are on site from around 6am) and late afternoon (after 3.30pm), when they feed locally, so you're strongly advised to visit at those times; during the day they often range further afield (beyond the boundaries of the reserve) and are much harder to spot. The trail winds past **unrestored ruins** and a cenote in which many Maya skeletons were found, and where there's a little Maya shrine, lovingly tended. In the middle of the reserve is a big, brackish lake where you can rent kayaks (M$60) and paddle around looking for herons and crocodiles. This is very much a community project; some of the local women sell handicrafts at a small shop and there's a simple lakeside restaurant. To reach the area you'll need a car or taxi, though some tours from Tulum, Cancún, Playa del Carmen and Valladolid (see p.153) include a visit to the reserve. Alltournative, for example, have an impressive zip-line here (☎ 984/803-9999, ⓦ www.alltournative.com).

The Sian Ka'an Biosphere Reserve

Sian Ka'an means "the place where the sky is born" in Maya, which seems appropriate when you experience the sunrise in this stunningly beautiful part of the peninsula. The nature reserve is a huge, sparsely populated region sprawling along the coast, south of Tulum. Most of the thousand or so permanent residents here are fishermen and subsistence farmers, gathered in the village of **Punta Allen** and in an experimental agricultural settlement called El Ramonal.

Created by presidential decree in 1986 and made a World Heritage Site in 1987, the Sian Ka'an Biosphere Reserve is one of the largest protected areas in Mexico, covering 1.3 million acres. It contains all of the principal ecosystems found in the Yucatán Peninsula and the Caribbean: approximately one-third of the area is **tropical forest**, one-third fresh- and salt-water marshes and **mangroves** and one-third marine environment, including a section of the Mesoamerican Barrier Reef. The variety of flora and fauna is astonishing. All five species of Mexican **wild cat** – jaguar, puma, ocelot, margay and jaguarundi – live in the forest, along with spider and howler monkeys, tapir and deer, though all of these are very elusive. More than three hundred species of **birds** have also been recorded (including fifteen types of heron and the endangered wood stork, the largest wading bird that breeds in North America), and the coastal forests and wetlands are important feeding and wintering areas for North American migratory birds. The Caribbean beaches provide nesting grounds for four endangered species of **marine turtle**, while some extremely rare West Indian manatees have been seen offshore. Morelet's and American **crocodiles** lurk in the swamps and lagoons.

Although you can enter the park unaccompanied (M$25), most easily on the Punta Allen road south from Tulum's zona hotelera, you will benefit more from an organized tour (from around M$950), which is easily arranged in Tulum (see p.119). Most include knowledgeable guides who will introduce you to the diverse ecosystems along with a choice of activities – nature walks through the mangroves, swimming in cenotes, boat rides across the lagoons and the ancient Maya canals and maybe fly-fishing or snorkelling around Punta Allen. Whatever you choose, it's a beautiful trip around the fringes of the reserve's vast open spaces, with excellent opportunities for birdwatching, especially on the sunset tour. There are also less ecofriendly jeep safaris to Punta Allen with mainstream operators, with stops en route and lunch and snorkelling in Punta Allen. If you're doing it yourself, you can stop and swim at deserted beaches almost anywhere along the way, and there's a **Visitor Center** about 9km inside the reserve where you can rent kayaks, follow nature trails and arrange boat trips around the lagoons (from around M$1000 per boat).

Accommodation is available at Punta Allen (see opposite), or at the rigorously ecofriendly *Boca Paila Camps* (☎ 984/871-2499, ⓦ www.siankaan.org; ❺), located just before the Visitors' Center. The camp's sturdy "tent cabins" are hidden among the trees in a prime location beside the beach; guests share bathrooms (with composting toilets), and water is heated with solar and wind power. The staff are very informed about the reserve, and the inexpensive **restaurant** is worth the long drive from Tulum for its sunset view across the jungle. Note that although there are many enticing stretches of sand along the road south from the Tulum hotel zone, biosphere regulations **prohibit camping** on the beach to control erosion – which is not to say it's not done, unfortunately.

Punta Allen

Right at the tip of a narrow spit of land, with a lighthouse guarding the northern entrance to the **Bahía de la Ascensión**, the remote fishing village of **PUNTA ALLEN** is not the kind of place you stumble across by accident. With a population of just five hundred, it's the largest village inside the reserve. Bonefish, permit, snook and tarpon in the bay are a draw for active travellers; layabouts come for the feeling of being entirely cut off from the world. This really is the end of the road – its sandy streets empty, the atmosphere languid: the beach is more for hammock-lounging than swimming, though, as there's lots of sea grass and, depending on the currents, a fair bit of rubbish. The road south from Tulum's zona hotelera has traditionally helped maintain Punta Allen's special quality and can still be rough going; reckon on anything from an hour and a half to three hours for the 42km drive from the reserve entrance, depending on its current state (at the height of the rainy season, it may be completely impassable). A *colectivo* leaves Tulum daily at 2pm (departing from near the taxi office; M$200), heading down this road unless conditions are really bad, in which case it may take the alternative route via the highway south and a bone-rattling track to Vigia Chico (also called El Playón), from where a small boat ferries you across the lagoon to Punta Allen. **Leaving** Punta Allen with public transport requires an early start, and hence a couple of nights stay if you are actually to spend any time here: the Tulum *colectivo* will collect you from your accommodation at 5am (sign up the night before to reserve your space). However you get here, bring plenty of cash (there's no bank); and note that the local electricity grid is switched off around midnight to conserve energy.

Entering Punta Allen from the north, the first sign you'll see is to the *Hotel Casa de Ascension* (T 984/801-0034, W www.casadeascensionhotel.com; ❹), a new place with just four rooms but a generator for 24-hour power, air conditioning, cable TV, wi-fi and a small bar/restaurant. *Cuzan Guesthouse* (T 983/834-0358, W www.flyfishmx.com; ❹), on the beach towards the southern end of the village, is the longest-established place here, with a wide variety of wooden cabañas and tepees, all with hot water, some with solar lighting, at a range of prices (backpacker beds from M$200). The bar and restaurant are great, too, and there's internet access for a fee. *Serenidad Shardon* (T 984/876-1827, or T 616/827-0204 in the US, W www.shardon.com; ❾), the next place south, offers everything from extremely comfortable cabañas and two-bedroom beach-houses to camping space on the beach (M$50 per person, or in fully-equipped tents with power and beds, from M$200 per person) and dorm beds (low season only; M$200), all with access to showers and communal kitchen.

There are a number of **restaurants** along the beach serving simple meals and fresh seafood; *Bonefish* is good, as is *Muelle Viejo*, by the plaza (at both, watch out for the vicious *salsa de chile habanero*). There's also a small **supermarket**, Casa Viejo Chac, a couple of other stores and two **internet** cafés, but no cell-phone signal. All of the hotels above offer **fishing tours** – indeed many of their guests will be here on inclusive deals – and these can also be arranged through the local tourism co-op for around M$3000 for the day (per boat); book at the office signed 'tourist info', beside the beach as you enter the village. They can also arrange nature tours of the Sian Ka'an lagoons (around M$1650). If fishing is your sole reason for coming here, you might also want to check out the dedicated fly-fishing lodges in the vicinity, with all-inclusive rates for longer stays – try for example *Pesca Maya* (☏998/848-2496, ⓦwww.pescamaya.com) or the *Palometa Club* (☏1-866/723-7776 in the US, ⓦwww.palometaclub.com).

On land, for a great view over the bay, you can simply follow the trail south from the village to the **lighthouse**, 2km away, or find your way west, where some broken-down watchtowers offer great birdwatching opportunities over the lagoon.

Chunyaxché

Heading south from Tulum, the highway narrows as it runs along the west edge of the Sian Ka'an reserve. After about 20km, you reach the ruins of **Chunyaxché** (daily 8am–5pm; M$31, plus M$40 to follow the boardwalk to the lagoon), also known as **Muyil**. Take any second-class **bus** from Tulum to Chetumal, or a *colectivo*, and ask to be dropped at the gate to the ruins. Despite the size of the site – probably the largest on the Quintana Roo coast – and its proximity to Hwy-307, you're likely to have the place to yourself, as few visitors to the Yucatán venture further south than Tulum.

Archeological evidence indicates that Muyil was continuously occupied from the Pre-Classic period until after the arrival of the Spanish in the sixteenth century. There is no record that the inhabitants came into direct contact with the conquistadors, but they were probably victims of depopulation caused by European-introduced diseases. Most of the buildings you see today date from the Post-Classic period, between 1200 and 1500 AD. The tops of the tallest structures, just visible from the road, rise 17m from the forest floor. There are more than one hundred mounds and temples, and around the central cleared area it's easy to wander and find dozens of buildings buried in the jungle; climbing them is forbidden, however.

The centre of the site was connected by a *sacbé* to the small **Muyil lagoon,** 500m away at the edge of the Sian Ka'an reserve. This is joined to the large Chunyaxché lagoon, and ultimately to the sea at **Boca Paila,** by an amazing **canalized river** – a route used by ancient Maya traders. Wildlife scatters as you follow the boardwalk that leads through the mangroves to the lagoon. At the end of the path you might find a fisherman offering a boat tour into the reserve, where you'll come across even less-explored Maya sites (there are said to be over twenty small sites within the reserve), some of which appear to be connected to the lagoon or river by **underwater caves**. If you want to be sure of entering the reserve this way, however, it's easiest to do so by arranging it in advance through one of the Sian Ka'an tour operators in Tulum (see p.119).

Leaving the site, particularly if you're making your way up to Tulum, should be easy enough; continuing south could prove a little more difficult, however, as buses to Chetumal run only every couple of hours, and *colectivos* are often full when they pass.

The Costa Maya
and the Río Bec

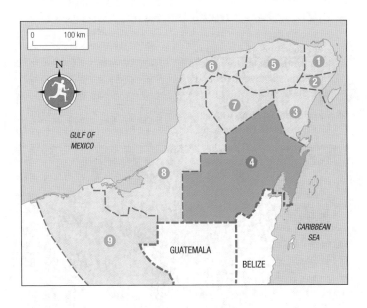

CHAPTER 4

Highlights

* **Mahahual** Rebuilding after the ravages of Hurricane Dean, Mahahual remains a beach bum's fantasy, with a string of cabaña camps and a few friendly restaurants. See p.130

* **Banco Chinchorro** Scores of ships have dashed against this large coral atoll 30km off the coast, creating a vast playground for scuba divers. See p.130

* **Laguna Bacalar** As clear and gloriously coloured as the Caribbean, this 45-kilometre-long freshwater lake is home to a huge variety of birds and fish. See p.133

* **Río Hondo** Team up with a tour operator in Chetumal to go rafting along this seldom-visited river, which forms Mexico's border with Belize. See p.140

* **Kohunlich** Giant monster masks, a sprawling palace complex with fantastic views and parrots swinging among the enormous fan palms are the main draws at this archeological site. See p.141

* **Calakmul Biosphere Reserve** Centred on Calakmul, the largest (and one of the most spectacular) Maya cities in the Yucatán, the biosphere shelters a vast array of wildlife as well as other ancient cities, including Balamkú. See p.146

▲ Spider monkey, Calakmul Biosphere Reserve

The Costa Maya
and the Río Bec

South of Tulum, Quintana Roo State changes character: the jungle creeps up against the narrow highway, now just two lanes with the merest whisper of a hard shoulder, and margaritas are in very short supply. The one exception is the growing beach-bum community of the **Costa Maya**, south of the Sian Ka'an Biosphere Reserve – where **Mahahual** is an unlikely but popular cruise ship destination, while **Xcalak** is a laidback fishing and diving centre. The once isolated beachfronts around these two are rapidly being bought up by wealthy Mexicans and foreigners. For the most part, though, the true personality of this part of the peninsula is found in the inland towns and villages. **Felipe Carrillo Puerto**, a crossroads on the way to Valladolid and Mérida, with strong Maya roots, was the centre of the **Zona Maya**, the semi-independent area established during the decades-long Caste Wars that marked the second half of the nineteenth century, when years of grand campaigns and small uprisings finally succeeded in earning the Maya some measure of autonomy.

Ancient Maya history, too, is everywhere in evidence along the southern border of Mexico, reached by heading due west out of Chetumal on Hwy-186. The jungle to the south of this narrow road – which was laid down only in the latter half of the twentieth century – is some of the densest and richest in the country, and either side of the highway are several wondrous Maya ruins, collectively known as the **Río Bec sites**. These tumbledown cities continue well into Campeche State, making for a fascinating archeological tour in an area that's little affected by tourism and barely populated. With mostly second-class buses plying the roads, and relatively few places to bunk, the Río Bec can be a difficult and pricey place to explore (taxis provide the only transport to many ruins), but it's extremely rewarding if you make the effort.

On the way, southern Quintana Roo can offer the seldom-visited Maya ruins of **Chacchoben** and the wetlands around beautiful **Laguna Bacalar**, an important destination for birds and the people who love them. The impeccably clear lake is also popular with Mexican vacationers. Hwy-307 ends at **Chetumal**, the state capital and the gateway to Belize. A small, enjoyable city situated on a wide bay, with a multicultural border-town feel, Chetumal is a good point from which to explore the surrounding lakes, rivers and wetlands, and to rest up before the Río Bec.

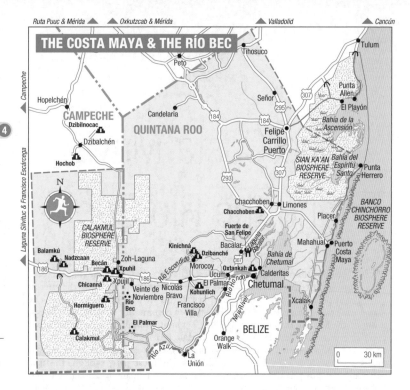

Felipe Carrillo Puerto

The first settlement of any size beyond Tulum – a good 100km south – is **FELIPE CARRILLO PUERTO**, a crossroads with the route to Valladolid and Mérida. The place has an intriguing history as the capital of the Zona Maya in the nineteenth and early twentieth centuries (see box, opposite). Although the original town was all but destroyed during the wars, this is still an important cultural and spiritual centre for the modern Maya.

You can visit the **Santuario de la Cruz Parlante**, built on the site of the Talking Cross, though since the remnants of the cross itself have been moved to a village nearby, there's not a great deal to see. Nonetheless the sanctuary retains an air of mystic power, with the altar topped with several crosses "dressed" in *huipiles* in the distinctive Yucatec Maya way. Turn west off the main street at the Pemex station, up Calle 69; the complex is at Calle 62. The other, more imposing relic of the religion is the **Iglesia de Balam Na**, which dominates the main plaza. In a tidy bit of table-turning, the Cruzob forced white interlopers they'd captured in the jungle to build the first Maya temple of the post-Columbus era, beginning in 1851. Despite its pagan roots, it is almost indistinguishable from a conquistador Franciscan church, with its arched roof and single-nave layout. It was consecrated as a Catholic church only in 1948.

Practicalities

Felipe Carrillo Puerto is laid out on a straightforward grid of numbered streets. A **Pemex station** on the highway (Calle 70 or Avenida Juárez), surrounded by food

The Talking Cross movement

The Talking Cross movement in 1850, after the first wave of the Caste Wars ended in the defeat of the Maya at Mérida, a group of rebels led by **José María Barrera** (himself a mestizo) retreated into the forests of Quintana Roo. There they set up camp near a cenote and discovered a cross, embedded in a tree, that spoke to the group and encouraged them to fight on against their oppressors. The apparition was not unique – such talking crosses and statues, known as way'ob, are common in Maya mythology as conduits through which disincarnate spirits speak.

Galvanized by the cross's directions (delivered through a "translator", Manuel Nahuat), and armed with weapons supplied by the British via neighbouring British Honduras, the **Cruzob**, as the fighters called themselves, began conducting raids all around the central peninsula. The encampment by the cenote grew into a formal town named **Chan Santa Cruz** ("little holy cross"), which functioned as the Cruzob's capital. They established control of territory as far north as Tulum and well inland, and they enforced it ruthlessly: light-skinned non-Maya were typically shot on sight or captured and enslaved. After the rest of the peninsula was subdued, the Cruzob continued their guerrilla struggle; even after 1901, when the British withdrew support and Mexican armies occupied and gutted Chan Santa Cruz, the rebel Maya held a large patch of the jungle, later negotiating with the Wrigley's chewing-gum company to grant access to chicle trees and making a good bit of money in the process. In 1935 they finally signed a treaty, carefully worded to emphasize that they were not conceding, only allowing the Mexican government to rule them. Around the same time, Chan Santa Cruz was resettled and given an innocuous new name, **Felipe Carrillo Puerto**, after a former governor of the Yucatán. Though they've since stowed the guns, many of the Maya in this area maintain the syncretic religious practices – which meld Catholic elements such as baptism with ancient healing and prayer rituals – that were born out of this violent era.

stalls (some of them excellent), marks the heart of town, though the main **plaza** (bounded by calles 65, 66, 67 and 68) and **bus station** (on the plaza at the corner of calles 65 and 66) are a couple of blocks southwest. There's an **ATM** by the Pemex station and a couple more at the bus station. **Colectivos** for Tulum and points north leave from the bus station; for Chetumal, from a tiny separate terminal one block south at Calle 63.

Plenty of through traffic ensures numerous **hotels and restaurants**, mostly along Juarez. The best choice if you are staying, though, is the *Hotel Esquivel* on the plaza (main entry at the rear on C 63, between 66 and 68; ☎983/834-0344, ⓔesquivel hotel@yahoo.com.mx; ❸), marginally more expensive than most but a big step up in quality, with fan or air-conditioned rooms. The hotel restaurant, the *Parilla Galerias*, is reasonably priced, with an unrivalled position for people-watching; *La Placita Maya*, two blocks south of the bus station on Calle 66, serves excellent tacos.

For more **information**, and tips on visiting nearby nature spots and villages, check out Xiimbal Tours, on the plaza at Calle 65 (☎983/834-1073, ⓦwww .xiimbal.com), which organizes trips to small Maya communities and visits to local attractions, or call in at the small tourist office, on Juarez at Calle 59 (Mon–Fri 9am–4pm; ☎983/267-1452).

Towards Valladolid and Mérida

Heading northwest from Carrillo, a well-paved, arrow-straight road leads into the densely forested interior and eventually to Valladolid. Along the way you may want to stop off at the scenic **Laguna Azul** lake, 7km from the traditional Maya village of **Señor**, or in **Tihosuco**, where the small but engaging **Museo de la**

Guerra Castas (Tues–Sun 10am–6pm; M$5) tells the story of the Maya rebellion (in Spanish). The Franciscan church here is particularly dramatic, its crumbling nave open to the sky and overgrown with vines and weeds. The church was torched during one of the many battles in this town between 1848 and 1865, and until recently stood empty, still blackened by the fires that destroyed it. Now a good part of the interior has been whitewashed and reclaimed for regular church services. At the front on the plaza stands a weathered monument to native son Jacinto Pat, one of the Caste Wars' great leaders.

Colectivos provide the most frequent service to Señor, Tihosuco and Valladolid, departing every hour or so from the Carrillo market, on the northwest corner of the central traffic circle. But you may find it difficult to hop from village to village, as the shared vans are often packed full.

The Costa Maya

The beaches that line the 250km of coast between the southern edge of the Sian Ka'an reserve and the Belize border, while not as scenic as those in Tulum, are quite beautiful in their sheer emptiness. Because of this, the **COSTA MAYA**, as this area is known, has become an object of fascination among those seeking a truly remote getaway, and for people hoping to make some money on this relatively untouched patch of Caribbean-front property (the latter group includes investors in a lavish cruise ship pier, Puerto Costa Maya). Development was temporarily halted in 2007 by **Hurricane Dean**, one of the most powerful hurricanes ever recorded over land, which saw winds of up to 200mph (320kph) ravage **Mahahual**, closing the port for a year. Regeneration is pretty much complete however, and as many as five cruises a week now call in. The rest of the time the region has a very end-of-the-road feel, and those looking for solitude can certainly find it at **Xcalak**, while even in Mahahual the fleeting crowds are easy enough to avoid. Watersports enthusiasts will want to make the trek to **Banco Chinchorro**, most easily reached from Mahahual; a divers' playground with more than a hundred shipwrecks, encrusted with rainbow-hued coral, that was designated a biosphere reserve in 2003.

Mahahual

MAHAHUAL, 60km east of Hwy-307 via a fast, dead-straight highway, has a bizarre split personality, caught between cruise-ship glitz and back-of-beyond

Costa Maya transport: getting there and away

Poor transport is one of the factors that have helped keep the tourist droves at bay. ADO **first-class buses** to Mahahual leave Chetumal (2hr 30min) at 5.30am and 7.30pm; they return at 7.30am and 6.30pm. There's also direct service from Cancún at 7.30am (6hr; return at 5.30pm) and from Mérida at weekends (11.30pm Fri–Sun; 7hr). **Second-class** Caribe buses, which continue along the coast from Mahahual to Xcalak (dropping off at Mahahual's beach hotels), depart Chetumal at 6am and 4pm daily; return journeys from Xcalak set out at 5.30am and 2pm. You can connect with the Caribe bus at the town of Limones (7.30am and 5.30pm), where most first class services on the main highway should stop. Additional buses may run at weekends and peak Mexican holiday times. You can also get a **taxi** from Limones for about M$300–500, depending on your bargaining skills and final destination, and there are **colectivos** from Chetumal which will stop here for you if they have space. If you're **driving**, there's a Pemex station on the main road just outside Mahahual, the only fuel locally.

somnolence. The wooden shacks that dot the narrow beach are increasingly shadowed by multistorey, concrete and glass structures. A new **malecón** (seafront promenade) winds through town, and on cruise days – most weekdays in high season – is lined with stalls, bars and beach clubs; for a few hours, jet skis buzz the beach, there are Hobie cats on the water, and all sorts of tours and activities are on offer. Yet few of these open at all if there's no ship in dock, and all close as the passengers leave, so that by 7pm only a handful of places to eat or drink remain open. To get the best out of Mahahual, consider staying on the beach to the south – where the lifestyle is still idyllically Robinson Crusoe.

The main activity in Mahahual is hanging out on the **beach**. If you want to add a bit more purpose to this, there's also wonderful **snorkelling** and **diving** around the pristine offshore reef. The sand itself can't match the immaculate white of Tulum, and in front of town there's lots of sea grass in the water; better, quieter beaches can be found further afield, both north and south along the coast road. South, past Mahahual's beach hotels, is easier and closer, but if you have transport you can head north. Having passed the cruise ship terminal and Nuevo Mahahual (with a Hard Rock Café and the tackiest souvenir shops you could hope to find; open only for the cruise trade), **Placer**, about 20km north (or 30km by the paved inland route) has some great sand. Beyond lies the southern perimeter of the **Sian Ka'an Biosphere Reserve** (see p.122). An extremely poor road heads on through the reserve, with spectacularly empty beaches alongside almost all the way, as far as **Punta Herrero** (another 25km or so, but likely to be two hours' driving); in the tiny community at the end you may find a fisherman who can take you on a boat tour, or a shack where they'll cook fresh fish for you, but there's no guarantee of either, so bring plenty of water and other supplies. There's **wildlife** outside the reserve, too, with mangroves and small lakes behind the coast road in both directions.

Accommodation

We give addresses for places in town below, thought the only street signs you'll find are on the malecón (where each cross-street is named); Huachinango is the main street through town. Virtually everything is here or on the malecón. Prices are even more seasonal than normal in Mahahual, and many places have higher rates at weekends, when it's a popular Mexican escape.

Balamku Coast road south at Km. 5.5 ☎ 983/839-5332, ⓦ www.balamku.com. Ecofriendly outlook, recycling greywater, generating solar power and keeping natural landscaping around its attractive white stucco, thatch-roof cottages. Wi-fi and kayaks included. ❻

Caballo Blanco Malecón between Martillo and Coronado, mobile ☎ 983/126-0319, ⓦ www .hotelelcaballoblanco.com. Pricey new place with a couple of stunning rooms overlooking the beach, including one with a huge terrace. Sky TV, a/c, fridges in rooms and a tiny plunge pool on the roof. ❻

Las Cabañas del Doctor Coast road immediately south of town ☎ 983/832-2102, ⓦ www .lascabanasdeldoctor.com. Sturdy cabañas (en suite, but no hot water) and rooms (with hot water), across the road from the beach and in easy walking distance of the centre. Also camping from M$50 per person. ❷–❸

Los 40 Cañones Between Huachinango and the malecón, close to the southern edge of town, mobile ☎ 983/123-8591, ⓦ www.40canones .com. The fanciest hotel in town, with a lovely, airy bar and a/c rooms on two floors around a courtyard, most with at least partial sea views. Wi-fi too. ❺

Hotel Maya Luna Coast road south at Km. 4.5 ☎ 983/836-0905, ⓦ www .hotelmayaluna.com. The first true escape as you head south: idyllic studios right on the beach (no a/c but cool), with private roof terraces for stargazing, plus a couple of smaller apartments. The restaurant here serves Dutch/Indonesian/ Mexican fusion and excellent breakfasts (included for guests). Primarily solar-powered; pets welcome. ❻

Mayan Beach Garden At Placer, on the coast 20km north, mobile ☎ 983/132-2603,

Ⓦ www.mayanbeachgarden.com. Beautiful spot on an empty beach, though the isolation is gradually being encroached on by surrounding villas; lovely, well-equipped cabañas and units with kitchens, some with a/c. Wi-fi, kayaks and snorkel gear included; excellent meals available. ➐

Posada Pachamama Huachinango between Martillo and Coronado, mobile ☎ 983/134-3049, Ⓦ www.posadapachamama.net. Six very comfortable rooms with a/c, wi-fi and friendly Italian owners, plus access to the beach club next door – no views though. ➏

Eating and drinking

Only a few places in town are reliably open when there's no ship, but many hotels, especially those on the coast road, have restaurants.

Colonial Café Sierra between Huachinango and the malecón. Busy little place for breakfasts and snacks; tortas, hamburgers and *licuados*.
La Dolce Vita Malecón between Coronado and Robalo. Italian-run place with good coffee, smoothies and ice cream; you can grab a slice of takeaway pizza next door at *Alfa Pizza* too.
Fernando's 100% Agave Huachinango between Sierra and Cherna. Sand-floored, palapa-roofed place that's the best in town for simple Mexican meals; just about every visitor and local hangs out at the bar here in the early evening. Closed Sun.
Ki'i Taco'o Huachinango at Cherna. Serves nothing but prawn and fish tacos, but it's hard to believe something so simple can taste so good;

check out the *gambas al ajillo*. If you can find space, add to the appreciative customer graffiti on the walls.
Sak-Ha Northern end of the malecón. Simple palapa beachside bar (and beach club by day), directly underneath the lighthouse – take an evening stroll here along the malecón and, while sipping a margarita, watch the lit-up cruise ships leave.
🏃 Travel in' Coast road south at Km. 6. A popular meeting place for the local expat community with great food from an eclectic menu, home-made pita bread and frequent theme nights – tapas on Wed, for example, and regular fondue sessions. Open Tues–Sat (plus Mon in high season) from 5.30pm.

Listings

Diving Numerous dive centres in town: Dreamtime Dive Centre, about a kilometre south of town on the coast road (☎ 983/124-0235, Ⓦ www.dreamtimediving.com), is a reliable place with regular trips to Chinchorro.
Internet V@mos, on Cherna between Huachinango and the malecón.

Money It's wise to bring plenty of cash: there are at least three ATMs (at V@mos internet, the Pemex station and Hotel Luna de Plata), but they are frequently out of order.
Taxis Hang out at the corner of Sierra, just beyond the bus station; around M$60 to the beach hotels or *Travel in'*.

Xcalak

The only other community in the area, **XCALAK** is some 40km south of Mahahual, very near the Belize border. The coast road eventually becomes impassable: instead turn inland after about 30km (or sooner) to join the paved route that turns off the main road into Mahahual, near the Pemex station. At the tip of the isthmus that stretches like a finger towards Belize, Xcalak was once the largest town in Quintana Roo, but is today a desolate village that never really recovered from being flattened by a hurricane in 1955; steady electricity was restored only in 2004, and Hurricane Dean did further damage. Although there's a fair amount of new building along the beach – mainly private villas – Xcalak is definitely at the back of the queue when it comes to government investment; roads in the village, and along the coast, are severely potholed. There are no real beaches to speak of here, so the main reasons to visit Xcalak are for superb diving, salt-water fly-fishing and snorkelling. The reef offshore is easy to visit, and most local hotels offer fishing trips, kayaks and snorkel gear.

Practicalities

Much the best accommodation is along the coast road, but in town you will find a couple of general stores and an **internet** and phone caseta, in the village's main street, one block back from the beach. There are also a couple of great **places to eat**. ★ *The Leaky Palapa* (lunch & dinner Nov–May Sat–Mon, weekends July & Aug, ⓦwww.leakypalaparestaurant.com), on the northern edge of the village, would be great anywhere, but here it's really exceptional. They have drinks, cappucinos, wi-fi and a library of books to borrow, but the innovative, inexpensive cooking (and warm welcome) really mark the place out; lunch is relatively simple – hamburgers, sandwiches, gourmet quesadillas – but at dinner you'll find delights like crab-stuffed local mero fillet with salsa, or chipotle pork 'osso buco' with risotto mexicana, for around M$180. When they're closed, check out *Toby's*, on the inland street, where local cooking is served in Toby's front room.

Heading north out of town, you cross a small bridge that leads to what is sometimes grandly referred to as the zona hotelera. Among the comfortable options here is *Costa de Cocos* (ⓦwww.costadecocos.com; ❼), a long-established, laidback fly-fishing and diving centre with its own fishing boats and dive instructor, plus good snorkelling right off the dock; accommodation is in old-fashioned, but cool and comfy, wooden cabañas and there's also a popular restaurant, where a buffet breakfast is included in the rates. ★ *Tierra Maya* (mobile ⓣ983/839-8012, ⓦwww.tierramaya.net; ❻), a little further north on a lovely stretch of sand, is a bit more beachfront-lux, with comfortable ocean-view rooms and another good restaurant; nearby, solar-powered *Casa Carolina* (ⓣ1-610/616-3862 in the US, ⓦwww.casacarolina.net; ❻) has four plush rooms with simple kitchens. These last two both include bikes and kayaks in the rates, along with breakfast.

Finally, the excellent dive shop XTC (ⓣ983/831-0461, ⓦwww.xtcdivecenter .com), just north of the bridge, organizes **fishing** expeditions (half-day US$175), runs **snorkelling and birdwatching trips** (US$20–50) and a day-trip (or transfer) to **San Pedro, Belize** (from US$50). They also offer diving and dive courses and have a licence to dive at Banco Chinchorro.

Laguna Bacalar and around

Glimpsed through the trees to the east as you continue south along Hwy-307, the gorgeous **Laguna Bacalar** resembles the Caribbean Sea, sparkling clear and ranging in colour from palest aqua to deep indigo. The reeds and trees around the water host a variety of **birdlife**, and in the lake you'll find freshwater snails and huge fish that reach nearly 2m in length. At 45km long and, on average, 1km wide, Laguna Bacalar is the second largest lake in Mexico (after Lago de Chapala, south of Guadalajara), linking with a series of other lakes, and eventually, the Río Hondo and the sea.

Chacchoben

Near the northern end of the lake, about 15km south of Limones, a rather grand intersection marks the way to the ruins of **Chacchoben** (daily 8am–5pm; M$41), 9km west of the highway. For somewhere so little known, the "place of red corn" is remarkably impressive and, provided you don't coincide with a cruise-ship tour, you are likely to have the place to yourself. Unfortunately, a visit does really require your own car (or taxi from Bacalar or Limones), as it is almost impossible to get here by bus. The road beyond Chacchoben continues towards Mérida, via the sites of the Ruta Puuc (see p.204).

Populated from around 250 BC to 1200 AD, Chacchoben flourished above all in the Early Classic period (250–600 AD); it was only rediscovered in the 1970s. The two main excavated areas are separated by a vast Gran Plaza; once paved, this is now totally overgrown, but its extent can be appreciated from above, by climbing the pyramid at the far end. A residential area, barely excavated, lies alongside the plaza, and there are many more unexcavated structures nearby. Of those which have been cleared, the first complex you reach, around Plaza B, had a dual purpose – temple at the front (with stucco decoration of butterflies), administrative area behind. The buildings at the far end are more striking, including the Gran Basamento, a Petén-style, rounded corner pyramid raised high above its surroundings on a platform. This temple served an astronomical as well as a religious purpose, with portals on top through which the rising sun would shine on significant dates. Palapa thatch protects more stucco decorations.

Bacalar

More Maya remains dot the southern end of the lakeshore, around the town of **Bacalar**, which was a key point on pre-Columbian trade routes. The *Chilam Balam* of Chumayel, one of the Maya's sacred books, mentions it as the first settlement of the Itzá, the tribe that later occupied Chichén Itzá. Now it's a quiet place to stop for a day or two, enjoyed by naturalists as a base for birdwatching and kayaking on the glassy lake. The town is pretty spread out, but its centre clusters on a slope above the water, and most of what you'll need is here, within a couple of blocks of the main plaza and the fortress.

The **Fuerte de San Felipe**, overlooking the lake immediately below the plaza, is Bacalar's only real "sight". Built by the Spanish in the 1730s for protection against British pirates based in Belize (then British Honduras), the fort became a Maya stronghold during the Caste Wars and, in 1901, was the last place to be subdued by the government. Today it is a small, enjoyable **museum** (Tues–Thurs & Sun 9am–7pm; Fri & Sat 9am–8pm; M$23) that displays some of the Maya relics found here, as well as the trappings of pirate days. On the lake a couple of blocks north of here is the **Balneario Magico** (M$5), a pleasant swimming area with a restaurant and palapas (M$30 rental) for lounging; they also have space for camping (M$50 per person). At the far southern end of the lakeshore road, just where it rejoins the highway, you can have more watery fun at the inky-blue "bottomless" **Cenote Azul** (daily 9am–6pm). Although free, you can only get to the cenote through the restaurant of the same name, so at the very least you'll have to pay for a drink; at weekends the place is busy with local swimmers and dive-bombing teens, entertained by live musicians, and it's a great place for a lunch stop any day of the week.

Back in town several **restaurants** along the lakeshore road capitalize on the lake view at weekends, but more reliable for good local food is the basic yet satisfying *Orizaba*, serving inexpensive Mexican classics and a daily comida corrida on Av 7, one block north of the plaza, then one-and-a-half long blocks west. Closer to the plaza are *Gaia* (Tues–Sun 8am–4pm), an excellent vegetarian restaurant with fine breakfasts and a very good value comida, overlooking the lake from Av 3 just off the southeast corner; and *La Palapa* (6–11pm, closed Tues), off the northeast corner on Av 5, for better home-made pasta and pizza than you might expect here, plus sandwiches and Mexican dishes.

For **overnight stays**, check out a number of options strung out along the water. Best of the places in town is 🏂 *Casita Carolina* (☎ 983/834-2334, ⓦ www .casitacarolina.com; ❷), a friendly American-owned guesthouse, a little over a block south of the fort, with seven assorted units, dotted around a lovely garden that slopes down to the water. Accommodation ranges from pretty basic rooms to large apartments that share a kitchen, all with fans, bathroom and hot water. Another block further south, *Hotelito El Paraiso* (☎983/834-2787, ⓦwww .hotelitoelparaiso.com; ❹) has more conventional lakeshore rooms, with wi-fi and air conditioning, as well as a jetty for swimming and kayaks to hire. The **lakeshore outside town** also offers numerous opportunities to stay, often in a somewhat wilder setting, with endless opportunities for birdwatchers: *Villas Ecotucan* (mobile ☎983/120-5743, ⓦwww.villasecotucan.info; ❹), 5km north of town, has large stone cabañas in agreeably landscaped grounds, sandwiched between the lake and acres of uncleared forest; rates include breakfast and the use of kayaks. There's solar power only, so limited power and no fans or air conditioning. They also offer camping (M$50/person, plus M$100 if you need a tent) and rental of kayaks and bikes (M$120 a day) and hand-crafted Hawaiian-style canoes (M$300); if you just want to visit for a swim and to climb their observation tower, it's M$20. *Colectivos* and second-class buses can drop you off on the highway near the entrance. *Laguna Azul* (mobile ☎983/114-7002, ⓦwww.laguna-azul.de), at the northern extremity of the lake (3km down a track immediately south of Pedro Santos, between Limones and the turn to Chacchoben), is still more remote but wonderfully welcoming, with a great little restaurant and bar; choose from sturdy en-suite cabañas (❸) or camping space (M$50), and rent a kayak to explore the lake.

Second-class **buses** from Chetumal drop off and pick up on Av 5 just off the plaza; southbound services on Av 7, a block uphill. First-class buses will drop you on the highway; not all stop here, especially those heading south. There's an **ATM** in the centre of the plaza and various locations offer **internet** access, including one just beyond the *Orizaba* restaurant. Wonderful **tours** are offered by Active Nature (mobile ☎983/120-5742, ⓦwww.activenaturebacalar.com), based at *Villas Ecotucan*, ranging from two-hour jungle walks or lake trips (in kayaks or Hawaiian-style outrigger canoes) to two- or four-day kayak camping trips around the local lakes, rivers and rapids. An excellent local web portal, ⓦwww .bacalarmosaico.com, offers information on all the above and more.

Chetumal and around

If you're heading south to Belize or Guatemala, you can't avoid **CHETUMAL**, 15km from the Belize border and capital of the state of Quintana Roo. Until 1898, when the Mexican navy established the frontier outpost of **Payo Obispo** (Bishop's Point) on this spot, no official border ran through the Bahía de Chetumal, which forms the city's southern edge. Today, elements of the neighbouring country's culture still linger in the little clapboard houses and the amount of English spoken. The city has very few "sights" to speak of. Indeed, it's largely oblivious to tourists and dedicated almost entirely to unglamorous cross-border commerce. Mexicans come to visit the **duty-free zone** between the two countries, a dilapidated mini-mall area accessible by bus, where shops flog everything from Dutch cheese to Taiwanese boom boxes, fake Ralph Lauren to Scotch whisky. Likewise, vendors of appliances and cheap lingerie line the main avenue. Despite all this Chetumal retains a certain old-fashioned tropical graciousness, especially palpable in the evenings, when the bay boulevard is filled with lovers and families.

You probably won't want to stay long, but Chetumal does make a decent one- or two-day stop to rest and restock; everything from food to internet access is easily and inexpensively available here. From the city, you can also make day or overnight trips to the Río Bec archeological sites or to nearby beaches and fascinating rivers

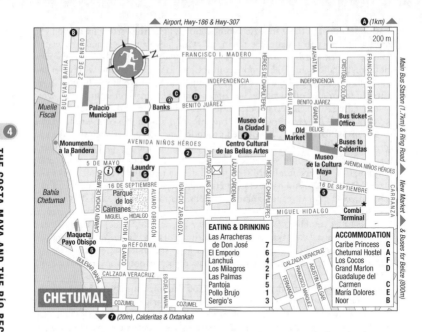

Map labels:

Airport, Hwy-186 & Hwy-307

A (1km)

0   200 m

Main Bus Station (1.7km) & Ring Road ▶

New Market ▶

& Buses for Belize (800m)

FRANCISCO I. MADERO

MAHATMA

CRISTÓBAL COLÓN

FRANCISCO PRIMO DE VERDAD

HÉROES DE CHAPULTEPEC

22 DE ENERO

BULEVAR BAHÍA

INDEPENDENCIA

INDEPENDENCIA

AGUILAR

BENITO JUÁREZ

Muelle Fiscal

B

Palacio Municipal

@

Banks

C

D

BENITO JUÁREZ

❶

Museo de la Ciudad

@

Old Market

BELICE

GANDHI

Bus ticket Office

E

Buses to Calderitas

Monumento a la Bandera

AVENIDA NIÑOS HÉROES

Centro Cultural de las Bellas Artes

❷

PLUTARCO ELÍAS CALLES

LÁZARO CÁRDENAS

Museo de la Cultura Maya

AVENIDA NIÑOS HÉROES

CARRANZA

5 DE MAYO

❸

i❹

Laundry

❻

HÉROES DE CHAPULTEPEC

16 DE SEPTIEMBRE

16 DE SEPTIEMBRE

Bahía Chetumal

CARMEN OCHOA DE MERINO

ÁLVARO OBREGÓN

Parque de los Caimanes

IGNACIO ZARAGOZA

MIGUEL HIDALGO

❺

Combi Terminal

Maqueta Payo Obispo

❻

MIGUEL HIDALGO

OTHÓN P. BLANCO

REFORMA

BULEVAR BAHÍA

CALZADA VERACRUZ

ESCUELA NAVAL

COZUMEL

COZUMEL

CALZADA VERACRUZ

FRANCISCO FERNANDO

AGUSTÍN MELGAR

FERNANDO

AGUSTÍN MARQUEZ

EATING & DRINKING

Las Arracheras de Don José	7
El Emporio	6
Lanchuá	4
Los Milagros	2
Las Palmas	F
Pantoja	5
Pollo Brujo	1
Sergio's	3

ACCOMMODATION

Caribe Princess	G
Chetumal Hostel	A
Los Cocos	F
Grand Marlon	D
Guadalupe del Carmen	C
Maria Dolores	E
Noor	B

CHETUMAL

❼ (20m), Calderitas & Oxtankah

---

and wetlands (the latter most easily done on a tour). Be warned, though, that car rental (see p.138) is the one thing in Chetumal that's not a great deal.

Arrival and information

Chetumal's main **bus station** is on the north side of town, a short taxi ride from the centre (M$20); locker rental costs M$5 per hour, and there are ATMs, as well as *colectivos* outside to many local destinations. The **airport** – currently offering only domestic flights to Mexico City – is 2km west of town. The heart of Chetumal, certainly for tourists, is Niños Héroes as it runs down from the Museo de la Cultura Maya and old market to the bay. The main **tourist information** office, on 5 de Mayo at Carmen Ochoa de Merino (Mon–Fri 9am–5pm; ☎983/832-2031), is friendly enough but not particularly knowledgeable. There are also information kiosks at the bus station and on the malecón at Hidalgo.

Accommodation

Most of Chetumal's **hotels** are on or near Niños Héroes, in the few blocks back from the malecón; virtually all have off-street parking.

Caribe Princess Obregón 168 ☎983/832-0900, ⓦwww.caribeprincesschetumal.com. The pimped-up lobby doesn't reflect the state of the rooms here; nonetheless they're a step up from the real budget places, clean, quiet and with a/c. It's popular with Mexican business travellers. **❹**

Chetumal Hostel Sicilia 262 at San Salvador ☎983/832-8317, ⓦwww.chetumalhostel.com. Very friendly hostel with four- to eight-bed dorms (M$135) and shared kitchen. The only problem is

the location, in the west of the city a couple of kilometres from the centre or bus station; you really need to use taxis if you're staying here, though these are very good value (M$20 from the bus station or to centre).

Los Cocos Niños Héroes 134 ☎01-800/719-5840, ⓦwww.hotelloscocos.com.mx. The pick of the downtown deluxe hotels with large, comfortable rooms (the "premier" category is worth the upgrade), a pool and a sprawling terrace bar and restaurant. Also very pleasant suites. **❻**

Grand Marlon Juárez 88 ☎983/285-3287, ⓦwww.hotelesmarlon.galeon.com. Modern business hotel with very comfortable, quiet rooms (though not quite as fancy as the designer exterior may lead you to expect); it's worth paying a little extra for an executive room. There's also a restaurant and small pool. *The Marlon*, an older sister hotel directly opposite, is a step down in both price and quality. ❺

🔧 Guadalupe del Carmen Zaragoza 226 ☎983/832-8649. Clean and tidy two-storey courtyard hotel, a little roomier than budget competitor *María Dolores*; some rooms have a/c. ❸

María Dolores Obregón 206 ☎983/832-0508. Basic budget offering that's popular with backpackers. Rooms are cramped but clean, and there's a good restaurant downstairs. ❷

Noor Bahía at José María Morelos ☎983/835-1300, ⓦwww.hotelnoor.com.mx. Beautiful bay views from your room are the chief attraction at Chetumal's newest hotel; designer furnishings, too, plus pool, restaurant and wi-fi. ❻

The City

Chetumal is a mishmash of modern concrete buildings and the few old wooden houses with porches that survive from the settlement's earliest days. The only major tourist attraction, on Avenida Niños Héroes at the northern edge of the city centre, is the large, modern **Museo de la Cultura Maya** (Tues–Thurs & Sun 9am–7pm, Fri & Sat 9am–8pm; M$55). Architecturally spectacular, the museum is in desperate need of refurbishment – it's dark, the air conditioning rarely works and most of the interactive displays are broken. In this state, the flowery text describing the natural world of the Yucatán, as well as the ins and outs of ancient Maya society, mathematics and cosmology, can seem something of a triumph of style over substance. Nonetheless there are a few insightful displays – including a full-scale replica of the mural-filled room at Bonampak (see p.255) – and there's an auditorium with independent film screenings and free modern art displays. On the street in front of the museum, the *Alegoría del Mestizaje* **sculpture** is one of the most striking depictions of the popular theme of the intermingling of Spanish and indigenous cultures, showing modern Mexico born of a conquistador and a Maya woman (see "Oxtankah", p.139). Immediately south is a little warren of shops and *loncherías* – what's called the "old" **market** (the newer, larger one, where most of the fresh produce is sold and buses for Belize gather, is 1km northwest along Calzada Veracruz).

A few blocks south of the old market on Niños Héroes, the **Centro Cultural de las Bellas Artes**, in an impressive 1936 neo-Maya-style school, now houses the **city museum** (Tues–Sun 9am–7pm; M$55), with a collection of romantic memorabilia – from locally made Raleigh bicycles to ladies' hand fans – reminiscent of Chetumal's swashbuckling days, when it was a city of *vaqueros sin caballos* ("cowboys without horses"). The state schools for the performing arts are also located here, offering free live performances several evenings a week; check out the noticeboards for these and other events in town.

Niños Héroes continues down to the bay and the **malecón**, popular for fishing and evening strolls. A few blocks east, behind the modern Palacio Legislativo, a small Caribbean-style wooden house contains the fascinating **Maqueta Payo Obispo** (Tues–Sat 9am–3pm, Sun 9am–2pm; free), a hand-carved scale model of the town as it looked in the 1920s. The small adjacent museum tells the story of the lighthouse barge *Chetumal*, with which the Mexican army helped establish the town and the country's border with British Honduras, in order to stop the flow of arms to the rebels defending the Zona Maya. The town was renamed after the barge (itself named after a Maya lord of the sixteenth century) in 1936.

Eating and drinking

The area around the intersection of avenidas Niños Héroes and Obregón has the highest concentration of restaurants in Chetumal, while the **market stalls** south of the Museo de la Cultura Maya have good, inexpensive fare at lunch. **Nightlife** isn't particularly vibrant, but on weekend evenings the malecón is busy with food stalls, and locals flock to the bars and restaurants strung out along Bulevar Bahía, east of the centre.

Las Arracheras de Don José Blv Bahía, between Cozumel and Josefa Ortiz. The speciality of this sprawling terrace restaurant, very popular on weekend nights, is meat tacos of every kind (stuff yourself for M$100), served with an array of fresh salsas. You can also get good-value steaks, stuffed baked potatoes and pastas.
El Emporio Carmen Ochoa de Merino, between Hidalgo and Reforma. An excellent Uruguayan restaurant in a historic wooden house – steaks (from M$160) are served with lashings of garlicky *chimichurri*, and there are great empanadas, along with a good selection of South American wines. Follow the smell of grilled meat up the street.
Lanchuá 5 de Mayo 33, between Othon Blanco and Carmen Ochoa de Merino. Simple, plastic-table pasta, salad and steak restaurant, housed in a pink-painted wooden clapboard house. Mon–Fri 2–9pm, Sat buffet, 1–7pm.
Los Milagros Zaragoza, between Niños Héroes and 5 de Mayo. Tasty, inexpensive food

(breakfasts are especially good) at this little sidewalk café, popular with local journalists. Busy day and night.
Las Palmas In *Los Cocos* hotel. Not the cheapest food in town (mains from M$100), but Mexican dishes are prepared with care. A mix of tourists and dressed-up locals makes for a convivial scene. Open till 1am Fri and Sat.
Pantoja Gandhi at 16 de Septiembre. Good comida corrida, a favourite with the locals, and hearty dishes like *mondongo* (tripe stew) and *chilaquiles* for breakfast. Closed Sun.
Pollo Brujo Obregón, between Juárez and Niños Héroes. Roasted chicken and nothing else, served fast and hot. Daily 10am–7pm
Sergio's Obregón 182 at 5 de Mayo. Upscale but reasonably priced Italian-style restaurant (most mains are less than M$100) with a few veggie options, such as soups, pizzas and salads; well-prepared steaks, too. Open all day till late, starting with breakfast from 7am.

Listings

Banks There's a cluster of banks with ATMs around the junction of Juárez and Obregón
Belizean consulate Genova 369 (☎983/285-3511); open to the public Mon–Fri 9am–noon.
Car rental Expensive in Chetumal; try the travel agents below, Continental (☎983/832-2411, ⓦ www.continentalcar.com.mx), in the lobby of the *Holiday Inn*, or Europcar, Niños Héroes 129, opposite *Los Cocos* hotel (☎ 983/833-9959), and at the airport (☎ 983/107-9008).
City tour A two-hour bus tour leaves from outside the Museo de la Cultura Maya, Tues–Sat noon & 3pm, Sun 11am (M$20).
Internet Plenty of options, including Arba, with branches in the old market and opposite, on Aguilar, and C@lix, on Juárez near the *Hotel Guadalupe del Carmen*.
Laundry Lavandería Centro, Othon Blanco between 16 de Septiembre and 5 de Mayo (daily 8am–8pm; M$13/kg).

Post office Plutarco Elias Calles at 5 de Mayo (Mon–Fri 8am–6pm, Sat & Sun 9am–12.30pm).
Tour operators Not plentiful in Chetumal and often need advance notice to arrange something for you. On the plus side, because there are not yet many fixed routes, you can often tailor a trip precisely to your tastes. Mayan World Adventures, 5 de Mayo 110 between Lázaro Cárdenas and Calles (☎983/833-2509, ⓦ www .mayanworldadventures.com.mx), is much the most organized, with one- to four-day tours to the Río Hondo and the Río Bec sites, including kayaking, cycling and camping options. See also Active Nature at Bacalar (p.135).
Travel agencies Bacalar Tours, Obregón 167 opposite the *Caribe Princess* (☎983/832-3875), has car rental as well as tours and general travel agency services; Premier, Juárez 83 by the *Marlon* hotel (☎983/832-3096), is a handy place for Belize boat tickets.

Around Chetumal

Near Chetumal are several refreshing escapes. At weekends, the town descends en masse on **CALDERITAS**, a small seaside resort just 6km north around the bay. Much the best **place to stay** here is the *Yax-Há* RV park (☎983/834-4127, ⓦ www.yaxha-resort.com; ⑥), which has very comfortable air-conditioned

You can buy tickets for ADO and many others in the centre at the **downtown office** on Belice, between Gandhi and Colón: some second-class buses, including Mayab services to Cancún, actually depart from the dusty yard adjacent to this office. From the main **bus station** there are very frequent services to Cancún via Tulum and Playa del Carmen, running at least hourly on ADO, with a couple of ADO GL services (5am & midnight) and numerous second-class buses. For the **Río Bec** area (Xpujil or Escárcega) there are at least a dozen buses daily. For **Mahahual**, ADO runs twice daily (5.30am & 7.30pm) most of the year, but adds a couple of buses in August; Caribe goes twice (6am & 4pm), continuing to Xcalak. For **Mérida**, ADO goes four times a day, and there are at least ten second-class services (Clase Europea, Mayab). OCC runs to destinations in **Chiapas**, such as San Cristóbal de las Casas via Palenque (3 daily, all late at night); ADO GL goes once a day at midnight), and ADO goes to **Villahermosa** (7 daily).

For nearby destinations, the **Terminal de Combis** on Hidalgo at Primo de Verdad is easier to reach; services include **Bacalar** (every 30min; 45min) and **Nicolás Bravo** (4 daily; 1hr 15min), for the Río Bec sites nearby. Interjet (☎01-800/011-2345, ⓦwww.interjet.com.mx) has six **flights** a week to Mexico City from the airport, 2km west of the centre.

To Belize and Guatemala

Buses run frequently between Chetumal and **Corozal** (1hr), the closest town across the border, though you must get off the bus and walk over the bridge at Subteniente López, 8km west of Chetumal. Citizens of the UK, US, Canada, Australia and New Zealand do not need a visa to enter Belize; if you are planning to return to Mexico, make sure to keep your tourist card, or you will have to purchase another.

The cheapest, very rattle-trap buses leave from the *mercado nuevo*, a kilometre north of the centre on Calzada Veracruz, from roughly 4am to 5pm, (more frequently in the morning); you can get over the border for about M$20 – a few of these continue to **Orange Walk** (2hr 30min) and **Belize City** (5hr). First-class services on Linea Dorada, San Juan and Premier Lines depart from the main bus station (5 daily; 3hr to Belize City). Note that cars rented in Mexico cannot generally be driven into Belize. There's no air travel straight from Chetumal, but there are **water-taxi** services from the *muelle fiscal* on the downtown waterfront to San Pedro on Ambergris Caye, with rival boats operated by San Pedro Water Taxi (☎501-2/26-2194 in Belize, ⓦwww.sanpedrowatertaxi.com; daily at 3pm, US$35) and San Pedro Belize Express (mobile ☎983/839-2324, ⓦwww.sanpedrobelizeexpress.com; daily at 3.30pm US$30); you can buy tickets at the dock, or from many travel agents in town.There are at least two buses a day from the ADO to Flores in **Guatemala** (for Tikal, via Belize), one or more in the early morning (6am) and another at lunchtime (12.45pm).

---

cabañas for up to four people and a large picturesque garden with a swimming pool right on the seafront. You can hire a **boat** at the adjacent *El Rincón de las Tortugas* bar (☎983/834-4220) for various day outings: to the beaches on the nearby empty island of Tamalcab (M$400 for 6–8 people); a tour around the bay to look for manatees (M$1500; 3hr); or to several other nature spots. **Buses** to Calderitas leave frequently from Cristóbal Colón, west of Héroes and behind the museum.

Seven kilometres north of Calderitas, the small Maya site of **OXTANKAH** (daily 8am–5pm; M$35) is what remains of a maritime city that was occupied principally in the Classic period (200–600 AD) and was developed to exploit maritime resources – specifically salt. Oxtankah is also allegedly the site of the original *mestizaje*, the intermixing of Spanish and Indian races that literally gave birth to modern Mexico. The legendary first couple were Gonzalo Guerrero, whose ship was wrecked off the coast in 1511, and Za'azil, a high-ranking woman in the Maya tribe that took Guerrero in. Guerrero assimilated, had three children – the first mestizos – and even fought against the Spaniards who arrived a few years later. There's a small museum (Spanish labels only) and two main groups of buildings: the Plaza Abejas is the larger, with an altar at the centre overlooked by a temple, a palace and a building known as Estructura IV. Two tombs were found in the temple – you can enter them round the back – and one beneath the altar, while Estructura IV has stucco decorations protected by a huge palapa. The Plaza Columnas consists of a palace, two temples and other unexcavated structures, while a small side path leads to a *chultun*, a bottle-shaped underground cistern. In the middle of it all is a **Franciscan chapel** built by the Spanish. The site is peaceful and wooded, with trees and other flora neatly labelled. You'll need your own transport to get there (follow the shoreline north through Calderitas) or a taxi (M$200 round-trip with waiting time).

West and south of Chetumal, the winding, deep-green **Río Hondo**, which forms the border between Mexico and Belize, is an area rich in wildlife, from furry capybaras to massive numbers of bats. It's hard to visit on your own, thanks to poor roads and little infrastructure, but well worth a guided trip with one of the tour operators in Chetumal.

The Río Bec and Calakmul

The road that runs across **the south** of the peninsula, Hwy-186 from Chetumal to Francisco Escárcega, passes through some of the emptiest areas of the Yucatán. Many trees have been – and still are being – cleared through subsistence farming practices, or felled for logging or cattle-ranching, but the forest becomes thicker as you travel west toward Campeche State, where a vast tract of land on both sides of the highway is given over to the **Calakmul Biosphere Reserve**, which encompasses the densest jungle on the peninsula.

The area, known as the **Río Bec**, is rich in Maya ruins, most of which have been open to the public only since the mid-1990s. Populated during the Classic era, this land forged a link between the Petén cities to the south and the younger settlements just being established in the Chenes area to the north. The enormous site of **Calakmul**, located west of the other sites in Campeche State, deep in the wilderness near the border with Guatemala, is the highlight of this area; the view from its main pyramid, the largest in the Maya world, takes in a pure sea of green from horizon to horizon. However, the other sites are also fascinating and substantial, evidence of a land that was vastly more populated a thousand years ago than it is now. Travellers typically arrange tours to the ruins and find accommodation at Xpujil (see box below), on the border between Campeche and Quintana Roo states. Tourist services are rudimentary in this area, but you will often be able to enjoy the ruins and the untamed forest in virtual solitude, the antithesis of a visit to Chichén Itzá.

Dzibanché and Kinichná

About 65km out of Chetumal, the first sites you reach are Dzibanché and Kinichná. A well-signed turn-off 5km past the town of Morocoy leads some 15km north to a joint ticket office (8am–5pm; M$41); from here each site is a further kilometre or so. If you're travelling by taxi, specify that you'll be visiting both sets of ruins: it takes little more than an hour to tour everything.

Dzibanché is the earliest city in the area, thought to be the base for the influential Snake Kingdom (Kaan) clan before it ascended to rule in Calakmul in the early seventh century. Because of its early date, the city is not truly a Río Bec site – the buildings are relatively simple and show none of the later ornate detail. It's a good place to start, though, as the plain buildings, sparse trees and dry soil make a sharp contrast to the sites further down the road and deeper in the jungle. You also get a good idea of the scale of these cities – the inhabitants of Dzibanché were spread over an area of some forty square kilometres around the ceremonial centre, and you pass a large, semi-excavated plaza on the drive up from the ticket office. Entering the site you come first to Edificio 6, or the **Edificio de los Dinteles**, named for the original wood lintels that were found in the two rooms at the top of the pyramid. The northern one has been replaced, but the southern one remains, dating from the 700s. In the Plaza Gann beyond are several more impressive buildings, among which **Edificio 13** is particularly notable for its stairs carved with the figures of war prisoners. The tallest structures, edificios 1 and 2, lie beyond here on the Plaza Xibalba – each housed tombs of important personages.

At the small site of **Kinichná**, which was most likely a territory of Dzibanché, the centrepiece is a hulking **pyramid**, built layer upon layer by succeeding leaders. Each of its three levels is built in a different style, reflecting three different eras. Sixty-six tall, steep steps lead to the top, but it's well worth the climb for the stunning views in every direction. From here the strategic significance of the site, and of Dzibanché, the tops of whose structures you can just make out, is clear – each occupies an area of higher ground above the endless plain. You can also see the progress of modern land clearance, with most of the surrounding country given over to ranches or the cultivation of corn. The face of the pyramid was originally decorated with giant masks, and though most of the detail has gone (as the result of erosion or theft), you can still make out where these would have been.

Kohunlich

The expansive ruins of **Kohunlich** (daily 8am–5pm; M$49) are beautifully situated a few kilometres past the turn for Dzibanché, then 9km south from the village of Francisco Villa, in a dense jungle of near-prehistoric proportions that's

---

Visiting the Río Bec sites

The typical strategy for visiting this string of ruins is to spend the night in Xpujil, hire an early-morning taxi to visit Calakmul and Balamkú, and return to Xpujil to see the ruins in town in the late afternoon. You can then take a late bus to Chetumal or Campeche (see p.220). If you have the time, though, it will be a more rewarding and relaxing visit if you take at least two days and allow yourself to see more. Renting a car in Campeche or Chetumal affords the most flexibility, but taking taxis can cost about the same amount, leaving you the option of continuing on a loop route rather than returning your car.

Using Xpujil as a base, **taxis** can be arranged through the hotels, though you'll usually get a slightly better rate if you deal directly with the drivers gathered at the crossroads in town. Rates vary depending on the number of people and your bargaining skills, but reckon on paying from M$700 for one person to M$1200 for four to go to Calakmul and Balamkú or to Kohunlich and Dzibanché, half that for Chicanná, Becán and Xpuhil, including waiting time. If you're not in a hurry, it's also possible to start off sightseeing from Chetumal by taking a *combi* to the town of Nicolás Bravo, hiring a taxi from there to visit Dzibanché and Kohunlich, and then flagging down a second-class bus to Xpujil.

Alternatively, there are organized **tours** to Calakmul from Campeche (see "Listings", p.228) and elsewhere.

home to green parrots and enormous lurid butterflies. Allow about an hour and a half to visit all of the buildings, spread out among the towering fan palms and linked by a loop trail. The buildings range from the late Pre-Classic to the Classic periods (100–900 AD), and the majority are in the Río Bec architectural style (see box, opposite). But, to quote the early writer and adventurer John L. Stephens, the site is a perfect example of "a strong and vigorous nature…struggling for mastery over art", as even the buildings that have been excavated in the last few decades are once again being consumed by the creeping foliage and moss.

The most famous structure here, the **Templo de los Mascarones**, is named after the five two-metre-high stucco masks that decorate its facade, facing west to the setting sun. Disturbing enough now, these wide-eyed, open-mouthed gods once stared out from a background of smooth, bright-red-painted stucco. Quite whom they represent is a subject of some debate, but most probably they are Kinich Ahau, the sun god, with the features of members of the ruling family. The temple is one of the oldest here, dating from around 500 AD; at some point around 700 AD another pyramid layer was constructed over it (helping preserve the masks), but this has mostly been cleared by excavation.

Other structures, following recent reconstruction efforts, include a ball-court, the moss-covered Pixa'an palace and an elite residential area called the **27 Escalones**, worth the detour to see the great views over the jungle canopy from the cliff edge on which it is built (prime real estate was just as prized 1400 years ago, it seems). Look out throughout the site, too, for evidence of the complex drainage system that collected rainwater in *aguados*, or cisterns. There are also small, square pools to collect water; similar structures were found alongside Maya roads in the forest to provide drinking water for messengers and other travellers.

The intimate, honeymoon-lux *Explorean* resort (T 01-800/504-5000, W www .theexplorean.com; ⑨), halfway up the winding road to the site, is a beautiful place, with classy, thatch-roof cabins scattered through extensive grounds. Its pool, **restaurant** and **bar** are open to non-guests, and the view over the jungle canopy can be worth the price of a post-ruins drink.

Río Bec

Despite giving its name to the entire region, the scattered buildings of the city of **Río Bec**, 10km east of Xpujil and south of an *ejido* (community) named 20 de Noviembre, are frustratingly inaccessible. The area is still under excavation and usually closed to visitors, though some years it opens for a few months in the spring. Ask in the tourist office in Xpujil about arranging an expedition on horseback, perhaps, as otherwise only four-wheel-drive vehicles can tackle the dirt tracks here. If you do visit, you will see the most extreme example of the Río Bec false-pyramid style: as at Xpuhil, the "steps" on the site's twin towers were never meant to be climbed, with risers that actually angle outwards.

Xpujil

Thanks solely to its location halfway between Chetumal and Escárcega, the one-street village of **XPUJIL** (also spelled "Xpuhil"), straddling Hwy-186 at the border of Campeche and Quintana Roo states, is the main base for exploring the Río Bec region. In this it is at least efficient, with food and accommodation all gathered within walking distance, though none is of very high quality. Of the **places to stay** in town, the best choice is the *Hotel Calakmul* (T 983/871-6029), west of the centre, with pleasant, modern, air-conditioned rooms around a garden (④) and some very basic cabañas with shared bath (②). Alternatively,

El Mirador Maya (☎ 983/871-6005, ✉ mirador_maya@hotmail.com; ❸), at the top of the hill on the western edge of town, has decent wooden cabañas with porches, though the noise of trucks struggling up the slope is noticeable at night. Both have adequate **restaurants**, which are significantly more expensive, however, than simpler places along the highway (including a great place for roast chicken). *El Mirador Maya* also offers money **exchange** and arranges taxi tours to the sites. Around the bus station are several phone casetas and the Mundo Maya **internet** café; the local **gas station** is 5km east of town. Xpujil also boasts an unofficial **tourist information** office (☎ 983/871-6064, ⓦ www.ecoturismocalakmul.com), at the eastern edge of town. Maintained by a dedicated ecotourism group that also operates a campsite near Calakmul (see p.147), they can arrange a variety of **tours**, including horseriding and visits to traditional villages, as well as jungle and archeological expeditions. However, the office keeps irregular hours, since they're often at the campsite, so advance notice is recommended; not all the staff (or guides) speak English.

As an alternative to staying in Xpujil, the tranquil village of **Zoh-Laguna**, 10km north, is an attractive option. Here 🍴 *Cabañas y Restaurant Mercedes* (☎ 983/114-9769 or 9933; ❶) offers spotless cabins with private baths, and the kindly owners can fix tasty meals on request. You may fall asleep to the sound of your neighbour's satellite TV, but you'll wake to the sound of turkeys, pigs and the other village livestock. The only problem is that the place is increasingly popular, so it's safest to book; should you turn up and there's no space, there are a couple of newer alternatives in the village. If you don't have your own car, you can hire a taxi from Xpujil (around M$40 one-way), or hop on a *colectivo* if your timing is right – though this will drop you on the main road, about 700m from the hotel itself.

Leaving Xpujil, note that virtually every bus is *de paso*, so you may not always be able to secure a seat; the first-class buses, in particular, can be packed with through travellers. There are three ADO and four Mayab **buses** a day to Chetumal, plus at least four more second-class services, a couple of which continue all the way to Cancún. In the opposite direction there are around fifteen departures in total to Escárcega, many of them continuing to Villahermosa.

The Río Bec style

While Río Bec is the name of a specific archeological site, it also refers to a characteristic **architectural style** common to all of the sites found in this area. Río Bec buildings, most built around 600 AD, were influenced by neighbouring Petén, a region notable for its massive pyramids with rounded corners and the commemorative stelae dotting its plazas.

The Río Bec style's most distinctive feature is a dramatic distortion of the great early pyramids of the Petén. In the Río Bec, the shape of the steep Gran Pirámide at Tikal, for instance, is further elongated to form a tall, slender tower with an unclimbable steep-stepped facade. These are usually built in pairs and topped with temples that are impossible to reach and generally filled in with solid rock; narrow roofcombs add another level of ornamentation to these purely decorative structures. In the lower register, the central doorway is often adorned with the gaping mouth of a god – typically thought to be the ancient deity **Itzamná**, the god of night and day – whose teeth frame the opening. The remaining surfaces of Río Bec buildings are covered with smaller masks of Itzamná and other gods, all hooked noses, curling tongues and rolling eyes, alternating with intersecting crosses and inset stone squares forming checkerboard patterns, another distinctive motif of the region. Tour all the Río Bec sites in a day or two, and you'll come away dizzy from the intertwining grotesquery.

Second-class buses also run north out of town, past the Chenes sites (p.231) towards Hopelchén; most continue to Campeche, though some head for Mérida via the Ruta Puuc (p.204).

Xpuhil ruins

The smallest of all the sites in the area, the Xpuhil **ruins** (8am–5pm; M$37) are less than 1km west along the highway from the bus stop in Xpujil village – spellings of the two places are to an extent interchangeable, but most commonly they are spelt as we have here. Much of the stone carving at this ancient settlement, which was probably a satellite of Becán to the west, is in excellent shape, and you need about half an hour to see it all. The path leads first past a small residential complex, then to the main building, a long, low structure studded with three striking towers (unusual, as other Río Bec buildings have only two); the central one faces west, the other two, east. The stairs up the ersatz pyramids are purely decorative, as they are almost vertical. A narrow, almost equally steep internal staircase leads partway up the south tower, providing a bit of a view over the neatly cleared grassy plaza that fronts the structure.

Hormiguero

Only the most dedicated Mayaphiles make the effort to reach **Hormiguero** (8am–5pm; free), a small site with excellently preserved decoration. It's a bumpy, forty-minute, 22-kilometre drive south from the crossroads in Xpujil, for a visit that takes only half an hour or so (no buses run this way; taxis charge around M$200 round-trip with waiting time). However, the effort is rewarded by some remarkable, beautifully preserved stone decoration and by it being almost certain that you'll have the place to yourself; even the caretaker is rarely to be seen. Just two structures, tucked in deep forest, have been completely excavated, but plenty of others are visible among the trees. Both the main buildings show a combination of features typical of the Río Bec style: the distinctive monster mouths, later used extensively in the Chenes sites (see p.231), and the impossibly steep towers (although the temples at the tops of these are actually functional, unlike those at Xpuhil). Keep your eyes on the forest floor here as you explore – Hormiguero has its name ("ant hill") for good reason.

Becán

Though it covers a relatively small area, **Becán** (daily 8am–5pm; M$41), 6km west of Xpujil and then 500m north on a signed track, is a very impressive site with several details that set it apart from its neighbours; allow about an hour and a half for a basic tour. The most remarkable feature is the dry **moat**, 16m wide and 5m deep, which surrounds the entire site. This moat and the wall on its outer edge form one of the oldest known defensive systems in Mexico and are unique among Maya sites. The structure has led some to believe that this, rather than present-day Flores in Guatemala, was the site of Tayasal, early capital of the Itzá. Becán was first occupied in 600 BC and reached its peak between 600 and 1000 AD, when it apparently functioned as a regional capital and trade centre.

Unlike many of the excavated sites in the northern Yucatán, most of the buildings here seem to have been residential rather than ceremonial; in fact, the tightly packed buildings – with rooms stacked up and linked with corridors and unusual, winding internal staircases – create a strong sense of dense urbanism, akin to modern apartment blocks.

Enter the ruins through a break in the east wall, and you face an alleyway overhung with a narrow, typically Maya, vaulted arch; passing through, you reach the **Plaza Central**, dominated by the massive 32-metre-high **Structure IX** and the temple-palace complex **Structure X**, topped with the gaping mouth of Itzamná. At its far south end, a glass box protects a beautiful stucco **mask** of the sun god, Kinichná. Though it's nowhere near as large as the Kohunlich masks, the work is marvellously intricate, with much of the original pigment remaining.

Whereas the area around the Plaza Central feels crowded, the raised **Plaza Oriente** exudes a more orderly grandness and was clearly an elite residential area. **Structure I** sports some of the tallest, steepest towers of all the Río Bec sites, topped with small galleries probably used as observatories, and **Structure II** exhibits another typical decorative technique: small limestone cubes inset to form checkerboard patterns and crosses, which represent the cardinal points. Because much of the site was excavated only in the last few decades, the restoration process is meticulously marked throughout: small chips of stone set in the plaster walls mark the edges of the buildings as they were first found; everything above this line is recent restoration. You can climb several of the buildings, and from the tops of the tallest ones, you can just make out the towers of Xpuhil to the east.

Chicanná

Two kilometres west of Becán, **Chicanná** (daily 8am–5pm; M$37) is south of the highway, across from the *Chicanná Ecovillage Resort*. For most of its history, Chicanná was a dependency of Becán, and given the quality of the building and the richness of the decoration, many believe that it was the home of that city's elite. Entering the site, you first reach the large **Structure XX**, topped with a second tier made of stacks of heads traditionally identified as the rain god, Chac, though more recent scholarship suggests they actually depict Itzamná. You can walk inside some of the rooms to see surviving stucco details, such as small human faces. **Structure VI** preserves part of its original roofcomb; all the buildings here, and indeed at most of the surrounding sites, would originally have had similar roofcombs, decorated with depictions of their gods and rulers. Following the path around, you eventually come to the impressive **Structure II**, the design of which gives the site its name ("House of the Serpent Mouth"). Its massive square doorway forms a face and gaping mouth, complete with spiky teeth, thought to be the god Itzamná due to the distinctive crossed eyes and round earrings. The rest of the building is covered in smaller masks of hook-nosed Chac (or Itzamná), made up of intricately carved mosaic pieces of limestone. Many of these are still painted with red stucco, in a style that was developed in this area and the adjacent Chenes cities, then picked up and refined by later builders in the Puuc region to the north.

After visiting the site, you can stop for a drink and a dip in the pool at *Chicanná Ecovillage Resort* (T 981/811-9191, W www.chicannaecovillageresort.com; ❼), which also offers the most comfortable rooms around (though the "eco" label isn't particularly applicable). A bit further west on the highway, *Río Bec Dreams* (W www.riobecdreams.com) is a smaller **lodging** option offering cosy wooden "jungalows" with shared bath (❸), or larger private-bath cabañas for families (❺). *Dreams* is also a great travellers' resource: the owners are archeology buffs who can advise on the latest site openings and arrange good tours. Non-guests can call in at the **restaurant**, with its varied (non-Mexican) menu.

Calakmul

The vast ruined city of **CALAKMUL** (daily 8am–5pm; M$41), a UNESCO World Heritage Site, is one of the best Maya ruins for quiet contemplation of the culture's architectural legacy. The site lies 58km west of Xpujil on Hwy-186, then 60km south, in the heart of the **Calakmul Biosphere Reserve**, which encompasses more than 1.7 million acres of jungle. The reserve's entrance gate on the highway opens at 7am (M$40/car, plus M$28/person, to enter the reserve), and it takes over an hour, on a paved but narrow road, to reach the ruins.

If you arrive early, or better still stay late, you'll almost certainly catch plenty of **wildlife** at the site itself and on the ride down – ocellated turkeys, white-tailed deer, peccaries, woodpeckers, hummingbirds and toucans are common, while jaguars roam the forest by night. In total there are said to be 235 species of bird within the reserve and more than ninety mammal species. Even if you don't see anything, you'll certainly hear the jungle life: booming **howler monkeys** and raucous **tree-frogs** as well as the ubiquitous birds. At about Km 27, a short nature trail leads down to a swampy area; the path is not well maintained, but you don't need to go far to reach the water, in which there are said to be crocodiles – there's also a good chance that spider or howler monkeys will be in the trees overhead.

The site

Although the ruins were spotted from the air in the 1930s, excavation has been going on only for the past three decades; every year new discoveries yield more revelations about the city's historical significance. At the very least, Calakmul is probably the biggest archeological zone in Mesoamerica, extending for some seventy square kilometres; at its peak, it was home to over fifty thousand people, with some two hundred thousand within its immediate sphere of influence. The central area alone contains nearly seven thousand buildings and more stelae and pyramids than any other Maya city. The city's **treasures** are on display in the archeological museum in Campeche (see p.226), and include two hauntingly beautiful jade masks. Also at the museum, you can see the first mummified body ever found in Mesoamerica, unearthed inside **Structure XV**.

Calakmul was founded as early as the sixth century BC, when many of the larger structures were erected, setting out the basic plan of the place. The many stelae – around 120 have been found in all – mostly date from the city's peak of power in the Classic era, around 600 AD; the city's importance can also be judged by the frequency with which it is referred to in hieroglyphs at other cities, more than any of its rivals. Calakmul was finally abandoned by 900 AD, after fourteen centuries of occupation.

Unlike its neighbours, Calakmul's primary focus, for trade and culture, was to the south, to the great cities of the Petén. Thus Calakmul is not considered a true part of the Río Bec; its architecture is much more akin to that of the Petén. The city's great rival – and inspiration – was Tikal in modern Guatemala, with which it had an often violent rivalry. The two cities' ruling dynasties were in almost continual conflict, fighting for prestige, and for control over lucrative trade routes. Recent hieroglyphic translations reveal how the greatest leader of the ruling Snake dynasty, Yuknoom Che'en II, who reigned between 636 and 686 AD, came to control many smaller cities and outposts through puppet kings. Decades of struggle finally led to a bloody rout of Tikal in 657, but this led in turn to recrimination, and Yuknoom's son, Yich'aak K'ak' (also known as Jaguar Paw), suffered his own staggering defeat in 695, all but ruining Calakmul.

A choice of three **routes** – *larga*, *media* or *corta* (long, medium or short) – wind through the excavated areas, with even the shortest loop taking at least ninety minutes (it's a twenty-minute walk just from the car park to the first set of buildings). You could easily spend the better part of a day here, as long as you were well-stocked with bug repellent, snacks and water. While at times the paths seem to lead away from the buildings, bear with them: all will eventually bring you to the most impressive structures.

There are two main building complexes, the Gran Acropolis (not visited on the *via corta*) and the stunning Gran Plaza, plus many other buildings and smaller groupings scattered through the jungle. What you don't see, or see little of, is the network of roads and reservoirs that sustained the population and made the whole thing possible. While not all the buildings are individually spectacular, the scale of the place is always impressive, as are the many stelae scattered throughout the site, and in particular standing sentinel around the **Gran Acropolis**. Of the lesser areas, seek out especially the **residential section** to the east, where a tight warren of private rooms is built against a section of a large defensive wall that enclosed this elite district of the city.

The real highlights come towards the end of the tour, though. It's at this point that you'll reach **Structure I**, a 50m high pyramid. Over one hundred tall steps lead to the top, where no sign of civilization is visible through the jungle canopy in any direction, save for the tops of some of the other neighbouring structures. Nearby is the **Gran Plaza**, where the **Gran Pirámide** (Structure II) is located – this is one of the largest known Maya buildings, with a base covering almost fifteen thousand square meters. From the plaza below it's impossible to see the top (just a couple of metres lower than Structure I), as it recedes in stacked layers of construction, each one added by a new leader. Two giant monster masks flank the central stairway, and one of the temples contained the tomb of Jaguar Paw. Daunting as it may be, the climb yields another awe-inspiring view of nothing but jungle. On a clear day, you can just make out the square top of the Danta pyramid, at El Mirador in Guatemala; it's off the back of the pyramid, slightly to the right.

Accommodation at Calakmul

Just off the highway, by the entrance to the reserve, you'll see signs to the *Hotel Puerta Calakmul* (☎ 998/892-2624, ⓦ www.puertacalakmul.mx; ❸), a lovely, upmarket "ecological" retreat with a pool, large cabañas and a westernized restaurant that's open to anyone. Some 7km further down the access road, 700m up a rough track, *Yaax' Che* could hardly be a greater contrast; a very basic jungle **campsite and restaurant** run by Servidores Turísticos Calakmul (mobile ☎ 983/134-8818, ⓔ www.ecoturismocalakmul.com; see p.143). Here the eco claims are for real, with no electricity (paraffin lamps in the tents and restaurant), composting toilets and showers provided by an oil-drum of water and a gourd to scoop it over you. Accommodation is in tents with comfortable mattresses (M$200/person) and it's a truly back-to-nature experience. The staff can point you to **nature trails** within the reserve, bikes are available for rent (M$150 a day) and anyone can stop for a **meal**, though as the kitchen uses all local products, it may not have provisions on hand in slow seasons.

Balamkú and Nadzcaan

Most organized tours to Calakmul stop at **Balamkú** (daily 8am–5pm; M$39), just a couple of kilometres west of the turn-off to the larger city and 3km north of the highway. The main draw at this small site is a beautifully preserved seventeen-metre-long stucco **frieze**, located in a cluster of buildings furthest from the entrance and protected in a concrete shed embedded inside the central palace; the caretaker should be around to let you in. The embellished wall, crawling with toads, crocodiles and jaguars, seems to undulate in the dim light, and the rolling eyes of the red-painted monster masks, though smaller than those at Kohunlich, are perhaps more alarming here. The elaborate iconography establishes a parallel between the rising and setting sun, as it dips into the underworld, and the dynastic cycle, as kings ascend to the throne, then die and settle in the maw of the earth. Likewise, the frieze's very location inside and under a public space is suggestive of the underworld, although originally it was on the outside of a pyramid, and is preserved so well because another was later built over the top of it. Balamkú is again surrounded by thick forest and full of wildlife; there's often a large troupe of spider monkeys in the trees, especially in the late afternoon.

Just before the Balamkú turn a dirt road leads 15km north to a sizeable collection of pyramids (some 50m tall), plazas and ball-courts: the city of **Nadzcaan** (daily 8am–5pm; free), which once linked the Petén cities with Edzná further north (see p.228). Stelae found inside the temples are dated around 650 AD. The perimeter of the area contains caves and quarries where limestone was excavated for building. Serious archeological work began here only around 1999, and there's little in the way of services or signage – you're free to thrash around on your own in the untamed undergrowth. The solitude is fantastic, but a visit is advisable only for those with sturdy cars.

5

Valladolid and Chichén Itzá

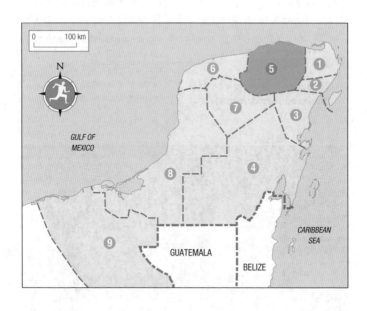

CHAPTER 5

Highlights

✳ **Casa de los Venados** Plan ahead to visit this private collection of Mexican folk art, in a renovated mansion with a modern edge. See p.154

✳ **Iglesia de San Bernardino de Siena** Valladolid's Franciscan mission is the oldest permanent church in the Yucatán. See p.154

✳ **Cenote X'keken** This spectacular cave is lit by a transfixing beam of sunlight through a hole in its ceiling on to glowing blue water. See p.157

✳ **Ek-Balam** Some of the best-preserved stucco decoration in the Maya world is on display here. See p.158

✳ **Ría Lagartos Biosphere Reserve** This strip of marsh along the coast is the place for birdwatching or simply lazing on the empty beaches. See p.160

✳ **El Castillo** The giant pyramid that towers over the ruined city of Chichén Itzá is the symbol of Maya power in the Yucatán Peninsula. See p.164

✳ **Convento de San Antonio de Padua** This massive monastery looms over the plaza in the small, scenic town of Izamal. See p.169

▲ Convento de San Antonio de Padua, Izamal

Valladolid and Chichén Itzá

econd only to the beaches around Cancún, the biggest tourist draw in the Yucatán Peninsula is **Chichén Itzá**, the ancient Maya ruins due west from the coast along Hwy-180 (two hours on the toll highway, three on the free road). The towering Pyramid of Kukulcán also known as El Castillo, and the most iconic of all the Maya pyramids, dominates the site. The area is huge, and if you attempted to visit on a day-trip, you'd be rushed, as well as crammed in with busloads of other visitors. Better to stay overnight nearby, as an early start gives you a chance to see the site without crowds, and maybe spot some of the colourful birds in the forest surrounding the ruins.

You can stay in a luxury hotel within walking distance of the site, or in a budget guesthouse in the neighbouring village of **Pisté**. But if you're as interested in contemporary Maya culture as in the ancient remains, you can't do better than **Valladolid**, 40km east and connected to the ruins by frequent bus and *colectivo* service. Many visitors often miss this predominantly Maya city that exemplifies the distinct atmosphere and structure of the inland towns built during the Spanish colonial period. Here you'll see the basic blueprint – a central plaza dominated by a cathedral (plus vendors, strolling lovers, taxi drivers and stray dogs) – that's endlessly repeated, on varying scales, in the villages and cities throughout the rest of Yucatán State.

Valladolid is also a good base for visiting the Maya ruins of **Ek-Balam**, north of town. The place is distinct from Chichén Itzá in its decorative style, with rare and perfectly preserved stucco adorning the main building. The setting in rolling grasslands is a change, too, as is the lack of crowds. From Valladolid, Hwy-295 continues north to the Gulf coast, running through the travel hub of **Tizimín**, a larger city than Valladolid but less scenic. If you're getting around by bus, you change here to carry on to the **Ría Lagartos Biosphere Reserve**, a sixty-kilometre-long strip of marshland that harbours more than 330 species of birds, including a large flamingo population. The raucous pink creatures are most easily visited from the town of **Río Lagartos**, directly north from Tizimín. Beach lovers can get their fix at the remote towns of **San Felipe**, west on a narrow road along the coast from Río Lagartos, and **Las Coloradas** to the east.

From Chichén Itzá or Valladolid, Hwy-180 continues west, with the free and toll roads merging at the town of Kantunil. At this point, you can carry straight on to Mérida, or you can make the detour north to **Izamal**, one of the region's

VALLADOLID & CHICHÉN ITZÁ

0   25 km

QUINTANA ROO

Cancún

YUCATÁN

QUINTANA ROO

GULF OF MEXICO

RÍA LAGARTOS BIOSPHERE RESERVE

PARQUE NATURAL SAN FELIPE

Bocas de Dzilam

El Cuyo

Las Coloradas

Río Lagartos

San Felipe

Dzilam de Bravo

Santa Clara

Dzidzantún

Temax

Telchac Puerto

Telchac

Dzemul

Xcambó

Motul

Bocobá

Cacalchén

Hacienda San José

Aké

Tahmek

Tekit

Ekmul

Acancéh

Cuzamá

Tixkokob

Mérida

Tekal de Venegas

Buctzotz

Sudzal

Izamal

Kantunil

Sotuta

Yaxcabá

Libre Unión

Cenote Yokdzonot

Yokdzonot

Pisté

Chichén Itzá

Grutas de Balankanché

Uaymá

Tizimín

Colonia Yucatán

Felipe Carrillo Puerto

Nuevo X-Can

X-Can

Ideal

Punta Laguna

Reserva de Monos Arañas de Punta Laguna

Cobá

Tulum

Chemax

Temozón

Ek-Balam

Cenote Suytun

Valladolid

Chichimilá

BIOPARQUE XLA'KAJ

Xocén

Dzitnup

Cenotes X'Keken & Samulá

Tihosuco & Felipe Carrillo Puerto

180

180

80

180

176

295

281

80

most beautiful small towns, notable for its egg-yolk-yellow buildings, its enormous Franciscan mission church and its strong craft tradition.

Valladolid and around

About 160km west of Cancún, **VALLADOLID**, the second oldest town in the Yucatán State (after Mérida), took a bashing when the Caste Wars began here in 1847. But the city's revolutionary spirit ultimately survived: a bold anti-*hacendado* statement by Maya rebels in Valladolid is credited with being the spark (*chispa*) that ignited the Revolution of 1910 (see Contexts, p.280).

The town has a strong colonial feel, with towering churches dotting the city grid. Unlike Mérida, with its cosmopolitan bustle, or Campeche's museum-piece, multicoloured centre, Valladolid exudes the quieter, less pretentious attitude of a rural capital, busy with the farmers and ranchers who live in the surrounding counties. Village women gather in the plaza to sell their hand-embroidered *huipiles* and other craftwork. Along with excellent traditional food, it's a quintessential slice of Yucatecan life. Moreover, the city has great-value hotels and is well situated for day-trips: to Chichén Itzá, certainly, but also up to the north coast or south to Punta Laguna (see p.121), or to nearby cenotes and other sights, easily reached by bicycle.

Arrival, information and tours

Valladolid's main **bus station** is on Calle 39, between calles 44 and 46, a block and a half west of the plaza. If you come from Izamal on a Centro bus, you're deposited at an old terminal on Calle 37 at Calle 54; it's a fifteen-minute walk or M$20 taxi to the plaza. The **tourist office**, on the southeast corner of the plaza (Mon–Fri 9am–9pm, Sat 9am–8pm, Sun 9am–7pm; ☎985/856-2529), has plenty of information, including free maps. For information and **day-trips**, visit the excellent MexiGO Tours (C 43 no. 204-C, between C 40 and C 42; ☎985/856-0777, ⓦwww.mexigotours.com), on the block behind the cathedral. The team runs small-group outings to the ruins, Río Lagartos, Punta Laguna and more. One particularly good trip is a bike tour to a nearby Maya village (M$350/9hr); you can also **rent bicyles** here (M$90/day) and do a self-guided trip.

Accommodation

Valladolid's budget **hotels** are perfectly serviceable, but prices are low enough here that you might choose perks like a swimming pool or a mansion setting. Then again, the one **hostel** in town, *La Candelaria* (☎985/856-2267, ⓔhostel-valladolid @hotmail.com), on Parque la Candelaria, on Calle 35, between calles 44 and 42, offers spotless dorms (M$110) and private rooms (❷), a garden, laundry, an outdoor kitchen and bike rental. And *Genesis Retreat*, an affordable eco-lodge in Ek-Balam (see p.159), is less than half an hour outside town.

La Aurora C 42 at C 37 ☎985/856-1219, ⓔla.aurora.hotel@hotmail.com. Great mix of old colonial style and new features: clean and sparkling rooms around a central courtyard and pool, all built new in 2010, but retaining the building's old tile floors. Free wi-fi. ❸

Casa Hamaca C 49 at C 40, southwest corner of Parque San Juan ☎985/856-5287,

ⓦwww.casahamaca.com. In a garden packed with fruit trees, this quiet B&B has eight expansive rooms decorated with elaborate murals. There's also a pool, and the expert owner can arrange massages and nature tours. On Sun mornings, you get breakfast at the local market. A few mature budget travellers are welcome in a shared hammock room (US$45, including the hammock). ❼

Casa Quetzal C 51 no. 218, between C 50 and C 52 ☎985/856-4796, ⓦwww.casa-quetzal.com. A pleasant alternative to the plaza hotels, *Casa Quetzal* is a very comfortable guesthouse near the San Bernardino church with a big pool. ❺

Lili C 44 no. 192, between C 37 and C 39 ☎985/856-2163. One block off the plaza, this small, homely hotel rents 21 basic rooms (those upstairs get a little more light) at reasonable rates. ❶

María Guadalupe C 44 no. 198, between C 39 and C 41 ☎985/856-2068, ⓔhotel_guadalupe@hotmail.com. The best of Valladolid's cheapies, with well-kept rooms featuring private baths and optional a/c in a small, two-storey 1960s building

with a little curvy flair. *Colectivos* for Cenote X'keken leave from outside. ❷

El Mesón del Marqués C 39 no. 203, on the plaza ☎985/856-2073, ⓦwww.mesondelmarques.com. Lovely hotel that started in a mansion, then expanded into neighbouring buildings. It's where most tour groups stay, but the quality is quite high. It has a wonderful palm-fringed pool, and one of the best restaurants in town (see p.156). ❺

🏃 Zací C 44 no. 191, between C 37 and C 39 ☎985/856-2167. Pleasant, modern three-storey hotel with a quiet courtyard; the big rooms have either a fan, or, for a few dollars more, a/c and TV. A pool makes it a great bargain. ❸

The city

Valladolid is compact, and even the farthest site, the Iglesia de San Bernardino de Siena, is only a short walk from the centre. Each of the town's seven central neighbourhoods is named after an elegant church.

Around the plaza

The two white towers of the eighteenth-century **Catedral de San Gervasio** rise gracefully over the south side of the **Parque Principal**, bounded by calles 39, 40, 41 and 42. The pretty, peaceful plaza is at its finest at dusk, when the curving love seats are filled with chatting couples and the bubbling fountain, topped with a statue of a woman in a traditional Yucatecan *huipil*, is lit from below. During the day, you can walk upstairs in the **city hall** (*ayuntamiento*; on the southeast corner) to see murals and photos of Valladolid's history, including a wall of portraits of city leaders.

East of the plaza on Calle 41, a smaller historic church has been converted to the **Museo de San Roque** (Mon–Sat 9am–8pm; free). It's a bit dusty, and signage is only in Spanish, but you can see objects from the site of Ek-Balam (see p.158), embroidery and other craftwork from nearby villages and contemporary Maya altars to the rain god Chac.

Far more impressive is **Casa de los Venados** (☎985/856-2289, ⓔjavenator1@gmail.com; M$60), on Calle 40 just off the southeast corner of the plaza. The home of an enthusiastic American couple, the modern renovation of a seventeenth-century mansion contains a truly boggling collection of modern Mexican folk art. It's a treat to see such fine work up close, outside of the confines of a museum, and the house-proud owners are delighted to answer questions. To be sure of seeing the place, pre-arrange a visit by email. If that's not possible, drop by at 10am, the default tour time if the owners are home and people are interested.

Iglesia de San Bernardino de Siena

The sixteenth-century **Iglesia de San Bernardino de Siena**, 1km southwest of the plaza (Wed–Mon 9am–8pm, Mass daily at 6pm), is one of the oldest in the Yucatán, from around 1545. The church buildings, which include a large monastery, were once on the very edge of town, so the Franciscans could minister to both the Spanish city residents and the Maya villagers in the countryside. In 1848, Maya rebels briefly took control of the city, sacking the church (and much of the rest of the town) in the process. Despite this, a fine Baroque altarpiece from the eighteenth century remains, as do some striking seventeenth-century paintings on the side walls.

The monastery on the north side is now a **museum** (Mon–Sat 9am–6pm; M$30), where you can see weapons that were dredged up from the on-site cenote, and other

Cuota entrance, Ek-Balam & Río Lagartos

VALLADOLID

Laundry

Parque Candelaria

CALLE 33

CALLE 35

Centro Terminal

CALLE 37

Chichén Itzá & Mérida

Mercado Municipal

CALLE 54
CALLE 50
CALLE 48
CALLE 46
CALLE 44
CALLE 42
CALLE 40
CALLE 38
CALLE 36

Cenote Zaci

Bus Station

Bazar de Artesanías

CALLE 39

Colectivos to Chichén Itzá

El Rey de Béisbol

CALLE 41

Parque Principal

Bank

Ayuntamiento

Museo de San Roque

Catedral de San Gervasio

Casa de los Venados

CALLE 41-A

CALLE 43

MexiGO Tours

CALLE 45

Cancún

ACCOMMODATION
La Aurora	B
La Candelaria	A
Casa Hamaca	H
Casa Quetzal	G
Lili	D
María Guadalupe	F
El Mesón del Marqués	E
Zací	C

Cenotes X'keken & Samula

Iglesia de San Bernardino de Siena

CALLE 47

CALLE 49

CALLE 51

0   250 m

EATING & ENTERTAINMENT
El Bazar	4
Las Campanas	5
Casa Italia	1
Conato 1910	8
Hostería El Marqués	E
Oasis	9
Squimz	3
Taberna de los Frailes	7
Yepez II	6
Zací	2

Parque San Juan

Iglesia de San Juan

CALLE 49

N

Cinema

VALLADOLID AND CHICHÉN ITZÁ | Valladolid and around

relics from the revolution. You can also see the beautiful structure that houses the water wheel over the cenote, and the sprawling gardens where the self-sufficient monks grew their own food. For a brief period in the seventeenth century, one of the monk's cells was used as a lock-up for the infamous pirate Lorencillo (legend has it he was lured inland by a beautiful Valladolid resident who had been a passenger on a ship he attacked). Lorencillo's crew rescued him in a raid before he could be executed.

To reach the complex, take scenic Calle 41-A (also called Calzada de los Frailes), which runs diagonally southwest, starting two blocks west of the plaza. While you're down this way, you can also see the seventeenth-century **San Juan** church on Calle 40 at Calle 49.

Cenote Zací

For a refreshing break, head northeast from the plaza to **Cenote Zací**, on the block formed by calles 34, 36, 37 and 39 (daily 8am–6pm; M$15). It was the water source for the former Maya stronghold of Zací ("white hawk"), from where the fierce Cupul clan fought against the first conquistadors. Broad stairs lead down into a huge cavern where the air is cool, and light reflects off the green water and glimmers on the walls. It's also home to lots of catfish. Swimming is permitted, but not encouraged – there are no changing rooms, though you could tidy up in the open-air restaurant at the top, so long as you order something.

The markets

As the *huipil*-clad statue in the plaza's fountain suggests, Valladolid is a good place to purchase craftwork. In addition to the women selling their embroidery in halls next to *El Mesón del Marqués* on the plaza, you can also visit the main **craft market** (*bazar de artesanías*) on Calle 44 at Calle 39. The city vegetable market, the **Mercado Municipal**, is on Calle 32, between calles 35 and 37.

Eating and entertainment

Overall the quality of food in Valladolid is very high, and the prices relatively low – most of these **restaurants** would qualify as "author picks" in less-culinarily-inclined towns. And the good stuff is all handily located on or near the plaza. For **nightlife**, though, there's nothing much beyond people-watching at the park, though *Las Campanas*, on the southwest corner of the plaza, occasionally has live music (and reasonably good food as well). A **cinema** on Calle 51, between calles 38 and 40, shows first-run American hits.

El Bazar Northeast corner of the plaza. A sort of food court with a fine selection of inexpensive, always busy *loncherías* and pizzerias. It's also about the only place in town aside from *Hostería El Marqués* where you can eat after 9pm.

Casa Italia Parque Candelaria. Sweet family-owned Italian restaurant that's both delicious and cheap (pizzas about M$100, pastas just M$50). The atmosphere in the evening is great, as it draws local families as well as tourists, and there are seats outside on the city's prettiest small plaza.

Conato 1910 C 40, between C 45 and C 47. This *restaurante histórico* occupies a few rooms in an old house, furnished with antique oddities and vinyl booths. The food is eclectic, home-made, a little on the natural side (lots of salads), plus a few rich sweets, such as a rich coconut pudding. With mains for just M$60 and up, it's a family place, but still has a special atmosphere, with teens on dates and girlfriends sharing those fine desserts. Dinner only; closed Sun.

🏃 **Hostería El Marqués** C 39 no. 203, in *El Mesón del Marqués*. Valladolid's best (and quite reasonably priced) restaurant is set in an interior courtyard on the plaza. Don't be put off if you find a tour group has packed the place – the excellent traditional menu features *sopa de lima*, *poc-chuc* and *escabeche de Valladolid* (chicken in a spicy vinegar broth). Open till 10.30pm daily.

Oasis C 36 at C 47. A bit away from the plaza, and more of a locals' place because of it, *Oasis* does Mexican food with a healthy twist–the "Oasis special" sandwich bursts with vegetables.

🏃 **Squimz** C 39, between C 44 and C 46. A cute, somewhat stylish restaurant-café: pastries and coffee up front, and full dinners (and slightly breezier and quieter seating) in back. The core of the menu is Yucatecan, but often presented in a new way: heavy *queso relleno* (cheese stuffed with spiced meat) is rendered here as a delicious, surprisingly light lasagne, for instance.

Taberna de los Frailes C 49 at C 41-A ☎985/856-0689. The chic rehabbed colonial building and attentive service make this Valladolid's fanciest restaurant, but it's not prohibitively priced – mains run from M$160 to M$250 and include traditional tastes and more modern ones, such as a salad of grilled watermelon and cheese.

Yepez II C 41, between C 38 and C 40. Friendly open-air bar and restaurant opposite the Museo de San Roque with live music after 9.30pm, as well as very cheap Mexican snacks (*queso fundido* for M$25). Families come for dinner, but the crowd becomes predominantly male (not too rowdy, though) once the music starts. Open daily till 2am.

Zací C 36, between C 37 and C 39. The restaurant at the cenote is very reasonably priced (mains M$65) and features some hearty Yucatecan food, such as ultra-smoky *longaniza* sausage, and handmade tortillas. The setting is cool and shady. Closes at 6pm.

Listings

Banks Bancomer, which changes travellers' cheques and has an ATM, is next door to the post office on the plaza. There's another ATM in El Bazar. **Bicycle rental** Available from MexiGO Tours (see p.153), as well Rudy Tours, on C 40 just north of

the plaza. For sheer character, though, see the Rey de Béisbol sports shop, C 44 no. 195, between C 39 and C 41, owned by Antonio "Negro" Aguilar, a one-time professional baseball star who is also a great source of local

Moving on from Valladolid

Oriente, Mayab, Noreste and ADO **buses** leave from the central bus station on Calle 39, between calles 44 and 46. The most frequent departures are for **Cancún** (roughly every 45min, 6am–3.15pm; 2hr–3hr 30min) and **Mérida** (roughly every 30min, round-the-clock; 2hr 30min–4hr), on second- or first-class service. ADO's **Chichén Itzá** service is frequent (16 daily, 3.20am–9.15pm; 40min). Mayab buses run to **Cobá** (3 daily at 9.30am, 2.45pm & 5.15pm; 1hr 30min). These continue to **Tulum**, while ADO buses go there direct (5 daily, 9.15am–8.10pm; 2hr). For Río Lagartos, head first to **Tizimín** (roughly hourly, 5.30am–8pm; 1hr). There's one **Chiquilá** bus, for Holbox (2.45am; 3hr 30min). You can also go as far as **Campeche** (1 daily at 1.35pm on ADO; 6hr) and **Chetumal** (3 daily at 5.20am, 7.30am & 2.20pm; 8hr), via Carrillo Puerto and Bacalar. For **Izamal**, there's only one Oriente bus (at 12.50pm) from the main terminal, but plenty more (10 daily, 4.15am–2.45pm; 1hr 30min) from the Centro terminal (the old Oriente terminal), on Calle 37 at Calle 54. **Colectivos** are handy for nearby towns and sights, such as Tizimín, Ek-Balam and Dzitnup. Most depart from marked points along Calle 44 just west of the plaza. For Chichén Itzá, Servicio Plus vans leave from Calle 39, between calles 44 and 46; these can be faster than buses in the morning, and much cheaper (M$20 compared with M$48). The same company also goes to the X'keken and Samula at 8am.

information. Rates everywhere are less than M$100/day.

Laundry None immediately in the centre; the closest is C 40 at C 33.

Parking Sometimes parking is limited on the plaza and hard to find on side streets. On the east side of the plaza, look for an alley directly north of the city hall; this leads to a large free lot, usually patrolled.

Post office On the plaza, C 40 near the corner of C 39 (Mon–Fri 9am–3pm).

Shopping In addition to the craft markets (see opposite), Valladolid has a few more refined shops: Coqui Coqui (C 41-A no. 207), a perfumer using local ingredients and recipes from Franciscan monks; Dutzi (C 47 at C 40), which sells hip burlap bags, designed by a German and made by local women; and Yalat (C 40 at C 39), for local foodstuffs, soaps and locally made clothing.

Telephone and internet A couple of cafés on C 41 west of the plaza (daily 7am–10pm), and a Ladatel *caseta* on the plaza also has computers (daily 7am–10pm).

Sights around Valladolid

Perhaps the most photogenic swimming hole in the Yucatán, the remarkable **Cenote X'keken**, also called Dzitnup like the nearby village (daily 7am–6pm; M$52), is 7km west of Valladolid on Hwy-180 *libre*. Visitors descend through a cramped tunnel into a huge vaulted cave, where a nearly circular pool of crystal-clear turquoise water glows under a shaft of light from an opening in the ceiling. A swim in the ice-cold water is a fantastic experience. Across the road, at the equally impressive **Cenote Samula** (daily 8am–5pm; M$52), the roots of a huge tree stretch down into the pool.

Colectivos run direct to the cenotes (signs say "Dzitnup") from outside the *Hotel María Guadalupe* in Valladolid (M$15; see p.154). Alternatively, any westbound second-class **bus** will drop you at the turn-off, 5km from town; then it's a 2km walk down a signed track. You could also take a taxi or, best of all, **cycle** on the paved bike path; the most scenic route is down Calle 41-A to San Bernardino, then along Calle 49, which eventually connects to Avenida de los Frailes, then the old highway and the *ciclopista*. If you **drive**, you can also keep an eye out for the excellent hammocks sold at the local jail, on Hwy-180 a few kilometres west of the turn to the cenotes.

Just northwest of Valladolid, 13km along the road to Izamal, is the village of **Uaymá**, notable for its dramatically painted red-and-blue **church**, unique in the

Yucatán for its fresco ornamentation, a mix of geometric patterns that look inexplicably like a combination of Islamic geometric patterns and northern European folk decorations. The church, once in ruins, was recently restored, and repurposed stones from Maya buildings hold pride of place above the door. You can get here on a Centro bus to Izamal (see p.168).

South of Valladolid, it's a slightly longer trip to **Bioparque Xla'kaj** (M$10), 5km south of town, then 2.2km east on the road to Xocén. Despite the grand name, the destination is simply a huge, open-air **cenote** with easy access on stone stairs. The surrounding grounds, maintained by the nearby farm community of Chichimilá, are a bit enthusiastically manicured, but there are also refreshments for sale, as well as several nice palapas for **overnight** guests (no tel; ❷). These go for a bargain rate, considering they have individual bathrooms and ceiling fans. The place is busy on weekends, when locals come for the day (and rent the palapas for lounging), but empty during the week. Cycling here is possible, if not as nice as the route to Dzitnup – follow the bike path which begins on the south end of town, off Calle 42, then take the well-signed 2.2km ride east.

East of Valladolid about 7km, **Cenote Suytun** (9am–6pm; M$25) doesn't merit a special trip, but it makes a fine break if you happen to be driving this way. The admission price covers two pools: Suytun, which is set in a large cave, and a more open sinkhole that's nicer for swimming. They're less splendid than X'keken, but also less crowded.

From Ek-Balam to the Gulf coast

From Valladolid, most traffic heads straight west to Mérida, or east to Cancún. North, however, is less explored and makes a nice detour for wildlife: flamingo colonies at **Río Lagartos** are the main draw. You can also visit the small but flawless site of **Ek-Balam** 25km north. If you want to go all the way to the coast as a day-trip, you'll need to make an early start – the last bus from Río Lagartos for Tizimín leaves at 5pm. You'll have to return at least to the bus-transfer point of **Tizimín** to continue on to Mérida or (less conveniently) to the Caribbean coast.

Ek-Balam

Little visited but well excavated, **EK-BALAM** (daily 8.30am–5pm; M$89) is notable for the high quality and unique details of its sculpture. Enclosed by a series of defensive walls, the compact site is really only the ceremonial centre; the entire city, which was occupied from the Pre-Classic period through the Spanish Conquest, spreads out over a very wide area, punctuated by *sacbeob* (Maya roads) heading out in all directions.

The entrance is along one of these ancient roads, leading through a freestanding four-sided arch. Beyond are two identical temples, called **Las Gemelas** (the Twins), and a long **ball-court**. The principal building, on the far side of the plaza, is the massive **Acrópolis**, the stones along its two-hundred-metre-long base adorned with bas-reliefs. Thatched awnings protect the site's finest treasure, an elaborate stucco frieze fully uncovered only around 2000; 85 percent of what you see is original plaster from the ninth century that didn't even require retouching once the dirt was brushed away.

A staircase leads up the centre of the building. On the first level, two doorways flanking the steps display near-matching designs of twisted serpents and tongues; in the right-hand carving, the snake's tongue is emblazoned with a glyph thought to represent the city of Ek-Balam. Just below the summit, a **Chenes-style doorway** in the form of a giant gaping mouth is studded with protruding teeth. This is the **entrance to the tomb** of Ukit-Kan-Lek-Tok, the city's powerful king in the mid-ninth century. The lower jaw forms the floor, while the skulls, lilies, fish and other symbols of the underworld carved below reinforce its function as a tomb gateway. Of the detailed human figures that surround the door, one's disproportionate limbs and deformed hands and feet suggest it is a portrait of a real person – one theory holds that this deformity was a result of inbreeding in the royal class. The figure at the top centre of the mouth is thought to be the king himself. Back on the ground, in the plaza, an exceptionally well-preserved **stele** depicts a king receiving the objects of power from Ukit-Kan-Lek-Tok, the smaller figure at the top of the stele, seated with one leg folded under. Given the rich detail at the site, it's worth hiring a **guide** for about M$250 for a small group. Juan Canul, who has worked on many excavations, is recommended; ask for him at the ticket desk.

In the parking area at the site, you'll find someone selling tickets to **Cenote Xcanché** (daily 9am–5pm; M$30), a seemingly bottomless pool that's a two-kilometre walk from the ruins. You can rent a bike to ride there, as well as do rappelling, kayaking or other activities at the cenote. There's a small **restaurant** too.

Practicalities
There is no bus service to the site – you'll have to catch a **colectivo** on Calle 44 just west of the plaza (M$50). Look specifically for taxis from the nearby village of Ek-Balam – these are cheaper than a Valladolid car. But unless most of the people in the car are headed to the ruins, the *colectivo* will drop you at the start of the access road to the site, about 1km from the entrance. A round-trip taxi from Valladolid costs about M$250 with waiting time.

In the village of Ek-Balam itself, ⚏ *Genesis Retreat* (☎985/852-7980, ⓦwww .genesisretreat.com; ❸) is a beautiful, value-priced **eco-lodge** with a big garden and a bio-filtered pool. The hospitable Canadian owner, who built the place herself, is also dedicated to responsible cultural tourism – she arranges a "meet the neighbours" trip around the village to learn about local food and crafts. She also organizes periodic nature tours, led by visiting experts, and has a separate piece of property for birdwatching and other outings. The **café** here also makes a good stop after the ruins, with treats like rich crêpes of spinach-like *chaya*. To reach the lodge, turn north just outside the gate to the ruins; when you hit the village plaza, turn right, then left, and follow signs off the far corner of the square. If you're taking a taxi to the place, be aware that some drivers may attempt to take you to another, less savoury cabaña lodge around the corner – *Genesis* has a doghouse labelled "Concierge" out front.

Tizimín
If you are travelling by bus from Valladolid to Río Lagartos, you will have to transfer 51km north in **TIZIMÍN**, the unofficial capital of Yucatán's cattle country. It's a little rowdier than Valladolid (kids from there head north for nightlife), and pleasant enough, but travellers rarely come this way – even though it is a handy transport hub for northeastern Yucatán – you can go straight from here to Mérida or Cancún, for instance, without returning to Valladolid. One seasonal draw: the **Feria de los Tres Reyes**, which takes place during Epiphany in early January. The fair's festivities draw both Catholic pilgrims and cowboys (who relish showing off their barbecue skills).

The rest of the year, it's worth arranging your schedule to pass through Tizimín at lunchtime, when you can have lunch at one of the region's best restaurants, ⚏ *Tres Reyes*. From the hand-patted, chewy tortillas to the succulent meats, the fresh food here is the very soul of Yucatecan cooking. It's open only until late afternoon, and located on the plaza, at calles 50, 51, 52 and 53. This is an easy walk from the two **bus stations**, which are around the corner from each other at Calle 46 and Calle 47, very near the **market**. If you do find yourself here overnight, the best of the modest **hotels** in the centre is *Hotel San Carlos*, on Calle 54, between calles 51 and 53 (☎986/863-2094; ❸), while *Posada Maria Antonia*, on Calle 50, just off the plaza between calles 53 and 51 (☎986/863-2384; ❷), is a decent cheap choice. Tizimín also has direct **bus** services to and from Mérida and Cancún.

Río Lagartos

The village of **RÍO LAGARTOS**, 100km due north of Valladolid, is set on a small spit, surrounded on three sides by water and protected from the open sea by a barrier island. The resulting shallow inlet is inhabited by tens of thousands of **pink flamingos**. Spanish explorers mistook the inlet (*ría*) for a river (*río*), and resident crocodiles for alligators (*lagartos*). The former error, at least, has been corrected, and now the area of marshy flatland along the water in either direction from the town is the **Ría Lagartos Biosphere Reserve**, home to almost four hundred bird species. Though there's not much in the town itself, the flamingos alone make a visit worthwhile, and the best time of year to see them is the spring nesting season, from April to July.

A day-trip from Valladolid is manageable, but if you want to **stay the night**, *Cabañas Escondidas* (☎986/862-0121; ❸) has a few simple cabins, all with private bath, facing the waterfront on Calle 14 just south of Calle 19. For air conditioning and other comforts, there are two decent choices: waterfront *Villa de Pescadores* (☎986/862-0020; ❸), at the end of Calle 14, and *Tabasco Río* (☎986/862-0116; ❹), at Calle 12 no. 91. There is **no bank or ATM** in town, so plan accordingly. **Buses** from Tizimín make the 1hr 30min trip nine times a day (4am–7.45pm).

As soon as you arrive at the **bus station** (on C 19 just east of the main north–south street through town) or get out of your car, you'll be approached about boat tours. Several experienced guides operate in town: ask for Ismael Navarro and Elmer Canul of Río Lagartos Expeditions (☎986/862-0452) at the *Restaurante Isla Contoy*, on the waterfront on the west side, or Diego Nuñez at *Las Palapas de la Toreja* restaurant, on the north malecón, near Calle 14. Both operations run **boats** to visit the many feeding sites; a two-hour tour usually costs about M$700 for a maximum of seven people. As well as flamingos, you're likely to see fishing eagles, spoonbills and, if you're lucky, one of the very few remaining crocodiles after which Río Lagartos was (mis)named. A three-hour trip includes a "Mayan spa treatment", in which you get to slather your skin in clay in some nearby mud flats. Arrive early if you're interested in joining up with others to fill a boat. Though it's usually not a problem with these guides, do make sure your boat captain doesn't drive too close to the birds for the sake of photos; also, never pay for the tour before you go out – it's a bad sign if your captain demands it.

San Felipe and Las Coloradas

Twelve kilometres west of Río Lagartos, **SAN FELIPE** sports especially clean streets lined with tidy, colourfully painted, tin-roofed houses and a beautiful **beach** on an offshore spit. All but one of the **buses** from Tizimín to Río Lagartos come out here as well; the last daylight bus leaves from Río Lagartos at 5.15pm. There's one good **hotel**, *San Felipe de Jesús,* Calle 9, between calles 14 and 16 (☎986/862-2027; ✉hotelsf@hotmail.com; ❺), which also has a decent restaurant; the water views here are beautiful and worth the small upgrade in price. To get to the beach, take a boat (M$15/person) from the east end of the malecón, where you can also get **tourist information** and buy tickets for various birdwatching and nature tours (from M$250 for up to five people). At Mexican holiday times – July, August and Semana Santa – the beach is crowded; the rest of the year, though, it's deserted, and you can **camp** here. If you do, be sure to bring protection against mosquitoes. Of the handful of seafood **restaurants**, *Pescadería Danilu*, on the main street, is popular, as is *Vaselina*, on the waterfront.

Twenty kilometres east of Río Lagartos, **LAS COLORADAS** isn't a good end point as it has no hotels – though you can **camp** on the windy beach. But the road out to the village passes through the nature reserve, and past Sendero Peten Tucha, a 2.5km **trail** through the marshlands that is ideal for birders (Km 8, south side of the road). The road then continues past a long stretch of beach that's the core of the reserve (camping is prohibited here), behind a buffer of yucca and century plants. The reserve abruptly ends at the edge of a vast industrial **salt** operation, followed shortly thereafter by the village itself – this is the end of the road, and it really feels like it. Three buses come out here from Tizimín (10.30am, 12.30pm & 7.50pm); from Río Lagartos, you can take the 12.30pm bus.

Chichén Itzá and around

The most famous, the most extensively restored and by far the most visited of all the Maya sites, **CHICHÉN ITZÁ** lies conveniently along the main highway from Mérida to Cancún, about 200km from the Caribbean coast. Regular bus services make it feasible to visit as a day's excursion from Mérida, or en route to the coast, or even as a day out from Cancún, as many tour buses do. But to do the ruins justice, you need to make an overnight stop – either at the site itself or in the nearby village of **Pisté** or in Valladolid, which is both convenient and inexpensive (see p.153).

Arrival and information

Arriving at Chichén Itzá, Hwy-180 *libre* curves around the site to the north, making an arc that merges with the site access road (the original highway straight through) at both ends. All first-class buses drive right up to the site entrance. All buses stop in Pisté as well, at one or both **bus stations**, on the east end of town (all buses) or the west end (second-class buses only). The rather grandly named Chichén Itzá International Airport, north of the ruins, is in fact a small **airstrip** that receives charter flights from the Caribbean coast.

The main **entry to the site** (daily winter 8am–5pm; summer 8am–6pm, last entry an hour earlier; M$166) is on the west side. A huge **visitor centre** (open until 10pm) houses a museum, restaurant, **ATM** and shops selling souvenirs, film, maps and guides. **Guided tours** of the ruins can be arranged here: private tours in one of four languages (Spanish, English, German or Italian) cost approximately M$480 and last ninety minutes; group tours cost a little less. You can also buy tickets and get in at the **smaller eastern gate** by the *Hotel Mayaland*. Here you can book two-hour **horseback trips** around the wilder, southern part of the site, Chichén Viejo (M$500 with guide), and across the road at *Hacienda Chichen*, naturalist Jim Conrad leads **plant walks** in the surrounding forest (ask at reception; price varies). A **sound-and-light-show** in Spanish runs nightly (7pm in winter, 8pm in summer; included in price of day entrance ticket, or M$69 alone). It's a bit of a yawn, but it does briefly recreate the shadow-serpent effect

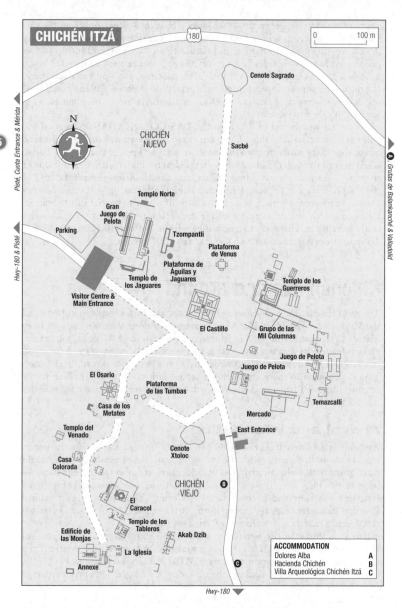

CHICHÉN ITZÁ

180

0   100 m

N

Cenote Sagrado

CHICHÉN
NUEVO

Sacbé

Templo Norte

Gran
Juego de
Pelota

Parking

Tzompantli

Plataforma
de Venus

Plataforma de
Águilas y
Jaguares

Templo de los
Guerreros

Templo de
los Jaguares

Visitor Centre &
Main Entrance

El Castillo

Grupo de las
Mil Columnas

Juego de Pelota

El Osario

Juego de Pelota

Plataforma
de las Tumbas

Casa de los
Metates

Temazcalli

Templo del
Venado

Mercado

East Entrance

Casa
Colorada

Cenote
Xtoloc

CHICHÉN
VIEJO

B

El
Caracol

Edificio de
las Monjas

Templo de los
Tableros

Akab Dzib

La Iglesia

Annexe

C

ACCOMMODATION
Dolores Alba   A
Hacienda Chichén   B
Villa Arqueológica Chichén Itzá   C

Pisté, Cuota Entrance & Mérida

Hwy-180 & Pisté

A, Grutas de Balankanché & Valladolid

Hwy-180

(see p.165) on the stairs of El Castillo, and it's the only thing to do in the evening; wear lots of bug spray.

About 3km west of Chichén Itzá, **Pisté** is a rather scraggly village strung out along the road. Its main function is providing visitors with accommodation (see opposite), so they can get up early enough to beat the buses that arrive at the ruins around 10.30am. There's an **internet** café here, opposite the **bus station** at the east end of town.

Accommodation

Visitors to Chichén Itzá have a choice of staying in a handful of more expensive **hotels** immediately **east of the ruins** (all but one are on the short access road off Hwy-180, signposted "Zona Hotelera"), or along the main street in the town of **Pisté**, to the west of the site. In Pisté, most hotels are on the main road, between the village and the ruins, so it's easy to shop around for the best deal – though quality can be low and occupancy high; the reliable *posadas* have only a few rooms apiece. You can **camp** or hang a hammock at the *Pirámide Inn* (M\$50). You could also stay in Yokdzonot (see p.167), though in this case, it helps to have a car.

Near the ruins

Dolores Alba Hwy-180 *libre* Km 122, 2km east of Chichén Itzá east entrance ☎985/858-1555, ⓦwww.doloresalba.com. The best-value hotel on either side of the ruins, with clean, colourful rooms, a good restaurant (see below) and two swimming pools, one built out of a natural spring. Transport is provided to the site (but not back); rates include breakfast. ❹

Hacienda Chichén Off Hwy-180, near the east entrance to the ruins ☎985/920-8407, ⓦwww.haciendachichen.com. Of the two luxury choices at the Chichén Itzá site (*Mayaland* is the other), this place has a more gracious feel, with wrought-iron furniture and plenty of greenery, as well as some small ruins within its grounds, and a resident naturalist who gives tours. Some rooms are in individual cottages that housed Carnegie Institution archeologists in the 1920s. ❾

Villa Arqueológica Chichén Itzá Off Hwy-180 *libre*, near the east entrance to the ruins ☎985/856-6000, ⓦwww.villasmex.com. Not as lavish as its neighbours, but comfortable enough, and handy to the site. The snug, thick-walled rooms (each with a double bed and a single bed) and suites (two small rooms) are set round a patio enclosing a pool and cocktail bar. ❺

In Pisté

Felix Inn Just west of *Posada Chac-Mool* ☎999/851-0033, ⓔhotelfelixinnchichenitza @hotmail.com. A welcome addition to Pisté's somewhat dreary hotel scene, the *Felix* is a sensible and sunny alternative to the hotels by the ruins. Clean a/c rooms are laid out around a pool, plus a restaurant, an internet café and wi-fi. ❹

Pirámide Inn Hwy-180 *libre* at the west end of town ☎985/851-0115, ⓦwww.chichen.com. Good rates, a pool and big gardens – but all fairly dilapidated (one-bed rooms have new mattresses at least). Recommendable only for its location – an easy walk to ruins, and right next to the bus station. ❸

Posada Kary West end of Pisté; from the bus stop, turn right off Hwy-180 *libre* just before the central intersection and plaza ☎985/851-0208. Look for the pink trim on this building with six sunny rooms – walls are a little smudged, but good value, and a choice of fan or a/c. ❷

Posada Maya West end of Pisté, next to *Posada Kary* ☎985/851-0211. Just past *Kary* on a side street, this place, with eight rooms, is an even better deal – though you don't get a toilet seat. Rooms can be a little dark but are livened up with groovy wood-block prints on the pastel walls. ❷

Posada Olalde On C 6 south of the main road ☎985/851-0086. The basic rooms, with fans and hot water, can be a bit dim, but they're clean. This is one of the quieter spots, since it's off the main road. Calle 6 is about two-thirds of the way through town coming from the east-side bus stop; turn left (south) across from *Posada Carrousel*. ❷

Eating and drinking

For refreshment near the ruins, the **restaurant** at the *Dolores Alba* is good and affordable, and diners can use the pool. Across the road is the package-tour stop *Parque Ikkil* (daily 8am–6pm; M\$60), which is more appealing for its large Sagrado Azul **cenote** than its massive buffet restaurant. If you have your own car, or don't mind hopping on a second-class bus, you could also visit **Cenote Yokdzonot** (see p.167) and its small restaurant, a little west of Pisté.

In Pisté, the best dining options include *Restaurante San Antonio*, opposite the east-end bus station – it serves a daily stew special and has nice outdoor seating. *Las Mestizas*, farther west, on the south side of the road, serves some good regional cuisine. At the west end of town, several *loncherías* serve comida corrida for about M$45; they're also open in the evenings, with lighter meals. For **coffee** and sandwiches, *La Casa del Caffé*, on the north side of the road on the west side of town, is a surprising little oasis of urban cool, with decent espresso.

The site

Though in most minds **Chichén Itzá** represents the very image of the Maya, it's actually the city's sharp divergence from Maya tradition that makes it archeologically intriguing. Experts are fairly certain that the city was established around 300 AD and began to flourish in the Terminal Classic period (between 800 and 925 AD). The rest of its history, as well as the roots of the Itzá clan that consolidated power in the peninsula here after 925, remain disputed. Much of the evidence at the site – an emphasis on human sacrifice, the presence of a huge ball-court and the glorification of military activity – points to a strong influence from central Mexico. For decades researchers guessed this was the result of the city's being invaded and conquered by the Toltecs, a theory reinforced by the resemblance of the Templo de los Guerreros to the colonnade at Tula, near Mexico City. They also found Toltec-style pottery remains and numerous depictions of the Toltec god-king, the feathered serpent Quetzalcoatl (Kukulcán to the Maya).

Work since the 1980s, however, supports a theory that the Itzá people were not Toltec invaders, but fellow Maya who had migrated from the south (which explains why their subjects refer to them as "foreigners" in texts). The Toltec artefacts, this view holds, arrived in central Yucatán via the Itzás' chief trading partners, the **Chontal Maya**, who maintained allegiances with Toltecs in Central Mexico and Oaxaca.

The old highway that used to pass through the site is now a path dividing the ruins in two: the Itzá-era **Chichén Nuevo** (New or "Toltec" Chichén) to the north and Terminal Classic **Chichén Viejo** (Old Chichén) to the south. If it's still reasonably early in the day, head first to the north.

Chichén Nuevo

Most buildings in this area, including the central **Castillo** pyramid, the **Templo de los Guerreros** and an enormous **ball-court**, date from the city's peak, sometime during the Post-Classic period, between 925 and 1200 AD. They have all been very well excavated and restored, though the methods employed in the 1920s by the Carnegie Institution's archeologists relied perhaps a bit more on imagination than academic rigour, according to contemporary critics.

El Castillo

The main path leads directly to **El Castillo** (also called the Pyramid of Kukulcán), the structure that sits alone in the centre of a great grassy plaza. At 25m high, it doesn't compare with larger structures at Cobá and Calakmul, but its simple lines and monumental stairways ascending each face (two of which are restored) rise precipitously to a temple at the top. (Visitors are not allowed to climb, unfortunately.)

The design's simplicity is deceptive, however, as a numerological analysis of the building suggests that it is the **Maya calendar** rendered in stone: each staircase has 91 steps, which, added to the single step at the main entrance to the temple, amounts to 365, the number of days in a solar year. On each face, the central staircase divides 9 terraces into 18, the number of months in the Maya solar year. Additionally, 52, the number of stone panels on each face, is deeply symbolic, representing the number of years required for the two Maya calendar systems (the solar year and the 260-day year) to align and repeat. Most remarkably, the stones are set so that near sunset on the spring and autumn equinoxes, the great heads of the feathered serpent Kukulcán, which are carved into the foot of the main staircase, are joined to the carved tails at the top of the building by an undulating shadow resembling a snake's body. This event lasts just a few hours and draws spectators and awed worshippers by the thousands.

Inside El Castillo an **earlier pyramid** survives almost intact, and at the top of it, in a sort of hidden sanctuary, archeologists discovered one of the greatest treasures at the site: an **altar**, or perhaps a throne, in the form of a jaguar, painted bright red and inset with jade "spots" and eyes.

The "Toltec" plaza

El Castillo marks one edge of a **plaza** that formed the focus of Chichén Nuevo, and in addition to a *sacbé* leading to **Cenote Sagrado**, all its most important buildings are here, many displaying a strong Toltec influence in their structure and decoration. The **Templo de los Guerreros** (Temple of the Warriors), lined on two sides by the **Grupo de las Mil Columnas** (Group of the Thousand Columns), forms the eastern edge of the plaza. These are the structures that most recall the great Toltec site of Tula, both in design and in detail – in particular the colonnaded courtyard (which would have been roofed with some form of thatch) and the use of Atlantean columns representing battle-dressed warriors, their arms raised above their heads. The temple is richly decorated on its north and south sides with carvings and sculptures of jaguars and eagles devouring human hearts, feathered serpents, warriors and, the one undeniably Maya feature, masks of the rain god Chac, with his curling snout. On top (now visible only at a distance, as you can no longer climb the structure) are two superb examples of figures called **Chac-mools**, once thought to be introduced by the Toltecs: offerings were placed on the stomachs of these reclining figures, which are thought to represent either the messengers who would take the sacrifice to the gods or perhaps the divinities themselves. The "thousand" columns alongside originally formed a square, on the far side of which is the building known as the **Mercado**, although there's no evidence that this actually was a marketplace. Near here, too, is a small, dilapidated ball-court.

Walking west across the plaza from El Castillo, you pass the **Plataforma de Venus**, a raised block with a stairway up each side guarded by feathered serpents. Here, rites associated with Quetzalcoatl when he took the form of Venus, the morning star, would have been carried out. Slightly smaller, but otherwise identical in design, the adjacent **Plataforma de Águilas y Jaguares** features reliefs of eagles and jaguars holding human hearts. Human sacrifices may have been carried out here, judging by the proximity of a third platform, the **Tzompantli**, where victims' heads likely hung on display. This is carved on every side with grotesque grinning stone skulls.

The Gran Juego de Pelota and the Templo de los Jaguares

Chichén Itzá's **Gran Juego de Pelota**, on the west side of the plaza, is the largest known ball-court in existence, with walls some 90m long. Its design is a capital "I" surrounded by temples, with the goals, or target rings, halfway along each side. Along the bottom of each side runs a sloping **panel** decorated with scenes of the game. Although the rules and full significance of the game remain a mystery, it was clearly not a Saturday afternoon kick-about in the park; for more on the game's significance, see p.288. On the panel, the players are shown proceeding from either side towards a central circle, the symbol of death. One player, just right of the centre (whether it's the winning or losing captain is up for debate) has been decapitated, while another holds his head and a ritual knife. Along the top runs the stone body of a snake; heads stick out at either end. The court has a whispering-gallery effect, which enables you to be heard clearly at the far end of the court, and to hear what's going on there.

The **Templo de los Jaguares** overlooks the playing area from the east side. At the bottom – effectively the outer wall of the ball-court – is a little portico supported by two pillars, between which a stone jaguar stands sentinel. The outer wall panels, the left and the right of the interior space, are carved with the images of Pawahtuns, the gods who supported the sky and who are thought to be the patrons of the Itzá people. Inside are some worn but elaborate relief carvings of the Itzá ancestors inserted in the Maya creation myth – a powerful demonstration of their entitlement to rule.

Cenote Sagrado

The **Cenote Sagrado** lies at the end of the *sacbé* that leads about 300m off the north side of the plaza. It's an almost perfectly round hole in the limestone bedrock, some 60m in diameter and more than 30m deep, the bottom third full of water. It was thanks to this natural well (and another in the southern half of the site) that the city could survive. It gives Chichén Itzá its name, which is literally "at the edge of the well of the Itzá". The well was regarded as a portal to the underworld, called Xibalba, and the Maya threw in offerings such as statues, jade and engraved metal disks (a few of them gold), as well as human sacrifices – all of them boys, recent research has shown. People who were thrown in and survived were believed to have prophetic powers, having spoken with the gods.

Chichén Viejo

The **southern half of the site** is the most sacred part for contemporary Maya, though the buildings here are not in such good condition. They were built for the most part prior to 925 AD, in the architectural styles used in the Puuc and Chenes regions. A path leads from the south side of El Castillo to the major structures, passing first the pyramid **El Osario** (the Ossuary; also called the High Priest's Grave), the only building in this section that shows Toltec-style detail. Externally it is very similar to El Castillo, but inside a series of **tombs** was discovered. A shaft, first explored at the end of the nineteenth century, drops down from the top through five crypts, in each of which was found a skeleton and a trap door leading to the next. The fifth is at ground level, but here too was a trap door, and steps cut through the rock to a sixth chamber that opens onto a huge underground cavern: the burial place of the high priest.

Follow the main path and you arrive at **El Caracol** (the Snail, for its coiled shape), a circular, domed tower standing on two rectangular platforms and looking remarkably like a modern-day observatory. The roof has slits aligned with various points of astronomical significance. Four doors at the cardinal points lead into the tower and a circular chamber. A spiral staircase leads to the upper level, where observations were made.

Immediately to the south, the so-called **Monjas** (Nunnery) palace complex shows several stages of construction. Part of the facade was blasted away in the nineteenth century, but it is nonetheless a building of grand proportions. Its **annexe**, on the east end, has an elaborate facade in the Chenes style, covered in small heads of Chac that combine to make one giant mask, with the door as a mouth. By contrast, **La Iglesia**, a small building standing beside the convent, is a clear demonstration of Puuc design, its low band of unadorned masonry around the bottom surmounted by an elaborate mosaic frieze and roofcomb. Masks of Chac again predominate, but above the doorway are also figures of the four mythological creatures that held up the sky – a snail, a turtle, an armadillo and a crab.

South of Las Monjas, a path leads, after about ten minutes, to a further group of ruins that are among the oldest on the site, although they are unrestored; this is a good area for birdwatching, with few people around to disturb the wildlife. Just east of Las Monjas, is the **Akab Dzib**, a relatively plain block of palace rooms that takes its name ("Obscure Writings") from undeciphered hieroglyphs found inside. Red palm prints – frequently found in Maya buildings – adorn the walls of some of the chambers. Backtrack along the main path to the building opposite El Osario, the **Plataforma de las Tumbas**, a funerary structure topped with small columns; behind it is a jungle path that heads back to the main east–west road via the site's other water source, Cenote Xtoloc.

Around Chichén Itzá: Grutas de Balankanché

Just 1.6km east of the *Dolores Alba* hotel (see p.163), the **Grutas de Balankanché** are a refreshingly cool way to pass an hour. These damp caverns were reopened in 1959, when a sealed passageway was discovered, revealing a path to an underground altar to Chac. Tours with taped commentary (in English daily 11am, 1pm & 3pm; M$95) lead past an underground pool, stalagmites and stalactites to a huge rock formation that resembles a ceiba, the Maya tree of life. Around its base lie many of the original Maya offerings, such as clay pots in the shapes of gods' faces. Second-class **buses** between Valladolid and Mérida will drop you at *las grutas*, or you can catch a **colectivo** from Calle 44 in Valladolid. A taxi from Pisté should cost about M$50.

West to Mérida

Moving on from Chichén Itzá and Pisté, the most direct route to Mérida is along Hwy-180, where you pass through the village of **Yokdzonot**, known for its appealing cenote. Or you can make a detour to **Izamal**, dominated by a beautiful sixteenth-century Franciscan mission, and past the ruins of **Aké**, set on a working henequen plantation.

Yokdzonot

Fourteen kilometres west of Pisté on the *libre* road on Hwy-180, the village of **Yokdzonot** is known for its well-kept **cenote** (9am–6pm; M$60). It has excellent facilities, with good showers and restrooms. You can rent snorkel gear (M$25), dine at a small **restaurant** serving excellent *poc-chuc* and *panuchos*, take a **bike tour** to another cenote (M$60; 1hr) and even **camp** overnight (M$200, tent included). If you have a car, this is an easy refresher after the ruins; by bus, it's not quite as handy, but any second-class service will stop on request at the town plaza. The cenote is about 350m south.

On the north side of the road in Yokdzonot, signs point to another **lodging** option, *Yucatan Mayan Retreat* (Ⓦ www.yucatanmayanretreat.webs.com; ❹), a small operation with something for everyone: a surprisingly plush apartment (for up to six people), a rustic palapa (for up to four) and a comfy tent with an airbed (for two). Rates are great for groups or families, as you're not charged more for extra people; you must book ahead online.

Izamal

The exceptionally scenic small town of **IZAMAL** makes a fine day visit or overnight stop, for its historic monuments, gracious feel and strong crafts tradition. It also has some kind of festivity happening for most of October through December. If you prefer the country to the city, Izamal can also be a good alternative to Mérida as a base for sightseeing. In this case, though, it's nice to have a car, as Izamal is served only by slow second-class buses.

Driving from Pisté, head west on Hwy-180 *libre* to Kantunil (where the *cuota* and the *libre* merge), then 18km north. To turn north, you actually have to follow signs for the *cuota* to Cancún, then make an awkward U-turn. If you're on the *cuota* heading west, look for a direct right turn off the highway immediately before Km 68. If you miss the turn (easy to do), you can continue to Hoctún, then backtrack from there. **By bus** from Chichén Itzá or Pisté, you must go to Valladolid (see p.157 for connecting bus times) or Mérida (see p.188), then transfer.

Arrival and information

Arriving at Izamal's **bus station**, on Calle 32 at Calle 33, you're one block back from (and within view of) one of the two central plazas, set corner-to-corner – walk straight out (east), and you're headed in the right direction. The **tourist office** (9am–6pm; ☎988/954-0096) is at the next corner (C 31 at the plaza); here and at most hotels, you can pick up a good **map** of the town. Also on the main plaza is a **post office** (Mon–Fri 8am–2.30pm), and in the north plaza is a Banorte **bank** with ATM. An **internet café** is on Calle 32, just south of the bus station. A **laundry** is on Calle 30 two blocks north of the north plaza. **Horse-drawn carriages** lined up around the plaza will take you for a pleasant *paseo* around the town (45min; M$100).

Leaving Izamal, buses run to Mérida (1–2hr) nearly every thirty minutes until 7.30pm; Oriente service is preferable to Centro because its terminal is closer to Mérida's centre. Buses go hourly to Valladolid (1hr 30min) and Cancún (5am–1am; 5hr).

Accommodation

As Izamal has become more of a tourist destination, quite a few hotels have opened, but the longer-established ones still offer the best value. The couple of hotels on or quite near the plaza are not great – the better ones are at least a few blocks away, and may require a taxi if you arrive by bus with lots of luggage.

Macan Ché B&B C 22, between C 33 and C 35 ☎988/954-0287, Ⓦ www.macanche .com. An assortment of comfortable cottages tucked among rambling gardens a few blocks east of the main plaza, with a small pool and space for yoga. Breakfast is included in the rates, and you can order dinner as well. ❹

Posada Flory C 30 at C 27 ☎988/954-0562. A bargain, with ten welcoming, if somewhat small, rooms; a/c is an option in a few. Very homely feel, with a chatty, hospitable woman owner. Look for it a block north off the north plaza. ❷

Posada Los Arcos C 30 at C 23
☎988/954-0261. Formerly the town's no-tell motel, this place was renovated in 2010 and is great value, as it has a pool. Rooms are a bit basic and fluorescent-lit, but all have a/c and fan. ❷

Santo Domingo C 18, between C 33 and C 35
☎988/967-6136, �🖥www.izamalhotel.com. This collection of rooms and palapa-roof bungalows (the latter with shared bath) has a great rural feel (goats and horses roam the grounds), as well as a pool, restaurant and wi-fi. It's near the southeast edge of town – still walkable to the centre, but perhaps better with a car. Breakfast included. ❹

The Town

The most immediately striking thing about Izamal is that all of its buildings are painted a rich ochre, which positively glows in the setting sun. Ancient Izamal was an important religious centre for the Maya, where they worshipped **Itzamná**, mythical founder of the ancient city and one of the gods of creation, at a series of huge pyramid-temples of the same name. Most are now no more than low mounds in the surrounding country, but several survive in the town itself and are fascinating to see right in the middle of the residential grid; some businesses on the plazas have pyramids literally in their backyards. The largest pile, the partly restored **Kinich Kakmó** (daily 8am–8pm; free), dedicated to the sun god, is a couple of blocks north of the two central plazas.

Early in the colonial period, the Franciscans sought to establish Izamal as the centre of their religious leadership. In 1552 Fray Diego de Landa (later responsible for the vicious inquisition and auto-da-fé in Maní) lopped the top off a pyramid and began building the grand **Convento de San Antonio de Padua** (daily; free). Its porticoed yard occupies some 24,000 square metres and looks down over the town's two plazas: the main one at the front (the west side), and a second one north of the convent.

When the complex was completed in 1561, de Landa consecrated it with one of two statues of the Virgin that he had brought from Guatemala. Several years later, when church leaders from Valladolid attempted to claim the statue, it is said to have become impossibly heavy, and they were forced to leave it in Izamal. In light of this and numerous other presumed miracles, a cult developed that draws pilgrims from all over the peninsula, even though the original statue burned in 1829 and had to be replaced by its twin. She is now the official patroness of the Yucatán; on a visit to the town in 1993, Pope John Paul II gave her a silver crown. During the **fiesta** dedicated to the Virgin on December 8, penitents climb the monastery's staircase on their knees, and worshippers sing in the church the entire night before. The statue is on view in the *camarín*, a chapel around the back of the main altar. Next to the chapel, the **Museo Santuario de Nuestra Señora** (Tues–Sat 10am–1pm & 3–6pm, Sun 9am–4pm; M$5 donation) includes many elaborate gowns that have clothed the statue, including a silver lamé number from 1974. In the evenings, a **sound-and-light show** (Mon–Sat at 8.30pm; M$85) is projected on the front facade of the main church. Fray Diego looks on from his post on a pedestal in the plaza on the north side of the monastery.

The town's artisans – master wood-carvers, papier-mâché artists, hammock-weavers and more – have become an attraction in themselves, thanks to a well-organized programme that promotes their work. The core of the project is the beautifully done **Centro Cultural y Artesanal** (Mon–Sat 10am–8pm; M$20), where a museum showcases craftwork from all over Mexico, organized by medium, with a wing devoted to Yucatecan specialities. It houses a small café (peek behind to see some pyramid remnants), a quiet, perfumed back room where you can get a foot massage and a nice shop. You can also **rent bicycles** (M$40/2hr) here, for visiting the various **artists' workshops** around town, all signposted and marked on the tourist-office map. It's all a very casual arrangement, and a great opportunity to chat with some talented locals, such as the charming Don Esteban, on Calle 26 at Calle 45, who makes jewellery from henequen spines, and Agustín Colli, on Calle 19, between calles 24 and 26, whose double-weave hammocks are positively luxurious (and well worth the M$700 or so).

If you've caught craft fever, also check Hecho a Mano, a particularly good craft and **folk-art shop** stocked with everything from Mexican wrestling masks to Huichol yarn paintings. Hours (Mon–Sat 10am–2pm & 4–7pm) can be erratic, however.

Eating and drinking

For lunch, the palapa-roof *Kinich* on Calle 27, between calles 28 and 30, is a good traditional **restaurant**, even if it is a top tour-group destination. Women pat tortillas by hand, and the Yucatecan dishes like *poc-chuc* are very well priced. In the evening, *El Toro*, on Calle 30 just east of the convent, also has a hearty traditional menu of dishes like *chaya* tamales and *queso relleno*. Of the **snack bars** on the north plaza, *Los Arcos* makes enormous tortas and delicious fresh fruit drinks. From morning till mid-afternoon, the **market**, off the south side of the main plaza, is busy with snack stands, a few of which serve a comida corrida.

Aké

Midway between Izamal and Mérida on the back road via Cacalchén, the **Aké ruins** (9am–5pm; M$37) are interesting to see because they're partially integrated into an inhabited village and working henequen plantation. Aké was probably in alliance with the old city of Izamal, as it is linked to it by one of the peninsula's largest *sacbeob*. The most impressive building here is the **Edificio de las Pilastras**, a large platform topped with more than twenty stone pillars. The Maya rubble intermingles with San Lorenzo de Aké, a henequen **hacienda**, which, though a bit run-down, is still a fine example of neo-French architecture from the end of the nineteenth century. You're welcome to wander through the machinery to see the fibre-making process. North of the henequen plant, a church has been built on top of one of the old Maya temples. An Auto Centro **bus** makes the 45-minute trip from Mérida or Izamal, passing by the ruins six times daily, roughly every three hours; the last bus to Mérida is theoretically at 8pm, but be sure to confirm this before setting off. If you're driving from Izamal, turn south in Euan. From Hwy-180, there's now a direct route off the north side, opposite Tahmek.

Coming from Izamal, before you reach Aké, about 6km west of the village of Cacalchén, you pass *Hacienda San José* (☎999/910-4617, ⓦwww.luxurycollection .com; ⑨), good for a lavish **lunch** and a nice spot to take in the excellent birdlife in this area. It's also a gorgeous place to **lodge**.

6

Mérida and around

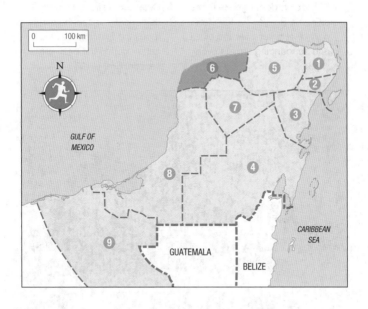

CHAPTER 6

Highlights

✳ **Catedral de San Ildefonso**
The first cathedral built in the
Americas is the site of a major
pilgrimage in September and
October. See p.181

✳ **Palacio de Gobierno** Inside
the Yucatán governor's offices
in Mérida, Fernando Castro
Pacheco's stirring modernist
murals depict local history.
See p.182

✳ **Mérida en domingo** Be in the
city on a Sunday for the street
party that takes over the plaza
and surrounding streets every
week. See p.187

✳ **Dzibilchaltún** The temple at
this Maya ruin north of Mérida
aligns perfectly with the
sunrise on the equinoxes.
See p.190

✳ **Gulf coast beaches** All of
Mérida decamps here in the
summer, but the rest of
the year you'll probably
have the sand to yourself.
See p.191

✳ **Celestún** Visitors flock
here mainly to see the thirty
thousand flamingos that
gather during the peak winter
season. See p.193

▲ Palacio de Gobierno, Mérida

6

Mérida and around

The capital of Yucatán State and the largest city on the peninsula, Mérida is modern and prosperous, but it is also distinctly proud of its past and its mix of Maya and Spanish heritage. Its historic central district, filled with old courtyard houses, is well kept without feeling like a museum piece, and the oldest cathedral in the Americas stands proud by the plaza. As the region's cultural centre, it has a busy schedule of music and dance (both traditional and modern), as well as the best weekend street party – every weekend – anywhere on the peninsula.

Even with all the activity, it's a far more sedate and relaxing city than you might expect – it's hardly the teeming Mexican metropolis of the imagination. There's enough to occupy you for at least four days, if not longer, and it serves as a great base for easy day- or weekend trips – aided by a non-stop flow of buses in and out.

Most visitors use Mérida as a base for trips to the great Maya sites of Uxmal and Chichén Itzá (see p.200 & p.161) as well as the scenic Maya ruins along the Ruta Puuc that loops south of the city (see p.204). But the city's also near the beach. About a half-hour's drive straight north, the resort town of **Progreso** functions as Mérida's collective patio in the summertime and during Semana Santa. Otherwise, it's virtually a ghost town, with green water lapping at the shore and only a few travellers lolling on the sand; some "snowbird" Americans maintain winter retreats here, but mostly this is not a heavily touristed area.

The whole **Gulf coast**, a bit to the west but largely to the east, is dotted with vacation homes and a few fishing villages. The ancient Maya settled here in cities like **Dzibilchaltún**, where the temple is aligned with the rising equinox sun. On-site is a sophisticated museum, which displays a collection of Maya and Spanish art and artefacts that show a powerful picture of the interaction between the two peoples from the Conquest to the present. Thanks to the *salinas*, or salt flats, in this marshy area, the ancient Maya were able to harvest and trade one of the great treasures of their time. The area is also rich with birdlife. All along the coast highway in the evening, flamingos and great herons wing home. You'll see even more flamingos if you go west of Mérida to the **Ría Celestún Biosphere Reserve**, a long strip along the west-coast Gulf waters where the pink birds roost year-round.

Mérida

In every sense the leading city of the peninsula, **MÉRIDA** bears the nickname "La Ciudad Blanca" (the white city) even though its sprawl of one- and two-storey buildings, once bare white limestone, are now covered in peeling layers of gem-coloured paint. Bus traffic rumbles down its stone streets, but it

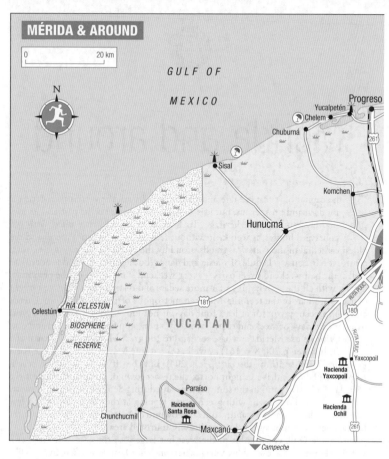

somehow remains a calm and likeable place, with a small-town geniality despite its population of more than a million. Come dusk, the curving loveseats that dot the numerous parks fill with pairs of lovers, young and old. But don't mistake Mérida for a sleepy backwater: the cultural scene ranges from free traditional entertainment every night of the week to avant-garde dance festivals, foreign films, contemporary art exhibitions and lively theatre performances. The events draw young people and older ones, often in Mérida's version of formalwear – the embroidered *huipil* for ladies and the white guayabera shirt for gents.

This winning combination of cosmopolitanism and graciousness (and cheap real estate) has appealed to expats and Mexicans fleeing larger, more chaotic metro areas. Many of them come to live the dream of renovating one of the fine old buildings in the historic centre – which, in practical terms, means there's a vast selection of B&Bs. But even as Mérida develops as a "hot" scene, the city retains the grace and manners of the past. Seemingly every street in the centre boasts a well-maintained colonial church or museum, and locals still ride in the little horse-drawn taxis that gather by the plaza in the evenings.

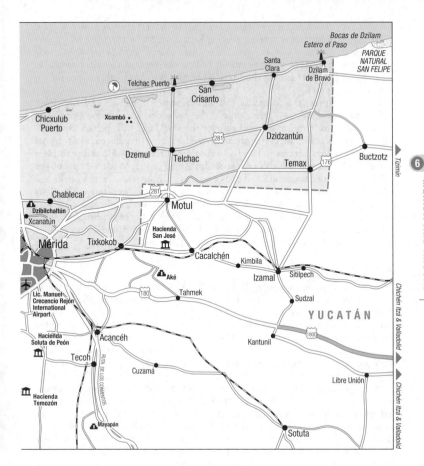

Some history

Founded on January 6, 1542, by conquistador **Francisco de Montejo the Younger** (who also established Campeche), Mérida was the product of a bloody, drawn-out struggle between the Spanish and the local Maya. It was built over, and partly from, the ruins of a Maya city known as **T'hó**, or Ichcansihó, and was intended from the start to be the Spanish capital in the Yucatán. Despite some impressive initial construction around the plaza, however, the city was never a jewel in Spain's crown, largely because the Yucatán contained no gold or other natural wealth. Colonists struggled along with what resources they had: land and forced Maya labour. They established sugarcane and maize plantations outside the city, and looked longingly back to Europe for influence.

It was the *meridanos'* desperate squeezing of the Maya people that sparked the **Caste Wars**, beginning with small uprisings in 1847 and gaining momentum in the spring of 1849, when, in a surprise attack, rebel Maya armies besieged Mérida. They were within a hair's breadth of capturing it and thus regaining control of the peninsula (most of the Spanish populace fled to Sisal on the coast, hoping to board ships and return to Europe), but, according to legend, the Maya peasant fighters decided they could no longer neglect their fields and left the siege lines to plant corn. In truth, historians have no real explanation for why the Maya let victory slip from their grasp. The Yucatecan elite, once spared, quickly arranged a deal with the central Mexican government, ceding the peninsula's independence in exchange for support against the Maya rebellions, which nonetheless ground on for some fifty years.

In the meantime, the *hacendados* (plantation owners) finally found the riches they'd been seeking, in "green gold": the henequen plant, which produced valuable fibre for rope, in demand all over the world (see box, p.200). By 1900, Mérida had become an extraordinarily wealthy city, influenced more by its European trading partners (a standard French ship route was Marseilles to New York via Havana and Mérida's port at Sisal) than by central Mexico. Many of the houses built in the nineteenth and early twentieth centuries use French bricks and tiles, brought over as tradable ballast in ships that exported henequen. The city's wealthy fancied themselves living in "the Paris of Mexico", and commonly sent their children to be schooled in Europe. Today, even with the henequen trade all but dead (it petered out around World War II, when nylon became the material of choice), the city remains elegant, bustling and intellectual.

Arrival

Mérida is laid out on a simple **grid**: like all Yucatán towns, even-numbered streets run north–south and odd from east to west, with the central **Plaza de la Independencia** bounded by calles 60, 61, 62 and 63. Mérida has two main **bus stations**, both on the southwest side of town. The **Terminal CAME**, reserved for express and first-class services from ADO, ADO GL and ADO Platino, is on Calle 70, between calles 69 and 71. You'll arrive here if you're coming directly from Cancún, Campeche or Chichén Itzá. The **TAME** (officially the Terminal de Segunda Clase), across the street on Calle 69, between calles 68 and 70, deals with ATS, Mayab, Sur and some Oriente buses. The latter station has **luggage-storage** service (at a window outside, facing the CAME entrance), and both have **tourist information** booths. Some deluxe buses from Cancún arrive at the **Fiesta Americana** hotel, north of the centre off Paseo de Montejo at Colón. City buses don't go all the way from the bus stations to the Plaza Mayor; a **taxi** costs about M$30, or it's a twenty-minute walk. Bus lines not mentioned here arrive at smaller terminals around the city – see box, p.188 for details.

The Lic. Manuel Crecencio Rejón **airport** (☎999/946-1530, ⓦwww.asur.com.mx) is 7km southwest of the centre and has a **tourist office** (usually open late to meet the last arriving flights), major car-rental outlets, an ADO ticket booth and a post office, plus long-distance phones and ATMs. To get downtown, take a taxi from the stand at the front: buy a ticket (M$140 to the centre) at the desk outside; you may be asked to share with another passenger, but the ticket price is for the whole car, not per person. You could also walk straight out and across the parking lot and wait for bus #79 ("Aviación"; M$6); it runs only every 45 minutes or so, though not reliably after 7pm. *Combis* (marked "Uman") run more frequently along the main road outside the airport, but it's a 500m walk (bear right outside the airport), and they have little room for luggage; look for the stop immediately to your right when you reach Avenida Itzáes. Both the *combis* and the #79 bus drop off at Parque San Juan, about a ten-minute walk from the central plaza.

Information and tours

Yucatán State's main **tourist offices** (daily 8am–9pm; ☎999/924-9290, ⓦwww.yucatan.travel) are in the Palacio de Gobierno, on the plaza, and in Teatro Peón

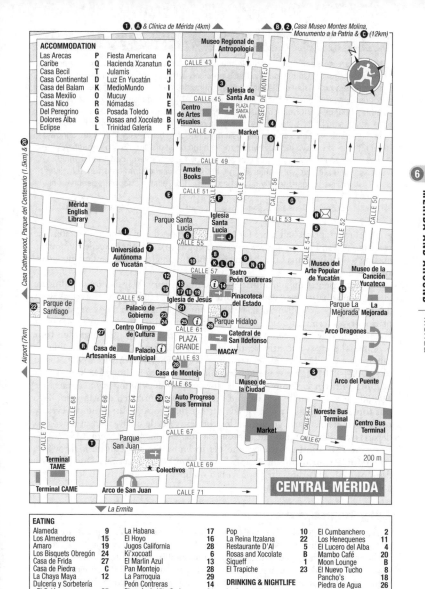

ACCOMMODATION

Las Arecas	P	Fiesta Americana	A
Caribe	Q	Hacienda Xcanatun	C
Casa Becil	T	Julamis	H
Casa Continental	D	Luz En Yucatán	J
Casa del Balam	K	MedioMundo	I
Casa Mexilio	O	Mucuy	N
Casa Nico	R	Nómadas	E
Del Peregrino	G	Posada Toledo	M
Dolores Alba	S	Rosas and Xocolate	B
Eclipse	L	Trinidad Galería	F

CENTRAL MÉRIDA

0   200 m

EATING

Alameda	9	La Habana	17	Pop	10
Los Almendros	15	El Hoyo	16	La Reina Itzalana	22
Amaro	19	Jugos California	28	Restaurante D'Al	5
Los Bisquets Obregón	24	Ki'xocoatl	6	Rosas and Xocolate	B
Casa de Frida	27	El Marlin Azul	13	Siqueff	1
Casa de Piedra	C	Pan Montejo	28	El Trapiche	23
La Chaya Maya	12	La Parroquia	29		
Dulcería y Sorbetería		Peón Contreras	14	**DRINKING & NIGHTLIFE**	
El Colón	25	Pizzería de Vito Corleone	21	La Casa de Todos	7

El Cumbanchero	2
Los Henequenes	11
El Lucero del Alba	4
Mambo Café	20
Moon Lounge	1
El Nuevo Tucho	8
Pancho's	18
Piedra de Agua	26
La Quilla	3

Contreras, on Calle 60 (enter on Calle 57-A). There's usually at least one English-speaker on hand, and the staff are equipped to answer the most obscure questions. The city has its own, slightly less savvy tourism bureau (Mon–Sat 8am–8pm; Sun 8am–2pm; ☎ 999/942-0000, ext 80199, ⓦ www.merida.gob.mx/turismo), in the municipal building on the west side of the plaza. For general info, though, a free copy of the very thorough *Yucatán Today* magazine (ⓦ www.yucatantoday.com)

The only scam in the Yucatán?

People are so genuinely friendly in the Yucatán that it's easy to lose your normal traveller's guard. Unfortunately, that's precisely what the craft salesmen of Mérida are counting on. They circle the blocks around the park, introducing themselves to tourists as students or government employees. They'll usually mention that there's a Maya dance performance that night, or some other event, then make quite a bit of other small talk before mentioning there's a good craft shop nearby, run by some village women's cooperative. And it's about to close – for lunch, for Sunday, for a three-day Maya holiday, whatever – so the pressure's on! Soon enough you're in some second-floor room crammed with low-grade, overpriced tourist trinkets. As scams go, it hardly qualifies as one, but it is a nuisance that unfortunately gives this otherwise tourist-friendly city a bad name. For reliable shopping destinations, see p.184.

provides maps, prices and more for Mérida and most destinations in the state. The website Yucatan Living (Ⓦ www.yucatanliving.com) is another excellent resource, posting a weekly events calendar and commenting on local bars, restaurants, news and cultural items.

For basic orientation and a little architectural history, Mérida's tourism bureau gives an informative **free walking tour** (though the guide appreciates tips) every day but Sunday, at 9.30am; make reservations at the office, on the west side of the plaza. Or you can rent headsets for a self-guided **audio tour** anytime (M$80). If you're curious what's behind all the brightly painted facades, take a **garden tour** of some the city's recently renovated mansions, run by the Mérida English Library, on Calle 53, between calles 66 and 68 (Nov–April Wed 9.45am; Ⓣ 999/924-8401, Ⓦ www.meridaenglishlibrary.com/tours.htm; M$200). A tour by **horse-drawn carriage** (*calesa*) is slow-paced but relaxing; typical rates are M$250 for a 45-minute trip around the centre and up Paseo de Montejo. Two **bus tours** cover similar routes, going further than you'd walk: avoid the eyesore red double-deckers and go instead for the festive little open-sided number that departs from Parque Santa Lucía (Mon–Sat 10am, 1pm, 4pm & 7pm; Ⓣ 999/927-6119; M$75). Another great way to get to know the city culture is through a **street-food tour** with the deeply knowledgeable chef at Los Dos (Ⓦ www.los-dos.com; US$195; 5hr); you visit a number of excellent stalls, the market and a *cocina económica* for lunch.

City transport

Driving a **car** in Mérida is more trouble than it's worth – parking is scarce, and virtually everything is in walking distance of the centre. You can probably get by without using a **bus** either – the system is remarkably convoluted. The only buses you're likely to take advantage of are those that run up Paseo de Montejo (look for them on Calle 56 north of Calle 55 – most will say "Gran Plaza" on the windscreen). In general, you can flag down buses at any corner; fares are posted on a green sticker by the door – usually M$6. A small free bus called the Circuito Enlace makes a loop around the centre, clockwise on calles 59, 54, 69 and 64, starting from Parque Hidalgo and stopping at the market, the city museum and Parque San Juan; unlike other buses, it stops only at dedicated points. For **taxis**, those waiting at Parque Hidalgo, Parque San Juan and other stands around town use zone fares; anywhere within the centre, as far as Avenida Itzáes, is M$40. Other, roving cars (marked "Taximetro") use meters, so they can be cheaper for short trips; you can hail them on the street or call for one at Ⓣ 999/928-3030.

If you're accustomed to riding in traffic, a **bicycle** can be an excellent way to see the city – catch a little breeze, and get to the furthest sights with ease. For an easier, car-free excursion, join the Sunday-morning **Bici–Ruta**, when many of the streets downtown, as well as Paseo de Montejo, are closed, and the streets fill with bike riders, performers and more. Bikes are available for rent on the plaza, just for the morning; the rest of the time, contact La Bicicletería (☎999/928-2383 or mobile 999/234-3325).

Accommodation

Although Mérida can get crowded at peak times, you should always be able to find a room. Unless you have a very early bus to catch, there's no point in staying in the grimier area near the **bus stations**, nor in the generic upmarket hotels on **Paseo de Montejo**. The more desirable options are all within a few blocks of the central plaza. In addition to the usual hotels, Mérida has a glut of excellent **B&Bs** and smaller inns in converted old homes complete with vintage tile floors and lofty ceilings. A glamorous option is to stay in a **rental house** from Urbano Rentals (⊛www.urbanorentals.com); they vary in price, but can be quite reasonable if you're travelling with a group or family. A more rural alternative is to stay outside town in a **hacienda**. The closest one is listed here; you may also consider the guesthouse at *Hacienda Yaxcopoil* (see p.198). **Hostels** come and go in Mérida, but long-established *Nómadas* (☎999/924-5223), on Calle 62 at Calle 51, is still backpacker heaven, with clean dorms (M$110) and private rooms (❷), plus music every night, organized tours, even a pool.

Las Arecas C 59 no. 541, between C 66 and C 68 ☎999/928-3626, ⊛www.lasarecas.com. Small, colonial-style guesthouse (one of the few run by a *meridano*) that's a fantastic bargain. Rooms around the small garden courtyard are simply furnished, but four of the five have a/c, and there's wi-fi throughout the house. ❸

Caribe C 59 no. 500, Parque Hidalgo ☎999/924-9022, ⊛www.hotelcaribe.com.mx. One block from the plaza, on a pretty, small square of its own. Rooms don't have any particular flair, but the views of the cathedral and plaza from the rooftop pool are lovely. There's also a travel agency and (paid) parking on site. ❹

Casa Becil C 67 no. 550-C, between C 66 and C 68 ☎999/924-6764, ⊛www.hotelcasabecil.com.mx. This small hotel needs a fresh coat of paint, but the staff are helpful, and it's close to the main bus stations. A few rooms have a/c, and there's a kitchen guests can use. ❷

Casa Continental C 47 at C 56 ☎999/924-1401, ⊛www.hotelcasacontinental.com. Going just a bit farther from the plaza (still easily walkable, though), you get much more for your money at this modern-Maya-look business-class hotel with big, smartly designed rooms. Free wi-fi, continental breakfast; no pool, though. ❺

Casa del Balam C 60 no. 488, at C 57 ☎999/924-8844, ⊛www.hotelcasadelbalam.com. Good combo of colonial-house style – tiled floors, dark-wood furniture – with the amenities of a large hotel. Rooms have fridges and bathtubs, and there's a shady pool, a cosy bar and free parking. Full breakfast. ❼

Casa Mexilio C 68 no. 495, between C 57 and C 59 ☎999/928-2505, ⊛www.casamexilio.com. One of Mérida's real treasures, this long-established B&B is a fascinating labyrinth of individually decorated rooms, tranquil gardens, sun terraces and a pool. Excellent full breakfast. ❺

Casa Nico C 63, between C 66 and C 68 ☎999/286-8944, ⊛www.hostelcasanico.com. Nominally a hostel (beds in two dorms from M$135), but the eleven simple private rooms win out here. The setting is a colonial house with a pool in the centre. Definitely the best option near the bus station. ❷

Del Peregrino C 51 no. 488, between C 54 and C 56 ☎999/924-3007, ⊛www.hoteldelperegrino.com. A quiet, beautifully remodelled house, with an especially nice outdoor kitchen, *Del Peregrino* has tidy, simply furnished tile-floor rooms. Breakfast. ❹

Dolores Alba C 63 no. 464, between C 52 and C 54 ☎999/928-5650, ⊛www.doloresalba.com. Popular midrange place situated around two courtyards (one colonial-style, and one sporting a dazzling array of mirror glass) and a large swimming pool. Rooms in both sections have TV, phone and a/c. With parking, laundry facilities and more, you get a lot for your money, but the place is a bit out of the way. **④**

Eclipse C 57 no. 491, between C 58 and C 60 ☎999/923-1600, ⓦwww.eclipsehotel.com.mx. On colonial overload? Mérida's sole hip-and-modern hotel has spare white rooms, each with a different theme suggested with fabric accents and accessories (a lava lamp, a Warhol print). A glittery-tile pool sits in the centre, and a café was slated to open in early 2011. A/c, wi-fi and flatscreen TVs, of course. **⑤**

Fiesta Americana C 60 at Colón ☎999/942-1111, ⓦwww.fiestaamericana.com. Mérida's top business-class hotel, just off Montejo, is perfectly nice but a bit too far from the centre. We mention it primarily as a landmark – car rental agencies and a bus terminal are here too. **⑧**

Hacienda Xcanatun 12km north of Mérida on the road to Progreso ☎999/930-2140, ⓦwww .xcanatun.com. This eighteenth-century plantation house on lush grounds has been remade as a small, exclusive hotel with luxurious suites – some with baths hewn from local rock, some with hot tubs. There's also a full spa and a very good restaurant (see p.186). **⑨**

🏃 **Julamis** C 53 at C 54 ☎999/924-1818, ⓦwww.hoteljulamis.com. Owned (and decorated by) two Cuban artists, *Julamis* is a great opportunity to stay in a colonial house, for barely more than less-inspiring "budget" hotels. The six rooms and one apartment all have a/c, and mix modern style (sleek bathroom fixtures) with soaring ceilings and old tiled floors. Perks include free beers in the in-room fridges, and a plunge pool on the roof. Breakfast included. **④**

🏃 **Luz En Yucatán** C 55 no. 499, between C 58 and C 60 ☎999/924-0035, ⓦwww .luzenyucatan.com. Delightful rambling place with fifteen rooms to suit every traveller: studios, kitchenettes, private terraces or patios (and even a whole rental house just down the street). Pool,

wi-fi, kitchen – and owners who were once tour guides, so well attuned to guests' needs. **⑤**

MedioMundo C 55 no. 533, between C 64 and C 66 ☎999/924-5472, ⓦwww.hotelmediomundo .com. Well-travelled owners have created this hospitable guesthouse, distinguished by eclectic furnishings from around the world. Ten sunny tile-floor rooms (fan or a/c) have pillow-top beds and huge bathrooms. **⑥**

Mucuy C 57 no. 481, between C 56 and C 58 ☎999/928-5193, ⓦwww.mucuy.com. Quiet and well run, with kind staff, good-value rooms (choice of fan or a/c), a small pool and wi-fi in the lobby. Housekeeping isn't always as diligent as it should be, but overall it's tidy and the best of the non-hostel budget spots. **②**

Posada Toledo C 58 no. 487, at C 57 ☎999/923-1690, ⓔhptoledo@prodigy.net.mx. A rambling old family compound, with an air of faded elegance. Singles are a little cramped and light on character, but the high-ceiling doubles are grand (if a bit fluorescent-lit); all have beautiful tile floors and antique furniture. **③**

Rosas and Xocolate Paseo de Montejo 480 at C 41 ☎999/924-2992, ⓦwww.rosasandxocolate .com. Built in the shell of a grand Montejo mansion, this is Mérida's only luxury boutique hotel, and the design – all eye-popping pink and sleek lines – is stunning. The bar and restaurant are a scene in themselves. A minor drawback: room windows don't open. **⑨**

🏃 **Trinidad Galería** C 60 no. 456, at C 51 ☎999/923-2463, ⓦwww.hotelestrinidad .com. Eccentric hotel crammed full of bizarre artefacts, sculptures and paintings. Rooms upstairs are lighter and more spacious; all have cool mosaic bathrooms (some have a/c). Also: pool, wi-fi and a breakfast café. Its sister hotel, *Trinidad* (C 62 at C 55), has some cheaper rooms with shared bath (**②**), and guests can use the *Galería* pool. **④**

The City

Mérida sprawls further than most visitors will ever see – particularly up **Paseo de Montejo** (called Prolongación de Montejo in its northern stretch), where chain stores and slick restaurants start to appear. But the centre (*centro histórico*), which radiates out from the main **Plaza de la Independencia**, is dense with historic attractions and other entertainment. Most sights, from the main market on the south side to the broad boulevard of Paseo de Montejo to the north, are easily reached on foot from the plaza.

The Plaza de la Independencia

Usually called simply the *plaza grande* or *plaza mayor* and formed by calles 60, 61, 62 and 63, the **Plaza de la Independencia** is a hub of the city's life, particularly in the evenings, when couples meet on the park benches and bands of *trovadores* in

Originally, street corners here (and in many colonial cities) were marked not by a written name, but by a statue – most commonly of an animal, but also of objects such as a clenched fist or a flower – mounted on top of the building. This cleared up language confusion in the Spanish–Maya city with a universally identifiable "elephant corner" or "cat corner", for example. Corners also came to be known for residents or even abstract ideas, such as "La Libertad" (freedom), the origins of which are now lost to time. Today, small red-and-white **plaques** have replaced the original figures, but often many of the surrounding business names still reflect the old corner designation, and in some cases, the city has devised new designations, such as "El Motór Eléctrico" (the electric motor) on a corner near a repair shop. A few of the plaques, such as "La Ermita" (the hermitage), are the last remaining evidence of major buildings that used to serve as landmarks. And the *peón* (serf) on the corner of calles 62 and 63, is a bit of a historical joke – this was the former home of the exceedingly wealthy Peón family, who were hardly peasants.

white guayaberas wait to be hired for serenades – or, less traditionally, families gather around laptops to watch YouTube videos streamed on the park's free wi-fi.

On the east side of the plaza is the **Catedral de San Ildefonso** (daily 6am–noon & 5–8pm). Construction began in 1562 and finished before the end of the century. Singularly vast and white, it is almost severe in its simplicity, reflecting the trend toward crisper Renaissance design and away from the ornate Spanish style, inspired by Gothic forms. On its facade, the entwined eagle and snake, symbol of the Mexican republic, is a later addition, replacing the Spanish empire's two-headed Hapsburg eagle, which was removed in 1822. Most of the church's valuables were looted in 1915, though in a chapel to the left of the main altar, people still venerate the **Cristo de las Ampollas** (Christ of the Blisters), a crucifix carved from a tree in the village of Ichmul that burned for a whole night without showing the least sign of damage. Later, in 1645, the parish church at Ichmul burned down, and the crucifix survived, though blackened and blistered. It is entirely likely that the original statue was also destroyed in 1915, but whether the existing statue is a reproduction is irrelevant – it remains the focal point of a local **fiesta** from mid-September to mid-October, when each day a different professional group, or *gremio* (taxi drivers, bakers and so on), pays its respects at the church, then parades on the plaza.

Beside the cathedral, separated from it by the Pasaje San Alvarado, the old bishop's palace has been converted into shops, offices and the **MACAY** (Museo de Arte Contemporáneo Ateneo de Yucatán; Wed–Mon 10am–6pm; free). The museum has the best modern art collection in southern Mexico, with permanent displays featuring the work of internationally acclaimed Yucatecan painters Fernando Castro Pacheco, Gabriel Ramírez Aznar and Fernando García Ponce. Ponce's enormous, multilayered collage paintings are particularly striking. Temporary exhibitions range from local photographers to European masters on loan from Mexico City museums.

On the south side of the plaza, the **Casa de Montejo** was built in 1549 by Francisco de Montejo, a captain under Hernán Cortés and the first conquistador to attempt to bring the peninsula under Spain's control. His first effort, in 1527, failed, as did several later forays. His son, Francisco de Montejo the Younger, did what the father could not, securing the northern part of the peninsula in the 1540s. But not long after the father built his triumphant palace, he was stripped of his titles and recalled to Spain; his son moved in, and his family occupied the place until 1970, finally selling it to Banamex. Most of the interior is office space, but during weekday business hours, visitors can look at a couple of lavishly restored rooms off the Moorish-feeling courtyard. Above a staid doorway of Classical columns, the facade is decorated in the manically ornate plateresque style (probably the first instance of it in the New World), with conquistadors depicted trampling savages underfoot. The woolly men with clubs are similar to figures decorating the Colegio de San Gregorio in Valladolid, Spain, where the Montejos hailed from.

Across the plaza from the cathedral, the **Palacio Municipal** is another impressive piece of sixteenth-century design, with a fine clock tower and a large painting upstairs depicting the *mestizaje*, the birth of the first mixed-blood Mexican. Next door, the modern **Centro Olimpo de Cultura** contains an auditorium and an art gallery featuring local works and travelling exhibits. In the basement is a **planetarium** (shows Tues–Sat at 7pm, with additional programmes on weekends; M$30); narration is in Spanish, but the air conditioning can be a treat on a hot day.

Completing the square, the nineteenth-century **Palacio de Gobierno** (daily 8am–10pm) is a showcase for huge modernist murals by Fernando Castro Pacheco. They cover the walls on the ground floor and in the large front room on the second floor, powerfully depicting the violent history of the Yucatán and the trials of its indigenous people, including a period in the nineteenth century when the Maya were sold as slaves to Cuban plantation owners.

North of the plaza

Most of the remaining monuments in Mérida lie north of the plaza, bordering Calle 60 and Paseo de Montejo. Calle 60 is one of the city's main commercial streets, lined with its fancier hotels and restaurants. It also boasts a lovely series of colonial buildings, starting one block north of the plaza with the seventeenth-century Jesuit **Iglesia de Jesús**, on the corner with Calle 59, between Parque Hidalgo and Parque de la Madre. If the doors are open, peek inside – the lavish chandeliers and frescoes are an opulent surprise in such a spare church. The building is made of stones from the original Maya city of T'hó, and a few pieces of decorative carving are visible in the wall on Calle 59.

On the same block of Calle 59, the **Pinacoteca del Estado Juan Gamboa Guzmán** (Tues–Sat 9am–5pm, Sun 10am–5pm; M$31) houses a collection of nineteenth-century portraits of prominent Yucatecans and Mexican leaders – Austrian-French Emperor Ferdinand Maximilian, executed less than three years into his reign, looks particularly hapless among the crowd of presidents. Back on Calle 60 and continuing north, you reach **Teatro Peón Contreras**, a grandiose Neoclassical edifice built by Italian architects between 1900 and 1908, in the heady days of Porfirio Díaz, the Mexican dictator whose decadence inspired the Revolution. A gallery off the north side of the lobby often has good contemporary art exhibits. Across the street stands the **state university** (UADY, or Universidad Autónoma de Yucatán), a highly respected institution that has existed, under various names, since 1624.

One block north of Teatro Peón Contreras, the sixteenth-century **Iglesia Santa Lucía** stands facing the elegant plaza of the same name – a small colonnaded square that used to be the town's stagecoach terminus. Three blocks further on is **Plaza Santa Ana**, a modern open space, bordered by a small cluster of market stalls. The surrounding neighbourhood is the heart of a small-scale contemporary art scene – see what's on at the **Centro de Artes Visuales** (Mon–Fri 9am–10pm, Sat & Sun 9am–7pm; free), the exhibition space for the state university's arts programme. Up and down the block, and further north, are several private galleries displaying a huge range of work, from conceptual sculpture to figurative painting (look for the free Mérida Art Map, published by

Yucatan Living, in shops and tourist offices). Head east from here a couple of blocks to reach the south end of Paseo de Montejo.

Paseo de Montejo

Running north from Plaza Santa Ana (C 58 at C 45), **Paseo de Montejo** is a broad boulevard designed for strolling, its sidewalks dotted with trees and modern sculptures by Yucatecan and foreign artists. It's also lined with the magnificent mansions of the henequen-rich grandees who flaunted high-European style around the end of the nineteenth century. One of the most striking, the Palacio Cantón, at the corner of Calle 43, houses Mérida's **Museo Regional de Antropología** (Tues–Sat 8am–5pm; M$41). The Beaux Arts palace, grandly trimmed in wrought iron and marble, was built at the beginning of the twentieth century for General Francisco Cantón, a railway tycoon and the former state governor, and set off a competitive building boom along the avenue. The **walk to the museum** from the plaza takes about half an hour, or you could try a city bus (see p.178) or a horse-drawn **calesa** (about M$150 from the centre to the museum).

Given the archeological riches found near Mérida, the collection can seem a bit skimpy, but it's a useful introduction to the surrounding sites nonetheless, with displays (most in both English and Spanish) covering everything from prehistoric stone tools to modern Maya religious custom. You'll find sculptures and other objects from Chichén Itzá and elsewhere, but more interesting are the attempts to give some idea of what it was like to live in a Maya city. Topographic maps of the peninsula, for example, explain how cenotes are formed and their importance to the ancient population, while a collection of skulls demonstrates the practices of skull lengthening, teeth filing and dental inlay with turquoise. Other displays cover jewellery, ritual offerings and burial rites, as well as the workings of the Maya calendar. Upstairs, temporary exhibits examine Mérida's history and specific archeological sites. The **bookshop** offers leaflets and guidebooks in English to dozens of ruins in the Yucatán and the rest of Mexico.

A few blocks further north brings you to the **Casa Museo Montes Molina**, between calles 35 and 33 (⊕www.laquintamm.com; tours in English Mon–Fri 9am, 11am & 3pm; M $50). Built for a Cuban businessman by the same architects who designed Teatro Peón Contreras, the building is a shiny white confection of excess, and its interior is similarly grand. A guided tour leads through its halls, wine cellar and servant quarters, a pitch-perfect rendition of a European manse.

Another ten minutes' walk north on Paseo de Montejo, past scores of other old mansions that now contain banks and insurance companies, brings you to the 1956 **Monumento a la Patria**. It is a titan, covered in neo-Maya sculptures relating to Mexican history. Beyond the monument, the street continues under the name Prolongación de Montejo and leads into "new" Mérida, the district of glossy shops and chain restaurants frequented by the younger, wealthier population.

East of the plaza

If you want to flesh out your impressions of the *centro histórico*, head several blocks east of the plaza to a couple of interesting museums and a generally quieter atmosphere. The first exhibition you reach on Calle 57, just before Calle 50, is the **Museo del Arte Popular de Yucatán** (Tues–Sat 9.30am–6.30pm, Sun 9am–2pm; M$20, free on Sun), a small but flawless collection of Mexican craftwork. Likewise, the gift shop is small but very nicely stocked. The museum faces a little park, named for the former monastery of **La Mejorada**, on Calle 59 at Calle 50. The monastery, along with Las Monjas (a convent) on Calle 63 and the now destroyed San Francisco de Mérida monastery (the old market and former post office are built on its ruins), housed the city's devout Franciscan community.

Behind La Mejorada, on Calle 57, before you reach Calle 48, the **Museo de la Canción Yucateca** (Mon–Fri 9am–5pm, Sat & Sun 9am–3pm; M$15, free on Sun) details the diverse musical influences on the local *trovadores*, from pre-Columbian traditions to Afro-Cuban styles. The presentation, except for one "interactive" room with music clips, is very old-fashioned, with hall upon hall full of vitrines of memorabilia and walls hung with oil portraits of the great composers and singers of the *trova* tradition. The gift shop is an excellent place to pick up some romantic tunes.

A few blocks south of this area and just east of Calle 50, you can also spy two of the old city's entrance **arches** (thirteen of them once marked the major streets from the sixteenth to the early nineteenth century). The Arco del Puente, at Calle 61, sports an adjacent walkway, a 1.2-metre-high tunnel for single-file pedestrians. A third arch, the most elegant, stands on the south side of town, on Calle 64 by the Parque San Juan, marking the former Camino Real ("royal road") that linked the city to Campeche and carried on to Mexico City during colonial times.

South of the plaza

The blocks south of the plaza are a bit scruffier than the rest of the centre, the streets getting more crowded and the shops more jumbled as you head towards Mérida's huge main **market**, between calles 65, 69, 54 and 56, where more than two thousand vendors ply their trades. It's a wild scrum of consumer goods, from freshly hacked-up beef to hand-tooled leather belts to more varieties of bananas than you can count on one hand – usually, but not reliably, divided into rough districts. Arrive before noon to see the most bountiful food; **craft shops** (many in a separate wing on C 56 at C 67) are open all day.

On Calle 65 at Calle 56, the grand **Museo de la Ciudad** (Mon–Fri 9am–8pm, Sat & Sun 9am–2pm; free) occupies the beautiful old central post office. The exhibits trace city history from ancient Maya times through the henequen boom (text in Spanish and English). The building also contains a gallery of local contemporary art.

West of the plaza

On Calle 59 just west of Calle 72, **Casa Catherwood** (Mon–Sat 9am–2pm & 5–9pm; M$50) displays an exhibit of English artist Frederick Catherwood's etchings of crumbling Maya ruins, made during his excursions with John Lloyd Stephens in the mid-1800s. The works became the illustrations for Stephens' *Incidents of Travel in Yucatán* (see p.290). The courtyard houses a pretty café too. After some refreshment, push on a few more blocks to the sprawling green space of **Parque del Centenario**, on the edge of the *centro histórico* at Avenida Itzáes. It contains a **zoo** (Tues–Sun 6am–6pm; free), with a very full aviary. The park is a little scrappy, but it's a change from the historic area, and a nice place to see modern Mérida at leisure. It also has lots of room for children to run around, and other kids for them to run around with. There are boats for paddling about a tiny lake, a mini-chairlift ride and a small-scale train (Tues–Sat 10am–2pm & 3–5pm; M$1) that runs through the zoo area.

Shopping

For **crafts**, prices in the market are no great shakes, unless you're an unusually skilled and determined haggler. Before buying anything, head for the **Casa de Artesanías** (Tues–Sat 9am–8pm, Sun 9am–1.30pm), in the Casa de la Cultura on Calle 63 two blocks west of the plaza. Run by a government-sponsored organization, the shop sells consistently high-quality crafts, including delicate silver filigree jewellery; the clothing options are somewhat limited, though.

One of the most popular Mexican souvenirs is a **hammock** – and Mérida is probably the best place in the country to buy one. Head to Tejidos y Cordeles Nacionales, a top specialist very near the market at Calle 56 no. 516-B, just north of Calle 65; a *doble* (about the smallest you can realistically sleep in) starts at M$250. Similar stores nearby include the respected El Aguacate, on Calle 58, near Calle 73, and La Poblana, at Calle 65 no. 492, near Calle 60.

Clothing is good value here as well, in particular men's pleated guayabera shirts, which both Cubans and *meridanos* claim to have invented. Guayaberas Cab, on Calle 60, between calles 65 and 67, does especially fine versions in pure cotton or linen, and will make shirts to measure, in about a week, for M$600 and up. Less expensive guayaberas, in polyester-blend fabrics, are found in shops around the market. For *huipiles*, the embroidered smocks, as well as *rebozos*, the checked scarves Maya women wear, see some of the same shops that sell hammocks in the market area, such as La Poblana. Mérida's distinctive *trova* **music** is available in many gift shops on CD; it's especially cheap at the weekly serenade on Parque Santa Lucía, where vendors sell remastered classics or newer songs in the same vein. You can also try the gift shop at the Museo de la Canción Yucateca (see opposite).

There are a few quite refined shopping options in Mérida as well. Check out hip women's **fashion** and pop-culture artefacts at Vintage Retro Style (Mon–Fri 10am–2pm & 5–9pm, Sat 11am–2pm & 5–8pm), on Calle 60, between calles 47 and 49. On Calle 55 near Calle 62, opposite Parque Santa Lucía, Coqui Coqui (Mon–Sat 10am–2pm and 4–8pm) sells its own **perfumes**, as well as jewellery and bags. And there are more **antiques** shops in the city than can be covered here; start at J&K Antiques, on Calle 66, between calles 55 and 57 (afternoons only), and look for more on the Mérida Art Map (see p.182).

Eating

Restaurants are plentiful in the centre of Mérida, though the best are open only for lunch. At dinner, many restaurants are a bit overpriced and cater largely to foreigners; locals tend to frequent the **snack stalls** on Plaza Santa Ana (C 60 at C 47) and Parque de Santiago (C 59, between calles 70 and 72) for *panuchos*, *salbutes* and *sopa de lima*. As usual, cheap eats are best at the *loncherías* in the **market**, and you can also easily make a late lunch out of the *botanas* (snacks) served free with beers at traditional afternoon bars – see p.187.

For breakfast, the **bakery** *Pan Montejo* is most central, at the corner of calles 62 and 63 on the plaza, and *Jugos California*, next door, does all the regular juices; a couple of blocks down, *La Parroquia* (C 62, between calles 65 and 67) serves cinnamon-laced chocolate milk, fruit plates and yogurt. For **groceries**, head to the state-run Isstey store on Calle 60, between calles 47 and 49, or to the mega Super Bodega on Calle 63, between calles 54 and 56.

Cafés and snacks

Alameda C 58, between C 55 and C 57. This old-fashioned lunch café, a popular Lebanese hangout, serves *garbanzos* (hummus) and other Middle Eastern standards. Daily 7.30am–5pm.

Dulcería y Sorbetería El Colón C 61, on the north side of the plaza. Popular spot for fruit sorbets; try a *champola*, a big scoop in a tall glass of milk. Another branch on Paseo de Montejo,

between C 39 and C 41, is a good stop after the archeology museum.

La Habana C 62 at C 59. Mérida's older bohemian intellectual crowd doesn't come around this coffee shop much now that the national smoking ban is in effect. But the black-and-white-clad waiters still dish out Mexican-style diner fare, 24 hours a day. There's free wi-fi and decent coffee.

El Hoyo C 62, between C 57 and C 59. A hip student hangout in the evening, buzzing with both conversation and the hum of blenders and espresso machines, whipping up all kinds of juices and caffeinated drinks. It also serves pressed sandwiches, and good breakfasts until 1pm. Closed Sun.

Ki'xocoatl C 55, between C 60 and C 62. Chocolate junkies head here for frothy, cinnamon-spiked hot chocolate and other local cacao products. Closed 2.30–4.30pm.

Peón Contreras C 60, adjacent to the Teatro Peón Contreras. A bit expensive (M$50 for a beer), but you're paying for a fine sidewalk seat, just off C 60. All the action's outside (with live music in the evening), but don't miss the glamorous interior of the café. Food is average – stick to easy things like queso fundido (melted cheese).

Pop C 57, between C 60 and C 62. A good cheap breakfast joint with vintage 1960s decor, popular with students at the nearby university. Also serves hamburgers, spaghetti and Mexican snacks. Daily 7am–midnight.

Restaurants

Los Almendros C 50, between C 57 and C 59, in the Plaza Mejorada. A venerable Yucatecan restaurant, marred by inconsistency, but when it's on, it serves delicious, moderately priced food. The dressier wing, Gran Almendros, with a separate entrance around the corner, has slightly higher prices, but can be fun on a busy Sun afternoon.

Amaro C 59 no. 507, between C 60 and C 62. Set in a lovely tree-shaded courtyard with a fountain and a romantic guitarist Wed–Sat. A little overpriced (mains from M$80), but interesting veggie options, such as crepas de chaya, are novelties for non-meat-eaters tired of quesadillas.

Los Bisquets Obregón C 62 at C 61. At the corner of the plaza, this chain diner serves good Mexican standards, but it's best at breakfast, for a frothy café con leche poured tableside, and a huge assortment of pastries. Open till midnight, and 1am Fri and Sat.

Casa de Frida C 61 no. 526 at C 66 ☎999/928-2311. Specializing in chiles en nogada (chiles stuffed with sweet-savoury beef and topped with a creamy walnut sauce; M$120), this eclectic little restaurant is painted in candy colours and romantically lit, sporting a cosy back patio. Dinner only Mon–Fri, lunch and dinner weekends.

Casa de Piedra In Hacienda Xcanatun ☎999/941-0273. Yucatecan-French fusion is the speciality at this elegant place 12km north of town. Dishes like

duck glazed with xtabentun (a Yucatecan liqueur) and bitter orange (M$200) are served in the hacienda's old machine-house, warmed by the glow of candles. Also open for breakfast and lunch, but no dinner Sun.

La Chaya Maya C 62 at C 57. An inexpensive, sparkling-clean restaurant with a thorough menu of Yucatecan specialities, with handmade tortillas and lots of chaya (a nutritious wild green), pumpkin seeds and other earthy flavours.

El Marlin Azul C 62, between C 57 and C 59. Long-time local favourite for excellent seafood (trucked in every morning from Celestún), including tasty fish tacos and perfectly fresh ceviche (from M$75). If there's no space in the main restaurant (under a blue awning), try the separate, unmarked dining room next door to the north. Mon–Sat 8am–4.30pm.

Pizzería de Vito Corleone C 59 no. 508 at C 62. Inexpensive pizza joint that also does takeaway. Head for tables on the upstairs balcony if you don't want to get roasted by the wood-burning oven.

La Reina Itzalana Parque de Santiago, C 59, between C 70 and C 72. This and a couple of other basic restaurants in the same park are some of the few places near the centre of town to get a casual, super-cheap dinner of panuchos, salbutes and sopa de lima. Packed with families until 10 or 11pm; also open for lunch.

Restaurante D'AI C 54 at C 53. A typical cocina económica serving hearty, stick-to-your-ribs daily specials (about M$30) on flowered tablecloths, but open into the evenings. Also, a rarity at this type of hole-in-the-wall restaurant: beer is served.

Rosas and Xocolate Paseo de Montejo 480, at C 41 ☎999/924-2992. The restaurant at the hip hotel is a double treat: excellent creative Mexican food (don't miss the crispy-fried octopus!) plus eye candy in the form of the upper-crust meridano crowd. Dessert (with lots of chocolate options, naturally) inspires plate-licking. Mains M$180–300.

Siqueff C 60 at C 35. One of Mérida's longest-running Lebanese haunts. Try kafta, kibi (fried balls of bulgur and meat, aka kibbeh) and hummus, with guacamole on the side. Historic note: this is the restaurant that invented the odd Yucatecan egg dish huevos motuleños in the 1920s. Lunch only.

El Trapiche C 62, between C 59 and C 61 ☎999/927-2320. Basic, budget-friendly Yucatecan restaurant, handily located just off the plaza and open for every meal, from fresh juices for breakfast to poc-chuc for dinner.

The historic centre hosts a party nearly every night of the week, all free and attended largely by locals. Many films and concerts happen at the **Centro Olimpo de Cultura**, on the northwest corner of the plaza. In addition, these are the recurring events:

Monday *Jarana* folk dances, in or in front of the *ayuntamiento* (city hall) on the west side of the main plaza. 9pm.

Tuesday Big band music, heavy on the mambo, Parque de Santiago (C 72 at C 59); *trova* at the Centro Olimpo. 8.30pm.

Wednesday Concert at the Centro Olimpo. 9pm.

Thursday Serenata Yucateca, traditional *trova* music, Parque Santa Lucía; classical music at the Centro Olimpo. 9pm.

Saturday Noche Mexicana, music from all over Mexico, at the start of Paseo Montejo, Calle 56-A; jazz, salsa and more on the Plaza de la Independencia. 8pm.

Sunday Car-free centre: in the morning (8am–noon), bicycles take over the streets for the Bici-Ruta. In the afternoon and evening, the plaza is filled with music, dancing, food stalls and more. There's also a flea market during the day in the Parque Santa Lucía.

Drinking, entertainment and nightlife

In addition to all the free entertainment (see above), there are **mariachi nights** in hotel bars and **salsa dancing** in nightclubs. On Fridays, the **Ballet Folklórico de la Universidad de Yucatán** presents a colourful performance of traditional Mexican and Maya ceremonies at the Centro Cultural Universitario, Calle 60 at Calle 57 (9pm; M$30). Also check the schedule at **Teatro Peón Contreras**, which hosts some excellent musicians, and tickets are usually very affordable; the symphony orchestra plays alternating Fridays and Sundays October–April. And you can always get a personal **serenade** at the central plaza from trios of *trovadores*, in their white shirts and pants – M$100 gets you three songs.

For **film**, twin-screen Cine Rex, on Parque de Santiago (C 59, between calles 70 and 72), shows first-run films, usually American, and ticket prices can be as low as M$28; schedules are at Ⓦ www.mmcinemas.com. Also check the schedule at Teatro Mérida on Calle 62, just north of the plaza; its small upstairs cinema often screens art films; the Centro Olimpo on the plaza shows free films too.

Distinguished from the hard-drinking men-only **cantinas** (there are plenty of these all over the city, including a couple on C 62, just south of the plaza), traditional **family bars** (*bares familiares*; look for signs saying "*100% familiar*") are a more mixed affair, with, yes, sometimes even kids. They're open only till about 6pm, serving beer accompanied by *botanas* – small-plate snacks delivered with each round – and often live music.

La Casa de Todos C 64 at C 55. Very small student bar – more of a clubhouse, really – with a strong leftist bent. Most nights there's a rousing folksinger or two on the tiny stage; other nights, young punk bands. Wed–Sun after 9pm.

El Cumbanchero Paseo de Montejo at C 39. More convenient than *Mambo Café*, this small salsa bar is owned by the son of the late Rubén González, of Buena Vista Social Club. Dancing starts around dinner time, with an older crowd at first, who then give way to younger dancers around 10pm. Also open for brunch on Sun.

Los Henequenes C 56 at C 57. Once you're past the giant plastic frog out front, this is really a traditional *bar familiar*, with a local clientele, two-for-one beer specials and live music.

El Lucero del Alba C 47 at C 56. TVs lend an unfortunate sports-bar feel in part of the space, but head out back to the palapa-roof area for a very mellow, very local afternoon bar scene.

Mambo Café In the Plaza Las Américas mall. Worth the cab ride (about M$50) if you're looking to mingle with salsa-mad locals in what's

Mérida has a profusion of **bus stations** – see below for details. CAME and TAME services overlap, and you may be able to get an equally fast bus for less at the TAME. For smaller towns mentioned later in this chapter, see the relevant section for bus details. Additional service to Izamal goes from the Centro terminal, Calle 65, between calles 44 and 46, but departures from the more central Noreste terminal are more convenient. Additionally, *colectivos* often provide more frequent service to

Terminal	Services
CAME (C 70, between C 69 at C 71) Long-haul first-class on ADO, ADO GL, Platino and OCC	**Campeche** (at least hourly, round-the-clock; 2hr 30min); **Cancún** (at least hourly, round-the-clock, including one on Platino at 5.55am; 4hr–4hr 45min); **Chetumal** (4 daily at 7.30am, 11am, 6pm & 11pm; 6hr); **Chichén Itzá** (3 daily at 6.30am, 9.15am & 12.40pm; 1hr 45min); **Escárcega** (6 daily, 8.30am–11.50pm; 4hr 15min); **Mexico City** (2 daily on ADO GL at 2pm & 5.30pm; 19hr); **Palenque** (4 daily at 8.30am, 7.15pm, 10pm & 11.50pm; 7hr 15min–9hr); **Playa del Carmen** (16 daily, round-the-clock, including 3 on ADO GL; 5hr 30min); **Tulum** (5 daily 6.30am–11.40pm; 4hr); **Valladolid** (at least hourly 5am–7.30pm; 2hr 15min); **Villahermosa** (21 daily, including 6 on ADO GL and 2 on Platino, 7.15am–1.35am; 8hr 30min)
Noreste (C 67 at C 50) Second-class LUS, Noreste, Oriente, to towns north, east, southeast and west of Mérida	**Cancún** via **Chichén Itzá** and **Valladolid** (17 daily, 6.20am–8.20pm; 4hr); **Tulum** via **Cobá** (2 daily at 5.20am & 2.50pm; 8hr); **Cuzamá** (14 daily, 7.45am–9pm; 1hr 30min); **Izamal** (16 daily, 4.45am–9pm; 1hr); **Maní** via **Acanceh** and **Tecoh** (11 daily, 5.30am–8pm; 2hr); **Río Lagartos** (3 daily at 9am, 4pm & 5.30pm; 6hr); **San Crisanto** (3 daily at 7.15am, 10.15am & 6.30pm; 1hr 45min); **San Felipe** (1 daily at 5.30pm; 6hr 30min); **Tizimín** (15 daily, 5.30am–8.20pm; 4hr)

considered one of the city's best nightclubs. Touring Dominican and Cuban bands often play here. Free on Wed; otherwise, cover is about M$50. Wed–Sat 10am–3am.

Moon Lounge Paseo de Montejo 480, at C 41. The first step is getting in: look for the spiral staircase hidden in the courtyard, then climb up to this terrace bar with a view down the avenue. Busier on weekends with locals; try the *limonada eléctrica*, fresh limeade with Midori.

El Nuevo Tucho C 60, between C 55 and C 57. The one traditional bar in a string of other, cheesier nightclubs on the main drag. Gets surprisingly loud (there's usually a band), but still wholesome.

Pancho's C 59, between C 60 and C 62. A steak restaurant with a pricey haute Mexican menu

(and a goofy theme: bandolier-draped waiters, no less), this sprawling space is better as a bar – considering it has two of them, plus tasty mojitos and margaritas. Try to hit the happy hour, 6–8pm Mon–Fri.

Piedra de Agua C 60, between C 59 and C 61. Head through the lobby of the hotel and out back to a comfortable garden area where you can drink a cold beer under the shadow of the cathedral just down the block. The wood-burning oven does good pizza too.

La Quilla C 60, between C 43 and C 45 ⓦwww.laquilla.blogspot.com. This artist-friendly café really takes off in the evenings – it often hosts bands, DJs, films and other cool events (cover M$20 or M$30), starting at 9pm or so. Even on quiet nights, it's a nice place to drink a beer.

destinations an hour or two outside the city, and to smaller villages. These, as well as small buses to Dzibilchaltún, Oxkutzcab and Ticul, congregate on **Parque San Juan** (C 62 at C 69). For Progreso, *colectivos* leave from the east side of Calle 60, between calles 65 and 67. **Flights** depart from the airport for Mexico City, as well as Houston. To get to the airport, catch bus #79 ("Aviación") from Parque San Juan, or take a taxi for about M$100.

Terminal	Services
TAME (C 69, between C 68 and C 70) Second-class on ATS, Clase Europea, Mayab, Sur, TRT and some Oriente buses Ruta Puuc and towns between Mérida and Campeche	**Campeche** via Maxcanú, Hecelchakán and Becal (every 30min, 4.15am–5pm; 4hr); **Cancún** (20 daily, most via Valladolid, 6am–midnight, 2 daily via Carrillo Puerto at 5.45am & 1.30pm; 4–8hr); **Chetumal** (8 daily, 7am–midnight; 6hr); **Chiquilá** for Holbox (1 daily at 11.30pm; 6hr); **Escárcega** (3 daily at 11am, 1.10pm & 3.40pm; 6hr); **Felipe Carrillo Puerto** (10 daily, 4am–11.55pm; 2hr 30min); **Hopelchén** via Santa Elena and Uxmal (5 daily; 2hr 30min); **Oxkutzcab** (12 daily via Ticul, 6am–6.30pm; 2hr); **Playa del Carmen** (6 daily via Cancún, 6am–11.35pm; 5–7hr); **Tulum** (6 daily via Cancún, 6am–11.35pm, 2 daily via Cobá at 5am & 9.55pm; 4–6hr); **Villahermosa** via Escárcega (3 daily at 11am, 7pm & 9pm; 9hr)
Fiesta Americana (C 60 at Colón, behind the *Fiesta Americana* hotel) First-class long-haul on ADO, ADO GL and Platino	**Campeche** (1 daily at midnight; 2hr 30min); **Cancún** (9 daily, including 3 each on ADO GL and Platino, 6am–8.30pm; 4hr 15min); **Cancún airport** (2 daily at 6.15am and 10am; 4hr 30min); **Villahermosa** (2 daily on Platino at 9.30pm & 11.40pm; 8hr 45min)

Listings

Airlines Aeroméxico, C 15, between C 22 and C 28, Colonia Altabrisa ☏ 999/167-9388; InterJet, Plaza Americana, *Fiesta Americana* ☏ 999/920-3414.

American Express Travelissimo travel agency, C 17 no. 287-A, between C 38 and C 60 (Mon–Fri 8am-7.30pm, Sat 9am–1pm; ☏ 999/944-5662, ☏ 999/944-5670).

Banks Most are around C 65, between C 60 and C 64; they have ATMs and are open 9am–4pm. The most centrally located is Banamex, in the Casa de Montejo on the south side of the plaza; it also has an ATM.

Books and maps Amate Books, C 60, between C 49 and C 51 (closed Mon), has an excellent selection of English-language titles on Mexican culture, plus Latin American literature, some magazines and guidebooks. Librería Dante, on the west side of the plaza and on C 59, between C 60 and C 62, has some guidebooks and its own line of field guides. The Conaculta bookshop adjacent to Teatro Daniel Ayala, C 60 just north of the plaza, carries art books, guides and music, mostly in Spanish. Alternatively, borrow English-language books from the extensive Mérida English Library, C 53, between C 66 and C 68. For maps, try Librería Burrel, C 59 opposite Dante, or Sanborns, in the *Fiesta Americana*.

Bullfights Plaza de Toros on Av Reforma (C 72) at C 25, once a month or so on Sunday at 3.30pm; tickets from M$40.

Car rental Family-run Mexico Rent a Car, with offices on C 57-A, between C 58 and C 60

(☎ 999/923-3637, ✉ mexicorentacar@hotmail
.com) and at at C 62 no. 483-A (☎ 999/927-4916),
has very good rates that include all insurance.
Otherwise, try the international agencies, either in
a strip on C 60, between C 55 and C 57, or in the
Fiesta Americana.

Consulates Opening hours are limited,
so phone ahead. Belize: C 58 no. 450, at C 35
☎ 999/928-6152, ✉ dutton@sureste.com; Cuba:
C 42 no. 200, between C 1-E and C 1-D, Fracc.
Campestre ☎ 999/944-4216, ✉ concuba
@prodigy.net.mx; US: C 60 no. 338-K, between
C 29 and C 31, Colonía Alcala Martín
☎ 999/942-5700.

Hospitals Mérida is the Yucatán's centre for medical
care. Clinica de Mérida hospital, Itzáes 242 at Colón
(☎ 999/942-1800, ⊛ www.clinicademerida.com.mx),
is accustomed to dealing with foreigners.

Internet and telephone Casetas are not
numerous; you're better off with VOIP at one of the
internet cafés which dot every street in the centre,
especially C 61 west of the plaza. There's free wi-fi
in most city parks.

Laundry Lavandería La Fe, C 64, between C 55
and C 57; Lavandería Aurea, C 57, between C 52
and C 54. Both closed Sun.

Post office C 53, between C 52 and C 54 (Mon–Fri
8am–4.30pm, Sat 9am–1pm). For packages, try
Mayan Mail shipping service, C 58, between C 57
and C 59 (Mon–Fri 8am–8pm, Sat and Sun
9am–2pm; ☎ 999/287-1795).

Tourist police Police-staffed information and help
kiosks are set up at the plaza (☎ 999/942-0060).

Travel agents and tours Adventures Mexico
(☎ 999/925-1700, ⊛ www.adventures-mexico
.com) does a good day-long bike trip to the ruins of
Aké and an outing to the cenotes at Chunkanán.
Ecoturísmo Yucatán (☎ 999/920-2772, ⊛ www
.ecoyuc.com.mx) runs day-trips as well as
multi-day camping trips. Red de Ecoturismo de
Yucatán, C 56-A no. 437, near the Monumento a la
Patria (Mon–Fri 10am–2pm, Sat 4–6pm;
☎ 999/926-7756, ⊛ www.redecoturismo.com.mx),
is a network of small community eco-adventure
projects, offering activities like bike trips and
camping excursions.

The Gulf coast

From Mérida to the port of **Progreso**, the closest point on the coast, is just 36km,
or about 45 minutes to the north by bus. The drive out of Mérida follows Paseo
de Montejo through wealthy suburbs and shopping malls before reaching the flat
countryside and the ancient ruins of **Dzibilchaltún**, about halfway to the coast.
East and west of Progreso lie near-empty beaches.

It's easy enough to visit Dzibilchaltún on the way to Progreso from Mérida. Get
a **combi** to Chablecal from Parque San Juan (C 62 at C 69) about every half-hour,
or a Chablecal-bound bus from Calle 59, between calles 58 and 60. From the ruins,
you can walk or hitch a ride back to the main highway, where you can flag down
a Progreso bus.

Dzibilchaltún

The archeological importance of the ruins of the ancient city of **Dzibilchaltún**
(daily 8am–5pm; M$107) is hardly reflected in what you see. The area was
settled from 1000 BC right through to the Conquest – the longest continuous
occupation of any known Maya site. More than eight thousand structures have
been mapped, but unfortunately, little has survived, in particular because the
ready-dressed stones were a handy building material and therefore used in
several local towns and in paving the Mérida–Progreso road. In addition, there
is virtually no descriptive labelling on the buildings, so it's worth hiring a **guide**
(M$250 for up to six people) at the main entrance. Dzibilchaltún features an
excellent museum, and the area is part of an **eco-archeological park**, where
birders can catch the rough-winged swallow and the Yucatán woodpecker.
Allow about two hours to see everything.

Just past the site entrance, the small but smartly done **Museo del Pueblo Maya**
(daily 8am–4pm) provides an overview of Maya culture and the history of the

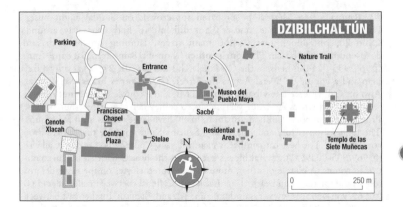

region up to the present. The exhibits place special emphasis on the continuity of Maya culture and art under Spanish rule, with some beautiful examples of colonial-era wood carvings – including a *retablo* (altarpiece) salvaged from Mérida's cathedral after the Revolution-era fire – as well as samples of *huipiles* from across the Maya world.

From the museum, a meandering nature trail leads to the **Templo de las Siete Muñecas** (Temple of the Seven Dolls). Originally a simple square pyramid, it was subsequently built over with a more complex structure. Later still, a passageway was cut through to the original building and seven deformed clay figurines (dolls) were buried, with a tube through which their spirits were meant to commune with the priests. The structure is remarkable for being the only known Maya temple to have windows, and for having a tower in place of the usual roofcomb. On the **equinoxes**, the sun shines straight through the tower doors, in a display of ancient astronomical savvy that draws crowds of tourists. In conjunction with the buildings that surround it, the temple is also aligned with other astronomical points, so it could have been an observatory.

One of the ancient causeways that linked the city's major points runs dead-straight from the temple to another cluster of ruins around a plaza. In the centre of the grassy field sits the shell of a Franciscan chapel built around 1600, and the gates of a cattle ranch from the next century still stand to the west. A little further west, **Cenote Xlacah**, in addition to providing the ancient city with water, was of ritual importance to the Maya: more than six thousand offerings – including human remains – have been discovered in its deeper end (44m down), which connects to an underground river system. It's also home to a species of spiny fish found only in the Yucatán.

Progreso and around

When Mérida residents talk lovingly of **PROGRESO**, they're usually thinking of their summer homes in the area. The town itself, a working port with a six-kilometre-long concrete pier, is not particularly appealing, and it tends to be crowded with carousers in summer and desolate in winter. But the beach is long and broad, with fine white sand, and it makes for a pleasant enough, non-touristy day out from Mérida.

Buses depart Mérida every thirty minutes from the AutoProgreso station (C 62, between calles 65 and 67), arriving in Progreso forty minutes later at the **bus station** on Calle 29 (running east–west, four blocks south of the water) at Calle

82. Returning to Mérida, be prepared for crowds on Sunday-night buses. Progreso is a small place, and it's not difficult to find your way around. Calle 80, one block east, is the main street, running north–south and dead-ending at the beach. The **tourist office** (Mon–Fri 8am–2pm, Sat 8am–1pm; ☎ 969/935-0114) is here, in the Casa de la Cultura at Calle 27; it has only a free map and a couple of flyers. Across the street, Global **rents bikes** (M$50/day). Also on Calle 80 are a few **banks** with ATMs, and a couple of **internet** cafés.

Hotels in town range from very seedy to somewhat overpriced, but because Progreso is a popular family destination, many have large rooms ideal for groups. The high season is July and August and Semana Santa; outside that, prices drop considerably. The best bargain bet is *Hotel Progreso*, Calle 29 no. 142, at Calle 78 (☎ 969/935-0039; ❷), several blocks back from the beach, with clean, air-conditioned rooms. A couple of other, more upscale hotels cluster on the east side, just off the end of the main beach: *Casa Isidora*, on Calle 21, between calles 58 and 60 (☎ 969/935-4595, ⓦ www.casaisidora.com; ❹), and *Yakunah*, further east between calles 48 and 50 (☎ 969/935-5600, ⓦ www.hotelyakunah.com.mx; ❺), are both set in old houses, with pretty tiled floors and a pool.

For **eating**, try lively *Eladio's*, the best of the beachfront restaurants, at Calle 80. You can make a good meal just of the generous *botanas* that come free with beers; mains are about M$90. Several more basic seafood restaurants are on Calle 80 in the block before the beach. All of these places set out tables on the beach across the road as well. *Loncherías* in the centre of the town's **market**, on Calle 80 at Calle 27, are a source of cheap meals. The other lively area is around the **plaza** at calles 80 and 31, where there are coffee and snack spots, and a mega-grocery store.

East of Progreso

Heading **east from Progreso**, it's best to have a car to explore, as the pleasures along this coast come more from poking along the ever-narrowing road rather than heading for a particular destination. At Km 15 on the highway, east of Chicxulub Puerto, stop at the **viewing platform** (*mirador turística*; free) over the Uaymitún inlet to spot the **flamingos** that settle here, especially just before the 6pm closing time. A bit south of the highway, just west of Telchac Puerto, **Xcambó** (8am–5pm; free) is an Early Classic Maya salt-trading outpost. A thatch-roof chapel, built from the ruins' stones in the 1950s following a reported apparition of the Virgin, sits astride some old foundations, and a *huipil*-dressed cross stands atop the tallest building. In San Crisanto, 9km east of Telchac Puerto, a village group runs **mangrove tours** for just M$40 per person – you navigate canals on a paddle-boat, winding up at a cenote for a swim. The whole trip lasts an hour and a half, and the last tour goes at about 4pm. Look for the office (☎ 991/959-7205) one block south of the main intersection, by the baseball field.

At the end of the road, from Dzilam de Bravo, you can visit the Parque Natural San Felipe, a state nature reserve of coastal forests, marshes and dunes. The **Bocas de Dzilam** are freshwater springs on the seabed; the nutrients they provide encourage the wide biological diversity found here. The Sayachuleb cooperative, a block east from the north edge of the square, runs tours (M$800 for up to five people; 5hr). You can also get to Dzilam de Bravo directly from Mérida on a second-class **bus** from the Noreste terminal (C 67 at C 50); morning departures are at 5am, 7.15am and 9am. The last bus back to Mérida is at 6.30pm.

For **food**, you could have a big fried-fish lunch at one of the rustic restaurants in remote **Santa Clara**, or a more diverse seafood meal at *Restaurante Moctezuma* (aka "Los Barriles", for the giant wood barrels that form its front entrance) in **Chicxulub Puerto** (where, incidentally, a massive meteor crashed 65 million years ago, permanently altering the Earth's atmosphere and likely causing the extinction of the dinosaurs). All along the road, look out for stands selling coconut sweets.

You can easily cover this area as a day drive, but to stay overnight, Telchac Puerto has two decent **hotels**, tidy but basic *Libros y Sueños* (T 991/917-4125, W www .l-y-s.net; ❷) and, across the street, *El Príncipe Negro* (T 991/917-4004; ❸), which has air-conditioned rooms and a pool. If you get stuck in Dzilam de Bravo, *Jean Lafitte* (T 991/102-1543; ❸) will have to do.

West of Progreso

Venturing **west from Progreso** is not as promising, though in the 19km of coast road you will find a few more beach villages: **Yucalpetén**, **Chelem** and **Chuburná**, respectively fifteen, twenty and thirty minutes from Progreso and easy day-trips from Mérida, have clean, wide beaches and some **accommodation** and restaurants. *Hotel Sian Ka'an* (T 969/935-4017; W www.hotelsiankian.com; ❹), in Yucalpetén, is one good option, offering oceanfront rooms ideal for groups or families, with balconies and kitchenettes. *Costa Azul*, just down the road in Chelem, is a highly recommended fish **restaurant**.

Beyond Chuburná, the coast road, which was damaged by Hurricane Isidore in 2002, is not passable, and you'll have to turn inland again. It's not worth making a detour back to the coast at **Sisal**. It's hard to believe this was Mérida's chief port in colonial times (and gave its name to the henequen fibre that was exported from here), as now it's practically deserted.

Celestún

Were it not for its amazing flamingo-filled lagoon, **CELESTÚN** – 93km west of Mérida, at the end of a sandbar on the peninsula's northwest coast – would be little more than a one-boat fishing village. The place has become a very small-scale ecotourism destination, and its beach gets busy in summer as a getaway for Mérida residents.

To see the birds – most numerous from November to May, when blue-winged teal and shovellers also migrate – in the warm waters of the 146,000-acre **Ría Celestún Biosphere Reserve**, the easiest option is to hire a boat at the official *parador turístico*, just past the bridge on the main road into town. Ask the bus driver to drop you here, as it's a twenty-minute walk back from the main square (or M$20 for a *triciclo* taxi).

The standard tour (M$158; approx 1hr) stops at the flamingo feeding grounds and a freshwater spring amid mangroves; the longer trip (M$258; approx 2hr) also visits a "petrified forest" (really, a spooky swathe of salt-choked trees). Guides (M$300/1hr, M$400/2hr) are definitely recommended – all speak English and can identify most of the birds you'll see. You may be approached by unlicensed captains outside the *parador*; they will offer a competitive price, but their deep-keel boats are not designed for the inlet, and some passengers have found themselves pushing their craft out of the mud. For extended **birding** tours, contact Alberto Rodriguez Pisté, one of the expert guides at the *parador turístico* and a fluent English-speaker and longtime birder. If he's not here, ask at *Restaurant Celestún*, on the waterfront.

A few other ecotourism operations have opened in recent years. The best organized is **Manglares de Dzinitún** (T 999/232-5915), off the main road a bit west of the boat *parador*, and south about 1km. From here, you can take a circuit **bike-and-canoe tour** in about two hours (M$500), passing the flamingos and the petrified forest. There's also space to **camp** (M$100, with tent) and three solar-powered **cabañas** (❷).

Practicalities

Buses for Celestún depart sixteen times daily from Mérida's Noreste terminal (see p.188), beginning at 5.15am; the trip takes about two hours. In addition to the cabins at Manglares de Dzinitún (see p.193), the village has half a dozen **places to stay**, though there's virtually nothing going on at night. Beachfront *María del Carmen*, Calle 12 no. 111 at Calle 15 (☎988/916-2170, ✉mcrodriguez@hotmail .com; ❸), is the best bet, with balconies overlooking a wide beach (a/c is an option). If you want to settle in for a while, *Casa de Celeste Vida* (no tel, ⓦwww.hotelcelestevida.com; ❻) has three rooms with kitchens. On the upper end, the remote and lovely 🍴 *Eco Paraíso* (☎988/916-2100, ⓦwww .ecoparaiso.com; ❾) is 10km north of town. Operating primarily on wind and solar power, it has stylish cabañas, outdoor showers and a good restaurant. The real treat, though, is the utterly wild beach.

Of the several **seafood restaurants** along the beach, *La Palapa* is the biggest (and priciest) and generally more reliable than others in the centre, and *Los Pompanos*, north about 500m, is worth the trek. At night, *El Lobo*, on the plaza, is about the only place open, but fortunately it's good. For cheap home cooking, visit the *loncherías* by the small market (just off the inland side of the plaza). There's also a bakery, an **ATM** and a petrol station.

7

Uxmal and the Ruta Puuc

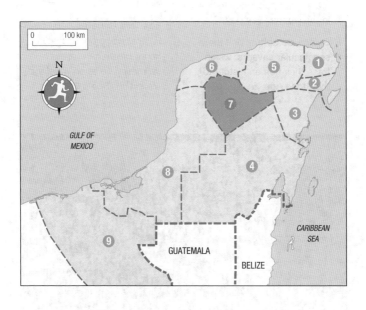

CHAPTER 7

Highlights

* **Haciendas** Stay at a restored nineteenth-century hacienda and get a sense of henequen plantation life. See p.198

* **Uxmal** Ranks with Chichén Itzá and Palenque as one of the great Maya sites of Mexico, with distinctive architecture. See p.200

* **Sayil** Trimmed with fine decoration, these vast ruins are also a good place to walk in the woods. See p.206

* **Grutas de Loltún** Visit these spectacular caverns, which trace their human history to the Stone Age. See p.208

* **Fortress churches** Built to awe the native population, the Franciscan churches along the Ruta de los Conventos have stood for centuries. See p.208

* **Acancéh** Virtually unknown, a hefty ancient pyramid stands alongside a huge colonial church in this rural town's main square. See p.211

* **Los Tres Cenotes** A trip back in time, riding on a rickety horse-drawn cart to visit swimming holes on a defunct plantation. See p.211

▲ Sculptured mask of the rain god Chac, Sayil

7

Uxmal and the Ruta Puuc

A bout 80km south of Mérida in the Puuc hills lies a group of the peninsula's most important archeological sites. Chief among them is **Uxmal**, second only to Chichén Itzá in size and historical significance, yet perhaps greater in its initial impact and certainly in the beauty and harmony of its unique architectural style. These are the first stop on the **Ruta Puuc**, as the driving route from Mérida to Uxmal and beyond is called. It runs along Hwy-261, on to the ruins of **Kabáh**, before turning east along a minor road to **Sayil**, **Xlapak** and **Labná**. Though Uxmal is firmly established on the tourist trail, these lesser Maya sites are surprisingly little-visited. If these places or their equivalents were in Europe or the United States, you wouldn't be able to move for tourists. Here, if you time your excursion right, you may get a vast site covering several square kilometres entirely to yourself. All this, and the Ruta Puuc is relatively accessible – particularly if you are coming from Mérida, the main city in Yucatán State. The sites are also very well restored, in comparison with many of the other ancient Maya cities.

Though the Puuc sites are the highlight, there are plenty of other attractions to blend into the mix when touring this area. The Ruta Puuc takes in contrasting **haciendas** at Yaxcopoil, Ochil and Temozón on the way to Uxmal, while beyond Labná it passes impressive caverns, the **Grutas de Loltún**. These are just outside the market town of **Oxkutzcab**, on the old main road from Mérida to Quintana Roo, and from here you can return to Mérida via **Ticul** and Muna, or take the fast new road past the Maya ruins of **Mayapán**.

The latter route, known as the **Ruta de los Conventos**, links a string of villages with gigantic fortified churches, relics of the early years of the Spanish occupation. The most impressive of these is the Franciscan monastery of San Miguel in **Maní**, and while the other villages en route are far less visited, many of them offer other attractions in the form of minor ruins, caves or **cenotes**, the latter especially impressive at Cuzamá, where a horse-drawn rail cart will take you to Los Tres Cenotes.

Southwest from Mérida

Between Mérida and Uxmal are few towns of any note, and Hwy-261 bypasses virtually all the settlements en route. But several restored haciendas offer compelling reasons to break your journey or even spend a night.

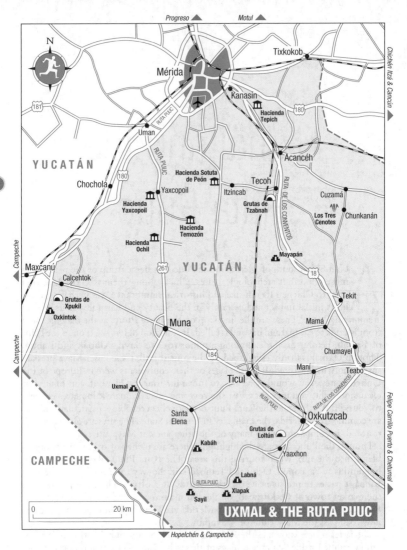

UXMAL & THE RUTA PUUC

   The first you reach, **Hacienda Yaxcopoil** (Mon–Sat 8am–6pm, Sun 9am–5pm; M$50, kids free) lies on the edge of the village of the same name, 32km south of Mérida. At its height, the place employed four hundred people, but now the main house stands in a state of picturesque disrepair – peeling walls, sagging ceilings and rooms full of mildewed tablecloths and faded pictures. If you're the only visitors, one of the employees will offer his services as a guide – this can be very illuminating (though only if you can understand Spanish).

   But it's also nice just to wander around the place, which is full of poignant corners. There's a water tank (used as a swimming pool) with changing rooms, a beautifully preserved old pumping engine by a well and lush orchards that you're free to wander, still watered by the original irrigation system. One room

The ideal way to visit this area is to **rent a car**, so you can explore all the key sites over two or three days, staying overnight around Uxmal or in Santa Elena, Oxkutzcab or Ticul. (For car rental agencies in Mérida, see p.189.) If your budget doesn't stretch to a car, your next best option is the **Ruta Puuc day-trip bus** (M$148), which departs daily from the second-class bus station in Mérida (C 69, between C 68 and C 70) at 8am, returning to Mérida at 3.45pm. It stops for twenty minutes at Xlapak, thirty minutes each at Labná and Sayil, fifty minutes at Kabáh and two hours at Uxmal. Since Uxmal is the last visited it's possible to stay longer and pay for a later bus back (though there is no service after the evening sound-and-light show). Alternatively, almost every travel agency in Mérida offers some kind of Ruta Puuc or Ruta de los Conventos trip that includes meals and a guide, with prices starting from around M$400 per person.

For **towns** along the Ruta Puuc, look for the service from Mayab (for Ticul, about 1hr, and Oxkutzcab, 2hr) and Sur (for Santa Elena, 1hr 15min, via Uxmal) – both go from the second-class station. The Ruta de los Conventos is a little more accessible by bus – these towns are all served by Lineas Unidas del Sur, departing from Mérida's Noreste terminal (C 67 at C 50). (For frequencies from Mérida, see box, p.188.) For the service between towns, ask around for **colectivos** – these often run more frequently than buses, and they're the only originating service in each town.

To travel on from the area, head for Ticul, the main transport hub, from where buses head to the Caribbean coast via Felipe Carrillo Puerto (10 daily; 4hr 30min). You can also get to Campeche (1 daily at 7pm; 3hr) via Hopelchén or to Chetumal (4 daily at 8.40am, 12.40pm, 6.40pm and 12.40am; 6hr).

is dedicated to Maya relics unearthed when the plantation was expanding, with ancient carved stones, *metates* (used for grinding corn) and pots. The old machine rooms are in a separate block – though beware of rocky floors and unprotected drops. If you really want to escape the crowds, there's a wonderful **room to rent** here, a huge, tiled, high-ceilinged space with two double beds, a fridge, coffeemaker, bathroom and terrace. You can cook over a fire or they'll bring meals in for you (T 999/900-1193, W www.yaxcopoil.com; ●).

Another 10km south and then 8km east from the highway, **Hacienda Temozón** (T 999/923-8089, W www.luxurycollection.com; ●) is one of the grandest of the haciendas that have been converted into a hotel. On its sprawling grounds you'll find two cenotes, a dramatic swimming pool and a gym in the old machine room. There is also a rather lavish international **restaurant** (7am–11pm) on the premises. Its breakfasts are not too expensive, and this makes a good early start to a trip to Uxmal, if you time it right.

Just west off Hwy-261, about 30km north of Uxmal, the attractively refurbished **Hacienda Ochil** (10am–6pm; T 999/924-7465, W www.haciendaochil.com) operates as a very good **restaurant** (standard meals for M$95), along with a small henequen **museum** displaying old photos and henequen at various stages of processing as well as a group of excellent *artesanía* stores and workshops. Some of the old narrow-gauge rail lines along which carts of henequen were transported have been restored to working order, and you can also see the plant being grown; occasionally there are demonstrations of the entire production process. A bonus for contemporary art fans: behind the restaurant, a cenote has been built into a beautiful amphitheatre by American land artist James Turrell. The hacienda entry fee of M$20 is waived if you're eating at the restaurant.

If you're travelling **by bus**, *Yaxcopoil* and *Ochil* lie right beside the road, so it's easy enough to be dropped here and flag down another to continue your journey.

7

Haciendas and henequen

The country all around Mérida is dotted with the crumbling remains of old **haciendas**, a number of which are restored as luxury hotels, restaurants or tourist attractions in one form or another. The oldest of them were established as early as the seventeenth century, when Spanish colonists took on vast landholdings to raise cattle or farm. The heyday of the haciendas was the end of the nineteenth century and the beginning of the twentieth, when the henequen boom brought vast wealth to their owners.

A type of agave cactus, **henequen** produces fibres that can be extracted for use as rope and twine. The fibre became known in English as sisal, after the port on the Yucatán coast from which it was originally shipped. The spiky leaves are harvested, just a few from each plant every year to prolong its life, then transported to the **machine house**, crushed and shredded to extract the individual fibres. Steam-powered machinery to do this initiated the boom, and at some of the haciendas you can see the original equipment.

Henequen is still grown and processed in the Yucatán, but only in small quantities, since the market for the "green gold" collapsed in the 1940s with the invention of artificial fibres. Before that, foreign competition and land redistribution after the Revolution dealt the first blows – but not before Mérida's Paseo de Montejo was lined with grandiose mansions from the profits. Many of the smaller towns in the Yucatán evolved out of a hacienda, and you can still see a towering smokestack or other remnants of the plantation buildings off one side of the central plaza.

Uxmal

The UNESCO World Heritage Site of **UXMAL** (pronounced "OOSH-mal", meaning "thrice-built") represents the finest achievement of the Puuc-region Maya. Rising to power when many southern cities were disintegrating, Uxmal fell into its ultimate decline near 1000 AD. Its spectacular buildings remain, however, encrusted all over with elaborate, sometimes grisly decoration. Admittedly, there has been a huge amount of reconstruction, primarily done in the 1930s and some of it quite haphazard. But most visitors will probably feel that the mix of accessibility and preservation has been judged about right, and it's a hard site not to enjoy. In fact, it's potentially more rewarding than a visit to Chichén Itzá, as the crowds are somewhat smaller, the decorative detail is fascinating, and you can still climb one of the pyramids.

Try to arrive close to opening time (the drive from Mérida takes about an hour). You can see the major buildings in a couple of hours; bus convoys start arriving by 10.30am. Even if you can't come this early, at least there's plenty of space for people to disperse once you get past the packs of guided tours around the largest pyramid.

Arrival and information

Several **buses** a day run direct from Mérida to Uxmal, and any bus heading down the main road towards Hopelchén will drop you just a short walk from the entrance. There's a pay **car park** (M$10) at the modern **entrance to the site** (daily 8am–5pm; M$166, where the small but handy **tourist centre** includes a basic museum (Spanish only), a Dante bookshop, a state-run craft store, a snack bar, phones, an ATM and an espresso vendor. You can hire a **guide** for M$550 for a small group. Uxmal's **sound-and-light show** (M$69, or free with day entry ticket) starts at 7pm daily in winter and 8pm in summer: the commentary is in Spanish and of dubious historical accuracy, but the lighting highlights the relief decorations on the walls beautifully. No inter-city buses run back to Mérida after the hour-long show.

Accommodation

Several **hotels** can be found close to the site, none in the budget category. Two are right at the site's entrance. *Villa Arqueológica Uxmal* (☎ 997/974-6020, Ⓦ www .villasmex.com; ❺) is the better value, with a pool and tennis courts, though the air-conditioned rooms are relatively small. *The Lodge at Uxmal* (☎ 998/887-2495, Ⓦ www.mayaland.com; ❾) is much more spacious, but grossly overpriced, at least officially; online booking can often get the rate under US$200. Across the main road from the site entrance (a 500m walk), the colonial-style *Hacienda Uxmal* (☎ 998/887-2495, Ⓦ www.mayaland.com; ❾) is a sister hotel to *The Lodge*, with similar rates. Other accommodation a short drive away includes budget options in Santa Elena (see p.204) or the ultra-lux *Hacienda Temozón* (see p.199).

The site

The main restored buildings are set out on a roughly north–south axis in a large cleared site. The alignment of individual buildings often has astrological signifi- cance, usually connected with Venus or the sun. As in all Maya sites in the

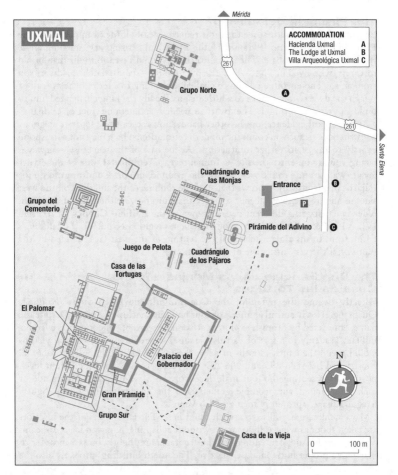

Yucatán, the face of **Chac**, the rain god, is everywhere. Chac must have been more crucial in this region than almost anywhere, for Uxmal and the other Puuc sites have no cenotes or other natural sources of water, relying instead on *chultunob*, jug-shaped underground cisterns, to collect and store rainwater. (Most have been filled in, to prevent mosquitoes breeding, but Kabáh has an extant one.)

Little is known of the city's early history, but what is clear is that the chief monuments, and the peaks of power and population, fall into the Terminal Classic period, 800–1000 AD. Though there are indications of settlement long before this, most of the buildings that you see date from this time.

After 900 AD the city began to decline, and by 1200 Uxmal and the Puuc sites, together with Chichén Itzá, were all but abandoned. The reasons are unknown, although political infighting, ecological problems and loss of trade with the Toltec site of Tula, near Mexico City, may have played a part. Later, the **Xiu Dynasty** settled at Uxmal, which, along with Chichén Itzá and Mayapán, became part of the League of Mayapán (see p.210). From Uxmal, in 1441, the rebellion originated that finally overthrew the power of Mayapán and put an end to any form of centralized Maya authority over the Yucatán.

The Pirámide del Adivino

Entering the site, you first see the most remarkable of all Mexican pyramids, the **Pirámide del Adivino** (Pyramid of the Magician), soaring at a startling angle from its unique oval base. The legend of the pyramid's creation tells that an old sorceress, who lived in a hut where the pyramid now stands, hatched a dwarf son from an egg and encouraged him to challenge the king to a series of tests – all of which the dwarf won, thanks to a little magic. Finally the king challenged him to build a pyramid overnight. The dwarf succeeded, and became ruler of Uxmal.

Archeological evidence, on the other hand, shows at least five separate stages of construction – six if you count the modern restoration, which may not correspond exactly to any of its earlier incarnations. At the base of the rear (east) stairway – facing you as you enter the site –a tunnel reveals **Templo III**, one of the earlier levels. Walk around to the west face of the pyramid into the **Cuadrángulo de los Pájaros** (named for the macaws that stud the roofline of the building on the west side) to admire the even steeper stairway that runs down either side of a second, older sanctuary in a different style. Known as the **Edificio Chenes** (or Templo IV), as it reflects the architecture of the Chenes region (see p.231), the building's entire front forms a giant mask. At the bottom of the west face, divided by the stairway, is the very first stage of construction.

The Cuadrángulo de las Monjas and the Casa de las Tortugas

Directly behind the pyramid, the **Cuadrángulo de las Monjas** (Nunnery Quadrangle) is a beautiful complex of four buildings enclosing a plaza. Despite the name, concocted by Spanish explorers, it wasn't a convent. Theories range from a military academy to a sort of earthly paradise, where intended sacrificial victims would spend their final months in debauchery. The four buildings, probably all constructed between 895 and 906 AD, are each set on a slightly different level, possibly representing the four main levels of the Maya universe. The facade of each is decorated with complex reliefs, and the quadrangle itself is a slightly irregular shape, apparently to align with Venus.

Maya architectural skills are at their finest here. The false vaults of the interiors are taken about as wide as they can go without collapsing, and wooden crossbeams provide further support. Moreover, the frontages are slightly bowed in order to maintain a proper horizontal perspective. The **north building**, probably also the oldest, has a strip of plain stone facade (from which doors lead into vaulted chambers) surmounted by a slightly raised panel of mosaics, featuring geometric patterns and human and animal figures, with representations of Maya huts above the doorways. The **west building**, which has been heavily reconstructed, boasts even more varied themes, and the whole of its ornamentation is surrounded by a coiling, feathered rattlesnake with the face of a warrior emerging from its jaws. The **east building** mirrors the west one in its proportions; its snake decorations, however, run in long horizontal bars.

An arched passageway through the middle of the **south building**, the lowest of the four, is directly aligned with the **ball-court** (ham-handedly rebuilt with cement) outside. Today a path leads through here, between the ruined side walls of the court and up onto the levelled terrace on which stand the Palacio del Gobernador (see below) and the **Casa de las Tortugas** (House of the Turtles). This very simple, elegant building, named after the stone turtles carved around the cornice, demonstrates another constant theme of Puuc architecture: stone facades carved to resemble rows of narrow columns. These, marked with bands of masonry, probably represent the Maya huts still in use today, with walls of bamboo or saplings lashed together.

The Palacio del Gobernador and the Grupo Sur

The **Palacio del Gobernador** (Governor's Palace) marks the finest achievement at Uxmal. Arriving at the then virtually unknown site in June 1840, explorer and writer John L. Stephens did not doubt its significance. "If it stood this day on its grand artificial terrace in Hyde Park or the Garden of the Tuileries," he later wrote, "it would form a new order...not unworthy to stand side by side with the remains of the Egyptian, Grecian and Roman art." The palace faces east, away from the buildings around it, probably for astronomical reasons – its central doorway aligns with the column of the altar outside and the point where Venus rises. Long and low, it is lent a remarkable harmony by the use of light and shade on the facade. Strong diagonals run through its broad band of mosaic decorations, particularly in the steeply vaulted archways that divide the two wings from the central mass, like giant arrowheads aimed at the sky. Close up, the mosaic shows excellent details: curly-nosed masks of Chac, the rain god, alternate with grid-and-key patterns and stylized snakes. The patterns vary in depth, lending the whole facade a rippling texture. Inside, by contrast, the chambers are narrow, gloomy and unadorned and, at the back, the rooms have no natural light source at all.

Behind the palace stand the ruinous buildings of the **Grupo Sur** (South Group), with the partly restored Gran Pirámide (Great Pyramid) and El Palomar (Dovecote, or Quadrangle of the Doves). You can climb the rebuilt staircase of the **Gran Pirámide** to see the temple on top, decorated with macaws and more masks of Chac – some of these have even smaller carved faces set inside their mouths. **El Palomar** was originally part of a quadrangle like that of the Nunnery, but the only building to retain any form is this, topped with the great latticed roofcomb that gives it its name: it looks somewhat like a dovecote.

The outlying structures are rather anticlimactic, but the scrub forest is the perfect place to spot some of the Yucatán's more distinctive birds, such as the turquoise-browed motmot, with its pendulum-like tail, particularly along the path that runs off the south side of the Palacio del Gobernador. The trail leads to an odd display of small **stone phalluses**, protected by a thatch roof – collected from all over the site, they're evidence of a fertility cult centred on Uxmal. (They're also worked into the back of the building on the west side of the Nunnery Quadrangle.)

Eating

La Palapa, the breezy **restaurant** and bar at *The Lodge at Uxmal*, is a convenient spot for a cool drink, though service can suffer when large groups arrive. Numerous other **restaurants** can be found along Hwy-261 towards Mérida, all catering mainly to tour groups. One decent, smaller-scale option is *Restaurante Cana-nah*, next to the otherwise dumpy *Rancho Uxmal* hotel, about 1.5km north of the site. The food is tasty and inexpensive, and diners are welcome to use the swimming pool. Or you can backtrack to *Hacienda Ochil* (see p.199), or press on to Santa Elena (see below).

⑦ The Ruta Puuc

From Uxmal, the **RUTA PUUC** continues south through the town of Santa Elena, a handy base for exploring this region. The road continues to the site of Kabáh, and shortly afterwards turns left (east) along a minor road to the market town of Oxkutzcab. The Maya sites of Sayil, Xlapak and Labná are all along this road, as are the Grutas ("caves") de Loltún.

If you're on a day-trip from Mérida, you can zip from the caves on the fast new highway via Mayapán (see p.210). But if you're taking things at a more leisurely pace, want somewhere to stop over or are reliant on public transport, then head for either **Oxkutzcab** or larger, livelier **Ticul**. (But if you prefer to stay overnight in a town rather than in the country, Oxcutzcab has a better hotel.)

Many of the organized **tours** cover this route in the opposite direction than described here, starting with a visit to the Grutas de Loltún and ending up at Uxmal in the late afternoon in time for a tour, followed by the sound-and-light show. So if you start out early, there's a good chance of seeing the smaller Puuc sites when very few other people are around.

Two things seem particularly striking when visiting the Puuc sites today. First, though each has its unique features, the overall impression is of a consistent **style**: the geometric patterns of Xlapak are echoed at Labná; the masks with the upward-curling noses that abound at Kabáh are also seen at Uxmal and all the other sites. The other striking factor is the extraordinary change in **population**. Today, along the entire route from Uxmal to Labná you'll see just one small town, Santa Elena. Twelve hundred years ago, several hundred thousand people lived here.

Santa Elena

The village of **SANTA ELENA**, 16km south of Uxmal and just 7km from Kabáh, is worth visiting mainly for the magnificent view from its large **church**, perched atop the only hill for miles around. Ask for the sacristan, who will open the door to the spiral staircase that leads to the roof. Beside the church is a morbidly interesting small **museum** (daily 8am–6pm; free) with displays on local funerary practices, including the two hundred-year-old mummified remains of four children that were discovered under the church floor in 1980. **Horseriding** tours around the area are available; ask at *The Pickled Onion* (see opposite) for details.

Three pleasant **places to stay** are located on Hwy-261 as it bypasses the village centre, making them particularly accessible – all are popular, so book ahead. *Flycatcher Inn* (☎997/978-5350, ⓦwww.flycatcherinn.com; ❺, breakfast included), is a B&B with seven rooms and a separate guest cottage, all decorated with local craftwork and furnished with lovely pillow-top beds; air conditioning is optional. A little further south on the highway is *The Pickled Onion* (☎997/111-7922,

As with Chichén Itzá, the **Puuc sites** were once thought to be the product of invading Toltecs from central Mexico, but are now accepted as being as authentically Maya as Tikal or Palenque. Though Uxmal is easily the best known today, the less celebrated sites were originally more important. The earliest significant examples of Puuc style are found at sites such as Oxkintok (see p.216) and Edzná (see p.228), but at the height of the Classic era it was the area around Kabáh and Sayil that dominated the region. Uxmal rose to dominance only at the end of the Classic period, around 800 to 900 AD, perhaps thanks to the city's relationship with the **Chontal Maya** of the Gulf coast lowlands, who became the Yucatán's most important trading partner by the Terminal Classic period (800–1000 AD). The Chontal Maya themselves traded extensively with Oaxaca and central Mexico and are thought to have passed on their architectural styles and themes to the Yucatán.

The distinctive **Puuc style** clearly evolved from themes in the Río Bec and Chenes regions. You'll see the same gaping monster mouths and facades decorated in mosaic-like Xs and checkerboards. In both cases, though, the techniques reflect a new strategy of mass production. The mask-covered front of the Codz Poop at Kabáh, for instance, is dotted with hundreds of consistently round carved eyes that form both a regular decorative pattern and individual images of the rain god **Chac**. A new core-and-veneer style of construction, rather than stone blocks stacked with mortar, yielded sounder buildings with a smoother appearance, which is highlighted by the tendency to leave the lower registers of buildings unadorned. Each Puuc site has its unique characteristics, but they also share architectural and artistic technique, religious symbolism, hieroglyphic writing and settlement patterns – scarcely surprising since there were also great causeways (*sacbeob*) linking the main centres.

Ⓦ www.thepickledonionyucatan.com; ❸, breakfast included) owned by a British expat who rents a handful of Maya-style cabañas. They're basic but comfortable (one is great for families), and there's a big pool. Around the next bend in the road, at *Sacbe Bungalows* (☎985/978-5158, Ⓦ www.sacbebungalows.com.mx; ❷), a hospitable Mexican-French couple offer basic but spotless bungalow rooms with porches, dotted about the spacious grounds; there's a cottage with a kitchen as well. Breakfast and supper are available. Buses from Mérida can drop you on the highway at all of these places on request.

For **meals**, *The Pickled Onion* (Mon–Sat 1–9pm, Sun 5–9pm) is also a good restaurant with an international menu (mains from M$95), plus good versions of local dishes, such as *lomitos de Valladolid*. Vegetarians will appreciate the fresh salads and the *chaya* soufflé, and all diners can use the pool. *El Chac Mool*, just north, does decent, inexpensive local food (closes at 8pm), while *La Central*, slightly further away in the village's main square, also offers good, simple meals.

Ticul

Eighty kilometres south of Mérida on Hwy-184, **TICUL** is another good base for exploring the Puuc region, though not especially scenic. Historically an important centre of Maya shamanism, it's also a shoe-manufacturing town. Streets here are lined with shoe shops, and there's an annual Feria de Zapatos (Shoe Festival) in the fall – if you're in the market for some totally impractical sparkly sandals, you've come to the right place.

The centre of town is around the junction of calles 25 and 26, with a large plaza to either side, plus a massive church and several **hotels** in the immediate vicinity. Simplest of these is the friendly *Sierra Sosa*, Calle 26 no. 199-A, between calles 23 and 21 (☎997/972-0008; ❶), where basic, if dark, rooms have a shower and fan (upstairs is better), though air conditioning and TV are available. A smarter alternative is the *Plaza*, Calle 23 no. 201, between calles 26 and 26-A (T 997/972-0484, W www.hotelplazayucatan.com; ●), with TV, telephone and air conditioning in all rooms. For a quieter night, go slightly further afield, to *Posada Jardín* at Calle 27 no. 216, between calles 28 and 30 (T 997/972-0401, W www .posadajardin.com; ●), which has four excellent-value cabins with separate sleeping and sitting areas, air conditioning, TV, fridge and coffeemaker, set in a lovely, bright garden with a small pool.

Ticul's best-known **restaurant**, *Los Almendros*, is famous for having invented the classic Yucatecan dish of *poc-chuc*. Unfortunately that's no guarantee you'll get a great meal, as the place is almost as famous for being wildly inconsistent. It's on Calle Principal, heading out of town towards Oxkutzcab, in a big building complete with a pool, and packed with families at weekends. Back in the centre, for an inexpensive *comida*, try *Restaurante & Cocktelería La Carmelita*, at the corner of calles 23 and 26. At night, don't miss the tortas at the front of the market on Calle 23, between calles 28 and 30.

Buses from Mérida and elsewhere use a station directly behind the church at the corner of calles 24 and 25-A. **Colectivos** for Mérida, as well as Santa Elena, Oxkutzcab and surrounding villages, set off when they're full from various points in the immediate vicinity of the bus station: for Mérida, from around the corner of calles 24 and 25; for other destinations, mainly from Calle 25-A, alongside the church. Other practicalities are also central – the **Banamex bank** facing the plaza on Calle 26, just off Calle 25, has an ATM; directly opposite is a good **internet café**.

Kabáh

The extensive site of **KABÁH** (daily 8am–5pm; M$37), meaning "Mighty Hand", stretches across the highway some 25km from Uxmal. Much of it remains unexplored, but the one great building, the **Codz Poop**, or Palace of Masks, lies not far off the highway to the east, near the main entrance. The facade of this amazing structure is covered all over, in ludicrous profusion, with goggle-eyed, trunk-nosed masks – to get into the doorways you need to tread over the masks' noses. Even in its present state – with most of the long, curved noses broken off – this remains the strangest and most striking of all Maya buildings, decorated so obsessively, intricately and repetitively that it almost seems the product of an insane mind. A couple of lesser buildings are grouped around the Codz Poop, directly in front of which stands a rare, working *chultun* (an underground cistern) with a concave stone floor gathering water into the underground chamber.

The other main buildings of the site lie across the highway. At first almost invisible through the trees, **La Gran Pirámide** is an unusual circular pyramid – now simply a green conical mound that, once you spot it, is so large you can't believe you missed it. It is believed that the building, erected on a natural elevation, functioned as a place where priests offered sacrifices or interpreted divine messages. Just beyond, a sort of triumphal arch marks the point where the ancient thirty-kilometre causeway, or *sacbé*, from Uxmal entered the city.

Sayil

A sober, restrained contrast to the excesses of Kabáh, the site of **SAYIL** (daily 8am–5pm; M$37) lies some 5km along a smaller road heading east off the highway, from a junction 5km beyond Kabáh. Once one of the most densely populated areas in the Puuc region, it is estimated that up to 17,000 people inhabited Sayil from 700 AD to 1000 AD. In the early part of that period, before Uxmal rose, Sayil was probably the foremost centre of the region.

Today the site is dominated by one major structure, the extensively restored, eighty-metre-long **Gran Palacio** (Great Palace), built on three storeys, each smaller than the one below. Although several large masks with protruding noses adorn a frieze around the top of the middle level, the decoration mostly takes the form of bamboo-effect stone pillaring – seen here more extensively than at any other Puuc site. The interiors of the middle level, too, are lighter and airier than usual, thanks to the use of broad openings, their lintels supported on fat columns. The upper and lower storeys are almost entirely unadorned, featuring plain stone surfaces with narrow openings. Water for the palace's inhabitants was once provided by eight *chultunes*.

Few other structures have been cleared, and those that have are widely scattered in the forest. The distances between cleared sites gives a strong impression of how big Sayil once was – it's a fifteen-minute walk from the Gran Palacio out to the farthest structures. But there's plenty of surviving tropical forest and wildlife. You'll see birds of all sorts, including hummingbirds, and there's a chance of spotting monkeys and other larger animals, such as the racoon-like coati.

From the Gran Palacio a path leads through the forest, past the piled stones of unexcavated remains, to **El Mirador**, a small temple with a roofcomb, and, in the other direction, to a large stele carved with the phallic figure of Yum Keep, god of fertility, now protected by a thatched roof. A signed turn-off leads to the **Templo de las Jambas Jeroglíficas**, named for the uninterpreted glyphs carved all around one half-buried doorway. At the end, the **Palacio Sur** is a large, little-restored structure with another characteristic bamboo facade, overlooking a ball-court, along with some unrestored mounds that make up the rest of the Grupo Sur and mark the end of the ceremonial *sacbé* through the site. You've actually been following this *sacbé* for much of your walk through Sayil, though there's little evidence of that fact to the untrained eye.

Xlapak and Labná

The minor road continues from Sayil past tiny **XLAPAK** ("Old Walls"; daily 8am–5pm; free), the smallest and least-visited of the Puuc sites. If you have time, stop to see the one restored building, a small, elegant palace with huge Chac masks above its doorways and geometric patterns on the façades. The remains of a *chultun* can be seen on the far side. There's almost no signage at all at Xlapak, and from the palace unmarked trails lead through the forest to other nameless, half-uncovered mounds, again characterized by geometric patterns.

Three kilometres after Xlapak, the ancient city of **LABNÁ** (daily 8am–5pm; M$37), historically far smaller and less important than Sayil, is in many ways a more impressive site. There has been more excavation here, so the main buildings can all be seen as part of a harmonious whole. The **Palacio**, near the entrance, is similar to, though less impressive than, that of Sayil. Traces of sculpture include a crocodile-snake figure with a human face emerging from its mouth – thought to symbolize a god escaping from the jaws of the underworld.

Remnants of a raised *sacbé* lead from here to the **Arco de Labná**. Originally part of a complex linking two great squares, like the Nunnery at Uxmal, it now stands alone, richly decorated on both sides: on the east with geometric patterns; on the west (the back) with more of these and niches in the form of Maya huts or temples. Nearby **El Mirador** is a barely restored temple mound topped by the well-preserved remains of a tall, elaborate roofcomb. An inner passageway at one time led to the site's principal temple. Many of Labná's buildings were originally adorned with human figures; you can still see the lower half of one standing by the roofcomb of El Mirador as well as painted stucco remnants inside the "huts" atop the arch. The last of the main structures, the **Edificio de las Columnas**, is a long, low building, its facade punctuated by five doors, characterized by the classic Puuc-style bamboo column decoration from which it takes its name.

Grutas de Loltún

The **Grutas de Loltún** (daily 9am–5pm, accessible only with guided tours, at 9.30am, 12.30pm & 3.30pm; M$111) are the most impressive caves in the Yucatán, at least among those that are developed and lit for visitors. The two-hour tour (for which you can request an English-speaking guide) concentrates on strange rock formations and the patterns seen in giant stalactites and stalagmites. There's also plenty of fascinating history: mammoth bones discovered here attest to prehistoric periods of climate change, and the caves were revered by the Maya as a source of water long before they built their cities. At the entrance, a huge bas-relief warrior guards the opening to the underworld, and throughout are traces of ancient paintings and carvings on the walls. The surrounding jungle is visible through the collapsed ceiling of the last gallery, and ten-metre-long tree roots have anchored themselves on the cavern floor.

Across the road is a decent **restaurant**, *Lol-tún*, with *panuchos* and other standard items. From Oxkutzcab (see below), you can take a **colectivo** or truck; they leave from Calle 51 next to the market, and if you get there by 8.30am you may be able to catch the truck taking the cave employees to work. **Getting back** is less easy, as the trucks are full of workers and produce, but if you wait something will turn up. The short taxi ride from the town will cost you approximately M$50. If you're **driving** back to Mérida, the fast route is Hwy-18, which starts just north of the caves.

Oxkutzcab

At the heart of Yucatán's citrus orchards, **OXKUTZCAB** doesn't look like much unless you visit early in the morning (or wake up here), when its huge daily **market** is bustling. In addition to all the usual snacks, housewares and vegetables, fruits and flowers are sold wholesale, piled high by the crate and sack, all under a resplendent mural of Yucatecan farmlands and orchards. It's right at the centre of town, at the junction of calles 51 and 50, where the main plaza sits next to a hefty Franciscan church, established in 1581 and not completed until 1699. Railway fans can also seek out the old depot, built of old Maya stones in a faux-Puuc style, on Calle 45 at Calle 54.

Buses to Mérida via Ticul (2hr) leave about every hour from the **bus station** on Calle 51 at Calle 56; *colectivos* come and go from Calle 51, beside the market. One basic **hotel**, *Hospedaje Duran* (☎997/975-1748; ●), is centrally located on Calle 51, opposite the market, but the *Hotel Puuc*, at calles 55 and 44, on the way out of town towards Labná (☎997/975-0103; ●), is more preferable and only marginally more expensive. Its bright, clean rooms have TV, wi-fi and optional air conditioning; there's even a pool. The Banamex **bank** on Calle 50, opposite the plaza, has an ATM, and there's an **internet café** at the corner of calles 51 and 52. **Restaurants** and *loncherías* skirt the market area, and the *Hotel Puuc* has a restaurant as well.

The Ruta de los Conventos

The **Ruta de los Conventos** ("Convent Route"), Hwy-18 between Oxcutzcab and Mérida, is a natural extension of the Ruta Puuc. It also makes an easy day outing from Mérida, best if you get an early start, then end with a leisurely late lunch at one of the destination restaurants along the way. The route itself is something of a recent invention by the tourist authorities, for although it's true that almost all the villages along the way do have impressive, fortified churches or monasteries – above all at **Maní** – the same can be said of towns and villages

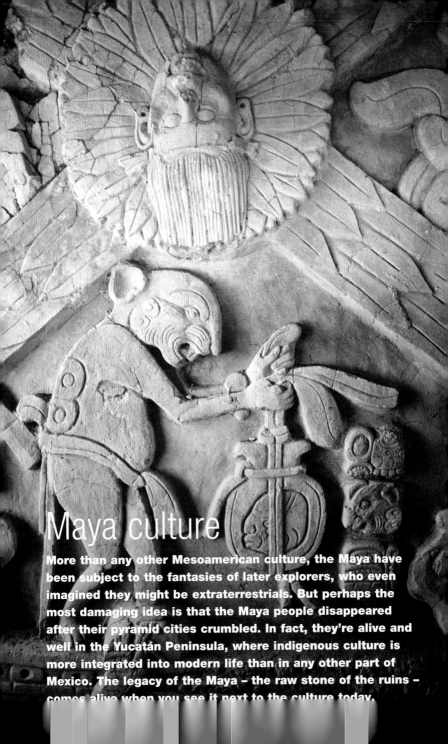

Maya culture

More than any other Mesoamerican culture, the Maya have been subject to the fantasies of later explorers, who even imagined they might be extraterrestrials. But perhaps the most damaging idea is that the Maya people disappeared after their pyramid cities crumbled. In fact, they're alive and well in the Yucatán Peninsula, where indigenous culture is more integrated into modern life than in any other part of Mexico. The legacy of the Maya – the raw stone of the ruins – comes alive when you see it next to the culture today.

Maya then and now

At its peak a thousand years ago, the ancient Maya empire had a population of some two million, based around at least forty substantial cities, including Chichén Itzá, Calakmul and Uxmal. Eventually the empire splintered, and, after the **Conquest**, collapsed. But despite the best efforts of the Spanish Catholics, the culture persisted, and the ancient religion even helped fuel a rebellion in the nineteenth century. The **Caste Wars**, as the decades-long resistance came to be known, were the only really

Celebrating the Day of the Dead, or Hanal Pixan ▲

A Maya incense burner, Palenque ▼

The Grutas de Loltún were used by ancient Maya ▼

Touring the sites

Travellers often aspire to "do" the major Maya sites of Chichén Itzá, Uxmal, Palenque and Calakmul in a single trip. But it's more realistic to focus on one and explore the surrounding smaller ruins, giving you time to appreciate living Maya culture, too. Not far from Chichén Itzá lie **Ek-Balam** and **Cobá** (an excellent place to spot wildlife), but be sure to also stop in the town of **Valladolid** (see p.153), where Maya women from surrounding villages come to sell their embroidery. South of Mérida, **Uxmal** anchors the **Ruta Puuc**, a circuit that passes several smaller but equally ornate ruins, as well as the **Grutas de Loltún** (see p.208), a network of caves where the ancient (and not-so-ancient) Maya conducted rituals. South from **Palenque**, along the border with Guatemala, sits **Bonampak** and riverside **Yaxchilán**, reachable only by boat. You may see offerings and incense at the altars in these remote yet vibrant spots. Also stop in Palenque town's small **textile museum** (see p.247) to see the variety of weaving produced by the Maya group in Chiapas. The most remote site of all is **Calakmul**. Once you've gone that far, don't miss the odd towers of the **Río Bec** sites (see p.140) to the west.

Ancient Maya art

Apart from the ruined buildings themselves, the most famous Mesoamerican artworks are the **Jaina figurines**, a collection of small clay animals and people found on the Maya burial ground of Isla de Jaina (see box, p.219). Thousands of the statuettes depict everyone from queens to village governors to weavers, and their timeless, expressive features give a clear impression of the Maya as people, rather than just as pyramid-builders. Most museums in the area have a few of the figurines, with the largest collection in Hecelchakán (see p.219). Other art forms, seldom seen at ruined sites, are **plaster sculpture** and **fresco painting**. Because plaster is so fragile, little of either kind of work has survived, but the elaborate figures at **Ek-Balam** (see p.158) and the murals at **Bonampak** (see p.255) are a reminder that the ancient world was much more ornate and colourful than the grey stone we see today.

▲ *Jarana* dancers at Mérida's Sunday party

▼ A Maya woman cooking tortillas

▼ Traditional Maya dress, near San Cristóbal de las Casas

successful indigenous uprising in Latin America. The Maya fought for more than fifty years, and even succeeded in briefly establishing an **independent state** that was recognized by the British.

Now there are some six million Maya, spread throughout the Yucatán, Tabasco, Chiapas and neighbouring Belize and Guatemala. They're barely visible in Tabasco but vibrant in Chiapas, home to the Lacandón, Tzeltal, Tzotzil and Chol Maya. On the peninsula itself, the majority are **Yucatec Maya** – that is, related to or current speakers of the Yucatec variation of the Maya language, which is spoken everywhere and often incorporated into Spanish as slang. In the Yucatán the culture is most visible, a point of regional pride even among those who have little or no Maya roots.

Fresco of a Maya feast at Bonampak, Chiapas ▲

A mother with her daughters in Chiapas ▼

Beyond the ruins

After you've toured the archeological sites, check out these other ways to experience Maya culture in the Yucatán Peninsula and Chiapas.

Party down

Town fiestas highlight the *jarana* dance. For a list of festivals in the Yucatán, see p.35, and ask at the tourism office in Mérida for smaller events.

Camp out

After visiting Bonampak, stay the night with the **Lacandón** in their village near the ruins. This most remote of the Maya groups has a vast knowledge of the surrounding forest. See p.256.

Take to the water

At the ruins of **Muyil**, hire a small boat to tour the canals that early Maya traders dug between the mangroves. They link the inland forest with the sea. See p.124.

Pay respects

Visit the rustic shrine of the **Talking Cross** in the town of Felipe Carrillo Puerto, the stronghold of the Maya resistance during the nineteenth-century Caste Wars. See p.128.

Meet the neighbours

Guests at *Genesis Retreat* in the village of Ek-Balam can **visit local Maya** houses, where they meet artisans and home-makers – try your hand at making tortillas and weaving an intricate hammock. See p.159.

Visit the artists

In Izamal, open workshops show embroidery, jewellery-making and other skills the Maya have honed for centuries. The folk-art museum rents bikes to make the tour easier. See p.168.

Eat up

The **food** on your plate – with ingredients such as turkey, achiote, pumpkin seeds and fiery *habañero* chiles – was probably eaten by Maya millennia ago too. See p.29 & p.302 for menu items.

throughout the Yucatán. Nevertheless it's an enjoyable excursion, with a fascinating and wholly Yucatecan mix of churches, minor Maya ruins, caves and cenotes, set against a backdrop of small towns and villages that see relatively few tourists. If you follow Hwy-18 you can turn off to any town en route and find a hulking, centuries-old church, but the highlights of the route are the late Maya site of **Mayapán**; **Los Tres Cenotes**, where, as the name suggests, three cenotes lie along the tracks of a hacienda's old rail system (the journey itself is much of the attraction); and **Acancéh**, with its Maya remains in the middle of town.

The **churches** themselves date mainly from the seventeenth century or earlier, when the Spanish were trying to establish their control. They were built so huge partly to impress, partly as symbols of Christianity's domination over traditional gods (often on the site of Maya temples, using the stones from the older buildings) and partly as fortresses and places of refuge in times of trouble – windows are few, high and narrow, and interiors are relatively plain.

If you're starting in Mérida (going backwards on the route as described below) and travelling **by car**, the easiest route out is Calle 69 east to the *periférico* (ring road), then following signs to Mayapán. This takes you to the improved highway, **Hwy-18** – it bypasses all of the towns and villages mentioned below, but they're all well signposted and only a short way from the new road. Virtually all **bus** services to the area depart from Mérida's Noreste terminal, Calle 67 at Calle 50; the primary company is Lineas Unidas del Sur.

Maní and around

Twelve kilometres north of Oxkutzcab is the small town of **MANÍ**. Founded by the Xiu after they abandoned Uxmal, it was the largest city the Spanish encountered in the Yucatán, though almost no trace now survives. Avoiding a major confrontation, Maní's ruler, Ah Kukum Xiu, converted to Christianity and became an ally of the Spanish. In 1548, one of the earliest and largest **Franciscan monasteries** in the Yucatán was founded here; this still stands, surrounded now by Maya huts. About the only evidence of Maní's past glories are the ancient stones used to construct it and the walls around the town. In front of the church, in 1562, Bishop Diego de Landa held an infamous auto-da-fé, in which he burned the city's ancient records (because they "contained nothing in which there was not to be seen the superstitions and lies of the devil"), destroying virtually all surviving original Maya literature in one conflagration. The monastery itself offers an enjoyable wander through courtyards and cloisters full of plants, flowers and old wells, while the church has some fine, elaborately carved altars and saints in niches. Maní has little else to offer beyond an entrancingly slow pace of life. Méridans often come down here on day-trips to dine at ✱ *El Príncipe Tutul-Xiu* (Tues–Sun 11am–7pm), on Calle 26, between calles 25 and 27, a festive palapa-roof **restaurant** that has been serving Yucatecan standards for more than thirty years.

Continuing north from Maní along Hwy-18, there's a string of villages distinguished by their huge fortress-like churches, plain on the inside save for carvings of saints. Most see few tourists and have no facilities apart from the odd general store. Many of the women here still dress daily in elaborately embroidered *huipiles*, and there's a real sense of traditional rural life. The churches are generally open during the day, though there's no guarantee of this. Just across the highway (northeast) from Maní, **Teabo** has a monster-sized church, while **Chumayel**, up the road, has the rather smaller Templo de la Purisima Concepción, with a brightly gilded altar set off by whitewashed walls. In **Mamá**, the vast, crumbling fortress of a church is cathedral-like in scale, and probably the oldest on the route. Dedicated to the Virgin (celestial images around the intricately carved entrance represent the Queen of Heaven), it dates originally from the sixteenth century, but has been much altered and added to during the centuries since. If you can get in, be sure to look at the beautiful wall-paintings in the room behind the altar, as well as the cloister-style garden courtyard around a well. In **Tekit**, a village otherwise devoted to farming, there are some good carved-wood saints in its church.

Mayapán

Roughly halfway between Maní and Mérida, the ruins of **MAYAPÁN** (daily 8am–5pm; M$31) lie right beside the road. (Don't confuse them with the village of Mayapán, east of Teabo.) The most powerful city in the Yucatán from the thirteenth to the fifteenth century, Mayapán was, according to Maya chronicles, one of the three cities (the others being Chichén Itzá and Uxmal) that made up the **League of Mayapán**, which exercised control over the entire peninsula from around 987 to 1185. The league dissolved when the **Cocom** dynasty of Mayapán attacked and overwhelmed the rulers of an already declining Chichén Itzá, establishing itself as sole controller of the peninsula. Archeological evidence tells a different story, as Mayapán does not appear to have been a significant settlement until the thirteenth century. The rival theory has Mayapán founded around 1263, after the fall of Chichén Itzá.

Whatever its history, Mayapán became a huge city by the standards of the day, with a population of some fifteen thousand on a site covering five square kilometres, in which traces of more than four thousand buildings have been found. Rulers of subject cities were forced to live here, perhaps even as hostages, where they could be kept under control. This hegemony was maintained until 1441, when Ah Xupan, a Xiu leader from Uxmal, finally led a rebellion that succeeded in overthrowing the Cocom and destroying their city, thus paving the way for the fractured tribalism that the Spanish found on their arrival and which greatly facilitated the Conquest.

What can be seen today is in some ways a disappointment, and certainly no match for the Classic Maya sites. The buildings, by Maya standards, are relatively crude and small, at best poor copies of what had come before. Only a few of the other structures have been restored, so a visit doesn't take long. The scale of the place has led to the dismissal of the Mayapán society as "decadent" and failing, but a powerful case can be made that it was merely a changing one. As the priests no longer dominated here (hence the lack of great ceremonial centres), what developed instead was a more genuinely urban society: highly militaristic, no doubt, but also far more centralized and reliant on trade than any previous Maya culture.

The site has its undeniable attractions, too. If you've already been to Chichén Itzá, you may experience déjà vu: the main structure, the so-called **Castillo de Kukulkán**, looks like a miniature rendition of the Castillo at the larger site. Steep, narrow steps lead to an unshaded platform from where there's a seemingly infinite view across the plains. Low down at the rear of the building are stucco reliefs of decapitated warriors – there's a niche where their heads would have been, where perhaps the heads or skulls of real enemies were displayed. Elsewhere are rows of columns, again similar to Chichén Itzá, as well as gaping snake heads protruding from staircases. Scattered throughout are numerous frescoes, carvings and stuccos (look under the thatched shelters), many with their original colours still visible. Keep an eye out also for the cenote – it's not one you can swim in (it's tucked underground, the entrance shaded by banana palms) but it's one of no fewer than 26 similarly small springs scattered across the ancient city.

Tecoh and Hacienda Sotuta de Peón

The next stop north along the route, **TECOH** has another vast, fortified church on its plaza, at calles 30 and 29. It's on a small rise because it was built on the foundations of a great pyramid. But Tecoh's main claim to fame is an extensive cave system, the **Grutas de Tzabnah** (8am–5pm; M$40), containing as many as thirteen cenotes. This is a trip only for the cave enthusiast: there's no lighting except for the flashlights you and your guide will carry, and the caves are slippery, dark, low-ceilinged and full of bats. Taking the full tour (about 2hr) involves crawling through tight, muddy passageways as well as various steep inclines where you need a rope. There are some impressive caverns along the way, and at the far end a welcome swim in the tenth cenote, but you'll get muddy and sweaty again on the way out – at least until plans to put in a staircase and lighting are realized. The caves are about 500m south of town, on Calle 28; if you come in from the highway from the south, you'll pass them on your right.

In Tecoh, you'll also see signs pointing west to **Hacienda Sotuta de Peón** (daily tours at 10am & 1pm; ☎999/960-8551, ⓦwww.haciendatour.com; M$300, kids M$150), just outside of Itzincab. In terms of dilapidation, it's the polar opposite of Yaxcopoil (see p.198), although fortunately it's not so well groomed that it's no fun. Set up as a sort of living history museum, the grounds are actually in use as a henequen plantation. A guided tour on a horse-drawn rail cart takes you to each point in the processing. Entrance is a bit pricey, but this also includes access to a cenote and a large swimming pool. As such, it's a good alternative to the cenotes at Cuzamá if you have smaller children. Reservations are advised, as it's often full with groups.

Acancéh

The next town north from Tecoh, **ACANCÉH** (pronounced "ah-kan-KAY") is somewhere that could exist only in Mexico. This town, with its extraordinary mix of Maya, modern and colonial architecture, almost entirely ignored by tourism, encapsulates Yucatecan history. Penetrating through the scrappy outskirts of what is a sizeable town, you arrive abruptly at the central plaza, where, beside the church – a sixteenth-century Franciscan construction that in any other setting would command your attention – is a large Maya **pyramid** (daily 8am–5pm; M$31). Behind this is a second smaller pyramid, and nearby there's a third – all of them surrounded by people's backyards and the everyday life of the town. At the top of the large pyramid, protected under thatched shades, are four huge stucco masks. It's not known exactly whom they represent, but they are old (Early Classic or before) and some of the finest of their kind that survive: some say that the features show Olmec influence. Acancéh was an important Maya centre before many of its better-known neighbours were, reaching its high point in the Early Classic period (300–600 AD) before gradually declining in the face of the rising power of nearby Mayapán.

The ancient Maya **Palacio de los Estucos** is about four blocks away, behind the market (get directions from the booth at the main pyramid). Though fenced, it seems to be open all day and is usually deserted save for some truly huge iguanas. A long, low building, the palace may have been an elite residential complex as its name suggests, or possibly an administrative centre. At the top is a corbel-arched passageway and, under cover, the stuccos from which the palace takes its name. These are far from complete, but there are plenty of easily identifiable figures, animals and glyphs.

Los Tres Cenotes

The trip to **LOS TRES CENOTES** ("The Three Cenotes") is a significant detour off the Ruta de los Conventos, and a time-consuming one likely to take at least four hours, including the drive from the main highway. The starting point is **Chunkanán**, a tiny village south of Cuzamá (which is east of Acancéh). The village was originally built as a hacienda, and the cenotes lie in the semi-abandoned henequen fields, reached by the old narrow-gauge rail lines. To reach the pools, you hire a *truk* (or *carrito*), a rickety, wooden, horse-drawn rail carriage (M$200/*truk*). These can seat four or five in some discomfort, with no brakes or suspension, and little padding on the seats. The journey is roughly 45 minutes each way, plus as long as you choose to spend at the cenotes. You get a real sense of journeying back in time as you leave the road behind and head off along the wobbly tracks through the fields. You'll want to bring swimming gear, towels and perhaps a picnic, as locals do on weekends.

The first two cenotes, **Chelentún** and **Chansinic'ché**, are partially enclosed and have steep stairways down to the water. The first is more appealing in the morning, when the sun still hits the water. The third, **Bolonchoojol**, is a somewhat different beast, an entirely enclosed cave that is reached by a ladder that appears to drop down into infinite blackness. In fact, it leads to a large wood platform from where, once your eyes adjust, you see a sparkling blue pool, lit only by a shaft of light piercing through the stone ceiling.

The process of hiring a *truk* has gotten slightly complicated by the fact that two competing groups now offer them. Coming from Cuzamá, you first pass a large parking area off the right side of the road, liberally signed for Los Tres Cenotes and often staffed with an enthusiastic greeter who will flag you down. This is the upstart organization, run by people from Cuzamá and greatly resented by the people of Chankanán, who have always run the *truk*s and have no other income in their village. If you press on to Chunkanán, less than 1km down the road, you will find the original operation, in front of an enormous, multi-storey palapa structure. This happens to be a superb **restaurant**, ⚔ *El Dzapakal* (daily 10am–6.30pm), with hearty Yucatecan food (avoid the other stuff), beautifully presented and very reasonably priced (mains M$45–75). If you're in a taxi or *triciclo* from Cuzamá, you'll of course get steered to the first, Cuzamá-run *truk* stop; if you want to go to Chunkanán without raising a fuss, you can always say you're headed for the restaurant.

You can **spend the night** in Chunkanán at the wonderful little hideaway of ⚔*Sac-Nicté* (no tel, ⓦwww.mayanvillagerental.com; ➐), an authentically Maya-style compound, where one small palapa hut houses two hammocks (with mosquito nets), another has a toilet and bathtub and another has a kitchen and another hammock, if you need it. Out back is a pool. Once you've come this far, you'll probably want to take advantage of the three-day package, which includes meals and tours to other cenotes, caves and ruins.

Getting to the cenotes from Mérida on a **bus** is possible, but requires a full day. LUS buses run fifteen times a day (first at 7.45am, then 9.15am; 1hr 30min) from the Noreste terminal, or you can take a *combi* from the Parque San Juan (this usually takes closer to two hours). You'll then need to take a *triciclo* to Chunkanán, another M$15 or so. If you're already in the area, look for *combis* in Acancéh.

Hacienda Tepich

Just 5km before Mérida's ring road on Hwy-18, **Hacienda Tepich** is the old henequen plantation in the town of Tepich Carrillo. The main house has been renovated just enough to be a functioning and reasonably tasty **restaurant** (noon–7pm) that specializes in rabbit dishes – the simple grilled preparation (M$100) is the best. Squeamish diners should probably go somewhere else, but anyone who appreciates locally grown food will also appreciate the fact that the live, pre-dinner rabbits are raised right on the grounds, along with a lot of the chickens. There are other traditional Yucatecan dishes, too, whose ingredients are somewhat less conspicuous. Before or after your meal, you can stroll the vast, overgrown grounds. The hacienda entrance is on the east side of the main plaza, not well marked. Don't be deterred if the gates are closed – this is usually just to keep the horses in.

Campeche

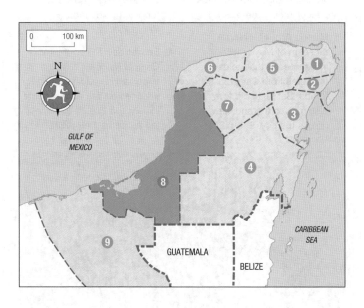

CHAPTER 8

Highlights

* **Caves** Riddled with cave systems, the area includes two of the Yucatán's largest at Calcehtok and X'tacumbilxuna'an. See p.218 & p.232

* **Campeche's centro histórico** Surrounded by brash modern Mexico, this fortified colonial settlement, beautifully preserved as a UNESCO World Heritage Site, conjures past glamour. See p.224

* **Museo Arqueológico** A museum of Maya relics in Campeche that holds treasures from Calakmul's tombs. Set in an old fort, it also gives a grand view across the city. See p.226

* **Edzná** The Maya's mastery of the land is evident at this great site, whose ancient population was dependent on an elaborate system of drainage and irrigation. See p.228

* **Chenes sites** Home to a wildly decorative architectural style, in which buildings look like monsters or gods, complete with doorways forming gaping mouths. See p.231

* **Sea turtles** The southern Campeche coast is an important breeding ground for endangered sea turtles; come in July and August to witness the hatching. See p.233

▲ The Templo de los Cinco Pisos (Five-Storey Temple on the Gran Acrópolis), Edzná

8

Campeche

The third of the three states that make up the Yucatán Peninsula, Campeche is far less visited than its neighbours, even though its capital city is a UNESCO World Heritage Site and the area's importance in the ancient Maya world grows clearer with every year of new excavation. The ruins of **Edzná**, **Oxkintok** and the **Chenes sites**, notably **Hochob**, are magnificent, but it is the city of **Campeche** that is the region's highlight – a place that evokes an era when pirates were a constant threat and the wealth of the Americas flowed through on its way to Spain. It combines the feel of Old Spain in its superbly preserved colonial centre, the chaos of modern Mexico in its raucous outskirts and the hot, heady atmosphere of a tropical port that's half-asleep in the mid-afternoon.

Campeche State is located on the southwest part of the Yucatán Peninsula, where the coast of the Gulf of Mexico curves from a north-south direction to east-west. Its beaches are functional, but seldom a destination, and the few towns along the water see hardly any tourism, as they're more concentrated on industries like shrimp (in **Champotón**) and oil (**Ciudad del Carmen**). The more interesting sights are inland, whether just off the **main route** from Mérida to Campeche (Hwy-180) or along the more leisurely alternative, the meandering Hwy-261, via Uxmal and Hopelchén and a number of seldom-visited ruins, often referred to collectively as the **Chenes sites**. There is a very good **bus service** on the major highways (most buses to Villahermosa and Palenque go through the junction town of Escárcega, in the southern part of the state), but away from these routes the service is far less frequent, and you'll need a car if you want to stop at more than one town or set of ruins in a day.

Mérida to Campeche via Hwy-180

First-class buses and all *directo* services take the direct road from Mérida to Campeche, **Hwy-180**, which follows the line of the old colonial Camino Real, the Spanish trade route connecting Gulf ports with central Mexico. This is a fast, flat drive of 160km or so, but you need to turn off to make the most interesting stops on the way, such as the Maya site of **Oxkintok** and the hat-producing town of **Becal**. Entering the state of Campeche, there's a further worthwhile detour to **Hecelchakán,** where a small archeology museum displays figures from nearby Isla de Jaina (the island itself is not publicly accessible).

The longer route follows **Hwy-261** for almost 250km past Uxmal and Kabáh (see Chapter 7), entering Campeche State near **Bolonchén de Rejón**. Much

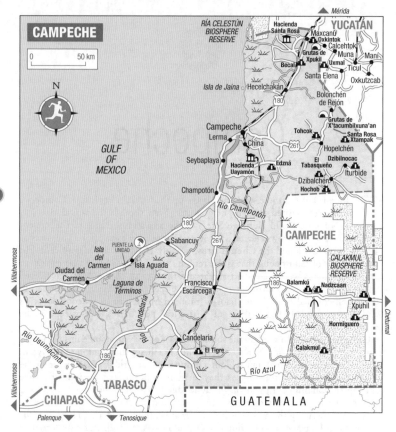

slower as it winds through the hills inland, this is also a far prettier route with a number of possible stops. Uxmal and Kabáh themselves could take the best part of a day, while several of the smaller Chenes sites are reached from **Hopelchén**. As you approach Campeche, Edzná is also not far off this road. It's easy going if you're driving, of course, and a bit slower – but still feasible – by bus. With an early start you should be able to go this way, take in at least one site and continue the same day. Only Uxmal and Kabáh lie directly on the road.

Oxkintok

Only recently excavated, **OXKINTOK** (daily 8am–5pm; M$37), in Yucatán State, is a large and beautifully maintained site, set on a low ridge with beautiful views. The ruins are signed off Hwy-180, a few kilometres along a minor road that leads to Muna and Uxmal and then a dusty white track to the site itself. They are not easily reached by bus – you'd have to get to Maxcanú and take a *triciclo* taxi for several kilometres from there. Similarly, there are no facilities or shops of any kind nearby, so be sure to bring some water and perhaps pack a lunch; there are picnic tables under palapa shades near the entrance and further into the site.

Oxkintok was probably the dominant city in the region during the Early Classic period (c.250-600 AD), thanks in part to a strategic position among low hills which command the route from the coast at Celestún to Uxmal and Sayil, and also to Dzibilchaltún and the salt lagoons to the north and west. It is among the earliest of the Puuc sites, and although power later passed to the better-known cities further south, Oxkintok continued to be inhabited right through the Classic Maya era.

The site features three main groups of buildings: Ah Dzib, to the right as you enter; Ah Canul, to the left; and Ah May, directly ahead of you. Tzat Tun Tzat, the so-called "**Maya labyrinth**", is behind the Ah Dzib group, to the right of Ah May. All of the structures here are old – older than most you'll see at other Puuc sites – and for that reason are on the whole smaller, less decorated and perhaps a little cruder than those at the great sites. Nonetheless, this proto-Puuc style contains many of the seeds of the architectural forms that would reach their height at Uxmal. The **Ah Dzib** group is the oldest of all, dating mainly from the Pre-Classic era (c.300 BC–250 AD). The small ball-court here was equipped with a *temazcal*, a steam-bath similar to those still used by the Maya today, where players would undergo ritual purification before a game.

Sadly, the labyrinth – El Laberinto or **Tzat Tun Tzat** – the most famous individual structure here, is closed to the public, so you can no longer explore its sixteen rooms on three levels and numerous dimly lit passageways. Off to the right of the main path, it is a highly unusual building for this era, with its tiny windows and rooms: locals claim that there are tunnels, as yet undiscovered, linking the labyrinth to other buildings here, or even to nearby caves. This fits neatly with ancient myths that at Oxkintok there was an opening to Xibalba, the Maya underworld.

Between the labyrinth and the Ah May group, a damp depression, alive with plants, cacti and butterflies, marks the site of an ancient cistern, or *aguada*. Scattered around the site are also numerous underground *chultunes*, their openings usually blocked with flat stones or metal discs. The **Ah May group** itself offers great views of the surrounding countryside, studded with unexplored mounds. Structure MA-9 was built later than most at the site: its dressed-stone walls with simple bamboo-column decoration overlook a large plaza, very reminiscent of the style at other Puuc sites.

The **Ah Canul** group is the largest and perhaps most impressive of all. Most of the facade of El Palacio Ch'ich (CA-7) has crumbled, but a couple of columns survive, carved with human figures that still stand sentinel over the plaza in front of them. In the centre of the plaza, you can make out the opening to a large *chultun*, while adjacent to the building lies the Palacio del Diablo, of which almost nothing remains save the column from which it takes its name, carved with a figure with two holes in the top of its head. The Spanish thought that horns had sprouted from these – hence the name. There were once many other human figures adorning these buildings, but neglect and easy access mean this site has been very heavily looted. The Palacio Pop (CA-3) is among the oldest structures at the site: on its floor, remnants of a painted palm mat design have been found (a palm mat, or *pop* in Maya, was a symbol of authority).

Around Oxkintok

More than twenty **cave systems** lie under the countryside around Oxkintok – some are single caverns, others huge interconnecting areas that have not yet been fully explored. They appear to have been used by the local population since prehistory, for living, refuge (including as recently as the nineteenth century, during the Caste Wars; see p.278) and worship. You may well be accosted at the entrance to Oxkintok by a local guide offering to take you to one of these caves, and if you have the time and are prepared for a bit of walking over rough ground, it's an opportunity worth taking (the guide will almost certainly speak no English, though).

The best known of the local caves, and possibly the largest system in the Yucatán, are the **Grutas de Calcehtok** (also called the Grutas de Xpukil). They're near the village of the same name, farther along the same road that leads to Oxkintok. You must go in with a guide, as there are no paths or lighting – just an alarmingly rickety metal ladder leading down into a hole, from which a cool breeze emanates. The basic tour ("Go in clean, come out clean" is the guide's promise) lasts about an hour (M$100) and explores some impressively large vaulted caverns. The two-hour *paseo aventura* (M$120) will leave you pretty dirty (the guides love to claim that the mud you are covered in is actually bat guano, which may be, in part, true), as you have to slide through muddy passages and clamber on ropes as you see quartz crystals and ceremonial objects left behind by the Maya over many centuries. The longest trip, the so-called *paseo extremo*, is for potholing enthusiasts only, involving a great deal of climbing, sliding and squeezing through narrow gaps, though you do get to see human skeletons in some of the deepest caverns. Prices depend a bit on the number of people in your group, and it helps to call ahead to make sure a guide will be available (mobile ☎ 997/102-3641), though if you go in the morning, you should find someone around.

Maxcanú, Becal and Hecelchakán

The new highway has been routed around all the towns it used to pass through, so you'll need to turn off to visit any of the following, and of course you'll find more interesting places to eat and sleep than you do on the highway, where the clientele is long-haul truckers and families with kids who need a rest stop. **MAXCANÚ**, the nearest town to Oxkintok, is sizeable, but you'd probably only stop in to break up your journey or get something to **eat**. You could take a look at the recently renovated church of San Miguel on the main plaza, and directly opposite the church's main doors is the pleasant, nicer-than-it-needs-to-be *Restaurant Oxkintok*, the kind of place that's a destination for city people on Sunday drives. If you want to **stay** in this region, just about the only option is the gorgeous *Hacienda Santa Rosa* (☎ 999/910-0088, ⓦ www.luxurycollection.com; ❾). Some of the eleven rooms here have their own private gardens and plunge pools, and there are extensive grounds with native plants as well as a beautiful main pool. You could also call in here for a meal, though since it's so small it would be wise to phone in advance to let them know. The hacienda, in the village of Santa Rosa, is hard to find; it's off Hwy-180, near Maxcanú, about 10km down unmarked roads, past Granada. (For a more affordable hacienda option, press on south to *Hacienda Blanca Flor*; see opposite).

About 20km further, **BECAL**, just across the border in Campeche State, is famous for the manufacture of baskets and, above all, the ubiquitous Yucatecan **jipis**, or "Panama" hats (genuine Panama hats, confusingly, come from Ecuador). Like Maxcanú, this is a hot, slow-moving place where little seems to happen, but it's interesting to see a village so consumed with a single cottage industry – a fountain made of concrete hats even graces the town square. If you pull over, you're likely to be approached by a friendly local offering to show you round, which basically means being taken to a nearby hat shop – though you may get a short tour in the back of a *triciclo* thrown in, with a stop at one of the town's many *cuevas*, the cool, damp cellars in which the villagers traditionally make and store their hats, to keep them soft and flexible. Ask your guide to point out a *jipi*, too, the fibrous plant from which the hat-making material is extracted. There doesn't seem to be a great deal to choose from among the many hat shops; they all sell similar products at prices ranging from around M$120 to M$1200, depending on quality, which is determined by the fineness of the fibres and tightness of the weave. The best ones (unfortunately hard to come by even here at the source) can be crumpled into a ball and spring back into shape.

A little under halfway from Becal to Campeche, **HECELCHAKÁN** lies just off the highway, where a road to **Isla de Jaina** turns off. Despite the tempting signs, there's no public access to the archeological site or the island itself, and the surrounding coast is windswept and entirely lacking in facilities. But you can view some of the original Jaina figurines (see box, below), as well as many other objects from local sites, in Hecelchakán's small and well-kept **Museo Arqueológico del Camino Real** (Tues–Sat 9.30am–5.30pm; M$31), housed in an elegant old mansion on the main plaza. Signage is in Spanish only, but the wonderfully detailed and quirky figurines speak for themselves. The other side of the vast colonial square that marks the centre of town is presided over by the impressive church of San Francisco de Asís, a sixteenth-century foundation whose dome and towers are later additions.

On the plaza, among elaborate topiary hedges, a couple of *loncherías* serve tacos, tortas and juices for a quick lunch. If you're looking for **accommodation** around here, ✱ *Hacienda Blanca Flor*, a short way north of Hecelchakán near the village of Poc-Buc (at Km 85.5 on the highway; ☎999/925-8042 or 996/827-0266, ⓦwww.blancaflor.com.mx; ❽) has sixteen large, comfortable rooms with air conditioning in a converted seventeenth-century hacienda. It was one of the first

The Jaina figurines

The **Isla de Jaina** (which means "the place of the house on the water" in Maya) is the source of thousands of beautiful, detailed **clay figurines** that grace the collections of museums around the world. Typically just 10–20cm tall, the figures have been a key to research on the everyday life of Maya people in ancient times: what people wore, how they altered their appearance, what they did for entertainment. The figures were placed in the graves of the people they depicted, often held in their hands or laid on their chests. Many of them also work as rattles or whistles, and clearly they were meant to accompany their owners to the underworld, perhaps as offerings or companions, or to make a noise to attract attention or ward off evil spirits.

Over twenty thousand tombs have been counted on the island, and it seems likely that Jaina was some kind of necropolis for people from all over the region. Its western location may have been symbolic of the setting sun, or the island may have marked an entrance to **Xibalba**, the Maya underworld. Initially, perhaps, this was an elite burial place: early interments have few figurines, but of very high quality. Later, it appears the burial location gained in popularity, and the quality of the figures declined, increasingly made in moulds rather than by hand, and they began to feature ordinary people as well as members of the upper class.

In many ways, it is these "lesser" figurines that are of most interest. They depict people going about their daily activities: weavers with their waist-looms, ball players at the doors of temples, dwarfs, musicians, the sick, the blind. And they show clothing in great detail, revealing clearly that what people wore was dependent on their social status. They also record ancient Maya physical characteristics – short stature, hooked noses and straight hair – as well as artificial features such as intentionally deformed skulls and dental ornamentation.

The island was occupied throughout the Classic Maya period, from as early as 250 AD to as late as 1000 AD, though whether it was purely a ritual centre or a city in its own right is a matter of some disagreement. In order to build here, the ancient Maya were forced to transport materials from the mainland: they did so in sufficient quantity to construct two substantial pyramids, as well as many lesser buildings.

hacienda hotels (opened in 1988) and shows its age a little, especially in the bedroom decor, but it's set on a beautiful working ranch, complete with a lambs, goats and horses. Simple but excellent meals are available.

If you're driving, you may also want to stop outside the prison about 12km north of Campeche – stalls along the road here sell excellent-value **hammocks**, all woven by inmates.

Campeche

Capital of the state that bears its name, startlingly beautiful **CAMPECHE** is one of Mexico's finest colonial gems. At its heart, relatively intact, lies a historical port town still surrounded by hefty defensive **walls and fortresses**; within them, interspersed with the occasional grand Baroque church, are elegant eighteenth- and nineteenth-century houses painted in pastel shades, hundreds of which have been restored to their former glory. Nonetheless, the place doesn't feel like an outdoor museum, as appliance stores and internet cafés occupy many of the historic shopfronts. Around the old **centre** are the trappings of a modern city that is once again becoming wealthy, while the **seafront**, built on land reclaimed from the sea, provides a thoroughly modern vista.

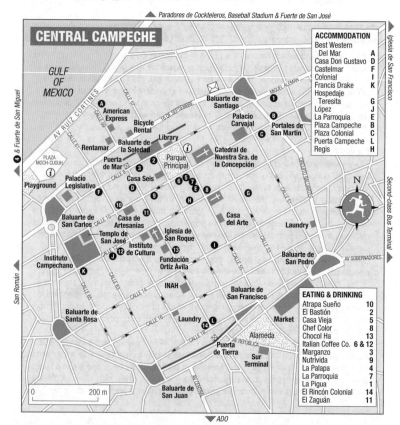

▲ Paradores de Cockteleros, Baseball Stadium & Fuerte de San José

CENTRAL CAMPECHE

Iglesia de San Francisco ►

GULF OF MEXICO

ACCOMMODATION

Best Western Del Mar	A
Casa Don Gustavo	D
Castelmar	F
Colonial	I
Francis Drake	K
Hospedaje Teresita	G
López	J
La Parroquia	E
Plaza Campeche	B
Plaza Colonial	C
Puerta Campeche	L
Regis	H

& Fuerte de San Miguel ◄

AV RUIZ CORTINES

CALLE 51

CALLE 49

16 DE SEPTIEMBRE

MIGUEL ALEMÁN

Baluarte de Santiago

American Express

Bicycle Rental

Palacio Carvajal

Portales de San Martín

Library

Rentamar

Baluarte de la Soledad

PLAZA MOCH-CUOUH

Puerta de Mar

Parque Principal

Catedral de Nuestra Sra. de la Concepción

Palacio Legislativo

Casa Seis

CALLE 55

BENITO JUÁREZ

CALLE 51

N

Playground

Casa del Arte

Laundry

Second-class Bus Terminal ►

Baluarte de San Carlos

Casa de Artesanías

Templo de San José

Iglesia de San Roque

Instituto de Cultura

Instituto Campechano

Fundación Ortiz Ávila

CALLE 53

Baluarte de San Pedro

AV GOBERNADORES ►

San Román ◄

INAH

CALLE 12

CALLE 14

CALLE 63

Baluarte de San Francisco

Baluarte de Santa Rosa

CALLE 16

Laundry

Market

EATING & DRINKING

Atrapa Sueño	10
El Bastión	2
Casa Vieja	5
Chef Color	8
Chocol Ha	13
Italian Coffee Co.	6 & 12
Marganzo	3
Nutrivida	9
La Palapa	4
La Parroquia	7
La Pigua	1
El Rincón Colonial	14
El Zaguán	11

Alameda

AV REPÚBLICA

Puerta de Tierra

Sur Terminal

0   200 m

Baluarte de San Juan

▼ ADO

In the past, few travellers stopped here, preferring to sweep by en route to Palenque or Villahermosa, though more visitors – almost entirely European – are beginning to spend at least a few days in the tranquil streets which compare favourably with Mérida's. Campeche so far remains unblighted by tourist overkill, and though the city is growing, it's still the sort of place where businesses shut down for the afternoon. Here, *campechanos* live up to their reputation as some of the most gracious and friendly people in Mexico.

Some history

In 1517 a crew of Spanish explorers under Francisco Hernández landed outside the Maya town of Ah Kin Pech, only to beat a hasty retreat on seeing the forces lined up to greet them. Not until 1540 did the second-generation conquistador **Francisco de Montejo the Younger** found the modern town – which he named Villa de San Francisco de Campeche – and from here set out on his mission to subjugate the Yucatán. From then until the nineteenth century, Campeche was the chief port on the peninsula, exporting goods from throughout the region, but above all **logwood** (*Haematoxylum campechianum*, a tree also known as *palo de campeche* or *palo de tinte*), the source of a red dye called haematein, which attracted huge prices in Europe. Although logwood was planted – and still grows – throughout the Caribbean, the finest is said to be from Campeche. The wealth made Campeche an irresistible target for **pirates** (see box, p.222) until locals prevailed upon the Spanish authorities to fortify the city. Construction of the **walls**, with their eight massive *baluartes* (bulwarks), began in 1686 after a particularly brutal massacre of the local population, and the original defences were completed in 1704.

Arrival

Campeche has two **bus stations**, one each for first- and second-class services, as well as a separate small terminus for local and rural buses. The **first-class ADO** station is about 2km from the centre on Avenida Central; taxis line up outside (M$40 to the centre), as do buses and *colectivos* (M$5; look for "Mercado" or "Centro"). The **second-class** terminal is 600m northeast of the centre on Gobernadores; to get downtown, either walk (turn left on Gobernadores) or cross the street in front of the station and take a city bus, also marked "Centro" or "Mercado". All of these buses head to the market, just outside the city wall on the landward side. Some buses from **Edzná** and other local destinations such as Champotón use Sur's local terminal on República just south of the market and a block from the Puerta de Tierra.

To get from the **airport**, about 10km southeast of town, you'll have to take a **taxi** (M$80). **Drivers** coming from Mérida are routed off Hwy-180 well north of the city and onto a seafront road that takes several kilometres to arrive in the centre.

Information and tours

Campeche's **state tourist office** (daily 8am–8pm; ☎981/127-3300, ⓦwww.campeche.travel) is in the tent-like building on Plaza Moch-Couoh, on the seaward side of the very mod Palacio Legislativo. There's usually someone there who speaks English, and you can pick up brochures on attractions throughout the state, as well as the monthly *Cartelera Cultural*, for events listings. The city map it dispenses is more fanciful than functional, though. They also have a list of independent **guides** (speaking various languages) who lead tours of the city and archeological sites. The **city tourist office** is on the north side of the plaza; it's less organized and has fewer resources. Smaller **information booths** at the bus

The pirates of Campeche

As the Spanish colonies grew wealthy in the sixteenth century, they became an inevitable target for **pirates**, and the Campeche coast, especially the sheltered waters and unpopulated islands of the Laguna de Términos around modern-day Ciudad del Carmen, was a popular hideout. Despite their swashbuckling and violent reputation, the majority of pirates were authorized by the English, Dutch and French governments to seize Spanish shipping in return for a share of the loot. Such raiders described themselves as **privateers** rather than pirates; many were former or future naval officers.

Cargos of gold, silver and jewellery sailed from Campeche, as did less exotic but equally valuable goods like cotton, feathers, hardwoods and, above all, Campeche logwood. To deter pirates, by the late sixteenth century the Spanish authorities had begun to send cargos in fewer, more heavily armed ships and assemble convoys in Caribbean ports to sail to Spain under armed escort.

But as the privateers were prevented from plying their trade at sea, they turned their attention to **raiding coastal towns**. Wealthy as a port and from its trade in local wood and tobacco, the isolated and poorly defended Campeche became a favourite target. As early as 1568 the port was attacked by a group of pirates whose members included the English captains John Hawkins and Francis Drake, and for the next hundred years the frequency and severity of the **attacks** increased, as privateers banded together to create formidable fleets for joint assaults. In 1663 some 1500 English, French and Dutch buccaneers – commanded by Christopher Myngs and including the notorious Henry Morgan – attacked Campeche, seizing twelve Spanish ships and over 150,000 pesos in treasure. Four years later a band under Lewis Scott occupied the town for three days, stripping it of almost everything that could be moved, then demanding a ransom not to burn the place down.

In 1685, a force under the French pirate Laurent de Graff invaded the town silently by night. They rang the bells of the church of San Francisco to signal the population of Campeche to assemble, then imprisoned virtually everyone inside the church – after which they proceeded to systematically and savagely sack the town. The following year, the Spanish began to fortify the city and, though raids on shipping continued into the nineteenth century (when privateers operated under the flag of the Texan navy), Campeche itself was never seriously threatened again.

stations, in the Baluarte de San Pedro and in the Casa Seis, are not always manned, but do have leaflets and maps and details.

For a concise overview of the city, you can take a **walking tour** starting at the city tourist office on the plaza (daily 9am & 5pm; reserve ahead), or the **tranvía tour**, with commentary in Spanish and English, departs from the main plaza (hourly 9am–1pm & 5–9pm; M$80), taking a pleasant 45-minute tour around neighbourhoods beyond the walls. It's especially nice in the evening, when the doors of the historic churches you pass are all flung open.

Accommodation

Campeche's **hotels** are just beginning to match tourist demand. There are relatively few to choose from; some are dismal, but a couple are outstanding. The few decent budget options are within a couple of blocks of the main plaza, and some upmarket choices are just outside the old city walls. In any case, avoid rooms overlooking the street, as Campeche's narrow lanes magnify traffic noise. There are several **hostels**, though all are scruffy, and none have air conditioning, making them brutal in the summer; at the time of research, *La Parroquia* (☎981/816-2530, ⓦwww.hostalparroquia.com; M$95), on Calle 55, between calles 10 and 12, was only marginally better than the others. At the other end of the price band, the city now supports two super-luxury hotels; in this latter category, you might also consider *Hacienda Uayamón* (see p.230), 21km out of town on the way to Edzná.

Best Western Del Mar Ruíz Cortines 51, between C 57 and C 59 ☎981/811-9191, ⓦwww .delmarhotel.com.mx. Of the two big hotels on the seafront (the other is the *Baluartes*), this one is in better shape. It's bland and modern, but might show up as a very good deal with online booking. ❻

Casa Don Gustavo C 59 no. 4, between C 8 and C 10 ☎981/811-2350, ⓦwww.casadongustavo .com. A new competitor for *Puerta Campeche* (and not quite so stratospherically priced), this grand colonial place is distinguished by lovely staff and a slightly more local feel. ❾

🏃 **Castelmar** C 61 no. 2-A, between C 8 and C 10 ☎981/811-1204, ⓦwww .castelmarhotel.com. Renovated colonial-style place, with old floor tiles, a large courtyard and soaring ceilings. Modern touches include a pool, a/c, satellite TV and free wi-fi. Continental breakfast included. ❻

🏃 **Colonial** C 14 no. 122, between C 55 and C 57 ☎981/816-2222. The only attractive budget place in town, and one of the best hotels in the Yucatán: an airy courtyard building with conscientious owners who keep the place immaculate and running just as it did fifty years ago, only now with a/c in a few of the rooms, painted Easter-egg hues. It's vintage in the best way; book ahead. ❶

Francis Drake C 12 no. 207, between C 63 and C 65 ☎981/811-5626, ⓦwww.hotelfrancisdrake .com. This small hotel in a renovated colonial building has lavish rooms and a few suites (though they lack the high ceilings of *Plaza Campeche* and *Castelmar*). The staff here are particularly helpful. ❹

Hospedaje Teresita C 53, between C 12 and C 14 ☎no tel. This oldest of the old-school family-run

guesthouses, has dingy, jail-cell-basic rooms with shared bath (at M$125, firmly in the ❶ category); an extra M$30 gets you a private bath. 11pm curfew. Only vaguely an option because Campeche's hostels are so uninspiring.

López C 12 no. 189, between C 61 and C 63 ☎981/816-3344, ⓦwww.hotellopezcampeche .com. A nicely renovated hotel catering to Mexican business travellers with free wi-fi and a newspaper in the morning. Modern a/c rooms are in a pretty Deco-era building with open halls (though bathrooms can be musty). There's even a small pool. ❹

Plaza Campeche C 10 at Circuito Baluartes ☎981/811-9900, ⓦwww.hotelplazacampeche .com. Outside the old wall on the north side, the *Plaza Campeche* is a colonial-look high-end place with friendly service. Large rooms have marble baths and dark-wood furniture and there's a tiny pool, a bar and wi-fi. The same management's *Plaza Colonial* (C 12, just inside the walls) has smaller, slightly cheaper rooms. ❼

Puerta Campeche C 59 no. 61, between C 16 and C 18 ☎981/816-7508, ⓦwww.luxurycollection .com. Just inside the Puerta de Tierra, Campeche's finest hotel is set in the shell of a colonial home that sprawls down most of the block. The pool winds through crumbling walls, but the rooms, with soaring ceilings, are appointed with every modern touch. ❾

Regis C 12 no. 148, between C 55 and C 57 ☎981/816-3175. Seven very large rooms, all with a/c as well as fans, arranged around a small patio – a decent alternative to the *Colonial* or the *López*, and about halfway between the two in price. ❷

The City

Perhaps the greatest pleasure to be had in Campeche is simply wandering around the old streets and seafront – especially in the early evening, as the air cools, the lights come on behind the grilled windows of the old homes and locals come out to stroll, or to jog, bike or blade along the waterfront **malecón**, which runs for several kilometres north and south of the centre. Museums, churches, mansions and fortresses punctuate each block, though only the **archeological museum** in the Fuerte de San Miguel could really be described as a "must-see" (note that it, and several other museums, are closed on Mondays).

Even-numbered **streets** run parallel to the sea, starting inside the ramparts with Calle 8; odd-numbered streets run inland. The **plaza**, which locals call the *parque principal*, is bordered by calles 8, 10, 55 and 57. Outside the ring of the old city wall, the grid system is less strictly adhered to; the **market**, immediately outside the wall on the landward side, is as far as you're likely to need to venture into the modern city except when you arrive or leave. Much of the city wall has been demolished and replaced by a ring road – **Avenida Circuito Baluartes** – but two substantial sections survive, along with seven of the eight original *baluartes* (bulwarks). The city defences were completed by two large fortresses, overlooking the city from hills along the coast in either direction: the **Fuerte de San José** to the north, and the **Fuerte de San Miguel** to the southwest. With the exception of the forts, everything that follows is within easy walking distance of the central plaza.

The plaza

Campeche's central plaza is at its best on weekends, when the streets are closed to car traffic and food vendors set up. Musicians play, and crowds flock to the *lotería* tables – Campeche's variation of this game of chance is more complex than most, with a much larger pool of cards. Just off the corner of the square, a musical fountain provides a pretty light show.

Chief among the monuments here is **La Catedral de Nuestra Señora de la Concepción**, established in 1540 along with the town, and one of the oldest churches on the peninsula. The bulk of the construction took place much later, and what you see today is a wedding-cake Baroque structure; look in the adjacent **museum** (11am–5pm; donation) for a seventeenth-century statue of Christ, interred in a dark wood and silver catafalque, among other relics. Directly across the plaza, the **Centro Cultural Casa Seis** (daily 9am–9pm; M$10) has an elegant permanent display of Baroque interiors (with an optional audio tour for M$15). Under the central patio is a giant cistern: rain that fell on the house was collected and could be drawn up from the well-like structure in the centre. This building hosts art exhibits and cultural performances, including musical *serenatas* most Thursday evenings, and there's a good café in the back, as well as a tasteful craft shop.

On the seaward side of the plaza, the **Baluarte de la Soledad** incorporates the **Museo de la Arquitectura Maya** (daily 9.30am–5.30pm; M$31). Its small but informative collection of columns, stelae and stone details from Edzná and other local Maya sites are arranged by regional style, such as Chenes, Puuc, etc. Likewise, its presentation of a sketch outline of the decoration next to most of the carved stone helps train your eye to see the details. Just to the north, in front of the city wall, a beautiful building contains the well-used public **library** (with a good reference section that's open to anyone), formerly the city's main barracks.

Around the plaza

Elsewhere in the old city streets, a number of other grand old homes have been converted to schools, hotels or offices, and you can peek inside. The Moorish-style **Palacio Carvajal**, on Calle 10, between calles 51 and 53, was the city home of the fabulously wealthy owners of *Hacienda Uayamón* (see p.230) and now houses government offices (Mon–Fri). On Calle 59, between calles 12 and 14, the **Fundación José Ortiz Ávila**, in the former home of an ex-governor of the state, contains Ávila's library and a huge collection of guns. Opening hours are a bit erratic, but entry is free and it remains open till late in the evening. The state offices of **INAH** (the national archeology commission) occupy a pretty old home in the next block of Calle 59, between calles 14 and 16 – a nice shop sells reproduction Maya pottery, and there's a small exhibit on central Campeche's zoning and preservation. On Calle 55, between calles 12 and 14, look for the **Casa del Arte** – not as remarkable a building, but its rooms are turned over to art exhibitions, with free admission.

The numerous colonial churches are open sporadically for services. Among the finest is the **Templo de San José**, on Calle 63 at Calle 10. It dates to the mid-seventeenth century, but its striking tiled facade is from the end of the eighteenth. One of the mismatched towers also incorporates Campeche's original lighthouse. The church is now part of the Instituto Campechano, so you can get in during school hours; you'll often find temporary exhibitions here. Another elegant sight is the church and monastery of **San Roque** (Mon–Fri 8am–9pm, Sat & Sun for special events and church services only), also known as San Francisquito, on Calle 12, between calles 59 and 61. The beautifully restored red gilt altars crowd the walls of the narrow chapel. The monastery portion has been converted into the **Instituto de Cultura**, set around a courtyard where occasional art displays and concerts are staged.

The city wall and museums

Heading southwest along the old city wall from the Baluarte de la Soledad (the one facing the plaza) takes you past the flying-saucer-like Palacio Legislativo to the **Baluarte de San Carlos**, which has cannons on the battlemented roof and, underneath, the beginnings of a network of ancient tunnels that runs under much of the town. Sealed off now, the tunnels provided refuge for the populace from pirate raids, and before that were probably used by the Maya. The *baluarte* contains Campeche's **Museo de la Ciudad** (daily 8am–8pm; M$31), a tiny but rather lovely collection of local memorabilia that includes models of ships, an ancient compass and the like.

From here you could walk right around the old centre following the line of the wall, but it's more interesting to cut through the old streets. Those on this southwest side, calles 57, 59 and 61, for example, are less commercial than those around the plaza, with more of a sense of history. Calle 59 leads eventually to the **Puerta de Tierra** (daily 9am–4pm), the main gate on the landward side, in the middle of the other well-preserved stretch of wall. Just to the north, at the **Baluarte de San Francisco**, you can pay M$10 to climb up to the ramparts and walk a little way along the top of the wall and look over the old town on the one side and the newer, less preserved city on the other, typified by the **market** and the **Alameda Francisco de Paula Toro**, the Havana-inspired promenade next to it. Downstairs in the bulwark is a **piracy museum** (Mon–Fri 9am–5pm, Sat & Sun 9am–4pm; M$40), though it has very few physical objects and relies instead on about an hour of audio commentary provided in headsets, probably appealing for pirate obsessives only. Far more interesting is the **sound-and-light show** (Thurs–Sun 8pm; M$50, or M$80 with translation), which starts from the Puerta de Tierra and includes a walk along the wall in the company of the "soldiers" guarding it.

Beyond the city wall

If you take the city *tranvía* tour (see p.222), you'll see much of what's interesting outside the city wall. Perhaps most striking is the way that, to the northeast especially, the *barrios* of San Martín, San Francisco and Guadalupe are like less glamorous versions of the UNESCO-burnished walled centre. Indeed, these are some of the oldest parts of the city. A little over 1km north, the Iglesia de San Francisco marks the site of the first Mass given in Mexico, in 1517, in what was then the Maya settlement of Ah Kin Pech.

Just off the north side of the centre, the **Baluarte de Santiago** stands alone in a traffic island. It has been adapted to house the **Jardín Botánico Xmuch'haltún** (Mon–Sat 9am–9pm, Sun 9am–4pm; M$12), with a small collection of native plants – nothing grand, but a good basic introduction. Originally, this and the other sea-facing city defences dropped straight into the water, but now they face a reclaimed strip of land on which stand the bizarrely modern Palacio de Gobierno and state legislature and striking **sculptures** representing various aspects of the city. The area has been made less severe with the installation of a vast **playground** next to the state tourist office. It's a wild sight in the evening, when it's crawling with local kids. Another good evening destination is the neighbourhood of **San Román**, especially its massive church, where the altar is dominated by an enormous black crucifix, originally set in place in 1565, when the church was first built. Head south on Calle 10 and look for the blue bell tower.

Substantially further from the centre, north and south along the coast, the two outlying **forts** require transport to get to. Each is wonderfully preserved, with a dry moat and cannons that still seem ready to blast approaching ships out of the water. The **Fuerte de San Miguel**, overlooking the coast some 4km southwest of the centre, contains one of the city's chief attractions: the impressive **Museo Arqueológico** (Tues–Sun 9.30am–5.30pm; M$37). Though the information provided is in Spanish only, the relics, from all over the peninsula, are beautiful alone. Maya artefacts from Edzná and Jaina predominate, including delicate Jaina figurines, fine sculpture and pre-Hispanic gold. But the highlight is the treasure – jade death masks, jewellery and more – from the tombs at Calakmul, the most important of which is thought to be the Calakmul ruler Jaguar Paw (see p.146). If you go late in the day, you can take in the sunset from the ramparts. To get here, you can take a city **bus** along the coast road (look for "Lerma" or "Playa Bonita"), but that will leave you with a stiff climb up the hill to the fort.

The **Fuerte de San José** (Tues–Sun 9.30am–5.30pm; M$31), completed in 1792, occupies a similarly superb defensive position, uphill from the *paradores de cockteleros* (see below) on the north side. Its museum contains armaments, scale models of the city and ships and sundry items salvaged from shipwrecks, such as centuries-old Dutch gin bottles (signage is in Spanish only). Although this museum is not as compelling as the other fort's, the view north to the green swathe of protected marshland is striking; also look south for the mammoth modern statue of Benito Juárez, Mexico's great reform president of the mid-1800s, on the next ridge. To get to the fort, look for buses marked "Bellavista", starting from in front of the Alameda, just south of the market – they make the climb all the way up the hill so you don't have to, going within a block of the entrance. A **taxi** from the centre to either museum costs about M$25.

Eating and drinking

Restaurants abound in the centre, especially along calles 8 and 10. **Seafood**, available almost everywhere, is a good bet; try the *pan de cazón* (tortillas layered with shredded shark meat) or shrimp in tomato sauce. For breakfast, the cafés along Calle 8 near the government offices offer everything from tacos to fresh juices and pastries. Later in the day, the café in the centre of the plaza serves excellent coffee and home-made ice cream. The blocks around the Instituto Campechano (C 10 at C 63) hold numerous snack joints catering to students, and Campeche's **market**, just east of the walled city, is surrounded by *comedores* offering cheap and tasty lunches. Another local favourite is the stretch of *paradores de cockteleros* on the malecón – these seafood-vending kiosks are open until around 4pm (a taxi costs about M$30). At **night**, people snack at the restaurants at Portales de San Martín, just north of the walls between calles 10 and 12. Bars aren't open late, but on Friday and Saturday, stop by the rooftop bar at the hotel *Puerta Campeche* (see p.223) for the gorgeous view.

Atrapa Sueño C 10, between C 59 and C 61. Vegetarian snacks from M$40, alongside handicrafts.

El Bastión C 57, on the plaza. Best place to eat with a plaza view (and you can compare then and now, with the old-photo wallpaper inside), though the traditional *campechano* menu (mains M$100-140) isn't quite as good as others.

Casa Vieja C 10 no. 319, on the plaza. Cuban-owned restaurant with well-appointed balcony overlooking the main square that serves decent international cuisine (mains M$120 and up) – but it's really about the classy setting and the rum cocktails.

Chef Color C 55 at C 12. Cafeteria-style service and plastic folding chairs give this little lunch spot the feel of a church basement, but the home-made food – hearty dishes like pork with beans – is delicious, fast and cheap. Lunch only.

Chocol Ha C 59, between C 12 and C 14. Fresh fruit juices and hot chocolate (from local cacao) make this café special. There's wi-fi and mellow music too. Mon–Sat 9am–noon and 6–11pm.

Italian Coffee Co. C 10, on the plaza. This slick café satisfies cravings for espresso as well as less traditional drinks, such as Oreo frappés. Grilled sandwiches are also available, though they're not cheap. A larger space is on C 12 between C 61 and C 63. Free wi-fi draws local teens and laptop drones.

Marganzo C 8 no. 267, between C 57 and C 59. Somewhat touristy but still pleasant and not as expensive as it looks. The varied menu includes tasty crab quesadillas and generous *botanas* (bite-size snacks).

Nutrivida C 12 no.157, between C 57 and C 59. Health-food store serving vegetarian and whole-grain snacks, sandwiches, juices and the like. Mon–Fri 8am–2pm & 5.30–8.30pm, Sat 8am–2pm.

La Palapa Resurgimento, 2.5km south along the malecón from the city centre. A good goal for a waterfront stroll, this large bar is right on the water, and delicious *botanas* are served with every drink.

La Parroquia C 55 no. 8, between C 10 and C 12. High ceilings echo with the clink of dishes and buzz of conversation at this big open-front diner. Staff can be scattered (check your bill: ten percent for service is sometimes added, sometimes not), and the food is inconsistent – but at least it's cheap (breakfast for M$50 or so). Open 24 hours, with free wi-fi.

La Pigua Miguel Alemán 179-A ☎ 981/811-3365. Follow C 8 north to find one of the city's most legendary restaurants, a pretty, somewhat elegant spot with exceptionally delicious seafood, such as creamy shrimp soup and fresh filets with garlic and herbs (M$120 and up). Open for lunch and dinner; reserve nights and weekends if possible.

El Rincón Colonial C 59 at C 18. A charming old-fashioned men's cantina, complete with swinging doors and ceiling fans. Women get relegated to the ladies' lounge next door – not quite as picturesque, but it is a/c.

El Zaguán C 59 no. 6, between C 10 and C 12. Small, friendly bar-restaurant, with tables in wooden booths, serving inexpensive but good local and Mexican specialities, including *pan de cazón* and *mole poblano*. From 4pm; closed Sun.

Listings

Airlines Aeroméxico, López Mateos 201, Colonia Prado ☎ 981/812-8904.

American Express Inside the VI-PS travel agency, C 59, between Ruíz Cortines and 16 de Septiembre, near the *Best Western Del Mar*. Mon–Fri 9am–5pm, Sat 9am–1pm; ☎ 981/811-1010.

Banks HSBC, C 10 at C 55, is just off the main square and has an ATM; Banorte is on the southeast corner of the plaza.

Baseball The minor-league Campeche Piratas play at the Estadio Nelson Barrera Romilón, on the malecón north of the centre, just inland from the *paradores de cockteleros*. Good seats cost about M$100.

Bicycle rental Buena Ventura, on 16 de Septiembre behind *Hotel Del Mar*, rents cruisers with baskets (M$50/2hr or M$150/24hr) and even has a couple of tandems. Rentamar (☎ 981/811-6461, ✉ rentamar@aol.com), on C 59 around the corner, rents mopeds (M$100/hr).

Car rental Europcar, at the airport (☎ 55/5207-5572, ⊕ www.europcar.com); Localiza (☎ 981/811-3187), in the *Hotel Baluartes*; Maya Car Rental (☎ 981/816-0670), in the *Best Western Hotel Del Mar*.

Internet access There are internet cafés on virtually every street in the centre of Campeche, most charging approx M$10/hr.

Laundry Klar, C 16 no. 305 at C 61; Lave Klin, Circuito Baluartes Nte, between C 14 and C 16. Both charge about M$10/kg (Klar has a 3kg minimum).

Post office 16 de Septiembre at C 53 (Mon–Fri 8.30am–3.30pm, Sat 9am–1pm).

Shopping Casa de Artesanías Tukulná, C 10 no. 333, between C 59 and C 61, is a particularly well-stocked craft shop, with items like horn combs, fine Panama hats and Campeche-style *lotería* sets. Casa Seis, on the plaza, has a smaller but also quite fine selection. (With these options right at hand, the large Bazar Artesanías, near the convention centre on the malecón, is not worth the walk.) The Librería Levante, C 12, between C 59 and C 61, next to the Instituto Cultural, has glossy art books, though almost everything is in Spanish.

Taxis Within the city, these are inexpensive, but sometimes not plentiful. Look for them at taxi stands around the centre or call ☎ 981/816-2363, 816-2359 or 816-2355.

8

CAMPECHE | Campeche

The **first-class bus station** has ADO, OCC and some ATS services. Buses leave at least hourly for **Ciudad del Carmen** (2hr), **Escárcega** (2hr), **Villahermosa** (5hr 15min–7hr 15min) and **Mérida** (2hr 30min). A direct bus goes to the **Mérida airport** five times a day (5.45am, 7am, 10am, 12.30pm & 3pm; 2hr 20min). You can also get as far as **Chetumal** (1 daily at 2pm; 6hr 30min) via **Xpuhil**, **Palenque** (4 daily at 11am, 9.45pm, 12.30am & 2.20am; 4hr 45min–6hr 30min) and **Cancún** (4 daily, 5.45am, 9.35am, 11pm & 11.30pm; 6hr 45min). For tickets without a trek to the station, visit Edzná Tours travel agency on Circuito Colonias at Calle 8. City buses to the station are marked "Av Central" or "ADO".

You'll need Sur or ATS services at the **second-class terminal** for stopping buses on Hwy-180, for towns such as **Hecelchakán** (every 30min 3.45am–9.15pm; 1hr); Mérida via **Uxmal** (5 daily at 6am–5pm; 2hr 15min); and **Hopelchén** (hourly 6am–12.30am; 1hr 30min). **Colectivos** for most of the same destinations depart from Gobernadores as well – you'll pass the marked stops on the walk to the bus station. City buses marked "Gobernadores" run past this terminal.

For **Champotón**, Seybaplaya or Sabancuy (hourly 7.30am–5.30pm), go to the auxiliary **Sur terminal** on República just inland from the Puerta de Tierra.

Driving out of town can be a little tricky. The two main arteries are Gobernadores, running northeast out to Hwy-180, and Avenida Central, which runs more due east. Where it joins with Hwy-180, jog north a few hundred metres for the direct route to Edzná and Hwy-261 (the back way to Mérida), or turn south to continue to Champotón. The safer bet is to follow the seafront road straight south, and eventually wind up at the old Hwy-180; if you want the fast toll road (*cuota*) south to Champotón, turn left at the Pemex and backtrack a few kilometres to the highway entrance.

Tours Xtampak Tours, C 57 no. 14, between C 10 and C 12 (Mon–Sat 8am–3pm & 5–9pm; ☎981/811-6473, ✉xtampac_7@hotmail.com), runs trips to Edzná (M$200 half-day, transport only; or M$850 with guide, lunch and other stops), as well as Calakmul and the Chenes sites. Campeche Tours, 16 de Septiembre, in *Hotel Baluartes* (☎981/816-5452) runs kayaking trips to the *petenes*, the marshlands north of the city (M$700; 4hr). Nómadas, Ruíz Cortines 61, San Román (☎981/816-2935, ✇www.nomadastravel.com.mx), is a good all-purpose, student-friendly agency.

Edzná and the Chenes sites

Some 50km from Campeche lie the ruins of **Edzná**, the only local site reasonably accessible by bus and a surprisingly large and richly decorated site, given how little it is known to tourists. Beyond Edzná, Hwy-261 leads towards Hopelchén and the so-called **Chenes sites**: the ruins of Hochob, Dzibilnocac, El Tabasqueño and Santa Rosa Xtampak, which share a similar style of architecture (see box, p.230). These other sites are tough to get to unless you have your own transport, and often have just one important structure. But the buildings are spectacular, and there's a real sense of adventure in getting there – especially as you may well be the only visitor.

Edzná

Yet another Maya site that's far more impressive than its relative obscurity might suggest, **EDZNÁ** (daily 8am–5pm; M$41) reached the height of its power very early, in the Pre-Classic period from around 250 BC to about 150 AD. At this time, the flood-prone, marshy valley in which Edzná lies was transformed by a drainage system of canals, reservoirs and aqueducts (one stretching 12km) into terraced agricultural land that supported a population of thousands. Handily located on major trade routes between the coast and the Maya highlands, Edzná effectively ruled the region. After 150 AD, however, possibly as a result of war, the city declined and there was virtually no more building until the height of the Classic era, from 600 AD onwards. Most of what you see now dates from around 700–900 AD, and shows elements of the Chenes style, as well as Río Bec, Classic Maya and Puuc design. Allow a minimum of an hour and a half to visit.

The main plaza of Edzná is dominated by the raised **Gran Acrópolis**, atop which stands the site's largest structure, the great **Templo de los Cinco Pisos** (Five-Storey Temple). A stepped palace-pyramid more than 30m high, each of its storeys contains chambered "palace" rooms. While solid temple pyramids like this are relatively common, as are multi-storey "apartment" complexes, it's rare to see the two combined in one building. At the front, a steep monumental staircase leads to a three-room temple, topped by a roofcomb. It's a hot climb, but the view from the temple is one of the finest in the peninsula. On the way, notice the hieroglyphic inscriptions (as yet undeciphered) on the first four steps and, halfway up,

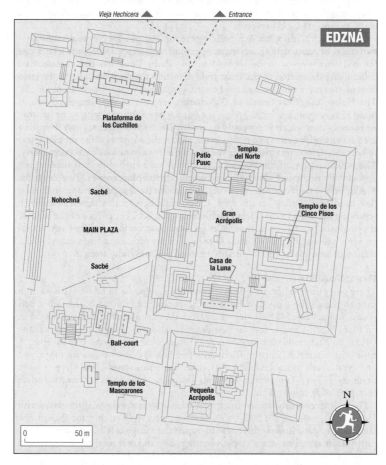

The Chenes style

Chenes **architecture** is characterized by highly decorative facades, often on relatively small structures. Above all, it features buildings on which the doorways form the mouth of a giant mask, created out of stone reliefs. The design often takes up the entire front of the building. No one is quite sure who the mask is meant to be – some contend it represents Itzamná, the Maya creator god, in the form of a giant serpent, while other say it is a *witz*, a deity representing mountains and earth. *Chen* means "well" in local Maya and is a fairly common suffix to place names in this region, where towns have grown up around these sources of water. The Maya cities were no doubt equally dependent on wells, but they're not in evidence at any of the sites.

three giant, crumbling masks. At the top, looking out over two plazas, the further of which must have been capable of holding tens of thousands of people, it is easy to imagine the power that the high priest or king commanded. Beyond lie the unexcavated remains of other large pyramids, and behind them, the vast flat expanse of the Yucatán plain. Inside the west-facing temple a stele of the god of maize was illuminated by the setting sun twice a year, on the very dates when maize was planted and harvested.

Descend back to the Gran Acrópolis, where the **Templo del Norte** demonstrates two stages of construction: an original pyramid with stepped sides, and a later one finished with sloping stone. Behind it, the **Patio Puuc** has the characteristic column-like decoration of the Puuc style. Down in the main plaza itself, the clear lines of two ceremonial *sacbeob* can be seen leading away from the Gran Acrópolis. The **Nohochná** (*Casa Grande* or Big House), across from the Gran Acrópolis, is some 55m long and includes a room used as a *temazcal* (sauna), with stone benches and hearths over which water could be boiled. The steps on its front may have been used as seating for events and rituals in the plaza – the acoustics at the site allow you to hear announcements made from the top of the Templo de los Cinco Pisos clearly. The buildings around the **Pequeña Acrópolis** are rather older and smaller, but impressively decorated, above all the **Templo de los Mascarones** (Temple of the Masks), where two haunting stucco masks represent the Sun god – rising on the east (left-hand) side, setting on the west. If you walk beyond this main cleared area, following the signs to the **Vieja Hechicera**, you'll get a better idea of the scale of the original city, and also of the challenges faced by its builders – there's a great deal of water and marshy ground here. At the end of the path, some five minutes' walk, is another large plaza, with a partially restored pyramid rising from it.

Practicalities

There's no public transport that gets you from Campeche to Edzná with enough time to return the same day. But the Campeche State tourist board runs a **bus** (Tues–Sun at 9am; M$150), departing from the parking lot in front of the office on Plaza Moch-Couoh. It gives you about two hours at Edzná, then stops at the Grutas de Xtacumbilxuna'an (see p.232) before returning to the city by 3pm. A **tour** with Xtampak Tours in Campeche (see p.228) doesn't cost a lot more, and gives you a little more flexibility with time. The **sound–and–light show** is quite dramatic (Thurs–Sun, 8pm; M$116), but wear bug spray. Xtampak offers transport-only tours for this as well.

The only **accommodation** closer than what's in Campeche is at the wonderful *Hacienda Uayamón* (℡981/813-0530, ⓦ www.luxurycollection.com; ⓞ), off the fast road to Edzná (follow this route to bypass the village of China). Founded as a cattle ranch as early as the sixteenth century, its vast lands were raided by pirates in the seventeenth, but it reached its height in the nineteenth century, when its production of sugar, logwood and, above all, henequen, made it one of the largest, wealthiest and most famous haciendas in the country. Most of the rooms – many with a private outdoor terrace and plunge pool – are in the old workers' housing scattered throughout the extensive grounds. There's exuberant birdlife here, and armadillos and other small animals are often seen around the rooms. Amenities from horseriding to massage are on offer. The hacienda's **restaurant** is a good option for a romantic dinner (you can have a table set up on the terrace overlooking a centuries-old ceiba tree, its split trunks intertwining), or just an excuse to poke around the grounds. Call ahead for a dinner reservation.

The Chenes sites

Most of the ruins that exhibit undiluted Chenes style – colonnaded facades and monster-mouth doorways, evolved from the Río Bec further south – are accessible only with a car or exceptional determination. They are near the village of **Hopelchén**, about 90km east of Campeche, notable for the large number of Mennonite farms nearby; they make a good semi-hard cheese that's available in stores and restaurants here. Hopelchén itself has basic facilities, including a branch of Bancomer with an ATM around the corner from the plaza, next to the town hall, and a simple **hotel**, *Los Arcos* (☎996/100-8782, ✉hiram_aranda@hotmail .com; ➊), on the corner of the plaza at Calle 23, near where the buses stop. You might also want to check out the interesting wood altar in the eighteenth-century Church of San Antonio de Padua. A good road heads south from Hopelchén all the way to Xpuhil; if you take it, be sure to fill your tank here, as it's almost 200km with very few services.

The closest of the archeological sites is **Tohcok** (daily 8am–5pm; free), right beside the highway, immediately outside Hopelchén as you approach from the west. It's no more than a single unrestored building, but it's worth a few minutes; the friendly site guardian will point out the main features in rapid-fire Spanish. The more significant sites lie off the road to the south. **El Tabasqueño** (daily 8am–5pm; free), reached by a 4km track from the village of Pakchén, and about 30km from Hopelchén, has a temple with a doorway in the form of the mouth of a monster, surrounded by hook-nosed masks as well as a tower, which is unusual. The most beautiful of the Chenes sites, **Hochob** (daily 8am–5pm; M$31), can be found 15km down a paved side road that turns off just outside Dzibalchén. Even this is very modest – it consists of a lovely little hilltop plaza with one very elaborately decorated building. Other structures are buried, almost imperceptibly, in the dense forest all around. The decorated building (romantically named "Structure 1") is a three-room temple (low and fairly small, as are most Chenes buildings) with a facade entirely covered in richly carved, stylized snakes and masks. The central chamber is surmounted by a crumbling roofcomb, and its decoration takes the form of a huge mask, with the doorway in the shape of a gaping mouth: hooked fangs frame the opening, while above are the eyes and to either side elaborate decoration on the ears. Surrounding the plaza are other small structures (including one with part of a roofcomb), their facades softly carpeted with green moss.

Dzibilnocac (daily 8am–5pm; free), the Place of the Painted Vault or of the Great Painted Turtle, is something of a contrast – a very large, flat site that is undergoing substantial restoration. It doesn't match the beauty of Hochob, but there are plenty of elaborate facades and masks typical of the Chenes style, and one very pretty little pyramid with a temple on top. Dzibilnocac is also the one large Chenes site that you could get to by bus, with planning. It's 1km east of the small town of Iturbide (or Vicente Guerrero, according to many road signs), which gets second-class bus service from Campeche; then you'll need to walk or take a *triciclo*. To be on the safe side, set out early (morning buses are hourly from 7.45am) and check return times as soon as you get there.

In the other direction from Hopelchén, Hwy-261 heading north towards Mérida passes one other Chenes site at **Santa Rosa Xtampak** (daily 8am–5pm; M$31), 32km off the highway on a rough paved road. It mirrors Edzná in size and importance, as well as in its history, as it developed very early, around 800 BC – Xtampak means "old walls". Its style, too, is predominantly Chenes, but with Puuc and a variety of other influences. In its heyday there were no fewer than ten ceremonial plazas here, built across a naturally raised but artificially levelled platform. Numerous semi-ruined structures can still be explored, the most important of them being a three-storey palace. As at all of these sites, curly-nosed masks and doorways in the form of mouths are constant motifs.

Back on the main highway, you pass the **Grutas de X'tacumbilxuna'an** (Tues–Sun 10am–5pm; M$50, or M$80 with translation) shortly before Bolonchén de Rejón. This cave system is an impressively vast hole, some 350m deep. A sound-and-light show relates a tale of a wronged Maya princess and tantalizing descriptions of other parts of the cavern that you unfortunately never get to see. If you can muddle along with the Spanish commentary, it's an interesting diversion; paying the extra for simultaneous translation places it in the realm of overpriced. **Bolonchén** itself is an attractive little town, with nine decorative wells outside its church (in fact, Bolonchén means "nine wells").

South from Campeche

South of Campeche, Hwy-180 splits into free (*libre*) and toll (*cuota*) roads. The free seafront route is winding and scenic, alternating between rolling hills fuzzy with sea grass and reeds, and striking vistas of the green Gulf waters. But it can be very slow, given the likelihood of tailing an underpowered delivery truck servicing the small towns along the way. The toll highway (M$56), however unremarkable, is straight, fast and easy. It ends just outside **Champotón**, a sleepy port that's famous for its seafood cocktails. From here, Hwy-261 heads due south to **Francisco Escárcega**, where it meets cross-country Hwy-186: to the east this takes you past the Río Bec sites to Chetumal and the Riviera Maya; west it heads to Palenque and Villahermosa, with the opportunity to turn off for **Candelaria** and the site of **El Tigre**, both in the wildlife-rich, little-visited valley of the Candelaria river. Hwy-180 meanwhile heads southwest to the steamy oil port of **Ciudad del Carmen**, via an alternative route to Villahermosa along the coast.

Along the coast

Leaving Campeche on the free **coast road** you head first through **Lerma**, the city's port, with major oil facilities and a sizeable fishing fleet. Immediately south are the town beaches at Playa Bonita (pretty enough, but usually either overcrowded or desolate), then a long inland stretch of road winds around the hills, with occasional access points to the sea. From here on, southern Campeche State is low, flat, hot and monotonous. The white sand **beaches** frequently look tempting, but they're less attractive close up, with coarse sand and shallow water that smells none too clean.

Nonetheless, the beaches along this stretch of coast, down to Ciudad del Carmen, are important breeding grounds for endangered green, Kemp's Ridley and hawksbill **turtles**. There are a number of places where the turtles are protected and where, in nesting season (May–Sept, but busiest in July and Aug), you may be able to witness the young turtles making their way to the sea. One such spot is **Xpicob** (mobile ☎981-131-6958, ⓦwww.xpicob.com), where you can also rent kayaks – look for the turn between Playa Bonita and **Seybaplaya**. The latter town is a torpid place, home to dozens of small fishing boats and thousands of pelicans and other seabirds. Just to the south, the one really appealing seafront **hotel** in the area is *Tucán Siho Playa* (☎982-596-1817, ⓦwww.tucansihoplaya.com; ❼), set on a high bluff over the water – it's the best place to get in some beach time near Campeche.

The free and toll roads come together again near **Champotón**, a fishing town at the mouth of the broad Río Champotón. Here in 1517 a Spanish force under Francisco Hernández de Cordoba landed – having been driven away from Campeche and caught in a storm – to replenish their stocks of fresh water. They were surprised by a Maya force and heavily defeated; Hernández de Cordoba died of his wounds a few days later, and the place became known as the Bay of the Bad Fight. Today it's more famous for delicious and fabulously cheap shrimp cocktails and *ceviche*, served up at *cocktelerías* all along the water, especially in a clutch of palapas on the north edge of town. Trips upriver, where there's kayaking, fishing and a chance to visit a couple of crumbling haciendas, can also be organized, most easily at one of the tour agencies in Campeche. If you do want to arrange one locally, enquire at one of the local **hotels**, the *Snook Inn* (☎982/828-0018, ⓦwww.hotelsnookinnchampoton.com; ❹), a modern, motel-style place with a pool, TV, air conditioning and wi-fi, or the *Hotel Geminis* (☎982/828-0008; ❸), somewhat older, simpler and cheaper, but also with a pool and optional air conditioning. Both are on Calle 30 close to the main road, on the south side of the river's mouth, right by the bus station and market.

Most visitors turn inland at Champotón, on their way southeast towards Escárcega for Chetumal or Palenque. If you're driving to Villahermosa, however, you could opt for the improved highway to **Ciudad del Carmen**. Although it isn't really a compelling destination, the drive down the coast is fast and pretty. You pass pleasant **Sabancuy**, perched on a glassy green inlet 2km from the coast; you can tour by boat with the fishermen moored by the village's little waterfront plaza. Further along, **Isla Aguada** is another beachy spot that sees few visitors outside of Easter vacation; it also has a sea-turtle nesting site. Both towns have very basic hotels. Sabancuy is served by regular buses from Campeche, and you can get off at Isla Aguada on any second-class bus – you'll know you're there when you reach the Puenta de la Unidad (M$54 toll), which crosses the eastern entrance to the Laguna de Terminos, joining the Isla del Carmen to the mainland. If you're driving, be careful not to exceed the 50kph speed limit; traffic cops posted at either end of the bridge are notorious for demanding heavy fines on the spot. Locals fish off the bridge, and in the evening you'll often see kids holding up strings of fish for sale.

Ciudad del Carmen

The only town of any size on the 35-kilometre-long Isla del Carmen, **CIUDAD DEL CARMEN** doesn't merit a special trip except perhaps during Carnaval (the week before Lent), which it celebrates with gusto, and its lively **fiesta** in the second half of July, celebrating the town's namesake, Our Lady of Carmen. The first real settlers, in 1633, were pirates, but nowadays, the money's in oil and shrimp (a giant bronze prawn presides over one central traffic circle). The oil industry has forced prices up, so you won't find any bargains. Moreover, the city sprawls and is knotted with terrible traffic, and if you arrive on a **bus**, you're stuck at a station on the ring road, a long way from the centre.

If you do penetrate as far as the seafront **Plaza Central** (bounded by calles 24 and 22, parallel to the shore, and by calles 31 and 33), however, there's a small-town Mexican feel, hot and bustling. North on Calle 22, near Calle 41, a small **museum** (Mon–Fri 9am–6pm; M$15) charts the history of the city; fittingly, there's also an exhibit about the wonders of petroleum, plus a small-scale pirate ship where kids can walk the plank. The main beach in town is **Playa Norte**, due north of downtown, about ten minutes in a taxi. The broad swathe of sand is very lively on weekends, though not particularly scenic.

The **tourist desk** (Mon–Sat 9am–9pm) in the modern government offices on the malecón, in front of the central plaza, is helpful (when it's staffed). **Banks** are on Calle 24, just south of the plaza. There's a handy **internet café** in the Plaza Delfín, on Calle 20, across from the Plaza de Artesanías y Restaurantes – a good **place to eat**, with a dozen operations serving ice cream, coffee and a distinctive mix of Yucatecan food laced with the spicier flavours of the state of Tabasco. Also seek out *La Fuente*, at calles 20 and 29, on the waterfront, a traditional Mexican café serving simple food round-the-clock. Most of the accessible budget **accommodation** in town is around the plaza, near the water-front. At fiesta time places fill up, so book ahead. The big, basic *Hotel Zacarias* (☎938/382-3506; ❸), on the plaza at the corner of calles 24 and 31, has rooms with a choice of air conditioning or fan. More luxurious is the *Hotel del Parque* (☎938/382-3066; ❹), on Calle 33, between the plaza and the waterfront, where all rooms have air conditioning, TV and a phone.

Francisco Escárcega

A dusty town straggling along the road and old train tracks, **FRANCISCO ESCÁRCEGA** (usually just called Escárcega) is not an ideal stopover, but you may need to change buses here (and there's bearable lodging if you do get stuck overnight). The ADO **first-class bus station** is at the west end of town, at the junction of Hwy-261 and Hwy-186; from there, it's 1.5km east to the east end and the Sur **second-class bus station** (you can buy tickets for all services at ADO). You'll find an **ATM** in the next block south of the Sur station. The **food** options are basic, but a little better closer to the ADO station. Try the 24-hour *La Teja*, southwest across the traffic circle. If you need to **stay**, the gaily painted *Hotel Escárcega*, on the town's main drag (☎982/824-0186, ✉hotelescarcega@hotmail .com; ❷), has tidy enough rooms with air conditioning or fan, but if you definitely want your climate controlled, *Gran Hotel Colonial del Sureste*, a bit further east (☎982/824-1908; ❸), is better value. **Getting out of town** is relatively easy: there are thirteen first-class buses to Villahermosa (4–5hr), though half of those are after midnight; six to Palenque (3hr), with only one, at 12.50pm, during the day; and four to San Cristóbal de las Casas (8hr), also very late or early. Six buses run daily to Mérida (4hr 45min) and thirteen to Campeche (2hr 30min). Services to Xpujil (2hr 15min) go four times daily – you're better off with Sur (second-class) for this destination; services to Chetumal (4hr) go six times during the day, with several more services in the middle of the night.

9

Tabasco and Chiapas

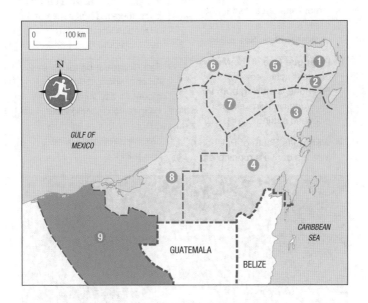

* **Wildlife** You don't have to travel far for exotic wildlife, but the finest spotting opportunities are in the protected wetlands of the Pantanos de Centla and the unspoilt tropical forests that crowd the Guatemalan border. See p.239 & p.254

* **Parque La Venta** Don't miss the massive, Olmec-carved stone heads salvaged from the remote site of La Venta, now easily accessible in the heart of Villahermosa. See p.244

* **Palenque** One of the Maya's greatest achievements, Palenque is striking both for its evocative ruins and its dramatic setting. See p.250

* **Waterfalls** South of Palenque, a series of rivers running off the mountains forms a string of spectacular waterfalls, most famously at Agua Azul and Misol-Há. See p.254

* **Bonampak** Over a thousand years old, the still-vivid murals here provide a unique insight into ancient Maya culture. See p.255

* **Yaxchilán** Set on the riverbank in the midst of thick forest, and accessible only by boat, there's a real sense of adventure about a journey to this Maya site. See p.257

* **San Cristóbal de las Casas** An enchanting colonial mountain city surrounded by villages rich in indigenous culture, with a delightfully diverse travellers' scene. See p.264

▲ Giant basalt Olmec head, Parque La Venta

9

Tabasco and Chiapas

Though not technically part of the Yucatán, the adjoining states of Tabasco and Chiapas are culturally and historically bound to the peninsula. Here we cover only the highlights most easily accessible from the Yucatán; you'll find more extensive details in *The Rough Guide to Mexico*. The states' eastern sections, with slow-moving **tropical rivers** making their way to the Gulf, provided vital trade routes for the ancient Maya, as well as for the Olmecs before them. In **Chiapas** the great Maya site of **Palenque**, which sits on the very edge of the vast plain of the Yucatán, is intimately connected to the Yucatán Maya sites, and one of the most impressive of all to visit. There are also important Maya sites at **Bonampak** and **Yaxchilán**, on the banks of the mighty **Río Usumacinta**, as well as at **Toniná**, higher in the mountains near the town of **Ocosingo**. All of these, as well as the magnificent **waterfalls** that tumble down alongside the road from Ocosingo to Palenque, can easily be visited on day-trips if you're based at Palenque. Further into the Chiapas highlands there's less obvious connection with the Yucatán, but **San Cristóbal de las Casas** lies at the heart of an area where Maya tradition survives particularly strongly among the local population, as well as being a wonderful place to visit in its own right – beautiful and surprisingly cosmopolitan.

Villahermosa, capital of **Tabasco**, is by far the largest city in the region, busy and wealthy from the oil that's extracted all over the state. It's also a virtually unavoidable road junction, especially if you're travelling by bus. At its supreme attraction, the Parque La Venta, you'll find the most important objects from the Olmec site of La Venta (including the giant basalt heads for which the Olmec culture is primarily known) displayed in a steamy jungle setting. This is one of the very few opportunities to see anything created by the Olmecs, the predecessors of the Maya. Not far from Villahermosa, the Maya site of **Comalcalco** lies en route to the coast. Here, an abundance of clay and shortage of stone meant that the Maya constructed their pyramids from bricks, making for an extraordinary and unexpected site. The **coast** itself, with alternating estuaries and sand bars, salt marshes and lagoons, is well off the beaten track.

This area is also exceptionally rich in **wildlife**, which you'll experience above all if you visit Bonampak or Yaxchilán, off the Frontier Highway at the edge of Mexico's last unspoilt tropical forests. Though development is making inroads at a frightening pace, vast tracts of forest are protected, and a little adventure will guarantee some exotic sightings. Monkeys are common at many of the sites, as are birds of every description and crocodiles basking on the banks of the Río Usumacinta. As they approach the sea, the rivers come together to form vast flood plains where natural reserves have been established, most accessibly at the Pantanos de Centla Biosphere Reserve, to protect the unique flora and fauna.

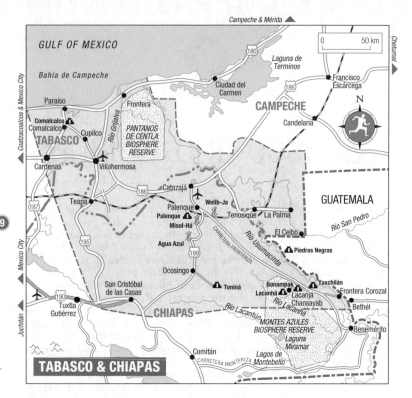

Campeche & Mérida ▲

Chetumal ▶

GULF OF MEXICO

Bahia de Campeche

Coatzacoalcos & Mexico City ◀

Laguna de Terminos

Ciudad del Carmen

Paraíso

Frontera

Francisco Escárcega

CAMPECHE

Comalcalco
Comalcalco

Cupilco

PANTANOS DE CENTLA BIOSPHERE RESERVE

Candelaria

TABASCO

Cardenas

Villahermosa

Catazajá

Palenque
Palenque

Welib-Ja
Tenosique

La Palma

GUATEMALA

Teapa

Mexico City ◀

Misol-Há

El Ceibo

Río San Pedro

Agua Azul

CARRETERA FRONTERIZA

Piedras Negras

Río Usumacinta

Ocosingo

Toniná

Bonampak
Lacanhá
Lacanjá
Chansayab

Yaxchilán

Frontera Corozal

San Cristóbal de las Casas

Tuxtla Gutiérrez

Juchitán ◀

CHIAPAS

Río Lacantún

Río Lacanhá

Bethél

Benemérito

MONTES AZULES BIOSPHERE RESERVE

Comitán

CARRETERA FRONTERIZA

Laguna Miramar

Lagos de Montebello

TABASCO & CHIAPAS

Frontera and the Tabasco Coast

Though there are few major attractions, the little-travelled coast road makes for a beautiful drive, passing through areas of wetland teeming with wildlife: mangroves and lagoons are covered with flocks of feeding water birds, and if you look hard enough you may spot the odd crocodile. However, if it's beaches that you've come for, you are likely to be disappointed – the sand is grey-brown and, though generally clean, there are almost always oil facilities in sight out in the Gulf. There are few hotels along this stretch, but plenty of spaces for **camping** – if you can stand the swarms of mosquitoes and sandflies.

Baking and half-asleep, **FRONTERA** is a pleasant, if uninspiring, working town and port about 90km west of Ciudad del Carmen. Once the main port for southern Mexico, when river steamers provided the only access to the roadless interior, it has changed little since Graham Greene visited in 1938, and wrote about the place (in less than flattering terms) in *The Lawless Roads*. If you **arrive** by second-class bus, turn left out of the bus station and walk two blocks along Madero to reach the plaza or, from the first-class bus station, left along Zaragoza, then right, and walk three blocks down Madero from the other direction. **Buses** for Villahermosa or Ciudad del Carmen leave every one or two hours during daylight hours, and four buses daily go to Veracruz. Everything you'll need is around the tastefully modern plaza, including a couple of nondescript **hotels**; the renovated *Marmor Plaza* (☎913/332-0001, ⓔ hotel_marmorplaza@hotmail.com; ❸) at Juárez 202, just left of the delicate

Gothic-style church, is the best option, with reasonable-value rooms equipped with air conditioning. For tasty shrimp or a hearty comida corrida, try *El Conquistador*, in an old colonial building, at Juárez 8.

The Pantanos de Centla Biosphere Reserve

The sole reason most people stay in Frontera is to visit the 17,200-square-kilometre **Pantanos de Centla Biosphere Reserve**. Among the more exotic species protected here (few of which you are actually likely to encounter) are jaguar and tapir, osprey and tiger heron, and, in the water, manatee and crocodile; the mangrove forests are also full of rare orchids and bromeliads.

To **get into the reserve**, you will almost certainly need your own transport, unless you're lucky enough to catch one of the few *combis* to Jonuta – head through Frontera and continue west on the highway a few kilometres, then take the Jonuta road, just before the huge bridge over the river. Ten kilometres south, on the riverbank, the Desarrollo Ecoturístico Punta Manglar (☎913/398-1688; open daily, but most activities available only at weekends) offers guided walks, canoe and ferry trips, and other educational **activities** in the reserve, plus it has a small **restaurant** for refreshment. A few kilometres further down, the Centro de Interpretación Uyotot-Já (Tues–Sun 9am–5pm; M$20 admission includes a guided tour; ☎913/131-3274) is a larger tourist centre with an observation tower, restaurant, boat trips (from about M$500 for up to ten people) and walkways over the marshy riverbanks. There are also a few cabañas here for **spending the night**, plus a restaurant.

Paraíso

A weekend escape for Villahermosa residents, **PARAÍSO** is a sleepy place with some beaches nearby – pleasant enough if you need to wind down, and a better place to spend the night than Frontera. Paraíso's ADO **bus station** is 1km south of the centre along Benito Juárez, the main road. Turn right out of the station and keep walking: eventually you'll see the town's most distinctive monument – the twin-towered colonial church – across the river up ahead. The main second-class station, with departures for points along the coast, is north of the centre and well served by *combis*; to make the fifteen-minute walk, turn south (left) and aim for the church towers. One quality **hotel** is *Sabina*, on the east side of the plaza (☎933/333-2483, ⓦwww.hotelsabinaparaiso.com; ❸), with freshly painted, clean air-conditioned rooms with TV, private bathrooms and drinking water. There are plenty of juice bars around the plaza and a couple of decent, moderately priced **restaurants**: *Real de la Costa* on the east side is good, with a wide selection of Mexican food, meats, pastas and seafood dishes. The nearest beach, **Playa Limón**, where locals go for picnics on weekends, is a twenty-minute *combi* ride north of Paraíso. **Taxis** to the beaches cost M$30, and there are a couple of daily first-class buses to Frontera.

Comalcalco and the cacao region

The Classic-period site of **COMALCALCO** (daily 8am–5pm; M$41 including museum), 58km north of Villahermosa, is the westernmost known Maya site. Occupied around the same time as Palenque (250–900 AD), it shares some features with the better-known city, and may have been ruled by some of the same kings. The area's lack of building stone forced the Chontal Maya to adopt a distinctive form of construction: kiln-fired brick. As if the bricks themselves were not sufficient to mark this site as different, the builders added mystery to technology: each brick was stamped or moulded with a geometric or representational design before firing, with the design deliberately placed facing inwards, so that it could not be seen in the finished building.

Most **buses from Villahermosa** take an hour and a quarter; you'll likely be dropped off at or near the ADO terminal on the main highway outside town (Comalcalco is west of the road). Green *combis* (M$5), found outside the ADO terminal, ply the route to the ruins, and any second-class bus heading north (to or from Paraíso) will also pass by. Ask the driver for "ruinas", or get off after about five minutes, when you see the sign. The ruins are on the right along a long straight paved road; some *combis* go all the way there and taxis charge M$20, but otherwise it's a fifteen-minute walk. There's a small **restaurant** and toilets at the site, and on the highway plenty of buses back to Villahermosa (look for TRT buses, which take the fast route via Cárdenas, every 45 minutes, or Allegro and Comalli buses, which go via Cupilco) or on to Paraíso (20min).

The museum

You can see the astonishing designs on the bricks in Comalcalco's marvellous **museum**, though the labels are in Spanish only. Animals depicted include crocodiles, turtles, frogs, lizards, dogs and mice, while those portraying the sculpted faces of rulers display an advanced level of artistic development. One of the most amazing figures is of a skeleton that appears to be leaping out at you from the surface of the brick. The abundant clay that provided such a versatile medium for architects and artists here also formed the basis for many more mundane artefacts. Comalcalco means "place of the *comales*" – fired clay griddles for cooking tortillas – and these and other clay vessels have been excavated in great numbers. Some of the largest jars were used as **funerary urns** and several are on display here, including one with an intact skeleton.

The site

Though there are dozens of buildings at Comalcalco, only around ten or so of the larger ones have been restored. Because the brickwork is so fragile, you're not allowed to enter or climb on many of them, but you can follow a path up to Structure 3 and around the Palacio. Entering the site, you first come to **Temple I**, the main structure of the **North Plaza Cluster**, a tiered pyramid with a massive central stairway. Originally, the whole building (like all of the structures here) would have been covered with stucco made from oyster shells, sculpted into masks and reliefs of rulers and deities, and brightly painted. Only a few of these features remain – the exposed ones protected from further erosion by shelters, while others have been deliberately left buried. Facing Temple I at the opposite end of the site is the **Gran Acrópolis**, a complex of buildings, some still being excavated, raised above the plaza. Here you can climb up to **El Palacio** for some excellent close-up views of the brickwork, including a series of massive brick piers and arches that once formed an enormous double corbelled vault, 80m long and over 8m wide – one of the largest enclosed spaces the Maya ever built. There's a fine stucco mask of Kinich Ahau, the Maya sun god, on **Temple VI**, and at the side of **Temple V** a small, corbel-arched room contains stucco reliefs of nine, richly dressed, half-life-size figures apparently in conversation or even argument – they may represent the **Lords of Xibalba**, the Maya underworld.

Around Comalcalco

The area between the coast and Villahermosa is the heart of Tabasco's **cacao-growing region**. Just a couple of kilometres out of Comalcalco, en route to

Paraíso, is **Hacienda Cholula** (☎933/334-3815, ⓦwww.fincacholula.com.mx), a small business producing organic chocolate in the old-fashioned way. There are guided tours (daily 9am–4pm; M$30) and a shop where the end product, traditional Mexican drinking chocolate, is for sale. It's also something of a nature trek – there's a large troupe of howler monkeys here as well as innumerable birds (and thousands of mosquitoes), and alongside the cacao the hacienda grows coffee, cinnamon and bananas.

Towards Villahermosa, the slower route winds through countless *tope*-strewn towns via **Cupilco**, notable for its roadside church, the **Templo de la Virgen de la Asunción**. Exuberantly decorated in gold and blue with floral patterns, it's a beautiful example of the distinctive *tabasqueño* approach to sacred spaces.

Villahermosa

Huge, hot, noisy and brash as only a Mexican city can be, **VILLAHERMOSA** – or "Beautiful Town" – could at first sight hardly be less appropriately named. For travellers in this area, though, it's not just something of an inevitability – its position at the junction of road and bus routes means that sooner or later you're almost bound to pass through here, especially if you hope to see Palenque – but also a unique experience, far more like a big city than Mérida or anywhere else in the Yucatán, and after a while the place can start to grow on you. Quite apart from the **Parque La Venta** and sudden vistas of the broad sweep of the **Río Grijalva**, there are attractive plazas, quiet old streets, impressive ultramodern buildings and several art galleries and museums. In the evening, as the traffic disperses and the city cools, its appeal is heightened, and strolling the pedestrianized streets around the **Zona Luz**, as the historic downtown core is known, or the lively malecón, where everything stays open late, becomes a genuine pleasure. Villahermosa's modern commercial centre, **Tabasco 2000**, 2km northwest of the Zona Luz, is a smart area of government buildings, a conference centre and high-end hotels, where oil-industry business travellers hang out.

Arrival and information

Villahermosa's busy regional **airport** lies about 13km east of the centre on the main road towards Escárcega and Palenque. No buses run to the centre from here; a taxi will set you back around M$200. The **bus stations** are pretty close to each other northwest of the Zona Luz: the **first-class station** (known as El ADO – pronounced *ah-day-oh*) is a modern building on Javier Mina just off Ruíz Cortines. There's luggage storage and an information booth, usually unstaffed. *Combis* ply the road outside, but to **get to the Zona Luz** requires changing at the market – it's less hassle (and less confusing) to take a taxi (M$20). Walking takes around twenty minutes: head east on Merino or Fuentes for six or seven long blocks, and then turn right (south) at Madero. The main **second-class** terminal, the Central de Autobuses, is on Ruíz Cortines. To walk into the centre, turn left on Ruíz Cortines, follow it to its junction with Madero and turn right.

Villahermosa's humidity might make you consider taking **taxis** to get around – rates are M$20 within most of the city. The **local bus** system comprises a confusing jumble of *combi* minivans, with the **Mercado Pino Suárez** acting as the main hub. Fares are a standard M$5.

Despite the growth in visitor numbers in recent years, there's no handy **tourist office**. Booths at the airport, history museum, malecón, Parque La Venta and ADO bus station have erratic opening hours and can offer only leaflets, while the main state and federal office (Mon–Fri 8am–6pm, Sat 8am–1pm; ☎993/310-9700 ext 5238, ⓦwww.visitetabasco.com), on Avenida de los Ríos south of Paseo Tabasco in Tabasco 2000, is too far away from the centre to be of much use.

Accommodation

Hotels in Villahermosa are not great value at the low end: most **budget** options are on Avenida Madero or Calle Lerdo de Tejada, close to the heart of things, though none is particularly praiseworthy. A few of the more **upmarket** hotels, on the other hand, are actually very well priced when compared with more touristy cities, though a steady stream of Pemex employees and conventioneers can keep the rooms full. With a couple of exceptions, these pricier places are located in the Tabasco 2000 district, about 2.5km west of the centre along Paseo Tabasco, not far from La Venta.

Best Western Madan Madero 408 ☎993/314-0518, ⓦ www.madan.com.mx. Excellent-value midrange option, with quiet a/c in the well-kept modern rooms and exceptionally nice staff. The café downstairs is a busy meeting place. If you need a place near the bus stations, try the equally good *Best Western Maya Tabasco* on Ruíz Cortines, midway between the two (ⓦwww .hotelmaya.com.mx). ⑤

Hostel La Chonita II Abelardo Reyes 217 ☎993/312-2053, ⓦwww.hostelachonita.com. Not a bargain hostel (M$150/person in small dorms), but clean and friendly, with bikes, wi-fi and a/c. Handy location near the bus stations; look for the lurid paint job.

Miraflores Reforma 304 ☎993/358-0470, ⓦwww .hotelmiraflores.com. A bit cheaper than the *Madan*, this independent hotel has all the same amenities (parking, a lobby bar and café, lobby wi-fi), though they're not quite as slick and new. Rooms all have balconies, and the staff are friendly. ④

Olmeca Plaza Madero 418 ☎1-800/201-0909, ⓦwww.hotelolmecaplaza.com. Much the most luxurious downtown option, with slick modern rooms and a swimming pool; offical rates can seem steep, but there's often a promotion which can halve the cost. ⑦

Oriente Madero 425 ☎993/312-0121, ⒺHotel-oriente@hotmail.com. The best of the budget options, with big, clean tile-floor rooms with firm beds and decent bathrooms. Most are internal, so quiet; some with a/c. ②

Quality Inn Cencali Paseo Tabasco at Juárez ☎993/313-6611, ⓦwww.qualityinnvillahermosa .com. The best-value spot in the Tabasco 2000 area. Set in quiet, luxuriant gardens on the shore of a lagoon, the *Cencali* has an inviting pool, comfortable, well-furnished rooms with a/c and suites with beautiful tiled bathrooms; upstairs rooms have balconies. Parque La Venta is a 1km walk. ⑥

Quinta Real Paseo de la Choca 1402 ☎993/310-1300 ⓦwww.quintarealvillahermosa.com.mx. The best of the city's luxury hotels, done up in grand mansion style, with vast rooms and two pools. It's 5km west from the centre, but right by the city's outer ring road, making it easily accessible for drivers, yet not too far from Parque La Venta. ⑧

San Rafael Constitución 240 ☎993/312-0166. A bit tatty, but notable for its very cheap fan-only rooms, and, perhaps more importantly, its splendid old tiled floors, soaring ceilings and brilliantly painted walls. A few rooms have a/c and TV, but for that, you're better off elsewhere. ①

The city

Most visitors to Villahermosa head straight out to **Parque La Venta**, the obvious highlight of the city, but the **Zona Luz** in the old centre also warrants some exploration. The narrow streets contain several absorbing museums and galleries, particularly the **Museo de Historia de Tabasco**, housed in one of the state's most ornate buildings. If you have more time, it's worth heading out to **Yumká**, an enjoyable safari park and ecological research centre.

Downtown

The oldest part of Villahermosa can be found **downtown**, in the **Zona Luz**, where vestiges of the nineteenth-century city (the original colonial buildings were built mostly of wood and have perished) survive on streets busy with shoppers and commerce. Many of the main shopping blocks are now

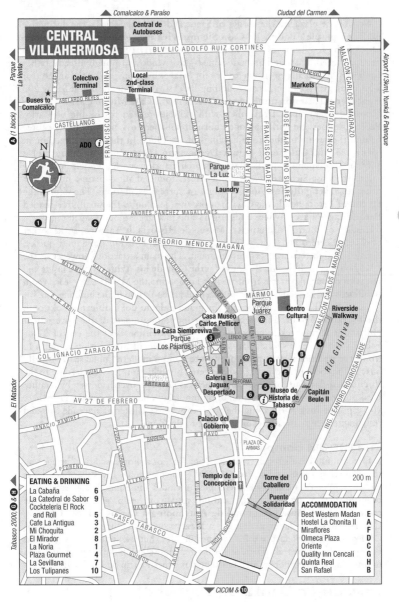

CENTRAL VILLAHERMOSA

Central de Autobuses

BLV LIC ADOLFO RUIZ CORTINES

Colectivo Terminal

Local 2nd-class Terminal

Markets

Buses to Comalcalco

ADO ⓘ

ABELARDO REYES

CASTELLANOS

HERMANOS BASTAR ZOZAYA

DONA FIDENCIA

JUAN ALVAREZ

PEDRO FUENTES

CORONEL LINO MERINO

Parque La Luz

Laundry

ANDRES SANCHEZ MAGALLANES

❶   ❷

AV COL GREGORIO MÉNDEZ MAGAÑA

MATAMOROS

GALEANA

2 DE ABRIL

CHIAPULTEPEC

SAENZ MARSAL

ALDAMA

MÁRMOL

Parque Juárez

Centro Cultural

Riverside Walkway

Casa Museo Carlos Pellicer

La Casa Siempreviva

Parque Los Pájaros

COL IGNACIO ZARAGOZA

IGUALA

GUAL

ARTEAGA

Z O N A

L E R D O   D E   T E J A D A

@ L C U D Z

REFORMA

Galería El Jaguar Despertado

AV 27 DE FEBRERO

Museo de Historia de Tabasco

Capitán Beulo II

ⓘ

Palacio del Gobierno

IGNACIO RAMIREZ

PEDRO FUENTE

PLAN DE AYUTLA

BARRERA

N BRAVO

PLAZA DE ARMAS

ALLENDE

PEDRERO

Templo de la Concepción

Torre del Caballero

Puente Solidaridad

0   200 m

MANUEL DOBALDO

PASEO TABASCO

QUINTIN

ARENAS

INDEPENDENCIA

RIO GRIJALVA

MALECON CARLOS A MADRAZO

ING. LEANDRO ROVIROSA WADE

EATING & DRINKING

La Cabaña	6
La Catedral de Sabor	9
Cockteleria El Rock and Roll	5
Cafe La Antigua	3
Mi Choquita	2
El Mirador	8
La Noria	1
Plaza Gourmet	4
La Sevillana	7
Los Tulipanes	10

ACCOMMODATION

Best Western Madan	E
Hostel La Chonita II	A
Miraflores	F
Olmeca Plaza	D
Oriente	C
Quality Inn Cencali	G
Quinta Real	H
San Rafael	B

Parque La Venta

A (1 block)

El Matador

Tabasco 2000, ⑥ & ⑪

FRANCISCO JAVIER MINA

INSURGENTES

DON CASTILLO

VENUSTIANO CARRANZA

JOSE MARIA PINO SUAREZ

FRANCISCO MADERO

AV CONSTITUCION

AMADO NERVO

MALECON CARLOS A MADRAZO

Airport (13km), Yumká & Palenque

▼ CICOM & ⑩

pedestrianized, and the buildings along them are gradually being cleaned up and restored. At the northern end of the Zona, Parque Juárez, at the junction of Madero and Zaragoza, is bustling in the evenings, as crowds swirl around watching the street entertainers. Facing the plaza on the east side, the futuristic glass **Centro Cultural de Villahermosa** (Tues–Sun 10am–8pm; free) presents changing exhibitions of art, photography and costume, as well as film screenings and concerts – stroll by and check out the schedule.

West of the plaza, on the corner of Sáenz and Lerdo de Tejada, the distinctive pink and purple paint on **La Casa Siempreviva** immediately catches the eye. One of the few fully restored houses from the early twentieth century, it has beautiful tiled floors and arched stained-glass windows, though already rather rundown: it's usually open as a gallery for local exhibitions, and is the anchor for a bit of an arts scene in the surrounding blocks. Almost next door at Sáenz 203 is another old mansion turned into a museum – the **Casa Museo Carlos Pellicer** (Tues–Sun 9am–5pm; free), filled with exhibits related to the life of Carlos Pellicer, a poet and anthropologist born in Villahermosa and the driving force behind the rescue of the stone carvings of La Venta. In the other direction, at Sáenz 117, the **Galería El Jaguar Despertado** (Tues–Sun 9am–5pm; free) is another state-sponsored gallery in a restored mansion, with a similar lurid paint job to the Casa Siempreviva; the side streets round about contain a number of other small **art galleries** – look for signs of current exhibitions. The steps at the far end of Lerdo, beside the Casa Siempreviva, lead up to the small, tree-shaded **Parque Los Pájaros**, where budgerigars sing in a large, globe-shaped cage.

Heading on south, Villahermosa's **Museo de Historia de Tabasco**, at the corner of 27 de Febrero and Juárez (Tues–Sun 9am–5pm; M$30), provides a quirky, detailed account of the state's development. The main attraction, however, is the 1915 building itself, popularly known as the **Casa de los Azulejos**, tiled inside and out with colourful patterns from all over Europe and the Middle East – each room is different and dazzling. There's an excellent art bookshop in the building too.

A couple of blocks further south, the grand **Palacio del Gobierno** looks onto the **Plaza de Armas**, although the most interesting aspect of the government building is at the back, where a modern glass extension faces the end of 27 de Febrero and there's a spectacular, vast modern statue, lit from within at night. In front, the traditional civic plaza opens into a more modern public space, usually busy in the cool of the evening, when there's often live music. Steps lead up to the **Puente Solidaridad** footbridge over the Río Grijalva, overshadowed by a rather bleak square tower, its observation deck unreliably open to the public. From here you can head back north along the river, to where a cluster of riverside bars and restaurants occupy the **malecón**, adjacent to the Zona.

The CICOM complex

A fifteen-minute walk south from the Zona Luz, or a short *combi* ride, brings you to Villahermosa's cultural centre, **CICOM** – the Centro de Investigaciones de las Culturas Olmeca y Maya. The complex includes museums, a concert hall, a beautiful theatre, research library and fine restaurant (see p.247), along with the centrepiece, the **Museo Regional de Antropología Carlos Pellicer Cámara**. Unfortunately, the latter is shut for a massive overhaul; the vast collection of Olmec and Maya artefacts is due to reopen in 2011, but ask at the history museum before you make the trek. There are other small museums in the complex (devoted to music and contemporary art), but they don't merit a trip on their own.

Parque La Venta and around

A visit to Villahermosa's **Parque La Venta** (daily 8am–5pm; M$40) could easily fill half a day. The most important artefacts from the Olmec site of La Venta, some 120km west of Villahermosa, were transferred here in the late 1950s, when they were threatened by Pemex oil explorations. Little is known about the **Olmec culture** (see p.287), referred to by many archeologists as the mother culture of Mesoamerica; that it developed and flourished in the unpromising environment of the Gulf coast swamps 3200 years ago only adds to its mystery.

Just inside the entrance, a display familiarizes you with what little is known about the Olmecs, as well as the history of the discovery of La Venta. The most significant and famous items in the park are four gigantic **basalt heads**, notable for their African-looking features. Additionally, there's a whole series of other Olmec stone sculptures. To conjure a jungle setting, monkeys, agoutis (large rodents) and coatis (members of the racoon family) wander around freely, while crocodiles, jaguars and other animals from the region are displayed in sizeable enclosures. The mosquitoes add an unplanned touch of reality. You can also visit the park at night for a rather good **sound-and-light show** (Tues–Sun 7, 8 & 9pm; M$100) that involves strolling from monument to monument, dramatically illuminated amidst the shadowy trees. For this event, you must buy tickets and enter at a second gate about 250m southwest along Paseo Tabasco.

Parque La Venta is set inside the much larger **Parque Tomás Garrido Canabal**, which stretches along the shore of an extensive lake, the **Laguna de Ilusiones**. There are walking trails here and boats for hire, or you can climb the Mirador de los Águilas, a tower in the middle of the lake. Also in the park, opposite the La Venta entrance, the small **Museo de Historia Natural** (Tues–Sun 9am–5pm; M$15) features displays on the animals and plants of Tabasco, focusing on the interaction between humans and the environment.

To get to La Venta, take a taxi or hop on one of the *combis* that pass on Avenida Madero in the city centre ("Tabasco 2000", "Circuito 1", "Parque Linda Vista", "Fracc Carrizal", among others); they also run along the highway from the second-class bus terminal. A taxi from the centre costs M$40.

Beyond La Venta, many of the *combis* continue down Paseo Tabasco to the **Tabasco 2000** area. This extension of the city is an impressive, if soulless, example of modern Mexican architecture, with concrete shopping malls, government buildings and a planetarium, as well as a number of large hotels.

Yumká

Villahermosa's major ecological attraction, **Yumká** (daily 9am–5pm, last entry 4pm; M$50, kids M$25 Ⓦ www.yumka.org), named for the Chontal Maya dwarf-god who looks after forests, is an enjoyable combination of safari park and environmental studies centre. The park covers more than six square kilometres, so after a guided walking tour of the Tabasco jungle, complete with monkeys, you board a train for a trip round paddocks representing the savannahs of Africa and Asia. Elephants, rhinos, giraffes and antelopes are rarely displayed in Mexico and almost never in such spacious surroundings. After a stop at the **restaurant**, you can take a boat tour of the lagoon (M$20), where, in addition to hippos, there are good opportunities for birdwatching.

Yumká is 14km from the centre of Villahermosa, very close to the airport. *Combis* leave regularly from along Calle Amado Nervo behind the market at the top end of Avenida Constitución, and a park-operated **shuttle bus** (M$15) runs from Parque La Venta (by the sound-and-light show ticket office; Sat & Sun 9am, 11am, 12.30pm & 2pm). A taxi will set you back M$200.

Eating and drinking

The Zona Luz boasts only **fast food** or bland hotel fare, with a couple of exceptions noted below. For the former, head for Aldama, north of its junction with Lerdo de Tejada: at this junction there's a *Flor de Michoacan* ice-cream place, and heading up Aldama you'll find half a dozen taco and pizza joints. Try also the *Plaza Gourmet*, an outdoor food court on the malecón, opposite the end of Lerdo de Tejada. As ever, the **market** – here, a vast, tidy two-storey complex trimmed in white wrought-iron trellises – is good for fruit, bread and cheap tacos. It's several blocks north of the Zona

Luz on Avenida Constitución. For **nightlife**, check out the various clubs on the malecón around Avenida 27 de Febrero and to the north, some facing the water and others on structures jutting into the river – all far smarter than you might expect.

Cafe La Antigua Lerdo de Tejada 608, on the steps by Casa Siemprevira. A pleasant spot for good coffee, smoothies and sandwiches, plus more substantial food including a M$45 *comida*. There's often live music in the evening.

La Cabaña Juárez, opposite the Casa de los Azulejos. Traditional café where local gents linger over their coffees and conduct their business. Food is served, though it's rather pricey.

La Catedral de Sabor Independencia, adjacent to the Templo de la Concepción. Cool down with a refreshing *horchata de coco* – a Tabasco speciality – at this little sidewalk stand. You can also sit down inside, in a more formal café.

Cockteleria El Rock and Roll Reforma 307. A bustling place with excellent seafood cocktails (M$80), *ceviche* and prawns, accompanied by, yes, blaring rock-and-roll from the jukebox. There's slightly quieter seating upstairs.

Mi Choquita Javier Mina 304-A. No-frills local place handy for the bus station, with plastic tables and chairs. Good breakfasts from M$39 and regional dishes in a typical Tabascan style as well as Spanish/Castilian classics like roast lamb – there's a decent *menu del día* for M$55.

El Mirador Madero 105. Seafood restaurant with river views and a slightly time-warp classiness. Prices are not unreasonable – a full dinner runs about M$300 per person. Mon–Sat noon–8pm.

La Noria Gregorio Méndez 1008. Comfortable a/c restaurant serving inexpensive Lebanese and Middle Eastern restaurant; tastes you are unlikely to find elsewhere in the state.

La Sevillana Madero, just north of *El Mirador*. Swanky little gourmet shop with a takeout deli (lots of Spanish ham) and liquor store, plus a sit-down café serving expensive but tasty sandwiches.

Moving on from Villahermosa

Villahermosa is a regional transport hub, with excellent air and bus connections to every corner of the country and state.

To get to the **ADO bus station** from the centre, catch a *combi* from the malecón heading for "Chedraui". From here, ADO, OCC and TRT operate dozens of services to all major destinations. The front of the station deals with services originating here; tickets for *de paso* services are sold in a separate complex behind. Services include **Campeche** (19 daily; 6hr), **Cancún** (19 daily; 12–14hr), **Frontera** (29 daily; 1hr 10min), **Mérida** (19 daily; 8–10hr), **Mexico City** (21 daily; 11hr), **Oaxaca** (3 daily, in the evening; 13–14hr), **Palenque** (12 daily; 2hr 30min), **Tenosique** (13 daily; 3hr 45min), **Tuxtla Gutiérrez** (19 daily, most via Hwy 187; 4–5hr) and **Veracruz** (23 daily; 6–9hr). For San Cristóbal (6–7hr), there are just three direct services; it's often easier to change at either Tuxtla or Palenque. TRT has minibus departures to **Comalcalco** (1hr 15min) every ten minutes.

The **Central de Autobuses** (the main second-class terminal) has buses to virtually everywhere in the state and all the main cities beyond, including **Tenosique** ten times a day (5am–5.30pm; 4hr), **Teapa** every half-hour (5am–9pm; 1hr), and **Coatzacoalcos** (for La Venta, every half-hour 5am–9pm; 2hr 30min). There's another, more dilapidated **second-class terminal near the ADO**, off Eusebio Castillo near Zozaya, with frequent buses to **Frontera** and **Paraíso** (1hr 30min), as well as **Palenque** (3hr) and **Escárcega** (5hr 30min). Several companies run buses to **Comalcalco** (1hr 15min), the best of which is Comalli Bus, on Gil y Sáenz above Abelardo Reyes, not far from the ADO (4.45am–10pm). Just south of here on Gil y Sáenz, **combis** run to **Nacajuca** (for Cupilco; 30min), and pale yellow **colectivos** go from Castellanos, just east of Gil y Sáenz. **Shared taxis** are usually faster and not that much more expensive; the terminal is just north of the ADO on Abelardo Reyes. Taxis leave when full for Palenque, Paraíso and Frontera, taking four or five people, but you won't have to wait long, at least in the morning.

From the **airport** (☎993/356-0157), flights depart for Mérida, Mexico City, Poza Rica and Veracruz. Continental flies to Houston, Texas, once a day. There's an ADO office at the airport where you can buy bus tickets, notably for the six daily **direct buses from the airport to Palenque**.

Los Tulipanes In the CICOM complex. A lovely riverfront restaurant, a bit formal and unstinting on the a/c. Come here to sample delicious renditions of Tabasco cuisine: shrimp with coconut and passionfruit salsa, fresh corn tortillas stuffed with seafood, crab soup. Very well priced, considering the massive portions. Open till 6pm.

Listings

Airlines Villahermosa is served by Aeromar (ⓦ www.aeromar.us), Aeroméxico (ⓦ www.aeromexico.com, ☎ 1-800/021-4000), Continental (ⓦ www.continental.com, ☎ 1-800/900-5000), Interjet (ⓦ www.interjet.com.mx) and VivaAerobus (ⓦ www.vivaaerobus.com).

Banks and exchange There are branches of all major banks, with ATMs, at the airport and throughout the centre, especially on Madero and Juárez downtown; any will change cash and travellers' cheques.

Internet access Try Inet at Aldama 520 or G&C on Zaragoza.

Laundry Lavandería La Paz, Coronel Lino Merino 403, near Madero (Mon–Sat, 8am–8pm Sun 8am–2pm; M$18/kg).

Post office The main post office is in the Zona Luz at Sáenz 131 on the corner of Lerdo (Mon–Fri 9am–3pm, Sat 9am–1pm).

River trips The *Capitán Beulo II* makes hour-long trips on the Grijalva river (Wed–Fri at 5pm; weekends at 12pm, 2.30pm, 5.30pm ad 7.30pm; M$90; ⓦ www.olmecaexpress.com); information and tickets from the *Hotel Olmeca Plaza* or from a kiosk on the malecón before sailings.

Travel agents and tours There's no shortage of travel agencies in the Zona Luz, and all the big hotels have a tour desk to arrange domestic flights and trips to Palenque. Creatur, Paseo Tabasco 1404, on the right just beyond Ruíz Cortines (☎ 993/310-9900, ⓦ www.creaturviajes.com), is the best in the region, with multilingual staff.

Palenque

Set in thick jungle buzzing with insects, in the foothills of the Chiapas mountains, **PALENQUE** is hauntingly beautiful. For many, it is the finest of Mexico's Maya sites: less crowded than Chichén Itzá, larger than Uxmal, with a far more spectacular setting than either. It is not a huge site – you can see everything in a morning – but it is a fascinating one, strongly linked to the lost cities of Guatemala yet with a distinctive style of its own.

Nine kilometres east of the ruins, the **town of Palenque** has every facility a visitor might need. An excellent base for exploring the ruins and the waterfalls in the nearby hills, it is lively enough, with music in the turquoise-painted plaza most evenings, but – save for a small **museum** on the plaza devoted to the textiles and embroidery styles of Chiapas (Mon–Fri 9am–1pm & 5–9pm; M$5) – it has no real intrinsic appeal. As there are a number of excellent camping sites, cabañas and hotels near the ruins, you may prefer not to stay in town at all.

Arrival and information

Arriving on any long-distance bus, you'll be at one of two nearly adjacent **bus terminals** on Avenida Juárez, just off the main highway through town. If you know when you're leaving it's worth buying your onward ticket as soon as you arrive – or at any rate as soon as possible – as buses out of Palenque can be very crowded, particularly the more popular first-class services towards Mérida or San Cristóbal de las Casas. Both bus stations have lockers if you want to leave your stuff while you head for the ruins – marginally cheaper at second class. Palenque's three main streets, avenidas Juárez, 5 de Mayo and Hidalgo, all run parallel and lead straight up to the **plaza**, the Parque Central.

The **tourist office** (Mon–Sat 9am–9pm, Sun 9am–3pm; ☎ 916/345-0356) is in the Plaza de Artesanías on Juárez at the corner of Abasolo, a block below the plaza;

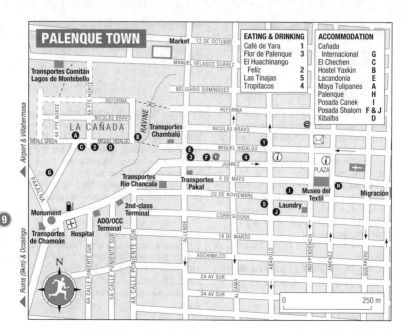

PALENQUE TOWN

EATING & DRINKING		ACCOMMODATION	
Café de Yara	1	Cañada	
Flor de Palenque	3	Internacional	G
El Huachinango		El Chechen	C
Feliz	2	Hostel Yaxkin	B
Las Tinajas	5	Lacandonia	E
Tropicatos	4	Maya Tulipanes	A
		Palenque	H
		Posada Canek	I
		Posada Shalom	F & J
		Xibalba	D

the staff will very sweetly give you wrong information, and a street map if you're lucky. There's another booth on the east side of the plaza, with sometimes sharper staff. You'll generally get better **information** from local tour operators (see "Listings") or at your hotel.

Accommodation

In Palenque town, there are plenty of **hotels** on the rather noisy streets leading from the bus stations to the plaza, especially Hidalgo and 20 de Noviembre. A quieter option is **La Cañada**, a neighbourhood named for the ravine that divides it from the town centre. With brick-paved streets and soft lighting, it feels a little like a chic subdivision, but set in a swathe of trees (birds and monkeys are audible in the morning) and only a short walk from the action. You'll also find a host of places lining the **road to the ruins**, in every category from luxury hotel to campsite, though the latter options are becoming fewer. Note that high season here is Mexican vacation times – July, August, Christmas and Semana Santa; outside that time, rates can drop significantly.

In town

Lacandonia Allende 77 at Hidalgo ☎916/345-0057, ©hotel-lacandonia@hotmail.com. Plant-covered balconies around an internal courtyard set a pretty tone at this midrange hotel; the twenty rooms have wrought-iron furniture, a/c and fans. There's a café downstairs, as well as parking. ➍

Palenque 5 de Mayo 15 ☎916/345-0188, ⓦwww.hotelpalenque.com.mx. Just off the plaza, the *Palenque* is a comfy hotel with a groovy Sixties feel, complete with two-tone green rooms –

bathrooms are new, and there are plenty of facilities including pool, bar and restaurant. Breakfast included. ➍

Posada Canek 20 de Noviembre 43 ☎916/345-0150, ©maizdemexico @hotmail.com. One of several *posadas* along this street, *Canek* is great value, with dorm beds in shared rooms from M$70 (peak times only). The friendly staff look after solo travellers like family. Double rooms, some with a/c, private bath and a street-side balcony, are huge. Free wi-fi, and internet, meals, luggage storage and tours all available. **②**

Posada Shalom Juárez 156 ⓣ916/345-0944, and Corregidora near Abasolo ⓣ916/345-2641, ⓦwww.posadasshalom.com. Twin hotels, both with scrupulously clean, if cramped, rooms with cable TV, tiled private bathrooms and optional a/c. Free wi-fi, and luggage storage and laundry service available. **③**

In La Cañada

Cañada Internacional Juárez 1 ⓣ916/345-2094, ⓦwww.hotelcanadapalenque.com. Big, good-value rooms with heavy wood furniture in a modern building, with a/c, wi-fi and a small pool. **④**

El Chechen Merle Green at Hidalgo ⓣ916/345-1008. Just sixteen rooms, all with private bath, a/c and fans; run by a conscientious family. Basic, but clean and good value. **③**

Hostel Yaxkin Hidalgo at 5ta Poniente ⓣ916/345-0102, ⓦwww.hostalyaxkin.com. Welcoming new hostel with excellent communal areas featuring kitchen, games, TV, wi-fi and Italian restaurant. Accommodation is a little more basic, in eight-bed dorms (M$134), tiny shared bathrooms, cabañas or a/c, en-suite rooms. **①–③**

Maya Tulipanes C Cañada 6 ⓣ916/345-0201, ⓦwww.mayatulipanes.com.mx. Very comfortable if rather dull business-style hotel with a/c rooms, shady grounds, a tiled pool and decent café. **⑦**

Xibalba Merle Green at Hidalgo ⓣ916/345-0411, ⓦwww.hotelxibalba.com. Pretty white rooms are accented with green and brown, giving a vaguely natural feel, even if rooms are not very large. Staff are friendly, and there's a good restaurant, roof terrace and helpful travel agency. **④**

On the road to the ruins

Chan Kah Resort Village 4km from town, on the left ⓣ916/345-1100, ⓦwww.chan-kah.com.mx. Luxury brick and stone cabañas, rather tightly packed in a lovely forest and river setting, humming with birdlife. Amenities include three huge stone-lined swimming pools and a restaurant. Big discounts often on offer. **⑧**

Mayabell The closest place to the ruins, inside the park 6km from town, just before the museum ⓣ916/341-6977, ⓦwww.mayabell .com.mx. A great favourite with backpackers and adventure-tour groups, this camping spot and trailer park has something for everyone: palapa shelters for hammocks, vehicle pads with electricity and water, and very comfortable private cabañas with hot water. The shared showers have hot water, and there's also a *temazcal*, spa, laundry and decent freshwater swimming pool (with occasional fish), plus frequent live music in the restaurant. Rates vary: hammock rental (M$20), tent camping (M$50), RV (M$170). Basic cabañas **①**, with a/c **⑤**

El Panchán 5.1km from town, on the left, just before the park entrance ⓦwww.elpanchan.com. A large complex incorporating a number of different cabaña operations, separated by screens of trees and sharing a couple of restaurants and other facilities including bike rental, body-piercing, travel agent and more. The vibe might be a little too nouveau-hippie for some, but most places are excellent deals. It's easy to take a *combi* here and then compare rates by walking around to the various options. *Margarita and Ed's* (ⓣ916/348-4205; **②–③**) is the cleanest and best-value of the places here, with thatched cabins or conventional double rooms with a/c. *Jungle Palace* (ⓣ915/348-0520; **①**) has lovely, but tiny, shared bath cabañas with terraces above the stream; also some en-suite versions. Avoid the places closer to the centre, near *Don Mucho's*, if you want to go to bed early – there's live music and fire-spinning at night.

Quinta Chanabnal 2.2km from town, on the right ⓣ916/345-5320, ⓦwww .quintachanabnal.com. Stunning luxury hotel whose vast, ochre-toned rooms are furnished in purpose-built hardwood furniture and antique Guatemalan fabrics in a fusion of European, Far Eastern and Mexican styles. The owner – originally from Italy – is an expert in Maya iconography and modern Maya glyphs throughout the complex tell his story and that of the hotel. There's a pool, restaurant, small lake alive with birdlife and it's great value for the quality. **⑧**

Eating and drinking

Food in Palenque town is fairly basic, and most restaurants serve up similar dishes, often just pasta and pizza, to customers who've really only come for the ruins. There are also several places along the road to the site – some of which cater mainly to tour groups – including a couple in *El Panchán*. **Avenida Juárez** also has several budget options between the bus stations and the plaza, while **Hidalgo** has more Mexican-style food, with several taco places and even a couple of seafood restaurants. There's a good Mexican **bakery**, Flor de Palenque, on Calle Allende, next to the *Hotel Lacandonia*.

Don Mucho On the road to the ruins, 5.1km from town. The social centre of *El Panchán*, serving Mexican and Italian food in the evening, with live music nightly from 8pm. Great for breakfast (around M$40) or a leisurely lunch after visiting the ruins, though it can be a victim of its own success – so packed with tour groups that it can be hard to find a table. Happy hour 6–8pm.

El Huachinango Felíz Merle Green at Hidalgo. A bi-level restaurant in La Cañada that serves great fish and shrimp baked in banana leaves, among other seafood. Prices are reasonable (less than M$100), and the setting is pretty and quiet – a nice break from restaurants in town.

Las Tinajas 20 de Noviembre at Abasolo. Pleasant, family-run restaurant, open morning till night and popular for its vast menu of hearty meats, fish, chicken and pasta in addition to the usual Mexican fare. Probably the best of the places in the town, though that's not saying a great deal. Good-value breakfasts, and the substantial main dishes go for around M$85.

Tropitacos Juárez between Allende and Abasolo. Not much to look at, but the fast-food style tacos are delicious, served hot and fast to the constant drone of blenders whipping up fruit drinks. Go for the *tacos al pastor* pork or try a *torta de bisteck*, garnished with griddle-fried cheese, if you want something more substantial.

Café de Yara Hidalgo at Abasolo. Café culture comes to Palenque – try the cappuccino (from a proper espresso machine) and breakfasts especially. Dinner (about M$80) is also decent.

Listings

Banks Several banks along Juárez will change travellers' cheques and have ATMs. There's also an ATM at the first-class bus station.

Internet Most hotels here have terminals and wi-fi, and internet cafés are plentiful. They include Ciber-konqueror, just past the post office on Independencia at Nicolas Bravo, and Ciber Vlos, on Juárez next to *Posada Shalom*.

Laundry Gota de Agua, on Independencia between 20 de Noviembre and Corregidora.

Post office On Independencia, a block from the plaza (Mon–Fri 9am–6pm, Sat & Sun 9am–1pm).

Tours Walk the streets of Palenque and you'll be accosted by touts offering a huge variety of tours to local attractions, above all the waterfalls at Agua Azul and Misol-Há (p.259) and the ruins of Bonampak and Yaxchilán (p.255 & p.257). There are also trips to Guatemala and adventure tours, including kayaking and horseriding. Prices vary according to season (and even time of day if there's one seat left to fill) but start from around M$100 for the waterfalls, M$600 for a day-trip to Bonampak and Yaxchilán. Be sure to check what's included – entrance fees, meals and English-speaking guides most importantly. Two of the more reliable agents are Na Chan Kan (☎916/345-0263, ✉chiapastour@hotmail.com), with a small office on Juárez, just up from the bus station, and a main office on Hidalgo at Jiménez, and Viajes Shivalva, based at the *Hotel Xibalba* in La Cañada (☎916/345-0411, ✆www.hotelxibalba.com).

The ruins of Palenque

The **ruins of Palenque** occupy the top of an escarpment marking the northwestern limit of the Chiapas highlands. Superficially, the site bears a closer resemblance to the Maya sites of Guatemala than to those of the Yucatán, but ultimately it's unique – the **towered palace** and **pyramid tomb** are like nothing else, as is the site's abundance of reliefs and glyphic inscriptions. The setting, too, is remarkable. Surrounded by jungle-covered hills, Palenque stands right at the edge of the great Yucatán plain – climb to the top of any of the structures and you look out across an endless stretch of low, pale-green flatland. If you arrive early enough in the day, the mist still clinging to the treetops and the roaring of the howler monkeys lend an exotic ambience.

Founded around 100 BC as a farming village, it was four hundred years before Palenque began to flourish, during the Classic period (300–900 AD). Towards the end of this time the city ruled over a large part of modern-day Chiapas and Tabasco, but its peak came during a relatively short period in the seventh century, under two rulers, **Hanab Pakal (Jaguar Shield)** and **Chan Bahlum (Jaguar Serpent)**. Almost everything you can see (and that's only a tiny, central part of the original city) dates from this era.

Ruin practicalities

Getting to the ruins of Palenque, 9km from town, is no problem. Combis run at least every fifteen minutes (6am–6pm; M$10 one way), most operated by Chambalú and Joya de Tulúm, from their terminals on Allende, either side of Juárez. They will stop anywhere en route, including outside the bus stations or at any of the hotels and campsites along the road to the ruins. After 6pm, you'll have to either walk or take a **taxi** (M$60). There are also plenty of organized **tours** from town.

The **ruins** (daily 8am–5pm, last entry 4.30pm; M$51 including museum) are in the **Parque Nacional de Palenque**, for which there's an additional M$25 charge (if you're staying inside the park, at *Mayabell*, for example, you only have to pay once – just hold onto your ticket.) The main road first passes the site **museum**, where there's a good café and artesanías shop. It's possible to buy a site ticket here, after 9am (but not on Mon, when the museum is shut), then enter at the gate across the road, hiking up to the main part of the site via the waterfalls trail. But most people will press on to the main site entrance, at the top of the hill another 2km up a winding road. In this area, there's a small **café** and numerous souvenir stalls selling drinks, as well as toilets and some expensive lockers. Guides officially cost M$600 for groups of up to seven people, but that's open to negotiation. Even if you have your own **car**, you may still prefer to take a *combi*, as this enables you to exit on the downhill side of the site by the museum, and spare yourself the hike back up to your vehicle. If you do drive, know that there's very little space for parking at the main entrance on top of the hill.

El Palacio and around

As you enter the site, **El Palacio**, with its extraordinary watchtower, stands ahead of you. The path, however, leads to the right, past a row of smaller structures – one of them, the so-called **Tumba de la Reina Roja** ("Tomb of the Red Queen"), is open inside, and you can climb in to see a sarcophagus still in place. This is nothing, though, compared with the structure's neighbour, the enormous **Templo de las Inscripciones**, an eight-stepped pyramid, 26m high, built up against a thickly overgrown hillside. You are not permitted to climb the pyramid, so you just have to imagine the sanctuary on top, filled with a series of stone panels carved with hieroglyphic inscriptions relating to Palenque's dynastic history. Deep inside is the **tomb of Hanab Pakal** (615–683 AD). Discovered in 1952, this was the first such pyramid burial found in the Americas, and is still the most important and impressive. Some of the smaller objects found – the skeleton and the jade death mask – are on display at the Museo Nacional de Antropología in Mexico City, but the massive, intricately carved stone **sarcophagus** is still inside; you can see a replica at the site museum (p.253). In order that the deified king buried here should not be cut off from the world of the living, a psychoduct – a hollow tube in the form of a snake – ran up the side of the internal staircase, from the tomb to the temple.

The centrepiece of the site, **El Palacio**, is in fact a complex of buildings constructed at different times to form a rambling administrative and residential block. Its square **tower** is unique, and no one knows exactly what its purpose was – perhaps a lookout post or an astronomical observatory. Bizarrely, the narrow staircase winding up inside starts only at the second level, though you're not allowed to climb it. Throughout you'll find delicately executed **relief carvings**, the most remarkable of which are the giant human figures on stone panels in the grassy courtyard, depicting rulers of defeated cities in poses of humiliation. An arcade overlooking the courtyard held a portrait gallery of Palenque's rulers, though many of these have been removed.

9

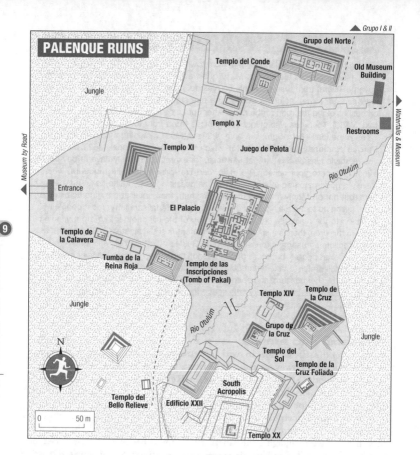

PALENQUE RUINS

Grupo I & II

Grupo del Norte

Templo del Conde

Old Museum Building

Jungle

Waterfalls & Museum

Templo X

Restrooms

Templo XI

Juego de Pelota

Museum by Road

Río Otulúm

Entrance

El Palacio

Templo de la Calavera

Tumba de la Reina Roja

Templo de las Inscripciones (Tomb of Pakal)

Templo XIV

Templo de la Cruz

Jungle

Río Otulúm

Grupo de la Cruz

N

Templo del Sol

Jungle

Templo de la Cruz Foliada

South Acropolis

Templo del Bello Relieve

Edificio XXII

0   50 m

Templo XX

South of El Palacio and adjacent to the Templo de las Inscripciones, a small path leads to the **Templo del Bello Relieve** (**Templo del Jaguar**). More temples are being wrested from the jungle beyond, but the paths are closed and you won't be permitted to pass much further into the forest without a guide. Even so, clambering around here, it's easy to believe you're walking over unexcavated buildings, as the ground is very rocky and some of the stones don't look naturally formed.

The Grupo de la Cruz and around

The main path then leads across the Río Otulúm, one of several streams that cascade through the site. In Palenque's heyday, the Otulúm was lined with stone and used as an aqueduct; the reinforcement also kept the stream from overflowing its banks and undermining the foundations of the surrounding buildings. On the way up the hill, structures are tucked back in the greenery – this area, the **South Acropolis**, is rarely open to the public, as there is ongoing excavation work here.

The path ends in the plaza of the **Grupo de la Cruz**, oddly oriented away from Palenque's more central buildings. The **Templo del Sol**, the **Templo de la Cruz** and the **Templo de la Cruz Foliada** are all tall, narrow pyramids surmounted by a temple with an elaborate stone roofcomb. All, too, contain carved panels representing sacred rites – the cross found here is as important an image in Maya iconography as it is in Christian, representing the meeting of the heavens and the underworld with the land of the living. On the right-hand side of the Templo de la Cruz, God L, one of the gods of the underworld, is depicted smoking tobacco – so far the oldest known image of someone smoking. A small path next to the Templo de la Cruz Foliada leads to the only open portion of the South Acropolis, a building with a replica relief carving, covered with elaborate glyphs and a triumphant king.

The Grupo del Norte and around

Following the Río Otulúm to the northern edge of the cleared site, you reach the lesser buildings of the **Grupo del Norte** and the **Juego de Pelota** (ball-court), on lower ground across a grassy area from El Palacio. Beyond them, two **paths** lead downhill towards the museum. One goes down some perilous stairs behind the Grupo del Norte, leading down via the buildings of **Grupo I** and **Grupo II**, intricate complexes of interconnected rooms. The other path follows the stream as it cascades through the forest and flows over beautiful limestone curtains and terraces into a series of gorgeous pools (no swimming allowed, sadly). It initially skirts **Grupo C**, a small cluster of buildings minimally restored and cleared. **Grupo B** is a small residential complex right on the path, located between the aptly named **Baño de la Reina (Bathing Pool of the Queen)** and a small waterfall on a second stream, the Arroyo Murciélagos. Beyond this, the **Grupo de los Murciélagos** is another residential area where you can see remnants of the original drainage systems as well as benches and stairways. The paths join again just after a suspension bridge crossing the river; eventually the route emerges on the main road opposite the museum. If you don't want to exit here, it's best to make a loop by going down via Grupo I and II – the steeper route – then making your way back up by the other, somewhat easier trail.

The museum

Palenque's excellent **museum** (Tues–Sun 9am–4.30pm; included in site entry), on the road 1.5km from the site entrance, will give you a good idea of the scale of

Moving on from Palenque

Leaving Palenque by **bus** it's extremely easy to get to **Villahermosa** (2hr 30min) – with around fifteen first-class and even more second-class services daily. You may find it easiest to head there and change for your onward journey. Other **first-class** departures from the ADO/OCC terminal can be very busy: they include ten daily to **Ocosingo** (2hr 30min) and **San Cristóbal de las Casas** (5hr); four daily to **Mérida** (8hr) via Campeche (5hr); five daily to **Cancún** via Chetumal and the coast (13hr; mostly overnight); one a day to **Oaxaca** (5.30pm; 15hr); and two overnight to **Mexico City** (13hr). **Second-class** buses run frequently to Ocosingo and San Cristóbal de las Casas (a dozen or more daily) and at least five times a day to Cancún.

Combis for many local destinations will drive past the bus stations, on the lookout for passengers if they have space. For **Ocosingo** and the **waterfalls** en route, El Nueve Volcán has constant departures from its terminal just off the main road between the two bus stations, on 5ta Poniente; though for a day-trip to Misol-Há and/or Agua Azul, a tour might be easier. Destinations along the Frontier Highway, including Bonampak, **Frontera Corozal** (for Yaxchilán) and beyond, are served by Transportes de Chamoán, on the west side of the traffic circle by the statue of the Maya head. You can also get **taxis**, from the plaza, and tours to any of these destinations.

There are three **flights** a week with Aerotucan to Tuxtla Gutiérrez and Oaxaca (Mon, Wed & Fri at 12.30pm; ☎916/341-7094, ⓦwww.aerotucan.com.mx).

Palenque, and a look at some of its treasures. Many of the glyphs and carved relief panels found at the site are on display, as well as examples of giant ceramic censers (incense-burners) in the form of gods or mythological creatures. An intricate model of El Palacio reveals how it would have appeared in the Classic period – with the tops of the buildings adorned with roofcombs – and there's a map of the entire site showing that only around a quarter of the structures have been excavated.

The back wing is devoted to a replica of Pakal's famous sarcophagus lid from the Templo de las Inscripciones – entrance is restricted to small groups, every thirty minutes or so. One of the most renowned iconographic monuments in the Maya world, the sarcophagus lid depicts Pakal at the moment of his death, falling into Xibalba, the underworld, symbolized by a monster's jaws. Above the dead king rises the **Wakah Kan** – the World Tree and the centre of the universe – with **Itzam-Ye**, the Celestial Bird, perched on top representing the heavens.

The Frontier Highway

Southeast of Palenque, the Carretera Fronteriza (**Frontier Highway**) provides access to the valley of the Usumacinta river and the Lacandón forest, and to the great Maya sites located here: **Bonampak**, famous for its murals, and **Yaxchilán**, a vast ruined city on the riverbank. Following the river (also the Guatemalan border), the remote highway has a reputation as a dangerous place – as recently as 2003, Mexican federal police would escort tourists in convoys. A steady military presence has made the area far more secure, however, and though it's still not advisable to drive the road after dark, it is no problem to travel this way in your own car during the day. Army checkpoints are frequent, so be sure to carry your passport.

Sadly, increasing human settlement has also meant the destruction of the forest. The road is now lined with tidy farm plots and occasional hamlets virtually all the way to Frontera Corozal. Further from the road, though, large areas are protected, and wildlife remains abundant, even if you need a keen eye to spot the howler monkeys or the toucans that hide in the treetops.

A growing tourism infrastructure has also made visiting the area significantly easier – though still one of the better adventures in this part of Mexico. It used to be that the only way to visit Bonampak and Yaxchilán was with a **tour** from Palenque (see p.250). That's still the easiest option, whether you go on a day-trip or overnight, with accommodation at the Lacandón Maya community of **Lacanjá Chansayab**. But it's no longer difficult to make the trip on your own, giving you the option of arriving at the remote sites relatively alone. Independent travel can also be substantially cheaper, although the final cost will depend on finding people to share the boat from the settlement of **Frontera Corozal** to Yaxchilán.

The starting point for **DIY trips** is the Transportes de Chamoán *combi* office in Palenque (see box, p.253). And if you have a chance, pick up an information sheet on the Lacandón community from **Casa Na-Bolom** in San Cristóbal (see p.265) before you set off. Should you intend to push on into **Guatemala**, you can get a boat from Frontera Corozal to **Bethél**, across the border a short distance upstream.

Welib-Ja

About 30km southeast of Palenque, the beautiful waterfalls of **WELIB-JA** (8am–5pm; M$10) are far less visited than Agua Azul or Misol-Há. And because they're only 500m from the road, they're also easier to reach by public transport (take the Chamoán *combi* and ask to be let off at the *cascadas*). A forest path alongside the river leads down to the base of a towering split cascade, close enough for the mist to spray over you. There are a few palapas for picnicking in the shade, as well as a protected swimming area for kids, upstream from the falls. Getting back to Palenque shouldn't be hard, as long as you start looking for a ride by 4.30pm or so – you can flag down the pick-up trucks fitted with bench seats as well as standard *combi* vans.

Bonampak and Lacanjá Chansayab

The outside world first heard of **BONAMPAK** ("Painted Walls") in 1946, when Charles Frey, an American conscientious objector to WWII who had taken refuge deep in the forest, was shown the site (though apparently not its famous **murals**) by the Lacandón. The first non-Maya to see these murals – astonishing examples of Classic Maya art – was the American photographer Giles Healey, who arrived shortly after Frey's visit, sparking a long and bitter dispute over exactly who was responsible for their discovery. Bonampak's actual buildings are small and not the most spectacular, but the murals definitely make it worth the visit – there is very little like them elsewhere in the Maya world, and even in their somewhat decayed state, the colours are vivid and the imagery memorable.

The site

At the **entrance to the site** (daily 8am–5pm; M$41) are toilets and a couple of huts selling snacks and souvenirs. Across the defunct airstrip, you emerge at the northwest corner of the main plaza, 110m long and bounded by low walls – the remains of some palace-style buildings. In the centre of the plaza **Stele 1** shows a larger-than-life **Chan Muan**, the last king of Bonampak, dressed for battle – you'll encounter other images of him throughout the site. At 6m, the stele is one of the tallest in the Maya world. Ahead, atop several steep flights of steps, lies the **Acrópolis**, built on at least two smaller structures underneath. On the lower steps more well-preserved stelae show Chan Muan with his wife, Lady Rabbit, preparing himself for blood-letting and apparently about to sacrifice a prisoner. From the highest point of the acropolis there's an impressive sense that you're surrounded by primeval forest – the Selva Lacandona – with just a small cleared space in front of you.

Splendid though all this is, however, the undoubted highlight of the site is the modest-looking **Edificio de las Pinturas**. Inside, on the walls and roof of three separate chambers, the renowned **Bonampak murals** depict vivid scenes of haughty Maya lords, splendidly attired in jaguar-skin robes and quetzal-plume headdresses, their equally well-dressed ladies, and bound prisoners, one with his fingernails ripped out, spurting blood. Musicians play drums, pipes and trumpets in what is clearly a celebration of victory.

Dated to around 790 AD, these paintings show the Bonampak elite at the height of their power: unknown to them, the collapse of the Classic Maya civilization was imminent. Some details were never finished and Bonampak was abandoned shortly after the scenes in the temple were painted. Though you can't enter the rooms fully, the vantage point inside the doorway is more than adequate to absorb what's inside; no more than three people are permitted to enter at any one time so queues are possible, but you shouldn't have to wait long. Having said that, time and early cleaning attempts have clearly taken their toll on the murals, and apart from a few beautifully restored sections, it takes some concentration and imagination to work out what you're looking at.

Room 2, in the centre, is the heart of the scene: it contains a vivid, gruesome depiction of battle and the defeat of Bonampak's enemies. Tortured prisoners lie on temple steps, while above them lords in jaguar robes are indifferent to their agony. A severed head has rolled down the stairs as Chan Muan grasps a prisoner (who appears to be pleading for mercy) by the hair, clearly about to deal him the same fate. The chambers to either side continue the story with celebrations of the victory and the arrival of rulers of vassal states to pay tribute. In **Room 1** an infant wrapped in white cloth (the heir apparent?) is presented to assembled nobility under the supervision of the lord of Yaxchilán, while musicians play drums, pipes and trumpets in the background. **Room 3** shows more celebration and the execution of captives, while **Lady Rabbit**, accompanied by noblewomen, prepares to prick her tongue to let blood fall onto the paper in a clay pot in front of her. The smoke from burning the blood-soaked paper will carry messages to ancestor-gods. Other gorgeously dressed figures, their senses probably heightened by hallucinogenic drugs, dance on the temple steps.

Practicalities and staying at Lacanjá Chansayab

Bonampak lies in a small national park controlled by the Lacandón, on the fringe of the much larger Montes Azules Biosphere Reserve. However you get here, you are permitted to enter the forest only via Lacandón transport. For Bonampak or the settlement of Lacanjá Chansayab, you need to get off the *combi* at **San Javier** (about 3hr and 132km from Palenque), where there's a large palapa on the right side of the road. Taxis usually wait here to take passengers to a parking area 3km down a side road, from where beat-up vans (M$70 per person return) cover the final 9km stretch to the ruins; alternatively the taxi can take you on to the village, a further 2.5km down the side road. You can also **rent a bike** (M$75) to ride up to the ruins, but the business is set up another 250m past the *combi* parking area, and the *combi* drivers may tell you the bikes don't exist.

If you want to spend the night, the easiest option is right by the parking area, a simple place called *Camping Margarito* (camping from M$70 per person, simple rooms ❶), which also runs a **restaurant**. But there are more − and preferable − **camping spots and cabañas** in and on the way to the village of **Lacanjá Chansayab**. It's easiest if you have a particular spot in mind − the village is too spread out to walk around comparing options. There are ten or so operations, few with phones and mostly set up for groups, but there's little chance you'll wind up with nowhere to sleep.

The first place you pass en route to the village is *Cueva del Tejon* (E cuevatejon @hotmail.com; ❷), where large concrete cabañas − with four beds in two rooms, bathrooms and power − are set by a broad section of the river. *Tucan Verde* is next, with riverside camping, friendly owners and a fancy website (W www.tucanverde .com), but badly neglected cabañas. *Ya'aj Ché*, pretty much in the centre of the village, and again next to the water, is much preferable: a few lovely shared bath wood cabins (❶) have good mosquito nets and porches by the water, or you can go for large concrete rooms with en-suite facilities (❸). By far the most organized place, though, is *Río Lacanjá* (booking essential through Explora in San Cristóbal, T 1-800/397-5072, W www.ecochiapas.com) about 1km beyond the village, at the end of the road to the left from the main village junction. It's popular with tours and has a big restaurant, but also a selection of great cabañas ranging from basic six-bed dorms (M$130) through simple riverside bamboo structures (❷) to comfortable rooms with private bath and terrace (❸). It also has a tiny waterfall and swimming hole and a 45-minute jungle nature walk on a well-signed path (M$20 for non-residents). Lacanjá really is remote, and the surrounding jungle alive with wildlife; any place here will be happy to arrange guided walks (from around M$200) to the gorgeous rivers and waterfalls in the forest. Top choices are the **Cascada Ya Toch Kusam** (M$35 entry), a magical waterfall, and the **Lacanhá ruins**. The hikes are wonderful in the dry season (Jan to late April) − be prepared for mud at other times.

The Lacandón

You may already have encountered long-haired **Lacandón Maya**, dressed in simple white robes and selling exquisite (and apparently effective) bows and arrows at Palenque. Until recently, they were the most isolated of all the Mexican Indian groups. The ancestors of today's Lacandón are believed to have migrated to Chiapas from the Petén region of Guatemala during the eighteenth century. Prior to that the Spanish had enslaved, killed or relocated the original inhabitants of the forest. The Lacandón refer to themselves as "Hach Winik" (true people). Appearances notwithstanding, some Lacandón families are (or have been) quite wealthy, having sold timber rights in the jungle, though most of the money has gone. This change has led to a division in society, and most live in one of two main communities: **Lacanjá Chansayab**, near Bonampak, a village dominated by evangelical Protestants, some of whom are developing low-impact tourist facilities (see opposite); and **Nahá**, where a small group attempt to live a more traditional life. In Lacanjá, at least, their traditions seem to be rapidly disappearing: only a few of the older generation, and those who work with tourists, wear traditional dress or keep their hair long; the kids, with their spiked hair and bikes, are indistinguishable from those in any other Mexican village.

Frontera Corozal

Fifteen kilometres beyond San Javier is the turn for the narrow paved road to **FRONTERA COROZAL**, on the Mexican bank of the Río Usumacinta. Frontera is the gateway to **Yaxchilán**, one of the most enigmatic Maya ruins in Mexico; the ancient city can only be approached by boat along the river.

The turn-off to Frontera (*combi* drivers call this the *crucero de Corozal*) is marked by a *comedor* and shop selling basic supplies. If your *combi* doesn't go further, you can pick up a taxi for M$20 for the ride 15km down the road to town. On the edge of town, a kiosk collects a "conservation fee" of M$15 per person. Your first destination is the *embarcadero* on the banks of the Usumacinta, where you catch the boats to Yaxchilán. Shortly before, you'll pass the community **museum** (7am–7pm; free) which showcases the history of the settlement, founded only in 1976, and the relationships between the Chol, Lacandón and Tzeltal people, along with local archeology (there are a few large stelae) and flora and fauna. The true centre of the village – a couple of scrappy **plazas** and a market – is about 400m south from the main paved road and 300m back from the river; *combis* usually pass this way.

Should you want **to stay**, there are a couple of attractive riverside options. *Escudo Jaguar* (☎00502/5353-5637, a Guatemalan number, ⓦwww.escudojaguarhotel.com; ❷ shared bath, ❹ private camping M$75 per person) is the longest-established, and though its rooms are clean, spacious and comfortable, they're also the top choice for every tour group and can fill up early. Their shocking-pink, concrete aesthetic may also not chime with your vision of ecotourism. *Nueva Alianza* (☎00502/4638-2447, a Guatemalan number, Ⓔctnuevaalianza@hotmail.com; ❷ shared bath, ❹ private dorm bed M$125, camping M$70 per tent), on the far side of the *embarcadero*, is more natural-feeling and less crowded, with many of its cabañas in a wooded area kept intentionally dark at night. Both hotels have decent **restaurants**, and there's one other very bare-bones operation selling fried chicken about 500m back along the main road.

Yaxchilán

A large and impressive site, **YAXCHILÁN** (daily 8am–5pm; M$49) was an important Classic-period centre. From around 680 to 760 AD, the city's most famous kings, Escudo Jaguar (Shield Jaguar) and his son Pájaro Jaguar IV (Bird Jaguar), led a campaign of conquest that extended Yaxchilán's sphere of influence over the other

Getting to Yaxchilán

To reach Yaxchilán, you need a *lancha* – a narrow riverboat with benches along the side and a tin roof for shade. A number of companies compete for business, but prices are all similar. If you're looking to share a boat to bring down the cost, your best bet is to head to the *embarcadero* at the riverfront. Fares here vary with group size, how busy they are and your bargaining skills: reckon on paying M$500–700 for one to five passengers, M$800–1000 for six up to the maximum of ten passengers.

You also need to buy your **site entrance ticket** (M$49) at the INAH office by the museum (or your boat company will send someone to buy it for you), as cash is not kept at the isolated ruins. You can also hire a **guide** here (M$280 for between one and three people), though only a few speak English; during high season (July, Aug, Christmas and Semana Santa), the guides wait at the site itself. Guides and *lanchas* can also be arranged through the *Escudo Jaguar* hotel (generally a bit more expensive), where they also offer a variety of river tours; Siyaj Chan (☎00502/5047-5908, a Guatemala number; ⓦwww.siyajchan.blogspot.com) can provide guides too, and also leads six-hour **hiking trips** for M$1000 to Gruta Tzolkin, a cave deep in the forest.

The **river trip** is fabulous in itself, down a broad, fast-flowing river with Mexico on one bank, Guatemala on the other; depending on the state of the river the journey downstream to Yaxchilán takes around half an hour; the return nearly twice as long. To allow enough time at the site, the latest you should get on a *lancha* is 2pm. If you're headed **back to Palenque** or Lacanjá Chansayab the same day, you'll have to go much earlier, as the last buses and *combis* leave from in front of the *embarcadero* at 5pm. The earliest you can leave for the site in the morning is 8am, when the INAH office opens.

Usumacinta centres and may have established alliances with Tikal and Palenque. The buildings occupy a natural terrace above the river, with others climbing steep hills behind – a superb natural setting. Not so many people make the trip to this evocative site, and you'll often be alone in the forest with nothing but moaning howler monkeys around you. Giant trees keep the site shady, but nonetheless the jungle heat can be palpable – bring plenty of water, as there are no services at the ruins.

From the entrance, the main path leads straight to the Gran Plaza, but if you have the energy for climbing, it's more rewarding to explore the wilder parts of the site first. Follow the branching path to the right leading up the hillside to the **Pequeña Acrópolis**, a set of thirteen buildings. A lintel on the most prominent ruin, known as **Edificio 42**, depicts Escudo Jaguar with one of his warriors. Walk behind here to find another narrow trail down through the jungle, over several unrestored mounds, until you reach a fork: to the right, the path climbs steeply once again, until it reaches **Edificios 39–41**, also called the Templos del Sur, 90m above the river level. These buildings probably had some kind of astronomical function. High above the main forest, this is also a good spot to look for canopy-dwelling birds like parrots, though the trees also obscure any view.

Retrace your steps to the main path, and continue until it emerges at the back of **Edificio 33**, the most famous building at the site, also known as El Palacio. It overlooks the main plaza from a high terrace. The lintels here are superbly preserved, and inside one of the portals is a headless statue of Pájaro Jaguar IV. In ancient times the building was a political court; more recently, it served as a religious site for the Lacandón Maya.

Descending 40m down the stairs in front brings you to the long **Gran Plaza**. Turn back to look up at the Palacio: with the sun shining through the building's roofcomb and tree roots cascading down the stairs, this is what you imagine a pyramid lost in the jungle should look like, especially if you've been brought up on Tintin. To your left, just above ground level, **Edificio 23** has a few patches of coloured stucco around its door frames – just one patch of many well-preserved paintings and relief carvings that appear on the lintels of buildings surrounding the long green lawn. Some of the best works were removed in the nineteenth century and are now in the British Museum in London, but the number and quality of the remaining panels is unequalled at any other Maya site in Mexico. Many of them show rulers performing ritual events. This can also be seen on **Stele 1**, right in the middle of the plaza, near the base of the staircase. It depicts Pájaro Jaguar IV in a particularly eye-watering blood-letting ceremony, ritually perforating his penis. **Stele 3,** originally sited at Edificio 41, has survived several attempts to remove it from the site and now lies at the west side of the plaza, where it shows the transfer of power from Escudo Jaguar to Pájaro Jaguar IV.

Heading back to the entrance, pass through **El Laberinto** (The Labyrinth) at the plaza's northeast corner, where you can walk down through dim passages and out onto the main path.

Frontera Corozal to Guatemala

Entering Guatemala from Frontera is relatively easy, with plenty of *lanchas* heading for **Bethél**, about a forty-minute boat ride upstream. You'll pay around M$350 for one to three people, M$450 for more than that. There's a Mexican **immigration post** 200m back along the main road into Frontera: if you're crossing permanently to Guatemala, you should surrender your tourist card here; if you're coming back, hold on to it. Guatemalan **immigration procedures** can be completed in Bethél, from where buses normally depart at noon and 5pm for **Flores** (for Tikal; US$5), a five-hour ride, mostly along dirt roads. Alternatively, you can **stay** in the simple but comfortable *Posada Maya* cabañas (❶), on the riverbank amid the small Maya **ruins of Bethél**. All of this can, if you wish, be pre-arranged through travel agents in Palenque.

Escudo Jaguar in Frontera can arrange trips **downstream from Yaxchilán** to the impressive ruins of **Piedras Negras** on the Guatemalan bank. If you go in a single, long day, it's M$3800 for one to five people; an overnight trip costs M$4400. There are rapids above the site, meaning you may well have to get out and walk along the bank at times. It's a beautiful journey, though, and well worth making if you have the time. Below the site the river speeds through two massive canyons.

Palenque to Ocosingo

South of Palenque, a series of stunningly beautiful **waterfalls** is the chief attraction on the winding mountain road that heads towards Ocosingo. The awesome cascades on the Río Shumulhá at **Agua Azul** and the exquisite falls at **Misol-Há** are usually visited on a day-trip from Palenque, but it's also possible to visit them independently and stay nearby, or to make this part of a more extended excursion into the Chiapas highlands. Pressing on up into the mountains past the waterfalls, a visit to **Ocosingo** and the nearby Maya site of **Toniná** will give you a sense of the Chiapas mountain heartland – a complete contrast to the relative lowlands of Palenque. The unrelenting winding road makes it a slow trip, but a fascinating one, through scores of tiny villages where women's colourful clothing changes with each ridge you cross.

Misol-Há and Agua Clara

Just 18km from Palenque, **Misol-Há** (M$15) is a much easier day-trip than Agua Azul if travelling by public transport, and in many ways more pleasant, with none of the development present at its more celebrated neighbour. A

25-metre waterfall provides a stunning backdrop to a pool that's safe for swimming, and a fern-lined trail leads along a ledge behind the cascade – refreshing from the spray and mist even if you don't swim. It's an easy 1.5km walk downhill from the road (though not so much fun in the other direction); there's an additional M$5 charge on the road if you arrive by car. Most tours arrive here early (around 9.30am) or at lunchtime and spend only an hour or so, so if you can visit mid-morning or mid-afternoon you'll find things much quieter – even more so midweek, as local families visit at weekends. The San Miguel *ejido* manages the area, offering a decent **restaurant** catering to tour groups, as well as inexpensive **accommodation** in some beautiful wooden cabañas (☏55/5151-3377, Ⓦwww.misol-ha.com; ❷); each cabin has a private bathroom and electricity, and some also have kitchens. The organization recommends advance reservations, especially during Mexican holiday times.

Pressing on up the winding mountain road, you reach the turn for **Agua Clara** (M$10), 56km from Palenque and 3km down a side road. This is a more recently developed river attraction that is also on many tour itineraries. Here the water is calmer and you can rent kayaks and small boats to explore the river, plunge from a precarious rope bridge, or trek a couple of kilometres through the forest to a quiet natural pool where the Tulijá and Shumulhá rivers join. There's also horse-riding. Check before visiting, however, as in recent years Zapatista activity has at times closed the access road.

Agua Azul

The impressive cascades of **Agua Azul** (M$25) lie in the Parque Nacional Agua Azul, around 70km from Palenque, a little over halfway to Ocosingo. Now a major tour-bus destination – and packed with locals at weekends – they're about 4km off the main road, where a car park marks the start of a string of souvenir stalls and snack vendors lining the river upstream. Though no individual fall is as impressive as that at Misol-Há, here there are dozens of small falls and rapids, stretching for 1km up the river. The whole area is tremendously picturesque, despite the commercialization.

If you come **by bus or** *combi* (not on a tour), you'll be dropped at the turn-off to the falls on the main highway, where taxis and vans wait to shuttle you down to the parking area (M$10). Villagers have set up two tolls along the road; at each (if manned), you'll be charged M$10. Add in the entry fee, toilets and changing rooms (M$5), and for drivers a fee to the kid who guards your car, and this can start to become an expensive visit.

If it's safe to walk upstream (it may not be in the rainy season), you'll come across a perilous-looking bridge over the river and eventually reach an impressive gorge where the **Río Shumulhá** explodes out of the jungle-covered mountain. At the right time of year, the river is alive with butterflies. Higher up, the swimming is a little safer, too – but don't go in at all if you're not a strong swimmer and sure it's safe. People drown here every year, and though a few signs warn of **dangerous currents**, they don't begin to mark all the perilous spots (and many were washed away in floods in 2010); the most secure place is in the marked pool, near the car park. Although you may want to get as far from the tourist scrum as possible, keep in mind that violent attacks have occurred here in the past. A heavy federal police guard has proved a major deterrent, but you're always safer with other people nearby.

Ocosingo

By the time you reach **OCOSINGO**, you're at an elevation where pines have replaced tropical trees and the evenings are distinctly cool. Its streets lined with single-storey, red-tiled houses and its air thick with the scent of wood smoke, Ocosingo makes a good place to escape the tourist crowds of San Cristóbal or Palenque. The town has stayed close to its country roots, with farmers in cowboy hats in from their ranches and local women selling *maíz* from great bubbling vats. Central to town life is the **plaza**, surrounded by *portales*, a big old country church on the east side and the modern *ayuntamiento* opposite. Not far away is the **market**, vast, old-fashioned and crowded with people from all sorts of different ethnic groups. Coming from the Yucatán, it's striking to see just how culturally different this area is.

The area around Ocosingo is something of a **Zapatista** stronghold; on the road here, and especially as you head out to Toniná or continue towards San Cristóbal, you'll see plenty of signs proclaiming Zapatista control in the region ("Pueblo Zapatista…el pueblo manda y el gobierno obedece" – "Zapatista town…the people command, the government obeys"). Also look out for some striking murals on buildings at the north edge of town. There are army checkpoints, and often Zapatista ones collecting money (much less scary than the army), but tensions are generally low, and the worst that should happen is a slight delay.

Practicalities

First-class **buses** use the OCC terminal on the highway as it passes through Ocosingo; second-class buses and *combis* all stop along the road nearby. To get to the plaza walk downhill for three or four blocks until you reach Calle Central, then turn right for a further three blocks. The plaza is at the junction of Calle Central and the broader Avenida Central; you'll find pretty much everything you need within a block or two of here.

Accommodation options are plentiful. The *Hotel Central* (☎919/673-0024; ❷) is hard to miss on the north side of the plaza, but though all rooms have fans, hot water and cable TV, none has air conditioning. *Hotel San José*, just off the northeast corner of the plaza on Calle 1 Ote Nte (☎919/673-0039; ❶), is a great budget option, with clean, comfortable rooms, some with cable TV and air conditioning. Colourful *Hospedaje Esmeralda* (☎919/673-0014, ✉info@ranchoesmeralda.net), a block north of the plaza on Calle Central Norte, has both en-suite (❷) and shared bathrooms (❶), pleasant if a bit small and dark. It's a popular travellers' meeting place, and the welcoming staff can offer guided horseriding trips (2hr; M$200) or trips by light aircraft for up to four people – sightseeing flights over Toniná (M$1000), visits to the isolated **Laguna Miramar** (M$5800 to be dropped and picked up a day or two later) or day-trips to **Bonampak** and **Yaxchilán** (M$6500). If you're travelling alone they can sometimes arrange shares, but it's best to book as there are only four rooms.

The *Esmeralda* also has a good **restaurant**, and several other budget **places to eat** are on the square. *El Desván*, on the south side of the plaza, is the fanciest and generally the busiest, open late and serving pizza as well as Mexican standards on its upstairs terrace. *El Campanario*, on the north side, is very friendly, with an English menu, hearty plates of Mexican classics (breakfasts M$30–40, tortas M$15). In the **food market**, indigenous women sell fruits, vegetables and local cheeses, including the round waxy *queso de bola* and the delicious creamy *queso botanero*. To get there turn right at the church for one block, then left along Avenida 2 Sur Ote for another four.

There are a couple of **ATM**s on the plaza, another just beyond *Hospedaje Esmeralda* on Calle Central Norte, and yet another at the bus station. An **internet** café, La Troje, can be found on the south side of the plaza between the *Hotel La Casona* and *Desván* restaurant.

Leaving Ocosingo is easy enough during the day, with at least a dozen first-class buses daily in each direction, to Palenque (2hr 40min) or to San Cristóbal de las Casas (2hr 10min) and Tuxtla Gutiérrez (3hr 20min). There are also second-class buses, plus *combis* leaving every twenty minutes or so throughout the day. The last *combis* and second-class buses leave around 7.30pm; after this, there are just a couple of first-class services.

Toniná

Some 14km east of Ocosingo, the Classic-period Maya site of **TONINÁ** (daily 9am–4pm, museum daily 8am–5pm; M$41) is large and impressive, and yet it sees few visitors. At its height, Toniná was a great regional power; it defeated Palenque and captured its ruler in 699 AD, and from then until after 900 AD, when it became the last of the great Maya centres to fall victim to whatever disaster led to them all being abandoned, it was probably the greatest power in the Usumacinta basin. It's also the place where the **latest Long Count date**, corresponding to 909 AD, was recorded.

At the site entrance is a good **museum**, which is well worth a look before heading off to the ruins. There's a helpful model of the site here, as well as drawings of some of the relief carvings still in place in the buildings – seeing these first will help you discern the images more clearly. The museum's collection ranges from exuberant images of the chocolate god to obscure details about skull shapes

Zapatistas and the Chiapas uprising

On New Year's Day 1994 an armed guerrilla movement known as the **Zapatista Army of National Liberation** (EZLN) took control of San Cristóbal de las Casas, Ocosingo and other municipalities in the state of Chiapas. The guerrillas were mainly indigenous villagers, and their action took the country almost entirely by surprise; they demanded an end to the feudal system of land tenure in Chiapas, free elections, the repeal of NAFTA (the North American Free Trade Agreement, which came into effect that very day) and the restoration of Article 27 of the constitution (concerning land redistribution). The government reacted with a predictable use of force, committing numerous human-rights abuses along the way, including the bombing of civilians and the torture and murder of prisoners, particularly in Ocosingo. Long hidden from the world, the repressive side of the Mexican state – together with the plight of the country's indigenous peoples – was front-page news throughout the world.

In fairness to the national government – and then president Carlos Salinas – a ceasefire was rapidly imposed and peace negotiations initially progressed with remarkable speed as the government made concessions to the guerrillas. The star of the talks was **Subcomandante Marcos**, the main spokesman for the Zapatistas. The Balaclava-clad, pipe-smoking guerrilla became a cult hero, his speeches and communiqués full of literary allusions and passionate rhetoric (he was later exposed as, allegedly, Rafael Guillén, a philosophy professor from Mexico City, though this did little to dent his popularity). Negotiations ended in March, when an accord was drawn together. The EZLN then sent the accord back to its community bases for them to vote on it, a process complicated by the inaccessibility of many villages and the different languages and dialects spoken. While the accord was being considered, the army and the guerrillas maintained an uneasy truce, and Mexicans were given ample time to dwell on events in Chiapas.

In June the EZLN rejected the accord with the government, and in July a leftist candidate for the governorship of Chiapas, Amado Avendaño Figueroa, met with a suspicious "accident" when a truck with no numberplates collided with his car, killing three passengers; Avendaño lost an eye. In national elections in August the PRI triumphed, helped by an electorate that had been shaken by the uprising. In **Chiapas**, however, where the PRI also claimed to have won the governorship, Avendaño declared himself "rebel governor" after denouncing the elections as fraudulent and as many as half the municipalities in the state refused to pay taxes.

of the various Toniná inhabitants, who came in two waves and practised very different rituals. You'll also see many of the sculptures and relief carvings that were removed from the exposed parts of the site and preserved indoors here. In ancient times Toniná was a major ritual site, and it displays an almost single-minded obsession with images of bound prisoners and decapitation – panel carvings show the process, and many statues have had their stone heads chopped off. Seeing them all packed together in the gallery space is a bit unnerving.

Approaching the **ruins** themselves, a five-minute walk from the entrance, you cross a broad grassy plaza once surrounded by smaller buildings and ball-courts. **Ball-court 1** exemplifies Toniná's preoccupation with prisoners; built around 699, possibly to celebrate the great victory over Palenque, it has representations of bound captives instead of the usual rings for the balls to pass through.

But the real focus is the **Acrópolis**, a series of seven artificial terraces built into the hillside, incorporating dozens of temples and other buildings on its various levels. This is the "house of stone" that gave the site its Tzeltal name. A flashlight is useful to explore the labyrinthine interiors – there are warrens of small rooms and even internal staircases ascending from one terrace to the next. As you climb

Both the **PRD** (the national left-wing alliance formed by Cuauhtémoc Cárdenas) and the EZLN supported his move. The EZLN warned that if the PRI candidate, Eduardo Robledo, was sworn in, the truce with the government would be at an end. By this point Chiapas was essentially in a state of **civil war**. Ranchers and landowners organized paramilitary **death squads** to counter a mobilized peasantry. Land seizures and roadblocks were met with assassinations and intimidation, and a build-up of federal troops in the state only made things worse. On January 8, 1995, new president Zedillo attended the swearing-in of the PRI governor of Chiapas. Ten days later, the EZLN deployed its forces, breaking the army cordon surrounding its positions and moving into 38 municipalities (it had previously been confined to four). That this was accomplished, as was their later retreat, virtually undetected, right under the noses of government troops, showed their familiarity with the terrain, their discipline and the folly of the "surgical strike" tactic that many in the military had been contemplating.

Meanwhile the EZLN continued to gain public and international sympathy, especially in view of its largely non-violent methods, and the government was forced to set up new negotiations. These eventually resulted in the **San Andrés Accords on Rights and Indigenous Cultures**, signed in February 1996. The accords guaranteed indigenous representation in national and state legislatures, but to this day they have not been fully implemented. For a while relations between the Zapatistas and the government hit a new low, while the remorseless increase of the military presence on the Zapatistas' perimeter appeared to give paramilitary groups even greater freedom to operate. This culminated in the December 1997 **Acteal Massacre**: 45 displaced Tzotzil Indians, 36 of them women and children, were murdered at a prayer meeting by forces linked to PRI officials. The killings brought worldwide condemnation, and at last some action from the government, with a purge of the local government and military.

In the twenty-first century, an uneasy peace continues to reign in Chiapas. Recent governments have made some progress at least in implementing the San Andres accords, but there's still a heavy military presence in the state, where the EZLN continue to wield a huge amount of influence. They have attempted to expand their non-violent campaigning methods across the country and to a broader spectrum of the population, allying with unions and urban groups on the left, as well as exploiting new media to generate worldwide solidarity.

the hill there's plenty to explore, but look out above all for the reliefs and stucco masks that survive in situ, easily spotted under their protective thatch or corrugated-iron roofs. The most extraordinary of these is the enormous (16m x 4m) **Mural de las Cuatro Eras**, on the sixth platform. This amazingly well-preserved stucco codex tells the story of Maya cosmology by following the eras of the world as they were created and destroyed. The worlds are depicted as decapitated heads surrounded by flowers. A grinning, skeletal Lord of Death presents a particularly graphic image as he cheerfully grasps a skinned human head.

The final two levels are crowded with temples, and the climb to the summit is by steep, narrow steps. At the top is the **Templo del Espejo Humeante** (Temple of the Smoking Mirror), built around 840 AD, where you will be rewarded with awesome views. In the foreground, the pasture that surrounds the cleared site is studded with unexcavated mounds.

To reach Toniná **from Ocosingo**, take one of the frequent *combis* (M$10) that leave from the market area – look for those marked "Predio/Ruinas". A taxi will cost around M$70 one way. Near the ruins, a small **café** sells packaged snacks, locally grown macadamia nuts and espresso, made from local coffee.

San Cristóbal de las Casas

Known by many locals as Jovel, **SAN CRISTÓBAL DE LAS CASAS** is around 90km from Ocosingo, though the winding roads and likelihood of army and Zapatista checkpoints can make for a slow journey. It's also around 1000m higher, at 2100m; even in August, the evenings are chilly. San Cristóbal's distinctive colonial charm, the fascinating **indigenous villages** nearby and, of course, its Zapatista cachet have made it a major stop on the travel circuit. But the city has held up to tourism well, with pedestrianized central streets and an unexpectedly sophisticated social scene, with plenty of small bars and restaurants, plus some exceptionally good-value accommodation. It's also a great base for studying at one of the numerous Spanish-language schools.

Arrival and information

Whether you arrive by first- or second-class **bus**, you'll almost certainly be just off the Carretera Panamericana (Hwy-190), which becomes Bulevar Juan Sabines Gutiérrez at the southern edge of town. For the centre, turn right out of the OCC **first-class terminal**, and it's seven blocks north on Insurgentes to the plaza. Most **second-class** services and *combis* stop along the highway to either side of the OCC terminal. **Taxis** within the centre should cost no more than M$20, though unless you're struggling with luggage, most places are in easy walking distance.

The helpful **tourist office** (daily 8am–8pm; ☎967/678-0665), in the Palacio Municipal, has free city maps, up-to-date lists of hotels, bus times and event information, as well as English-speaking staff.

Accommodation

Vast numbers of visitors and competition for business mean that San Cristóbal has some very good-value **hotels**. Nights can be pleasantly cool in summer, but cold in winter, so make sure there are enough blankets.

Barón de las Casas Belisario Domínguez 2 ☎967/678-0881, ✉hotelbaron@hotmail.com. Well-run budget hotel with a bit of colonial charm, one block east of the plaza. Simple rooms – tiled floors and clean bathrooms with plenty of hot water. TV is M$20 extra. The owners speak English. ❷

Casa Na-Bolom Vicente Guerrero 33 ☎967/678-1418, ⓦwww.nabolom.org. A special place with a special atmosphere (see below): luxurious rooms and suites have fireplaces and are decorated with local textiles and artefacts. Wi-fi, but it doesn't extend to every room. ❻

Casa Real Real de Guadalupe 51 ☎967/674-6991, ⓔhotelcasareal2009@gmail.com. Large rooms with double beds have only shared baths, but there is hot water, and a *pila* for washing clothes on the sunny, flower-filled rooftop terrace. It's M$100 per person, so very good value for singles. ❶

Diego de Mazariegos 5 de Febrero 1 ☎967/678-0833, ⓦwww.diegodemazariegos.com.mx. Set in two lovely colonial buildings, with spacious rooms – all featuring a fireplace, antique furniture and tiled bathrooms – arranged around attractive courtyards. Book ahead, as it's often busy with tour groups. ❼

Hacienda Los Morales Ignacio Allende 17 ☎967/678-1472, www.hotelhaciendalosmorales .com. Past an antiques-crammed lobby and restaurant, stone cabins sprawl up the hillside garden four blocks west of the plaza. Each rustic-feeling room has a fireplace and a porch or terrace for enjoying the views across town. Wi-fi and breakfast available. ❹

Holiday Inn 1 de Marzo 15 ☎967/678-0045, ⓦwww.hotelesfarrera.com/holidaysc. Never mind the association with a less-than-chic chain – this is the most luxurious place to stay in the centre, in an old hacienda with a pink-walled courtyard and beautifully decorated rooms. Significant discounts often available online. ❼

Posada México Josefa Domínguez 12, at Dr J F Flores ☎967/678-0014, ⓦwww.hostellingmexico .com. The HI-affiliated hostel is set around a grassy courtyard. There's a whole roster of activities, kitchen, games, TV, wi-fi and plenty of space to relax. Breakfast included. Dorm bed M$100, rooms, some en suite. ❷

Rossco Backpackers Hostel Real de Mexicanos 16 ☎967/ 674-0525, ⓦwww .rosscohostel.com. Arguably the best hostel in Chiapas, with enthusiastic English-speaking owners, a variety of dorms (M$119–150; including a women-only one) and rooms, some with private bath. It also has internet, breakfast, lockers, cable TV and X-Box in the common room, daily use of gym, salsa lessons and a cosy campfire in the garden every evening, all included in the price. ❷

Villa Real II Two locations on Benito Juárez 24 ☎967/678-4485, ⓔhvillareal2@hotmail.com. Comfortable, well-furnished, carpeted rooms all with private bath, wi-fi, cable TV and access to parking. *Villa Real I*, down the road at Juárez 8, is a category cheaper, but much less pleasant. ❸

The City

Plaza 31 de Marzo, usually referred to simply as *el parque*, is at the heart of the city, encircled by a cluster of attractive colonial mansions and the sixteenth-century **cathedral**, which boasts an ornate, pale orange facade, impressive *artesanado* ceiling and grand *retablo*. The finest of the mansions is **La Casa de las Sirenas**, now the **Hotel Santa Clara**, which boasts a very elaborate doorway around the corner on Insurgentes. In the middle of the plaza there's a bandstand and a café.

Cutting through the centre is the **Andador Eclesiástico**, a pedestrianized thoroughfare that connects the Templo del Carmen, south of the plaza beside the Arco del Carmen, once the gateway to the city, to the **Templo de Santo Domingo,** five blocks north. This is the most intrinsically interesting of San Cristóbal's churches, with a wonderfully elaborate Baroque facade. Inside, it's gilded everywhere – if you see the ornate pulpit in the evening, by the light of candles, you might well believe it's solid gold. To the left of the main entrance (beyond Sna Jolobil), the **Museo Centro Cultural de los Altos** (Tues–Sun 10am–2pm & 4–6pm; M$25, free Sun), tells the story of the city, with vivid portrayals of how the Indians fared under colonial rule.

San Cristóbal's daily market, the **Mercado José Castillo Tielemans**, lies beyond Santo Domingo along General Utrilla. Far bigger than it first appears, its chaos and the crowds in its souk-like lanes provide a dramatic change from the rather manicured centre of town.

Behind Santo Domingo, Chiapa de Corzo leads east towards the **Casa Na–Bolom** (daily 10am–5pm; tours in English at 4.30pm; M$40, M$50 with tour) at Vicente Guerrero 33. This was the home of Danish explorer and anthropologist Frans Blom, who died in 1963, and his Swiss wife, Gertrude, an anthropologist and

SAN CRISTÓBAL DE LAS CASAS

0   200 m

Combis to San Juan Chamula
Combis to Zinacantán

San Juan Chamula (10km) & Zinacantán (12km)

Tuxtla Gutiérrez & Toll Highway

EATING & DRINKING

Café El Kiosco	9	El Mirador II	10
Café El Puente	8	Normita	13
Café Museo Café	3	Normita II	15
La Casa de Pan	1	La Paloma	12
El Gato Gordo	4	Revolución	2
Iskra	7	Tierra Adentro	5
Madre Tierra	16	Tuluc	14
Makia	11	La Viña de Bacco	6

EDGAR ROBLEDO
Mercado José Castillo Tielemans
Museo Centro Cultural de Los Altos
DIAGONAL ARRIAGA
20 DE NOVIEMBRE
REAL DE MEXICANOS
ECUADOR
BRASIL
VENEZUELA
Río Amarillo
Sna Jolobil
TONALÁ
CHIAPA DE CORZO
COMITÁN
Casa Na-Bolom
Mercado Artesanías
Templo de Santo Domingo
TUXTLA
TAPACHULA
Casa Utrilla
ESCUADRÓN 201
5 DE MAYO
28 DE AGOSTO
DR NAVARRO
GENERAL UTRILLA
BELISARIO DOMÍNGUEZ
AV CRISTÓBAL COLÓN
1 DE MARZO
FLAVIO PANIAGUA
EJÉRCITO NACIONAL
HUIXTLA
AV BENEFAL
5 DE FEBRERO
Explora
12 DE OCTUBRE
16 DE SEPTIEMBRE
PLAZA
GUADALUPE VICTORIA
Catedral
Lavandería Talloncito
MARÍA ADELINA FLORES
NICOLAS RUIZ
AV IGNACIA LA CATÓLICA
DIEGO DUGELAY
AV VICENTE GUERRERO
Templo de Guadalupe
Museo del Ámbar
MATAMOROS
Palacio Municipal
REAL DE GUADALUPE
BERNAL DÍAZ DEL CASTILLO
AV ISABEL LA CATÓLICA
MAZARIEGOS
FRANCISCO LEÓN MADERO
PLAZA 31 DE MARZO
Lavandería Rossco
CUAUHTÉMOC
DR JOSÉ FELIPE FLORES
Templo de San Cristóbal
NIÑOS HÉROES
FRANCISCO LEÓN
Nichim Tours
Templo de San Francisco
Mercado de Dulces y Artesanías
HNOS DOMÍNGUEZ
ROSAS
IGNACIO ALLENDE
Sala de Bellas Artes
JULIO M CORZO
Templo del Carmen
Templo de Santa Lucía
ALVARO OBREGÓN
RAMON CORONA
Arco del Carmen
HIDALGO
PEDRO MORENO
AV BENITO JUÁREZ
Centro Cultural El Carmen
SARABIA
CARRETERA PANAMERICANA
HNOS PINEDA
Buses (2nd class)
OCC Bus Terminal
ORTIZ DE DOMÍNGUEZ
PANTALEÓN DOMÍNGUEZ
INDEPENDENCIA
N

Palenque & Comitán

ACCOMMODATION

Barón de las Casas	F
Casa Na-Bolom	B
Casa Real	E
Diego de Mazariegos	D
Hacienda Los Morales	H
Holiday Inn	C
Posada México	G
Rossco Backpackers Hostel	A
Villa Real I	I
Villa Real II	J

photographer who died in 1993. Today the house, set around a series of beautiful courtyards, is renowned as a centre for the study of the region's indigenous cultures, particularly of the isolated Lacandón Maya, with a fine library open to all; it's also a fascinating little museum of Blom's life and work and a tranquil hotel.

Finally, on either side of town, two churches perch on hilltop sites: the **Templo de Guadalupe** to the east and **Templo de San Cristóbal** to the west. Neither offers a great deal architecturally, but the climbs are worth it for the views – San Cristóbal, especially, is at the top of a dauntingly long and steep flight of steps. Best not to climb up to either of these relatively isolated spots after dark; we have received reports of women being subjected to harassment at San Cristóbal.

Eating and drinking

San Cristóbal has no lack of places to eat, with a huge variety of economical **restaurants** in the streets immediately east of the plaza, especially on Madero. Where the city really scores, however, is in lively places that cater to a somewhat bohemian crowd, above all on Hidalgo and Real de Guadalupe, lined with slick restaurants, bars and cafés.

Café El Kiosco In the plaza. In a great location under the bandstand, where you can enjoy a coffee at the outdoor tables and watch the world go by; there's often music and dancing in the evening.

Café El Puente Real de Guadalupe 55. Popular café serving inexpensive salads, soups, sandwiches, cakes and an inviting organic vegetarian buffet (1.30–5pm; M$60); also acts as a cultural centre, with internet access, live music, lectures and films. Closed Sun.

Café Museo Café María Adelina Flores 10. Delicious coffee and some of the best *chocolate con leche* in town, served in the café of a small museum exploring the coffee trade in Mexico. Open Mon–Sat 9am–9pm.

La Casa de Pan Dr Navarro 10. A superb range of reasonably priced vegetarian food and baked goods, made with local, organic ingredients. Open from morning till night, the place serves as a meeting place for expat development workers, and there's often live music at night. Tues–Sun 8am–10pm.

El Gato Gordo Real de Guadalupe 20. Inexpensive and deservedly popular backpacker place serving Mexican and international dishes with great-value specials and set meals from M$39. You can also read the newspapers, watch TV and listen to music. 1–11pm, closed Tues. Live music Fri & Sat from 8pm.

Iskra Real de Guadalupe 53. Micro-brewery with revolutionary trimmings. There's also live music nightly and a generally young party atmosphere.

Madre Tierra Insurgentes 19, opposite the Mercado de Artesanías. Restaurant in a colonial house with an international flavour: Mexican dishes plus home-made soups, salads and pastas. The late-night upstairs terrace bar has views of ancient walls and red-tiled roofs, plus regular live music, and the bakery and deli sell whole-wheat bread and carrot cake until 8pm Mon–Sat.

Makia Hidalgo at Mazariegos. Fashionable, dimly lit bar and club, with a good mix of locals and travellers. Thurs–Sat from 9pm.

El Mirador II Madero 16. The best cheap Mexican restaurant on Madero, with good meat-and-bean-filled tortas and comidas corridas.

Normita Juárez at José Flores. A great little restaurant serving Jaliscan specialities (try a *huarache*) and inexpensive breakfasts from M$30. Daily 7am–11pm. Normita II is on Niños Heroes between Insurgentes and Hidalgo.

La Paloma Hidalgo 3, just south of the plaza ☏ 967/678-1547. A sixteenth-century mansion houses this refined restaurant, classy *artesanía* store and hip upstairs coffeehouse with internet. The menu is broad, and ingredients are fresh, though some items border on bland – think of this more as an opportunity to relax in comfort for about M$150 for dinner. Open till 11.30pm.

Revolución 20 de Noviembre and 1 de Marzo. Zapatista chic is the style at this bar on the pedestrian street. Cocktails from M$36 and decent bar food. Open daily noon–midnight, happy hour noon–7pm, live music from 8pm.

Tierra Adentro Real de Guadalupe 24. Set around a large courtyard with leather chairs and free wi-fi, this café-cultural centre has everything from coffee and sandwiches to pizza and good value menus; round the outside of the courtyard are several arty bookshops and artesanía stores.

Local crafts

A major draw for visitors to San Cristóbal is the indigenous crafts tradition, with every village in the area specializing in a distinctive style of weaving, embroidery and more. Many of the salespeople in San Cristóbal are from nearby villages – in fact, many are so-called *expulsados*, evangelical Protestants who have been expelled from their communities for converting. To eke out an existence they have turned to craft-making, with tourists as their main source of income. As a result, the city is a textile collector's dream, with vibrant **woven blankets** and intricately **embroidered clothing**.

The plaza in front of Santo Domingo church, filled with **craft stalls**, is one great place to buy souvenirs, though there's also plenty of tat. Part of the former *convento* next door has been converted into a craft cooperative (**Sna Jolobil**) that sells textiles and other village products (Mon–Sat 9am–2pm & 4–6pm). The quality here is generally good, but the prices higher than elsewhere. The **Mercado de Dulces y Artesanías**, by the Templo de San Francisco on Insurgentes, is another worthwhile place to look.

There are also plenty of classy stores, above all in the upper reaches of Real de Guadalupe. As well as the traditional crafts, they do a brisk trade in **Zapatista chic** – T-shirts, posters, balaclava-clad dolls – and in works from other parts of Mexico. **Amber** is also found locally, and there's much fine amber jewellery to be found.

Moving on from San Cristóbal

First-class buses leave from the OCC terminal at the south end of Insurgentes, near the ring road, with **second-class** and *combi* services from a plethora of stops to either side along the main road. You can buy first-class tickets from the Boletotal office in the centre at Real de Guadalupe 24 (☎967/678-7623, daily 8am–9pm). **Tuxtla Gutiérrez** (1hr) has frequent first-class buses, and a constant stream of *combis*, which tout for customers outside. **Villahermosa** (7hr) is poorly served, with just a couple of late-night buses; it's easier to get any bus to Tuxtla and change there. For **Palenque** (5hr), there are eleven daily first-class departures. All buses going to Palenque call at **Ocosingo** (2hr 30min) and again there are dozens of *combis*: just go to the highway and someone will call out to you. OCC has the most comfortable service to **Ciudad Cuauhtémoc** via Comitán (5 daily; 2hr–3hr 30min) on the Guatemalan border. To Comitán only, you'll find any number of *combis* along the highway, with hourly departures. There are also buses to **Tapachula** (for the coastal route to Guatemala; 9 daily; 8hr) and three overnight services to Oaxaca (12hr); for more choice to the latter, head to Tuxtla. The first-class companies all have overnight services to Mexico City (9 daily; 14hr). For Campeche (10hr) and Mérida (13hr), there's a first-class service at 6.20pm. Buses for the Yucatán coast (4 daily) go via Chetumal (12hr), where you can catch connections to Belize, and make all major stops to Cancún (18hr).

Heading to Tuxtla's **airport** (the nearest in operation), there are three daily shuttles from the OCC terminal (at 9.30am, 1.30pm and 2.30pm; 1hr), or transfers can be arranged through local tour agencies. Travel agency Chincultik, Real de Guadalupe 34 (☎967/678-0957), runs a daily shuttle bus to **Guatemala**.

Tuluc Insurgentes 5. Popular restaurant with a good-value *comida* and tasty breakfasts (open from 6.30am, so ideal if you have to catch an early bus). The house speciality is a *parrillada* – a meaty mixed grill with accompaniments for M$140–150 for two.

La Viña de Bacco Real de Guadalupe 7. A snug little tapas bar that looks straight out of Spain – big selection of Mexican wines by the glass, as well as a platter of locally made cheeses, sausages and ham (M$80). You get a free bite-size *botana* with each glass, and snacks start at just M$5.

Listings

Banks and exchange Several bank branches (with ATMs) surround the plaza; most will exchange dollars and give cash advances (mornings only). HSBC is at Mazariegos 6.

Bike rental An enjoyable way to get out to the surrounding villages. Los Pingüinos, Ecuador 4-B (☎967/678-0202, ✆www.bikemexico.com /pinguinos), has well-maintained bikes for M$150/day, and leads day outings and multi-day tours. Croozy, Belisario Domínguez 7(☎967/114-2862), has bikes for similar prices and also scooters and motorbikes (M$260/390 a day).

Internet access It's scarcely possible to walk a block in the centre without coming across a place. Try Netcibercafé, Real de Guadalupe 15-D.

Laundry Lavandería Rossco, Juárez 4-A; Lavandería Talloncito, María Adelina Flores 19-A; and many others. From M$9/kg.

Post office Ignacio Allende between Diego Mazariegos and Cuauhtémoc (Mon–Fri 8.30am–7pm, Sat 9am–1pm); in addition, most hotels have Mexipost boxes, and many of the larger ones sell stamps.

Travel agencies and tours San Cristóbal has dozens of tour agencies, most doing the same standard tours to local villages, the Cañón del Sumidero, Lagos de Montebello and Palenque and Agua Azul. You can also arrange tours further afield to Bonampak and Yaxchilán, and transport to Guatemala. Horseriding tours can be arranged at Casa Utrilla, General Utrilla 33, leaving at 9am and 1pm (☎967/100-9611; M$150 to Chamula). Nichim Tours, Hermanos Domínguez 5-A (☎967/678-3520, ✆www.chiapastoursyexpediciones.com) has a broader range of tours than most; Explora (☎967/674-6660, ✆www.explorachiapas.com) specializes in trips to the Lacandón forest (see p.256).

Contexts

Contexts

History 271

Environment and wildlife 283

The Maya belief system 287

Books 290

History

The history of the Yucatán is inextricably linked with that of the surrounding territories. The indigenous Yucatec Maya, whose extraordinarily advanced culture and sphere of influence extended as far south as present-day Honduras, lived in a constantly changing pattern of local allegiances until the arrival of the Spanish in the early sixteenth century. Subsequently part of a loose political entity controlled from Spain – at times under the power of Mexico, sometimes thrown in with Guatemala and Central America – the Yucatán was, very briefly, an independent state, before being subsumed into the newly formed Mexico in the 1820s.

Prehistory

The exact date when human beings first crossed the Bering Strait into the Americas is debatable, but the earliest widely accepted figure is around 15,000 years ago. Successive waves of nomadic Stone Age hunters continued to arrive until around 6000 BC, pushing their predecessors gradually further south. Some of the earliest signs of human presence in the Yucatán can be found in the peninsula's many caves, such as the Grutas de Loltún, where prehistoric paintings can be seen.

The first signs of settled habitation – the cultivation of corn, followed by the emergence of crude pottery, stone tools and even some trade – seem to come from the **Archaic** period, around 8000 to 2000 BC. The first established civilization did not appear until the **Pre-Classic** or **Formative** era (2500 BC to 250 AD) with the rise of the Olmecs in the coastal jungles of Tabasco.

Still the least known of all the ancient societies, the **Olmecs** are regarded as the "mother culture" of Mesoamerica, inventors of the calendar, glyphic writing, a rain deity and probably also the concept of zero and the ball-game. What you see of them in museums today – above all at the **Parque La Venta** in Villahermosa – is a magnificent artistic style, exemplified in their sculpture and in the famous colossal basalt heads. These, with their puzzling "baby-faced" features, were carved from monolithic blocks and somehow transported over ninety kilometres from the quarries to their final settings – proof in itself of a hierarchical society commanding a sizeable workforce.

The Pre-Classic Maya

By the end of the **Pre-Classic period**, Olmec civilization was already in decline. La Venta, their most important cultural centre, seems to have been abandoned around 400 BC, and the other towns followed over the next few hundred years. As the Olmec weakened, new civilizations grew in strength and numbers, establishing cities throughout central Mexico at sites such as Monte Albán (near Oaxaca), Cuicuilco, in the great Valley of México (where Mexico City now stands) and above all **Teotihuacán** (northeast of Mexico City), the first truly urban society in Mesoamerica, whose architectural and religious influences reached as far south as the Maya heartlands of Guatemala.

The first identifiably **Maya** settlements appeared in the Guatemalan highlands from around 1500 BC. From here, over the next few hundred years, the Maya spread in all directions, including north to the lowlands of the Yucatán Peninsula.

Early villages were little more than temporary encampments, but gradually the cultivation of corn, beans, squash and chile allowed for the development of larger settlements. These were always near a water source, which in central Yucatán usually meant a cenote. The **spread of agriculture** allowed the population to grow, and with population growth came a society that was increasingly hierarchical and specialized. At this time, pottery replaced stone implements, woven cloth supplanted animal fur and writing, art and science began to flourish. Thatched huts, little different from those of the Maya of modern Yucatán, formed the basis of these early villages, but buildings of increasing size and complexity were soon constructed specifically for religious purposes.

By the late Pre-Classic period, some Maya settlements, above all in the Guatemalan highlands, were becoming very sophisticated indeed. In the Yucatán, development lagged behind, but even here cities of substantial size were growing up. Among the **early sites** are Calakmul, close to the Guatemalan centres, and Edzná, where a system of canals and moats helped drain agricultural land and defend the city. Along with Dzibilchaltún and Oxkintok, these early cities all lie on routes leading from the highlands to the Gulf coast, with its salt pans and trading opportunities.

The Classic period

It was in the **Classic period**, however, from around 250 AD to 900 AD, that the Maya reached their peak of power and achievement. While in Europe the Roman Empire was in decline, in Mesoamerica the Maya were embarking on six-and-a-half centuries of extraordinary technological, architectural, artistic and scientific advance. Without the use of metal tools, draught animals or the wheel, they built **city-states** that controlled hundreds of thousands of people, created intricate **statuary** and sculpture and devised a **mathematical and calendar system** far more advanced than those known in the "civilized" world. For more on Maya achievements, see p.287.

Again, the first great centres of the Classic period were not in the Yucatán but in the highlands further south – cities such as Tikal, Copán and Kaminaljuyú. The most celebrated cities of the Yucatán, on the whole, were latecomers: Palenque, Yaxchilán, Uxmal and Chichén Itzá all flourished towards the end of the Classic era. Which is not to say that Yucatán was not thriving, just that important sites like Calakmul or Sayil lived to some extent in the shadow of still greater powers further south.

Conflict and downfall

There was never a single Maya empire, but rather a series of independent – yet interdependent – city-states in an almost constant state of shifting **alliances, rivalry and war**. War was necessary not just for control over rivals and access to their resources, but also to increase a ruler's prestige and provide captives, preferably high-born, for ransom and sacrifice. Some cities, such as Calakmul and Tikal, or Yaxchilán and Palenque, seem to have been traditional rivals; others, like Yaxchilán and Bonampak, or Sayil and its Puuc neighbours, enjoyed long-standing alliances.

Among the major conflicts that we know about – mainly from carvings or even paintings (such as the famous Bonampak murals) created to celebrate the victory – the battles between the great centres of Tikal and Calakmul stand out. In 562 AD

Calakmul succeeded in putting together an alliance with Yaxchilán and others that inflicted a major and lasting defeat on Tikal. It was only when this alliance fell apart that Tikal was able to take its revenge, humiliating Calakmul and its ruler, Jaguar Paw, in battle in 695.

Further west, **Palenque**, under its rulers Hanab Pakal (Jaguar Shield) and Chan Bahlum (Jaguar Serpent), spent much of the seventh century asserting its authority over the Usumacinta basin, forcing Yaxchilán into subservience. A hundred years later, the roles were reversed, as **Yaxchilán** became the greater power – again under two kings, Escudo Jaguar (Shield Jaguar) and his son Pájaro Jaguar IV (Bird Jaguar) – and Palenque the subject. Similar swings of power affected central and northern Yucatán, too, where **Uxmal** and later Chichén Itzá rose to dominance at the very end of the Classic era.

Quite what caused the **downfall of Classic Maya civilization** remains the subject of fierce debate, yet what is certain is that societies throughout Mesoamerica suffered a similar fate at similar times. Teotihuacán, the great power of central Mexico, was abandoned as early as 750 AD (at the end of a long decline), and within a hundred years many of the important Maya centres, in particular those in the highlands, followed suit. Maya societies in the Yucatán were among the last to retain their authority, but by around 950 AD they too were in terminal decline, if not abandoned altogether. Only Chichén Itzá continued to thrive.

Numerous theories attempt to explain the Maya collapse, among them the notion that it was caused by invaders from the north, occupying a vacuum left by the fall of Teotihuacán. Certainly Teotihuacán's demise must have severely affected its trading partners throughout Mexico, possibly setting off a **chain of disasters** that had a cumulative effect. Natural causes would have been more likely than invasion, though, with the Maya paying the price for their success: overpopulation exacerbated by the failure of harvests, perhaps resulting from overexploitation of the land. Such events can easily be imagined spilling over into the political sphere in a rigorously structured society. A loss of faith in rulers and priests could have led to rebellion, or wars between cities may have broken out over increasingly scarce resources.

Post-Classic society

If the Yucatán saw the final flourish of Classic Maya civilization at sites like Uxmal, it also saw the most powerful surviving **Post-Classic societies** (900 to 1500 AD), above all at **Chichén Itzá**. This was the one city in the entire Maya land – or at least the only one we know of – that not only revived its former glory but, from around 1000 AD on, may even have surpassed it. For many years it was believed that this revival was the result of an invasion by the **Toltecs**, whose capital was at Tula in central Mexico. Certainly there are many apparent links between the two cities, not just in architecture, but in a new obsession with war and sacrifice, and with the legendary feathered-serpent god **Quetzalcoatl** (Kukulcán to the Maya). These days, though, most archeologists believe that Chichén Itzá remained under Maya control, albeit with strong trading and cultural links with the Toltecs. This theory sees not an invasion by a foreign power, but rather the arrival of a new Maya clan, the **Itzá**, driven north by the collapse of their cities in Guatemala.

Whatever their origins, the Itzá consolidated their influence, and Chichén Itzá remained the dominant power in the peninsula until it was abandoned in the first half of the thirteenth century. Shortly afterwards, around 1263 AD, the Itzá ruler

Kukulcán II founded a new city, **Mayapán**. A walled city with some ten thousand inhabitants, it led a broad alliance of small city-states that united the Yucatán for some two hundred years. Some of these were based at the old centres like Uxmal and Chichén Itzá, others were newly prosperous towns, especially on the Caribbean coast, such as Tulum, Xel-Há and Cozumel. What Mayapán lacked, however, was the great architecture and vast ceremonial centres of its predecessors – signs, perhaps, of a less hierarchical, more trade-based society. **Maritime trade** certainly flourished in the late Post-Classic age. Christopher Columbus himself (though he never got to Mexico) encountered a heavily laden boat of Maya traders, plying the sea between the Yucatán and Honduras.

Mayapán's supremacy ended in 1441 after an attack by the Xiu people, based at Uxmal. From then until the arrival of the Spanish, the Yucatán's city-states continued to form alliances and enmities, and apparently to prosper, but they remained disparate, with no central authority or dominant group.

The Spanish Conquest

Having heard tales of gold and empires to be claimed in the new territories ever since Columbus's accidental discovery of the Americas in 1492, the Spanish started to probe the Mexican coast from their bases in Cuba. The first expedition to land in the Yucatán was led by **Francisco Hernández de Cordoba** in 1517. Cordoba discovered Isla Mujeres, but after being driven away from Ah-Kin-Pech (Campeche) by hostile natives and caught in a storm, his team landed at the mouth of the Río Champotón to replenish their stocks of fresh water. There they were surprised by a Maya force under Moch Cuouh and heavily defeated. Cordoba died of his wounds a few days later, and the place became known as the Bay of the Bad Fight. The following year, **Juan de Grijalva** sailed round the Yucatán and up the coast as far as present-day Tampico, reporting back on the wealth of central Mexico.

The most notable Spanish invasion, of course, began with **Hernán Cortés's** landing on the coast near modern Veracruz on April 21, 1519. With him were just 550 men, a few horses, dogs and a cannon, yet in less than three years they had defeated the Aztecs and established control over central Mexico. Mopping up the rest of the Aztec Empire was a relatively straightforward task, but it took twenty more years to overcome the Maya.

The defeat of the Maya

Almost immediately after their campaigns in central Mexico, the Spanish turned their eyes south. During the 1520s Pedro de Alvarado and his brother Gonzalo conquered most of what is now Guatemala and the southern Mexican highlands of Chiapas. In 1526, **Francisco de Montejo**, a veteran of the Grijalva and Cortés expeditions, travelled to Spain to petition the king for the right to conquer the Yucatán. The following year he landed at Cozumel with about two hundred men, and from there crossed to the mainland. At first, his task seemed an easy one: most local chiefs, aware of the conquests elsewhere, swore loyalty to the Spanish Crown. However, as he advanced inland he found towns already deserted, and his troops began to suffer ambushes and attacks. In a pitched battle at **Aké** (near modern Tizimín) 1200 Maya warriors were killed, but Montejo also lost nearly half his force and the Maya refused to surrender. Leaving behind a small garrison, Montejo retreated to Veracruz to gather a larger army.

In 1531, Montejo returned with his son, **Francisco de Montejo the Younger,** and defeated the Maya at Campeche, setting up a base there. Montejo the Younger waged a successful campaign in northern Yucatán, making alliances and declaring Chichén Itzá his capital. Meanwhile, his father had travelled to Maní, where he established friendly relations with the **Xiu**, who a century earlier had brought about the downfall of Mayapán. Again, however, many Maya allies turned on the Spanish, and by 1535 the Montejos were forced to withdraw once more from the Yucatán, their troops demoralized by the fierce resistance and the lack of financial reward for their efforts.

The final chapter in the conquest of the Yucatán began in 1540, when Montejo the Younger returned to Campeche with a yet larger force, founding Mérida two years later. What really tipped the scales this time was the support of the Xiu, whose leader in **Maní** converted to Christianity. The Xiu dominated much of western and northern Yucatán and most of their subject cities followed their lead or were easily subdued. The east continued to resist, but armies led by Montejo's cousin (another Francisco de Montejo) gradually established power. By 1546, the Yucatán was firmly under Spanish control.

Colonial rule

Cortés was appointed governor of **Nueva España** (New Spain) in 1522, and there followed three hundred years of direct Spanish rule. The boundaries of the new territory initially stretched from present-day Panama to the western states of the US, although it wasn't long before internal struggles erupted over their control. In 1542, the state of **Guatemala** was formed, whose territory included the Yucatán, though 23 years later Guatemala found itself yet again a part of New Spain. Guatemala was ultimately re-established as a state in 1570, but this time the Yucatán was attached to Mexico. There it would remain throughout the colonial era, albeit never wholly absorbed thanks to the difficulties of communication with the centre.

For the Spanish, the initial colonial concerns were reconstruction, pacification and conversion. To this end they began building grand towns and constructing **churches**, often in areas that had been sacred to the Maya or on top of their pyramids. The cathedral in Mérida was built in 1561 on the ruins of a Maya temple; in Maní, the stones of the old temples were used in the construction of the monastery. Churches were built like fortresses, to awe the Maya population and to serve as refuges for the white population if necessary. Moreover, they were built in places sacred to the Maya, to encourage them to worship there and prove the superiority of the new god.

The most dramatic and immediate consequence of the Spanish Conquest and colonization, however, was the **decimation of the Maya population**, not through war or famine (though some died that way), but as a result of successive epidemics of infectious **diseases**, including smallpox and influenza, to which the New World had no immunity. It has been estimated that within a century, the native population of Mesoamerica was reduced by as much as ninety percent.

The Spanish Crown theoretically offered some protection to the surviving native population – outright slavery was outlawed, for example – but in practice Spanish authority was very distant. Indeed, many Maya were overseen by Maya chiefs, who collected tax and tribute on behalf of the colonial authorities. Some priests attempted to champion indigenous rights, notably **Bartolomé de las**

Casas in Chiapas, but they were few and far between. In the Yucatán, it was a Franciscan friar, **Diego de Landa**, later bishop of Mérida, who was responsible for one of the most notorious acts of all. In 1562 he held an auto-da-fé on behalf of the Inquisition, at which 42 local Indians were tortured and executed for heresy, and over twenty Maya codices (hieroglyphic books recording Maya history and beliefs) were burnt. This constituted virtually every known written Maya record at the time. Ironically, Landa, whose acts were condemned in Spain, is responsible for much of what we do know of the ancient Yucatecan Maya. Perhaps as an act of contrition, he later gathered all the information he could discover about the Maya, and compiled it in his famous book, *Relación de las Cosas de Yucatán*.

Pirates and traders

For much of the Yucatán, the colonial era settled into a pattern of semi-enslavement for the Maya population on vast landholdings granted to Spanish colonists. The region was far from the centre of Mexico and outside the mainstream of its politics; since it had few natural resources, it was largely left to itself. The exception was around the coasts, where persistent piracy led much of the population to flee inland. From bases in the uninhabited areas around the Laguna de Términos (near modern Ciudad del Carmen), pirates and privateers, many of them British, operated with impunity throughout the seventeenth century. They preyed on vessels travelling between Veracruz and Cuba, exploited local resources of logwood and mahogany, and frequently raided coastal towns, above all Campeche. Finally driven out at the beginning of the eighteenth century, they moved round the coast and, in 1763, with official British support and following numerous battles with Spanish fleets, founded **British Honduras** (now Belize) with the old pirate population as its basis.

What wealth there was in colonial Yucatán, and indeed throughout Mexico, was concentrated in the hands of a tiny local elite and the imperialists in Spain. The governing philosophy was that "what's good for Spain is good for Mexico", and towards that end all **trade**, industry and profit was exclusively aimed. No local trade or agriculture that would compete with Spain were allowed, so the cultivation of vines or the production of silk was banned. Heavy taxes on other products – coffee, sugar, tobacco, cochineal and silver and other metals – went directly to Spain. This didn't prevent the growth of a small class of extraordinarily wealthy **hacendados** (owners of massive estates or haciendas), whose money funded the architectural development of colonial towns like Mérida and Campeche. These were transformed from fortress-like huddles at the beginning of the colonial era to supreme examples of Baroque extravagance by its end. However, Spain's policies did stop the development of any kind of realistic economic infrastructure, or even of decent roads linking the towns. Throughout the colonial era there was no practical overland route from the Yucatán to central Mexico, for example.

Even among the wealthy there was growing **resentment**, fuelled by the status of Mexicans: only "**gachupines**", Spaniards born in Spain, could hold high office in the government or Church. Of course, such people constituted a tiny percentage of the population. The rest were **criollos** (creoles, born in Mexico of Spanish blood), who were in general educated, wealthy and aristocratic, and **mestizos** (of mixed race), who dominated the lower ranks of the Church, army and civil service, or lived as anything from shopkeepers and ranchers to bandits and beggars. At the bottom of the pile were the Maya.

Independence

By the beginning of the nineteenth century, Spain's status as a world power was in severe decline. In 1796, British sea power had forced the Spanish to open their colonial ports to free trade. At the same time, new political ideas were transforming the world, having inspired the French Revolution and the American War of Independence. Although the works of such political philosophers as Rousseau, Voltaire and Paine were banned in Mexico, the opening of the ports made it inevitable that their ideas would spread, especially via traders from the newly established United States. Literary societies set up to discuss these books quickly became centres of **political dissent**.

The spark, though, was provided by the French invasion of Spain, as colonies throughout Latin America refused to recognize the Bonaparte regime, and the campaigns of Bolívar and others in South America began. In Mexico, the *gachupín* rulers proclaimed their loyalty to Ferdinand VII (the deposed king) and hoped to carry on much as before, but creole discontent was not to be so easily assuaged. In Querétaro, the first leaders of the independence movement emerged from a literary society: **Father Miguel Hidalgo y Costilla**, a creole priest, and **Ignacio Allende**, a disaffected junior army officer.

When their plans for a coup were discovered, the conspirators were forced into premature action, with Hidalgo issuing the famous **Grito** (cry) of Independence – culminating in the rallying cry, *¡Méxicanos, viva México!* – from the steps of his parish church in Dolores on September 16, 1810. The mob of Indians and *mestizos* who gathered behind the banner swiftly took the major towns of San Miguel, Guanajuato and others to the north of the capital, but their behaviour – seizing land and property, slaughtering the Spanish – horrified the wealthy creoles who had initially supported the movement. In 1811, Hidalgo's army, huge but undisciplined, moved on the capital, but at the crucial moment Hidalgo decided to retreat, and his forces broke up as quickly as they had been assembled. Within months, Hidalgo, Allende and the other ringleaders had been captured and executed.

By this time most creoles, frightened at what had been unleashed, had rejoined the ranks of the royalists. But many *mestizos* and much of the indigenous population remained in a state of revolt, finding a new leader in the *mestizo* priest **José María Morelos**. Morelos was not only a far better tactician than Hidalgo, he was also a genuine radical. By 1813, after a series of highly successful guerrilla campaigns, he controlled virtually the whole of central and northern Mexico, with the exception of the capital and the route from there to Veracruz. At the **Congress of Chilpancingo**, he declared the abolition of slavery and the equality of all races. However, the royalists fought back with a series of crushing victories. Morelos was captured and executed in 1815, and his forces, now led by Vicente Guerrero, were reduced to carrying out the occasional minor raid.

Ironically, it was the introduction of liberal reforms in Spain, of just the type feared by the Mexican ruling classes, which finally brought about **Mexican Independence**. Worried that such reforms might spread across the Atlantic, many creoles pre-empted a true revolution by assuming a "revolutionary" guise themselves. In 1820, **Agustín de Iturbide**, a royalist general but himself a *mestizo*, threw in his lot with Guerrero; in 1821, he proposed the **Iguala Plan** to the Spanish authorities, who were hardly in a position to fight, and Mexico was granted independence.

The Yucatán declares independence

Always culturally, as well as geographically, distinct from the rest of Mexico, the Yucatán briefly attempted to go it alone as a nation. This was not as radical a notion as perhaps it sounds – Chiapas was in a similar situation, while Guatemala and the territories of Central America, after having been invited to join Mexico, chose to go their separate ways. Yucatán's independence initially lasted a matter of months, however, before both the Yucatán and Chiapas joined the new nation of Mexico.

The post-independence years were chaotic to say the least, with constant changes of government, and in 1835 a new regime in Mexico City under General Santa Ana attempted to impose far more control on the regions. Local discontent culminated in the **Mérida Congress** approving a declaration of independence for the Yucatán. At first, the governor, Santiago Méndez, blocked it, saying that the Yucatán would recognize the rule of the central government if the old constitution was reinstated. Promises were made but swiftly broken by President Santa Ana, and the Yucatán formally declared independence in 1841. Mexican flags were replaced by the flag of the **Republic of Yucatán** – five stars on a green field and one white horizontal stripe between two red.

Soon the Yucatán was suffering from loss of trade as Mexico blockaded its ports. Still more significantly, the Caste Wars broke out in 1847. Desperate for help, Méndez offered sovereignty over the Yucatán to any nation that helped defeat the rebellion. Although the US considered the offer seriously, it was the newly wealthy Mexican government, following the end of the Mexican-American War, that took him up, and the Yucatán was again reunited with Mexico on August 17, 1848.

The Caste Wars

The **Caste Wars** were one of the most successful indigenous uprisings in history, creating an autonomous Maya state that survived for over fifty years. Yet their origins were at least as much political, over land and labour rights, as they were racial. Initially, at least, the uprising was supported by poor *mestizos* as well as the Maya.

For all its promises, the effect of independence on most people in Mexico was simply a change of ruler, from the Spanish to locally born creoles. Indeed, for the lowest rungs of the population, this development actually made things worse: the protection of the Spanish Crown disappeared, and the liberalization of **land** laws allowed the privatization of previously communal land. Meanwhile, the power of the Church was barely diminished, but with a reduction of funds from the government the burden of tribute on the poor became even greater. At the same time, the loss of Spanish trade meant major changes to agriculture. **Henequen** was first planted in the 1830s, and by 1845 had become the Yucatán's chief export (see box, p.200); sugar cane was also widely introduced. As a result, forest that had previously been communal was taken over by the great haciendas and cleared. These supposedly unexploited forest areas were often sacred to the Maya, homes to their gods. Water, too, was sold off, with cenotes and springs that had been in communal use for centuries handed over to private owners.

In the battles for independence, and also in the internal struggles which had pitted Campeche against Mérida (a reflection of the wider struggles between liberals and conservatives across Mexico), many Maya had been recruited to **armed militia**, often with promises of land or freedom for their service. Such promises were rarely honoured, but the participants were taught the use of arms and military organization – training that the white elite of the Yucatán would come to regret.

The spark that ignited the Caste Wars is generally taken to be the execution, in July 1847, of rebel leader **Manual Antonio Ay** in Valladolid. That same year Valladolid, Tepich and Tabi were sacked by the rebels, and much of their white population slaughtered. By May 1848 a loose alliance of Maya forces, led by **Cecilio Chi** and **Jacinto Pat**, occupied almost the entire peninsula and advanced to within 24km of Mérida and 8km of Campeche, where the white population had taken refuge. Allegedly, the only reason the governor had not issued orders for a complete evacuation of the Yucatán was the shortage of paper in the besieged city. At the very point of victory, however, the spring rains came, and the Maya army evaporated as its soldiers went back to their fields to plant corn.

Within months, the Mexican-American War ended, the Yucatán accepted Mexican sovereignty and well-equipped **Mexican troops** poured in to suppress the rebellion. The rebels were pushed back into the southeastern corner of the state, in what today would be southern Quintana Roo, and both Chi and Pat were assassinated in 1849. The fighting had left perhaps two hundred thousand people dead or displaced in the Yucatán, and over the next ten years as many as two thousand Maya were arrested and sold as slaves in Cuba.

Chan Santa Cruz

In 1850, the **Talking Cross** appeared to a group of Maya (see box, p.129). They believed their gods had spoken to them through it, urging them to fight for independence. The same year, the town of Chan Santa Cruz (later Felipe Carrillo Puerto) was founded and would become the cultural, military and political capital of the ongoing Maya rebellion. From here the Maya administered a growing state, supplied with arms and other necessities from British Honduras, and launched occasional guerrilla attacks into Mexican territory. At its peak the **Maya nation of Chan Santa Cruz** controlled all the land from modern Playa del Carmen to the border of British Honduras, and inland as far as Tepich and Tihosuco; it was recognized by Britain (which benefited from the trade) as a de facto independent nation.

Chan Santa Cruz was never allowed to live at peace, however, and the Mexican government fomented rivalries with other Maya groups, supplying them with weapons and promising land rights. By the 1890s, the people and their leaders grew weary, and with the dictator Porfirio Díaz in power in Mexico City, British relations with Mexico improved. Partly to protect their huge new investments (in rail construction for example), the British government recognized the sovereignty of Mexico and closed the border between Chan Santa Cruz and British Honduras, cutting off the Maya nation's main line of supply. In 1901, Mexican general Ignacio Bravo occupied the town of Chan Santa Cruz, destroying the Talking Cross and officially ending the war.

Isolated resistance to the Mexican republic continued for many years, with major incidents in 1917 in Vigia Chico and 1933 in Dzula, and outbreaks of rebellion reported even in the 1950s. Many of the original causes of the war, however, disappeared (at least in theory) when the victorious revolutionary armies marched into the Yucatán in 1915, bringing with them promises of land reform and the cancellation of debt labour.

Dictatorship and revolution

Distracted by the Caste Wars and as physically isolated as ever, the Yucatán was largely a spectator during the civil wars that tore central Mexico apart from 1855 to 1876. The liberal reforms that resulted – largely the achievement of **Benito Juárez**, a Zapotec Indian who had been adopted and educated by a priest – most notably the reduction of the power of the Church, reached the Yucatán late. In 1876 a new radical liberal leader, **Porfirio Díaz**, overthrew the elected government and proclaimed his own candidate president. The following year he assumed the presidency himself, and was to rule as dictator for the next 34 years. At first his platform was a radical one, but it was soon dropped in favour of a brutal policy of **modernization**.

In many ways the achievements of his dictatorship were remarkable: some 16,000km of railway were built (including the line from Mexico City to Mérida), industry boomed, telephones and telegraphs were installed and major towns, reached at last by reasonable roads, entered the modern era. In the countryside, Díaz established a police force, the notorious *rurales,* who stamped out much of the banditry (though later, their corruption made them almost as bad as the bandits). But the costs were high: rapid development was achieved by handing over huge swathes of the country to foreign investors, who owned the vast majority of the oil, mining rights, railways and natural resources.

This was also the era when the vast **haciendas** of the Yucatán reached their peak of power, wealth and privilege. Able to rely on the forced labour of a landless peasantry, whose serfdom was ensured by wages so low that they were permanently in debt to their employers, they had little interest in efficiency or in production for domestic consumption. By 1900, the entire land was owned by some three to four percent of its population. The rich became very rich indeed; Yucatán's poor had lower incomes and fewer prospects than they had had a century earlier.

With the onset of the **twentieth century**, opposition was growing to Díaz, not just among the poor, but also the educated middle classes, concerned above all by the racist policies of their government (which favoured foreign investors above native ones) and by the lack of opportunity for themselves. In 1910, **Francisco Madero** ran against Díaz for president. When he was imprisoned and the election awarded to Díaz, **revolutionary forces** took up arms. In the northern state of Chihuahua, **Pancho Villa** and **Pascual Orozco** won several minor battles, and in the southwest, **Emiliano Zapata** began to arm indigenous guerrilla forces. After numerous revolutionary successes, Díaz fled into exile, and on October 2, 1911, Madero was elected president.

Like the originators of Independence before him, Madero had no conception of the forces he had unleashed. He freed the press, encouraged the formation of unions and introduced genuine **democracy**, but failed to do anything about the condition of the peasantry or the redistribution of land. The renewed fighting between revolutionary factions continued, on and off, for nearly ten years. Even later, in the 1920s and 1930s, there were sporadic attempts at a Catholic counter-revolution.

Again, the Yucatán was only peripherally involved, with all the major battles taking place in northern and central Mexico. When **Salvador Alvarado** marched into Yucatán at the head of a revolutionary army in 1915, the resistance of the conservative local elite was swiftly overcome.

The Yucatán in modern Mexico

The first president who was in a secure enough position to start to make real progress towards the revolutionary ideals was **Plutarco Elías Calles**, elected in 1924. Work on large public works schemes began – roads, irrigation systems, village schools – and about eight million acres of land throughout Mexico were given back to the villages as communal holdings, *ejidos*. At the same time, Calles instituted a policy of virulent **anticlericalism**, closing churches and monasteries, and forcing priests to flee the country or go underground. The bleak years of the Depression, however, brought reform to a halt.

Lázaro Cárdenas, elected in 1934, revived the revolutionary momentum. As the spokesman of a younger generation, Cárdenas set up the single broad-based party that was to rule Mexico for the rest of the twentieth century, the **PRI** (Party of the Institutionalized Revolution). He set about an unprecedented programme of reform, redistributing land on a huge scale (170,000 square kilometres during his six-year term), creating peasant and worker organizations to represent their interests at a national level and incorporating them into the governing party. He also relaxed controls on the Church to appease internal and international opposition.

In 1938, he nationalized the **oil companies**, an act that has proved one of the most significant in shaping modern Mexico and bringing about its industrial miracle. For a time it seemed as if yet more foreign intervention might follow, but a boycott of Mexican oil by the major consumers crumbled with the onset of **World War II**, and was followed by a massive influx of money and a huge boost for Mexican industry as a result of the war.

In the Yucatán, the so-called Mexican miracle was slower to take hold, and the fifty years following the Revolution were ones, on the whole, of gradual decline. Though the lot of the peasantry improved thanks to land distribution and the break-up of the haciendas, in economic terms the region went backwards. Many of the haciendas had been damaged during the Revolution, and henequen production was also hampered by the confusion following land redistribution and the loss of much of the workforce to work their own fields. At the same time, new sources of henequen in Asia and South America were becoming available. With the widespread replacement of henequen products by artificial fibres in the 1940s, Yucatecan agriculture lost its final overseas markets. It was not until the 1970s that Yucatán began to embrace the modern world. There were two chief drivers: the selection of **Cancún** for massive government investment in tourism, and the exploitation of **oil** reserves off the Gulf coast of Campeche. Suddenly the area was wealthy again, and development since, above all in tourism, has been unrelenting.

The final decades of the twentieth century were traumatic for Mexico. Vast oil revenues and a one-party state proved an ideal breeding ground for **corruption**, which permeated every level of government. Despite the country's wealth, a huge foreign debt had been built up, and in the 1980s, falling oil prices and rising interest rates provoked a major **economic crisis**. Public faith in the governing party was further shaken by the 1985 **earthquake** that devastated Mexico City and again revealed widespread corruption, both in the distribution of aid and in the contracts that had been awarded to erect sub-standard buildings in the first place. The governing party was further damaged by the outbreak, in 1994, of the **Zapatista** rebellion in Chiapas (see p.262), a revolt that is still far from resolved. Finally there were **drugs**, with cartels smuggling vast quantities across the border into the US, protected by corrupt police and government officials. Their wealth and ruthless use of violence for many years made the cartels inviolate.

The end of the ejido?

Land reform was one of the great promises of the Mexican Revolution, and its most cherished legacy. Land redistributed after the Revolution was parcelled out in communal holdings, known as **ejidos**, which could not be sold as they belonged to the state. At a local level the land was held communally, divided up by the communities themselves, following the pre-Hispanic and colonial tradition. In the 1990s, however, the constitution was amended to allow the sale of *ejido* lands. Many peasants and indigenous communities feared that their landholdings would now be vulnerable to speculators or corrupt officials. And as most poor communities exist in a state of almost permanent debt, people believed that their land would be seized to cover outstanding loans, worsening their economic plight still further. All too often they have been proved right.

All these crises, and the loss of their traditional support (even though they could still rely on the party machine to deliver election victories, legitimate or not) forced the PRI into ever more **radical change**, and in the 1990s much of the party's ideology was torn up in the name of economic reform. Most significantly, the NAFTA free trade treaty was signed, and the *ejido* system (see box, above) was reformed. At the same time, the electoral system was cleaned up. For the first time, the PRI started to lose elections.

Into the new millennium

On July 2, 2000, **Vicente Fox Quesada**, the candidate of the right-wing PAN party, was voted in as president. It was a landmark event. Not only was he the first opposition candidate ever to have been democratically placed in power, it was also the first peaceful transition between opposing governments since independence. Furthermore, it was the end of seven decades of PRI rule and of the world's longest-surviving one-party dynasty. At a national level, the decline of the PRI continues: in the 2006 presidential elections, PAN candidate **Felipe Calderón** defeated the candidate of the left (with the PRI nowhere) by less than half a percentage point. The close and controversial result left Calderón weakened, though he has gradually established more authority. Most strikingly, a feature of his government has been an all-out military campaign against the drug cartels; with fifty thousand troops deployed, and almost 35,000 casualties in the first four years (the majority in turf wars between rival gangs). The figures are terrifying, but so far the Yucatán has barely been affected.

The ongoing violence, with little sign of improvement, has led to something of a PRI revival – although in the Yucatán, the party machine never really lost its grip. All three current state governors are members of the PRI (Ivonne Ortega in Yucatán, Fernando Ortega in Campeche and Félix González in Quintana Roo), and the legislatures are generally dominated by them, too. PAN made some inroads here but, if anything, their influence in the region seems to be in decline as the PRI reasserts itself. In 2010 they regained control of the municipality of Mérida, for example, when Angélica Del Rosario Araujo was elected mayor.

Environment and wildlife

The Yucatán Peninsula, Tabasco and the lowlands of Chiapas contain some of Mexico's richest wildlife areas, with particularly outstanding birdlife. Lush tropical forests in Chiapas and southern Yucatán contain the remaining populations of monkeys and large cats, as well as parrots and toucans, while the flat uplands and coastal areas of the Yucatán Peninsula host a fabulous collection of migrating birds, including large flocks of greater flamingos. Snorkelling or diving along the Mesoamerican Barrier Reef and islands in the Caribbean reveals schools of brilliantly coloured fish.

Unfortunately, as in many countries suffering economic hardship, much of this natural beauty is under threat either from direct hunting or from the indirect effects of **deforestation** and **commercialization**. It is imperative that visitors be respectful of the natural environment and support the vital educational programmes working to preserve it.

It should be stressed that not only is it extremely irresponsible to buy, even as souvenirs, items that involve wild animals in their production, but it is also generally **illegal** to bring them back to the US or the UK. This applies specifically to tortoiseshell, black coral, various species of butterfly, mussels and snails, stuffed baby crocodiles and cat skins. Trade in living animals, including tortoises, iguanas and parrots (often sold as nestlings), is also illegal, as is uprooting cacti.

Geography

The Yucatán Peninsula is a single limestone platform, one of the largest on the planet. An accretion of layers of decayed reefs, it's rarely more than a few feet above sea level. There's no visible sign of it now, but 65 million years ago, an enormous meteor slammed into the north Gulf coast near the town of Chicxulub Puerto; this is the meteor that is thought to have brought about a catastrophic climate change and the extinction of the dinosaurs. The climate here, fortunately, is more stable today. The region is entirely within the **Tropic of Cancer**, and rainfall varies across the landmass, though generally there are only two seasons: a hot, wet one, from mid-May to mid-November, and a temperate, dry one, through most of the winter and spring. Hurricanes are a risk between August and November, and, due to the lack of elevation, they have on occasion swept well inland. Hurricane Isidore did substantial damage to Mérida in 2002, and Hurricane Dean hit land on the Caribbean coast in August 2007, sweeping all the way from the south of the peninsula to the Gulf of Mexico.

Most of the Yucatán's geographic interest lies underground. Despite the total lack of visible rivers, a reserve of fresh water is trapped just below the limestone surface, occasionally exposed through sinkholes called **cenotes**, and filling vast and beautiful **caves**, some more than 100m deep. In 2001 and 2002, explorers discovered three human skeletons that are more than ten thousand years old in caves here; several prehistoric elephants and other giant Pleistocene animals have also been brought to light. Because limestone is so porous, however, the aquifer is very easily contaminated, and scientists are only now starting to advise the government on safe modes of growth and development.

By contrast, **Tabasco** is almost entirely a coastal plain, shot through with rivers that have their sources in the mountains of **Chiapas** and Guatemala. In the foothills in the south of the state, and all over more mountainous Chiapas, the rivers take the form of dramatic **waterfalls**. The extensive river system comes with its own liabilities, namely flooding. Eighty percent of the state of Tabasco was inundated in November 2007, after a particularly heavy rainy season caused the Usumacinta and Grijalva rivers to rise well beyond their banks. What laid the groundwork for the disaster – which displaced more than twenty thousand people – was that Tabasco's ground level has sunk in the last century, due to heavy petroleum extraction and other mining, as well as deforestation. There was more severe flooding in 2010, with landslides claiming numerous lives in Chiapas.

Vegetation

The Yucatán Peninsula's vegetation is influenced by its low elevation. No mountains provide runoff water, but the extensive coastline brings regular and fairly reliable rain along with year-round warm temperatures. The northern portion is primarily **dry deciduous scrub**, filled with tamarind and bay cedar. Much of the thorny scrub has been cleared to grow maize, citrus fruits and **henequen**, a variety of agave cactus used for the production of rope. A swathe of **seasonal tropical forest**, where many of the low acacias and ceibas lose their leaves in the dry season, covers the centre, mostly in Yucatán State. Bougainvillea, hibiscus and flame trees add dramatic colour in these areas. **Tropical rainforests** extend across the base of the Yucatán Peninsula and through Tabasco, containing mahogany, cedar, rosewood, ebony and logwood, as well as over eight hundred species of wild orchid. Extensive **mangrove forests** line much of the Gulf coast and the Caribbean. Throughout, though, charcoal cutting or slash-and-burn agriculture has substantially denuded the original forest. Similarly, tourism growth along the coast has eaten away at the mangroves – a short-sighted move, as runoff from the trees' root systems nourishes the coral reefs that draw travellers in the first place.

The tropical forests provide both **chocolate** (from the cacao trees of Tabasco and Chiapas) and **vanilla**. Also harvested are chicle, from the latex of the **sapodilla** tree (used to make chewing gum), and wild rubber and sarsaparilla. **Herbs** used in the medicinal or pharmaceutical industries include digitalis from wild foxgloves and various barks for making purges and disinfectants. **Dioscorea mexicana**, a wild yam unique to Mexico that flourishes in Tabasco and Chiapas, was the source of the first lab-created progesterone, enabling the invention of oral contraceptives.

Insects

Insect life is incredibly abundant and diverse, particularly in the southern tropical rainforests, which teem with everything from assorted **gnats** to long columns of fungus-eating **leafcutter ants** to swarms of carnivorous **army ants**, which can devour much larger insects, even giant **grasshoppers** (called *langostas*, or lobsters). Lovelier are the colourful **butterflies** that can, at peak times of year, fill the air like snow. But for the most part, insects make themselves known through the variety of bites and sores they inflict. **Mosquitoes** are particularly troublesome; malaria is still a small risk in jungle areas. The **garrapata**, a tenacious tick found everywhere livestock exists, readily attaches itself to human hosts. And while **scorpions** live throughout the Yucatán, they are generally not lethal (and are in fact eaten dried as a purported wart cure); **tarantulas** are also encountered in the drier areas, and they too are not poisonous.

Fish and reptiles

Because the Yucatán has few rivers above ground and only one substantial lake, freshwater fish are few. Only in Tabasco is there significant diversity. Of the more than one hundred species in Tabasco's Río Usamacinta, one of the most remarkable is the prehistoric-looking, sharp-toothed **pejelagarto**, a type of gar – its name, derived from the Spanish words for "fish" and "lizard", accurately describes its appearance. The Yucatán cenotes and lagoons contain two **endemic species**, the Mayan cichlid and the banded tetra, while deep in the underwater cave systems, several varieties of eyeless fish flourish.

Offshore, the waters contain over one hundred significant marine species. Among the more prevalent are **swordfish**, **snapper**, **bonefish**, **tarpon** and **mackerel**. **Shrimp** and **spiny lobster** are also important commercial species, and deep ocean beds and coastal irregularities provide rewarding fishing in the waters of the Campeche Bank on the Gulf of Mexico. The Laguna de Términos, near Ciudad del Carmen, hosts the country's largest fishing fleet. A variety of sharks cruise the reefs, but the most remarkable ones are the placid **whale sharks** that congregate off the coast of Isla Holbox at the end of every summer, in what is perhaps the largest community in the world.

As for **reptiles**, iguanas and smaller lizards are at home in the forests and at seemingly every archeological site, while crocodiles populate the mangrove swamps and other brackish lagoon areas. **Marine turtles**, including the loggerhead, green, hawksbill and leatherback, are still found off many stretches of undeveloped waters and shores on the Gulf and Caribbean coasts. Hunting of both adults and eggs is against the law, but numbers have been greatly reduced, as illegal hunting continues. Nonetheless, programmes to protect turtle nests have been established in many of the major tourist areas, which may help boost the population in the future. Outside the Chiapas jungle (where the fer-de-lance viper makes its home) the number of poisonous **snakes** is relatively few – only rattlesnakes are found in the scrub forests, and assorted large green tree snakes are much more common. Amphibian life is similarly abundant; varieties include salamanders, several types of **frog** and the massive **cane toads** that have invaded nearly every continent.

Birds

Between the marshes and scrublands of the northern Yucatán Peninsula and Tabasco, and the dense rainforests in the south and Chiapas, this region is a delight for birdwatchers. During the winter migratory season, some two billion birds pass through. Among the diverse species (more than five hundred in the jungles alone) are resplendent **red macaws** and **parrots**, which make a colourful display as they fly amongst the dense tree canopy. The cereal-feeding habits of the parrot family have not endeared them to local farmers, and for this reason (and their continuing capture for sale as pets), their numbers have also been seriously depleted in recent times. Red macaws are now seldom seen outside of the southern fringes of Chiapas. Larger **game birds**, such as curassow, chachalaca and especially the ocellated turkey (eaten by the Maya for millennia) can be seen on the ground. Keel-billed **toucans** can also be spotted in the southern jungles – Maya legend has it that the tips of their bills are red because they dipped them in the blood that covered the land during the nineteenth-century Caste Wars. Another distinctive species in the Yucatán is the large turquoise-browed **motmot** (*toh'* in Maya), called the clock bird (*pájaro reloj*) because it switches its long tail feathers rhythmically like a pendulum.

The most familiar large birds of Mexico, however, are the carrion-eating **turkey vultures**, which migrate from North America and are often seen soaring in large groups. The Yucatán is also one of the last remaining strongholds of the small **Mexican eagle**, depicted on the Mexican flag.

Large numbers of coastal lagoons serve as feeding and breeding grounds for a wide variety of aquatic birds, some of them winter visitors from the north. Foremost among these are the substantial flocks of graceful **flamingos** that can be seen at selected sites along the western and northern Gulf coasts.

Mammals

The central Yucatán forest has traditionally teemed with **agouti**, **opossums** and **coatimundis**, but these have been seriously depleted by overhunting. Long-legged **pacas** (*tepescuintle*) have suffered greatly, as they have a reputation for being particularly tasty; they, at least, are now being semi-domesticated. **Spider** and **howler monkeys** are still plentiful in the Chiapas jungle and around Calakmul, though their numbers are also decreasing as their territory shrinks.

The largest ground-dwelling mammal in the region is the **tapirs**, a distant relative of the horse, with a prehensile snout, usually found close to water. Two species of **peccary**, a type of wild pig, wander the forest floors in large groups seeking their preferred food (roots, palm nuts and even snakes), and there's the smaller **brocket deer**. The **jaguar**, so revered by the Maya, is severely endangered.

The drier tropical and subtropical forests of northern Yucatán produce a more varied ground cover of shrubs and grasses, which supply food for the **white-tailed deer** and abundant small rodents such as the spiny tree **rat**, which in turn provides food for a variety of predators such as the **margay** and **jaguarundi**. Other large mammals that can still be found in small numbers are large and small **anteaters** and **armadillos**. The reefs and lagoons that run along the Quintana Roo coast, as well as the brackish Laguna de Catazajá in Chiapas, have small colonies of the large aquatic **manatee** or sea cow, a docile creature that feeds on sea grass.

The Maya belief system

L ike so many ancient cultures, the Maya have been subject to the fantastical theories of explorers as well as the imaginings of armchair spiritualists: "The Maya were not aided by extraterrestrial beings," a sign at several archeological sights clarifies, "What they accomplished was due to their ingenuity and hard work." It doesn't help, though, that the archeological record is so spotty, partially due to the fragile limestone in which the Maya predominantly built, but more the fault of the Spanish conquerors who were not content just to destroy the physical symbols of the Maya but were also bent on systematically replacing the pagan culture with Catholicism.

Much of our knowledge of the ancient Maya, then, is derived from the surviving traditions, handed down through generations, often in secret to protect them from Spanish pillaging. The **Chilam Balam**, for instance, are cumulative records of lore and prophecy recorded in various villages in Latin script in the late seventeenth and early eighteenth centuries. Experts also draw on various Spanish contemporary accounts, as well as the sculpture, pottery and jewellery retrieved from tombs. Images carved into the ruins of buildings offer clues, while the breakthrough in decoding the hieroglyphic system, a success of just the past few decades, has contributed greatly to the historical record. Further hints come from other Mesoamerican cultures, as the Maya share a great deal with the Aztecs and Toltecs, as well as the earliest related culture with a strong archeological record, the Olmecs.

The Olmec influence

The cities of the **Olmecs**, formed a template that was traced by subsequent cultures, including the Maya. They were the first Mesoamerican civilization, and literally set their cosmology in stone, making a permanent record of their rulers and the gods and spirits with whom they communed. The Olmec place of creation was the mighty volcano of **San Martín**, in the south of modern Veracruz State, and they built a replica – a sacred artificial mountain, complete with fluted sides – in their city at **La Venta** in Tabasco. This was the original Mesoamerican **pyramid**, a feature that recurs in virtually every subsequent culture. Into the base of their volcano pyramid the Olmecs embedded huge **stelae**, flat carved stones portraying ruling dignitaries communicating with gods and spirits. These were the first stelae in Mesoamerica, and later versions fill the plazas of ruined cities in the Maya world and all over Central America.

One stele at La Venta depicts a **World Tree**, a symbol of the "axis mundi" at the centre of the Mesoamerican universe. With its roots in the earth and its branches in the heavens, the tree links the underworld of the dead with the earth and sky. Though this was perhaps the first such representation, World Trees have been found in cities all over Mesoamerica. Among the Maya, the World Tree is specifically the spreading boughs of the silk-cotton (ceiba) tree. At Palenque there are several images of the ceiba, including one on the lid of a ruler's sarcophagus, where the ruler is shown falling through a World Tree inscribed in the night sky – the Milky Way.

Opposite Mexico's first pyramid, the Olmecs built a **gateway** to the spirit world, home to a pantheon of gods, spirits and the souls of dead ancestors, in the form of a sunken, court-shaped plaza with an enormous pavement of blocks made of the mineral serpentine. They added two large platforms topped with mosaics and patterns depicting aquatic plants. Such symbols appeared all over Mesoamerica in the ensuing centuries, often decorating ball-courts or ceramics.

The Olmecs also developed the ritual **ball-game** that appears in every subsequent Mesoamerican culture. Usually played in a ball-court shaped like the letter "I", the game featured players, in teams of two or three, who scored points by using their thighs or upper arms to hit a ball through hoops, or at markers embedded in the court walls. Heavy bets were placed by supporters, and the penalty for losing the most important games was death (though there have been suggestions that the winners were sacrificed in some cities).

In general, the basic structure of Olmec society – a theocracy ruled over by a priestly and regal elite who communicated with and propitiated the spirit world through sacrifice and ritual blood-letting – would change little throughout Mesoamerica until the arrival of Cortés.

The calendar

For the Maya, the stars were embodiments of gods, and the constellations re-enactments of cosmic events; they regarded the three stars below the belt of Orion as the place of creation itself. Their interest in the constant shifting of the heavens was aided by the invention of the **calendar**, probably by the Zapotecs of Monte Albán in about 600 BC.

By the time of the Classic Maya (250–900 AD), the 260-day calendar, depicted as a wheel, had become the most significant tool in prediction and divination. Every number and day had its own meaning; each of the twenty-day names had a specific god and a particular direction, passing in a continuous anticlockwise path from one day to the next until a cycle of time was completed. This calendar was used alongside a 365-day calendar, roughly matching the solar year, but lacking the leap days necessary to give it real accuracy. This was divided into eighteen groups of twenty days plus an unlucky additional five days. Each twenty-day grouping and each solar year also had a supernatural patron. When the two calendars were set in motion and running concurrently, it took exactly 52 years for the cycle to repeat. The ending of one cycle and the beginning of another heralded apocalypse and, afterwards, a new age and a reassertion of the ordered world from the disordered and demonic; one symbol of this new age was the construction of new temples over the old every 52 years.

In addition to these two calendars, the Pre-Classic Maya developed what is known as the **Long Count**, recording the total number of days elapsed since a mythological date when the first great cycle began (August 11, 3114 BC, to be exact). Under this elaborate record system, all became sacred, and every event, from the planting of crops to the waging of war, had to occur at the correct spiritual time. The Maya Long Count will end on **December 23, 2012**, and there are many who believe that this date will herald the end of the world – though there's little evidence that the Maya themselves would have believed that.

The pantheon

The ancient Maya worshipped a staggering number of gods who represented virtually every facet of life, from specific activities (Ek Chuah oversaw trade and commerce, for instance) to places, such as the maize fields, where squat, mischievous *aluxes* were believed to stand guard. The deities' relative importance varied across the Maya world, but typically the Sun God, most often called **K'inich Ahau**, was considered the supreme deity. As the creator, he took several forms: by night, he became the Jaguar God, guarding the way to the underworld. Characterized by crossed eyes and buckteeth, he was one of the oldest gods in the Mesoamerican tradition, and was also worshipped by the Olmecs. After 900 AD, in the Post-Classic era, he was conflated with **Itzamná**, a powerful god credited with inventing writing and the tradition of scribes. Itzamná is often depicted with a toothless mouth (signifying his old age) and a hooknose, holding a pen; his consort is **Ixchel**, goddess of fertility. Also vital to the pantheon is the rain god **Chac**, who is widely identified with the many curly-nosed masks that adorn Maya temples and other buildings, though more recent scholarship suggests that these may actually represent Itzamná.

The Maya's relationship with their gods was not one of simple worship, but of struggle and outwitting. Life was not so much borrowed time as time won by trickery from the gods of death. Maya vases, buried with the dead, often depict scenes from the **Popul Vuh**, the creation epic of the Quiché Maya tribe, in which the **Hero Twins**, two proto-humans with godlike powers, defeated the **Lords of the Underworld** through a series of tricks and their expertise in the ball-game. The largest ball-court at **Chichén Itzá** is covered in bas-reliefs of aquatic plants, which are traditionally associated with an opening to the underworld.

In the Yucatán, this connection to the spirit world was made all the more tangible by the **caves** and **cenotes** that riddle the peninsula. These, it was believed, were open gateways to the underworld, and as a result many were considered sacred and were the site of numerous rituals. Though the ancient Maya were not as bloodthirsty as the Aztecs of central Mexico (whose cosmology rested on the gods' seemingly insatiable appetite for human hearts), their rituals do seem to have included **human sacrifice**. When the main cenote at Chichén Itzá was dredged, for instance, it was found to contain numerous skeletons, and Fray Diego de Landa recorded details of sacrifices in the mid-sixteenth century.

The Spanish conquistadors and the Franciscan priests who accompanied them toppled a pantheon that had been in place for centuries. Hundreds of thousands of books were burnt, priests executed and temples overturned. Such is the tenacity of the traditional beliefs of the Maya, though, that even five hundred years of effort have not been enough to eradicate them entirely, as anyone who has entered a rural church in the Yucatán or witnessed the rituals of the Day of the Dead – called Hanal Pixan by the Maya – can attest.

Books

exico has attracted more than its fair share of famous foreign writers, and has inspired a vast amount of literature and several classics. Until very recently, however, Mexican authors had received little attention outside the country, and few are well known north of the border; what translations exist are mostly published by small US presses. Most big US bookstores will have a huge array of books about, from or set in Mexico, plus a few novels. In the rest of the English-speaking world there's far less choice, though the best-known of the archeological and travel titles listed here should be available almost anywhere. Some of the books are out of print, but may still be found in specialist libraries or second-hand shops. Books with a 🎿 symbol are highly recommended.

Travel

🎿 **Graham Greene** *The Lawless Roads*. In the late 1930s, Greene was sent to Chiapas and Tabasco to investigate the effects of the persecution of the Catholic Church. The result was this classic account of his travels in a very bizarre era of modern Mexican history. *The Power and the Glory*, published later, is an absorbing fictionalized version, centred on the exploits of a "whisky priest" on the run from the authorities.

Michel Peissel *The Lost World of Quintana Roo*. In 1958, Peissel, then 21 years old, bushwhacked on foot through the virtually empty fringe of the peninsula. Definitely worth snapping up if you find a used copy, as it's a great depiction of an area that has changed rapidly in just a few decades.

Nigel Pride *A Butterfly Sings to Pacaya*. The author, accompanied by his wife and four-year-old son, travels south from the US border in a Jeep, heading through Mexico, Guatemala and Belize. Though the travels took place over thirty years ago, the pleasures and privations they experience rarely appear dated.

John Lloyd Stephens *Incidents of Travel in Central America, Chiapas, and Yucatán*. A classic nineteenth-century traveller, Stephens, acting as American ambassador to Central America, indulged his own enthusiasm for archeology. His journals, full of superb Victorian pomposity, make great reading. The best editions include the fantastic original illustrations by Frederick Catherwood; a Smithsonian edition combines some of these with modern photographs.

John Kenneth Turner *Barbarous Mexico*. Turner was an American journalist who travelled through nineteenth-century Mexico. This exposé of the workers' conditions in the Yucatán's plantations did much to discredit the regime of Porfirio Díaz.

Ronald Wright *Time Among the Maya*. A vivid and sympathetic account of travels from Belize through Guatemala, Chiapas and Yucatán, meeting the Maya of today. The book's twin points of interest are the ancient Maya and the recent violence involving the Zapatistas.

Fiction and poetry

Jorge Ibargüengoitia *The Dead Girls, Two Crimes* and others. One of the first modern Mexican novelists translated into English, Ibargüengoitia was killed in a plane crash in 1983. These two are both blackly comic thrillers, superbly told, the first of them based on real events.

Octavio Paz (ed) *Mexican Poetry*. Edited by Paz (Mexico's leading man of letters in the post-revolutionary era) and translated by Samuel Beckett, this is as good a taste as you could hope for of modern Mexican poetry. Some of Paz's own poetry is also available in translation.

Earl Shorris *In the Yucatán*. This novel, the story of a Mexican-American lawyer and a Maya mystic who bond in jail, has its flaws, but its background detail is excellent, providing a good dose of political commentary and cultural information about the Maya. Shorris is also the author of numerous non-fiction titles including *The Life and Times of Mexico*, a somewhat rambling history that's fascinating to dip into.

B. Traven Traven wrote a whole series of compelling novels set in Mexico. Among the best known are *Treasure of the Sierra Madre* and *The Death Ship*, but of more direct interest if you're travelling are such works as *The Bridge in the Jungle* and the other six books in the *Jungle* series. These latter all deal with the state of the peasantry and the growth of revolutionary feeling in the last years of Díaz's dictatorship, and if at times they're overly polemical, as a whole they're enthralling.

History

Inga Clendinnen *Ambivalent Conquests: Maya and Spaniard in Yucatán 1517 to 1570*. A product of meticulous research that documents the methods and consequences of the Spanish conquest of the Yucatán, Clendinnen's book examines events from the viewpoints of both the Spanish and Maya. In particular, she probes the extent to which the Maya ever truly converted to Christianity or believed themselves subjugated.

Bernal Díaz *The Conquest of New Spain* (trans J.M. Cohen). This abridged version of Díaz's classic, *Historia Verdadera de la Conquista de la Nueva España*, is the best available in English. Díaz accompanied Francisco de Cordoba and Juan de Grijalva on their initial forays into the Yucatán, then joined Cortés's campaign of conquest. It's a magnificent eyewitness account that makes compulsive reading.

Brian Hamnett *A Concise History of Mexico*. The book kicks off with a brief examination of contemporary issues and then jumps back to the time of the Olmecs. A combined chronological and thematic approach is used to analyse the social and political history of Mexico from then to the present day, making for a good general introduction.

Nelson Reed *The Caste War of the Yucatán*. Reed's book is the authority on this tumultuous and defining era in Yucatán history, with great detail on the Talking Cross movement. A must-read for anyone intrigued by this period.

Hugh Thomas *Conquest: Montezuma, Cortés, and the Fall of Old Mexico* (US); *The Conquest of Mexico* (UK). Same book, different title, but either way a brilliant narrative history of the Conquest by the British historian previously best known for his history of the Spanish Civil War. A massive work of real scholarship and importance but also humorous and readable, with appendices on everything from Aztec beliefs, history and genealogy to Cortés's wives and lovers.

The ancient Maya

Michael D. Coe *The Maya*. The best available general introduction to the Maya, now in its eighth edition: concise, clear and comprehensive. Coe has also written several more weighty, academic volumes. His *Breaking the Maya Code*, a beautifully written history of the decipherment of the Maya glyphs, owes much to the fact that Coe was present at many of the most important meetings leading to the breakthrough that demonstrated how the glyphs actually did reproduce Maya speech. Aside from anything else, it is a beautifully written, ripping yarn. In *Reading the Maya Glyphs*, co-authored with Mark van Stone, he attempts to teach you to do just that – to interpret the ancient writing that you encounter at sites and in museums.

David Drew *The Lost Chronicles of the Maya Kings*. Ignore the title – this is actually a very thorough yet accessible account of almost all aspects of the Maya in a single volume, by a British archeologist and broadcaster.

M.S. Edmonson (trans) *Heaven Born Merida and Its Destiny: The Book of Chilam Balam of Chumayel*. The *Chilam Balam* is a recollection of Maya history and myth, compiled by the Maya over centuries; this version was written in Maya in Latin script in the eighteenth century. Although the style is not easy, it's one of the few keys into the Maya view of the world; other translations of other versions of the *Chilam Balam* exist, but this is the most accessible.

Diego de Landa *Yucatán Before and After the Conquest* (ed William Gates).

A translation of the Franciscan monk's *Relación de las Cosas de Yucatán*. De Landa's prior destruction of almost all original Maya books as "works of the devil" makes his own account the chief surviving source on Maya life and society in the immediate post-Conquest period. Written in 1566 during his imprisonment in Spain on charges of cruelty to the Indians, the book provides a fascinating wealth of detail. Various other translations are available locally.

Simon Martin and Nikolai Grube *Chronicle of the Maya Kings and Queens*. A graphic approach to Maya history, replete with photo illustrations, timelines, hieroglyphics and the like, making the complex dynasties a little easier to grasp.

Mary Ellen Miller *Maya Art and Architecture*. An excellent survey of the artisanship of the Maya, organized by media, from stelae to pottery. Miller's *The Art of Mesoamerica: From Olmec to Aztec* gives a broader view.

Mary Ellen Miller and Karl Taube *An Illustrated Dictionary of the Gods and Symbols of Ancient Mexico and the Maya*. A superb modern reference on ancient Mesoamerica, written by two leading scholars. Taube's *Aztec and Maya Myths* is perfect as a short, accessible introduction to Mesoamerican mythology.

Linda Schele and David Freidel *A Forest of Kings: The Untold Story of the Ancient Maya*. At the forefront of the "new archeology" school, the authors

The music of the Yucatán

The Yucatán peninsula has historically looked to the Caribbean and Europe, rather than central Mexico, for culture. This is most strongly reflected in its music, particularly *trova yucateca*, which melds Cuban and European rhythms with local sounds, amounting to a music entirely unlike the brassy, boastful mariachi style associated with Mexico.

Instead, **trova yucateca** features dreamily sentimental ballads performed most typically by trios of string musicians. It came about as an outgrowth of Cuban music, which was fashionable in Mérida in the late nineteenth century. The city's upper class, rich from the surrounding henequen plantations, loved nothing better than to dance the elegant, romantic *habanera* and *guaracha,* imports from Cuba. At the same time, to reinforce Mérida's self-made reputation as "París en miniatura", children were groomed for French salon society, with music lessons as part of their acculturation.

Some of these youngsters grew up to be composers, adapting Cuba's vibrant dance music to the Yucatecan setting. This meant incorporating the Spanish-inspired rhythm of the **jarana**, danced in the Maya towns during fiestas, and penning heartfelt paeans to local Maya women. The singers conveyed their gallantry and sensitivity with oiled hair, limpid eyes and starched shirts. By the 1920s, *trova yucateca* was in full flower, and the songs of this era, such as "Caminante del Mayab", "Ojos Tristes" and "Beso Asesino", are often compiled on albums and performed today by succeeding generations.

Though you may see trios made up of instruments other than the usual guitar, *mandolín* and *tololoche* (double bass guitar), or solo lounge crooners with more modern tousled hair and unbuttoned shirts instead of guayaberas, today's *trovadores* still hold closely to tradition. This remains music of romance, nostalgia and seduction. In Mérida, you can experience it every night of the week if you like, as *trova* trios gather on the Plaza de la Constitución and can be hired for a single serenade or an entire evening's entertainment.

Back home, you'll find plenty of **recordings** if you search online, mainly compilations and including such greats as Guty Cárdenas (who was assassinated in 1932 but is still revered). You can also listen to a number of great free samples on ⓦwww .yucatanliving.com, and in Maya at ⓦwww.indemaya.gob.mx. Locally there's plenty of choice, thanks to a tradition of home CD production by current *trova* artists; most markets will have a wide selection.

have been personally responsible for decoding many Maya glyphs, thereby revolutionizing and popularizing Maya studies. Although the authors' writing style, which frequently includes recreations of scenes inspired by their discoveries, is controversial to some fellow professionals, it has also inspired a devoted following. *The Blood of Kings*, by Schele, Mary Ellen Miller and others, continues the story, detailing how the ancient Maya were ruled by hereditary kings, lived in populous, aggressive city-states and engaged in a continuous entanglement of alliances and war. *Maya Cosmos: Three Thousand Years on the Shaman's Path*, by Schele, Freidel and Joy Parker, is perhaps more difficult to read, but continues to examine Maya ritual and religion in a unique and far-reaching way. *The Code of Kings*, written in collaboration with Peter Matthews and illustrated with Justin Kerr's "rollout" photography of Maya ceramics, examines in detail the significance of the monuments at selected Maya sites.

Robert Sharer and Ioa Traxler *The Ancient Maya*. The classic (and weighty) account of Maya civilization, now in its sixth edition. Required reading for archeologists, it also provides a fascinating reference for the non-expert.

Popol Vuh The Quiché Maya bible, a fascinating creation myth from the only ancient civilization to emerge from rainforest terrain, is available in two main translations (many others can also be found): the classic version by Dennis Tedlock is arguably still the most readable; Allen J Christenson's two-volume approach gives a literal translation as well. The Maya obsession with time can be well appreciated here, where dates are recorded with painstaking precision.

Society, politics and culture

Rick Bayless *Rick Bayless's Mexican Kitchen*. Aimed at ambitious chefs, this tome has more than 150 recipes but no photos. The country's gastronomic heritage is explored in detail with a special focus on the myriad types of chile that form the heart of Mexican cuisine. More accessible is his *Mexico One Plate at a Time* (though it features no Yucatecan dishes, unfortunately), with careful instructions and thorough coaching.

Fernández de Calderon Candida *Great Masters of Mexican Folk Art*. A grand and gorgeously photographed coffee-table book produced by the cultural wing of Banamex, with portraits of the artisans alongside their works.

Macduff Everton *The Modern Maya: A Culture in Transition*. Everton's black-and-white photographs document Maya village life with affection and an eye to socio-economic issues.

Nancy and Jeffrey Gerlach *Foods of the Maya: A Taste of the Yucatán*. A solid introduction to the Yucatecan culinary tradition, very well tested for non-Mexican kitchens.

John Gibler *Mexico Unconquered: Chronicles of Power and Revolt*. A history of Mexican revolution set against the background of current events; the Zapatista uprising and protests in Oaxaca. Combining travelogue, reportage and manifesto, this is an unashamedly political account.

Diana Kennedy *The Essential Cuisines of Mexico*. Kennedy was a pioneer in bringing the multifaceted cuisine of Mexico to the attention of Americans when she published her first cookbook in 1972. This book is an almost overwhelming reference, but compiled with love. Pair with *From My Mexican Kitchen: Techniques and Ingredients* if you're completely new to Mexican cooking.

Elena Poniatowska A pioneer in the field of testimonial literature and one of Mexico's best-known essayists and journalists. To write *Here's to You, Jesusa!* Poniatowska befriended and interviewed her real-life cleaning lady. Narrated in the first person, the text is compelling, lively and at times ribald; Jesusa herself is now a celebrity on the literary circuit. Other works available in English include *Massacre in Mexico*, a collage of testimonies by people present at the 1968 massacre of students in Tlatelolco.

John Ross *Zapatistas: Making Another World Possible: Chronicles of Resistance 2000–2006*. Ross is a journalist who was close to the Zapatistas from the beginning – this book chronicles the continuing rebellion, rarely mentioned in the outside world but, in Ross's view, "changing the World without taking power".

Guiomar Rovira *Women of Maize*. Rovira, a Mexican journalist, witnessed the Zapatista uprising in Chiapas on New Year's Day, 1994. Interweaving narrative, history and the personal recollections of numerous women involved in the rebellion, this book provides extraordinary insight into the lives of indigenous people.

Chloë Sayer *The Arts and Crafts of Mexico*. Sayer is the author of numerous books on Mexican arts, crafts and associated subjects, all of them worth reading. *The Skeleton at the Feast*, written with Elizabeth Carmichael, is a wonderful, superbly illustrated insight into attitudes to death and the dead in Mexico.

Joel Simon *Endangered Mexico: An Environment on the Edge*. Eloquent and compelling study documenting the environmental crisis facing Mexico at the end of the twentieth century. Now slightly dated, but still essential reading for those wanting to know how and why the crisis exists – and why no one can offer solutions.

Other guides

Carl Franz, Lorena Havens and Steve Rogers *The People's Guide to Mexico*. Not a guidebook as such: more a series of anecdotes and words of advice for staying out of trouble and heading off the beaten track. Perennially popular with old hippies of all ages (2006 saw the publication of the thirteenth edition), and deservedly so.

Joyce Kelly *An Archaeological Guide to Mexico's Yucatán Peninsula*. Detailed and practical guide to more than ninety Maya sites and eight museums throughout the peninsula, including many little-known or difficult-to-reach ruins; an essential companion for anyone travelling purposefully through the Maya world. Kelly's "star" ratings – based on a site's archeological importance, degree of restoration and accessibility – may affront purists, but they do provide a valuable rubric when deciding where to go.

Richard and Rosalind Perry *Maya Missions*. One in a series of expertly written guides to the sometimes overlooked treasures of Mexico's colonial religious architecture; *More Maya Missions* covers Chiapas. Both are illustrated by the authors' simple but beautiful drawings. These specialist offerings, ideal for travellers who want more information than most guidebooks can provide, are not widely available, though you can usually find them in tourist book stores in the areas they cover.

Jules Siegel *Cancun Users Guide*. Siegel, a freelance journalist, moved to Mexico in 1981, then worked for the tourism ministry in the nascent resort city. His self-published tome is as much an ode to this underappreciated city and the people who built it as it is a practical guide, with shopping and eating recommendations. Affectionate, opinionated and guaranteed to change your outlook on Cancún.

Wildlife

Rosita Arvigo *Sastun: One Woman's Apprenticeship with a Maya Healer*. The author established an organic herb farm in Belize and then studied with the region's best-known medicine man for five years. Her story is fascinating for anyone interested in herbal treatments; more detail can be found in her *Rainforest Home Remedies*.

Les Beletsky *Travellers' Wildlife Guides Southern Mexico*. An excellent, if rather bulky, field guide, with colour plates of birds, fish, reptiles and mammals found through out the Yucatán, Oaxaca and Chiapas.

Ernest Preston Edwards *A Field Guide to the Birds of Mexico and Adjacent Areas: Belize, Guatemala, and El Salvador*. Some 850 species are shown in colour plates, with names in English, Latin and Spanish.

Steve Gerrard *The Cenotes of the Riviera Maya*. This self-published full-colour guide is hard to come by outside Mexico, but it's worth tracking down if you'll be doing any cave diving, as it's meticulously thorough.

Steve Howell and Sophie Webb *The Birds of Mexico and Northern Central America*. A tremendous work, the result of years of research, this is the definitive book on the region's birds. Essential for all serious birders.

Paul Humann and Ned DeLoach *Snorkeling Guide to Marine Life: Florida, Caribbean, Bahamas*. A handy, spiral-bound field guide to corals, fish, plants and other underwater life off the Caribbean coast, with 280 colour photos. The same authors have hefty individual titles on *Reef Fish Identification* and *Reef Coral Identification* if you're after the ultimate authority.

Thor Janson *Maya Nature: An Introduction to the Ecosystems, Plants and Animals of the Mayan World*. A good complement to an illustrated field guide, as the 196 colour photographs show animals in their natural habitat.

Victoria Schlesinger *Animals and Plants of the Ancient Maya: A Guide*. More than a field guide, this book also examines the cultural significance of the over one hundred species that were present in ancient Maya times.

Language

Language

Mexican Spanish 299

Rules of pronunciation 299

Useful words and phrases 299

Food and drink terms 302

Glossary 307

Mexican Spanish

Once you get into it, **Spanish** is actually a straightforward language, and in Mexico, people are eager to understand and help even the most faltering attempt. **English** is widely spoken, especially in the tourist areas, but you'll get a far better reception if you at least try to communicate with people in their own tongue. You'll be further helped by the fact that Mexicans speak relatively slowly (at least compared with Spaniards) and that there's none of the awkward lisping pronunciation.

Rules of pronunciation

Relative to English, the rules of **pronunciation** are clear-cut and strictly observed. Unless there's an accent, words ending in D, L, R and Z are stressed on the last syllable; all others, on the second last. All vowels are pure and short.

A is between the A sound of "b**a**ck" and that of "f**a**ther".

E as in "g**e**t".

I as in "pol**i**ce".

O as in "h**o**t".

U as in "r**u**le".

C is soft before E and I, hard otherwise: *cerca* is pronounced "SER-ka".

G is a guttural H sound (a little softer than the ch in "loch") before E or I, and a hard G elsewhere: *gigante* pronounced "hi-GAN-te".

H is always silent.

J is the same sound as a guttural G: *jamón* is pronounced "ham-ON".

LL sounds like an English Y: *tortilla* is pronounced "tor-TEE-ya".

N is generally as in English, but in the Yucatán is often pronounced M at the ends of words ("Yuca-TAM").

Ñ with the tilde (accent), spoken like NY: *mañana* is pronounced "ma-NYA-na".

QU is pronounced like an English K.

R is rolled, RR doubly so.

V sounds more like B: *vino* is pronounced "BEE-no".

X has an S sound before consonants; an H sound between vowels in place names, like México ("MEH-hee-ko"). In Maya words, X sounds like SH: Xel-Há is pronounced "shel-HA".

Z is the same as a soft C: *cerveza* is pronounced "ser-VAY-sa".

Useful words and phrases

Although we've listed a few essential words and phrases here, if you're travelling for any length of time some kind of **dictionary** or **phrasebook** is a worthwhile investment. *The Rough Guide to Mexican Spanish* is an excellent practical guide, correct and colloquial, and will have you speaking the language in no time. One of the best small Latin American Spanish dictionaries is the University of Chicago version (Pocket Books), widely available in Mexico, although the Langenscheidt pocket dictionary is handy because its yellow plastic cover holds up well. If you're using an older dictionary, bear in mind that CH, LL and Ñ are traditionally counted as separate letters and are listed after the Cs, Ls and Ns respectively; most current dictionaries, however, follow more familiar alphabetizing procedures, though Ñ retains its own section.

Basics

Yes, No	Sí, No	Big, Small	Gran(de), Pequeño/a
Open, Closed	Abierto/a, Cerrado/a	This, That	Éste, Eso
Please, Thank you	Por favor, Gracias	More, Less	Más, Menos
Push, Pull	Empujar, Tirar	Cheap, Expensive	Barato/a, Caro/a
Where?, When?	¿Dónde?, ¿Cuándo?	Today, Tomorrow	Hoy, Mañana
With, Without	Con, Sin	Yesterday	Ayer
What?, How much?	¿Qué?, ¿Cuánto?	Now, Later	Ahora, Más tarde
Good, Bad	Buen(o)/a, Mal(o)/a	Out of order	Descompuesto
Here, There	Aquí or Acá, Allí or Allá		

Greetings and pleasantries

Hello, Goodbye	¡Hola!, Adiós	What's your name?	¿Cómo se llama usted?
Good morning	Buenos días	I am English	Soy inglés/inglesa
Good afternoon/night	Buenas tardes/noches	...American*	...americano/a
How do you do?	¿Qué tal?	...Australian	...australiano/a
See you later	Hasta luego	...Canadian	...canadiense
Sorry	Lo siento/disculpeme	...Irish	...irlandés/irlandesa
Excuse me	Con permiso/perdón	...Scottish	...escocés/escocesa
How are you?	¿Cómo está (usted)?	...Welsh	...galés/galesa
Not at all/You're welcome	De nada/por nada	...New Zealander	...neozelandés /neozelandesa
I (don't) understand	(No) Entiendo		

*Mexicans are from the Americas too, so describing yourself as American can occasionally cause offence. Another option is "estadounidense" (or, more simply, "de Los Estados Unidos", from the United States) if you are a US American.

Do you speak English?	¿Habla (usted) inglés?
I (don't) speak Spanish	(No) Hablo español
What (did you say)?	Mande?
My name is...	Me llamo...

Hotels, transport and directions

I want...	Quiero...	Do you have...?	¿Tiene...?
I'd like...please	Quisiera...por favor	...the time	...la hora
Do you know...?	¿Sabe...?	...a room	...un cuarto
I don't know	No sé	...with two beds/	...con dos camas/
There is... (Is there...?)	(¿)Hay...(?)	...double bed	...cama matrimonial
Give me... (one like that)	Deme... (uno así)	It's for one person (two people)	Es para una persona (dos personas)

...for one night (one week)	...para una noche (una semana)
It's fine, how much is it?	¿Está bien, cuánto es?
It's too expensive	Es demasiado caro
Don't you have anything cheaper?	¿No tiene algo más barato?
Can one...?	¿Se puede...?
...camp (near) here?	¿...acampar (cerca de) aquí?
Is there a hotel nearby?	¿Hay un hotel cerca de aquí?
How do I get to...?	¿Por dónde se va a...?
Left, right, straight on	Izquierda, derecha, derecho
This way, that way	Por acá, por allá
Where is...?	¿Dónde está...?
...the bus station	...la camionera central (or el ADO)

...the nearest bank	...el banco más cercano
...the ATM	...el cajero automático
...the post office	...el correo
...the toilet	...el baño (or el sanitario)
Where does the bus to...leave from?	¿De dónde sale el autobus para...?
I'd like a(return) ticket to...	Quisiera un boleto (de ida y vuelta) para...
What time does it leave (arrive in...)?	¿A qué hora sale (llega en...)?
What is there to eat?	¿Qué hay para comer?
What's that?	¿Qué es eso?
What's this called in Spanish?	¿Cómo se llama éste en español?

Numbers and days

1	un/uno/una
2	dos
3	tres
4	cuatro
5	cinco
6	seis
7	siete
8	ocho
9	nueve
10	diez
11	once
12	doce
13	trece
14	catorce
15	quince
16	dieciséis
17	diecisiete
20	veinte
21	veintiuno
30	treinta
40	cuarenta
50	cincuenta
60	sesenta
70	setenta

80	ochenta
90	noventa
100	cien(to)
101	ciento uno
200	doscientos
500	quinientos
700	setecientos
1000	mil
2000	dos mil
first	primero/a
second	segundo/a
third	tercero/a
fifth	quinto/a
tenth	decimo/a
Monday	lunes
Tuesday	martes
Wednesday	miércoles
Thursday	jueves
Friday	viernes
Saturday	sábado
Sunday	domingo

Yucatec Maya basics

Yucatec is the variant of Maya spoken throughout the Yucatán Peninsula and northern Belize. (Maya in Chiapas and Guatemala speak other variants: Tzotzil, Tzeltal, Quiché and others.) An estimated one million people speak Yucatec, whether in small villages in central Yucatán State (which has the highest number of native Yucatec speakers) or on the city streets of Mérida. Most Maya are also at least conversant in Spanish, but they will generally appreciate any effort you make to communicate in their language. If you are interested in learning more, look for Gary Bevington's *Maya for Travelers and Students*, which provides a good introduction to the structure of the language, with a basic dictionary, as well as commentary on Maya culture, or John Montgomery's smaller *Maya Dictionary and Phrasebook*. In Mexico, you may be able to find *Metodo Fácil para Leer, Escribir y Hablar la Lengua Maya*, by Jésus Rivero Azcorra and published in Mérida; it has English translations as well, and supplies more complete phrases than Bevington's book, though many are obscure – "Clean out that iguana", for instance.

For pronunciation, spelling here reflects the modern academic style, and is fairly phonetic. An X is spoken as "sh", and an apostrophe is a light glottal stop, or pause. Draw out double vowels, and try to keep stress equal on all syllables.

What's up?	Ba'ax ka wa'alik?	**See you tomorrow**	Samaal
Not much	Mixba'al		
How are you?	Biix a beel?	**Yes**	He'le'
I'm fine	Ma'aloob	**No**	Ma'
Where are you going?	Tu'ux ka bin?	**I**	Ten
		You	Tech
I am going to Mérida	Inka' bin a Ho	**Is there...?**	Yan he'...?
		There is...	Yan...
What's your name?	Ba'ax a k'aaba'?	**There is no...**	Mina'an.../ Na'am...
My name is...	In k'aaba'(e)...		
Where are you from?	Tu'ux ka tah?	**What's that?**	Ba'ax lela'?
		How much?	Bahuux?
Let's go	Ko'osh	**Thank you**	Dyos bo'otik
See you later	Ka'ka't(e)	**You're welcome**	Mixba'al
		Bon appétit!	Hach ki' a wi'ih!

Food and drink terms

On the table

Azúcar	Sugar	**Pimienta**	Pepper
Cuchara	Spoon	**Queso**	Cheese
Cuchillo	Knife	**Sal**	Salt
Cuenta	Bill/check	**Salsa**	Sauce
Mantequilla	Butter	**Servilleta**	Napkin
Pan	Bread	**Tenedor**	Fork

Cooking terms

A la parilla	Grilled over charcoal	**A la tampiqueña**	Thin strips of meat served with guacamole
A la plancha	Grilled on a hot plate		

A la veracruzana	Stewed with tomatoes, onions, olives and chile	Empanizado/a	Breaded
		En mojo de ajo	Fried with slow-cooked garlic
Al horno/horneado	Baked		
Asado/a	Broiled	Frito	Fried
Barbacoa/pibil	Wrapped in leaves and herbs and steamed/cooked in a pit	Poco hecho/a punto/ bien cocido	Rare/medium/well-done
Con mole	In rich *mole* sauce; *mole poblano* (with bitter chocolate) is the most common		

Breakfast (desayuno)

Chilaquiles	Tortilla strips with shredded chicken and tomato sauce	...motuleños	...fried, served on a tortilla with tomato sauce, ham, cheese and fried sweet plantains
Huevos...	Eggs...		
...a la mexicana	...scrambled with tomato, onion and chile	...rancheros	...fried, on a tortilla, smothered in a red chile sauce
...con jamón	...with ham		
...con tocino	...with bacon	...revueltos	...scrambled
		...tibios	...lightly boiled
		Pan dulce	Pastries

Soups (sopas) and starters (entradas)

Botana	Any snack served with drinks; given free at traditional bars	Pozole	Stew of hominy (soft, hulled corn kernels) and pork
Caldo	Broth (with bits in)	Sopa...	Soup...
Ceviche	Raw fish pieces, marinated in lime juice and mixed with tomato and coriander	...de fideos	...with noodles
		...de frijoles	...creamy black-bean soup
		...de verduras	...vegetable soup
Entremeses	Hors d'oeuvres		

Snacks (antojitos)

Burritos	Wheat-flour tortillas, rolled and filled	Flauta	Small, filled, fried tortilla
		Huarache	Chewy, thick oblong corn tortilla topped with assorted meats
Chile relleno	Mild green chile stuffed with meat or cheese and fried in batter		
		Molletes	Split roll covered in beans and melted cheese
Enchilada	Rolled-up taco, covered in chile sauce and baked	Panucho	Like a *salbute*, but with black beans as well
Enchilada suiza	As above, with green chile and cheese	Quesadilla	Toasted or fried tortilla stuffed with cheese

Queso fundido	Melted cheese, served with tortillas and salsa	Taco dorado	Deep-fried meat taco
Salbute	Crisp-fried tortilla topped with shredded turkey, lettuce, avocado and pickled onions	Tamal	Corn husk or banana-leaf packet of steamed corn-meal dough with a savoury or sweet filling
Taco	Soft corn tortilla with filling	Torta	Bread roll filled with meat, lettuce and avocado
Taco al pastor	Taco filled with spicy pork, often served with a slice of pineapple	Tostadas	Flat crisp tortillas piled with meat and salad

Fish and seafood (pescados y mariscos)

Calamares	Squid	Corvina	Sea bass
Camarón	Prawn	Filete entero	Whole, filleted fish
Cangrejo	Crab	Huachinango	Red snapper
Caracol	Conch	Langosta	Rock lobster
Cazón	Baby shark	Merluza	Hake
Coctel	Seafood served in a tall glass with spicy tomato sauce and avocado	Ostión	Oyster
		Pez espada	Swordfish
		Pulpo	Octopus
		Sábalo	Tarpon

Meat (carne) and poultry (aves)

Alambre	Kebab	Filete	Tenderloin or fillet
Albóndigas	Meatballs	Guisado	Stew
Arrachera	Skirt steak	Hígado	Liver
Barbacoa	Barbecued meat	Lengua	Tongue
Bistec	Steak (not always beef)	Lomo	Loin (of pork)
Cabeza	Head	Milanesa	Breaded escalope
Cabrito	Kid	Pata	Foot (usually pig's)
Carne...	Meat	Pato	Duck
...de res	Beef	Pavo/Guajolote	Turkey
...adobado	Barbecued or spicily stewed meat	Pechuga	Breast
		Pierna	Leg
Carnitas	Pork cooked with garlic until crispy	Pollo	Chicken
		Salchicha	Sausage or hot dog
Cerdo	Pork	Salpicón	Shredded beef and sliced radishes seasoned with vinegar
Chivo	Goat		
Chorizo	Spicy sausage		
Chuleta	Chop (usually pork)		
Codorniz	Quail	Ternera	Veal
Conejo	Rabbit	Tripa	Tripe
Cordero	Lamb	Venado	Venison
Costilla	Rib		

Vegetables (verduras)

Aguacate	Avocado	Flor de calabaza	Squash blossoms
Arroz	Rice	Frijoles	Beans
Betabel	Beetroot	Huitlacoche	Corn fungus
Calabacita	Zucchini (courgette)		("Mexican truffles")
Calabaza	Squash	Jitomate	Tomato
Cebolla	Onion	Lechuga	Lettuce
Champiñones/	Mushrooms	Lentejas	Lentils
hongos		Nopales	Cactus leaves
Chícharos	Peas	Papas	Potatoes
Col	Cabbage	Pepino	Cucumber
Elote	Corn on the cob	Rajas	Strips of mild green
Espárrago	Asparagus		poblano pepper
Espinacas	Spinach	Zanahoria	Carrot

Fruit (fruta) and juice (jugo)

Albaricoque/	Apricot	Melón	Melon
chabacano		Naranja	Orange
Cherimoya	Custard apple	Papaya	Papaya
	(sweetsop)	Piña	Pineapple
China	Orange (only in	Pitahaya	Dragonfruit, a type of
	Yucatán)		cactus fruit
Ciruela	Plum	Plátano	Banana/plantain
Coco	Coconut	Sandía	Watermelon
Durazno	Peach	Toronja	Grapefruit
Frambuesa	Raspberry	Tuna	Prickly pear, a type of
Fresa	Strawberry		cactus fruit
Guanábana	Soursop	Uva	Grape
Guayaba	Guava	Zapote	Sapodilla, fruit of the
Higo	Fig		*chicle* tree; similar to
Limón	Lime		*mamey*
Mamey	Fruit with sweet		
	pink-orange flesh		

Drinks (bebidas)

Agua...	Water	Licuado	Blended fruit drink
...mineral/con gas	Sparkling water	(Mi)chelada	Beer with (spicy) lime
...normal/sin gas	Still water		juice, ice and salt
Café de olla	Mexican-style coffee	Horchata	Creamy rice-milk
	brewed in a clay pot		drink, sometimes
			with coconut
Cerveza	Beer	Té	Tea
Jamaica	Cold drink of steeped	Vino	Wine
	hibiscus flowers		

Sweets (dulces)

Cajeta...	Caramel confection, often served with...	**Ensalada de frutas**	Fruit salad
...crepas	...pancakes	**Flan**	Crème caramel
...churros	...cinnamon-covered fritters	**Helado**	Ice cream
		Nieve	Sorbet
Champola	Ice cream or sorbet in a tall glass filled with milk	**Paleta**	Fruit popsicle/ice lolly
		Raspada	Shaved ice with fruit syrup

Yucatecan specialities

Achiote	Spice paste made with orange annatto seeds, cloves, onion and garlic	**Puchero**	Meaty stew with sweet potato, seasoned with cinnamon and allspice
Adobo	Chile-based spice paste similar to *achiote*	**Queso relleno**	Round of Dutch cheese hollowed out and filled with a spicy fruit-meat filling, topped with cream sauce
Brazo de reina	Large tamale filled with hard-cooked eggs and green pumpkin-seed paste		
Cochinita pibil	Suckling pig seasoned with *achiote*, wrapped in banana leaves and slow-roasted in a pit	**Sikil-p'aak**	Spicy ground-pumpkin-seed dip
		Sopa de lima	Broth with shredded chicken or turkey, tortilla strips and *lima*, an especially fragrant lime-like citrus
Habañero	Small, extremely hot chile pepper, made into red and green salsas		
Mondongo kabic	Tripe stewed in *achiote* and bitter orange and green onions	**Tikin xic**	Fish with *achiote* and spices wrapped in banana leaves and grilled
Papadzules	Enchiladas filled with hard-cooked eggs, topped with green pumpkin-seed sauce	**Xnipek**	Raw *habañero* salsa; literally, "dog's nose" for the sweat it induces
Poc-chuc	Pork marinated in citrus juice, then grilled		
Pollo en relleno negro	Chicken in a black, slightly burnt chile sauce		

Glossary

Ahorita diminutive of *ahora* (now) meaning "right now", but seldom applied as literally as a visitor might expect.

Artesonado intricate ceiling design, usually of jointed, inlaid wood.

Atlantean pre-Hispanic column in the form of a warrior.

Auto-da-fé a public act of repentance, usually involving punishment or execution, and a product of the Inquisition; see p.276.

Ayuntamiento city hall and/or city government.

Azulejo decorative glazed tile, usually blue and white.

Barrio area within a town or city; suburb.

Cambio foreign-currency exchange operation.

Camino blanco unpaved rural road, so called because it is paved with white limestone gravel.

Cantina bar, usually men-only.

Caseta telephone office.

Ceiba large tropical silk-cotton tree; also, the sacred tree of the Maya that represents the world.

Cenote natural sinkhole and underground water source.

Chac Maya god of rain.

Chac-mool stone statue of a recumbent figure who may represent a sacrificial victim or a messenger to the gods.

Chultun underground cistern.

Churrigueresque highly elaborate, decorative form of Baroque architecture (found chiefly in churches), named after the seventeenth-century Spanish architect José Churriguera.

Colectivo shared van that provides service between towns.

Colonia neighbourhood or district.

Comal large, round, flat plate made of clay or metal and used for cooking tortillas.

Combi van that runs on fixed routes, much like a city bus.

Comedor cheap restaurant, literally "dining room"; also called a *cocina económica*.

Convento convent or monastery.

Corbel arch the distinctive Maya "false" arch, in which overlapping stones are stacked to meet at the top, forming a narrow, triangular shape.

Cruzob Maya followers of the Talking Cross, a nativist political movement founded during the Caste Wars of the nineteenth century.

Descompuesto out of order.

Don/Doña Sir/Madam (titles of courtesy used chiefly in letters, for professionals or when addressing the boss).

Ejido communally owned farmland or village property.

EPR Ejército Popular Revolucionario (the Popular Revolutionary Army), a guerrilla group not allied with the Zapatistas.

Escudo shield, coat-of-arms or shield-shaped decoration.

EZLN Ejército Zapatista de Liberación Nacional (the Zapatista Army of National Liberation).

Feria fair or market.

FONART government agency to promote crafts.

FONATUR government tourism agency.

Fray friar.

Gringo/a white man or woman, used chiefly of North Americans, not necessarily intended as an insult; thought to originate with US troops, either because they wore green coats or because they sang "Green grow the rushes oh!".

Guayabera embroidered Cuban-style shirt, usually for men.

Güera/o blonde; also, a Westerner, a white man or woman; though often shouted after women in the street, not usually intended as an insult.

Hacienda plantation estate or the big house on it.

Hacendado plantation owner.

Henequen variety of agave cactus whose fibres are used to make rope.

Huipil Maya women's embroidered white smock dress or blouse, worn over a white petticoat.

IVA fifteen percent value-added tax (VAT).

Jarana popular dance blending Maya and Spanish styles.

Kukulkán Maya name for Quetzalcoatl, the feathered-serpent god.

Ladino (of people) Spanish-influenced as opposed to Indian; used chiefly with reference to clothing or culture rather than race.

Licenciado common title, literally "graduate" or "licensed"; abbreviated Lic.

Malecón seafront promenade.

Mariachi quintessentially Mexican music, with lots of brass and sentimental lyrics; originated in northern Mexico, and not particularly widespread in the Yucatán; see *trova*.

Maya people who inhabited Honduras, Guatemala, Belize and southeastern Mexico from around the second millennium BC, and still do.

Mestizaje the process that created mestizos: the birth of the first child to a Spaniard and a Maya, synonymous with the creation of modern Mexico.

Mestizo mixed race; of Indian and Spanish descent.

Metate flat stone for grinding corn; used with a *mano*, a grinding stone.

Milpa small subsistence farm plot, tended with slash-and-burn agricultural practices.

Mirador lookout point.

Mudéjar Spanish architectural style strongly influenced by Moorish forms.

Muelle jetty or dock.

NAFTA North American Free Trade Agreement.

Palacio mansion (not necessarily royal).

Palacio de Gobierno headquarters of the state or federal authorities.

Palacio Municipal headquarters of the local government.

Palapa palm thatch; also, any thatched-roof hut.

PAN Partido de Acción Nacional (National Action Party), a conservative party that took power when Vicente Fox became president in 2000, though it is now losing momentum.

Paseo broad avenue; also, a ritual evening walk around a plaza.

PEMEX Mexican national oil company.

Pila font or water basin; also commonly found in domestic buildings.

Planta baja ground floor; abbreviated PB in lifts.

Plateresque decorative style of the Spanish Renaissance, named for its resemblance to fine work in silver (*plata*).

Porfiriato the three decades of Porfirio Díaz's dictatorship.

Portal arcade; plural *portales*.

PRD Partido Revolucionario Democrático (Party of the Democratic Revolution), the left-wing opposition formed and led by Cuauhtémoc Cárdenas, which has the second largest number of seats in Congress.

PRI Partido Revolucionario Institucional (Party of the Institutional Revolution), the ruling party for eighty years until the PAN upset in the 1999 elections.

PT Partido del Trabajo (Workers' Party), a small party with opposition seats in Congress.

PVEM Partido Verde Ecologista de México (Green Party), a small opposition party.

Quetzalcoatl feathered-serpent god of the Toltec and Aztec civilizations.

Roofcomb decorative structure above the roof of a building, common in ancient Maya architecture.

Sacbé ancient Maya road, paved with limestone; plural *sacbeob*.

Stele freestanding carved monument; plural *stelae*.

TLC Tratado de Libre Comercio, the Spanish name for NAFTA.

Toltec people who controlled central Mexico after the Teotihuacán and before the Aztecs.

Tope speed bump or other barrier for slowing traffic on rural roads.

Trova romantic Yucatecan song style popular in the early twentieth century and still played by *trovadores*.

Tzompantli Aztec skull rack, or "wall of skulls".

Small print and

Index

A Rough Guide to Rough Guides

Published in 1982, the first Rough Guide – to Greece – was a student scheme that became a publishing phenomenon. Mark Ellingham, a recent graduate in English from Bristol University, had been travelling in Greece the previous summer and couldn't find the right guidebook. With a small group of friends he wrote his own guide, combining a highly contemporary, journalistic style with a thoroughly practical approach to travellers' needs.

The immediate success of the book spawned a series that rapidly covered dozens of destinations. And, in addition to impecunious backpackers, Rough Guides soon acquired a much broader and older readership that relished the guides' wit and inquisitiveness as much as their enthusiastic, critical approach and value-for-money ethos.

These days, Rough Guides include recommendations from shoestring to luxury and cover more than 200 destinations around the globe, including almost every country in the Americas and Europe, more than half of Africa and most of Asia and Australasia. Our ever-growing team of authors and photographers is spread all over the world, particularly in Europe, the US and Australia.

In the early 1990s, Rough Guides branched out of travel, with the publication of Rough Guides to World Music, Classical Music and the Internet. All three have become benchmark titles in their fields, spearheading the publication of a wide range of books under the Rough Guide name.

Including the travel series, Rough Guides now number more than 350 titles, covering: phrasebooks, waterproof maps, music guides from Opera to Heavy Metal, reference works as diverse as Conspiracy Theories and Shakespeare, and popular culture books from iPods to Poker. Rough Guides also produce a series of more than 120 World Music CDs in partnership with World Music Network.

Visit www.roughguides.com to see our latest publications.

SMALL PRINT

Rough Guide credits

Text editor: Tim Locke
Layout: Ankur Guha
Cartography: Animesh Pathak
Picture editor: Natascha Sturny
Production: Rebecca Short
Proofreader: Anita Sach
Cover design: Nicole Newman, Dan May
Photographer: Dan Bannister, Sarah Cummins
Editorial: London Andy Turner, Keith Drew, Edward Aves, Alice Park, Lucy White, Jo Kirby, James Smart, Natasha Foges, James Rice, Emma Beatson, Emma Gibbs, Kathryn Lane, Monica Woods, Mani Ramaswamy, Harry Wilson, Alison Roberts, Lara Kavanagh, Eleanor Aldridge, Ian Blenkinsop, Charlotte Melville, Joe Staines, Matthew Milton, Tracy Hopkins; **Delhi** Madhavi Singh, Jalpreen Kaur Chhatwal, Dipika Dasgupta
Design & Pictures: London Scott Stickland, Dan May, Diana Jarvis, Mark Thomas,

Nicole Newman, Rhiannon Furbear; **Delhi** Umesh Aggarwal, Ajay Verma, Jessica Subramanian, Pradeep Thapliyal, Sachin Tanwar, Anita Singh, Nikhil Agarwal, Sachin Gupta
Production: Liz Cherry, Louise Minihane, Erika Pepe
Cartography: London Ed Wright, Katie Lloyd-Jones; **Delhi** Rajesh Chhibber, Ashutosh Bharti, Rajesh Mishra, Jasbir Sandhu, Swati Handoo, Deshpal Dabas, Lokamata Sahu
Marketing, Publicity & roughguides.com: Liz Statham
Digital Travel Publisher: Peter Buckley
Reference Director: Andrew Lockett
Operations Coordinator: Becky Doyle
Operations Assistant: Johanna Wurm
Publishing Director (Travel): Clare Currie
Commercial Manager: Gino Magnotta
Managing Director: John Duhigg

Publishing information

This third edition published September 2011 by
Rough Guides Ltd,
80 Strand, London WC2R 0RL
11, Community Centre, Panchsheel Park, New Delhi 110017, India
Distributed by the Penguin Group
Penguin Books Ltd,
80 Strand, London WC2R 0RL
Penguin Group (USA)
375 Hudson Street, NY 10014, USA
Penguin Group (Australia)
250 Camberwell Road, Camberwell, Victoria 3124, Australia
Penguin Group (NZ)
67 Apollo Drive, Mairangi Bay, Auckland 1310, New Zealand
Rough Guides is represented in Canada by Tourmaline Editions Inc. 662 King Street West, Suite 304, Toronto, Ontario M5V 1M7
Cover concept by Peter Dyer.
Typeset in Bembo and Helvetica to an original design by Henry Iles.

Help us update

We've gone to a lot of effort to ensure that the third edition of **The Rough Guide to Cancún and the Yucatán** is accurate and up-to-date. However, things change – places get "discovered", opening hours are notoriously fickle, restaurants and rooms raise prices or lower standards. If you feel we've got it wrong or left something out, we'd like to know, and if you can remember the address, the price, the hours, the phone number, so much the better.

Please send your comments with the subject line "**Rough Guide Cancún and the Yucatán Update**" to @mail@uk.roughguides.com. We'll credit all contributions and send a copy of the next edition (or any other Rough Guide if you prefer) for the very best emails.

Find more travel information, connect with fellow travellers and book your trip on ⓦwww.roughguides.com

Acknowledgements

Zora O'Neill: I would like to thank my usual excellent local informants, Jim and Ellen of YucatanLiving.com and Rob and Joanne Birce at Alma Libre Books (who also offered me hospitality); "Nanbec" (Nancy Manahan and Becky Bohan) for hospitality at Nauti Beach; Denis Larsen at Casa Hamaca, who introduced me to some great new food and people; the lovely staff at Ecoparaiso in Celestún; mi madre, Beverly, for being a trooper; my father, Patrick O'Neill, who gave me a good reason to slow down and put on the snorkel gear; Tim Locke and Keith Drew, for pulling it all together; and all the readers who took the time to send in corrections, tips and criticism.

John Fisher: my thanks for their assistance in updating this edition go to Justa and family in Mahahual, Rubi at Puerta Calakmul, Ricardo Romano, Massimiliano Palli, Jose Martin, Raphael Tunesi, Carolien van Santvoord, Sarah Evans and Carlos Sanchez Lira. Also to my indefatigable co-author Zora, and as ever to A and the two Js.

Photo credits

All photos © Rough Guides except the following:

Title page
Celebration flags © Ricardo De Mattos

Fullpage
Horse and carriage © Danita Delimont

Introduction
Flamingos © Minden Pictures/Superstock
Boys diving © Eye Ubiquitous/Superstock
Grinning wooden skulls © DC Premiumstock

Things not to miss
01 Palenque ruins © Michele Falzone/Alamy
02 Hacienda Temozon © Jean-Pierre Lescourret/Corbis
03 Mérida © Jean-Pierre Lescourret/Corbis
04 Sian Ka'an Biosphere Reserve © Andoni Canela/Superstock
05 Whale sharks © Reinhard Dirscherl/Alamy
06 Playa del Carmen nightlife © travelstock.ca/Alamy
07 Uxmal © Marek Zuk/Alamy
08 Campeche © John Elk III/Alamy
10 Cochinita pibil © David Sanger Photography/Alamy
11 Cenote Dzitnup © Richard T. Nowitz/Corbis
12 Hammocks © Zora O'Neill
14 Textiles © Melvyn Longhurst/Alamy
15 Yaxchilán © Zora O'Neill
16 Calakmul © Leonardo Diaz Romero/Superstock
17 Scuba diving © Michele Westmorland/Corbis

Yucatán food section
Taco shop © Frans Lemmens/Corbis
Salbuches © dbimages/Alamy

Chile sauce bottles © Stefano Paterna/Alamy
Produce market near Progreso © Amanda Friedman/Getty Images
Dutch cheese © Zora O'Neill
Candies © Zora O'Neill
Woman with tortillas © Paul Harris/Corbis

Maya culture section
Maya hieroglyph, Chiapas © Adalberto Szalay/Robert Harding
Day of the Dead © Zora O'Neill
Incense burner © Werner Forman/Corbis
Grotas de Loltún © Bruno Perousse/Superstock
Dancers in Mérida © Deborah Waters/Alamy
Maya woman cooking tortillas © Melvyn Longhurst/Corbis
Traditional Maya dress © Superstock
Fresco at Bonampak © Gianni Dagli Orti
Maya woman and daughters © Frans Lemmens

Black and whites
p.78 Crocodile lagoon © Danita Delimont/Getty Images/Gallo Images
p.106 Snorkeling at Xel-Há © Macduff Everton/Corbis
p.126 Spider monkey © Thane/Superstock
p.150 Convento de San Antonio de Padua © Cosmo Condina/Getty Images
p.172 Palacio de Gobierno, © Cosmo Condina/Getty Images
p.196 Mask of Chac, Sayil © DEA/C. Sappa/Getty Images/De Agostini
p.214 Edzná © DEA/C. Sappa/Getty Images/De Agostini
p.236 Olmec head © José Fuste Raga/Corbis

Index

Map entries are in colour.

A

Acancéh 196, 211
accommodation 27–29
addresses 26
Agua Azul 260
Agua Clara 260
airfares, international 19
airlines 21, 23
airpasses 21
Aké 170, 274
Aktun Chen 110
Akumal 109
alcohol 31
Allende, Ignacio 277
all-inclusive resorts 28
Alvarado, Salvador 280
ATMs 46
Ay, Manuel Antonio 279

B

Bacalar 134
Bahía de la Ascensión ... 123
Bahía Soliman 111
Balamkú 147
ball-game 288
Banco Chinchorro
    .... 126, 130
bargaining 40
Barrera, José María 129
baseball 37, 65, 98, 227
beaches 9, 61
Becal 218
Becán 144
Belize City 139
Belize, transport to 139
bikes 26
Bioparque Xla'kaj 158
birds 285–286
birdwatching ....
    37, 71, 75, 100, 122, 133,
    134, 159, 160, 285
black coral 81, 283
Boca Paila 124
Bocas de Dzilam 192
Bolonchén 232
Bonampak 236, 255
books 290–296
border crossings 21
bribery 42

British Honduras (Belize)
    .... 129, 276, 279
bullfights 34
buses 21, 23, 26

C

cabañas 29
cacao 239–241, 284
Calakmul 16, 126,
    146, *Maya culture* colour
    section
Calakmul Biosphere
    Reserve 126, 146–148
Calderitas 138
Calderón, Felipe 282
Calles, Plutarco Elías 281
calling cards 46
CAMPECHE 14, 214,
    220–228
Campeche State 216
Central Campeche 220
    accommodation 222
    airport 221
    buses 221, 228
    eating and drinking 226
    history 221
    tourist information 221
    tours 222, 228
camping 29
CANCÚN 53–66
Cancún, Isla Mujeres & Isla
    Holbox 54
Downtown Cancún 57
Zona Hotelera 60
    accommodation 56–58
    addresses 56
    airport 55
    arrival 55
    beaches 61
    buses 56, 65
    downtown Cancún 58
    eating 61–63
    entertainment and nightlife
    .... 58, 63–65
    history 55
    listings 66
    ruins 59
    shopping 66
    sport 65
    tourist information 56
    tours 60, 66
    transport 56
    watersports 60–61
    zona hotelera 59–61

Candelaria 232
car rental 24
Cárdenas, Lázaro 281
Carnaval 33–34
Carretera Fronteriza 254
Caste Wars 116,
    129, 175, 278–280, *Maya
    culture* colour section
cave diving 36, 111
caves 36, 90, 208, 211,
    218, 232, 289
ceiba tree 287
Celestún 10, 172,
    193
cenotes 14,
    36, 84, 90, 106, 110, 111,
    119, 121, 134, 155, 157,
    158, 159, 167, 191, 196,
    211, 283, 289, 296
    Azul (Bacalar) 134
    Azul (Tulum) 111
    Boca del Puma 84
    Bolonchoojol 212
    Carwash 119
    Chansinic'ché 212
    Chelentún 212
    Choo-Ha 121
    Cobá 121
    Cristal 119
    Cristalino 111
    Dos Ojos 110
    Dzitnup 157
    Escondido 119
    Gran Cenote 119
    Hidden Worlds 110
    Jardín del Edén 111
    Las Mojarras 84
    Los Tres Cenotes 211
    Manatí 111
    Multún-Ha 121
    Ox Bel Ha 111
    Ruta de los Cenotes 84
    Sagrado Azul 163
    Sagrado 166
    Samula 157
    Siete Bocas 84
    Suytun 158
    Tak Be Ha 110
    Tankah-Ha 121
    Verde Lucero 84
    X'keken 157
    Xcanché 159
    Xel-Há 110
    Xlacah 191
    Yokdzonot 167
    Zací 155
Chacchoben 133–134
Champotón 233

Chan Bahlum.... see Jaguar Serpent
Chan Muan................255
Chan Santa Cruz
.... 129, 279
chaya.......31, Yucatán food colour section
Chelem 193
Chenes sites...........16, 231
Chenes style.........205, 230
CHETUMAL 135–139
Chetumal.....................136
 accommodation 136
 airport............................. 136
 buses 136, 139
 duty-free zone................. 135
 eating and drinking........137
 market............................ 137
 tourist information...........136
 tours 138
Chi, Cecilio 279
Chiapas 237
Chiapas & Tabasco 238
Chicanná 145
CHICHÉN ITZÁ
.... 15, 161–167, 273
Chichén Itzá................162
 accommodation 163
 airport............................. 161
 buses 167
 eating 163
 entrances 161
 tourist information...........161
 tours 161
Chicxulub Puerto 192
Chilam Balam 119, 134, 287, 292
children, travelling with... 40
chiles ....29, Yucatán food colour section
chocolate...........................
 241, 284 & Yucatán food colour section
Chuburná.....................193
Chumayel 209
Chunkanán 211
Chunyaxché 124
Ciudad del Carmen
.... 233–244
climate change..............20
climate......................9, 283
Cobá ....
 5, 106, 119–121, Maya culture colour section
Cocom Dynasty............210
coffee.......31, Yucatán food colour section
colectivos 24
Colombia Deep 101
Colombia Shallows
..............................78, 101

Comalcalco 239
combis...........................26
Congress of Chilpancingo
...................................277
Conrad, Jim.................161
consulates 43
Convento de San Antonio de Padua, Izamal
.... 2, 150, 169
cookbooks....................294
coral reef etiquette 37
Cordoba, Francisco Hernández de............274
corn 30
Corozal, Belize 139
Cortés, Hernán 274
Costa Maya
.... 127, 130–133
Costa Maya & the Río Bec, The 128
costs.......................27, 41
Cozumel ...see Isla Cozumel
crafts 15, 39, 267
credit cards 46
crime.............................41
cruise ships 21
Cruzob...............128, 129
culture and etiquette 38
Cupilco 241
currency.........................45
Cuzamá 211
cycling 26

Day of the Dead ....34, Maya culture colour section
de Landa, Diego
..........169, 209, 276, 292
de las Casas, Bartolomé
...................................275
dengue fever 44
dialling codes 46
Díaz, Porfirio 280
disabilities, travellers with
....................................48
diving..... 16, 36, 61, 71, 83, 90, 101, 111, 133
drink.............................31
driving licences.............25
driving..........................24
drug-running.................281
drugs 42
Dzibanché....................140
Dzibilchaltún 172, 190
Dzibilchaltún 191

Dzibilnocac..................231
Dzilam de Bravo 192

E

Ecopark Kantun-Chi.....110
eco-resorts 28
Edzná..........214, 228–231
Edzná 229
ejido 282
Ek-Balam.............150, 151, 158, Maya culture colour section
El Tabasqueño..............231
El Tigre 232
electric current 42
embassies 43
emergency numbers.......42
environment.................283
Escárcega....................234

F

Faro Celarain Eco Park, Cozumel 78, 99
Felipe Carrillo Puerto
...................................128
festivals 33–35
fiestas 33–35
fish and marine life.......285
fishing 36, 75, 83, 110, 123, 133, 233
Flamingos 75, 160, 192, 193
flights, internal...............23
flights, international.........19
food.................................
 29–32, 302–306, Yucatán food colour section
food and drink terms.........
 302–306
football...........................37
fortified churches
...........................196, 208
Fox Quesada, Vicente
...................................282
Francisco de Montejo
...........................181, 274
Francisco de Montejo the Younger 175, 181, 221, 275
Francisco Escárcega...234
Frontera Corozal... 257–259
Frontera, Tabasco.........238
Frontier Highway 254

G

gay travellers 43
geography 283
glossary 307
Grutas de Balankanché
.....................................167
Grutas de Calcehtok
............................214, 218
Grutas de Loltún........196,
208, *Maya culture* colour
section
Grutas de Tzabnah.......211
Grutas de
X'tacumbilxuna'an 214,
232
Grutas de Xpukil
.... 214, 218
Guatemala 139, 275
guayaberas 39, 174

H

haciendas 12, 28, 170,
179, 196, 197–200, 276,
280, 281
  Blanca Flor......................219
  Chichén.................. 161, 163
  Cholula............................241
  Chunkanán......................211
  Mundaca 69
  Ochil...............................199
  San José 170
  San Lorenzo de Aké 170
  Santa Rosa 218
  Sotuta de Peón 211
  Tabi.................................256
  Temozón.........................199
  Tepich.............................212
  Uayamón 230
  Xcanatun 180
  Yaxcopoil........................198
hammocks.........15, 39, 66,
157, 170, 185, 220
Hanab Pakal ..... *see* Jaguar
Shield
health.............................43
Hecelchakán................219
Henequen 199, 200, 278
Hidalgo y Costilla, Father
Miguel 277
Hidden Worlds..............110
hiking 37
history 271–282
  Caste Wars...............278–280
  Classic period 272
  colonial rule....................275
  dictatorship 280
  independence 277, 278
  modern Yucatán...............281
  Post-Classic society 273
  Pre-Classic Maya.............271
  Prehistory 271
  revolution 280
  Spanish Conquest 274
  twentieth century 280–282
  twenty-first century 282
hitching...........................26
Hochob..................14, 231
holidays, public 46
Hopelchén....................231
Hormiguero...................144
hostels 29
hotels.............................27
huipiles 39, 174
human sacrifice............289
Hurricane Dean 130, 283
hurricanes.................9, 283

I

Iglesia de San Bernardino
de Siena 150, 154
independence, Mexican
....................................277
independence, Yucatán
....................................278
insects 284
insurance......................44
Internet access.............44
Isla Aguada..................233
Isla Contoy............52, 61,
71
ISLA COZUMEL 94–104
  accommodation 96
  airport............................. 95
  beaches and beach clubs
 99–101
  Carnaval........................... 95
  Colombia Shallows 101
  cruiseships 94, 95
  diving...................... 99, 101
  drinking and nightlife 103
  eating 102
  Faro Celarain Eco Park...... 99
  ferries 95
  history 94
  museum 97
  Parque Chankanaab 99
  reefs 101
  ruins 100
  San Gervasio................... 100
  San Miguel 97
  snorkeling 99, 100,
  101, 102
  tourist information............. 95
  transport..................... 95, 96
Isla de Jaina 215,
219, *Maya culture* colour
section
ISLA HOLBOX 73–76
  accommodation 74
  buses 73
  eating and drinking 75
  ferries 74
  fishing.............................. 75
  snorkelling....................... 75
  whale sharks 75, 76
ISLA MUJERES.......66–73
Isla Mujeres...................67
  accommodation 68
  diving............................... 71
  eating and drinking 72
  ferries 67
  Punta Norte...................... 69
  snorkelling....................... 71
  tourist information............. 67
  transport........................... 67
Isla Pájaros 75
Iturbide, Agustín de......277
Itzá..............................273
Izamal .... 168–170, *Maya
culture* colour section

J

Jaguar Paw 146, 147,
226
Jaguar Serpent.....250, 273
Jaguar Shield 250, 273
Jaina figurines 219,
226, *Maya culture* colour
section
jarana 33, 187, 293,
Maya culture colour
section
Jardín Botánico Dr Marín
.....................................84
Juárez, Benito 280

K

Kabáh 206
Kantun-Chi 110
Kinich Kakmó, Izamal
....................................169
Kinichná........................141
kiteboarding..............36, 61
Kohunlich..............126, 141

L

La Quinta Avenida.........78,
89, 92
Labná...........................207

Lacandón Maya.......... 257,
   Maya culture colour
   section
Lacanhá ruins............... 256
Lacanjá Chansayab..... 256,
   257
Laguna Bacalar.......... 126,
   133–135
language classes............. 45
Las Coloradas 161
laundry............................ 45
League of Mayapán..... 202,
   210
Lerma 226
lesbian travellers............. 43
Los Tres Cenotes 211
Luxury hotels................. 82

M

Madero, Francisco 280
Mahahual..... 126, 130–132
mail................................. 45
malaria........................... 44
Mamá............................ 209
mammals...................... 286
mangroves........ 12, 60, 84,
   122, 124, 192, 193
Maní..................... 209, 275
maps.............................. 45
marine life.................... 285
markets........................... 40
Maxcanú....................... 218
Maya beliefs 287
Maya calendar...... 164, 268
Maya gods.................... 288
Mayapán............... 210, 274
meals (times) 31
media............................ 33
MÉRIDA 173–190
Mérida, Central 177
Mérida & around... 174–175
   accommodation 179
   airport............................ 176
   bicycles 179
   buses 178, 188
   dance 187
   drinking, entertainment and
      nightlife 12, 187
   eating 185
   history 175
   Museo de Antropología
      183
   Plaza de la Independencia
      180
   shopping 184, 189
   tourist information.....176–178
   tours......................... 178, 190
   transport......................... 178

Mesoamerican Barrier Reef
   .... 16, 81
mestizaje........ 137, 139,182
"Mexican time".............. 38
Misol-Há.............. 236, 259
mobile phones............... 46
money............................. 45
monkeys 13, 121, 122,
   126, 146, 258, 286
Morelos, José María..... 277
museums
   Baluarte de San Francisco,
      Campeche 225
   Casa Catherwood, Mérida
      184
   Casa de los Venados,
      Valladolid 154
   Casa Museo Montes Molina,
      Mérida........................... 183
   Centro Cultural de las Bellas
      Artes, Chetumal........... 137
   Centro Cultural y Artesanal,
      Izamal 169
   Centro de Artes Visuales,
      Mérida........................... 182
   CICOM 244
   Fuerte de San José,
      Campeche 226
   MACAY, Mérida.............. 181
   Maqueta Payo Obispo,
      Chetumal....................... 137
   Museo Arqueológco,
      Campeche 226
   Museo Arqueológico del
      Camino Real, Hecelchaká
      219
   Museo de Arte Popular,
      Mérida........................... 183
   Museo de Historia de Tabasco,
      Villahermosa.................. 244
   Museo de la Arquitectura
      Maya, Campeche 224
   Museo de la Canción
      Yucateca, Mérida.......... 184
   Museo de la Ciudad,
      Campeche 225
   Museo de la Ciudad, Mérida
      184
   Museo de la Cultura Maya,
      Chetumal 137
   Museo de la Guerra Castas,
      Tihosuco 129
   Museo de la Iglesia de San
      Bernardino de Siena,
      Valladolid 154
   Museo de la Isla de Cozumel
      97
   Museo de San Roque,
      Valladolid 154
   Museo del Pueblo Maya,
      Dzibilchaltún 190
   Museo Regional de
      Antropología, Mérida.... 183
   Pinacoteca del Estado Juan
      Gamboa Guzmán, Mérida
      182

music 293
Muyil 124

N

Nadzcaan 148
newspapers.................... 33
Nueva España 275

O

Ocosingo 260
oil industry............ 233, 281
Olmecs 236, 244,
   271, 287
online flight booking....... 21
opening hours 46
Orange Walk, Belize 139
Orozco, Pascual 280
overland travel............... 20
Oxkintok 216
Oxkutzcab 208
Oxtankah 139

P

Paamul 108
PALENQUE.................. 11,
   236, 247–254, 273, *Maya
   culture* colour section
Palenque Ruins 252
Palenque Town 248
   accommodation 248
   buses 247, 253
   eating and drinking 249
   museum (ruins)................ 253
   ruins 250–254
   textile museum................ 247
   tourist office 247
   tours 250
panama hats.......... 39, 218
Pantanos de Centla
   Biosphere Reserve
   ....236, 239
Paraíso 239
Parque Chankanaab,
   Cozumel 99
Parque de las Palapas,
   Cancún 52, 58
Parque La Venta,
   Villahermosa 236, 244,
   271
Parque Punta Sur......... *see*
   Faro Celarain Eco Park

Pat, Jacinto 130, 279
Payo Obispo.................135
pharmacies....................43
phones.........................46
photography 47
pirates.....69, 221, 222, 276
Pisté....................161, 167
Placer 131
PLAYA DEL CARMEN
........................13, 86–94
Playa del Carmen 87
Playa del Carmen &
  Cozumel 80
    accommodation 88
    airstrip 88
    beaches..............................90
    bicycles 88
    buses 88, 93
    diving..................................90
    drinking and nightlife 13,
      92–93
    eating 91
    ferries 88, 95
    kiteboarding 90
    Playacar 90
    shopping 93
    tourist information...............88
Playa Delfines, Cancún
........................52, 61
Playa Limón 239
Playa Xcacel........106, 111
Playacar.........................90
police...........................42
Popol Vuh 294
post 45
PRI.......................281, 308
price codes....................27
Progreso 173, 191–192
Puerto Aventuras..........107
PUERTO MORELOS
................................80–86
Puerto Morelos 83
    accommodation 81
    bars 85
    buses 81, 85
    cenotes 84
    crafts 83, 84
    diving..................................83
    eating and drinking 85
    fishing.................................83
    snorkelling..........................83
    tourist information...............81
Puerto Morelos Reef 83
Punta Allen 106, 123
Punta Bete.....................86
Punta Cancún................59
Punta Cancún 62
Punta Herrero 131
Punta Laguna 106, 121
Punta Norte....................70
Puuc architectural style
.... see Ruta Puuc

R

radio stations.................33
rain............................9, 283
rainfall, average 10
religion...........................38
reptiles.........................285
Reserva de Monos Arañas
  de Punta Laguna 106,
  121
revolution, Mexican 153,
  280, 282
Ría Celestún Biosphere
  Reserve.................10, 193
Ría Lagartos Biosphere
  Reserve.............150, 160
Río Bec sites....................
  16, 127, 140–145, Maya
  culture colour section
Río Bec.......................142
Río Grijalva 241
Río Hondo 126, 140
Río Lagartos 160
Río Secreto....................90
Río Shumulhá.............. 260
Riviera Maya.......9, 79, 107
rules of the road 25
Ruta de los Cenotes.......84
Ruta de los Conventos ....
  196, 197, 199, 208–212
Ruta Puuc........................
  16, 199, 204–208, Maya
  culture colour section

S

Sabancuy 233
salsa ....see Yucatán food
  colour section
San Crisanto................192
**SAN CRISTÓBAL DE LAS
  CASAS** 15, 264–268
San Cristóbal de las Casas
........................266
    accommodation 264
    bicycles 268
    buses 264, 268
    crafts 267
    eating and drinking
   266–268
    Templo de Santo Domingo
   265
    tourist information............264
    tours 268
San Felipe....................160
San Gervasio, Cozumel
....................................100

San Miguel, Cozumel
....97
San Miguel, Cozumel 98
Santa Elena 204
Santa Rosa Xtampak
....232
Santo Domingo de
  Palenque.... see Palenque
Santuario de la Cruz
  Parlante 128
Sayil....................196, 206
scuba.................see diving
sea turtles.............70, 106,
  111, 214, 233
senior travellers 47
Señor 128
Seybaplaya....................233
shopping.........................39
**Sian Ka'an Biosphere
  Reserve**......12, 122–124,
  131
Sisal 193
smoking.........................39
snorkeling........36, 99, 101,
  102, 110, 111
soccer............................37
Spanish language
........................297–306
sport 36
Stephens, John Lloyd
..........142, 184, 203, 290
study tours 45
Subteniente Lopez 139

T

Tabasco 237
Tabasco & Chiapas 238
Talking Cross movement
..........128, 129, 279, 291
Tankah 111
taxis...............................26
Teabo............................209
Tecoh............................210
Tekit 210
Telchac Puerto..............193
television 33
temperatures, average
....10
Teotihuacán 271
tequila............................32
Ticul 205
Tihosuco 129
Tikal 120, 146, 272
time zones 47
timekeeping...................38
tipping 39

I

INDEX

Tizimín 159
Tohcok 231
toilets 47
Toltecs 164, 165, 273
Toniná 262–265
tour operators................ 22
tourist cards 43
tourist offices................. 47
travel agents.................. 22
trova yucateca 184, 185,
   293
trovadores 59, 180, 187,
   293
Tulum 106, 111–119,
   Maya culture colour
   section
Tulum & around 108
Tulum Area................... 112
Tulum Ruins 115
Tulum Town.................. 113
   accommodation 113
   beach 114
   bicycles.......................... 118
   buses 118
   cenotes 119
   diving............................. 118
   eating 117
   listings............................ 118
   nightlife.......................... 117
   orientation 112
   ruins 115
   snorkelling 115
   tourist information............ 112
   tours........................ 115, 119
   town 114
turtles..........*see* sea turtles

U

Uaymá 157–158
UXMAL...............................
   13, 196, 200–204, *Maya
   culture* colour section
Uxmal 201
Uxmal & the Ruta Puuc
   198
   accommodation 201
   buses 200
   eating 204
   information...................... 200

V

VALLADOLID 39,
   153–157, 279, *Maya
   culture* colour section
Valladolid...................... 155
Valladolid & Chichén Itzá
   152
   accommodation 153
   buses 157
   cenotes 155, 157
   colectivos to Chichén Itzá
   157
   eating 156
   Iglesia de San Bernardino de
      Siena........................... 154
   markets 156
   tourist information............ 153
   tours 153
vegetarian food 31
vegetation 284
Villa, Pancho................ 280
VILLAHERMOSA ... 241–247
Villahermosa, Central ... 243
   accommodation 242
   airport............................ 241
   buses 241, 246
   eating and drinking ... 245–247
   Parque La Venta.............. 244
   tourist information............ 241
   tours 247
   Yumká 245
visas 42
volunteering.................... 45

W

waterfalls 236, 253, 254,
   256, 259
weather.............*see* climate
websites 47
Welib-Ja........................ 254
whale sharks 13, 71, 75,
   76, 285
wildlife 8, 37, 71, 122,
   131, 140, 146, 160, 193,
   236, 237, 283–286, 295
wine 32
women travellers 48

World Tree 287
wrestling 37

X

Xcacel 106, 111
Xcalak 132
Xcambó 192
Xcaret 90
Xel-Há.................. 106, 110
Xel Ha (ruins) 110
Xiu Dynasty 202, 209,
   210, 274, 275
Xlapak........................... 207
Xpicob 233
Xplor 90
Xpu-Ha 109
Xpuhil (ruins)................ 144
Xpujil (town) 142–144

Y

Yaxchilán 16,
   236, 257–259, 272, *Maya
   culture* colour section
Yich'aak K'ak'... *see* Jaguar
   Paw
youth hostels................. 29
Yucalpetén.................... 193
Yucatán, Republic of 278
Yucatán peninsula 6–7
Yucatec Maya
   .... 302, *Maya culture*
   colour section
Yucatecan cuisine 30,
   Yucatán food colour
   section

Z

Zapata, Emiliano........... 280
Zapatistas............. 261, 262
Zoh-Laguna................. 143
Zona Maya 127

Map symbols

maps are listed in the full index using coloured text

▬▬▬	International boundary	∩	Park entrance
▬▬ ▬▬	Province boundary	⊠	Gate
▬ ▬ ▬	Chapter divisions boundary	⚓	Boat
▬▬▬	Motorway	⧫	Point of interest
══════	Major road	ⓘ	Information office
═══	Minor road	ℂ	Telephone
═══	Pedestrian road	@	Internet access
───	Unpaved road	★	Transport stop
⊞⊞⊞⊞	Steps	✈	Airport
▪▪▪▪▪▪	Track	⛽	Petrol station
▪ ▪ ▪ ▪	Path	⊞	Hospital
───	River	⊠	Post office
─ ─	Ferry route	P	Parking
▬▪▬▪▬	Railway	⛳	Golf course
▬▬▬	Wall	⛺	Camping
⌣	Bridge	⚡	Lighthouse
→	One-way arrow	⬭	Baseball field
ﻟﻟﻟﻟﻟﻟ	Reef	▢	Market
⚵	Waterfall	⊞	Church
⩊	Cenote	▬	Building
⌂	Cave	⊞	Cemetery
∴	Ruins	▨	Park/reserve
⚙	Maya site	▨	Beach
🏛	Hacienda	▨	Swamp

So now we've told you about the things not to miss, the best places to stay, the top restaurants, the liveliest bars and the most spectacular sights, it only seems fair to tell you about the best travel insurance around

 WorldNomads.com
keep travelling safely

Recommended by Rough Guides